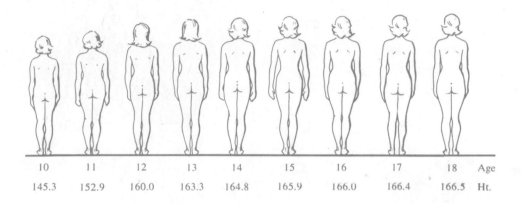

10	11	12	13	14	15	16	17	18	Age
145.3	152.9	160.0	163.3	164.8	165.9	166.0	166.4	166.5	Ht.

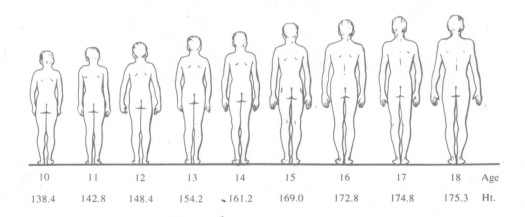

10	11	12	13	14	15	16	17	18	Age
138.4	142.8	148.4	154.2	161.2	169.0	172.8	174.8	175.3	Ht.

4th edition

chi

dren

Development AND Relationships

Mollie S. Smart
UNIVERSITY OF RHODE ISLAND

Russell C. Smart
UNIVERSITY OF RHODE ISLAND

Macmillan Publishing Co., Inc.
NEW YORK

Collier Macmillan Publishers
LONDON

To the Memory of Clem Hill

Macmillan Publishing Co., Inc.
866 Third Avenue, New York, New York 10022

Collier Macmillan Canada, Ltd.

Library of Congress Cataloging in Publication Data

Smart, Mollie Stevens.
  Children: development and relationships.

  Bibliography: p.
  Includes index.
  1. Child development. I. Smart, Russell Cook.
II. Smart, Laura S. III. Title.
RJ131.S56 1982   155.4   81-5969
ISBN 0-02-411910-5   AACR2

Printing:1 2 3 4 5 6 7 8   Year:2 3 4 5 6 7 8 9

Photo Acknowledgments

The authors wish to express their appreciation for permission to reproduce photographs from the following sources. (When two or more photographs appear on a page, the sources are listed in order: top to bottom and right to left.)

P. 5, Erika Stone/Peter Arnold, Inc.; p. 13, Mimi Forsyth/Monkmeyer Press Photo Service; p. 23, Suzanne Szasz; p. 43, George Zimbel/Monkmeyer Press Photo Service; p. 53, Mimi Forsyth/Monkmeyer Press Photo Service; p. 78, Erika Stone/Peter Arnold, Inc.; p. 90, Arthur H. Parmelee; p. 96, Suzanne Szasz; p. 101, Halvar Loken; p. 102, Gloria Karlson, Massey University and Glaxo Co.; p. 103, Arthur H. Parmelee; p. 105, Massey University and Glaxo Co.; p. 107, Stanley Summer; p. 119, Erika Stone/Peter Arnold; p. 120, Margaret Hamilton; p. 122, Kenneth Karp, Gloria Karlson; p. 123, Massey University and Glaxo Co.; p. 135, Arthur H. Parmelee; p. 137, Margaret Hamilton, Erika Stone/Peter Arnold, Inc.; p. 148, Margaret Hamilton; p. 150, Massey University and Glaxo Co.; Margaret Hamilton; p. 151, Erika Stone/Peter Arnold, Inc., Ken Heyman; p. 165, Donna J. Harris and the Merrill-Palmer Institute; p. 168, Margaret Hamilton; p. 171, Ken Heyman; p. 172, Robert Burgess; p. 174, Massey University and Glaxo Co.; p. 178, Gloria Karlson (both); p. 183, Tina Sanghui; p. 184, Ray Clayton, *The Narragansett Times*; p. 187, Margaret Hamilton; p. 206, Victor W. Sidel; p. 211, Stanley Summer; p. 213, Stanley Summer; p. 214, Donna J. Harris and the Merrill-Palmer Institute; p. 217, Donna J. Harris and the Merrill-Palmer Institute; p. 224, Donna J. Harris and the Merrill-Palmer Institute; p. 232, Ray Clayton, *The Narragansett Times*; p. 233, Edward C. Devereux; p. 240, Daniel G. Dunn, *The Narragansett Times*; p. 247, Tina Sanghui; p. 254, *The Narragansett Times*; p. 275, Donna J. Harris and the Merrill-Palmer

Writing a textbook is something like having a child, especially if you write several editions. A child develops, and so does a book. At some ages and stages, a child seems well integrated and in balance; at other times, the child seems to be growing in all directions. We think that our fourth edition of *Children: Development and Relationships* is integrated and balanced. Most of it has been rewritten. We have cut down on details and summarized more. Much is new, but we have retained and sometimes retrieved from earlier editions old findings and ideas that are sound and significant today. The format is new. In keeping with the increasingly visual aspects of communication, we have placed certain illustrations and photos in the margins. We hope that these will be educational, attractive, and mnemonic.

Our basic orientation has not changed; we are still committed to child development, the study of the child as a feeling person with a body as well as a mind, growing in the context of family, community, nation, and world. Why do we not confine our book to child psychology, when child development requires delving into so many different fields of study? We have written on child development because it offers basic knowledge for working with and for children and families, as well as for teaching and research. Solutions to many contemporary problems require knowledge of child development. The sources of child abuse, for example, include the physical organism of the victim, family interaction, neighborhood networks, and societal values and institutions. Likewise, adolescent childbearing has roots and repercussions in the physical, emotional, and mental areas of the developing child, and in family, community, and society. Problems of school failure and adjustment to family disruption also involve the whole child in a social context. Child developmentalists deal not only with children's problems, but with positive life situations, and for such work they also need a broad and deep understanding. For example, child developmentalists can contribute to the shaping of government policy, legal proceedings, and plans of towns, school boards, industries, and social agencies.

Chapter 1 shows the sources of the subject matter of child development in terms of fields of study. It covers some of the great people who have worked in this area and presents some of their ideas and achievements. Chapter 2 summarizes the theories upon which the book is organized. (The instructor may prefer to assign parts of it at different times rather than assigning it all at once.) As in the first three editions, Erikson and Piaget are used to structure material on personality and intellectual development. In the present edition, Bronfenbrenner's ecological concepts are used to organize discussions of the physical and social environment in which the child interacts and develops. We think that the ecological concepts contribute unity and clarity to our consideration of the child-in-context. Chapters 3 through 15 are organized on an age-level basis, dealing with infancy, the young child, the school-age child, and the adolescent. Each age-level section includes all aspects of the individual developing in a physical and social environment but features some aspects especially significant to that age level. For example, attachment is especially important in infancy, play in early childhood, school in the middle years, and sexuality in adolescence.

When we think about indebtedness to colleagues, our memories go far back to some of the people mentioned in Chapter 1 and to their less famous but no less revered contemporaries. And then we remember our co-workers through the years, in Canada, India, and New Zealand, and the People's Republic of China, as well as in the United States, and hosts of students who provided challenges and testing grounds. We are grateful to those who have done criticisms and reviews in order to help us with the preparation of this book: Nancy Busch-Rossnagel, Thomas Chibucos, Duwayne Keller, Cosby Rogers, Bernard Slatko, James Walters, and the four anonymous reviewers at Iowa State University.

Like all child developmentalists, we are indebted to our children and our families, who taught us the most fundamental lessons in human living. Now that our children are grown, we have a new set of teachers, our grandchildren (Sarah is new in this edition). Our youngest child, Laura S. Smart, a teacher of family studies and adolescent development, is now our colleague. She has written the last chapter, "The Self and Sociosexual Development."

Our photographers are acknowledged separately. We also want to thank John Beck, Hurd Hutchins, and Frances Long, and all of the Macmillan staff who have worked on the production of this edition.

Saunderstown, Rhode Island   M. S. S.
                                                                      R. C. S.

Contents

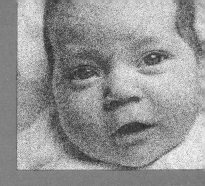

The Back- ground of Child Develop- ment

1
Roots: The Sources of Child Development

One day, when Mary Catherine was playing, she fell down and skinned her knee. Her playmate asked, "Shall we go to your house or mine to get it fixed?"

"Let's go to your house," said Mary Catherine. "Uncle Larry is so good at fixing hurts."

Mary Catherine, the daughter of Margaret Mead and Gregory Bateson, was seeking comfort and a bandaid from Lawrence K. Frank, knowing that Uncle Larry would respond immediately to her needs. Among many others who received tender care from Larry Frank was Erik Erikson. Newly arrived from Europe, Erikson went by himself to a professional meeting in New York. As he entered the room, his eye was paining him because of something that had got in it. While he was blinking and rubbing his eye, a voice said, "Come over by the window. Let me get the cinder out of your eye." And Larry Frank removed the offending cinder from Erik Erickson's painful eye. It was the beginning of an association that promoted Erikson's brilliant career in the United States.

Lawrence K. Frank: Research, Teaching, Service to families

Larry Frank administered funds that financed the first child development institutions in the United States and Canada in the 1920s and 1930s. He cared deeply about the well-being of children and families. He knew that feeling and thinking were based in physical bodies. Frank had the rare combination of vision, caring, imagination, and money. He promoted programs of research, teaching, and service to children and families because he realized that research-based information was needed in real-life situations, and that application provided a feedback to research. He regularly gave suggestions and inspiration to the nutritionists, psychologists, social workers, sociologists, nurses, physicians, and others who worked in the new child development institutions at the Merrill-Palmer School in Detroit, and at the Universities of California, Cornell, Georgia, Iowa, McGill, Minnesota, and Toronto. Until his death in 1968 he continued to encourage human developmentalists everywhere to do good work, giving out ideas and references to anyone who would listen. We ourselves have received postcards from Larry Frank, telling us something new and important to read and urging us to keep writing and studying on certain topics.

Why did Larry Frank found institutes of child development in order to serve children and families? Psychologists had been studying children for years. So had physicians, teachers, and other professionals, but they had not put their knowledge and efforts together. They had worked together neither in research, teaching, nor service In the child development institutes a variety of specialists cooperated to see a child as a whole person, interacting within a family that was part of a community. In this book we take a child development point of view. But first of all, we want to show the main roots of child development in the various fields that contribute to it. We will describe some of the founding fathers and mothers in those fields, and some of their distinguished present-day descendants, but one chapter cannot be a very full history of child development.

1. What is the field of child development?
2. Which fields of study contribute to understanding of children's growth and behavior?
3. Who are some of the outstanding persons who have influenced the field of child development?
4. What are some of the basic theories, concepts, and research studies of child development?

QUESTIONS TO THINK ABOUT WHILE READING THIS CHAPTER

We use the terms *growth* and *development* interchangeably, to refer to increases in size and/or complexity in either physical or psychological characteristics. Some authors make a distinction between *growth* and *development: Growth* refers to increases in size, *development* to increases in complexity. We, however, do not make this distinction.

The field of growth and health sciences is very broad, including everything concerning the child's body and its development in health and illness. This section discusses contributions from pediatrics and growth research. However, practitioners in growth and health sciences include

Growth and Health Sciences

Growth/Development = Increase in size and/or complexity

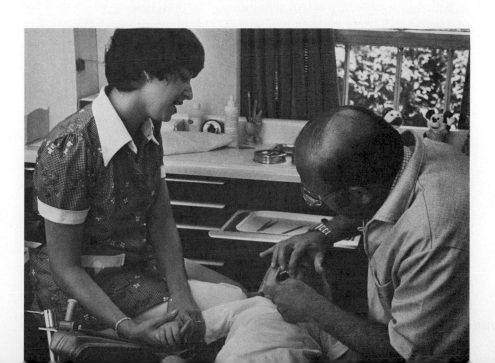

physicians, nurses, dentists, physical educators, and nutritionists, who give care and treatment to children in all conditions of health and illness, handicaps and wholeness. Pediatricians, physicians who specialize in childhood, draw knowledge from medicine, nutrition, immunology, growth research, and psychology. Some physicians specialize in a segment of life even smaller than childhood. Fetologists deal only with the fetus. There are also nurses and dentists who specialize in work with children. Dentists monitor jaw growth and tooth eruption, and of course treat dental diseases. Although sometimes parents have been excluded from hospitals and dental treatment rooms, pediatric practitioners usually realize that their success depends upon working with parents as well as children. Great pediatricians, such as Holt, Aldrich, Spock, and Brazelton, focus on parent-child relationships as major determinants of child and family health.

Pediatrics

One of the first American pediatricians, Emmett Holt, became the leading pediatrician in the 1890s. Holt's concern for mothers and babies led him to develop safe methods of artificial feeding for infants. Housework was burdensome in the large families that were typical then. Holt often saw mothers exhausted from overwork, because they could neither hire help nor get help from relatives. He therefore started a program for training nursemaids and wrote a book, *The Care and Feeding of Infants*, which went through twelve editions and seventy-five printings [25]. Holt told mothers and nursemaids to feed infants promptly every four hours. He believed that overburdened mothers would be helped by organizing their time around regular feedings, and that infants' digestions and characters would be benefited by immediate exposure to order and discipline. Holt dominated child care for several decades. Mothers tried to establish and maintain infant schedules. Many felt guilty when they fed the baby early or when they rocked a crying infant who was supposed to be sleeping.

C. Anderson Aldrich, working in the 1930s, prepared the way for a changed conception of infants. He was interested in life-span development, believing strongly in the continuity of personality. In *Babies Are Human Beings*, Aldrich and his wife, Mary, argued that the natural bodily wisdom of infants should determine when and how much they ate [2]. Aldrich influenced professionals and some colleagues, but it remained for his colleague, Benjamin Spock, to change the ideas and practices of large numbers of parents.

Today's students know Spock as a political activist, a crusading grandfather who went to jail for his beliefs. Spock has a long history of crusading for his ideas, beginning as early as 1940. As a member of a group revolting against rigidity in child care, Spock championed freedom from schedules. He wrote about parents and for parents, always respecting the feelings, needs, individuality, and growth potential of parent and child. Like Holt, he wrote an enormously popular book that went through sev-

Holt

Aldrich

eral editions and many printings. The first edition was *The Common-sense Book of Baby and Child Care* [38]. Also like Holt, he gave directions as to how to cope with physical problems and behavior. Spock, however, told parents to trust themselves and their feelings.

Berry Brazelton is distinguished for his interdisciplinary cross-cultural research and his ability to make information available and useful to parents. His book, *Infants and Mothers: Differences in Development*, contrasts with Holt's how-to approach [9]. Brazelton showed the individuality of each mother, each baby, and each mother-baby pair. He promotes the notion that there are many satisfactory ways of relating and developing, that cultural and family settings open certain paths, and that interacting persons work out modes of behavior with each other.

Each of these pediatricians is both a product of his historical time and a leader in it. Each used the current philosophy and science to meet the needs of children and parents. Through his actions, each changed existing beliefs and practices of child rearing.

Growth Research

Although a father in France began in 1759 to make a yearly record of his son's height, the first longitudinal growth study published in the United States appeared over a century later. The 1920s saw a blossoming of research on physical growth, with comprehensive longitudinal studies in progress at several universities, including Harvard, Yale, Iowa, and California at Berkeley. These studies involved large numbers of children, seen repeatedly over a stretch of years, and many physical measurements done with the utmost care. The measurements included weight, standing height, sitting height, chest, hips, fat, X rays, muscular strength, and number of teeth. Photographs were taken and used to rate posture and development of sex characteristics. A publication from the Harvard Growth Study, in 1938, gave results of 155,791 physical measurements, 33,837 mental measurements, and background information on 1,553 children [11]. Standards and tests of growth resulted from the large studies. The height and weight tables derived from the Harvard Growth Study are still used widely. The California Scales of Motor and Mental Development form the basis of Bayley's Scales of Infant Development, a modern revision used throughout the world. Data from the Berkeley Growth Study are still being analyzed. *Somatic Development of Adolescent Boys* [39] was published in 1951, but it was not until 1977 that *Somatic Development of Adolescent Girls* [16] appeared.

Longitudinal study — Subjects measured repeatedly

Cross-sectional study — Subjects measured once

Growth data are used not only in assessing American children's growth and health, but in building theories that show interrelationships, in answering questions about the influence of heredity and environment, in research on nutrition, infection, exercise and stimulation, in cross-cultural studies, and in addressing such problems as the effects of climate, light, and air pollution. Growth data from all over the world are used in a study of secular shifts, or changes in growth patterns over time [32].

Among the growth researchers who have built our present body of

Secular shift: Pattern of changes over a period of time

knowledge, James Tanner stands out as an integrator of information. Working at the Institute of Child Health in London, Tanner writes on child growth in a style understandable to persons not familiar with the methods of growth research. In his book *Foetus into Man: Physical Growth from Conception to Maturity*, Tanner [41] deals with growth curves and standards, processes of regulation, sex differentiation, puberty, the endocrines, the brain, heredity, and practical applications of growth norms and standards. For students of child development, who will be working professionally with children, knowledge of children's bodies is essential. And so is the application of that knowledge.

Developmental Psychology

Developmental psychology = Genetic psychology = Child psychology

When we (M.S.S. and R.C.S.) were undergraduates in psychology majors, we took a course called genetic psychology. *Genetic* meant that it was about development through the life span, mostly of human beings, but with some information about other living creatures when that information had something to say about psychological development. Genetic psychology was sometimes informally called child psychology. Because change is one of children's most outstanding attributes, development is implied in child psychology. Gradually, the name of the field changed to developmental psychology. We are going to take a historical approach, showing the sources of theories and research methods that form the basis of modern child development. Perhaps because psychology is our professional home base, it is harder to describe only a limited number of important ideas and persons in this field than it is in the other fields we describe.

Baby Biographers

Every parent is, to some degree, an observer of child development. When a parent is also a psychologist, philosopher, or biologist, the stage is set for carefully observing his own child and publishing the results. Famous nineteenth-century baby biographers were Wilhelm Preyer in Germany, Charles Darwin in England, and Millicent Shinn in the United States. Shinn wrote a biography of her niece as her Ph.D. thesis and later published the biography as a book [36]. Baby biographies served as source material for genetic psychologists and stimulated them to think of more objective research methods. Parents and aunts were naturally biased toward their own babies. Not only did they tend to observe behavior that did credit to their subjects, but they were likely to have unusual subjects, highly advantaged babies. Psychologists began to ask how typical were the behaviors of these favored infants.

G. Stanley Hall, Father of Child Psychology

President of Clark University at the turn of the century, Hall was an innovator in child psychology in the United States. Realizing that observations of individual children were not enough, he gave questionnaires to hundreds of children, parents, teachers, and others. Hall theorized that children, in growing up, live through the stages that the human species went through in its evolution. He applied this theory, as well as ideas about health to children's education. Hall created the concept of adolescence that persists today. He founded the American Psychological Association and several journals. He introduced Freud to North America, adopting Freud's psychoanalytic principles and notions on sex. Some of Hall's colleagues were shocked at his acceptance of sexuality.

Hall's use of questionnaires was a *cross-sectional* approach, because he gathered data from a number of people at one time. The baby biographies were *longitudinal*, because they gathered information from the same subjects repeatedly, over a period of time, and *observational*, because they recorded what was seen and heard. Present-day research uses cross-sectional and longitudianl methods, sometimes in combination; it uses observations and questionnaires, but in refined and complex forms. Accuracy of observation is aided by films, tapes, and timing devices, and the use of two or more observers. Questionnaires are tested and retested, refined, and applied to samples chosen with statistical aid. The structured interview is an interview guided by a list of key questions or topics. These refinements of method represent answers to the criticisms of bias that were leveled at the baby biographers and to Hall's critics, who said that his questionnaires were "unscientific" (uncontrolled).

John B. Watson and Behaviorism

During and after World War I, Watson founded *behaviorism*, a psychology that required working in the laboratory, using scientific, experimental methods, measuring behavior. Watson maintained that three basic emotions, love, fear, and anger, were present at birth, and that these were responses to specific stimuli, stroking, loud noise, and restraint, respectively. The particular stimuli are unconditioned stimuli. Other responses were learned, Watson said, through conditioning, or association of a neutral stimulus with an unconditioned stimulus. Watson conditioned 11-month-old Albert by sounding a loud noise (the unconditioned stimulus) when Albert reached with interest toward a white rat. The noise was sounded each time the rat was presented until Albert showed fear of the rat without the noise. At that point the rat became a conditioned stimulus. Fear of the rat transferred to other furry objects, even a Santa Claus beard. Mary Cover Jones, Watson's student and colleague, used Watson's methods of conditioning to *remove* fears from Peter, a 3-year-old who was afraid of animals.

Watson is famous for his advice on child rearing to parents in his book *Psychological Care of Infant and Child:*

> Never hug or kiss them and never let them sit on your lap. If you must, kiss them once on the forehead when you say goodnight. Shake hands with them in the morning. [44, pp. 81–82]

His strict, authoritarian ideas fitted in with those of Holt, whose word

Watson: Importance of experience, three basic emotions, classical conditioning, parental strictness

was still law on the care and feeding of children. Parents of the day did pay attention to Watson, and so did the Children's Bureau of the United States government. *Infant Care*, published in 1914, contained the advice, "The rule that parents should not play with their children may seem hard, but it is without doubt a safe one" [27]. Some modern developmental psychologists think that Watson had a very destructive effect on child rearing, through his influence on the Children's Bureau and through his own writing [35]. Mary Cover Jones says that Watson was later sorry that he wrote *Psychological Care of the Infant and Child*. Watson was willing to criticize himself. He would probably have grown beyond his rigid and extreme pronouncements to parents if he had not been forced to resign from his academic job because of his divorce, a great scandal in those times.

Although Watson's advice to parents became obsolete, his push toward strict scientific procedure continues and his behaviorism lives on in the many research studies and applications that have been made from behaviorism. His influence is seen in the work of widely differing scholars, such as B. F. Skinner and Albert Bandura.

Watson's method of pairing an unconditioned stimulus with a neutral stimulus is called *classical conditioning*. *Operant conditioning* (also called instrumental conditioning) developed by B. F. Skinner, is a method of controlling the learning of behavior by responding to tiny segments of behavior. Starting with the child's spontaneous behavior, the experimenter reinforces it positively if he wants it to be repeated and negatively if he wants it to be eliminated. Positive reinforcements such as giving food or toys, smiling, paying attention, saying "good," and so on, are events valued by the child. Negative reinforcements are events with no value to the child. For example, temper tantrums or swearing may be eliminated from a child's behavior when other people pay no attention to them, thus offering no reinforcement. Because behavior is changed in small steps toward a goal, the process is called *behavior shaping* or *behavior modification*. Thus operant conditioning has had many practical applications in changing children's behavior. It has been applied to making children more socially acceptable, to teaching language and concepts in school settings, and to behavior within the family.

Social learning theories also consider behavior changes in terms of stimulus, response, and reinforcement, but they include other people as sources of stimulation and reinforcement. Learning or acquisition of new behavior often takes place in social situations through interaction with other people or through observation of others.

Robert Sears used concepts from behaviorism and psychoanalysis (to be mentioned later in this chapter) to develop his social learning theory. According to Sears, innate drives, such as hunger, promote action and response to cues or stimuli. The hungry baby responds to a nipple. The responses to primary drives are reinforced positively by satisfaction and negatively by frustration. The response and reinforcement take place largely within the social unit of mother and child. Secondary drives de-

Instrumental conditioning used in behavior modification

Sears: Social learning; socialization; primary and secondary drives

velop in a social situation, as when the child comes to want the presence of the mother. Having given positive reinforcement in the context of primary drives, the mother herself becomes reinforcing. The parents *socialize* the child, reinforcing culturally approved behavior in the areas of feeding, toilet training, dependency, aggression, competition, and identification. The child-rearing methods used in socialization are related to the child's learning of behavior patterns. Sears and his colleagues published a classic study, "Patterns of Child Rearing," in 1957 [34a].

Albert Bandura has documented the power of observational learning. Children often acquire great chunks of new behavior without observable repeated reinforcements, by simply watching other people and imitating them. A little boy imitates his father shaving. An older child becomes leader of the club and performs the rituals that he has seen carried out by the previous leader. It is common knowledge that children learn to be polite and gracious by following the examples set by their parents and siblings. Bandura suggests that children acquire knowledge and new responses by watching and listening to others, but that the performance of those behaviors is determined by motivation and reinforcement. A child might see her friend kicking and screaming with anger and yet never do the same. If the child did not experience extreme anger, she would probably not be motivated to kick and scream. If she did not perceive her friend as being rewarded for the tantrum, she would not be influenced by vicarious reinforcement. Bandura uses the term *vicarious reinforcement* to refer to the influence of seeing the consequences of another person's action. In a series of experiments he showed that children's use of behavior patterns is strongly influenced by what happens to the model who demonstrates the behavior.

Bandura: Observational learning; modelling; vicarious reinforcement; aggression

In a series of studies on aggression, Bandura showed child subjects either live or filmed models speaking aggressively and/or hitting a doll clown, named Bobo. In one of the studies, children saw a film of an aggressive model being either punished or rewarded or experiencing no consequences [5]. The children were then left in a room with the aggressed-against clown and the instruments of aggression, as well as other toys. Those who saw the model being punished did less imitating of his aggressive behavior than did those who saw the model being rewarded or experiencing no consequences. When the children were offered reinforcements for imitating the aggression, the difference between the groups disappeared. Boys imitated more aggressive acts than girls after seeing the model punished, but when rewards were given, the sex difference disappeared. Thus, it seems that children inhibit aggressive imitation when they see the model punished, but they learn the behavior just as readily. Girls are more inhibited than boys by punishment for aggression, but they learn the behavior just as well. Bandura says that one of the most interesting questions in regard to modeling is whether one can keep people from learning what they have seen [6]. Presumably the answer is "no."

Bandura theorizes as to what happens within the child during observational learning. First, *attention* regulates the perception of modeled actions. Second, what is observed is transformed into representations that are preserved in *memory*. Coding and symbolic rehearsal make these transformations. Memory keeps the symbolically represented actions available as guides to performance. Third, new response patterns are integrated from *motor* acts. Fourth, *incentive* or *motivational* processes govern the choice of action patterns to be used.

Thus, it is the *person* who actively observes, remembers, judges, decides, and creates a response. The person's own values are the context in which the processes of modeling occur.

Arnold Gesell and Maturation

A student of G. Stanley Hall's, Arnold Gesell, received an M.D. after his Ph.D. in psychology. He studied children's development from prenatal life through adolescence, with emphasis on infancy. Gesell disagreed with Hall on Freud and his theories [35]. He thought that Freud was unscientific, disliked his ideas about sex, and believed that it was wrong to observe and ask questions about sexual matters. Gesell was also against the ideas of his contemporary, Watson, because his interpretation of human nature was the direct opposite. Watson believed that behavioral change occurred through responses to stimuli from the environment, and that a child could therefore be shaped into any kind of adult desired; Gesell believed that each person is an individual from the beginning, that progress toward maturity is governed by an internal timetable. Watson and Gesell stood at the extremes of the maturation-learning, heredity-environment, or nature-nurture controversy, in which the relative importance of inner and outside influences on growth is debated.

Gesell defined maturation as "the intrinsic component of development (or growth) which determines the primary morphogenesis and variabilities of the life cycle" [18, p. 210]. Gesell recognized the fact that an organism has to have an environment in which to grow, and that the child develops in a family and in a culture, but he thought that the forces of maturation, *within* the child, were very influential in organizing the body and mind and in governing their development. From his view of development as orderly and controlled, he derived principles of development that applied to both physical and psychological growth.

Gesell carried on his research and writing at the Yale Clinic for Child Development. It was here that he invented the one-way vision screen, a device that all students of child development know as an aid to observing children without disturbing them. Another invention was a globular room with a movable camera with which he made film records of examinations long before films were used widely in research. Through repeated observations and tests, Gesell developed norms and standards of the development of behavior, especially in infancy. The Gesell Developmental Schedules have been used throughout the world for assessing infant behavior and as starting points for developing other infant tests. In

addition to his scholarly reports of scientific work, Gesell wrote books for parents, as did his antagonist, Watson. Gesell's books told parents what was normal behavior at each age, characterizing certain stages of growth. The message most parents got was that inner forces of growth would keep the child developing in his own way, that annoying behavior was only a passing phase, and that the role of parents was to nurture the child while he became his mature self. Gesell provided reassurance to parents who were uncomfortable with Watson's strict and controlling methods.

The relative importance of heredity and environment, or of maturation and learning, continues to be debated and studied. Today it is commonly acknowledged that, at any given moment, a person, or any living organism, is the result of interactions between that organism, including genetic influences, and the environment. Questions asked about heredity and environment are different from the questions asked in Gesell's day, but they still seek to understand the inner and outer forces. The topic is discussed further in this chapter, under the heading "Behavioral Biology."

The study of animals contributes to the understanding of human beings. Skinner's operant conditioning came from his work with pigeons. Gesell's principles of development were derived from research that had been done on simpler forms of life. Research with primates is especially suited to learning about social and emotional behavior of human beings, who are indeed primates, along with apes and monkeys. Primate family interaction is observed in the field, under natural conditions. Experiments are carried out in laboratory settings. The best-known experiments are those of Harry Harlow. A number of them were done in collaboration with his wife, Margaret Harlow.

Comparative Developmental Psychology

The Harlows, like John Bowlby (mentioned later), were interested in the nature of infant-mother love. Unlike Bowlby, who worked with human children, Harlow was able to manipulate the experience of his monkey subjects. He took newborns away from their mothers and gave them substitute mothers, of wire and cloth. The monkeys spent more time with cloth-covered mothers, even if the wire mothers gave milk and the cloth ones did not. Harlow concluded that "contact comfort" was more important than food in the growth of love. Rocking added to the attractiveness of the cloth mother. As far as the experimenter could tell at that point, the baby's attachment to the cloth mother was as strong as to a real mother, and the security gained from her presence was as great as from a real mother [23]. However, when the cloth-mothered babies grew to maturity, neither males nor females were interested in mating. The females who were impregnated and gave birth became indifferent or abusive mothers. They would avoid their babies, knock them down, step on them, beat them, and rub their faces on the floor. The implications for understanding child abuse are readily apparent. The Harlows went on to try methods of rehabilitating monkeys who had been deprived of mother love in infancy. They found that play with peers, especially younger peers, resulted in nearly normal social-sex behavior in monkeys who had been raised without real mothers [24]. Thus there were seen to be different affectional systems, infant-mother, peer, and heterosexual, all of which interacted.

Intelligence Testers

$$IQ = \frac{MA}{CA} \times 100$$

The IQ has been a powerful idea in American life, influencing school systems, teachers, parents, and politicians. It has entered the arena of ethnic and racial strife, being denounced by leaders of minorities. Minority children, they say, have been sorted by IQ tests, and given a raw deal in the schools. Where did the IQ come from?

The intelligence test came from France, from the genius of Alfred Binet, but Lewis Terman, a student of Hall's, and professor of psychology and education at Stanford University in 1910, devised the Stanford Revision of the Binet Scale. The Stanford-Binet has been widely used ever since, in research and in clinical practice. The Intelligence Quotient was (and is) the ratio between mental age and chronological age. Mental age is derived from a number of tests, grouped into age levels according to successes and failures of the children on whom the tests were standardized. The resulting IQ was thought to stay the same as a child grew up. In 1933 Florence Goodenough pointed out that the IQ does not remain constant for individuals or for groups, but even today the IQ is sometimes wrongly thought to be unchangeable [19].

Psychologists have always differed in what they thought intelligence to be. Terman said an individual is intelligent in proportion to his ability to carry on abstract thinking [19, p. 305]. The IQ, because it has a number value, tended to make people think that intelligence is a unitary quality or attribute that people have more or less of, rather like height and weight. Other intelligence tests are based on the idea that intelligence is the ability to respond effectively to new situations and to profit from experience. Thorndike thought that there were various kinds of intelligence. His intelligence test consisted of four tests, including arithmetic and vocabulary, and separate scores were given. Even though Terman measured arithmetic, vocabulary, and other areas, the scores were all put together into one, whereas Thorndike kept them separate. The concept of intelligence derived from Thorndike's work, then, is different from that suggested by IQ.

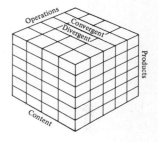

A modern development of a multifaceted model of intelligence is Guilford's [21]. He proposes three basic dimensions of intellect, operations, contents, and products. Five types of operations (intellectual processes) shown on one side of the cube act upon four types of content, shown on another side, yielding six types of products, shown on the third side. Each cell of the cube represents one factor of intelligence, making 120 in all. One of Guilford's contributions was his notion of operations including convergent and divergent thinking. Convergent thinking looks for the one right answer. (Who wrote *Paradise Lost*?) Divergent thinking produces new answers from an indefinite number of possible answers. (How might we regain paradise on earth?) Thus Guilford brought attention to the fact that IQ tests, and many other intelligence tests, were testing one kind of intelligence and ignoring creativity. Other workers have developed more creativity tests.

Many psychologists developed intelligence tests. Some yield only one score, but several give two, a verbal score and a performance score, as does the Wechsler Intelligence Test for Children. Some are performance tests only, such as the Raven Progressive Matrices, and some test language without requiring speech, such as the Peabody Vocabulary Test. Until psychologists came to realize that every child grows up in a particular culture, there were efforts to devise an intelligence test that would be free from cultural influences. The problem of comparing children from two cultures has not been entirely solved, but the present trend is to devise tests that will measure how well a child copes with tasks that are real and important within his own environment.

IQ tests and other intelligence tests have been useful in predicting school success, especially for children above and below average. Scores within the average range do not tell much about what children will do either in school or in later life. As for the extremes, success in life is not the same as achievement in school, and although highly intelligent children are likely to have more vocational and personal success, children classified as slow or dull have often succeeded as adults in supporting themselves and maintaining families.

It is possible for many retarded persons to learn skills necessary for homemaking, earning a living, and managing their own lives. Intelligence testing, as well as tests of specific achievement, can help in designing learning programs.

The use of intelligence tests and beliefs about intelligence are affected by historical events and the political and economic climate of the times. In times of inflation and/or depression, funds decrease for testing and special programs of education. The present multi-ethnic society of the United States is inhospitable to elitist notions. Parents of gifted (high IQ, variously talented) children have had quite a struggle to get special educational programs that would develop their children fully. Retarded, handicapped, and learning-disabled children have a better chance of getting appropriate education and treatment, although there is reluctance to segregate them from the mainstream. Streaming, or separation into ability (or IQ) or achievement levels, is generally unacceptable. At the same time, families of retarded children have united to form successful pressure groups, getting public funds and educational programs for their children.

Intelligence tests are used widely in research. IQs are important data in heritability studies. IQ changes are used to measure effects of various environments, environmental changes, educational techniques, and nutrition-supplement programs. Tests of divergent thinking, or creativity, have not been used nearly as much as tests of convergent thinking, which is what IQ tests are. Perhaps our society values creativity less, or perhaps the concept is less amenable to research.

Jean Piaget and Cognitive Development

We end our summary of highlights of contributions from developmental psychology with a giant figure who spans most of the years under review. Although he published some of his research on children's thinking in the 1920s, his work received little notice in the United States until the 1950s. True, few Americans could read his work in the original French, but even his chapters in the American publication, *A Handbook of Child Psychology* [31] did not make a great impression. Piaget's clinical methods were suspect. He observed his own children! Even when he used other subjects, he did not use statistics, large numbers of cases, and carefully selected samples. After Americans began to see the power of Piaget's theory, they started to do experiments in their own accepted ways. Meanwhile, back in Geneva, Piaget continued to develop his theories in research and books, most of which have been translated into English. The decades of the 60s and 70s saw hundreds of American experimental studies that validated Piaget's work. Applications of Piagetian principles were made to teaching, especially in nursery schools and kindergartens. Intelligence tests were created on Piagetian concepts, making a real break with the IQ tradition.

Piaget views the child as a biological organism that acts upon its environment, continually working toward establishing harmony or equilibrium between itself and the environment. The child, a very flexible organism, chooses to take parts of the environment into itself and to change in response to the environment. Piaget calls the first process *assimilation*, the second, *accommodation*. For example, children take food into the mouth and assimilate it, using it as energy and as body-buiding ma-

Adaptation = Assimilation + Accommodation

terials. They also choose what to take in through their sense organs and then use the sensory information to build mental structures, and to use the mental structures in behavior. The two processes, assimilation and accommodation, are the two parts of the process of *adaptation*. Adaptation results in growth and development. Thus Piaget sees the child as continually creating his own body and mind. This model of the child is very different from the behaviorist one, in which the environment acts upon the child.

Assimilation:Acting upon the environment

Accommodation: Changing the self

Piaget's theory deals with stages of cognitive growth, but he does not maintain that the regularity of behavior development is due to maturation (as Gesell did) but to the universality of the basic experience of infants. Piaget's student, Kessen, says, "What he's taught me, in part, is that there are such regularities in the environment that infants meet that they, with their own biological predispositions, are drawn to be the kind of child that one particularly sees at the end of 1 year or at the end of 2. Not that he could not be different, but this joint regularity almost guarantees certain emergent patterns." [35, p. 53]

Among the many scholars inspired by Piaget, Lawrence Kohlberg is outstanding. Using a cognitive approach to the development of moral reasoning, he has stimulated a great deal of research and thinking. Kohlberg's method and theory are described in "Moral Development" in Chapter 14.

Piaget's work will be discussed further in the appropriate places throughout this book. Some of the most interesting criticisms and revisions will be found in the sections on infants and on preschool children. Scottish developmental psychologist Margaret Donaldson, a student of Piaget's, gives some new insights into some of Piaget's findings [13].

Psychoanalysis

Many of Freud's concepts are widely accepted, used, and taken for granted today. Probably most people believe in the importance of childhood in shaping the adult years, in children's sexuality, in the importance of sex in motivation, and in the existence of the unconscious. Many people know something about the defense mechanisms of repression (forgetting painful experiences), sublimation (using the energy of a blocked drive in creativity), and regression (behaving in immature or primitive ways). Freud's concepts are basic to the present work of many or most child psychiatrists and play therapists.

Freud: Childhood shapes the adult; sexuality; the unconscious; defense mechanisms

Freud's Basic Concepts

According to Freud, personality develops in psychosexual stages, each of which uses a certain zone of the body for gratification of the *id* (the unconscious source of motives, strivings, desires, and energy). The *ego*, which mediates between the demands of the id, the outside world, and the superego, "represents what may be called reason and common sense,

Libido: Basic energy and
motivating force

Psychosexual stages: Oral,
anal, phallic or Oedipal,
latency, puberal or genital

in contrast to the id, which contains the passions" [17, p. 15]. The *super-ego* or ego ideal corresponds roughly to the conscience.

A basic energy, *libido,* is a motivating force throughout life. A new-born baby seeks only pleasure, which he gets from sucking and other feeding sensations, because his libido is centered on his mouth; he is in the *oral stage.* If gratification through feeding and mouthing is inadequate during the oral stage (the first year), frustration or conflicts may lead to later overeating, smoking, verbal aggression, or dependency. If all goes well, the child goes forward to the *anal stage,* in which the libido is centered on the anus. Gratification comes from processes of eliminating and controlling elimination. Frustrations and conflicts in the anal stage may lead to messiness and wastefulness or to compulsive cleanliness, order, and materialism.

Libido centers on the genital organs at about age 4, when the *phallic stage* begins. Pleasure comes from stimulating the genitals. The child notices differences between the sexes, asks questions about where babies come from, and develops the Oedipus complex. Sometimes the phallic stage is called the *Oedipal stage,* because of the importance of the child's desire for the opposite-sex parent and hostility to the same-sex parent. Problems rooted in this stage may lead to homosexuality, fixation on a parent, and other sexual problems.

From age 6 until puberty, during the *latency period,* the libido submerges and sexual cravings are repressed (made unconscious). The child identifies with the same-sex parent and peers. Puberty brings the *puberal stage,* with the libido again centered on the genital organs, and satisfaction sought in heterosexual activity.

Development of Psychoanalytic Theory

A neurologist, working with adult patients in Vienna, Freud came to see many problems as results of childhood experiences. He asked patients to tell him anything that came into their minds, and to tell about their dreams. He observed his own children and recalled his own childhood. Out of all this he developed psychoanalytic theory and his method of treatment, psychoanalysis. The theory revolutionized concepts of childhood, shocking his Victorian contemporaries, who believed that children were "innocent" of sexuality. The method revolutionized psychiatric practice. Play therapy for children was developed out of psychoanalysis. Freud's ideas and methods continue to influence theorists, researchers, and clinicians.

Recent studies in neurology have strengthened the notion of the id. The limbic system, located deep in the brain, is the seat of the following functions: *self-preservation,* including oral responses relating to feeding, expression of anger, defense behavior; *procreation,* including affectionate behavior and sexual arousal; *play; memory,* or connecting inner experience with outer; *personal identity; emotional vocalizations* [30]. This description makes the limbic system sound like the residence of the id, or the "seat of the passions." It seems that the limbic system, a physical structure, bears a relationship to Freud's idea of the id.

One of Freud's students is Erik Erikson, who came to the United States and created a grand theory of life-span personality development published in 1950 [15]. Ever since that time, Erikson has exerted a tremendous influence on American concepts of childhood, personality development, and child-family-society interaction. His theory, which will be described in the next chapter, integrates concepts of human development, mental health, and family interaction in a societal and historical framework. Erikson has continued to develop his theory, responding to the changing conditions and social movements of today.

Erikson: Person in context, development, interaction

The previous sections show that systems, theories, and their related practices come and go, usually leaving some influences or traces. The strict child care methods of Holt and Watson, buttressed by their researches, solved some problems that were current, but raised others. Holt's and Watson's ideas gradually gave way to those of Aldrich and Gesell, who solved some of the problems caused by Holt's and Watson's methods, but created a new set of problems. And now we are at a point where Piaget's theories do not explain children's cognitive development as completely as they seemed to do. The field of child development illustrates the dialectical process. Change is continuous. As soon as a problem is solved, its answer or solution creates new questions or problems. Piaget's theory stimulated experiments at the University of Edinburgh and elsewhere that required new explanations.

Family interaction is an example of the dialectic process. A person has only to recall being either a parent or a child to realize that a whiny child makes a parent feel irritated, or that a bossy parent will arouse resistance in a toddler. It is easy to imagine a sequence of interaction in either of these situations. Changes in the child make continually changing impacts on her family and friends. Changes in mother, father, and siblings also contribute to new interactions. Thus each person changes in response to himself/herself and to others. The family group changes as its members interact with each other and with their physical and social environment.

Interactions are reciprocal and circular. By reciprocal, we mean that each person influences the other; by circular, we mean that as the action goes back and forth in a reciprocal way, it builds up, each exchange influencing the next. For example,

TOBY: Hello, Mom. I'm home.
MOTHER: Hi, Toby. I just got home, too. I'm beat. How was your day?
TOBY: O.K. The teacher asked how many parents were coming to the meeting tonight.
MOTHER: Oh, I forgot about it. I just can't go! I'm too tired.

Dialectics: Child-Family-Network-Community-World Interactions

Dialectics: Change is continuous: Conflict ⟶ solution ⟶ conflict

TOBY: But I said you were going. I said you'd bring a cake, too.
MOTHER: How can you do this to me, you monster? I'm ready to collapse.
TOBY: The teacher will be mad at me if you don't go. Oh, please go, Mom.
MOTHER: Go and find a cake mix and do what it says. After dinner maybe I'll feel like going.

The example is one of a short-term sequence of interactions. An example of a long-term sequence might be Toby's quest for more and more autonomy or independence as he grows up. Each time his mother gives him freedom to make a new decision for himself, he becomes more autonomous, and she controls him less.

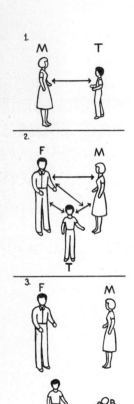

Toby and his mother are continuously changing through interactions with each other. They are a dyad, two interacting persons. Their dyadic relationship is represented in drawing no. 1 by a two-pointed arrow, linking T and M. In drawing no. 2 a father, F, has been added to the picture. Now we have a triad, three interacting persons. Not only will F have interactions with T amd M, but he will be influenced by the relationship between T amd M, and he will influence it. We have drawn a double-pointed arrow between F and T-M. Drawing no. 3 shows the same family with the addition of baby Belinda. Copy this drawing on a separate sheet of paper and on your copy draw arrows to show F's interactions with T and M and also with Baby Belinda. Add arrows between each character and the interaction arrows between pairs. The diagram becomes a fabric of threads running in many directions, but it gives only a slight idea of the complexity of family interaction. A gyroscope, or a mobile made of gyroscopes, would make a better model, because it would show continuous change and realignment of components. Even a gyroscopic mobile does not model the transformations in persons and groups that result from child-family interaction.

The diagram gives some notion of how difficult it is to do research on family interaction. It is enormously complicated to study even a dyad, but it is being done. Numerous studies of mother-infant and mother-young child interaction have been carried out during the past decade. A few researchers have focused on the father-infant dyad, and some on the mother-father-baby triad. One method of study is to record the behavior of child and parent on film and tape for later analysis by at least two persons, who must agree substantially with each other as to what they see. Or, observers may record the behavior directly, one observing the parent, one the child, and recording within time frames marked by a timing device. Later, the two records can be put together to show interaction. Family triads have also been studied by using games or discussion situations with older children, and by observing spontaneous actions when parents were observed with infants. Findings show that parents' interactions with their children are affected by the presence of the spouse. Because such large amounts of data are collected in child-family research, new statistical methods are needed to handle the load.

The term *personal-social network*, or just *network*, refers to people outside the household with whom an individual shares activities and exchanges [10]. A person's network usually includes friends, kin, neighbors, schoolmates, and fellow workers. Family members have overlapping networks, usually not exactly the same. Each family member interacts with his own network and is influenced by all the other networks in which family members are involved. In the example just given, we see Toby's network affecting his mother. Networks link each person to a wider outside world than that person would contact just through her or his own network. Networks often give support and assistance, as indeed the parent-teacher meeting might do for a parent, or a relative would do by baby-sitting and listening to troubles. Or a network member could compete for family time, by asking for help or company.

Network: Interaction, exchanges, support, sharing

Human interaction rests on a biological base, the body. Some aspects of the body have special significance for understanding the behavior of persons and groups. Biologists, sociologists, anthropologists, and psychologists are collaborating to study sociobiological questions involving heredity, evolution, intelligence, hormones, psychological states, and social behavior. Their findings and their questions have implications for the study of children and families.

Behavioral Biology

Behavior Genetics

The genes, the carriers of instructions in the cells of the body, are inherited by the child from the parents. The mechanisms of heredity will be discussed in the following chapter. Many physical characteristics and some behavior patterns are inherited according to known laws. However, inheritance of complex behavior cannot be understood in terms of the genes. A simple behavior, which can be explained by gene action, is tongue-rolling; a complex behavior, which cannot be explained in terms of genes, is intelligent action. Two genes control whether or not a person can roll the sides of her tongue up toward the roof of her mouth. An indefinite number of unknown genes are involved in solving a problem, but so also are an unknown number of other factors. For many years, psychologists have been intrigued by the contributions of heredity and environment to intelligent behavior, or, for short, to intelligence. The topic has stimulated heated discussions and disagreements.

Because heredity experiments cannot be done with human subjects, psychologists use natural experiments, to which they apply complex statistics. They measure the degree of similarity between persons of varying known degrees of relatedness, and of varying degrees of shared experience. Monozygotic (one-egg) twins reared together share the largest degrees of both relatedness and experience. Dizygotic (two-egg) twins reared together have very similar experience, but the same degree of relatedness as any pair of siblings. Adopted children have an experience very akin to that of siblings, but are not related genetically. Studies done over half a century have shown consistently that monozygotic twins reared to-

FIGURE 1–1
Median correlation coefficients for intelligence test scores showing degree of similarity between performances of people of varying degrees of relatedness under different and similar environmental conditions. (SOURCE: Data from L. Erlenmeyer-Kimling and L. F. Jervik. *Science*, 1964, **142**, 1477–1479.)

Category		Correlation	Groups included
Unrelated Persons	Reared apart		4
	Reared together		5
Fosterparent – Child			3
Parent – Child			12
Siblings	Reared apart		2
	Reared together		35
Twins / Two-egg	Opposite sex		9
	Like sex		11
Twins / One-egg	Reared apart		4
	Reared together		14

gether have highly correlated IQs. (Correlations are between 0 and 1, the 0 indicating no relationship and 1 a perfect relationship. A correlation of .5 indicates some relationship.) A recent study of 7- and 8-year-old twins shows the IQs of monozygotic twins correlate .86, of dizygotic twins, .45, and of siblings, .46. [46] (There is not a significant difference between .45 and .46.) These figures correspond closely with those found in earlier studies. Figure 1–1 shows correlations from a large number of studies of IQs of people varying in relatedness from monozygotic twins to unrelated persons, and of either being reared together or not. Thus the comparisons show the influence of both heredity and environment. When parents' and children's IQs are compared, they are found to be uncorrelated in infancy, low positive at the end of the second year, and moderate in childhood and thereafter [14]. Although an environmentalist might explain the growing similarity by the increasing time spent together, there is another piece of evidence that suggests heredity at work: The heights of parents and children correlate more as they grow older. What is more, attitudes toward authority, and vocational interests are also correlated between parents and biological children, but not between parents and adoptive children [34]. The connection may be through intelligence, because people of higher intelligence are likely to have less authoritarian attitudes than those of lower intelligence. Vocational interests may, however, have some basis in physiological characteristics that are genetically based.

While showing that genes play a role in the development of intelligence and attitudes, studies also show that experience is important. Correlations between siblings or parent and child are far from perfect, showing that heredity does not tell the whole story. An environmental improvement has greatest effects upon the IQs of children whose environmental change was greatest. When all have an excellent environment, then hereditary differences will account more for individual differences than when some have a good environment and others a poor one.

Every species has social behavior patterns that promote its survival in a particular environment. Planning and conscious effort to survive are not implied. The species simply would not survive if it did not have such patterns or behavioral systems. Reproduction is one of these systems that has obvious significance for species survival. Ethology is therefore concerned with, among other topics, the interactions between physiological and social patterns in sexual behavior, giving birth, and child rearing. Changes in these behavior patterns are studied from an evolutionary standpoint, looking at their form in a savannahlike environment, where simple hunting and gathering societies live, comparing it with modern industrial society, and with other forms of society. Ground-dwelling primates are also studied to discover social patterns between males and females and between parents and children.

Predispositions for behavior patterns are passed along to members of a species by way of genetics. Interaction patterns are developed in a social environment to which they are adapted. For example, infant-mother interaction has been studied from the standpoint of evolutionary adaptation. John Bowlby, an English psychiatrist, started in the 1940s to study "the nature of the child's tie to his mother." Eventually, he and his North American associate, Mary Ainsworth [1], defined the actions by which a baby becomes attached to the mother. These baby behaviors fit with mother behaviors in such a way that the two persons interact smoothly. The reciprocal behavior patterns are adapted to survival of the species, because they promote the survival and health of baby and mother. Another behavior pattern, wariness of strangers, is articulated with (fitted to) attachment behavior. The baby seeks the mother and clings to her when a stranger approaches. This pattern has survival value by protecting the baby from predators, or it did in the early history of our species [8]. Using their observations of infants with strangers, Bowlby and Ainsworth developed research techniques that have been very productive. The topic is discussed in Chapter 6.

It was not until the 1960s that the period immediately after birth was analyzed in terms of attachment, or bonding, as it was then called. John Kennell and Marshall Klaus, working with associates in Cleveland, found that mothers showed precisely patterned responses to their newborn babies [28]. During the first hours after birth, the infant and mother have reciprocal, interlocking behaviors that tie or bond them together—the baby's alert state, looking at the mother's face, and listening, and the mother's positioning the baby so as to look into her eyes, her patterned touching of the infant's body, and her elation. And then there is the whole interaction of feeding. By prompt bonding or locking together of the infant and mother, the newborn's survival and health are supported, thus promoting species survival. The findings of Kennell and Klaus have stimulated further research, as well as a revolution in obstetrical practices.

Mind, Hormones, and Social Behavior

Sex differences come from brain, body, hormones, and experience

Behavioral biologists are addressing one of the most fascinating of problems, the question of *sex differences*. What are sex differences, and what meaning do they have for men, women, children, and society? Sex differences have always been mysterious, ever since Adam and Eve, or before. The Women's Movement, in seeking equality, made a climate in which differences were minimized or denied. Differences between girls and boys, men and women, were explained in terms of child rearing, television, schooling, job opportunities, and legal inequities. Champions of men's liberation proved that men could take care of children and that babies liked playing with fathers as well as with mothers, if not better. They defended men's right to cry and otherwise behave in ways that used to be reserved for women. Even so, sex differences persisted.

In the meantime, during the 1960s, English scientists got together to study the biosocial aspects of fertility, sex differences, and race, and the American National Academy of Sciences sponsored a survey of life sciences [22]. A new perspective on sex differences was reported at some of these meetings. The relationship between nervous system and endocrines (brain and hormones) was seen to be a two-way street. The endocrines affect early brain development, making brains as well as bodies male or female. The brain, however, controls secretions of hormones by the endocrines, and the brain is affected by experience.

Sociologist Alice Rossi takes the viewpoint of behavioral biology in putting together biological and sociological findings of sex differences [33]. Rossi points out that there are behavior patterns that are easier for males to learn, and others that are easier for females to learn. The body, including the brain, of each sex is constructed under the influence of a genetic code, and the continuing influence of hormones and experience, interacting with each other. She suggests that a female is prepared to learn fine motor skills and to be interested in babies; it takes more effort for the average male to learn to do these things. A male is more prepared to run heavy machinery, because of his visual skill and shoulder strength, but some women have learned to operate back hoes. In the hunting and gathering societies that existed throughout most of Homo sapiens' history, reproductive success went to women who were good at childbearing, child rearing, and gathering food within a small area. The men who survived and reproduced were those who had the stature, shoulder strength, and visual acuity needed for hunting and defense. After thousands of years of selection for these characteristics and skills, males and females differ in certain propensities for learning. In many ways, socially prescribed gender behavior fits with existing tendencies.

Behavioral biology helps us to understand some of the roots of human behavior and then to deal with problems. Behavioral biology is relevant to many present-day problems in child-family-community interaction, including man-woman relationships, the relation of families to work at home and outside, child care, and teenage parenthood.

Cross-Cultural Child Development

Before the 1960's most child development research was focused on middle-class Caucasian children, who represent a tiny fraction of the children in the world. (*All* the children, including poor, middle-class, and rich, in the following regions made up only 25 per cent of the world's children in 1975 and will be 22 per cent in 2000: United States, Canada, temperate South America, Europe, the Soviet Union, Japan, Australia and New Zealand [47].) American research on American middle-class children, therefore, is very limited in what it can say about children in general, or even about American children from different ethnic groups in the United States. Cross-culture studies compare children from populations that differ in behavior and environment, looking for ways in which children are alike and ways in which they differ. Every culture is an example of the adaptations that a group of people have made to a certain environment, including their methods of passing knowledge and skills along to their children. By studying children and families in cultures other than middle-class American, researchers have found some constancies and some wide variations in the young of the human species. For example, several studies have shown village African babies to be greatly advanced in all aspects of development when measured by tests standardized on English and American babies. This finding has stimulated criticism of the ways in which birth and early infant care are conducted in England and the United States.

Emmy Werner states six main issues and questions that can be answered through research in cross-cultural child development [63].

Only a quarter of the world's children live in the industrialized countries

1. *Constancies in child behavior and development.* In what ways are children alike everywhere in their biological, psychological, and social characteristics and growth?
2. *Interrelationships among processes of development.* How is child development affected by interactions of biological, cognitive, and social processes?
3. *Effects of ecology and various social systems.* How are children and their caretakers influenced by ecology and economic, social, and political systems?
4. *Child-rearing goals and practices as adaptive to various environments.* How do beliefs about children and methods of caring for them fit into the culture?
5. *Changes in behavior of children and caretakers during periods of rapid social change.* How fast and in what ways do children and their parents change under changing conditions?

6. *Social policies and programs for children.* How do various programs affect children? How should programs be designed and timed? What can be expected from them?

In planning cross-cultural studies, investigators use all sorts of information that has been collected about the culture in which they are interested. Crossing a language barrier usually requires enlisting a native speaker for planning as well as carrying out experiments. Tests must be appropriate. The usual custom is collaboration by researchers from each of the cultures used in the cross. Werner emphasizes that knowledge from cross-culture studies should be implemented, especially when it means feeding and caring for children who do not have enough food and care for survival and health.

Studies on malnutrition, learning, and behavior illustrate Werner's second area of inquiry, interrelationships among processes of development. The importance of such studies can be appreciated by looking at Figure 1–2, which shows how many children throughout the world are not fed enough. Children who suffered serious malnutrition have been followed in several parts of the world to determine effects of malnutrition on later development. When studies were retrospective (dealing with subjects who were known to have been malnourished previously), it was impossible to separate the effects of what had happened in the meantime in the way of physical, social, and family interactions. Some of these difficulties have been met by including in the studies siblings who had not been malnourished. Both types of studies usually showed previously malnourished children as having some cognitive impairment at school age. Clearer results come from longitudinal studies, in which children are followed from birth or prenatal life into the school years. Several studies in Guatemala and Mexico have separated contributions of nutritional factors and social factors to different cognitive functions [45]. Nutritional history was related to perceptual-analysis tasks, somewhat to memory, and somewhat to language.

A logical next step from studying effects of malnutrition on development is to design and test programs of intervention. These efforts fit into

FIGURE 1–2
Number of children under age 15 with insufficient food energy levels, world regions, about 1975.
(SOURCE: Adapted from M. G. McHale, J. McHale and G. F. Streatfeild. *Children in the world.* Washington: Population Reference Bureau, 1979.)

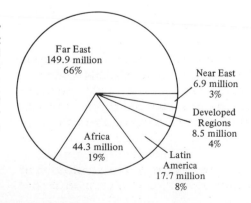

Werner's sixth area of inquiry. In longitudinal studies in Guatemala, nutritional supplements were given at different times during pregnancy, infancy, and childhood. The design of the studies, which included using four villages and two programs, made it possible to separate the results of food supplements during pregnancy from factors of gestation length and mother's age, stature, socioeconomic status, illnesses, and infections. One dramatic finding was that nutritional supplementation during pregnancy and lactation decreased infant mortality by almost a half. The next question, of course, is how policies and programs can be set up to act on this finding.

This example of cross-culture research illustrates two of Werner's issues and focuses on physical development in early life. Other studies deal with other issues, other age levels, and other aspects of development. Cross-culture research will be used throughout this book, in relation to various topics and age levels.

History of Childhood and Family Life

The new discipline of psychohistory is concerned with the personality and behavior of individuals and groups over time, looking for patterns and principles of development and interaction. Psychohistory gives perspectives on the present, suggests solutions to problems, and reveals sources of values, images, ideas, and behavior. Psychohistory deals with interactions between children, families, networks, communities, and nations.

To us, the most exciting idea to come out of psychohistory is that of Lloyd DeMause [12]. Extending Freudian psychology to groups (Freud worked with individuals), DeMause believes that common experiences in infancy and childhood are the basic source for later group beliefs and behavior. He deals especially with the fantasies and behavior that lead to war. He sees child rearing as the source of social change. It is promising to gain insight into causes of war, with the hope that understanding will lead to control. DeMause also gives support to child developmentalists when he shows the importance of infancy and childhood to every society and to the human world.

Historical studies of American children and families reveal views and practices that differ greatly from today's. For example, the doctrine of original sin was an important influence on the Plymouth colonists, who valued obedience and humility, and who believed that they must "break the child's will" and stamp out wickedness by strict discipline. The Victorian family is noteworthy for its idealization as a peaceful shelter, its conflicts over sexuality, and its development of the double standard. Victorian family life and child rearing were influenced not only by economics and religion, but by the medical and biological theories of the time [26]. The threats of venereal disease and hell were powerful modifiers of behavior.

The value placed on children, or on life itself, can be shown to be related to the resources and technology of a society, as well as to its religion and philosophy. This is what William Langer does in an essay, "Infanticide: A historical survey." Langer [29] points out that among non-Judeo-Christian peoples, since the beginning of known history, infanticide has been the usual procedure for disposing of not only sickly infants, but of all newborns that would strain the resources of family and community. The father usually made the decision as to whether a newborn was to be kept or not. Plato, Aristotle, Seneca, and Pliny the Elder accepted exposure of unwanted babies as necessary for population control, although Aristotle did suggest that abortion would be preferable. The Christian emperor, Constantine, in A.D. 318, declared the slaying of a son or daughter by the father to be a crime. At the same time, the Roman Empire, having suffered epidemics, famines, and disorder, was depopulated, and in need of increased fertility. By the end of the fourth century, infanticide in the Empire was made punishable by death. Infanticide persisted throughout the world, however, and persists even today, although to a much smaller extent. The widespread availability of birth control, including abortion, has reduced infanticide in recent years.

Some of the lessons of psychohistory are difficult or shocking. A student of child development finds it disturbing to read about infanticide. And it is hard to accept the ignoring of children's special needs. The value of studying psychohistory lies not only in a general broadening of perspective, but in giving insights into modern problems. For example, although there is abundant evidence to show that harsh punishment is harmful to child, family, and society, brutality persists. Psychohistory has much to say about the sources of violence.

History is also used to show how persons have been affected by the time-related environments into which they were born and through which they have lived. A *cohort* is a number of people born at the same time. It could be all of the children born during a certain period in a particular town, state, or country. The individuals in a cohort share many conditions and experiences because they encounter them at the same time of life. For example, people who were born in 1946 in the United States form a cohort of "baby-boom" children. They have experienced crowding in school, and later, competition for jobs. Effects of time-related events can be studied by comparing cohorts.

Definitions of Child and Childhood

What is a child? The answer can be biological or sociohistorical. There are two main biological landmarks, weaning and puberty (sexual maturity). Therefore, the three divisions of life, baby or infant, child, and adult are universal, or almost universal.

There seems to be no question that everybody recognizes a baby. A frequently used marker of the end of infancy is *weaning,* or the point at which the baby eats mainly solid foods instead of only milk from mother or bottle. The timing of weaning differs from one culture to another. The eruption of teeth may be taken as a sign that the infant is ready to chew food and can therefore be weaned. Or walking steadily may be regarded as marking the end of infancy. Talking is also used as an indication of the end of infancy. Through the use of language, imitation, and pretend play a child can represent objects and actions that are not present. These powers represent a changeover from the mental organization of infancy.

Philippe Ariès, in *Centuries of Childhood*, maintained that during the Middle Ages, European adults regarded and treated children like adults [4]. Using paintings, as well as documents and records, Ariès showed that children were depicted as small adults, wearing the same clothing as their elders, playing the same games, taking part in the same rituals. Presumably, adults thought that children shared their feelings, thoughts, and needs. A critic of Ariès points out that *mothers* can always tell the difference between babies, children, and adults [42]. The records of the Middle Ages, both written and graphic, were made by men who may have been quite distant from young children. Mothers neither wrote histories nor painted pictures, but they would have noticed the age of 7, just as do all people who have close contact with children.

Seven has been recognized by many cultures as the age of reason and responsibility. The Romans applied *infantia* to childhood under age 7. *Infans* means *unable to speak*. In Britain today, schools for children under 7 are called infant schools. First communion at age 7 has long been customary in the Roman Catholic Church. Piaget has shown that the child reconstructs his way of thinking at around age 7, when he begins to attain concrete operations. With concrete operations, the child's thinking is of the same kind that adults use a great deal of the time, perhaps all of the time in simple societies. Erikson describes the personality stage beginning around 7 as the development of the sense of industry, or duty and accomplishment. Thus the change at 7 involves new ways of thinking and new approaches to working. Although there is no physical changeover as dramatic as reaching sexual maturity, age 7 is marked by one obvious physical event, the loss of front baby teeth and their replacement by adult teeth.

If infancy is marked as ending at around 2 years, and 7 is seen as a change-over point, what is the time in between, roughly from 2 to 7? For many years, in North America, this stage has been called preschool, children between 2 and 7 being preschool children. The term no longer fits, because there are many schools designed for children this age, and the children are recognized as having much to learn. *Young child* is probably the most frequently used term. The young child learns through play, because of the ways in which his mind, body, and personality are organized. The Piagetian stage of preoperational thought is quite different from the concrete operations of the child over 7. The young child is not interested in sustained productive work, but in exploration and trying out different modes of action.

The attainment of sexual maturity is another universal landmark. In ancient societies, puberty usually signified adulthood. Girls married soon after puberty [20]. Boys began to work as adults, including serving

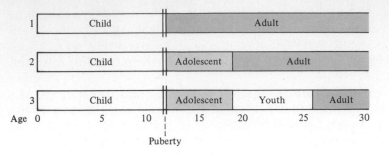

FIGURE 1–3
Definitions of maturity.

in the army or government. Upper-class Greek and Roman boys entered adult work roles at between 16 and 18 years of age. The Roman father, however, retained control over all of his grown children. A brief period of youth, between puberty and attainment of full adulthood, occurred in the upper classes in highly developed cultures. When there is much that an adult needs to know, a long period of schooling is required. Therefore, there must be an extended period of growing up socially, even though physical growth may have been completed. If the men are the professionals and executives whereas women are confined to homemaking and child rearing, then only the boys go through the prolonged period of education and youth.

Only in modern industrial society has adulthood been delayed for *all* children. Only in the twentieth century was adolescence a significant and usual stage of life. Although puberty may be acknowledged in some religious ceremonies, such as the Bar Mitzvah and confirmation, it does not mark adulthood in any practical sense. Laws require school attendance, usually until 16 years of age. Laws regulate the kinds of jobs at which adolescents can earn money, the ages at which they can drive cars, drink in public, and get married. Laws specify the penalties that can be applied to them. Such laws vary from state to state, making the legal definitions of adulthood in the United States variable. Full entrance into adult status depends on the society and family in which the adolescent lives. One family considers graduation from high school a mark of adulthood, whereas another believes that its members are adolescents until they finish college. Even college graduates are not always regarded as complete adults. A stage *of youth* may intervene between adolescence and adulthood. Exploration, experimentation, and enjoyment are the essence of youth. Figure 1–3 illustrates different definitions of maturity.

Adulthood is now seen as a period of change. Adults, as well as children grow through stages. Development continues throughout the life span.

Rights of the Child

The most basic right, life itself, depends upon when the organism is believed to be fully human. In the ancient world, the baby did not gain human status until the father accepted it. If the father rejected the baby, it died. In cultures where infant mortality is high, there may be customs that protect adults from becoming emotionally committed to the infant until there is some certainty that it will live. The baby may not be named for several months. It may be dressed in a way that does not define it as girl or boy.

Today, the infant's right to live is recognized throughout the world, but there is disagreement as to whether the fetus and even the embryo is a human being, with a consequent right to live, or whether a woman has the right to accept or reject the not fully human organism within her.

Throughout history there have been changes in the value placed upon children and childhood, and in the resulting conceptions of rights relating to children. The topic is of great contemporary concern, shown in the designation of the year 1979 as the International Year of the Child. In the ancient civilizations of Egypt, the Middle East, Greece, and Rome a dominant theme was the absolute rule of a father over his children [20]. Children were supposed to obey and honor their parents. Severe offenses against parents were punishable by death. In ancient times, as well as in many periods since then, parents used children as economic assets. Children could bring property into the family through marriage, and money through work. They were used as hostages, as security for debts, and as servants. Apprenticeship, a form of education and service, was begun during the Middle Ages and continued into colonial America. Children were sent away from home to another household, perhaps a relative's, to learn vocational skills and social customs. As far as we can tell there was no notion of children's rights as individuals.

Physical punishment has been used throughout history as a means of forcing children to obey adults. A new method was added in the seventeenth century, the use of guilt [20]. Self-control and moral righteousness were the goals. Jean-Jacques Rousseau introduced another concept of children's morality and a new educational philosophy in his book *Emile* in 1762. He maintained that the child was important in himself, that children are basically good, and that childhood is a special time of life in which children grow toward maturity in their own ways. He turned attention to the processes of growing up, and made parents feel that their functions were important. Rousseau changed concepts of the nature of childhood and of children's rights but it took a long time before resultant changes could be seen widely in the treatment of children. American schools changed under the influence of John Dewey, a contemporary and student of G. Stanley Hall. Dewey believed that children learn through their own actions of inquiring, exploring, analyzing, synthesizing, and evaluating. His point of view was the direct opposite of those who believed that memorizing and rote learning would produce educated people. "Learning through doing" is consistent with Piaget's theory of the ways in which children structure mind and experience. Dewey's concept of children, applied to education, was called "Progressive Education." There were always opponents, who clung to earlier notions of children as vessels into which knowledge could be poured, to concepts of obedience as a prime virtue, and to belief in the necessity for breaking the will. Dewey's concept of children is alive today, and so are the opposite concepts.

International organizations have made several declarations of the rights of children, beginning with one adopted by the League of Nations in 1925. In 1959 the United Nations adopted the Declaration of the Rights of the Child that formed the core of the International Year of the Child, 1979. A brief statement of the United Nations Declaration follows:

UNITED NATIONS DECLARATION OF THE RIGHTS OF THE CHILD

The right to affection, love, and understanding.
The right to adequate nutrition and medical care.
The right to free education.
The right to full opportunity for play and recreation.
The right to a name and a nationality.
The right to special care, if handicapped.
The right to be among the first to receive relief in times of disaster.
The right to learn to be a useful member of society and to develop individual abilities.
The right to be brought up in a spirit of peace and universal brotherhood.
The right to enjoy these rights, regardless of race, color, sex, religion, national or social origin.

The following statement of children's rights was made in the United States in 1969, by the Joint Commission on the Mental Health of Children [37].

STATEMENT ON CHILDREN'S RIGHTS BY THE JOINT COMMISSION ON THE MENTAL HEALTH OF CHILDREN

The right to be wanted.
The right to be born healthy.
The right to live in a healthy environment.
The right to obtain satisfaction of basic needs.
The right to receive continuous loving care.
The right to acquire the intellectual and emotional skills necessary to achieve individual aspirations and to cope effectively in our society.
The right to receive care and treatment through facilities that are appropriate to children's needs and that keep them as closely as possible within their normal social setting.

Statements of rights are not laws, but beliefs and goals. By focusing attention on these goals during 1979, many societies tried to move closer to them. Programs were carried out on all the continents of the world. Considering each of the rights listed, however, it is obvious that there are children throughout the world and in our own country and communities who do not possess the benefits to which they are entitled. In some places, the most pressing problem is shortage of food; in others, lack of social supports for parenting is a major deficit. Different rights require different kinds of implementation in different social contexts. Government programs and public policies provide some modes of protecting children's rights. The legalization of rights is a process, often a slow one.

The law works in two directions. First it confirms children's rights that have become accepted by a large proportion of the population. Second, it leads public opinion in establishing rights. Court decisions have defined children's rights in regard to school, family, and courts. The American Civil Liberties Union has published a handbook of laws and court actions dealing with young persons [40].

Children's right to education was asserted by making education free, beginning in Massachusetts in 1827, and by compulsory education laws that require all children to go to school. At present, some advocates for children think that compelling children to attend school is wrong, that children should be able to choose to go to school or not. Particularly for adolescents who dislike school, the right to work is sought. When laws were passed to regulate and prevent child labor, the purpose was to protect the rights of children to life and health. School attendance was substituted for work in factories and fields. Although too much work was unquestionably bad for children, no work at all may also be a deprivation.

Desegregation has been promoted in the schools, as one way of protecting the civil rights of children. Testing and ability grouping have been stopped in many school systems because they were judged unfair to some children. Suspension of students from school has been regulated by a court case in 1975, in which the court ruled that students must be told the charges and evidence against them and be given a chance to explain before being suspended. So far, the courts have not affirmed freedom from physical punishment, even though customs have changed considerably since the nineteenth century when teachers routinely whipped and beat children for misbehavior.

In Sweden physical punishment is outlawed, not only in the schools, but everywhere. The law concerning schools was passed first, and in 1979 when it was well accepted, a law was passed, "A child may not be subjected to physical punishment or other injurious or humiliating treatment." Even though the law will be difficult to monitor, the Swedes believe that it will be a deterrent to parents in punishing children physically. At the end of 1980, the law was reported to be working well [43].

Children's rights in relation to parents are in a process of redefinition. No longer does a father have complete jurisdiction over his children, because children are defined as persons with their own rights. The courts have recently been faced with the necessity of weighing parents' traditional rights against newly defined rights of children [7]. In the case of Wisconsin vs. Yoder, Amish parents wanted their children to stop going to school. Although the court upheld the rights of the parents, Justice William Douglas dissented, affirming the child's right to education and religious freedom. The courts have dealt with parent-child conflicts over a minor's right to have an abortion. In 1973 this right was affirmed under the constitutional right to privacy [7]. In the matter of child custody after divorce, judges are now paying more attention to what will be best for the child, instead of considering only the rights of the parents [3].

Revisions are also being made in children's rights when they break the law. Like compulsory education and child labor laws, juvenile courts were set up to protect children, but they have become obsolete in certain ways. In trying to maintain confidentiality, children were sometimes denied rights accorded to adult criminals. Furthermore, the increase in juvenile crimes has resulted in an overflow of children and adolescents in detention and treatment facilities. The problem facing our society is much more than that of children's rights in the justice system, because prevention of juvenile delinquency requires a rethinking of children's rights in the social systems of family, school, and related systems. Changes are going on right now. Recognition of children's rights in the future will result partly from the beliefs and goals of today's adults.

Throughout Western Europe and North America, children are becoming scarcer in relation to the rest of the population, while old people are becoming more numerous. Perhaps children will become more valuable to society as they decrease in proportion to adults. Perhaps more people will realize that children are sources of tenderness, fun, imagination, and new ideas. Adults may want to be with children more often, to watch, listen to, play with, enjoy, and nurture them. Children's rights would then be expanded and assured by adults who appreciate the special contributions that children can make to other people.

Summary

The field of child development is both theoretical and applied, drawing knowledge from many disciplines, and using it in many contexts.

In the growth and health sciences, a variety of practitioners specialize in childhood. In addition to treating illnesses, pediatricians have developed methods of child care and influenced parents to use those methods. Growth researchers have conducted studies, usually longitudinal research, that are basic to a variety of ongoing studies of theoretic and practical interest.

Developmental psychology deals with psychological development throughout the life span, with children as the primary focus, and animals also included. The first developmental psychologists studied their own infants. G. Stanley Hall introduced new research methods and founded child psychology in the United States. John B. Watson was the original behaviorist. Arnold Gesell emphasized maturation and individuality while developing new methods of observing children and creating tests. The Harlows, comparative psychologists, did ingenious studies of monkey love, especially of the infant-mother relationship. Lewis Terman started an American tradition of intelligence testing that has involved large numbers of psychologists and that has had wide effects upon children and the educational system. Jean Piaget's theories of cognitive development have had much influence, counteracting some of the ideas and practices stemming from IQ testing, and stimulating hundreds of research studies.

The psychoanalytic concepts of Sigmund Freud are part of the fabric of American thinking. His theory and methods are used widely in therapy. Freud's stages of psychosexual development were the base on which Erik Erikson built his powerful and productive theory of psychosocial development.

Sociobiological problems are studied by biologists, sociologists, geneticists and others looking for sources of behavior in heredity and environment. Topics include heredity-based interaction patterns, adaptations promoting species survival, sex-linked behaviors and their relation to social organization.

Cross-cultural child development prevents the bias that is likely with small, narrowly selected samples. It includes the study of constancies, processes, ecology, adaptation to social change, social policies and programs.

The history of childhood and family life gives another set of perspectives, showing roots of current concepts and practices, as well as broadening contrasts. Such history makes a good base from which to examine values, definitions, rights and laws concerning childhood.

References

1. Ainsworth, M. D. S. The development of infant-mother attachment. In B. M. Caldwell and H. N. Ricciuti (eds.). *Review of child development research.* Vol. 3. Chicago: University of Chicago Press, 1973.
2. Aldrich, C. A., and M. Aldrich. *Babies are human beings.* New York: Macmillan Publishing Co., Inc., 1938.
3. Alexander, S. J. Protecting the child's rights in custody cases. *Family Coordinator,* 1979, **26,** 377–382.
4. Ariès, P. *Centuries of childhood: A social history of family life.* New York: Alfred A. Knopf, Inc., 1962.
5. Bandura, A. Influence of models' reinforcement contingencies on the acquisition of imitative responses. *Journal of Personality and Social Psychology,* 1965, **1,** 589–595.
6. Bandura, A. Behavior theory and the models of man. *American Psychologist,* 1974, **29,** 859–869.
7. Bennett, W. M., and L. McDonald. Rights of children. *Family Coordinator,* 1977, **26,** 333–337.
8. Bowlby, J. *Attachment and loss.* Vol. 1: *Attachment.* New York: Basic Books, 1969.
9. Brazelton, B. *Infants and mothers: Differences in development.* New York: Delacorte Press, 1969.
10. Cochran, M. M., and J. A. Brassard. Child development and personal-social networks. *Child Development,* 1979, **50,** 601–616.
11. Dearborn, W. F., J. W. Rothney, and F. K. Shuttleworth. Data on the growth of public school children. *Monographs of the Society for Research in Child Development,* 1938, **3:**1.
12. DeMause, L. Historical group fantasies. *Journal of Psychohistory,* 1979, **7,** 1–70.

13. Donaldson, M. *Children's minds.* New York: W. W. Norton & Company, Inc., 1978.
14. Eichorn, D. H. Developmental parallels in the growth of parents and their children. *Newsletter of the Division on Developmental Psychology of the American Psychological Association,* Spring, 1970.
15. Erikson, E. H. *Childhood and society.* New York: W. W. Norton & Company, Inc., 1950.
16. Faust, M. S. Somatic development of adolescent girls. *Monographs of the Society for Research in Child Development,* 1977, **42:**1.
17. Freud, S. *The ego and the id.* New York: W. W. Norton & Company, Inc., 1962.
18. Gesell, A. Maturation and the patterning of behavior. In C. Murchison (ed.). *A handbook of child psychology.* 2nd ed. Worcester, Mass.: Clark University Press, 1933.
19. Goodenough, F. L. The measurement of mental growth. In C. Murchison (ed.). *A handbook of child psychology.* 2nd ed. Worcester, Mass.: Clark University Press, 1933.
20. Greenleaf, B. K. *Children through the ages: A history of childhood.* New York: McGraw-Hill Book Company, 1978.
21. Guilford, J. P. Intelligence: 1965 model. *American Psychologist,* 1966, **21,** 20–26.
22. Handler, P. (ed.). *Biology and the future of man.* New York: Oxford University Press, Inc., 1970.
23. Harlow, H. F. The nature of love. *American Psychologist,* 1958, **13,** 673–684.
24. Harlow, H. F., and M. K. Harlow. Social deprivation in monkeys. *Scientific American,* 1962, **207:**5, 136–146.
25. Holt, E. *The care and feeding of infants.* New York: Appleton, 1894.
26. Kern, S. Explosive intimacy: Psychodynamics of the Victorian family. In L. DeMause (ed.). *The new psychohistory.* New York: Psychohistory Press, 1975.
27. Kessen, W. The American child and other cultural inventions. *American Psychologist,* 1979, **34,** 815–820.
28. Klaus, M. H., J. H. Kennell, N. Plumb, and S. Zuelke. Human maternal behavior at the first contact with her young. *Pediatrics,* 1970, **46,** 187–192.
29. Langer, W. L. Infanticide: A historical survey. In L. DeMause (ed.). *The new psychohistory.* New York: Psychohistory Press, 1975.
30. MacLean, P. D. A mind of three minds: Educating the triune brain. In J. S. Chall and A. F. Mirsky (eds.). *Education and the brain.* The 77th Yearbook of the National Society for the Study of Education. Chicago: University of Chicago Press, 1977.
31. Piaget, J. Children's philosophies. In C. Murchison (ed.), *A handbook of child psychology.* 2nd ed. Worcester, Mass.: Clark University Press, 1933.
32. Roche, A. F. Secular trends in human growth, maturation and development. *Monographs of the Society for Research in Child Development,* 1979, **44:**3–4.
33. Rossi, A. S. A biological perspective on parenting. In A. S. Rossi, J. Kagan, and T. K. Hareven (eds.). *The family.* New York: W. W. Norton & Company, Inc., 1977.
34. Scarr, S., and R. A. Weinberg. Attitudes, interests and IQ. *Human Nature,* 1978, **1:**4, 29–36.
34a. Sears, R. R., E. E. Maccoby, and H. Levin. *Patterns of child rearing.* New York: Harper & Row, 1957.
35. Senn, M. J. Insights on the child development movement in the United States. *Monographs of the Society for Research in Child Development,* 1975, **40:**3–4.

36. Shinn, M. *The biography of a baby.* Boston: Houghton Mifflin Company, 1900.

37. Shore, M. F. Legislation, advocacy, and the rights of children and youth, *American Psychologist,* 1979, **34,** 1017–1019.

38. Spock, B. *The commonsense book of baby and child care.* New York: Duell, Sloan & Pearce, 1946.

39. Stolz, H. R., and L. M. Stolz. *Somatic development of adolescent boys.* New York: Macmillan Publishing Co., Inc. 1951.

40. Sussman, A. N. *The rights of young people.* New York: Avon Book, 1977.

41. Tanner, J. M. *Foetus into man: Physical growth from conception to maturity.* Cambridge, Mass.: Harvard University Press, 1977.

42. Tucker, N. *What is a child?* London: Open Books, 1977.

43. Vinocur, J. Sweden's antispanking law seems to be a success. *New York Times,* Oct. 19, 1980.

44. Watson, J. B. *Psychological care of the infant and child.* New York: W. W. Norton & Company, Inc., 1920.

45. Werner, E. E. *Cross-cultural child development: A view from the planet earth.* Monterey, Calif.: Brooks/Cole, 1979.

46. Wilson, R. S. Twins and siblings: Concordance for school-age mental development, *Child Development,* 1977, **48,** 211–216.

47. *World's children data sheet.* Washington: Population Reference Bureau, 1979.

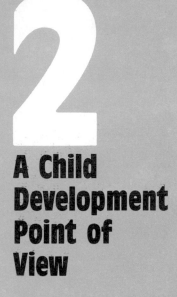

2

A Child Development Point of View

Mommy, are people really made out of dust?" asked David, the 4-year-old son of a minister.

"Yes," said his mother. "That's what the Bible tells us."

"Are babies made of dust?"

"Well, I suppose they are."

"Hurray," shouted David. "There'll soon be enough under my bed to make one."

We remember the woman who told us this story about her son many years ago. Since then we have heard it in other places and family settings. Whatever its source, the story opens up the age-old question of how does a tiny speck of substance get to be a baby and eventually a grown-up person.

The three main headings in this chapter deal with different aspects of the question of how the speck of life becomes a person. The first section considers the unique set of directions for development that are contained in each organism in the beginning. The second, concerning principles of growth, contains generalizations about the patterning of processes of development. In the third, we discuss various interactions between the child and the environment as sources of development. The most prominent contributor to concepts of principles of growth is Arnold Gesell. Concepts of interaction come chiefly from Jean Piaget, Erik Erikson, and Urie Bronfenbrenner.

QUESTIONS TO THINK ABOUT WHILE READING THIS CHAPTER

1. Why do we feel sure that every person in the world is unique?
2. What evidence supports the idea that genes continue to influence development throughout life?
3. What are the principles of growth?
4. In what ways does the individual interact with the environment?
5. What are Piaget's stages of cognitive development?
6. How does Erikson describe the healthy personality in each stage of development?
7. How does Bronfenbrenner represent the ecology of the child?
8. How do the three theorists, Piaget, Erikson, and Bronfenbrenner, use any or all of the principles of growth given in the first part of the chapter?

When a new organism is formed, its make-up is different from that of all other human organisms. When the egg and sperm unite to form a zygote (fertilized egg), the information in that zygote has only a minute chance of being identical to the information contained in any other zygote.

With the exception of the sperm and egg, every cell in the human body contains 46 chromosomes, the carriers of hereditary material. Each chromosome is made up of thousands of *genes,* each of which contains a chemical code that determines a particular cellular product and that directs a particular aspect of development [5].

The 46 chromosomes in human cells are arranged in 23 pairs, with one member of each pair being contributed by the father and one member of each pair being contributed by the mother. The sperm contributes 23 chromosomes to the zygote, as does the egg, to give rise to a zygote with the full count of 46 chromosomes. It is simply a matter of chance which of each pair of the mother's chromosomes is selected to go into the egg, and which chromosome of each pair of the father's chromosomes is selected to go into the sperm. Each zygote represents a different combination of chromosomes randomly contributed by each parent.

Further variation occurs during the production of sperm cells and egg cells through the mechanism of *crossing over.* If members of a pair of chromosomes exchange some of their genes, they are said to cross over to the other chromosome. The resulting chromosomes then differ in content from the chromosomes of either parent. An additional source of genetic variation lies in *mutation,* a change in a gene's chemical nature. Mutation, as well as crossing over, can take place during the production of sperm and egg cells.

Genes work in concert with each other. The simplest type of combination is one in which a pair of genes controls a single trait. When the more powerful or *dominant* gene is present, the trait it controls is shown; the less powerful, *recessive,* gene can express its trait only if it paired with another gene just like itself. A common example is eye color. Brown is dominant, blue is recessive. The action of eye-color genes is shown in Figure 2–1.

Genes work in more complicated ways, also. Sometimes one gene is modified by other genes; this kind of modification may occur in determination of skin color or, more commonly, numerous genes can be involved in producing a characteristic such as height. Height is the sum of the lengths of many different bones and pieces of cartilage, all of which are controlled by genes.

Considering all these sources of hereditary variation, to say "You're one in a million" is an understatement. Nobody is put together from the same genes as you unless you happen to be one of identical twins. Identical twins begin as one zygote which splits into two zygotes, each giving rise to an individual. Although such twins have the same set of genes, they do not grow up exactly alike. Their experiences and environments differ, even in the uterus, where one has a different position from the other, and one may get more adequate nourishment. One is born first.

Everybody Is Special: The Uniqueness of the Individual

Female   Male

Parents' Genes		Children's Genes				Children's Eye Color
● ●	● ●	● ●	● ●	● ●	● ●	All have brown eyes.
○ ○	○ ○	○ ○	○ ○	○ ○	○ ○	All have blue eyes.
○ ○	● ●	● ○	● ○	● ○	● ○	All have brown eyes
● ○	● ●	● ○	● ○	● ○	● ○	All have brown eyes.
● ○	○ ○	● ○	● ○	○ ○	○ ○	2 have brown eyes. 2 have blue eyes.
● ○	● ○	● ●	● ○	● ○	○ ○	3 have brown eyes. 1 has blue eyes.

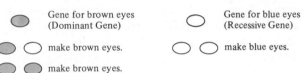

●	Gene for brown eyes (Dominant Gene)	○	Gene for blue eyes (Recessive Gene)
● ○	make brown eyes.	○ ○	make blue eyes.
● ●	make brown eyes.		

FIGURE 2–1
The action of dominant and recessive genes. The example shown here is for the inheritance of brown or blue eyes.

Identical twins doubtless experience more similarity in environment than do mere siblings, and siblings more than unrelated children. For each person, however, the world is different from anyone else's, and that person's genes continue to guide his or her interactions, resulting in a more and more differentiated person.

Development Is Orderly: Principles of Growth

Even though every individual is unique, she is like others in many ways. Because there are similarities in the ways in which children grow up, we can generalize about development. These generalizations are called *principles of growth*.

Normative Sequence

Growth and changes in the body and its parts take place in a certain order. A person grows bigger until adulthood and then smaller in old age. Baby skin and hair are fine and smooth, but coarsen as middle childhood approaches. Such physical changes are understood as under the laws of nature, as is the sequence of motor development. "A child must creepe ere he walke." Orderliness of mental development is also common knowledge. The "age of reason" comes after the "age of innocence." A normative sequence is a series of steps that everybody takes in a certain order. It is normal to progress from one particular condition or achievement to another and another.

Normative sequences have been found for locomotion, the use of the hands, language, problem solving, social behavior, and personality development. All development takes place through interactions with an environment. The same sequence or order will hold for persons in a similar environment, but when environments differ greatly, a developmental sequence may also differ from one environment to another. For instance, when babies move freely on the floor or ground, they creep before they walk, but when the ground is dangerous, an infant may be held in arms, on laps, in jumpers and swings, and never creep before learning to walk.

Environments for infants are, after all, pretty much alike; babies around the world are quite similar. The older one gets, the more differences can be found in environments and in what is held to be a normal sequence for development. Old people around the world are extraordinarily varied.

Differentiation and Integration

From large global patterns of behavior, smaller, more specific patterns emerge. Later the small, specific patterns can be combined into new, complicated, larger patterns. For example, the newborn baby will reach for a seen object, opening the hand before contact and closing it on contact, but too quickly for hand closure to have been released by the contact. The reaching and grasping form a unitary act. Reaching rarely occurs after 4 weeks, but reappears at around 20 weeks, in a different form. The infant can now reach without grasping and can also combine them. Reaching and grasping are differentiated. Either reaching or grasping can be corrected during the act instead of having to be corrected by starting again. Reaching and grasping are integrated. They are separate but combinable [1, pp. 150–166].

Examples can also be taken from purely intellectual fields, such as mathematics. At age 2 or 3, the child can count 2 or 3 objects, showing understanding of these numbers. Numbers beyond 3 are undifferentiated, as though the child regarded them as *a-lot-of*. A child may give the highest number he knows to represent a big set, just as adults may say *billion* or *trillion*. A step in differentiating further numbers is to give higher number to bigger groups, as for instance, sets of 5, 6, and 18 are called 7, 11, and 19, respectively. When the child can give accurate numbers for sets, he has differentiated numerosities out of a global concept. Using these differentiated concepts, the child next combines them in addition and subtraction to form new and more complicated concepts. Conceptual differentiation and integration are at work as the student moves up through algebra and geometry into higher mathematics. There remains an undifferentiated sphere where each person stops in his progress in mathematics.

Developmental Direction

Certain sequences of development take place in certain directions, in reference to the body. The motor sequence takes two such directions,

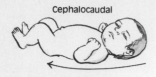

Cephalocaudal

Proximodistal

cephalocaudal (head to tail) and *proximodistal* (midline to outer extremities). Like all animals, the child grows a relatively large, complex head region early in life, whereas the tail region or posterior is small and simple. As he becomes older, the region next to the head grows more, and finally, the end region grows. Coordination follows the same direction, the muscles of the eyes coming under control first, then the neck muscles, then arms, chest, and back, and finally the legs. The motor sequence illustrates the proximodistal direction by the fact that the earliest controlled arm movements, as in reaching, are large movements, controlled mostly by shoulder muscles. Later the elbow is brought into play in reaching, then the wrist, and then the fingers.

Optimal Tendency

An organism behaves as though it were seeking to reach its maximum potential for development in both structure and function. Even though growth is interrupted, as in periods of inadequate food supply, the child (or organism) makes up for the lean period as soon as more and better food is available, returning to his characteristic pattern of growth. Only if the deprivation is severe, or if it occurs throughout a critical period, will he show permanent effects from it. During the deprivation period, the organism adapts by slowing growth and cutting down on the use of energy.

All sorts of adaptive arrangements are worked out when there are interferences with the normal course of development, as though the child is determined to reach his best potential by another route when one is blocked. The child with poor eyesight seeks extra information from his other senses. Babies with a tendency toward rickets drink cod liver oil freely if permitted to, selecting their own diets from a wide variety of simple foods [6]. For white children in the northern United States, the characteristics of the home were found to be most important in determining how well the child did at school, but for southern black children the characteristics of the school were more important than those of the home. "It is as if the child drew sustenance from wherever it was available. When the home had more intellectual stimulation to offer, it became more determining; but when the school could provide more stimulation than the home, then the school became the more influential factor." [3, p. 106].

Gesell has stated the principle of optimal tendency as follows. "Every breach in the normal complex of growth is filled through regenerative, substantive, or compensatory growth of some kind. . . . Insurance reserves are drawn upon whenever the organism is threatened. . . . Herein lies the urgency, the almost irrepressible quality of growth" [13, p. 165]. He also writes of a "profound stabilizing mechanism" [12].

Critical Periods

There are certain limited times during the growth period of any organism when it will interact with a particular environment in a specific way. The result of interactions during critical periods can be especially beneficial or harmful. The prenatal period includes critical periods for physical growth. The first three months are critical for the development of eyes, ears, and brain, as shown by defects in children whose mothers had rubella during the first three months of pregnancy. Apparently those organs are most vulnerable to the virus of rubella when they are in their periods of rapid growth.

Limited period of time for specific interaction between organism and environment

Experiments on vision with human and animal infants reveal critical ages for the development of visual responses, times when the infant will either show the response without experience or will learn it readily [9]. If the visual stimulus is not given at the critical age (as when baby monkeys are reared in darkness), the animal later learns the response with difficulty, or not at all.

Psychological development also shows critical periods in the sense that certain behavior patterns are acquired most readily at certain times of life. Critical periods in personality development include the period of primary socialization, when the infant makes his first social attachments [17] and develops basic trust [7]. A warm relationship with a mother figure is thought to be essential among the experiences that contribute to a sense of trust [2]. This type of critical period is probably not so final and irreversible as is a critical period for the development of an organ in the embryo. If the term *critical period* is applied to the learning of skills such as swimming and reading, then it should be understood that it signifies the most *opportune* time for learning and not the only one [14].

Growth takes place upon the foundation that is already there. New parts arise out of and upon the old. Although the organism becomes something new as it grows, it still has continuity with the past and hence shows certain consistencies over time. Through interactions with the environment, the organism continues to restructure itself throughout life, being at each moment the product of the interaction that took place in the previous moment between organism and environment. A toddler's body results from interactions of a baby's body with food, water, and air. The motor pattern of walking is derived and elaborated from creeping and standing. Writing is built from scribbling. Erikson's theory of personality development is epigenetic, each stage being built upon the preceding stages.

Epigenesis

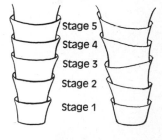

Stage 5
Stage 4
Stage 3
Stage 2
Stage 1

Epigenesis

Dynamic Interrelations in Growth

Growth measures are correlated

It would be surprising if different measures of growth were not related to each other. A tremendous number of studies have probed into the question of interrelationships of growth-controlling and regulating mechanisms.

Correlations between measures of growth can be between measures in the same field (physical–physical, mental–mental, and so on), or in different fields (physical–mental, mental–emotional). Skeletal development, assessed by X rays of the wrist, is at present the best indicator of physiological maturity, although if body proportions could be quantified and scaled in some manageable way, this might prove even more useful. Fat thickness in childhood is also a measure of general physiological maturity [11]. Sexual maturity and eventual height can be predicted with good accuracy from measurements of skeletal maturity. A general factor of bodily maturity operating throughout the growth period influences the child's growth as a whole, including his skeleton, size, physiological reactions, and possibly intelligence. Influencing factors of more limited scope operate independently of the general factor and of each other. One of these limited factors controls baby teeth, another permanent teeth, another the ossification centers in the skeleton, and probably several others regulate brain growth. This is why various measures of physical growth have low positive correlations with each other. If there were only one controlling factor, then the different measures would presumably all correlate highly or even perfectly with one another [18].

Studies of the relation between physical and mental growth show a small but consistent positive correlation, bearing out the hypothesis of a general factor that influences all growth processes. A positive relationship between height and measures of mental ability has been shown in childhood and adulthood, and in various countries [19, p. 149]. In all countries, students are the tallest group in the population. Mentally handicapped adults are, on the average, smaller than normal adults.

Variation in Rates and Terminals

Some people grow faster than others. Some people keep growing longer than others do. Within one individual organism, growth rates vary from one bodily system to another. There are sex differences in growth. These growth variations are common knowledge, and yet it is not enough to say that growth rates vary. In order to understand and predict a child's growth, we need information about patterns of growth that many children have shown. The body as a whole, as measured by height and weight, shows a pattern of velocity that is fast in infancy, moderate in the preschool period, slow during the school years, and fast in the beginning of adolescence. Figure 2–2 illustrates growth of four types of tissue, expressed at each age as percentages of the values for total growth. The general type of growth, which represents not only height and weight but muscles, skeleton, and most of the internal organs, is illustrated by a sigmoid curve, an elongated S. The brain and related tissues grow in a different pattern of velocity, very fast during the first 2 years, moderately until about 6, and very little after that. The growth curve for genital tissue is almost the reverse of that of neural tissue. The genital system grows very little during infancy and childhood and very fast in adolescence. The curve in Figure 2–2 represents the lymph system, designated by the small-dash line, which grows rapidly throughout infancy and childhood, reaches a maximum size just before puberty, and then decreases in size throughout adolescence.

Rates of growth vary from one individual to another. Some children

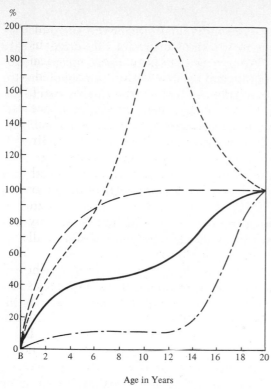

Lymphoid Type
  Thymus, Lymph-nodes,
  Intestinal Lymphoid Masses.

Neural Type
  Brain and Its Parts, Dura,
  Spinal Cord, Optic Apparatus,
  Many Head Dimensions.

General Type
  Body as a Whole, External Dimensions
    (with exception of head and neck)
  Respiratory and Digestive Organs,
  Kidneys, Aorta and Pulmonary Trunks,
  Spleen, Musculature as a Whole,
  Skeleton as a Whole, Blood, Volume.

Genital Type
  Testis, Ovary, Epididymis,
  Uterine Tube, Prostate, Prostatic Urethra,
  Seminal Vesicles.

Age in Years

FIGURE 2–2
Growth curves of the body as a whole and of three types of tissue. Values at each age are computed as percentages of values for total growth. (SOURCE: Reproduced by permission from J. A. Harris, C. M. Jackson, D. G. Paterson, and R. E. Scammon. *The measurement of man.* Minneapolis: University of Minnesota Press, 1930.)

Rates of growth vary between individuals, groups, sexes, bodily systems, and bodily organs

are fast growers, some moderate, and some slow in regard to the number of years taken to reach maturity. Periods of fast and slow growth vary as to when they occur and for how long. One child begins the pubescent growth spurt earlier or later than another, grows faster or slower during the spurt, and finishes sooner or later.

There are sex differences in rates. Early in fetal life, girls show evidence of maturing faster than boys, especially in skeletal development. At birth, girls are four weeks ahead of boys skeletally. Boys' skeletal development is about 80 per cent of that of girls' from birth to maturity [18, p. 43]. Girls are ahead of boys in dentition, as measured by eruption of permanent teeth. Although sex differences in height and weight before the preadolescent growth spurt are very slight, favoring boys, sexual maturity and its antecedent growth spurt occur in girls about two years before they do in boys. Therefore, there is a period of about two years when girls are taller and heavier than boys. At all ages, girls are more mature physiologically than boys.

It is obvious, yet it is essential in understanding growth, to recognize that for different people maturity comes at different points. You have only to walk down the street to observe that some people grow until they are over 6 feet tall, others stop at 5 feet, and most people stop in between. Measurable mental growth stops at different times for different individuals too. The average girl reaches height and weight terminals before the average boy. Little is known about mental growth terminals.

Life and Growth Require Interactions

From the first moment of life, the individual affects the surroundings and is affected by them. Some interactions maintain life; others create new structures and actions. After a brief look at the concept of homeostasis, or maintaining physiological balance within the organism, we shall describe three interactionist theories that deal with growth and development. Piaget's theory offers a way of conceptualizing mental development through the child's own activity and transactions with the world, and the people and objects in it. Erickson's theory deals with the development of the child as a feeling person within a family and a society. Bronfenbrenner's ecological model organizes the total environment in a way that clarifies the child's relation to the various parts of the social and physical world. Throughout the book, we draw upon concepts from Piaget, Erikson, and Bronfenbrenner in order to present the child's development as resulting from his own interactions within his world.

Homeostasis

Balance—Steady state

Homeostasis is a balance that the organism maintains within itself during the processes of living and as environmental influences affect its internal conditions. As the balance is continually upset and re-created, through a complex of interactions, it can be called a *dynamic equilibrium*. Through activities that are mostly unconscious, the individual keeps his blood sugar at a definite level, his water content within a given range, his oxygen content just so. Breathing and heartbeat speed up or slow down from their average rates to restore disturbed balances. The mechanisms of homeostasis regulate sleeping and waking states, activity and rest. Pressures and depleted tissues may register consciously as felt needs, leading to such purposeful interactions with the environment as eating, drinking, and eliminating.

Looming large in the life of a newborn infant, the problems of homeostasis dwindle throughout infancy and childhood. By about 3 months of age, basic physiological processes are well controlled. At any time throughout the life span, however, when the balance is seriously threatened, when biological demands become crucial or urgent, the individual drops his higher-order activities, such as giving a lecture or playing tennis, in order to restore the balance within his body.

Adaptation

Piaget, having been trained as a zoologist, sees the child as a biological organism, adapting to the environment. He considers intelligence as one way of adapting to the environment. Mental activity becomes differentiated out of total activity as the nervous system matures and the child interacts with the environment. The child's efforts are essential to mental development, just as the physical base in the nervous system is also essential.

Processes of Mental Development, According to Piaget [15, 16]. Living organisms interact with the environment by changing it and changing themselves. Piaget calls these processes of adaptation *assimilation* and *accommodation*, as we have already stated in Chapter 1. When a state of balance or harmony in interactions is achieved, the organism is in a state of equilibrium. When a state of equilibrium is upset, the processes of adaptation work to achieve a new state of equilibrium. Development, both mental and physical, takes place as the child moves through more and more complex states of equilibrium. Equilibrium can be upset by finding a new object, being asked a question, identifying a problem; in fact, by any new experience. Equilibrium is re-established by reaching a goal, answering a question, solving a problem, imitating, establishing an effective tie, or any other resolution of the difference between the new experience and the existing mental organization.

Scheme: Organization, structure, pattern, action

A *scheme* (or schema) is a pattern of action or thought. Piaget says, "A scheme is the structure or organization of actions as they are transferred or generalized by repetition in similar or analogous circumstances." [16, p. 4] The newborn infant already possesses some schemes that developed prenatally, such as sucking. A scheme is used for taking in the aspects of the world that it is able to deal with, or almost able to deal with. A child may assimilate an experience to a scheme, or she may change the scheme by accommodating it to fit reality. Sucking is an action-scheme that can assimilate liquids. When solids are introduced, the baby tries to suck them, but soon accommodates the sucking scheme to deal with solids. The result is a scheme of chewing. The following example describe the use of a thought-and-action scheme. A baby has a furry toy kitten that he knows as kitty. When given a small furry puppy he calls it *kitty*, strokes it and pats it, assimilating the puppy to an existing scheme. A new little horse on wheels requires accommodation, since it is too different to be assimilated into the scheme for dealing with *kitty*. It looks different; it feels different; it is not good for stroking and patting, but something can be done with the wheels that cannot be done with *kitty*. A new pattern of action is required. The child accommodates by changing and organizing existing schemes to form a scheme for dealing with *horsey*. Thus the child grows in his understanding of the world and his ability to deal with his experiences in meaningful ways. Assimilation conserves the structural systems that he has whereas accommodation effects changes through which he copes more adequately with his environment and behaves in increasingly complex ways.

When homeostasis presents no problems, such as hunger, thirst, or fatigue, a person looks for something to do, something interesting, a new experience. If equilibrium were completely satisfying in itself, then surely he would sit or lie quietly doing nothing. In looking for action, the child seems to be trying to upset his state of equilibrium, as though he enjoyed the processes of adaptation. And so he does! Activity is intrinsic in living tissue, brain cells included. The nervous system demands input, just as does the digestive system. Indications of human pleasure in mental activity include curiosity, exploration, problem solving, and striving for competence.

*Piaget's stages: Character-
istic structure or organization*

Piaget's Stages of Mental Development. Mental development takes place in three great periods or stages, according to Piaget's theory. There are substages within the main periods. Thinking is structured, and the structures are organized and reorganized through the processes of adaptation. Each stage has a characteristic organization. Each stage results from adapting, reorganizing, and building upon the previous stage. Thus Piaget uses the principle of epigenesis in his theory. The three great periods are these: the sensorimotor period; the period of concrete operations; the period of formal operations. Each child progresses through the stages and substages in the same order as other children, but some go through the stages and substages faster than others. The speed of mental development depends upon organic growth and upon experience in the social and physical world. The three stages and two of the substages will be described briefly. They will be discussed more fully in later chapters, where appropriate.

1. SENSORIMOTOR PERIOD (BIRTH TO 1½ OR 2 YEARS). The baby has neither language nor symbols, but a practical intelligence, consisting of action-schemes. Beginning with the reflex patterns present at birth, the infant adapts them into more and more complex schemes that cope more and more effectively with reality. Piaget distinguishes six substages of the sensorimotor period. These substages will be discussed in Chapter 5. The important achievements of the sensorimotor period are these: a scheme of the permanence of objects, through which the baby realizes that people and objects exist and move even when he is not looking at them; control of the body in space; beginnings of language and imitation, through which the child can represent reality.

2. CONCRETE OPERATIONAL PERIOD (1½ OR 2 YEARS TO 11 YEARS). Operations are actions carried out in the mind. The difference between this period and the sensorimotor period is that the child can represent objects mentally and can act upon them mentally. The period of concrete operations is divided into two large substages, the preoperational stage and the concrete operational stage.

The *preoperational stage* corresponds with early childhood, lasting until about 7 years. This stage is marked by the semiotic function and imitation. The semiotic function, often called *symbolizing*, is the use of an indicator or sign as distinct from the object or event to which it refers. For example, the bell that announces dinner is perceived as distinct from the food but as indicating food. Achievements show much use of his new representational abilities, in deferred imitation (imitation starting after the model has disappeared), symbolic play, drawing, mental images, and verbal representation. The child thinks that names are essential parts of the objects to which they refer. When he gives a reason, it is in terms of how he wants things to be. He sees no need to come to the same conclusions as anyone else because he does not realize the existence of viewpoints other than his own. Throughout this stage the child becomes more flexible in his thinking, more able to use past experience, and to consider more than one aspect of an event at a time.

The *concrete operational stage* from about 7 to 11 years of age is essentially the time when the child can think about real, concrete things in systematic ways, although he has great difficulty in thinking about abstractions. He orders, counts, classifies, and thinks in terms of cause and effect. He develops a new concept of permanence, called *conservation*, through which he realizes that amount, weight, volume, and number stay the same when outward appearances of objects or groups are changed. Although he finds it difficult to change his hypotheses, he learns to take other people's points of view and comes to feel that his reasoning and his solutions to problems should check with other people's. His thinking has become socialized.

3. FORMAL OPERATIONAL PERIOD. The period of formal operations or logical thought begins at about 11 and continues to develop until about 15, when the individual has the mental operations for adult thinking. Instead of having to think about concrete objects, he can think and reason in purely abstract terms. He can think systematically, combining all factors in a situation so as to exhaust all possibilities. He makes hypotheses and tests them. This type of thinking is basic to logic and to the scientific method. The limitation of this stage is a confusion of what could and should be with what is practically possible. The adolescent resists the imperfections in the world when he can construct ideal arrangements in his mind.

Formal operations: Abstract thought and systematic approach

Social Interactions

The processes of life and growth take place within a social environment, as well as a physical one. Without caregivers, an infant would die from lack of food, drink, protection, and stimulation. Without people who talked and played, the processes of adaptation would not have very much to work on. In order to grow up with human characteristics, a child must interact with other people. People are organized in social settings, small and large, some included in others, some overlapping. First, we are going to look at Erik Erikson's way of conceptualizing the child's development as a self and a social being, and then we shall describe Urie Bronfenbrenner's model of the social environment in which the child develops.

Psychosocial Development. Erikson uses Freud's stage concepts (see "Psychoanalysis" in Chapter 1) in his theory of psychosocial development, adding to the complexity of each stage and also adding three stages above the puberal, thus dealing with adulthood as a time for growth. Progress through the stages takes place in an orderly sequence. In making his stages psychosocial as well as psychosexual, Erikson recognizes the interaction between individual and culture as contributing to personal growth. Freud's theory has a great deal to say about pathology, but Erikson's offers a guide to both illness and health of personality. Thus, each stage is a critical period for the development of certain attitudes, convictions, and abilities. After the satisfactory solution of each crisis, the person emerges with an increased sense of unity, good judgment, and

Psychosocial stages: Crisis, solution, outcome

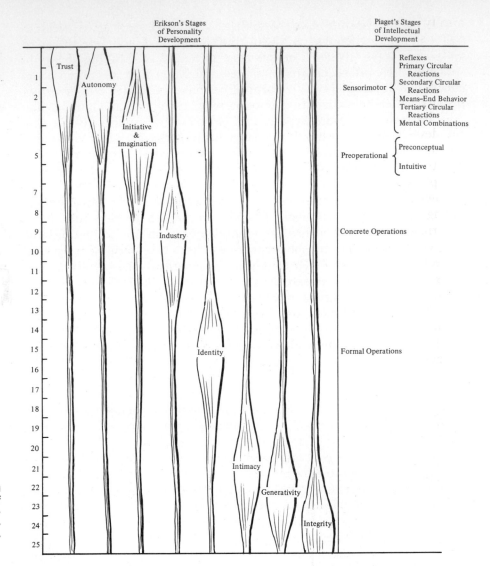

Erikson's Stages
of Personality
Development

Piaget's Stages
of Intellectual
Development

Trust

Autonomy

Initiative
&
Imagination

Industry

Identity

Intimacy

Generativity

Integrity

Sensorimotor

Reflexes
Primary Circular
    Reactions
Secondary Circular
    Reactions
Means–End Behavior
Tertiary Circular
    Reactions
Mental Combinations

Preoperational

Preconceptual

Intuitive

Concrete Operations

Formal Operations

FIGURE 2–3
Schematic representation of Erikson's stages of psychosocial development, with names of Piaget's stages of the development of intelligence.

capacity to "do well" [8, p. 92].   The conflicts are never completely resolved nor are the problems disposed of forever.   Each stage is described with a positive and negative outcome of the crisis involved.

Figure 2–3 shows the normal timing of Erikson's stages of psychosocial development.   The critical period for each stage is represented by a swelling to the rope that stretches throughout life.   The ropes indicate that no crisis is ever solved completely and finally, but that strands of it are carried along, to be dealt with at different levels.   As one rope swells at its critical period, the other ropes are affected and interact.   Solutions to identity problems involve problems in all the other stages.   The metaphor of the rope can also be extended by thinking of the personalities of a family's members as being intertwined ropes. When the parents' generativity strands are becoming dominant, the infant's trust strand is dominant. The ropes fit smoothly together, indicating a complementary relationship between the personalities of infant and parents. Erickson's stages of psychosocial development are summarized in the following paragraphs [7].

1. BASIC TRUST VERSUS BASIC MISTRUST. As in Freud's oral stage, the development of a sense of trust dominates the first year. Success means coming to trust the world, other people, and oneself. Since the mouth is the main zone of pleasure, trust grows on being fed when hungry, pleasant sensations when nursing, and the growing conviction that his own actions have something to do with pleasant events. Consistent, loving care is trust-promoting. Mistrust develops when trust-promoting experiences are inadequate, when the baby has to wait too long for comfort, when he is handled harshly or capriciously. Because life is never perfect, shreds of mistrust are woven into the fabric of personality. Problems of mistrust recur and have to be solved later, but when trust is dominant, healthy personality growth takes place.

2. AUTONOMY VERSUS SHAME AND DOUBT. The second stage, corresponding to Freud's anal period, predominates during the second and third years. Holding on and letting go with the sphincter muscles symbolizes the whole problem of autonomy. The child wants to do for him-

self with all of his powers: his new motor skills of walking, climbing, manipulating; his mental powers of choosing and deciding. If his parents give him plenty of suitable choices, times to decide when his judgment is adequate for successful outcomes, then he grows in autonomy. He gets the feeling that he can control his body, himself, and his environment. The negative feelings of doubt and shame arise when his choices are disastrous, when other people shame him or force him in areas where he could be in charge.

3. INITIATIVE VERSUS GUILT. The Oedipal part of the genital stage of Freudian theory, at 4 and 5 years, is to Erikson the stage of development of a sense of initiative. Now the child explores the physical world with his senses and the social and physical worlds with his questions, reasoning, imaginative, and creative powers. Love relationships with parents are very important. Conscience develops. Guilt is the opposite pole of initiative.

4. INDUSTRY VERSUS INFERIORITY. Solutions of problems of initiative and guilt bring about entrance to the stage of developing a sense of industry, the latency period of Freud. The child is now ready to be a worker and producer. He wants to do jobs well instead of merely starting them and exploring them. He practices and learns the rules. Feelings of inferiority and inadequacy result when he feels he cannot measure up to the standards held for him by his family or society.

5. IDENTITY VERSUS ROLE DIFFUSION. The Freudian puberal stage, beginning at the start of adolescence, involves resurgence of sexual feelings. Erikson adds to this concept his deep insights into the adolescent's struggles to integrate all the roles he has played and hopes to play, his childish body concept with his present physical development, his concepts of his own society, and the value of what he thinks he can contribute to it. Problems remaining from earlier stages are reworked.

6. INTIMACY VERSUS ISOLATION. A sense of identity is the condition for the ability to establish true intimacy, "the capacity to commit himself to concrete affiliations and partnerships and to develop the ethical strength to abide by such commitments". Intimacy involves understanding others and allowing oneself to be understood. It may be, but need not be, sexual. Without intimacy, a person feels isolated and alone.

7. GENERATIVITY VERSUS SELF-ABSORPTION. Involvement in the well-being and development of the next generation is the essence of generativity. While it includes being a good parent, it is more. Concern with creativity is also part of it. Adults need to be needed by the young, and unless the adults can be concerned and contributing, they suffer from stagnation.

8. EGO INTEGRITY VERSUS DESPAIR. The sense of integrity comes from satisfaction with one's own life cycle and its place in space and time. The individual feels that his actions, relationships, and values are all meaningful and acceptable. Despair arises from remorseful remembrance of mistakes and wrong decisions plus the conviction that it is too late to try again.

Human Ecology. Urie Bronfenbrenner, in his concern for the application of knowledge of child development and family relations, has created a model of the developing person in her social environment [4]. The model offers a systematic way of studying a person's interactions.

The child's ecology, the significant environment, consists of several structures. Bronfenbrenner suggests an image of these structures as *nested*, like a set of Russian dolls. The first structure is the immediate setting in which the child is, the home, the classroom, playground, and so on. Each of these immediate settings is a *microsystem*. A microsystem has three dimensions: physical space and materials, people in roles and relationships to the child, and activities that the people carry on with the child and with each other. The second structure, the *mesosystem*, consists of the interrelationships between two or more of a person's microsystems, such as the relationships between home and school, or home and peer group. The third structure, the *exosystem*, is one or more settings in which the child does not participate, but which affect him in one of his microsystems. A child's exosystems usually include his parent's job, and the school board. The fourth structure, the *macrosystem*, is similar to the concept, culture. The macrosystem consists of the patterning of micro-, meso-, and exosystems, along with ideology supporting them, in the subculture or culture. A macrosystem could be that of the United States, of Afro-Americans, of the working class, the Roman Catholic Church, and so on.

Microsystem has space and materials, people, interactions

Mesosystem is relationships between microsystems

Exosystem affects child in microsystem but has no participation by child

Macrosystem includes patterning of systems and supporting ideology

A child goes through an *ecological transition* when her position in the ecological environment changes because of a change in role, setting, or both. Examples of children's ecological transitions are being born, starting in school, having a new sibling, moving, having a grandparent die, traveling, joining a club, and being suspended from school. We know that ecological transitions are usually important events in a person's life. Using Bronfenbrenner's model, such events can be analyzed into manageable units for study. Ecological transitions are both results and causes of development of the person. Such a transition can involve changes in any or all four levels of the ecology. For example, starting to school adds a microsystem and enlarges the mesosystem, and opens the child to new influences from the macrosystem. In the next chapter, we discuss prenatal life and infancy in ecological terms, and birth as an ecological transition.

Ecological transition: Shift in roles and positions and shift in settings

An ecological approach is useful in tackling complex social issues, such as child abuse and adolescent pregnancy. A microsystems approach to child abuse might be to study parent-child interaction in order to find out what type of child behavior serves as a stimulus to parental violence. (Crying may be such a stimulus.) The child's exosystem could be examined for support or lack of support to the parent. If the mother has a network of helpful friends and relatives, she would be less likely to feel stress when with her child. If she has a tiring, low-paying job, then she will be more stressed as a parent. A study of macrosystem variables and child abuse found that abuse was more likely if mothers were poor, une-

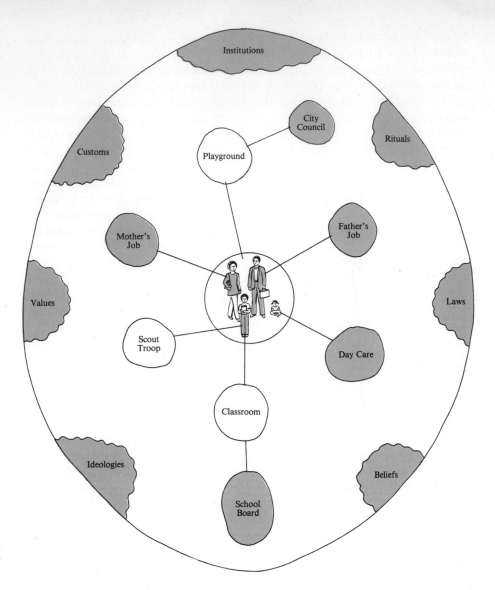

FIGURE 2–4
The ecology of a child. White circles show one child's microsystems; blue areas his exo- and macro-systems.

ducated, and lacking in support systems [10]. Another macrosystem variable in child abuse is cultural permission for physical punishment. Parents and teachers beat and whip children frequently in times and places where physical punishment is approved, and rarely when such punishment is disapproved and/or outlawed.

Summary

Every human being has a unique physical structure and a unique experience in growing up, and yet there are ways in which development is orderly and similar for all. Principles of growth, or generalizations about development include these: *Normative sequence*—physical, motor, mental, and social-emotional development take place in certain orders, even though speed varies from one individual to another; *differentiation and integration*—global patterns of behavior are broken into smaller ones, and smaller ones are put together into larger; *developmental direction*—growth in size and development of motor control take place in a cephalo-caudal, or head-to-tail direction, motor control also taking a proximodistal, or midline-to-extremities direction; *optimal tendency*—the organism grows as though seeking a target to be reached by using any available resources; *critical periods*—at certain limited times in its development, the organism is most able to make use of certain environments or experiences and most vulnerable to certain other environments and experiences; *epigenesis*—growth builds upon the organism that is already there, transforming it, but preserving some continuity; *dynamic interrelations*—different measures of growth correlate imperfectly with each other, suggesting some general overall controlling factors, and some independent controls; *variation of rates and terminals*—different velocities of growth, and different completed growth are shown by different tissues, by individuals, and by the two sexes.

Homeostasis is a physiological equilibrium that the organism maintains. For about the first 3 months of life the equilibrium is rather unstable. Adaptation, the process of achieving a mental state of balance, is basic to Piaget's theory of cognitive development. Adaptation consists of two complementary processes: assimilation, in which the organism takes something from the environment and uses it; and accommodation, in which the organism changes itself to fit the environment. Piaget's stages of cognitive development are these: sensorimotor, from birth to 18–24 months; concrete operational, from 1½ or 2 years to about 11 years; and formal operational, from 11 to about 15 years. A social environment is required for mental development, as well as for physical, social, and emotional development.

Erikson's theory of psychosocial development, built on Freud's theory, holds that personality growth occurs as the child interacts within a family in a culture. Each stage represents a critical period for solving a certain type of problem, the outcome of which affects ability to deal with subsequent problems. The problems that characterize each stage are these: basic trust versus basic mistrust, birth to 18 months; autonomy versus shame and doubt, 18 months to 3 years; initiative versus guilt, 3 or 4 to 6 or 7; industry versus inferiority, 7 to 11 or 12; identity versus role diffusion, 12 to 18-plus; intimacy versus isolation, the 20s; generativity versus self-absorption, 20s onward; ego integrity versus despair, adulthood.

In Bronfenbrenner's ecological model, the child's development is studied in terms of processes within the child and contributions of different levels of the environment to the child's interactions. The environmental levels or systems are as follows: macrosystem, or overall society, culture, or subculture, within which smaller systems are patterned, and the patterning supported by ideology; microsystem, a physical setting containing interacting people, in positions related to each other, and acting according to roles; mesosystem, or relationships and communications between microsystems; exosystems, the microsystems of the other persons in one's own microsystem, but from which one is excluded; social networks, or persons with whom one has regular face-to-face interactions and ongoing relationships, but not necessarily in one's microsystems.

References

1. Bower, T. G. R. *Development in infancy.* San Francisco: W. H. Freeman and Company, Publishers, 1974.
2. Bowlby, J. *Attachment and loss.* Vol. I. *Attachment.* New York: Basic Books, 1969.
3. Bronfenbrenner, U. *Two worlds of childhood.* New York: Russell Sage Foundation, 1970.
4. Bronfenbrenner, U. *The ecology of human development.* Cambridge, Mass.: Harvard University Press, 1979.
5. Burns, G. W. *The science of genetics.* New York: The Macmillan Company, 1969.
6. Davis, C. M. Self-selection of diet by newly weaned infants. *American Journal of Diseases of Children,* 1928, **36,** 651–679.
7. Erikson, E. H. *Childhood and society.* New York: W. W. Norton & Company, Inc., 1963.
8. Erikson, E. H. *Identity, youth and crisis.* New York: W. W. Norton & Company, Inc., 1968.
9. Fantz, R. L. The origin of form perception. *Scientific American,* 1961, **204,** 66–72.
10. Garbarino, J. A preliminary study of some ecological correlates of child abuse: The impact of socioeconomic stress on mothers. *Child Development,* 1976, **47,** 178–185.
11. Garn, S. M. Fat thickness and developmental status in childhood and adolescence. *Journal of the American Medical Association,* 1960, **99,** 746–751.
12. Gesell, A. Maturation and the patterning of behavior. In C. Murchison (ed.). *A handbook of child psychology.* 2nd ed. Worcester, Mass.: Clark University Press, 1933.
13. Gesell, A. *The embryology of behavior.* New York: Harper & Row, Publishers, 1945.
14. McGraw, M. B. Major challenges for students of infancy and early childhood. *American Psychologist,* 1970, **25,** 754–756.
15. Piaget, J. *Six psychological studies.* New York: Random House, Inc., 1967.
16. Piaget, J. and B. Inhelder. *The psychology of the child.* New York: Basic Books, Inc., Publishers, 1969.
17. Scott, J. P. *Early experience and the organization of behavior.* Belmont, Calif.: Brooks/Cole, 1968.
18. Tanner, J. M. *Education and physical growth.* London: University of London Press, 1961.
19. Tanner, J. M. *Foetus into man: Physical growth from conception to maturity.* Cambridge, Mass.: Harvard University Press, 1978.

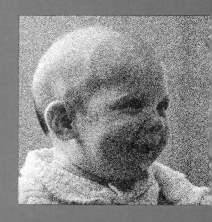

Prenatal
Life and
Infancy

3

From Egg to Baby

The ideal start for a human being is to be wanted by a young, healthy, adult couple who commit themselves to caring for their offspring. The ideal could be broadened to include a loving extended family of grandparents, aunts, and uncles, a sibling at least three years old who is eager for a baby, a helpful network of friends and neighbors, and a society that supports family life and health. Many conceptions occur under less than ideal conditions, and many healthy babies are born. The study of prenatal development will lead to more and more understanding of how to conduct a pregnancy that insures the best possible growth from egg to baby. This chapter is concerned with the development and ecology of the ovum, the embryo, and the fetus, and with the birth of the baby.

QUESTIONS TO THINK
ABOUT WHILE READING
THIS CHAPTER

1. What is an excellent environment for prenatal development?
2. How are the ovum, embryo, fetus, and baby distinguished from one another?
3. How does the development of the embryo illustrate the principles of development?
4. How does the fetus interact with its microsystem?
5. How is birth outcome related to the mother's age, physical adequacy, emotional life, and nutrition?
6. How can the fetus be safeguarded from damage?
7. How is the fetus influenced by the exosystem and macrosystem?
8. How does the macrosystem shape the conduct of labor and delivery?
9. What are some of the leading problems in birth outcome?
10. How can the conduct of pregnancy, labor, and birth be improved?

Stages of Prenatal Development

After the father contributes the sperm that fertilizes the mother's ovum, his only influence on the future baby is through the mother. The mother's bodily rhythms determine the timing of fertilization; the fetus determines the timing of birth.

From Fertilization to Implantation

At about the middle of each menstrual cycle (the thirteenth or fourteenth day of a 28-day cycle), a mature ovum reaches the middle of the Fallopian tube in its journey from the ovary to the uterus. Fertilization takes place

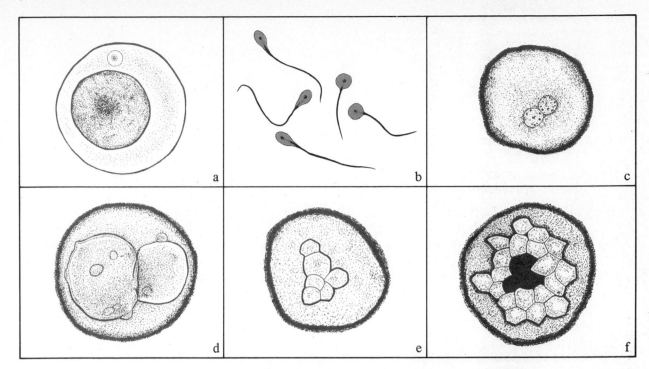

here, when a sperm penetrates the egg. If the sperm bears an X chromosome, a female is conceived, if a Y, a male.

The ovum is a little ball about the size of a dot that looks a lot like a chicken egg when viewed under a microscope. Figure 3-1 shows a greatly magnified human egg. A tough membrane encloses a layer of whitish fluid, inside which is a yolk-like central portion. The little ball inside the white layer is a polar body, containing unused chromosomes. Unable to move by itself, the ovum is swept down the Fallopian tube by suction, expansion and contraction of the tube, and hair-like parts of the tube that lash back and forth. The sperm that must meet the ovum partway down the tube if fertilization is to take place is one of 500 million, more or less, contributed by the father some time during the past 48 hours. Ever so much smaller than the egg, the sperm swims by lashing its long tail. Many sperm will probably bump against the egg before one succeeds in penetrating the egg's tough outer membrane. Although more than one sperm may penetrate the membrane, only one sperm's nucleus unites with the nucleus of the egg. The male and female nuclei lie side by side for a few hours before they merge to form the *zygote*, the fertilized egg. The egg splits into 2 cells. The 2 cells form 4 cells and the 4 cells 8. After 72 hours, the ovum has grown into 32 cells, and after four days, it consists of 90 cells. Note that there is a cavity in the center, and cells are clustered around it. It is in this state that the organism, now called a *blastocyst*, leaves the Fallopian tube and enters the uterus, where it floats for one or two days before settling itself into the lining of the

FIGURE 3-1
Fertilization and growth of the egg.
Top row: (a) A human egg, greatly magnified. (b) Male and female sperm cells. (c) A fertilized egg. Male and female nuclei lie side by side for a few hours before uniting.
Bottom row: (d) A few hours after the male and female nuclei merge, the egg splits into two cells. (e) During the first 72 hours of life, the ovum grows into 32 cells. (f) At four days of age, the ovum consists of about 90 cells. (SOURCE: After photographs by Landrum Shettles in E. H. Havemann, *Birth Control.* Time, Inc., 1967.)

FIGURE 3–2
These outlines, 60% of actual size, show the rapid growth of the human organism from ovum to fetus. The dot at the left represents the egg. The drawings show organisms at 1, 14, 16, 18, 20, 22, 25, 30, 42, 56, and 84 days of age. The period of the embryo ends with the 56th day. Only the largest and last drawing represents a fetus. (SOURCE: E. L. Potter, *Fundamentals of human reproduction.* New York: McGraw-Hill, Inc., 1948.)

Ovum: from fertilization to implantation 0–2 weeks

uterus. The outer layer of cells, the *trophoblast*, produces tendrils, or villi, that burrow into the uterine lining and connect the ovum with the uterine wall. This process, called *implantation*, marks the end of the stage of the ovum and the beginning of the stage of the embryo.

The Embryo

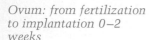

Embryo: from end of 2nd week to end of 8th week

The individual is called an embryo during the time that the various organs and tissues are being differentiated and formed, from the end of the second week to the end of the eighth week. Mosslike villi extend from the embryo into the blood spaces of the maternal uterus, forming a means of exchanging body fluids. Protective and supportive membranes, the *chorion* and *amnion*, take form. The amniotic sac enclosing the embryo begins to fill with fluid.

The head comes first in the developmental sequence. The head of the embryo is one-half of its total length; of the newborn, one-quarter, of the adult, one-tenth. These ratios illustrate the principle of developmental direction, described in Chapter 2, which holds for lower animals as well as for man and for function as well as for structure. The principle is that *development proceeds* from head to tail. The drawings in Figure 3–2 show the great speed of increase in prenatal height and weight. Figure 3–3 represents the development of the organs and systems at one month, greatly enlarged. The true size of a one month embryo is between that of the eighth and ninth silhouettes in Figure 3–2. From its appearance it is hard to tell a human embryo from any other embryo.

The Fetus

Fetus: from 8 weeks to birth

At eight weeks, the organism is beginning to look human, although changes are gradual. A new name is applied. From the end of the eighth week until birth, the individual is called *fetus* instead of embryo. Complete with face, neck, arms, legs, fingers, toes, some calcification of its bones, and functioning internal organs and muscles, the fetus is ready to build upon the basic form that has been laid down. Table 3–1 shows highlights of fetal development.

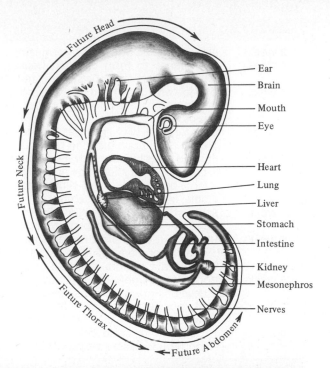

FIGURE 3–3
The month-old embryo has the foundations of many organs and systems. (SOURCE: After M. S. Gilbert. *Biography of the unborn.* Baltimore: Williams & Wilkins, 1938.)

The fetus at about seven weeks. This photograph is about three times life size. The face has eyes, ears, nose, and lips. The arms have hands, with fingers and thumbs. The legs have knees, ankles, and toes. (Courtesy of the Carnegie Institution of Washington)

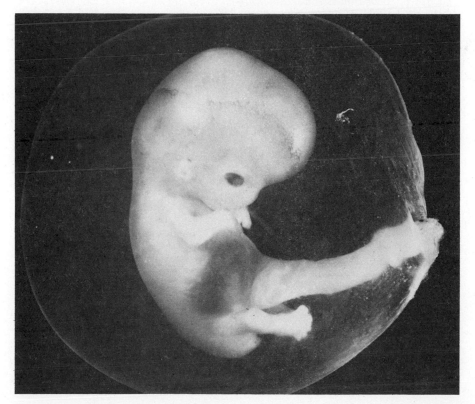

TABLE 3–1
Highlights of Development of Embryo and Fetus

Age	Developmental Characteristics
2 weeks	Flat embryonic disc with 3 germ layers.
3 weeks	Disc arches to form cylinder; beginnings of alimentary canal, kidney, heart, nervous system, and muscles.
4 weeks	C shape with large head end, tail, limb buds, gill slits, and bulging, beating heart; beginning of eyes, nose pits, ears, lungs, and jaws.
6 weeks	Face forming, with lips, eyes on sides, paddlelike limbs; cartilage beginning; brain growing rapidly, bending forward.
8 weeks	Embryo looks human, with jaws, ears, fingers, and toes; tail almost covered; head about half of total length; forehead bulges with large brain; ossification centers; testes and ovaries distinguishable; limbs move with trunk.
12 weeks	Sex distinguishable; eyelids sealed shut; buds for deciduous teeth; vocal cords; digestive tract, kidneys and liver secrete.
16 weeks	Head about one-third of total length; nose plugged; lips visible; fine hair on body; pads on hands and feet; skin dark red, loose, wrinkled; rapid brain growth.
20 weeks	Body axis straightens; vernix caseosa covers skin as skin glands develop; internal organs move toward mature position.
24–28 weeks	Eyes open; taste buds present; 6 layers of cerebral cortex. If born, can breathe, cry, and live for a few hours.
28–40 weeks	Fat deposited; rapid brain growth; nails develop; permanent tooth buds; testes descend. Fetus becomes viable.

Sources: G. S. Dodds. *The essentials of human embryology,* 3rd ed. New York: John Wiley & Sons, Inc., 1946. M. S. Gilbert. *Biography of the unborn.* Baltimore: Williams & Wilkins, 1938. B. M. Patten. *Human embryology,* 2nd ed. New York: McGraw-Hill Book Company, 1953. E. L. Potter. *Fundamentals of human reproduction.* New York: McGraw-Hill Book Company, Inc., 1948. H. V. Meredith. Somatic changes during human prenatal life. *Child Development,* 1975, **46**, 603–610.

The latter half of prenatal life is a period of preparation for birth and independent living. Most important is the maturing of the nervous system, which must organize and coordinate all the other systems. The establishment of breathing, the most precarious step into the outside world, will be determined largely by the condition of the nervous system.

Figure 3–4 shows growth in length and weight during the prenatal pe-

FIGURE 3–4
Mean length and weight of the human fetus from 10 weeks to birth. (SOURCE: H. V. Meredith. Somatic change during human prenatal life. *Child Development,* 1975, **46**, 603–610.)

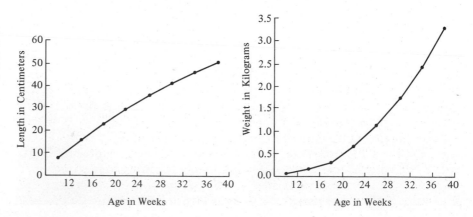

riod, along with some landmarks of development. Male fetuses grow faster than female. The male's placenta and the male fetus are larger than the female's placenta and the female fetus [35].

The Placenta and Cord

The *placenta,* an organ that serves the fetus' growth needs, is a part of the fetus that is discarded at birth. Derived from the *trophoblast,* which sends tendrils into the uterine lining of the mother, the placenta grows into an inch-thick disk, about 7 inches across. One side of it is attached to the mother's uterus and the other side to the fetus' umbilical cord. In the early stages of pregnancy, the placenta does the work of kidneys, intestine, liver, endocrines, and lungs, adjusting its function as the fetus grows its internal organs. Through the placenta the fetus gets nutrients and oxygen from its mother and sends carbon dioxide and other waste products into her body for disposal. The fetus' and mother's bloodstream do not mix, however, except for the occasional escape of small amounts of the fetus' blood into the mother's. They exchange products through the walls of tiny blood vessels that lie close to each other but do not run into each other. This system is the *placental screen.* Bodies carrying immunity pass through the screen from mother to fetus, thus giving the child some protection for several months after birth from the diseases to which the mother is immune. The placenta makes hormones that affect both fetus and mother, directing development of the mother's body in ways that nurture the fetus and prepare her body for birth and lactation. An inadequate placenta is likely to cause poor development in the fetus.

The umbilical cord is derived from the body stalk, which is differentiated out of the trophoblast. Connecting the placenta to the fetus, the cord in utero looks like a stiff rope or tube, about 20 inches long. Blood flows through the cord at a high rate. Since the cord in under pressure, it is not flexible enough to knot in the uterus. Only during the birth processes, when it becomes slack, is there any possibility of danger from the baby getting tangled in it. At that point, of course, the physician or midwife will take care of such an emergency.

Ecology of the Fetus

Extending Bronfenbrenner's ecological model of human development (described in Chapter 2), the mother *is* the microsystem in which the fetus lives. The mother's body is the physical setting. Unlike the child living in the microsystem of the home, the fetus never interacts with father and siblings, and never gets out to another microsystem, such as the school or playground. The fetus is in constant interaction with the mother microsystem, drawing nourishment from the food she has eaten, converted into nutrients and delivered through the placenta, taking in protective antibodies that she has manufactured in her blood, listening to her voice, her heartbeat, and intestinal rumblings, moving as she moves, and feeling the restricting walls of her uterus. The fetus gives off products into the amniotic fluid and via its blood, the placenta, and the maternal blood, to the mother's kidneys. The mother feels the fetus move, sometimes in response to experiences that she can identify, such as music, sudden loud noises, or a long period of inactivity on her part. The mother's body grows and develops throughout pregnancy in response to the growing fetus, which grows in response to her body. Her thoughts and feelings are also part of the microsystem, acting through her nervous system and blood to affect her own body and her fetus. Settings and persons that affect the mother microsystem constitute the exosystem of the fetus. Father, siblings, grandparents, and friends of the family are important parts of that exosystem. The macrosystem affects the fetus through its medical and health system, laws, welfare system, teachings on prenatal care, and the occupational system. Figure 3–5 illustrates the ecology of the fetus.

FIGURE 3–5
The ecology of the fetus. The fetus is in its only microsystem, the mother. The fetus's exosystem includes members of the mother's family, her friends, and her doctor. Significant parts of the macrosystem are shown around the outside of the diagram.

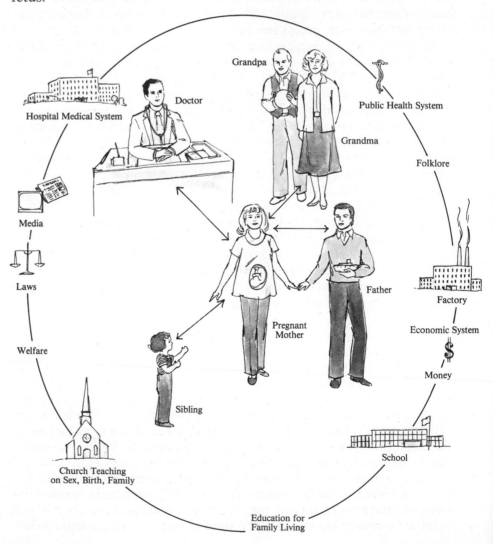

TABLE 3–2
Conditions Affecting the
Microsystem of the Fetus

Making for an optimal microsystem	Making for a less than optimal microsystem
Mother between 20 and 35 years old	Emotional disturbance
Mother well-nourished throughout life	Heavy physical labor
Mother in good health	Extreme heat
Previous baby 2 or 3 years old	Massive X rays
Socioeconomic status average or higher	Drugs, including tranquilizers, nicotine, alcohol, marihuana
Adequate nutrition	Polluted air
Prenatal care	Disease organisms
Rh treatment, if needed	

Mother Microsystem

What makes an optimal microsystem for a fetus? Mother microsystems are almost unfailing in providing body temperature, liquid surroundings, nutrients, antibodies, and hormones. Quality and quantity of nutrients vary. So do the type, quantity, and timing of hormones. Waste products are removed more or less adequately. The amniotic fluid and the placenta protect the fetus from harmful organisms and substances, but they cannot keep out certain ones if the mother ingests them. It is up to the mother to eat adequate foods, to avoid smoking, and ingesting alcohol, and all other drugs (unless medically necessary), and to avoid becoming infected with damaging diseases, such as rubella and syphilis. In addition to supplying the needed substances and keeping out the harmful ones, the mother must build and maintain her own health if she is to function as a good microsystem for her fetus. (See Table 3–2.)

Age and Parity. The only time a woman of 35 is considered elderly is when she is having her first baby. In this case, she is called an "elderly primipara" by the medical profession, a logical term in light of the fact that the childbearing period is more than two-thirds over.

Figure 3–6 shows the condition of babies at birth, according to the age and ethnicity of their mothers. The curves are based on Apgar scores, which combine five measures of well-being, heart rate, respiratory efforts, muscle tone, reflex irritability, and skin color. The graph shows percentages of births in which Apgar scores are less than 7, indicating poor condition. The heavy lines show scores for 1 minute after birth, the dotted lines for 5 minutes after birth. The figure shows that infants born to very young and very old mothers were more likely to receive poor Apgar scores than were infants born to mothers between 20 and 35 years of age, especially between 25 and 29. At all maternal ages, percentages of low-scoring babies were higher for black mothers than for white, suggesting the depressed economic status of black people [38a].

When risk to the baby is estimated, it makes a difference which portion of the first year of life is considered. Although death rates are stated in terms of the mother's age and parity (number of pregnancies she has had), it must be remembered that both age and parity have different signifi-

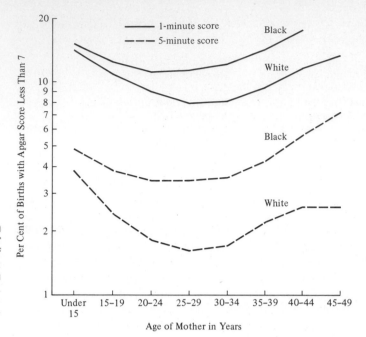

**FIGURE 3–6
Per cent of live births with 1- and 5-minute Apgar scores less than 7, by age of mother and race.** (Source: Querec, L. J. Apgar score in the United States, 1978. *Monthly Vital Statistics Report*, vol. 30, No. 1, Supplement. May 6, 1981.)

Birth risks vary with birth order, age of mother, and spacing

cance in different sociocultural settings. Stillbirths rise with increasing age and fall with parity up to the fourth pregnancy. The lowest rates are in the 20- to 24-year-age group and the highest is in mothers 35 and over. Death within the first month occurs most often with high parity in the youngest age group and next often to mothers of high parity in the oldest age group. The death rate between one month and 11 months rises with increasing parity and falls with increasing age. Prematurity rates are highest among mothers below 19, with the exception of first babies born to mothers over 35, who have the highest prematurity of all [24]. Older mothers are also more likely to produce children with Down's syndrome. Before age 30 the risk of having a baby with Down's syndrome is 1 in 1,000, whereas at age 40 it is 1 in 100. Older fathers have also been implicated in Down's syndrome [23a]. When defects of all kinds are counted, very young mothers and older mothers produce more impaired infants than do mothers in the ages in between [37].

In summary, the first birth carries an extra risk; aging and repeated births add risk. Close spacing is also risky. Babies born within one year of a previous gestation were matched with controls born two to five years after the previous gestation. Matching was done for sex, race, hospital of birth, and socioeconomic status [21]. Their gestation ages were equal, but when born within a year of an older sibling, babies averaged significantly smaller birth weights, lower scores on the Bayley tests at 8 months, and lower Stanford-Binet IQs at 4 years. At one year of age, the average baby in the experimental group had a smaller head and slower motor development than the average control baby.

When birth-order effects are studied in children and in adults, IQ is found to decrease with parity [3, 6]. Because the decrease is greater in poorer families, it is likely that prenatal deficits are made worse by the environmental handicaps of low socioeconomic status. The detrimental effects of closely spaced, frequent births are thought to be caused by depletion of the mother microsystem, shown by inadequacy of the placenta. Several sex hormones decrease with each birth, especially with closely spaced ones [29].

Physical Adequacy. How good an environment can the mother's body provide for the growing fetus? After she has delivered, the placenta can be examined for signs of adequacy, but in giving prenatal care, this method of judging adequacy is not available. Some ways of evaluating the mother microsystem have been developed by measuring stature [24].

Studies from several different countries have shown a relationship between height of mother and reproductive performance. Mothers judged poor in physique tended to be short and to have flattening of the pelvic brim. Short mothers are more likely to have complications of pregnancy and delivery, and to produce babies with lower birth weights, greater prematurity, more birth trauma, and more stillbirths. The relationship between stature of mother and physical well-being of baby is not thought to be a direct one, but, rather, both conditions are results of a socioeconomic environment. A poor environment, supplying inadequate food, housing, clothing, sanitation, and education, will stunt the physical and mental growth of children living in it. Short stature is thus associated with low education, early marriage, premarital pregnancy, premature delivery, longer labor, absence of family planning, frequent pregnancies, poor diet, poor housing, and poor use of information, health services, and social services [24].

General health can be evaluated in many other ways, in a physical examination given by a physician, supplemented by laboratory tests. Although not the custom at present, it seems to us that when planning to start a baby, the future mother could well get herself into the best possible physical shape before conceiving. Her nutritional condition at the start of pregnancy may be just as important as food intake during it.

Nutrition. The woman who starts her pregnancy in good nutritional condition is fortunate, because she can thus provide the optimal environment for her baby right from the beginning. A nutritional defect is difficult to correct when the demands upon the body are increased by pregnancy. The very fact of being well nourished shows that the woman has established a pattern of eating an adequate selection of foods in amounts suited to her. She will not have to change her ways of eating other than to increase the amounts slightly as pregnancy advances. The two main sources of fetal malnutrition are a *poor maternal diet* and *placental insufficiency* [47]. Animal studies show that a poor maternal diet before and/or during pregnancy results in fewer brain cells in the fetus and also increases the harmful effects of postnatal malnutrition on later brain growth. Placental insufficiency, according to animal experiments, may produce changes in enzymes and in the protein content of the cerebellum. Placental insufficiency may result from curtailment of cell division, in maternal malnutrition [34].

Adequate nutrition requires enough calories, as well as food elements in sufficient quantities. Weight gain, a rough index of nutrition, is related to birth weight. Although obstetricians used to try to limit a woman's weight gain during pregnancy, they no longer do so. It is important to gain enough weight. The best results are likely when a mother gains 10 to 12 kilograms (22 to 27 pounds), gaining 1 or 2 kilograms (2 to 4½ pounds) during the first trimester and averaging around 400 grams a week after that [38]. These recommendations and the following ones come from the chairman of the Committee on Nutrition of the Mother and Preschool Child, of the National Academy of Sciences–National Research Council.

Extra protein is needed beyond the 45 grams a day required by nonpregnant women. Estimates of the extra amount vary from 10 to 30 grams.[38]. Although salt used to be restricted for a pregnant woman,

FIGURE 3–7
Average weight gain in pregnancy. (SOURCE: After a drawing in N. Newton and C. Modahl. Pregnancy: The closest human relationship. *Human Nature*, 1978, **1**:3, 47.)

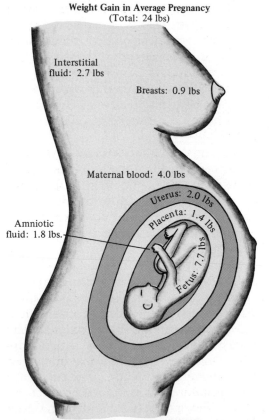

Weight Gain in Average Pregnancy
(Total: 24 lbs)

Interstitial fluid: 2.7 lbs

Breasts: 0.9 lbs

Maternal blood: 4.0 lbs

Uterus: 2.0 lbs

Placenta: 1.4 lbs

Amniotic fluid: 1.8 lbs.

Fetus: 7.7 lbs

Weight gain unaccounted for: 3.5 lbs

present thinking is that she needs a little more sodium than when not pregnant, and that taste should guide her in salting food. The fetus needs calcium and will take it from the mother's body if it is not supplied generously. The mother also needs extra calcium, probably in preparation for lactation. One quart of milk will provide the necessary 12 grams of calcium. A pregnant adolescent needs even more, because she is still growing. Because it is almost impossible for a pregnant woman to eat enough iron, supplements of 30 to 60 milligrams of elemental iron are recommended daily until three months after delivery. The need for folate doubles in pregnancy, making the requirement at least 800 micrograms. The need for vitamin B_6 increases .5 milligram beyond the 2 milligrams required ordinarily. Other vitamin requirements increase somewhat. Trace metals, especially zinc, chromium, and copper, are also important in reproduction. With the exception of iron and folate, all these nutrients can be provided by eating a varied diet rich in fresh foods and avoiding foods that are high in calories and/or additives but low in the nutrients here mentioned.

Because malnutrition of the fetus leads to low birth weight and poor mental and physical development, studies of nutritional supplementation have been carried out in many countries. As expected, if poorly fed women are given extra food during pregnancy, their babies weigh more at birth [8]. Examples of such programs follow.

Supplemental food is a benefit

In Taiwan, birth weights increased by an average of 150 grams when mothers were given additional proteins, vitamins, and calories. When Guatemalan mothers received an extra 20,000 calories, infant birth weights increased by 20 grams per 1,000 calories, no matter whether the calories were fed to the mother during the final trimester or throughout the pregnancy. Nutritional supplementation improved the condition of mothers and infants in a poverty area of New York City.

In Montreal, clinic patients were given measured amounts of supplementary foods in diets designed to fit each pregnant woman's individual needs, along with nutritional counseling and supervision [20]. Diets were adjusted in terms of pregnancy requirements, age, ideal body weight, actual weight, physical activity, degree of undernutrition, multiple fetuses, and stress. Included under stress were pernicious vomiting, pregnancies spaced less than one year apart, poor obstetrical history, failure to gain enough weight, and extreme anxiety from personal or family matters. For each stress condition, 200 calories and 20 grams of protein were added. The patients in this program had infants whose birth weights averaged 3,284 grams, or 276 grams more than those in a control group. Infants born to private patients in the same hospital averaged 3,276 grams at birth. Thus, the nutrition program erased the usual socioeconomic difference in birth weight. Another benefit to the group in the program was having fewer induced deliveries than did mothers in the control group. The United States has a supplemental food program for women, infants, and children that provides special foods, nutritional education, and some medical care [1]. The 1978 figures showed over 600 local programs and 720,000 participants, but as this book goes to press, the program is being reduced.

Emotional Well-Being.   Folklore says that a pregnant woman should be calm and happy, thinking positively, listening to good music, looking at beautiful scenes, and avoiding all disturbing experiences. This idea is valid, because research shows that the fetus and future child are affected by the mother's emotional experience during pregnancy. An experiment with positive experiences was conducted with women in their first pregnancy during the third trimester [16]. Deep muscle relaxation training was given for 7 weeks in addition to a regular course of training for childbirth. A control group had only the regular course. Infants of both groups were studied on the second day of life. The babies of the first group cried less. These results suggest that a relaxed mother microsystem is likely to produce a calm baby.

Maternal emotions affect fetus

There is little doubt that maternal emotional stress affects the fetus adversely. Depending on the timing and severity of the mother's upset, results may be the death of a fertilized ovum [40], bodily abnormalities [18; 44], physical complications of childbirth [18], and gastrointestinal malfunction and feeding problems in the newborn baby [9]. The health, development, and behavior of school-age children were related to prenatal stress by studying a cohort, all of the 1,300 children born during one year in a Canadian city [44]. Among children who had at least 20 per cent more illness than the cohort as a whole, the following conditions were present in their mothers during their prenatal life. The mothers suffered these conditions at least one and a half times as often as the average: respiratory illnesses; physical stresses such as standing all day or carrying heavy loads; and situational stresses, including fears about marriage, marital discord, money problems, shocks and worries over people or pets, and tensions involving people outside the family. Almost as high in frequency were other family tensions like being upset at moving away from her parents, not settled in her own home, not wanting the pregnancy, wanting an abortion, marital infidelity, out-of-wedlock conception, and having incurred heavy debts. In regard to situational stress, the investigators concluded that it was ongoing stress, or situations in which the pregnant woman felt trapped that resulted in damage to the fetus.

Protection from Physical and Chemical Damage.   The physical safety of the fetus depends upon keeping the mother microsystem free from all sorts of harm. She may be stressed by heavy labor or extreme summer heat. Massive X-ray doses are lethal or seriously damaging to the fetus. After World War II, the effects of atom bomb radiation on children who had been in utero at the time included increased defects and illnesses [51].

Many drugs taken by the pregnant mother can affect the fetus, some apparently temporarily and some drastically and permanently. Quinine can cause deafness. The tranquilizer thalidomide caused thousands of tragic births in Germany, England, and Canada, where its prenatal use produced babies lacking limbs or with limbs in early stages of embryonic development. Many other substances, including mild tranquilizers such as meprobamate (Miltown and Equanil), and chlordiazepoxide (Librium) [31] may cause deformities if taken during the period of the embryo when organs and systems are forming and growing rapidly. These findings illustrate the developmental principle of *critical periods*, described in Chapter 2.

When a pregnant woman smokes a cigarette, she reduces oxygen and nutrients going to the fetus, concentrates nicotine in her blood, and raises her blood pressure. An examination of fetuses at 8 months showed that all reacted within 30 minutes to their mothers' smoking, decreasing their chest movements and stopping breathing movements entirely for short periods [14]. Some of the outcomes of smoking during pregnancy are well known [37]. When pregnant women smoke, they are more likely to have a premature baby and/or a baby small for gestational age. These infants, of course, have a greater risk of dying, being ill, and having defects. Reports of research continue to confirm and extend these findings. A sample of several thousand British children were followed from birth to 11 years [7]. Physical and mental retardation were found more frequently in children whose mothers smoked during their prenatal life. Defects increased with the numbers of cigarettes smoked after the fourth month. Compared with children of nonsmokers, children of smokers of ten or more cigarettes per day were retarded in reading, mathematics, and social adjustment.

Heavy drinking during pregnancy has detrimental effects on birth weight and behavior of the newborn [11; 46]. Even the moderate amounts of alcohol consumed in social drinking can affect the baby's health adversely.

Marijuana may also endanger the fetus. It has been implicated in birth defects in children [42] and has been demonstrated to cause deformities and stillbirths in rats [52]. Hard drugs have different harmful effects on the fetus because they localize in different tissues, such as the thyroid, the pigment of the eye, the skeleton, and even in the yolk sac of the embryo [48]. A number of studies have shown withdrawal symptoms in babies born to addicted mothers [45]. Symptoms include irritability, excitability, tremulousness, excessive nervous system reactions, and great sensitivity to light. Death and defects also result from drugs such as heroin and barbiturates [19].

Oral contraceptives pose a threat to the embryo if conception takes place immediately after the woman discontinues her use of the pill. Like cigarette smoking, oral contraceptives induce high vitamin A levels in the blood [52]. The combination of smoking and taking oral contraceptives increases blood levels of vitamin A to greater heights. The interaction of drugs with nutrients is a new area of research that holds promise for giving more understanding of birth defects.

Pollution of air, water, and earth is a growing problem for everyone.

The fetus is especially vulnerable, because immature organisms are most easily damaged. Although the mother microsystem defends the fetus with the strength of the placental screen, many human-made substances can pass through it.

Protection from Invading Organisms. Certain organisms, especially viruses, are able to cross the placental screen. The embryo, being more immature than the fetus, is most likely to incur severe damage, but both embryo and fetus are at risk when the mother contracts rubella, rubeola, hepatitis, syphilis, smallpox, chickenpox, scarlet fever, tuberculosis, or malaria. A world-wide epidemic of rubella in 1964 left 20,000 to 30,000 defective babies in the United States. (European-derived people are more susceptible to rubella than many other ethnic groups [22].) A study performed on a sample of these children found that 40 per cent were premature and many of these were small for their gestational age [7a]. Only 20 per cent had no observable defect. Eleven per cent had defects in all major areas, hearing, visual, cardiac, and neurological. Over half of the children had psychiatric disorders, with various combinations of mental retardation and serious mental illness. Efforts are being made to treat these children and to help their families. Immunization campaigns have since reduced the likelihood of pregnant women contracting rubella. A family may choose to terminate a pregnancy that has only a 20 per cent (or even a somewhat larger) chance of producing a normal baby.

Preventing Damage from Hormonal and Blood Conditions. Endocrine problems, such as hypothyroidism and Addison's disease in the pregnant woman, require special medical care but can be managed [27, p. 32]. Diabetic women have higher chances of producing infants with defects, including hypoglycemia and heart, respiratory, and blood problems. Good medical care is important here. Administration of sex hormones during pregnancy has various and complex effects on fetal development.

Rh hemolytic disease of the newborn can be prevented, but about 7,000 babies are affected by it each year because the means of control are not fully applied [43]. The Rh factor occurs in the blood of most people. About 15 per cent of white women, lacking Rh, are Rh negative. When a negative Rh mother has a positive Rh baby, there is a chance that some fetal blood will get into the maternal blood and stimulate production of antibodies. If the mother has another Rh positive baby, these antibodies may destroy the blood of the fetus. If, however, the mother is inoculated with Rh-immune globulin (RhoGam) immediately after the birth of the first Rh positive baby, the next baby will be safe. Why has Rh hemolytic disease not been fully prevented? Some babies are still being born to women who were sensitized before the discovery of the RhoGam method in 1968. Other women do not receive the inoculation because it is expensive, perhaps $100. Sensitization can occur after an abortion, if the embryo was Rh positive and the mother negative. If the abortion has not been performed under conditions of good medical practice, then ignorance and neglect can lead to maternal sensitization and future hemolytic disease of the newborn.

Coping with Chromosomal Defects. Throughout the world every year, more than 700,000 infants are born with Down's syndrome (mongolism) or one of the other serious abnormalities due to a defective chromosome [30]. Although many of these children will die young, others will live as retarded children and adults. Chromosomal defects can be detected prenatally, and termination of the pregnancy considered. For those parents who give birth to a genetically abnormal child, life is difficult, and much is needed in support from their microsystems and exosystems. The medical system in the United States is more competent in caring for these children in early infancy than in giving lifelong care and family support [17].

Prenatal Care. Preconceptional care is desirable for all, though few receive it. Those who do are likely to be those with problems. Genetic counseling may be sought by couples who suspect or know that they have adverse heritable conditions. They can find out what are their chances of having a normal baby, and what are their options should they conceive a defective one. Infertile couples may look for diagnoses and treatments that will help them to conceive. Handicapped persons, such as diabetics, may ask for medical help in planning a pregnancy.

Prenatal care includes evaluation, monitoring, treatment, and education of the mother microsystem by someone skilled and knowledgeable in obstetrics. The caregiver also examines histories of both parents for genetic defects that pose risks. In many countries midwives are the chief caregivers, perhaps with physicians as consultants. In the United States, physicians are the main givers of prenatal care, but the popularity of nurse-midwives is growing. The sooner a pregnant woman gets prenatal care, the better for her and her embryo, fetus, and baby. For normally developing mother microsystems, the main part of prenatal care is education of the woman as to how to take care of herself and how to prepare for giving birth and breastfeeding. Weight gain is watched and nutritional advice given accordingly. The caregiver examines and tests repeatedly, watching for clinical signs of normalcy. Immediate attention to slight deviations can prevent bigger problems. Plans can be developed for a delivery suited to the mother-baby pair.

The American College of Obstetricians and Gynecologists recommends prenatal visits every four weeks for the first 28 weeks, every 2 weeks until 36 weeks, and weekly thereafter. A nationwide survey showed that only 17 per cent of mothers followed this plan [43]. When mothers made the recommended 13 or 14 visits, only 3 per cent of their babies had low birth weights of 1,200 grams or less. Among mothers making only one or two visits, 22 per cent of babies had low birth weights.

Preparation for birth is usually separate from prenatal visits. In a La-

Medical check-ups are important

Maze course, probably the most popular kind throughout the industrialized world, mother and father attend classes to learn how to work together in controlling labor and delivery. The couple also begin to prepare for parenting. In the process they usually grow closer to each other.

The Exosystem

The exosystem of the fetus includes all the systems in which the mother is involved. All of her face-to-face situations affect her in some ways, and so do the relations between these settings and people. Everything that affects the mother affects the microsystem of the fetus, including home, neighborhood, prenatal caregiver, and perhaps a job.

Home Exosystem. The home setting influences the fetus because it is so important in the well-being of its mother microsystem. The chief character in the home exosystem is usually the father. If he and the mother have a happy, satisfying relationship, then she is unlikely to be anxious or depressed. Niles Newton says, "When pregnancy begins with a rich emotional and sexual relationship, mother and fetus continue the pattern. Many psychological and physiological patterns learned in the parents' relationship with each other are carried over to create a bonding between parents and child" [33].

One of the father's important functions is to encourage the mother to attend classes to prepare her for childbirth and to go with her to the classes that include fathers. Mothers are unlikely to attend when fathers discourage them from going. The father is likely to be more helpful during labor when he has been to these classes. Therefore the mother is helped during labor by what she has learned in class and also by what her husband has learned [5a].

In cultures where mothers, daughters, and sisters are very close, as among the Akan of Ghana, or even in some American ethnic groups, the husband may not play such an important role during pregnancy. A pregnant woman's support may come from her mother, sister, or friend if not from her husband or partner, but it must come from someone if she is to be a good microsystem for her fetus. Support is physical: helping with the housework, carrying the groceries, and mending the broken step. Support is psychological: making plans for the baby, encouraging the expectant mother to take the outdoor exercise she needs, admiring her pregnant shape, and reassuring her when she is afraid.

If there are already children in the home, they may be burdens, as well as supports. If a child is 4 or 5, she will probably want a baby sibling and will be eager to share and help during the pregnancy. The younger the child, the more disturbance is likely to result from the new baby, and the more physical work must be borne by the mother.

Social Network. The mother's friends and relatives are also part of the exosystem of the fetus. These people give support, make demands, and share ideas. A mother often gets information, ideas, and values from her network. Friends tell all about their pregnancies and deliveries, making recommendations about prenatal care, what to buy for the baby's room, and what to eat. The mother-to-be often has a surge of warmth and closeness toward her own mother, as she realizes that they are sharing experiences they have not shared before. If members of the network disapprove of a pregnancy, as they often do with out-of-wedlock pregnancies, their responses may be more burdensome than supportive.

Job Exosystem. If a pregnant woman likes her job, and it is not physically stressing, then it probably has little effect on her fetus. Pregnant women need extra rest, however, especially during the first and last trimesters. If a mother is planning to return to her job, she may be anxious about holding the job and about managing both job and baby. Generous maternity provisions would help. The United States is not as advanced in the provision of maternity and paternity benefits as are many other countries, especially Sweden.

Prenatal Care Exosystem. The person who gives prenatal care is a very important person to the mother, and through her, to the fetus. The caregiver will most likely be a physician, assisted by nurses. It could be a midwife. It may even be a partner or friend. The mother gains confidence in herself as the microsystem when she develops trust and cooperation with her caregiver. A woman may have to be assertive in order to get the kind of prenatal care that makes her feel competent in the venture of childbirth. If she cannot assert herself enough, she can be helped by the father or a member of the network.

Macrosystem

Prenatal development and birth are greatly affected by the macrosystem in which they take place. Table 3–3 suggests the power of macrosystems to determine life or death for an infant. The table compares regions of the world on some indicators of social and economic conditions.

Every culture has its own way of patterning pregnancy and childbirth [50]. The rites of pregnancy, or formal acts established by custom and authority, give guidance and protection to the mother. They guide her through the physiological changes she is undergoing and through the change in social role, especially the transition into parenthood. Macrosystem influences include values, beliefs, laws, customs, and institutions. If pregnancy is believed to be an illness, and childbirth agonizing, then many mother microsystems will feel sick, tense, and afraid, and they will send upsetting biochemical substances through their bloodstreams, through their placentas, and into their fetuses. If meat and fish are thought to be too rich for pregnant women to eat, then those women will rarely eat enough protein to fuel the growth of a normal number of fetal brain cells. If the pregnant woman is entitled to special indulgence and care from her mother and family, as are many Indian women, then she may well produce a relaxed baby.

In the macrosystem of the United States there are three factors or conditions that have great significance to childbearing. They are the medical system, poverty, and adolescent childbearing.

Medical System. Childbirth has been medicalized, controlled by the medical profession and hospitals. A normal biological process has been treated as an illness. Men have become the authorities on childbirth. The system has worked well for ill and at-risk mothers and babies, who would die without expert and technical treatment. The system has promoted research and the development of instruments and procedures. Medicalized childbirth is very costly for all mothers, normal ones, as well as high-risk patients.

Beliefs and practices are changing. Some women are giving birth at home or in homelike birth centers, attended by family members, midwives, and perhaps a physician. Some hospitals have reorganized space and procedures to make normal births more rewarding and less frightening. There is some danger of losing the benefits of medicalized childbirth while shedding its restrictions. Prenatal care is still needed in order to guide normal pregnancies and to identify mothers and fetuses who need treatment. Even a normal delivery is facilitated by a skilled attendant.

Poverty. During the first 4 weeks of life, the baby of a very poor family is 1.6 times more likely to die than a baby born to a family above the poverty line [15]. If she lives in poverty, a mother is less likely to be an adequate microsystem to her fetus. Prenatal care, for example, is not

TABLE 3–3
Selected Indicators of Social and Economic Conditions, by Regions, About 1975

Indicators	World	World Regions						
		Northern America	Europe	U.S.S.R.	Oceania	Latin America	Asia	Africa
Life expectancy at birth (years)	60	73	71	69	68	62	58	46
Infant mortality (per 1,000 live births)	99	15	20	28	41	84	105	147
Birth rate (per 1,000 pop.)	29	15	15	18	21	36	30	46
% of calorie requirements met	107	134	130	136	127	107	97	91
Physicians (per 10,000 pop.)	8.8	16.5	16.6	29.7	11.0	7.3	3.1	1.1
Nursing and midwifery personnel (per 10,000 pop.)	22.7	63.6	37.5	59.8	31.1	7.4	7.5	7.0
GNP per capita (U.S. $)	1650	7850	4420	2760	4730	1100	610	440

Source: M. C. McHale, J. McHale, and G. F. Streatfeild. *Children in the World.* Washington: Population Reference Bureau, 1979. P. 29.

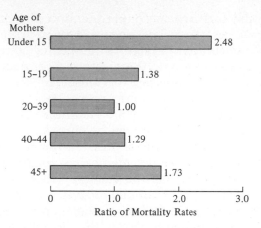

FIGURE 3–8
Ratio of infant mortality rate of mothers 20 to 39 years old to infant mortality rates of younger and older mothers. (SOURCE: R. J. Armstrong. *A study of infant mortality from linked records by birth weight, period of gestation, and other variables.* National Center for Health Statistics. Data from the National Vital Statistics System. Series 20, No. 12. DHEW Publication No. (HSM) 72-1055. Washington, D.C.: U.S. Government Printing Office, 1972.)

equally available to poor and not-so-poor mothers. A number of states do not provide prenatal care under Medicaid to women in their first pregnancies [15]. What is more, poor mothers are likely to be under stress from inadequate nutrition, crowding, extremes of temperature, pollution, and interpersonal problems. We have the knowledge necessary for improving the life chances of poor babies, but our society is not applying it fully.

Adolescent Childbearing. More than half a million babies are born each year to American teenagers. Births to teenagers are increasing as a proportion of all births [32]. Therefore an increasing proportion of infants are exposed to the risks of having an adolescent mother. With an unmarried teenage mother, the first birth is likely to occur at an earlier age than with a married one, increasing the risk to the baby. A government study found 332,000 teenage mothers living with their offspring. Over half had incomes below the poverty level. Over 80 per cent had less than 12 years of education. Unmarried teenagers are less likely than adults to receive adequate prenatal care. Therefore they run greater risk of having a premature baby or a baby of low birth weight. An infant born with such a handicap is especially vulnerable to living in poverty with only one parent of low educational level. Adolescents run a greater risk of having their babies die at birth than do women between 20 and 40, as shown in Figure 3–8.

The delivery date is calculated on the pregnant woman's first prenatal visit, by adding 280 days to the first day of her last menstrual period. This date is an approximation. Only 4 per cent of women deliver on the 280th day; 46 per cent deliver within a week of that date; and 74 per cent within two weeks of it. Being born and giving birth are physical crises for the two persons most concerned. The crises are emotional, also, for their family.

The Birth Process

Processes and Stages of Labor

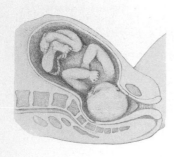

Labor is the work that the mother does in giving birth. Three distinct stages can be described. *The first stage*, requiring the major portion of the duration of labor, is the opening of the cervix or neck of the uterus. It begins with rhythmic uterine contractions, which are usually felt as pains. Two types of muscular forces work to enlarge the cervical openings. The uterus resembles a pear-shaped balloon whose walls are made of very strong muscle fibers. The fibers contract, exerting about 30 pounds of pressure on the fluids surrounding the fetus. The membranes enclosing the fluids press on the tiny opening in the lower end of the uterus. After the membranes break (the mother cannot feel this), the baby presses on the opening. At the same time another set of muscle fibers, which surround the tiny opening, are relaxing to allow the opening to enlarge. As these muscular processes continue, the tissues of the cervix are pulled back into the general roundish shape of the uterus. When the cervix is completely dilated, the diameter of the opening is about 10 centimeters. The first stage may take 2 to 16 hours or more [33].

The muscular processes of the first stage of labor are involuntary. The only way in which a woman can influence them is through relaxation. General bodily relaxation, due to the absence of fear, plus confidence, facilitates the relaxation of the muscle fibers surrounding the cervix; fear and tension increase their resistance to stretching and may result in pain. One of the purposes of education for childbirth is to induce relaxation. When a father prepares for childbirth and helps the mother during labor, she experiences less pain and more enjoyment [5a].

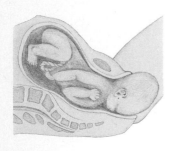

The second stage lasts from the time that the cervix is completely open until the baby emerges from the mother. For a first baby this stage usually lasts over an hour; for the second, it may take only a few minutes [33]. The uterus continues to push the baby out. The mother adds a bearing-down action to it, pushing with her diaphragm, but involving her whole body. Although she bears down spontaneously, without teaching or conscious thought, a great deal of this activity can be placed under conscious control. Education for childbirth includes teaching the mother to breathe, relax, and bear down in a manner calculated to facilitate the natural labor processes. The confidence factor is just as important in the second stage as in the first in promoting control and either eliminating pain, reducing it, or making it more bearable. The *third stage* is the expelling of the placenta and membranes. It lasts only a few minutes.

An overall average for the length of labor is about 14 hours, divided among the three stages about like this: first stage 12½ hours; second stage 80 minutes; third stage 10 minutes. The second stage requires about 20 contractions for a first baby and 10 or less for subsequent babies. For a first baby, half of the women in a study of nearly 15,000 cases took less than 11 hours; half took more. The most common length of labor was seven hours. Women who had already had at least one baby had shorter labors; half under approximately six hours and half over, with the most common length of labor being four hours [10].

When a normal birth is impossible or dangerous, the baby may be delivered by Caesarian section, a procedure of cutting the mother's abdomen and uterus to remove the baby and then, of course, the placenta. Although this surgical procedure used to be very dangerous, it now carries relatively slight risk. A Caesarian section is much safer for mother and baby than a difficult forceps delivery or a breech birth through a narrowed pelvis. Although there is no limit to the number of Caesarian births that one patient can have, each repetition means that the scar in the uterus is stretched by the pregnancy and hence runs a small risk of rupturing.

Medication for Pain of Labor and Delivery

Pain relievers have been used liberally in the United States. Perhaps American women have experienced higher pain levels at delivery than have women in cultures where childbirth is more natural than medical, where women deliver with the aid of gravity in an upright position rather than lying on their backs, and where the surroundings are familiar and familial, rather than cold and lonely. When mothers are given heavy doses of pain killers, sedatives, and/or general anesthesia, they and their babies (who receive the drugs through the placenta) usually sleep and drowse for hours or days. Their interaction with each other is delayed. Researchers are now asking whether obstetrical medication does permanent harm to infants.

Newborn infants' responses to obstetrical medication have been found to include delayed onset of respiration, poor muscle tone, irritability, drowsiness, and depressed sucking, consolability, and attention [2]. Developmental tests at 3 months [23] and visual tests at 4 and 5 months [12] have not shown effects of medications used at birth. Authors of the first study, which included Israeli and Uruguayan infants, as well as American, concluded that *light* obstetrical medication does not seem to affect newborn infant behavior significantly. Another question to consider is the effect of such medication on the reciprocal behavior of mother and infant immediately after birth.

Courses in preparation for childbirth may reduce the need for obstetrical medication. When a mother feels in control, confident that she knows what to do and that she will have skilled help and loving support, she may not want to have memory and consciousness blotted out. The moment of delivery may be extremely satisfying, even ecstatic. Even when a Caesarian section or other surgery must be done, local anesthetics make it possible for the mother to be awake to greet her baby. It seems desirable that childbirth customs in the United States change in the direction of giving lighter medications when drugs are needed to control pain.

The Baby During Labor

Labor marks the beginning of the ecological transition (see Chapter 2) out of the mother microsystem into the home microsystem, probably with a brief sojourn through the hospital. The change from fetus to baby is probably the biggest transformation a person ever experiences, except,

perhaps, for dying. The full-term fetus is prepared and equipped to make the journey out of the uterus through the birth canal. The largest part of the body, the head, is somewhat collapsible.

The important bones of the baby's head are separated by the sutures, membranous spaces that feel soft to the touch. Where several sutures meet, the space is called a *fontanelle*. During labor, the infant's head adapts by becoming narrower as the bones squeeze closer together. They may even overlap. The molding, or squeezing together, may result in a head that looks misshapen at birth, but within a few days, the head resumes a normal shape.

The fetal heartbeat responds to each uterine contraction by speeding up, slowing down, and then speeding up again. As labor progresses, the fetal heart beats very fast, slowly, or irregularly. During a strong uterine contraction, the fetal blood cannot get oxygen from the placenta. The increasing concentration of carbon dioxide stimulates the respiratory center and hence the beginning of breathing after birth. Amniotic fluid and mucus escape from the baby's air passages during expulsion of the baby, because of compression of its chest. The attendant may remove excess mucus from the mouth and throat, using a soft rubber syringe. Most babies begin breathing by themselves. If an infant does not breathe, slapping, cold water, and other stimulants are no longer used; instead a careful resuscitation is done [10].

Leboyer, a French obstetrician, maintains that the standard methods of treatment of newborns is very harsh and that a gentler transition to extrauterine life benefits the baby physically and emotionally [26]. He delivers the baby into a softly lighted room and places her prone on the mother's bare abdomen where she can feel warmth, softness, and rhythmic movement, the same as before birth. The mother feels satisfaction, too. The baby slowly relaxes and extends her limbs. After a gentle, rhythmic massage, the baby is put into a bath that is slightly warmer than body temperature. She moves her hands and feet and may smile.

Birth Injuries and Defects

With a big head (a result of a big brain), the human being often has a hard time being born. Kangaroos and bears, born when very tiny, do not run into the same problems. In spite of the wonderful ways in which mothers stretch and babies' heads narrow during the birth process, brain injuries sometimes occur. The infant is equipped to stand some deprivation of oxygen while being born, but when the oxygen deprivation is prolonged, the brain may be damaged. Many such injuries are very slight and their effects may not even be recognized later on. Other brain injuries are very severe, with death the final degree of severity. A multitude of birth injuries fall in between these extremes. From their many studies, Pasamanick and Knobloch [37] conclude that there is a "continuum of reproductive casualty." Some of the more serious results of complications of pregnancy and birth are mental retardation, cerebral palsy, epilepsy, and disorders of behavior, speech, and reading. The associated maternal conditions include toxemias; bleeding; premature birth; difficult, prolonged, or precipitate labor; malpresentation; and major illnesses. Neurological tests on the newborn can often detect minor, as well as major, injuries and can be used to guide caregiving. The degree to which a newborn is *at risk* is estimated by using combinations of tests and observations. Testing for metabolic disorders, such as PKU (phenolketonuria), is usually done soon after birth, because early treatment prevents much of the damage that would otherwise occur. Congenital anomalies (birth defects) and injuries re noted on the birth certificate. Table 3–4 shows incidences of anomalies and injuries, found in a nationwide survey. More anomalies are found in boys than in girls, in lightweight than in normal babies, in babies of older mothers, and in babies born within a year of a previous birth.

Fetology, the branch of medical science that deals with the fetus, has techniques for diagnosing and treating fetal illnesses and imperfections, thus making it possible to prevent many birth defects. One of its techniques is *amniocentesis*, the drawing off of amniotic fluid through a tube put through the mother's abdominal and uterine walls and into the amniotic sac. Analysis of the fluid can show genetic defects, such as Down's syndrome. The sex of the fetus can be determined, and this information may be important in a family that is known to have sex-linked defects, such as hemophilia. The fluid can also show if the fetus is ill and how ill it is from causes such as blood incompatibility. The fetus might be saved by a blood transfusion or a Caesarian delivery. Another diag-

	Anomalies per 100,000 births	Birth injuries per 100,000 births
Girls	678	179
Boys	955	251
Total	821	216

TABLE 3–4a
Congenital Anomalies and Birth Injuries per 100,000 Births

Condition	Anomalies per 100,000 births
Weight	
2,500 grams or less	1,894
More than 2,500 grams	727
Mother's age	
Over 40	1,710
25–29	779
Birth spacing	
Less than 1 year since previous birth	920
4 years since previous birth	788

TABLE 3–4b
Congenital Anomalies per 100,000 Births Under Differing Conditions of Weight, Mother's Age, and Previous Gestation

Source: S. Taffel, *Congenital anomalies and birth injuries among live births: United States, 1973–74.* Vital and Health Statistics: Series 21, Data from the National Vital Statistics System, Data on Nationality, Marriage, and Divorce: No. 31. (DHEW Publication No. (PHS) 79–109.) Hyattsville, Md.: National Center for Health Statistics, 1978.

nostic technique is examination with an *amnioscope,* an instrument for lighting and viewing the inside of the uterus from the birth canal. It is possible to draw a blood sample from the head of the fetus through the birth canal. Fetal surgery is performed by making a small opening in the mother's abdomen and uterus, inserting a catheter into the fetus or giving other treatment, and then closing the incision in the mother. Research on animals has demonstrated the possibility of much more complicated fetal surgery. Other techniques that have stimulated advances in diagnosis and treatment include *thermography,* a way of mapping the pregnant mother through heat waves, and ultrasonics, or mapping of the fetus by sound waves and electrocardiograms of the fetus.

Prematurity and Low Birth Weight

A baby is premature if the gestation period is less than 37 weeks, measured from the mother's last menstrual period. A birth weight of less than 2,500 grams indicates prematurity or inadequate prenatal growth, or both. More babies of low birth weight are born in poor countries than in prosperous ones, and in low socioeconomic groups than in higher ones. Low birth weight is also a danger signal, since 80 to 90 per cent of infant deaths in the United States are of babies who weigh less than 2,500 grams [27]. From one-third to one-half of low-birth-weight babies are probably not premature, but growth-retarded. The survival rate of growth-retarded infants is higher than that of prematures, but the former are more likely to have genetic defects [13]. When handicaps were asssessed at 10 years of age, in children whose birth weights were *very* low, under 1,500 grams, severity of handicap was related more strongly to birth weight than to gestation length [28]. In planning care for such infants, it is important to estimate gestation length as accurately as possible. Low socioeconomic status has a particularly depressing effect on mental development of low-birth-weight infants, especially if they are boys [49].

Growth-Retarded Infants. Infants who are small for their gestational age are also called "small-for-date babies." Whatever term is used, it implies that the fetus did not grow as fast or as much as the average fetus does during gestation.

Growth retardation is often associated with anomalies and mental and neurological impairment. Therefore, it is likely that genetic and early embryonic influences are important, although maternal malnutrition may also contribute to intrauterine growth retardation [27, pp. 110–124]. The mother's long-term prepregnant nutrition may have a greater effect than nutrition during gestation. Small babies usually have small placentas and sometimes defective placentas [13]. The size attained by the fetus is probably limited by the amount of placental tissue serving it. Twins are usually smaller than singletons, because their placentas (if fraternal) or placenta (if identical) do not allow them as much placental tissue as a singleton has. The smaller of a set of twins usually has had the smaller amount of placental tissue. One of the greatest threats to growth-retarded babies is hypoglycemia. Therefore, care includes monitoring of blood sugar levels.

Premature Infants. A baby who is premature but not growth-retarded has the development, both physical and behavioral, typical of his *gestational* age. Some of the best criteria used for diagnosing prematurity are evaluation of muscle tone and reflexes; only one or two transverse creases on the ball of the foot; scalp hair that is fine and fuzzy; ear lobes that are pliable and lacking in cartilage; small breast nodules; testes that are not fully descended, and a small scrotum [27]. Additional measures for estimating gestational age are head circumference and changes in the electroencephalogram. A promising new measure is that of measuring visual preferences [36]. The most serious threat to survival of a premature baby is hyaline membrane disease, which makes the lungs unable to expand [13]. In the United States, 25,000 premature infants die yearly from this disease. Preventive measures for it are being developed.

Causes of prematurity include obstetrical complications and environmental factors of cigarette smoking, high altitudes, toxemia, chronic vascular disease, rubella, syphilis, and malaria [13]. These conditions also apply to some cases of intrauterine growth retardation.

Because earlier studies of low-birth-weight children did not distinguish between prematurity and growth retardation, subsequent measures of the progress of these children group the two types together. Older studies found that infants of low birth weight grew into small children who continued to be smaller than average, but later studies showed that infants who weighed at least 2,000 grams at birth were not markedly below average as children [27].

A careful diagnosis of prematurity was made on the subjects of a longitudinal study in France and California [4, 5]. After the evaluation at 10 years, reports were made on the significance of prematurity and recommendations for care and education of premature children. One very positive finding was that the delays in mental development seen early in life had often disappeared entirely by 4 years, even in children born very early. There were persistent problems in behavior and emotional life that the authors traced to the basic problem of disturbed bodily-spatial relationships and concepts. A test of imitation of gestures surveyed a child's ability to imitate simple and complex gestures with hands and arms, ability to locate right and left in relation to self and others, body knowledge, and body image. A test of opposite gestures was one of the most highly diagnostic of the premature child. Failure on this test was highly related to IQ, drawing, reading, and speech articulation, all of which are significant for success in school. Remedial education can improve performance in all of these areas, especially if started early.

Prevention of Deficits in Premature Infants. Granted that the premature baby is born with some deficits as compared with full-term infants, much can be done to prevent further problems from developing while the baby completes growth to full-term level, and afterward. Indeed, a highly supportive, responsive environment seems to wipe out the effects of early complications; caregiving by deprived, stressed, poorly educated parents tends to make early problems worse [41].

Because the last two months of intrauterine life is the time when the fat is laid down under the skin, a premature baby looks red and wrinkled, as compared with a full-term baby. The head looks extra big for the tiny body. The very immature infant may not be able to suck and swallow. Feeding the right nutrients is a problem, even though mechanical devices can put the food into the baby's stomach. Human milk may be even more important for the premature infant than for a mature one. A premature baby may not be able to make *cystine,* an amino acid contained in human milk but not in cow's milk [13]. Even if the infant has to be kept in an incubator, the mother can express her milk, to be given by bottle or tube. By doing so she will not only feed the premature baby essential nutrients but will keep her milk flowing for the time when the baby can nurse. A milk bank may be used if the mother cannot produce her own milk.

Prematures need adequate stimulation

The question of adequate stimulation for the premature baby is important. As mentioned earlier, the fetus is constantly stimulated by the mother's movements and the sounds from her interior. The premature baby lies in an incubator or heated crib where there is little change, especially change of a rhythmic nature. Because the mother, as well as the infant, is deprived of opportunities for building bonds, new programs are bringing infants and their mothers together. Mothers, and fathers, too, are encouraged to visit and care for their babies. In one successful program, mothers systematically stroked their premature infants for 15 minutes and rocked them for another five minutes, four times a day for 30 days, beginning when the baby came home from the hospital [39]. Another effective treatment program used oscillating waterbeds [25]. Compared with controls, the infants showed greater neurological maturation, higher mental functioning, and greater weight gain.

Parental anxiety over the premature is one hazard to later development that may be minimized by acquiring expertise in the premature nursery. These parents need counseling and support even more than most new parents. A comprehensive child development service would be ideal in order to meet needs that will arise at later ages, as, for example, the premature child's need for motor education and help in developing bodily orientation to people and the world.

Improving Reproductive Performance

From the foregoing, it may seem as though having a baby is fraught with peril and problems both for parents and offspring. It might even appear that ignorance is bliss, since people have been having babies for ages without knowing about all the things that can and do go wrong. They have been blaming physical and mental handicaps on chance, nature, or even God's will, rather than upon the biological and environmental processes that are really responsible. A great deal is now known about how to produce healthy, well-developed children and competent parents. The problem is how to implement the knowledge at all levels of the ecology. As Figure 3–9 shows, the United States continues to improve in survival rates of infants. Infant mortality has decreased dramatically over the past 40 years. Survival rates for white infants compare well with those of the most advanced and prosperous nations, while rates for nonwhite infants resemble those of nations with centrally planned economies. Table 3–5 shows mortality rates in different types of countries. But there is much more to health than survival, as shown by the photograph on the following page of a healthy, normal, alert, beautiful newborn baby.

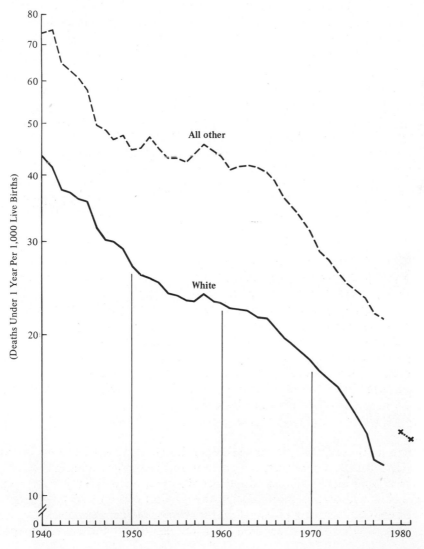

FIGURE 3–9
Mortality rates for white and nonwhite infants. The +··+ at far right represents mortality rates for all infants for 1980 to 1981. (Sources: Office of Health Research, Statistics, and Technology. Final mortality statistics, 1978. *Monthly Vital Statistics Report: Advance Report.* DHHS Publication No. (PHS) 80-1120. Vol. 29, No. 6. Supplement (2), Sept. 17, 1980. National Center for Health Statistics. Births, marriages, divorces and deaths, 1980. *Monthly Vital Statistics Report.* DHHS Publication No. (PHS) 81-1120 Vol. 29, No. 12, March 18, 1981.)

TABLE 3–5
Infant Mortality Around
the World, 1970–75

Country groups (number)	Deaths per 1,000 live births
Industrialized countries (20)	15
Developing countries	
High-income (20)	25
Upper-middle-income (23)	35
Intermediate-middle-income (30)	48
Lower-middle-income (22)	88
Low-income (25)	129
Centrally planned economies (7)	25

Note: The figures are median values of available data. The most recent infant mortality rate for the United States is 12.5, in 1980.
Source: World Bank. *World Atlas of the Child*. Washington: World Bank, 1979. Pp. 14–15.

Summary

A mature ovum in a Fallopian tube, during the middle of the menstrual cycle, is penetrated by a spermatozoon of either male or female type. The fertilized ovum is propelled to the uterus, where it implants itself into the lining and becomes an embryo. The basic forms of tissues and organs develop during the embryonic period. At 8 weeks of age, the organism is called a fetus, since its appearance makes it more recognizable as human. Structure and functions differentiate further. The head end is more advanced in development than is the tail. The fetus moves freely.

In the ecology of the fetus, the mother is the microsystem, enclosing, sustaining, and interacting with the fetus. The growth and health of the fetus depend upon her physical adequacy at the beginning of and

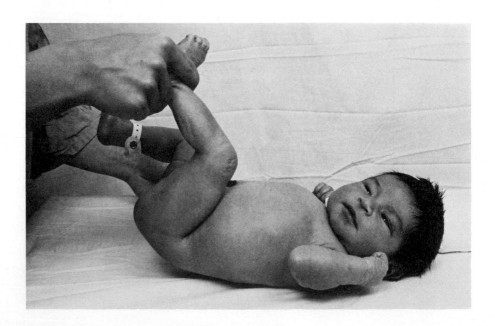

throughout pregnancy. Nutritive needs increase during pregnancy. Adequate weight gain is related to normal birth weight, normality, and survival. Maternal emotions and stress affect the fetus. Damage can occur from drugs, including nicotine and alcohol, from invading microorganisms, and from pollution. The mother microsystem is affected by her own microsystem, which is the exosystem of the fetus. This exosystem includes father and other family members, social network, prenatal caregiver, and perhaps a job. The macrosystem patterns the way in which pregnancy and childbirth are understood and managed. The macrosystem also structures institutions, laws, customs, and conditions that have direct and indirect influences on childbearing. Poverty, medicalized childbirth, and adolescent childbearing are especially relevant to childbearing in the United States.

Labor proceeds in three stages, the opening of the cervix, the expulsion of the fetus, and the expulsion of the placenta. The fetus is prepared to withstand the rigors of being born. Education for childbirth promotes relaxation in the first stage and controlled relaxation and action in the second stage. Self-confidence and trust in the assistants help to produce a positive emotional state. Some women, and some couples, experience tremendous joy in childbirth.

Through knowledge and techniques from fetology, obstetrics, and child development, many defects can be prevented and others diagnosed and treated early. Low-birth-weight babies are premature and/or growth-retarded. Careful diagnosis facilitates appropriate treatment. Prevention of deficits includes adequate feeding, stimulation, and emotional reactions in the family and throughout childhood, monitoring of development, support and education for parents, and psychomotor education.

References

1. Ade, W. Special supplemental food programs for women, infants and children. *Young Children*, 1978, **33:**6, 58–59.
2. Aleksandrowicz, M. K. The effect of pain-relieving drugs administered during labor and delivery on the behavior of the newborn: A review. *Merrill-Palmer Quarterly*, 1974, **20,** 121–141.
3. Belmont, L., and F. A. Marolla. Birth order, family size, and intelligence. *Science*, 1973, **104,** 1096–1101.
4. Berges, M., I. Lezine, A. Harrison, and F. Boisselier. The "syndrome of the post-premature child": A study of its significance, Part I. *Early Child Development and Care*, 1972, **1,** 239–284.
5. Berges, M., I. Lezine, A. Harrison, and F. Boisselier. The "syndrome of the post-premature child": A study of its significance, Part II. *Early Child Development and Care*, 1973, **2,** 61–94.
5a. Block, C. R., K. L. Norr, S. Meyering, J. L. Norr, and A. G. Charles. Husband gatekeeping in childbirth. *Family Relations*, 1981, **30,** 197–204.
6. Brown, B., and P. L. Nichols. Reversal of body weight trends in higher parity siblings. Paper presented at meeting of the Society for Research in Child Development, New Orleans, 1977.
7. Butler, N. R., and H. Goldstein. Smoking in pregnancy and subsequent child development. *British Medical Journal*, 1973, **5892,** 573–575.

7a. Chess, S. The influence of defect on development in children with congenital rubella. *Merrill-Palmer Quarterly*, 1974, **20**, 255–274.

8. Coursin, D. B. Maternal nutrition and the offspring's development. *Nutrition Today*, 1973, **8**:2, 12–18.

9. Dodge, J. A. Psychosomatic aspects of infantile pyloric stenosis. *Journal of Psychosomatic Research*, 1972, **16**, 1–5

10. Eastman, N. J., and L. M. Hellman. *Williams obstetrics*, 13th ed. New York: Appleton-Century-Crofts, 1966.

11. Fielding, J. E., and A. Yankauer. The pregnant drinker. *American Journal of Public Health*, 1978, **69**, 836–838.

12. Friedman, S. L., Y. Brackbill, A. J. Caron, and R. F. Caron. Obstetric medication and visual processing in 4- and 5-month-old infants. *Merrill-Palmer Quarterly*, 1978, **24**, 111–128.

13. General Clinical Research Centers Branch, National Institutes of Health. *How children grow*. (DHEW Publication No. (NIH) 72–166.) Washington: U.S. Government Printing Office, 1972.

14. Gennser, G., K. Marshall, and B. Brantmark. Maternal smoking and fetal breathing movements. *American Journal of Obstetrics and Gynecology*, 1975, **123**, 861–867.

15. Gortmaker, S. L. Poverty and mortality in the United States. *American Sociological Review*, 1979, **44**, 280–297.

16. Groom, G. L. An experimental study of prenatal events influencing postnatal behavior in the human infant. Paper presented at meeting of the Society for Research in Child Development, New Orleans, 1977.

17. Harvard Child Health Project Task Force. *Toward a primary medical care system responsive to children's needs*. Cambridge, Mass.: Ballinger, 1977.

18. Heinstein, M. I. Expressed attitudes and feelings of pregnant women and their relations to physical complications of pregnancy. *Merrill-Palmer Quarterly*, 1967, **13**, 217–236.

19. Heroin addiction in the newborn. *World Medical Journal*, 1972, **19**:3, 57.

20. Higgins, A. C., E. W. Crampton, and J. E. Moxley. *A preliminary report of a nutrition study of public maternity patients*. Montreal Diet Dispensary, 1973 (Mimeo).

21. Holley, W. L., A. L. Rosenbaum, and J. A. Churchill. Effects of rapid succession of pregnancy. In *Perinatal factors affecting human development*. Pan American Health Organization, Pan American Sanitary Bureau, Regional Office of World Health Organization, 1960. Pp. 41–45.

22. Honeyman, M. C., and M. A. Menor. Ethnicity is a significant factor in the epidemiology of rubella and Hodgkin's disease. *Nature*, 1974, **251**, 441–442.

23. Horowitz, F. D., J. Ashton, R. Culp, E. Gaddis, S. Levin, and B. Reichman. The effects of obstetrical medication on the behavior of Israeli newborn infants and some comparisons with Uruguayan and American infants. *Child Development*, 1977, **48**, 1607–1623.

23a. Horn, J. C. Fathers share the blame for Down's syndrome. *Psychology Today*, 1979, **13**: 4, 115–116.

24. Illsley, R. The sociological study of reproduction and its outcome. In S. A. Richardson and A. F. Guttmacher (eds.). *Childbearing—Its social and psychological aspects*. Baltimore: The Williams & Wilkins Company, 1975, pp. 75–141.

25. Korner, A. F., C. Guilleminault, J. Van den Hoed, and R. Baldwin. Reduction of apnea in premature infants through oscillating waterbed. Paper presented at meeting of the American Psychological Association, San Francisco, 1977.

26. Leboyer, F. *Birth without violence*. New York: Alfred A. Knopf, Inc., 1975.

27. Lowrey, G. H. *Growth and development of children*. New York: Year Book Medical Publishers, Inc., 1973.

28. Lubchenko, L. O., M. Delivoria-Papadopoulos, and D. Searls. Long-term follow-up studies of prematurely born infants. II. Influence of birth weight and gestational age on sequelae. *Journal of Pediatrics,* 1972, **80,** 509–512.

29. Maccoby, E. E., C. H. Doering, C. N. Jacklin, and H. Kraemer. Concentrations of sex hormones in umbilical-cord blood: Their relations to sex and birth order of infants. *Child Development,* 1979, **50,** 632–642.

30. McHale, M. C., J. McHale, and G. F. Streatfeild. *Children in the world.* Washington: Population Reference Bureau, 1979.

31. Milkovich, L., and B. J. van den Berg. Effects of meprobamate and chlordiazepoxide on human embryonic and fetal development. *New England Journal of Medicine,* 1974, **291,** 1268–1271.

32. Millman, S., and W. D. Mosher. Selected demographic characteristics of teenage wives and mothers. *Advance Data from Vital and Health Statistics of the National Center for Health Statistics.* No. 61. Sept. 26, 1980.

33. Newton, N., and C. Modahl. Pregnancy: The closest human relationship. *Human Nature,* 1978, **1:**3, 40–49.

34. Nutritional needs during pregnancy. *Dairy Council Digest,* 1974, **45:**4, 19–22.

35. Ounstead, M. Fetal growth. In D. Gairdner and D. Hull (eds.). *Recent advances in paediatrics.* London: Churchill, 1971.

36. Parmelee, A. H., C. B. Kopp, and M. Sigman. Selection of developmental assessment techniques for infants at risk. *Merrill-Palmer Quarterly,* 1976, **22,** 177–199.

37. Pasamanick, B., and H. Knobloch. Epidemiologic studies on the complication of pregnancy and the birth process. In S. Harrison (ed.). *Childhood psychopathology.* New York: International Universities Press, 1972.

38. Pitkin, R. M. What's new in maternal nutrition? *Nutrition News,* 1979, **42:**2, 5–6.

38a. Querec, K. J. Apgar scores in the United States, 1978. *Monthly Vital Statistics Report,* vol. 30, No. 1, Supplement. May 6, 1981.

39. Rice, R. D. Neurophysiological development in premature infants following stimulation. *Developmental Psychology,* 1977, **13,** 69–76.

40. Richardson, S. A., and A. F. Guttmacher (eds.). *Childbearing: Its social and psychological aspects.* Baltimore: The Williams & Wilkins Company, 1967.

41. Sameroff, A. J. Early influences on development: Fact or fancy? *Merrill-Palmer Quarterly,* 1976, **21,** 267–294.

42. Sharma, T. Marijuana: Recent research and findings, 1972. *Texas Medicine,* 1972, **68:**10, 109–110.

43. Stickle, G. The health of mothers and babies: How do we stack up? *Family Coordinator,* 1977, **26,** 205–210.

44. Stott, D. H., and S. A. Latchford. Prenatal antecedents of child health, development and behavior. *Journal of the American Academy of Child Psychiatry,* 1976, **15,** 161–191.

45. Strauss, M. E., R. H. Starr, and J. E. Lessen-Firestone. Influences of prenatal narcotics addiction on behavioral organization of the neonate. Paper presented at meeting of the Eastern Psychological Association, New York, 1975.

46. Streissguth, A. P. Maternal drinking and the outcome of pregnancy: Implications for child mental health. *American Journal of Orthopsychiatry,* 1977, **47,** 422–430.

47. Subcommittee on Nutrition, Brain Development and Behavior. Food and Nutrition Board, NAS. The relationship of nutrition to brain development and behavior. *Nutrition Today,* 1974, **9:**4, 12–13.

48. Ullbergh, S. Uptake and distribution of drugs in the fetus. *Acta Pharmacologica et Toxicologica,* 1971, **29** (Supplement 4), 81.

49. Welch, P., and K. N. Black. Biological and mental influences on early development in twins. Paper presented at meeting of the American Psychological Association, Toronto, 1978.
50. Werner, E. E. *Cross-cultural child development: A view from the planet Earth*. Monterey, Calif.: Brooks/Cole, 1979.
51. Yamazaki, J. N., et al. Outcome of pregnancy in women exposed to the atomic bomb in Nagasaki. *American Journal of Diseases of Children*, 1954, **87**, 448–463.
52. Yeung, D. Lecture at University of Guelph, Guelph, Ontario, Apr. 10, 1975.

4
Growth, Health, and Care

The newborn infant is closely connected to the mother, even after the cord between them is cut. The two members of the dyad are a working system, bound to each other, responding to each other and needing each other in order to carry out the functions for which they are prepared. The baby cannot live without the kind of care that a mother normally gives. (Such care can, of course, be given by another person.)

The infant's survival, health, physical growth, intelligence, language, and self are all products of the mother-infant system. As infant and mother live and interact with each other, health, growth, and development are continually affected. The infant-mother dyad functions in an ecology.

QUESTIONS TO THINK
ABOUT WHILE READING
THIS CHAPTER

1. How does the infant's ecology differ from that of the fetus?
2. In what ways do a mother and infant regulate each other?
3. In what ways does the infant's body adapt to the ecological transition caused by birth?
4. Of what significance are infant states to the family microsystem?
5. What sort of environment promotes optimal physical development?
6. What are the advantages and disadvantages of breast-feeding?
7. What are the primary responsibilities of caregivers to infants?
8. How can families be supported and assisted in caring for infants?

Ecology of the Infant

Comparing the ecology of the infant with the ecology of the fetus, one big difference is apparent. The microsystem of the fetus is the mother. The basic microsystem of the baby is the family. The baby has more than one microsystem, as shown in Figure 4–1. She goes visiting at Grandma's and Grandpa's, to the doctor's office or baby clinic, to parks, shopping center, and perhaps to day care. In her microsystems, she interacts with a variety of people, whereas the fetus interacts with the mother only.

The baby's exosystem is much larger than it was in her fetal days because all of her significant persons have their own microsystems, some of which influence the baby through those persons. Father catches cold from one of his co-workers and Baby gets it from him. Sister learns an action song at school and tries to teach it to Baby. Mother goes to a party, hears about a new kind of diaper, and tries it on Baby.

The macrosystem structures the infant's life through the family and

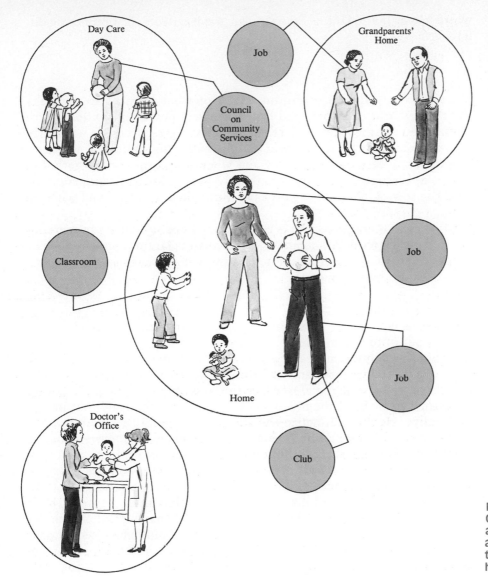

FIGURE 4–1
One infant's microsystems and exosystems. The blue areas indicate her exosystems. The white areas are her microsystems.

other microsystems, through exosystems, and all the patterning of institutions, values, beliefs, rituals, and customs that are part of the society. In this chapter, we are especially concerned with influences on growth, health, and care. The most basic measure of macrosystem influences on infants is the mortality rate. Birth weight and morbidity, or illness, are also crude overall measures. Different countries or regions of the world can be compared in terms of how many infants live and die in them. Table 3–3 in the previous chapter, gave infant mortality rates along with other macrosystem measures, such as availability of medical care. Figure 3–6 showed mortality rates during the first year for white and nonwhite babies in the United States. The graph reflects socioeconomic differences.

Transition to Infancy

Macrosystem variables determine much of what happens to the baby right after birth. Customs and rituals are very powerful. Official birth attendants, whether they be doctors, midwives, or relatives, do what they believe to be right for the mother and the baby. In traditional societies, there is no uncertainty as to how and when to cut the cord, whether to bury the placenta or eat it, whether to wash the baby immediately, whether to swaddle the baby or leave him naked, and how and when to feed.

Northern American society is going through many changes in methods of assisting the fetus into infancy. Agreement is far from universal. The following method is gaining more and more acceptance as the research base becomes better known.

Care Immediately After Birth

The cord is not cut until pulsation stops. With cord still attached, the baby is put onto the mother's bare abdomen and chest. This position seems to give comfort and satisfaction to both members of the dyad. The baby hears the heartbeat and breathing that he heard prenatally. The mother feels the weight and touch of the body that she felt inside her for many months. The baby now feels the outside of the body that he felt internally. He may recognize the smell and taste of the mother, especially when put promptly to the breast. If the birth has gone well and the baby is not drugged, the first hour or so after birth is a time of alertness. The baby responds to sounds, looks around, and fastens on faces and eyes.

When the mother locks eyes with her baby, she feels satisfied and excited. Films of mother-infant interaction within three hours of birth have revealed a normative pattern of maternal behavior [28]. With her naked infant lying on a heat panel beside her, the mother looked straight at him and began to touch his hands and feet with her fingertips. Gradually, she used her whole fingers, palms, and whole hands, moving from limbs to trunk and head. She touched him all over. She looked into his eyes, placing his face directly in front of hers. If his eyes were closed, she might ask him to open them. "Open your eyes. Oh, come on now, open up your eyes! If you open your eyes, then I will know you are alive."

Examination of the Newborn. At 1 minute and at 5 minutes of age, the birth attendant gives an Apgar test, by judging heart rate, breathing effort, muscle tone, reflex irritability, and color. Each item is given a rating of 0, 1, or 2. Scores from 7 to 10 indicate good condition; scores from 4 to 6 indicate some difficulty; scores from 0 to 3 indicate need for prompt treatment. Not only does the Apgar score show physiological adequacy. It is related to speed of infant learning [21].

Country and Ethnicity	Female	Male
Brazil		
White	3258	3397
Black	3204	3325
Canada	3320	3347
India	2880	2939
Indonesia	3048	3116
Jamaica	3070	3120
United States	3260	3400

TABLE 4–1
Mean Birth Weights (in Grams), by Sex, and Country.

Sources: A. M. deAuraújo and F. M. Salzano. Parental characteristics and birth weight in a Brazilian population. *Human Biology,* 1975, **47,** 37–43; S. M. Grantham-McGregor et al. A longitudinal study of infant growth in Kingston, Jamaica. *Human Biology,* 1972, **44,** 549–562; P. V. V. Hamill, T. A. Drizd; C. L. Johnson, R. B. Reed, and A. F. Roche. *NCHS growth curves for children birth–18 years.* Vital and health statistics: Series 11, Data from the National Health Survey; no. 165. (DHEW publication No. (PHS) 78-1650.) Washington: U.S. Government Printing Office, 1977. G. A. Harrison et al. *Human biology.* New York: Oxford University Press, 1964; Statistics Canada. *Vital Statistics Report,* vol. 1. 1972. Table 15, pp. 80–81.

Blood from the cord can be used for analyses for blood type, infections, genetic disorders, and anything else indicated by the baby's condition and history. A complete physical examination and a neurological examination are done. Behavioral examination may be done, using tests such as the Brazelton Assessment Scale or the Graham Scale.

Many changes take place within the first month of life, changes in weight, appearance, and functioning of internal organs.

Birth Weight. Weight at birth varies from one ethnic group to another, with geographic location and economic status. Table 4–1 illustrates some of these differences.

Birth weight is related to the weight of the mother and even more to the mother's birth weight, but not to the weight of the father [40]. The mother's body regulates the quantity of growth of the fetus. The mother's ability to constrain the growth of the fetus represents a safety mechanism for a small woman whose partner is a large man. Their child may be genetically large, but can be kept to a reasonable size before birth. After that, a catch-up mechanism takes over and the baby's growth speeds up to realize his inherited potential. [55, pp. 41–43]

Respiration. Breathing begins as the baby emerges or soon thereafter. It may take a day or two for the amniotic fluid and mucus to drain completely from the baby's breathing apparatus. Breathing is irregular, rapid, and shallow, involving the abdomen more than the chest. The neonate is often a noisy breather, wheezing and snuffling in a fashion that can be

Structure and Functions of the Newborn

alarming to first-time parents. During the first five days of life, the average respiration rate was found to be 46 breaths per minute [56].

Breathing reflexes are coordinated with and activated by the oxygen-carbon dioxide balance. The amount of air a baby breathes is regulated thus. Coughing, sneezing, and yawning are all reflexes with important survival value. Coughing and sneezing clear the air passages and lungs. Yawning gives a quick gulp of air when it is needed suddenly.

Circulation. The essential change in circulation immediately follows the change in respiration. Only a small quantity of blood goes to the lungs before birth, because it flows to the placenta to exchange products. After birth, blood is forced into the lungs, and the circulation to the placenta is cut off by the closing of the opening that leads from the fetal heart to the placenta. During fetal life, the right and left ventricles of the heart have an opening between them. Within the first week to ten days of postnatal life, the opening gradually closes. Another important change in the circulatory-respiratory combination is that the lungs expand gradually in the first two weeks. During that time, the blood includes almost twice as many blood cells per cubic millimeter as it does immediately after the lungs are fully expanded.

The heart rate decelerates during the birth process and quickly accelerates at birth. A peak heart rate of 174 beats per minute was found at two minutes after birth [59]. Heart rate at 6 weeks was found to be 153.6 when infants were awake and 141.2 when they were sleepy. At 12 weeks, rates were 150.2 while awake and 129.1 when sleepy [45]. Patterns of response become more stable during the first few months suggesting that important changes in control mechanisms take place during the first month of life [32]. Changes in heart rate are often used by experimenters as a means of measuring the infant's response to stimuli. Respiration is also used in this way.

Digestion and Excretion. The newborn changes from taking nutrients in through the placenta to taking food into the mouth and stomach. Hunger contractions and rooting, sucking, and swallowing mechanisms are present at birth. The small lower jaw and the fat pads in the cheeks facilitate sucking. The mother's breasts produce colostrum for the first two or three days of the baby's life, and then milk. Colostrum, a clear yellow liquid, supplies certain concentrated nutrients, prevents gastrointestinal infections, and probably acts as a laxative. Infant feeding will be discussed later in this chapter.

The first material evacuated from the colon is meconium, the material accumulated before birth from cellular breakdown, intestinal secretions, bile, mucus, and material swallowed with amniotic fluid. After three days, the stools assume a character that depends on the type of food, those of breast-fed babies differing noticeably from those of bottle-fed babies in appearance. Breast-fed babies usually have several bowel movements a day during the first few weeks, but after 1, 2, or 3 months they usually change to a pattern of infrequent movements, one a day or every other day. Bottle-fed babies have one to four, or even six a day at first and later the number decreases to one or two [53]. The kidneys excrete small quantities of urine before birth. Frequency of urination increases after the second day to an average of around 20 times a day, with a wide range of individual differences.

Metabolism. The newborn has a higher metabolic rate than the adult, but lower than the preschool child's. Immediately after birth, the temperature drops 2 to 5 degrees and then rises to 98 to 99 degrees after about 8 hours. Since mechanisms for maintaining a stable body temperature are immature, the neonate's temperature is unstable. Premature babies' temperatures are even more unstable than those of full-term infants. Heat loss is great through the baby's comparatively large surface, which is poorly insulated because skin and fat layers are thin. The newborn shows little diurnal change in temperature [51]. Thus, he gets along best in a controlled temperature, with clothing and bedding carefully regulated to maintain a steady temperature.

States

Infant behavior is organized into different states or conditions of alertness and activity, including sleeping, awake, and crying. States are important to parents, as well as to researchers. Crying is upsetting and disturbing to most, if not all adults [27], but especially to new parents. Researchers study infant states as important kinds of infant behavior, and as background information for setting up studies. For example, if cognitive capabilities are to be examined, they can be tested most readily during the state of alert inactivity. The classic research on infant states was done by Peter Wolff [64]. He defined six states: *regular sleep*, breathing smooth and even, little movement of face and body; *irregular sleep*, breathing irregular, movements of body and face, including rapid eye movements: *drowsiness*, less active than in irregular sleep but more active than in regular, eyes open and close, looking glazed, eyelids heavy; *waking activity*, silent or moaning, grunting, whimpering, spurts of diffuse motor activity, face relaxed or pinched, eyes open but not shiny, skin flushed in activity, breathing irregular; *crying*, vocalizing, grimacing, diffuse motor activity, red face; *alert inactivity*, body inactive, face relaxed, eyes open, bright and shining, respirations faster and more variable than in regular sleep. The infant's response to stimulation depends upon his or her state and upon the stimulus. For instance, in both kinds of sleep, infants were insensitive to touch; in alert inactivity, response to touch was increased motility; and in waking activity, touch stimuli resulted in decreased motility [64].

Time spent by 26 newborn infants in 5 categories of states is represented in Figure 4–3. Regular and irregular sleep have been classified together. Wolff's subjects steadily increased the amount of time spent in

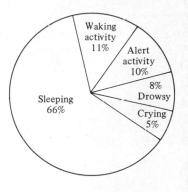

alert inactivity, the weekly averages of percentage of total time being, first week, 11; second, 17; third, 19; and fourth, 21 [62].

Variation in Patterning of States

From the moment of birth, infants differ in the amounts of time they spend in alert inactivity. During the first 6 hours, some of Wolff's subjects stayed awake and looked for 1½ hours or longer; others fell into a deep sleep as soon as they were cleaned and dressed [63]. Infants vary considerably in the duration of their sleep cycles and in the proportion of irregular sleep to other states [47]. Obstetrical medication and experience during delivery make a difference. A drugged baby is not likely to be alert. Nor is one who has undergone a prolonged and difficult delivery.

The temperature [58] and chemical composition [57] of the blood have been shown to be different in different states. Cortisol, a substance associated with stress in adults, was at high level in the blood of 3-day-old infants when they were crying or fussing. Cortisol levels were low during sleep. Thus, behavioral states have physical correlates in blood, as well as in the brain, muscles, and respiratory system.

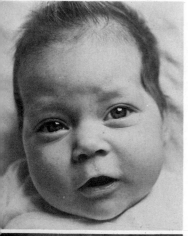

Sex Differences. Newborn girls had, on the average, longer periods of alert inactivity than boys [5]. Boys were more often awake and active, showing more facial grimacing and fussing than girls [43]. (Because circumsion has been shown to affect crying, sleep, and response to sound, uncircumcised boys were chosen for this study.) Boys seem to be more irritable and easily distressed than girls, perhaps because they are less mature at birth, and therefore less organized.

Ethnic Differences. State behavior of infants is different in different cultures. Reasons for differences are probably both genetic and environmental. Even though the infant is newborn, she has lived for 9 months in a prenatal environment, and has had the experience of birth. Both pregnancy and birth are, of course, influenced by macrosystem values and customs. Examples of ethnic differences come from a study of ethnic Chinese newborns and of Zinacanteco infants. A comparison of newborns of Chinese ancestry with Caucasian newborns showed that the Chinese babies were less likely to change back and forth between states of contentment and upset and that when they cried, they were much more easily consoled by being picked up [16]. In an isolated mountainous region in Mexico, Brazelton and his associates observed and tested Zinacanteco newborns [8]. Compared with American infants, the Zinacantecos stayed in quiet, alert states for long periods, moved slowly and smoothly from one state to another, and did not show deep sleep, intense crying, or intense sucking.

Because nobody likes to hear crying, a caregiver has a prompt desire to soothe and console the baby emitting the distressing noise. Even John B. Watson had to be very stern and firm with mothers to induce them to ignore their babies' cries. Parents sometimes want babies to be quietly alert in order to have exchanges of looking, smiling, and cooing. Or they may want a baby to go to sleep, in order to have time to do something other than caregiving. Researchers often want their infant subjects in the quiet alert state. The usual time for achieving smooth regulation of states is between 2 and 4 months. What can be done to help infants achieve and maintain states that bring ease, contentment, and mutual response to infants and their families?

Meanings of Crying. The first problem encountered by a new parent is usually figuring out why the baby is crying and then meeting the need expressed. The experienced caregiver knows how to interpret cries and how to apply the appropriate soother. The caregiver looks at the context of the cry. How long is it since the baby has been fed? Is she too hot or cold? Is her skin irritated? Has she been lying by herself in one position? The caregiver tries what seems like the most likely soother, and if the baby doesn't stop crying, she or he tries another.

Figure 4-2 shows spectograms of infant cries recorded in three contexts—hunger, pain, and boredom—by John Kirkland in New Zealand.

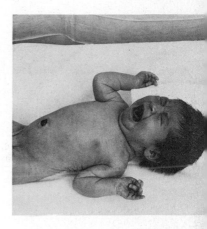

Boredom

F

FIGURE 4-2
Spectrograms of infant cries in three contexts: hunger, pain and boredom. (SOURCE: Reprinted by permission of John Kirkland, Massey University, New Zealand.)

Hunger

I

Pain

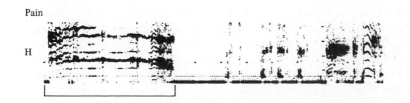

H

The three records look different, and sound different. We have played a tape of these sounds to several groups of people and asked them to guess why each baby was crying. The majority of listeners guessed (or discriminated) correctly, affirming what Kirkland and others have found in careful studies. A newborn infant has a repertory of cries that sound different from each other. Some meanings can be derived from them by some people.

Cry characteristics differ in abnormal infants. The cries of brain-damaged babies have a higher pitch than normal cries and show other differences. High-risk infants were found significantly different from normal infants in these ways: They needed more stimulation to elicit crying; they cried for shorter times; cries were higher pitched and showed timing differences [30].

The cries of premature infants are different from those of full-term ones. Parents respond differently to these two types of cry. Physiological tests and self-reports of mothers and fathers were used to examine responses to films and tapes of premature and full-term infants crying, to tapes of full-terms accompanied by pictures of prematures, and to tapes of prematures accompanied by films of full-terms [17]. All crying was irritating and disturbing, but the crying of prematures was much more so. Both mothers and fathers felt most sympathetic toward the normal baby with a normal cry. Mothers had least sympathy with the premature baby with the premature cry. This study has implications for explaining the fact that premature children are more likely than normals to be abused.

Soothing. When a baby is kept close to the mother's body, with continual access to her breast, crying is rare. The breast is probably the most certain soother, providing for sucking and contact comfort, as well as giving food. Few ecologies are organized to make such soothing constantly available, and so other methods have been found and tried. (Feeding will be discussed later.)

It is common knowledge that babies are likely to stop crying when fed and when picked up, cuddled, and rocked. The rocking chair and cradle as standard nursery equipment are evidence of this knowledge. Other soothers are patting, stroking, massage, pacifiers, and warm baths. Although used infrequently in North America, swaddling soothes infants in Russia and in other places where it is customary. Psychologists have investigated the conditions under which infants are soothed by sucking and being held and rocked. In attempts to soothe a baby, the most frequent methods used by mothers were found to be picking up and rocking. These methods succeeded 85 per cent of the time [4]. Vestibular stimulation (stimulation of the part of the ear that registers movements of the head) occurs when the baby is moved. Rocking results in a rhythmic, strong stimulation. Vertical rocking has been shown to be more effective than horizontal rocking. A fast pace (60 cycles per minute) was more soothing than a slower pace (30 cycles). A high amplitude had more effect than a lower one. By varying the dimensions of rocking, experiments have concluded that *acceleration* determines the effectiveness of rocking [42]. As the baby was moved through space, a greater acceleration would produce stronger vestibular stimulation and this, the authors hold, is what causes the infant to stop crying. Acceleration may also produce pleasurable sensations in other parts of the body. For example, taking off in a jet plane or a fast start on a motorcycle results in abdominal and chest sensations that are both satisfying and exciting to older individuals.

In cultures where babies are carried most of the time, the baby may ride in a string bag on his mother's back, in a shawl under her arm, or even in a plastic backpack. In any of these positions, the infant receives vigorous vestibular stimulation as his bearer's walking and bending accelerates his body in one direction and then in another. Contrast this richness with the experience of an infant lying in a stationary crib!

Soothing of crying may result in a change to a sleeping state or to a waking one. When mothers picked up their crying infants and held them to their shoulders, 77.5 per cent of a group of crying infants went into a state of visual alertness. Holding to the shoulder was also somewhat effective in eliciting visual activity in babies who had been sleeping [29].

Continuous stimulation increases the duration of quiet sleep in newborns [49]. Subjects in one study received two-hour sessions of continuous white noise, light, swaddling, and warmth; the control group received softer noise and light, loose clothing, and a cooler temperature [7]. The experimental group cried less, slept more, was less active, and had slower heart rates. The conclusion is that continuous stimulation reduces arousal level, both behavioral and physiological.

Sleep. Although persons unfamiliar with newborn babies often think that these infants sleep most of the time, the average sleep time of a group of 46 neonates was only between 16 and 17 hours in 24 [41]. By the age of 16 weeks, the average total sleep time had decreased to between 14 and 15 hours. The outstanding developmental changes are not in the number of hours spent in sleep but in the length of sleep periods and their timing during the 24 hours. Babies of 6 weeks sleep as long as five or six hours at a time. By 12 or 16 weeks, they are likely to sleep eight or nine hours at a time and to do so at night. There are occasional young infants, however, who sleep as little as 12 hours out of 24 and others who sleep as much as 21. Parents usually find it easier to take care of a baby who sleeps many hours rather than few. An awake infant, of course, has more varied and stimulating experiences than one who sleeps more. The sleep of the newborn may be affected by drugs received before or during birth.

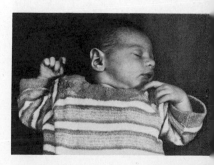

There are two main types of sleep, *active* or irregular and *quiet* or regular. Active sleep has been described as a "primitive anarchic state" and quiet sleep as a "more mature highly controlled state." As the central nervous system develops inhibiting and controlling mechanisms, quiet sleep increases. One of the distinctive differences between regular and irregular sleep is in the rapid eye movements that occur during irregular, active sleep. Characteristic brain wave patterns occur during each of the two kinds of sleep. During active sleep the brain-wave pattern is of low voltage and relatively fast; quiet sleep is typified by higher voltage and slower frequency waves [47]. Newborn infants spent a third of their time in active sleep and another third in quiet sleep. The proportion of active sleep diminishes as the brain matures. The total active-sleep time decreases from about 8 hours in the newborn period to 1 hour and 40 minutes in the adult. Active sleep in the newborn is different from that of the adult, but changes to an adultlike form at about 3 months of age. From 3 to 6 months, the infant stays awake more and more in the daytime, and sleeps longer at night. During the second year, most babies sleep through the night and take one or two naps during the day. The second nap drops out at some time in the second year.

Physical Development

Development and change are rapid during the first two years of life. After the first month, more or less, a baby really looks like a baby, like babies in advertisements and photograph albums, like other babies in the neighborhood—chubby, skin colored pink, golden, brown, or whatever it is destined to be, bumps smoothed out, and nose in shape. New, coarser hair comes in during infancy, replacing the fine black hair of the newborn (if he had it) and showing more and more the color it is going to be. Compared with an older child, a baby has a large forehead, large eyes, small nose, small chin, and plump cheeks. His hands and feet are chubby and his abdomen round; his delicate skin looks soft and fragile.

Babies differ in appearance, from one to another; the older they are, the more obvious the differences. They differ, of course, in coloring, facial features, amount and type of hair, height, and weight. They feel different, too. Firm muscles and good muscle tone give a solid impression, in contrast to the softness of slacker muscles or abundant fat. The baby's reactions to being held also add to the impression, according to whether the infant holds himself erect, pushes away, or yields to the arms that hold him.

Proportions and Measurements

Changes in shape and proportion continue along the lines charted prenatally, the head regions being most developed, the trunk and legs beginning to catch up, the center of gravity high in the trunk but descending. Birth weight is doubled by 4 or 5 months and tripled at 1 year. Height is doubled by about 4 years. Thus, the child starts life as a slender neonate, fills out to a round, plump infant during the first year, and then in the second year, he again becomes more slender, continuing this trend into middle childhood. A ratio useful for diagnosing malnutrition is that of head to thorax. After 6 months of age, the thorax is larger than the head in normal children. The difference in circumference between thorax and head increases with age. When a child is growing inadequately, his weight deficit is related to the difference between head and thorax [12].

Height and weight percentile tables (Tables 4–2 and 4–3) can be used to compare a baby with the babies in a sample of United States children. The long-term longitudinal study from which these figures are taken was chosen by the National Center for Health Statistics as the best, for a variety of technical reasons, that was available for inclusion in the Center's publication of growth data in the United States from birth to 18 years. The children were measured lying on their backs, with their knees extended as much as possible. Babies to be compared with the figures should be measured similarly.

When percentile tables are used, a score that falls anywhere between the 25th and 75th percentile is considered to be average. A point below the 25th percentile is low, and above the 75th, high. Therefore, even though the mean, or average, is a point in the middle, at exactly the 50th percentile, a child's height, weight, or any other measurement is considered to be average if it falls within the range stated. For example, Becky at 6 months measures 69.2 centimeters long and weighs 7.71 kilograms.

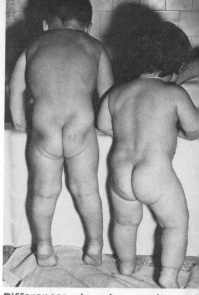

Differences in size and shape between a 2-year-old and a 1-year-old are shown here.

TABLE 4–2
Percentiles of Recumbent Length (in Centimeters) by Age and Sex.

| Sex and age | Percentile | | | | | | |
| | 5th | 10th | 25th | 50th | 75th | 90th | 95th |
	Recumbent length in centimeters						
Male							
Birth	46.4	47.5	49.0	50.5	51.8	53.5	54.4
1 month	50.4	51.3	53.0	54.6	56.2	57.7	58.6
3 months	56.7	57.7	59.4	61.1	63.0	64.5	65.4
6 months	63.4	64.4	66.1	67.8	69.7	71.3	72.3
9 months	68.0	69.1	70.6	72.3	74.0	75.9	77.1
12 months	71.7	72.8	74.3	76.1	77.7	79.8	81.2
18 months	77.5	78.7	80.5	82.4	84.3	86.6	88.1
24 months	82.3	83.5	85.6	87.6	89.9	92.2	93.8
30 months	87.0	88.2	90.1	92.3	94.6	97.0	98.7
36 months	91.2	92.4	94.2	96.5	98.9	101.4	103.1
Female							
Birth	45.4	46.5	48.2	49.9	51.0	52.0	52.9
1 month	49.2	50.2	51.9	53.5	54.9	56.1	56.9
3 months	55.4	56.2	57.8	59.5	61.2	62.7	63.4
6 months	61.8	62.6	64.2	65.9	67.8	69.4	70.2
9 months	66.1	67.0	68.7	70.4	72.4	74.0	75.0
12 months	69.8	70.8	72.4	74.3	76.3	78.0	79.1
18 months	76.0	77.2	78.8	80.9	83.0	85.0	86.1
24 months	81.3	82.5	84.2	86.5	88.7	90.8	92.0
30 months	86.0	87.0	88.9	91.3	93.7	95.6	96.9
36 months	90.0	91.0	93.1	95.6	98.1	100.0	101.5

Note: If a child is measured at an age different from one of those in the table, the approximate percentile ranking can be calculated by interpolation.

Source: P. V. V. Hamill, T. A. Drizd, C. L. Johnson, R. B. Reed, and A. F. Roche. *NCHS growth curves for children birth–18 years.* Vital and health statistics: Series 11, Data from the National Health Survey; No. 165. (DHEW publication No. (PHS) 78-1650.) Washington: U.S. Government Printing Office, 1977.

TABLE 4-3
Percentiles of Weight
(in Kilograms) by Age and
Sex.

Sex and age	Percentile						
	5th	10th	25th	50th	75th	90th	95th
	Weight in kilograms						
Male							
Birth	2.54	2.78	3.00	3.27	3.64	3.82	4.15
1 month	3.16	3.43	3.82	4.29	4.75	5.14	5.38
3 months	4.43	4.78	5.32	5.98	6.56	7.14	7.37
6 months	6.20	6.61	7.20	7.85	8.49	9.10	9.46
9 months	7.52	7.95	8.56	9.18	9.88	10.49	10.93
12 months	8.43	8.84	9.49	10.15	10.91	11.54	11.99
18 months	9.59	9.92	10.67	11.47	12.31	13.05	13.44
24 months	10.54	10.85	11.65	12.59	13.44	14.29	14.70
30 months	11.44	11.80	12.63	13.67	14.51	15.47	15.97
36 months	12.26	12.69	13.58	14.69	15.59	16.66	17.28
Female							
Birth	2.36	2.58	2.93	3.23	3.52	3.64	3.81
1 month	2.97	3.22	3.59	3.98	4.36	4.65	4.92
3 months	4.18	4.47	4.88	5.40	5.90	6.39	6.74
6 months	5.79	6.12	6.60	7.21	7.83	8.38	8.73
9 months	7.00	7.34	7.89	8.56	9.24	9.83	10.17
12 months	7.84	8.19	8.81	9.53	10.23	10.87	11.24
18 months	8.92	9.30	10.04	10.82	11.55	12.30	12.76
24 months	9.87	10.26	11.10	11.90	12.74	13.57	14.08
30 months	10.78	11.21	12.11	12.93	13.93	14.81	15.35
36 months	11.60	12.07	12.99	13.93	15.03	15.97	16.54

Note: If a child is measured at an age different from one of those in the table, the approximate percentile ranking can be calculated by interpolation.

Source: P. V. V. Hamill, T. A. Drizd, C. L. Johnson, R. B. Reed and A. F. Roche. *NCHS growth curves for children birth–18 years.* Vital and health statistics: Series 11, Data from the National Health Survey; No. 165. (DHEW publication No. (PHS) 78-1650.) Washington: U.S. Government Printing Office, 1977.

Table 4–2 shows that she is above the 75th percentile in length and therefore above average. She is close to the 90th percentile, at which point she would be longer than 90 out of 100 girls her age. Table 4–3 shows that Becky's weight is below the 75th percentile but above the 50th, placing her weight in the range of weights considered to be average. In spite of her chubby face and rounded abdomen, Becky is of linear shape when compared to baby girls of her own age.

Height and weight tables that give only averages have little use for the individual, although they are useful for comparing groups. Percentile tables, such as those shown here, give more information than mere averages. However, they take no account of body build nor do they consider heredity. The ideal weight for a short-legged, long-trunked child such as an Aleutian Islander would obviously be greater than for a white American of the same height. The expected height for the child of tall parents is greater than for the child of short parents. For example, for white Ohio sons of short parents, the average length at 1 year was 73.6 centimeters, at 2, it was 85.3; for sons of tall parents, the average 1-year length was 77.4, and at 2, it was 88.9 [18]. (The measurements in the article cited were in inches, and have been converted to metric units here.) Appendix A contains height-weight interpretation charts and directions for using them.

Skinfold thickness is a measurement that is useful for detecting inadequate nutrition in large groups of children, as in national surveys [25]. Accurate scales may not be available for weighing and exact ages may not be known. Exact age is not necessary when skinfold measurements are used between 1 and 5 years of age. Children with protein-calorie malnutrition are usually below the third percentile and almost always below the tenth.

Brain Development. The infant's brain grows rapidly in weight. At birth, the brain is 25 per cent of its adult weight, by 6 months, nearly 50 per cent, and at 2 years, 75 per cent [55]. Different parts of the brain grow at different rates, and different types of cell development occur at different times. Long before birth, in fact by mid-prenatal life, the cells that transmit impulses are formed, almost all 10^{12} (a million million of them). The neurons increase in size and complexity, contributing to the brain growth spurt of the first two years of life after birth. Much branching occurs in the projections that receive messages from other neurons, and connections between neurons multiply.

Neurons form before birth. From birth to 2 years, neurons enlarge and branch, glial cells form and enlarge, myelination takes place

The formation and growth of glial cells also contributes to the brain's growth spurt. The glial cells far outnumber the neurons, which they support and serve [14]. One of their functions is to link neurons with blood vessels. Another is to lay down a myelin sheath on the part of the neuron that sends impulses. Myelin, a fatty insulating substance, helps the nerve fiber to transmit impulses more quickly. Myelination is one sign of a neuron being mature enough to function well. Myelination of the brain continues at least into adolescence.

Every mammal has a brain-growth spurt during prenatal life and/or early infancy, in which glial cells multiply, myelin is laid down, and neurons grow in size and complexity. Experiments on animals have shown that severe malnutrition during this time will result in reduced brain growth and a smaller brain at maturity. Growth is not made up by abundant feeding after the growth spurt is over. After being malnourished during its growth spurt, the brain shows reduced numbers of cells, myelin, and connections between neurons, distorted proportions, and changed biochemistry. Behavioral changes include clumsiness, overreactions to stress, increased aggression, and learning deficits. Of course, the same experimental methods cannot be applied to human beings. Results from animal experiments are only suggestive. Human experiments are natural ones, in which malnourished populations are studied, and attempts made to compensate for deprivation already suffered. This type of research does indicate that brains stunted during infancy do not achieve normal size. Compensatory programs have, however, been successful in improving intellectual functioning when psychological programs were combined with nutritional [11].

Establishing Regularity of Basic Processes

Regularity increases in temperature control, breathing, eating, sleeping, and secreting

The body must stay within certain physical and chemical limits if it is to stay alive. In order to function optimally, it must stay within narrower limits. *Homeostasis*, the maintenance of steady states within these limits, is accomplished by integrated control of the nervous and endocrine systems. During the first 3 or 4 months of life, the mechanisms of homeostasis become more and more efficient. The baby settles down to an easier, more automatic supporting of life processes, his energies freed for a wider variety of activities.

Temperature regulation is one of the vital homeostatic processes. A certain constancy has to be kept in spite of heat loss and heat production. The baby regulates his temperature more adequately after the neonatal period than he does in the beginning. For example, the sweat glands become active at about a month of age. Even with temperature regulation improving, infants and young children are still highly susceptible to temperature fluctuation. Bodily temperature is likely to shoot up with active exercise, crying, emotional upset, or rise in surrounding temperature. Bodily temperature responds readily to chilling. Infants and young children, when suffering from infections, usually show higher temperatures than do older children. Although the average temperature at 3 months is 37.5°C, (99.4°F) about one-third of babies this age have temperatures above 37.9 or below 37.1. Temperature decreases after the first year and goes down steadily throughout childhood. Individual differences continue to exist, though, and an occasional child may have an unusually high (or low) temperature that is normal for that child [33].

Heat production increases with age throughout the growth period. The younger the child, the more he is likely to vary from the average and also to vary with himself from time to time [26]. The larger the body, of course, the greater is the absolute amount of heat produced. Taken in terms of heat production per unit of body weight, however, the 6-month-old baby produces more heat than anybody. Heat production builds up from birth to 6 months and then tapers off to adulthood. Considering what is known about temperature in children, it can be seen that good care includes protection against extremes of temperature and supervision that helps the child to regulate his own temperature. As infants and young children produce such large amounts of heat, they are likely to become overheated through active play or when wearing heavy clothing. They will show discomfort by a flushed face, perspiration, and perhaps irritability.

Respiration changes considerably during the first year. The rate slows down to about half what it was at birth. After 1 year, it continues to become slower. Breathing becomes deeper, too. At birth, the diaphragm does practically all of the work in breathing. The chest gradually comes into play during infancy, but thoracic breathing is not well established until the end of the preschool period [33]. A young baby's breathing sounds harsh, irregular, and shallow. Gradually his breathing becomes more regular and less noisy as he changes toward thoracic breathing, as his chest grows, and as the tissues covering his chest thicken and insulate the sounds.

The timing of eating, sleeping, and eliminating becomes regularized. By 3 or 4 months, even the baby who has made his own schedule (fed when hungry, allowed to sleep until he wakens) eats and sleeps at fairly predictable times. As eating and sleeping become regularized, bowel movements also tend to do so. By 6 months, one or two stools a day are most usual. Wide individual differences occur, however. About half of 2-year-olds have bowel movements at predictable times, and half are unpredictable [46].

Deterrents to Growth

Growth can be disrupted or distorted by malnutrition, infections, metabolic disorders, injuries, and deprivation of emotional and cognitive experience. Very often, a growth problem has more than one cause. Frequently there is interaction between factors deterring growth, as there is between malnutrition and infection. The malnourished infant is more likely to contract an infection, and to have it more severely. The infection, in turn, makes the child less able to eat and to utilize food, and therefore malnourishment increases. When diarrhea occurs with infection and malnutrition, the result may be death. This combination is the main killer of young children in the Third World [60, p. 54]. Figure 4–3 shows the difference in death rates for children between 1 and 4 years in selected countries around the world.

Malnutrition. In taking stock of children for the International Year of the Child, it was estimated that 10 million children under 5 were suffering from extreme malnutrition, and 90 million from moderate malnutrition [35]. Often the most important reason is that enough food simply is not available. Other reasons are ignorance and maladaptive customs, on all levels of the ecology. Figure 4–4 shows causes and effects of malnutrition.

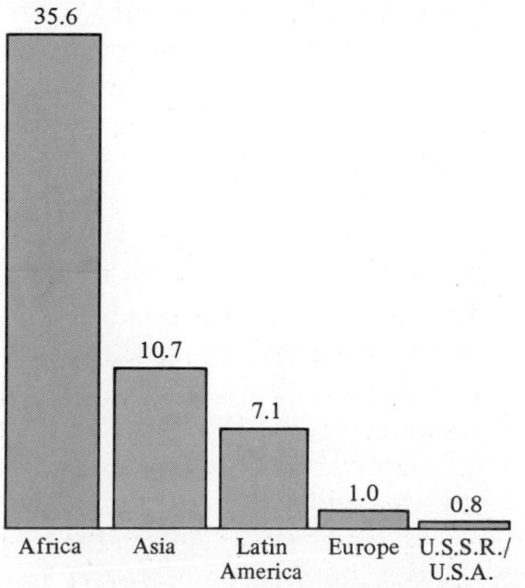

FIGURE 4–3
Annual death rates (ages 1–4), selected countries in world regions. (SOURCE: M. C. McHale, J. McHale, and G. F. Streatfeild. *Children in the world*. Washington: Population Reference Bureau, 1979.)

Causes and effects of childhood malnutrition

Insufficient food	Insufficient quality of food	Food spoilage	Lack of education/information	Poverty and deprivation	Poor sanitation
Thirty-seven countries most affected by food shortage have per capita grain production below 1969–71 levels. Thirty-four have a trend of falling per capital grain production.	• A young child's protein needs are proportionately 2½ times as great as an adult's. • For an adequate diet, the 32 poorest countries need to triple their production of meat and fish, and greatly increase production of milk, eggs, fruits, and vegetables.	• In many countries food spoilage runs higher than 30% of total food production. • Overall loss due to pests is about 20% of the world's food supply per year. • Rats, insects, and fungi destroy 33 million tons of food in storage per year.	• Insufficient and poor use of teachers, agricultural extension workers, community development agents. • Illiteracy: 800 million illiterates worldwide. In many countries half the population over 15 is illiterate, and the number is rising. • Non-reliance on breast-feeding. Breast-feeding can provide all that is required in first six months of life. • Unregulated fertility of mothers.	• In some Asian and African countries, daily per capita income is 20–24 U.S. cents. • Mothers, handicapped since early life by nutritional deficiency and environmental hazards, give birth to low weight infants, and are too exhausted to give adequate child care.	• Lack of clean water, safe environment, uncontaminated food and decent living space. • In 91 less developed countries, 71% of the population had no access to clean drinking water (1970); 83% of rural population had no safe drinking water available. • In some parts of the world, women and children spend half their time carrying water.

Susceptibility to infectious diseases → Susceptibility to vector-borne diseases → Susceptibility to gastro-intestinal diseases

Stunted physical and mental development

Early death, serious and permanent damage

Malnutrition: the biggest single contributor to illness and death among children in the less developed countries where 25% of the children die before age five (a rate 20–40 times higher than in the more developed world).

Half the deaths of children under five are caused by malnutrition.

Loss of body fluid and salt depletion from diarrhea leads to debilitation and death.

Five million children in the less developed countries are killed each year by diphtheria, whooping cough, tetanus, poliomyelitis, measles, and tuberculosis.

Vitamin A deficiency causes 20–100,000 children to lose their sight each year.

Water-related diseases kill approximately ten million people a year. The diseases are: water-borne, e.g., cholera, typhoid; water-washed, e.g., typhus, trachoma (a leading cause of blindness in young children); water-based, e.g., guinea worms; plus vector-borne, e.g., malaria; and those related to fecal disposal.

Figure 4–4
Causes and effects of childhood malnutrition. (Source: M. C. McHale, J. McHale, and G. F. Streatfeild. *Children in the world*. Washington: Population Reference Bureau.)

For the first year a baby needs about three times as many calories and two to three times as much protein per unit of body weight as an adult. Growth in height and weight of well-nourished children is rapid but slowing down in the latter half of the first year. At the same time, the rate of muscle growth increases. If the baby is getting supplementary foods, as most North American children are, a decreasing proportion of calories is coming from milk. If the infant is living in poverty, protein intake is drastically cut as he is weaned on to inadequate foods.

Marasmus and kwashiorkor are two severe diseases that are caused by malnutrition. *Marasmus* is a wasting away of body tissues. When suffering from marasmus, an infant is grossly underweight, with atrophy of muscles and subcutaneous fat but with no clinical edema. Marasmus is caused by undernutrition, resulting from insufficient food or from not utilizing food. It often is the result of early weaning from breast milk to an inadequate food, an unsuitable and unsanitary cow's milk formula or something that looks like milk but is not. It may be a gruel of tapioca or rice [3]. A severe emotional disturbance can cause the child not to eat or to be unable to utilize food adequately. A longitudinal study of children with marasmus was done in Chile, where a decline in breast-feeding produced some severe malnutrition in early infancy [39]. These babies were admitted to the hospital at ages 3 to 11 months with acute marasmus that had begun at some time between 1 and 5 months. Most of them weighed little more than they did at birth. They were treated to recovery and sent home with a steady and adequate supply of milk. At ages 3 to 6 years, all were clinically normal, with height far below average (lower than the 3rd percentile) for Chilean children. Their legs were short and their weights were all above the 3rd percentile, many close to the 50th percentile. Thus, weights were above normal for heights and some children looked obese. Head circumferences were below normal.

Kwashiorkor occurs most often in 1- to 4-year-olds whose diets are very low in proteins while being not so low in total calories. The biochemical changes in the body are quite different in the two diseases, kwashiorkor having more lasting effects after the acute stage is alleviated. Symptoms of kwashiorkor are swelling of face, legs, and abdomen because of water retention, growth retardation, wasting of muscles with some fat retained, apathy, or whimpering. The hair may be reddish and thin and the skin coarse, spotted, or with a rash or lesions. Liver damage is likely to occur [36]. A frequent beginning for kwashiorkor occurs when a mother weans her baby of a year or more because she has become pregnant [3]. She feeds him starchy foods and little protein.

There are malnourished children in all parts of the world, although nutrition problems are most severe in the poorest countries. Even in North America, where standards of living are generally high, two national nutrition surveys showed nutritional defects in children. Clinical assessments of Canadian children from birth to four years found 3.6 per cent of the general population and 9.2 per cent of Eskimo at risk in regard to protein-calorie malnutrition [48]. Biochemical assessments indicated sizable numbers at risk in regard to iron, serum folate, vitamin A, and vitamin C. The United States survey found low caloric intake in 14 per cent of white children between 1 and 5 years and in 23 per cent of black children the same age [1]. Significant deficiencies were also found in amounts of calcium, iron, and vitamins A and C, with black children often showing more severe deficiencies than white. A serious iron shortage was found in New York City infants of low-income families [37]. Some of these babies received too little food, some too much. From one month to one year, there was a steady increase in empty calories.

Infections. Respiratory infections are probably the most common type of illness in Northern American infants, with gastrointestinal upsets second. When parents smoke, their infants have a high incidence of bronchitis and pneumonia during the first year of life [10]. If only one parent smokes, the frequency of these diseases is halfway between the incidence when neither smokes and when both smoke. These findings are from a longitudinal study of 2,205 infants.

Protection by immunization is usual for infants in the United States and other industrialized countries. In the less developed countries, epidemics of whooping cough and measles still occur, and 5 million children under the age of 15 die each year from whooping cough, diphtheria, tetanus, poliomyelitis, measles, and tuberculosis [35]. Malaria has made a comeback, after being almost controlled. Water-related diseases (controllable by sanitation) affect many children living in poverty. Intestinal parasites damage children's digestive systems, deprive them of nutrients, and make them feel irritated and sick.

Metabolic Disorders. Some babies are born with genetic disability to process certain nutrients. For example, 70 per cent of Afro-Americans lack an enzyme required for converting a sugar in cow's milk to a kind that can be absorbed [19]. If an infant lacking the enzyme is fed cow's milk, he is likely to have severe diarrhea, pain, and growth retardation. He may die. Some children react to the gluten of wheat with intestinal changes that interfere with the absorption of nutrients and hence suffer growth retardation. Distorted growth can result from vitamin deficiencies and excesses. Early diagnosis and treatment minimize growth disturbance. For example, if vitamin D insensitivity (usually inherited) is detected before 6 months of age, bone deformities can usually be prevented.

Inadequate Reciprocal Interaction. Marasmus and failure to thrive are likely when an infant is isolated from human contact. Even under normal home conditions, mothers differ in the ways in which they feed their infants, and those differences are related to weight gain [44]. The appearance and behavior of the infant influence the mother's feeding techniques. Mothers were observed to try more to stimulate smaller babies to suck. If the baby does not suck well, and the mother does not encourage more sucking, then the baby is likely to gain poorly. If the nursing mother is not sufficiently stimulated by the baby's sucking, and/or she is malnourished herself, then she will produce less milk, and a negative cycle is set up. Other pressures, such as a heavy work load and caring for other children, may decrease the time and energy a mother has for affectionate stimulation of her infant. A failure-to-thrive syndrome occurs in about 3 per cent of infants [31]. Growth is slow and below normal limits. A feeding disturbance is usual, involving small food intake. In infants of less than 4 months of age, the symptoms of failure-to-thrive syndrome are unusual watchfulness, lack of cuddliness, little smiling, and few vocalizations. Between 4 and 10 months these infants are passive, showing deficient motor and vocal behavior and lacking the usual stranger-anxiety. This condition was called "hospitalism" by Spitz, who identified it and studied it in hospitalized children who were separated from their mothers [52]. Lipsitt, drawing conclusions from his research in the National Collaborative Perinatal Project, and from the research of others, suggests that a learning disorder is involved. Neonatal response patterns may be inadequate on which to build reciprocal relationships, or conditions may not support the building of interaction patterns that result in adequate food intake and stimulation. Although future research can be expected to give more insight as to how to help infants who fail to thrive, present knowledge at least indicates the need for helping and supporting the infant-mother pair in the family.

Failure to thrive is shown by slow growth, small food intake, low interaction, quietness, passiveness, solemnness

Injury. Planning and vigilance are needed to keep a baby safe from injury. Even a newborn infant can move by means of reflex crawling. The first time of turning over is not predictable. Therefore, minimum caution requires never leaving a baby unwatched on a table or bed without sides. Cribs and playpens are used in North America. In contrast, Umersingh, the baby we knew in India, was never left alone. He was held or carried by his mother, sister, or father. Or he lay on a cot with his father sitting beside him. In Africa, many babies are tied on their mothers' backs; in Mexico, they often ride in shawls tied in front. Siblings are frequent guardians and carriers of toddlers.

Safekeeping is insured by restraint and/or environmental design

Accidents account for a substantial number of infant deaths. A study of death rates found accidents responsible for 44 per cent of the deaths of year-old boys and 33 per cent of the year-old girls [13]. Designing the environment for a creeping or walking baby is an important part of parenting. American child-rearing values include freedom to explore and learn, along with safety from injury. Such a design includes physical limits indoors and out, removal of poisons, sharp instruments, breakable objects, and objects that can be knocked over, and lack of access to fire, electricity, and water. In this purged environment, there can be interesting objects and possibilities for activity, such as cupboards to open and shut, spoons, nesting bowls, muffin tins, paper bags, and other such toys and materials.

Child abuse accounts for some of the injuries suffered by infants. Both violence and neglect cause serious damage. Causes of abuse exist at all levels of the ecology and within the infant. When a newborn is difficult, interactions with mother and father are likely to be strained. Problems can arise from prematurity, small size, handicapping conditions, excessive crying, and inadequate sucking. Parents may be predisposed to abusing if they have experienced it themselves, if they are under stress and isolated from network and community interaction and support. The macrosystem may include customs, laws, and beliefs that sanction physical violence, including physical punishment of children.

Abused toddlers show characteristic behavior patterns that resemble those found in rejected infants [20]. Observed in a day care center and compared with nonabused babies between 1 and 3 years of age, these toddlers were more aggressive, more negative to friendly overtures, and more difficult.

Child abuse is presently being studied on all levels [9]. In order to treat abused children and their families, and even better, to prevent abuse, research and social action are both needed [54].

Feeding Infants

Feeding is social, a transaction between caregiver and infant. Human beings have devised an extraordinary number of variations of feeding children, in terms of what, how, and when.

Human Milk

Breast-feeding continues the intimate biological interaction of mother and baby that was established during pregnancy. The mother supplies the vast complex of materials that the baby needs for maintenance, growth, and resistance to disease, and the baby influences the mother to produce appropriate compositions and amounts of milk. When a baby sucks the mother's breast immediately after birth, her milk flow is likely to be established earlier than if sucking is delayed [38].

Uniqueness of human milk: Proportions, fat, protein, lactose, vitamins, minerals, responsive changes

Special Composition [24]. Every species of mammal, including woman, produces a unique kind of milk. Even the color is specific to the species. Human milk is bluish, cow's yellowish, and kangaroo's pink. A comparison of the gross constituents of human milk with cow's milk shows the former to have more calories per unit, less protein, more fat, more lactose, and less ash. When the biochemical and physical properties of these constituents are analyzed, the uniqueness of each kind of milk becomes more obvious. Not only is the amount of fat greater in human milk than in cow's milk, but its composition is different in having higher levels of essential polyunsaturated fatty acids and higher cholesterol levels. This feature of human milk is suited to the rapid brain growth that occurs in the human neonate, when fat makes up 60 per cent of the brain, and the myelinization of the nervous system is taking place. The type of subcutaneous fat produced from human milk differs from that made by cow's milk.

The protein of woman's milk makes a much softer curd in the baby's stomach than does the protein of cow's milk. Patterns of nitrogen-containing compounds are very different in the two milks. Human milk is richer in lactoferrin, a substance with disease-resistant properties that prevent gastrointestinal infections of the young baby.

Lactose, which is more plentiful in human milk than in any other milk, enhances calcium absorption, promotes the growth of lactobacilli in the intestine, and provides material necessary for brain growth. The patterning of vitamins is specific to human milk. Minerals, also, are constituted and patterned uniquely. Feeding with cow's milk produces babies who differ metabolically from those fed with woman's milk. Some of the extra weight gain in formula-fed babies may be caused by retention of sodium and water. Cow's milk places a greater load on human kidneys than does human milk.

The Changing Composition and Amount. Milk varies through one feeding, through the day, and through the total period of lactation. As we have seen, colostrum is the first product of the mother's breasts after the baby is born. It has less fat and less lactose, but more sodium and zinc than milk produced later.

At a given feeding, the first milk that flows is thin and watery. It gradually becomes more concentrated, carrying 4 or 5 times as much fat and 1.5 times as much protein at the end as at the beginning [22] Babies will stop nursing before one breast is empty and yet will readily nurse more from the other breast. Probably an apetite control mechanism is at work. For example, the increasing fat and proteins give a different taste as the breast empties. At a certain point in concentration, the baby rejects food, and yet he still needs more water, which the second breast supplies. The obesity more often seen in formula-fed babies is rare in babies fed on human milk, probably because of the changing composition of milk at each feeding. (As mentioned previously, some other properties of human milk also make obesity less likely.) An important part of the intake control mechanism is the baby's role in rejecting the breast and possibly accepting the other. If the mother, instead, made the decision to stop nursing or to change breasts, the control would be lost.

Disease-Resisting Functions. Infants are born with some temporary immunity to diseases to which their mothers are immune. They also receive such immunity while breast-fed. Human milk contains substances that confer resistance to gastrointestinal infections, especially infection by *E. coli*. Lactoferrin has already been mentioned. At least two human milk substances have been found effective against some viruses, including herpes virus. One of these, lysozyme (also present in tears) has been found to be as much as 5,000 times as great in human milk as in cow's milk. The intestinal floras of breast-fed babies are very different from those of formula-fed babies. Their stools differ in composition and odor. Also, when milk is regurgitated after feeding, the odor is more sour in a baby fed on cow's milk.

Trends in Infant Feeding

After pediatrician Holt (see *Growth and Health Sciences* in Chapter 1) developed safe methods of artificial feeding for infants, breast-feeding gradually gave way to formula-feeding among middle- and upper-class women in the Western World. Somewhat later, working-class and lower-class women followed the lead of the more privileged women. Only recently, poor women in the Third World have adopted bottle-feeding, with disastrous effects for many of their infants. At present the trend is to breast-feed among the middle- and upper-classes in the West. The best educated women have become convinced that human milk is best for human babies and that the emotional rewards of breast-feeding are great for mothers as well as infants. (See Figure 4–5.) Through education for childbirth, family-centered hospital care, and training and support for breast-feeding, some women have re-established breast-feeding as normal. A 1981 survey found 55 percent of United States mothers breast-feeding during the baby's first 6 months [15a].

There have always been mothers who could not breast-feed, and others who did not want to do so. Before safe formula feeding was developed, an infant was likely to die if not breast-fed. Although wealthy women

FIGURE 4–5
Per cent of babies who were breast fed, by year of baby's birth and mother's education: United States. (SOURCE: G. E. Hendershot. Trends in breast feeding. *Advance data from vital and health statistics of the National Center for Health Statistics,* No. 59. Mar. 18, 1980. D.H.E.W. Publication No. (PRS) 80-1250.)

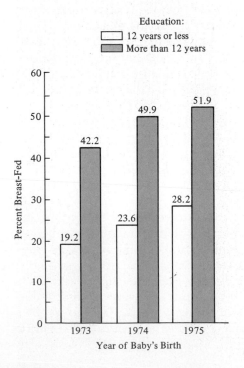

might hire wet nurses, the average mother would attempt unsafe formula feeding. Today, a mother does not have to breast-feed in order to give her infant safe, nutritious food. Researchers continue to improve formulas. Pediatricians and nutritionists try to suit the particular formula to the individual baby. Careful preparation and sanitation are important. An advantage of bottle-feeding is that fathers, siblings, grandparents, and others can feed the baby. And, of course, the mother is freer to carry responsibilities other than infant care, and to make more choices as to how she spends her time.

Ecology. "Would you breast-feed in public?" The cover of a recent *Parents' Magazine* featured this question. The article [65] assumes that mothers value breast-feeding, and goes on to tell them how to cope with the hostility that they are likely to encounter when breast-feeding in public. The hostility can be traced to macrosystem values and beliefs in which breasts are defined as sex objects rather than food-givers. Because breast-feeding is denigrated, many women are unable to lactate, even when they want to do so. Support groups for pregnant and lactating women are helpful, by generating confidence and positive feelings, as well as by teaching techniques of breast-feeding. The LaLeche League is an international organization devoted to breast-feeding. It cuts across macrosystems!

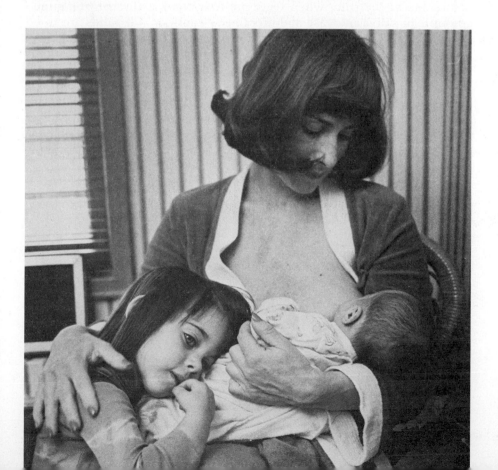

Most infant feeding takes place within the microsystem of the home, which is of course influenced by macrosystem values. The attitudes and behavior of fathers are extremely powerful in determining whether mothers are able to breast-feed. Siblings also contribute to the mother's feelings and hence to her performance. For example, a young child who feels displaced will show distress. Lactation is often influenced by grandmothers and friends who are supportive or destructive.

Transition to Solid Foods

Breast milk or well-prepared formula gives a baby enough nutrients during the first 3 to 6 months of life. Extra nutrients are likely to place a strain upon the kidneys and other organs. Excess calories may contribute to the laying down of extra fat cells, possibly leading to lifelong obesity [61]. On the other hand, inadequate supplements result in malnutrition and growth retardation. When milk intake declines, the quality of supplements is very important.

When new foods are introduced, they are accepted more readily if changes are gradual. The baby first uses the sucking movements that he uses with milk. The new cereal, fruit, or vegetable can be offered in a semiliquid form, in a very small quantity. The baby has time to accommodate to a new form and a new taste.

Table 4–4 shows the ages at which the deciduous or baby teeth erupt. Before and at the time when teeth are first coming through the gums, amounts of saliva increase and drooling is common. If solids are to be chewed, they have to be mixed with saliva and they must be ground between two teeth. The incisors, good for biting, begin to appear at 7 or 8 months, whereas molars can be expected at around 15 months. If these physiological indications of readiness for solids are taken seriously, then the offering of foods that need chewing will be delayed until the baby can chew them. However, babies make chewing movements with their gums while teething, and they seem to be comforted by chewing on hard rubber toys and foods that will not break off in pieces, such as a hard biscuit.

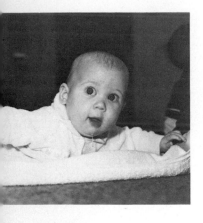

TABLE 4–4
Ages (in Months) for Early, Average, and Late Eruption of Deciduous Teeth.

Deciduous teeth	Early	Average	Late
Lower central incisor	5	7.8	11
Upper central incisor	6	9.6	12
Lower lateral incisor	7	11.5	15
Upper lateral incisor	7	12.4	18
Lower 1st molar	10	15.1	20
Upper 1st molar	10	15.7	20
Lower cuspid	11	18.2	24
Upper cuspid	11	18.3	24
Lower 2d molar	13	26.0	31
Upper 2d molar	13	26.2	31

Source: Data from S. L. Horowitz and E. H. Hixon. *The nature of orthodontic diagnosis.* St. Louis: The C. V. Mosby Company, 1966.

Weaning. Emerging resources include new ways of eating. Instead of getting all of his food by sucking liquids, the baby learns to bite and chew solids and to drink liquids from a cup. This particular changeover is called *weaning*. Weaning is also used sometimes to mean any gradual change from immature to mature behavior. In all contexts, weaning usually involves some pushing and encouraging of the child toward more mature behavior. As an older baby can hold his bottle and carry it with him, he can enjoy sucking and his autonomy at the same time, whereas with breast-feeding, the growing desire for independence may make him accept cup feeding more readily. The timing and techniques of weaning are related to personality development of the child and to macrosystem values.

The use of gradualness and gentleness is consistent with what is known about personality development during the first year. While developing the sense of trust, it is most helpful for the baby to be assured that the world and the people in it can be trusted. Traumatic experiences and major readjustments to life are injurious to the sense of trust and hence to the establishment of the foundations of a healthy personality.

An example from another macrosystem shows how weaning can be crucial to the sense of autonomy, rather than to the sense of trust, when weaning occurs at a time when the sense of autonomy is growing rapidly. A group of Zulu babies were studied before, during, and after weaning, which occurred between 15 and 24 months, at the average age of 19 months [2]. The day of weaning was a serious event, fixed months ahead. Bitter aloe juice was put on the mother's breast while the child watched. Then the breast was offered to him throughout the day. A charm was put around his neck to help him. On the day of weaning, all but one baby refused the breast after the first encounter with the aloe juice. Behavior changes followed a definite pattern of disintegration, followed by integration on a higher level. During the first two hours, the toddlers became more negativistic, aggressive, and fretful. They sucked their fingers and other objects. Some performed stereotyped actions. After the first day, relationships changed with everyone in the home. With their mothers, they first alternated attacking and ignoring, then tried to gain attention by illness, clinging, fretting, and crying, and finally paid little attention to their mothers, showing no anger and behaving with increasing independence. Sudden increases in mature behavior included helping with housework, imitating others, using new words, talking more distinctly, leaving home more often, and showing hospitality. Children also became more aggressive and mischievous, spilling water, playing with fire, and wasting food. Eating patterns changed, with preferences for adult food and greatly increased appetite.

These behavior changes can be seen as contributing to a growing sense of autonomy. Normal development during the second year, especially the latter half of the second year, involves establishing oneself as a separate individual. All of these six changes in behavior indicate increased independence, power in decision making, differentiation, and reorganization. The weaning experience apparently precipitated the second stage of personality growth. Thus, the method of sudden weaning, conducted differently and timed differently, had a very different result from weaning conducted American-style. Both methods of weaning can be seen to be functional in regard to the stage of personality growth during which they are conducted.

Autonomy in eating: Child determines how much

Self-regulation of Diet. Of great practical significance is the question of how competent the child is to select the quantity and quality of his food. "Does the baby know how much he ought to eat?" and "Does the baby know what is good for him?" Probably he would if he had been fed entirely on breast milk for most of the first year and then exposed at each mealtime to a wide selection of simple, nutritionally valuable foods and *no other foods*. Since it is impractical and even impossible to arrange these conditions at home, the baby needs to have a good diet selected for him and presented in small servings at regular times. If the atmosphere is pleasant, and autonomy in feeding encouraged, then most infants will be able to decide how *much* they should eat. If parents and caretakers develop trust in the baby's ability to decide when he has had enough, they will not be tempted to stuff unnecessary calories into him, nor will they set up the dining table as a battleground.

Caring for Infants

"I care for you" may mean "I love you," or it may mean "I give you and do for you the things you need in order to live and develop well." Infants need care in both its meanings, because affection is the setting in which physical caregiving has meaning and positive overall effects.

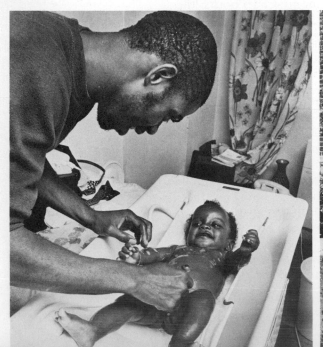

As mentioned in regard to states, the new infant-and-parent pair work toward regulation of states, toward less crying, more alertness, and longer sleep periods. With increasing homeostatic control, the infant's life becomes entrained or organized into a pattern that fits with the mother's life patterns and with the family's. The caregiver plays a vital role in interpreting the infant's signals and supplying what is needed at the right times and in the right amounts and qualities. Infant (and parental) personality develops as these transactions occur. The sense of trust is the crucial aspect of personality growth for at least the first year of life. Erikson [15, pp. 247–251] writes of the feeling of goodness that comes when the baby is helped to cope with his environment. The world must seem like a good place to be and the people in it trustworthy when he is fed before he is overwhelmed by hunger, when he is kept at a comfortable temperature, and when he receives a satisfactory amount of sensory stimulation. As he signals his needs and his caretaker responds, his sense of trust grows.

Care at Home

Although the mother is usually the first and primary caregiver, many fathers share in caring for their babies. In the United States, the father's traditional role in regard to a young baby is to help and support the mother, a very important function. Recent changes in men's roles now make men more free to give bottles and baths, to change diapers, and to carry babies in back packs or chest packs. In Sweden, men may take paternity leave in order to care for their infants. Chinese fathers and mothers share the care of babies and children. In parts of Africa, child nurses may be responsible for infant siblings for hours at a time. Various kinds of family organizations provide different patterns of caregiving. A grandmother may be an important, or even chief, caregiver. Care may be shared by sisters or by members of a communal group. Whatever the arrangement may be, primary responsibilities are these: keeping the baby safe from injury and illness; providing adequate food at appropriate times; keeping the baby clean; providing stimulation and interesting experiences; managing rhythms of daily life that make a good fit between the competencies of the baby and the optimal functioning of the family. Birth is an ecological transition. The microsystem of the home changes physically and socially to accommodate the new member. It continues to change as all the members develop and interact.

Basic infant care includes safety, food, cleanliness, stimulation, and timing

Sometimes a family cannot provide infant care. A friend or paid helper will be called into the home. *Sitter* is not a very accurate name for a paid caregiver, because much more than sitting is required. Caregivers may assume any or all of the primary responsibilities, but always the first one. Training has to be adequate for the skills needed. Even young infants react to changes in caregivers, although parents may not be aware that their baby can tell the difference between mother and sitter. Mothers' faces and voices may be distinguished as early as 5 weeks [6], and the smell of the mother's milk is distinguished as early as 6 days [34]. The emotional and physical comfort of the infant will be served by familiarizing caregivers with the baby, home, and routines before leaving a caregiver and baby alone together.

Day Care

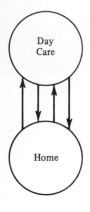

When a family needs regular help with caring for a baby, it is often more feasible to take the baby to a day-care center or to the home of a family day-care provider. Licensing of day care assures that certain standards are met, but some exploration is needed to find out which particular program will best suit a certain baby and family. The provider can be judged in terms of the primary responsibilities previously outlined.

The baby's mesosystem includes the relationship between home and day-care center or day-care home. The connection between these two vital microsystems is extremely important to the functioning of the infant. Well-being depends on all of the caregivers' knowing what is happening to the baby in both microsystems, and making bridges between them. The day caregiver makes a bridge by saying, "Karin ate such a big lunch. She may not be very hungry for her supper." The father makes a bridge as he arrives and says, "Ben was out with us last night and didn't get to sleep until late. He may be a bit cranky and ready for an early nap."

Macrosystems vary greatly in the caregiving support that they make available to families. Day care centers are more liberally provided when women's work is needed, as it is in China, and where family ideology and gender role equality are advanced, as they are in Scandinavia. At present in the United States, the demand for day care greatly exceeds the supply. Finding satisfactory day care is a serious problem to many working mothers and to fathers who bear major responsibility for caregiving.

Professional Health Care

Health care involves guidance, prevention, diagnosis, treatment

Children's health care includes four processes: monitoring and guidance of growth and nutrition; preventing illness by immunizations and hygiene; detecting and diagnosing illness and other physical problems; treating illnesses in such ways that health is restored and future complications prevented. An example of the fourth process is the prompt treatment of middle-ear infections, a common problem in early childhood that can result in loss of hearing. Children need frequent and consistent care from health professionals trained in child health.

Health care begins in the microsystem of the home, but the family cannot do the whole job. Another microsystem plays an important part in applying professional skills to children's health. The United States macrosystem places physicians, even pediatricians, in this role, although there are also well-baby clinics. North America has fewer people per physician than any region of the world except the U.S.S.R. [35]. Even so, the high cost of physicians' services is out of reach for many families. Instead of buying all four processes for their children, parents make do with the treatment of illnesses and probably also immunizations. Immunizations may be offered free or at low cost in clinics for those who cannot afford the fees in physicians' offices.

Other macrosystems structure child health care differently, in terms of both costs and delivery systems. A comparison of American and European systems yields the following conclusions [50]. Europeans provide more social support for families, including children's allowances, maternity allowances, and assistance with housing. Preventive and curative programs, often separate, are funded through taxes and insurances, with the patient paying a small part of costs in Scandinavia and France, a large amount in Belgium, and none in Great Britain. Holland, Sweden, and Finland, countries with excellent child health, share the following features of health system design: preventive services separate from but linked to curative; nurses important in preventive work and in linking preventive to curative; national standards and local control; strong supervision by the national health department.

Although European health care systems may set more feasible goals for the United States, it can also be instructive to look at the efficient system functioning in China [60]. All infants are frequently and regularly examined, weighed, and measured, and illnesses promptly treated. Immunizations are given during regular visits. The primary health caregiver is a neighbor, living close by, called a health aide or a "barefoot doctor." She or he has been chosen by peers in the factory, neighborhood, or commune, to receive very limited training. Further training is given to health workers chosen to become nurses and doctors to work in hospitals with serious cases. Prenatal care is given and normal deliveries assisted by midwives and barefoot doctors. High-risk cases are delivered in hospitals by more highly trained personnel. This system, financed by groups and not by individuals, is available to all children.

Children's health needs in the United States have been reviewed, and recommendations made, by the Harvard Child Health Project [23]. Services to all children should be increased, and especially to poor central city and rural children. More pediatric nurse practitioners and other nonphysicians should take part in giving health care. Financing, including government financing, should include preventive and follow-up work, not just treatment.

Summary

The ecological transition of birth brings the infant into a new microsystem, the family, and provides her with additional microsystems. Microsystems have varying influences on infants' birth weights, morbidity, and mortality, reflecting variation in opportunities for growth, health, and care. Methods of infant care change as a society changes, producing uncertainty at present for parents in North America.

An increasingly accepted method of caring for the newborn is to keep the baby close to the mother, permitting and encouraging mother-infant interaction. Physical and behavioral assessments indicate when medical intervention is needed. The transition from fetus to baby involves essential changes in respiration, circulation, digestion, and metabolism. Six behavioral states have been identified. Patterning of states varies between individuals, sexes, and ethnic groups. Regulation of states is a joint venture between infant and caregiver, crying being most problematic to caregivers.

Physical development includes rapid changes in appearance, length, weight, proportions, fat distribution, and brain structure. Height and weight tables can be used for assessing growth. Regularity of basic life processes is normally accomplished by 3 to 4 months.

Malnutrition, a widespread, serious problem, disrupts growth and makes infants susceptible to infections. Death is a likely result of the combination of malnutrition, infection, and diarrhea. Malnutrition results from insufficient food, food of poor quality or unsuitable for children, food prepared in inappropriate ways, and inadequate social interaction. Infants with metabolic disorders need special nutrition.

A substantial number of infant deaths occur from accidents and abuse. Constant supervision is necessary to keep a baby safe from injury. Care includes designing and maintaining a safe environment in which the baby is free to play and explore. Child abuse has complex roots in infant behavior, microsystems, networks, and macrosystems.

Breast-feeding is a biological and social interaction. The milk of each species is specific to the species and adapted to the growth characteristics of its young. The individual mother's milk continually adapts to the demands of her baby, in composition, amount, and immunizing properties. Macrosystem influences affect mothers' success in lactation, as do also family members, relatives, and friends. Transition to solid foods can be critical in very poor environments. Under prosperous conditions, questions of weaning are timing, gradualness, selection of nutritious foods, special preparation, and permitting choice and autonomy.

The family is the chief care-giving microsystem, with the mother usually the main caregiver. Fathers are assuming increasing responsibility for infants in North America, China, and some parts of Europe. Siblings are more often caregivers in Africa and Asia than in the West. Care is also given in other microsystems called day care centers or family day care homes. Macrosystems vary in the amount of available day care and other help to families. Medical or professional health care is given in various microsystems, structured differently in different macrosystems. European macrosystems have been found more adequate in providing preventive and regular health care to infants, although the American system makes skilled care available to newborn infants at high risk.

References

1. Abraham, S., F. W. Lowenstein, and C. L. Johnson. *Preliminary findings of the first health and nutrition survey, United States, 1971–72: Dietary intake and biochemical findings.* (DHEW Publication No. (HRA) 74–1219–1.) Washington: U.S. Government Printing Office, 1974.

2. Albino, R. C., and V. J. Thompson. The effects of sudden weaning on Zulu children. In W. Dennis (ed.). *Readings in child psychology.* 2nd ed. Englewood Cliffs, N.J.: Prentice-Hall, Inc., 1963. Pp. 128–148.

3. Barnes, R. H. Nutrition and man's intellect and behavior. Proceedings of the First Biological Congress of the American Institute of Nutrition, 1971, **30,** 1429–1433. In S. P. Raman (ed.). *Nutrition, development and learning.* New York: M.S.S. Information Corporation, 1974.

4. Bell, S. M., and M. D. S. Ainsworth. Infant crying and maternal responsiveness. *Child Development,* 1972, **43,** 1171–1190.

5. Berg, W. K., C. D. Adkinson, and D. D. Strock. Duration and periods of alertness in neonates. *Developmental Psychology,* 1973, **9,** 434.

6. Bigelow, A. Infants' recognition of mothers. Paper presented at meeting of the Society for Research in Child Development, New Orleans, 1977.

7. Brackbill, Y. Continuous stimulation reduces arousal level: Stability of effect over time. *Child Development,* 1973, **44,** 43–46.

8. Brazelton, T. B., J. S. Robey, and G. A. Collier. Infant development in the Zinacanteco Indians of Southern Mexico. *Pediatrics,* 1969, **44,** 274–293.

9. Chibucos, T. R. (ed.). Toward broader conceptualization of child mistreatment. *Infant Mental Health Journal,* 1980, **1:**4.

10. Colley, J. R. T., W. W. Holland, and R. T. Corkhill. Influence of passive smoking and parental phlegm on pneumonia and bronchitis in early childhood. *Lancet,* Nov. 2, 1974, 1031–1034.

11. Cravioto, J. Malnutrition in early childhood and some of its consequences for the individual and the community. General Foods Distinguished International Lectures on Nutrition. Toronto, Apr. 10, 1975.

12. Dean, R. F. Effects of malnutrition, especially of slight degree, on the growth of young children. *Courier,* 1965, **15,** 78–83.

13. Death rates from accidents among boys and girls aged one through four, and accidental deaths as a percent of all deaths. United States, 1972–73. *Statistical Bulletin,* 1975, **65:**5, 7–9.

14. Dobbing, J. Human brain development and its vulnerability In *Biological and clinical aspects of brain development.* Mead Johnson Symposium on Perinatal and Developmental Medicine No. 6. Evansville, Ind.; Mead Johnson & Co., 1975.

15. Erikson, E. H. *Childhood and society.* New York: W. W. Norton & Company, Inc., 1963.

15a. Emery, C. E. 36.5% of R.I. women breastfeed babies. *Providence Evening Bulletin,* July 8, 1981.

16. Freedman, D. G., and N. C. Freedman. Behavioral differences between Chinese-American and European-American newborns. *Nature,* 1961, **224,** 1227.

17. Frodi, A. M., M. E. Lamb, L. A. Leavitt, W. L. Donovan, C. Neff, and D. Sherry. Fathers' and mothers' responses to the faces and cries of normal and premature infants. *Developmental Psychology,* 1978, **14,** 490–498.

18. Garn, S. M. The applicability of North American growth standards in developing countries. *Canadian Medical Association Journal,* 1965, **93,** 914–919.

19. General Research Centers Branch, National Institutes of Health. *How children grow.* (DHEW Publication No. (NIH) 72–166.) Washington: U.S. Government Printing Office, 1972.

20. George, C., and M. Main. Social interactions of young abused children: Approach, avoidance, and aggression. *Child Development,* 1979, **50,** 306–318.

21. Groom, G. L., and T. McNichol. Relationship between perinatal factors and conditioned head turn responding in the very young infant. Paper presented at meeting of the Society for Research in Child Development, New Orleans, 1977.

22. Hall, B. Changing composition of human milk and early development of an appetite control. *Lancet,* Apr. 5, 1975, 779–781.

23. Harvard Child Health Project Task Force. *Toward a primary medical care*

system responsive to children's needs. Cambridge, Mass.: Ballinger Publishing, 1977.

24. Jelliffe, D. B., and E. F. P. Jelliffe. *Human milk in the modern world.* London: Oxford University Press, 1978.

25. Keet, M. P., J. D. L. Hansen, and A. S. Truswell. Are skinfold measurements of value in the assessment of suboptimal nutrition in young children? *Pediatrics,* 1970, **45,** 965–972.

26. Kelly, V. C., and J. F. Bosma. Basal metabolism in infants and children. In I. McQuarrie (ed.). *Brennemann's practice of pediatrics.* Vol. 1. Hagerstown, Md.: W. F. Prior, 1957.

27. Kilpatrick, A., and J. Kirkland. A neonatal pain-cry effect on caretakers and noncaretakers. *Journal of Biological Psychology,* 1977, **19:**2, 35–38.

28. Klaus, M. H., J. H. Kennell, N. Plumb, and S. Zuehlke. Human maternal behavior at the first contact with her young. *Pediatrics,* 1970, **46,** 187–192.

29. Korner, A. F. State as a variable, as obstacle and as mediator of stimulation in infant research. *Merrill-Palmer Quarterly,* 1972, **18,** 74–94.

30. Lester, B. M., and P. S. Zeskind. The organization of crying in the infant at risk. In T. M. Field, A. M. Sostek, S. Goldberg, and N. H. Shuman (eds.). *Infants born at risk.* New York: Spectrum, 1979.

31. Lipsitt, L. P. Critical conditions in infancy: A psychological perspective. *American Psychologist,* 1979, **34,** 973–980.

32. Lipton, E. L., A. Steinschneider, and J. B. Richmond. Autonomic function in the neonate. VII. Maturational changes in cardiac control. *Child Development,* 1966, **37,** 1–16.

33. Lowrey, G. H. *Growth and development of children.* 6th ed. Chicago: Medical Year Book, 1973.

34. Macfarlane, A. *The psychology of childbirth.* Cambridge, Mass.: Harvard University Press, 1977.

35. McHale, M. C., J. McHale, and G. F. Streatfeild. *Children in the world.* Washington: Population Reference Bureau, 1979.

36. McWilliams, M. *Nutrition for the growing years.* 2nd ed. New York: John Wiley & Sons, Inc., 1975.

37. Maslansky, E., C. Cowell, R. Caral, S. N. Berman, and M. Grussi. Survey of infant feeding practices. *American Journal of Public Health,* 1974, **64,** 780–785.

38. Mercer, J., and R. Russ. Variables affecting time between childbirth and the establishment of lactation. *Journal of General Psychology,* 1980, **102,** 155–156.

39. Mönckeberg, F. Effect of early marasmic malnutrition on subsequent physical and psychological development. In N. S. Scrimshaw and J. E. Gordon (eds.). *Malnutrition, learning and behavior.* Cambridge, Mass.: M.I.T. Press, 1968. Pp. 269–278.

40. Ounsted, M. Fetal growth. In D. Gairdner, and D. Hull (eds.). *Recent advances in pediatrics.* London: Churchill, 1971.

41. Parmelee, A. H., and E. S. Stern. Development of states in infants. In C. Clemente, D. Purpura, and F. Mayer (eds.). *Sleep in the maturing nervous system.* New York: Academic Press, Inc., 1972.

42. Pederson, R., and D. Ter Vrugt. The influence of amplitude and frequency of vestibular stimulation on the activity of two-month-old infants. *Child Development,* 1973, **44,** 122–128.

43. Phillips, S., S. King, and L. DuBois. Spontaneous activities of female versus male newborns. *Child Development,* 1978, **49,** 590–597.

44. Pollitt, E., M. Gilmore, and M. Valcarcel. Early mother-infant interaction and somatic growth. *Early Human Development,* 1978, **1:**4, 325–336.

45. Rewey, H. H. Developmental change in infant heart rate response during sleeping and waking states. *Developmental Psychology,* 1973, **8,** 35–41.

46. Roberts, K. E., and J. A. Schoelkopf. Eating, sleeping, and elimination: Practices of a group of two and a half year old children. *American Journal of Diseases of Children,* 1951, **82,** 121–152.

47. Roffwarg, H. P., J. N. Muzio, and W. C. Dement. Ontogenetic development of the human sleep-dream cycle. *Science,* 1966, **152,** 604–617.

48. Sabry, Z. I., J. A. Campbell, M. E. Campbell, and A. L. Forbes. Nutrition Canada. *Nutrition Today,* 1974, **9:**1, 5–13.

49. Schmidt, K. The effect of continuous stimulation on the behavioral sleep of infants. *Merrill-Palmer Quarterly,* 1975, **26,** 369–378.

50. Silver, G. A. *Child health: America's future.* Germantown, Md.: Aspen Systems Corp., 1978.

51. Smith, C. A. *The physiology of the newborn infant.* Springfield, Ill.: Charles C Thomas, 1959.

52. Spitz, R. A. Hospitalism. In *The psychoanalytic study of the child.* Vol. 1. New York: International Universities Press, 1945.

53. Spock, B. *Baby and child care.* New York: Pocket Books, 1968.

54. Starr, R. H. Child abuse. *American Psychologist,* 1979, **34,** 872–879.

55. Tanner, J. M. *Foetus into man: Physical growth from conception to maturity.* Cambridge, Mass.: Harvard University Press, 1979.

56. Tarlo, P. A., I. Valimaki, and P. M. Rautaharju. Quantitative computer analysis of cardiac and respiratory activity in newborn infants. *Journal of Applied Physiology,* 1971, **31,** 70–74.

57. Tennes, K., and D. Carter. Plasma cortisol levels and behavioral states in early infancy. *Psychosomatic Medicine,* 1973, **35:**2, 121–128.

58. Trnavsky, P. A. Tympanic temperature and behavioral state changes in newborns. Paper presented at meeting of the Society for Research in Child Development, New Orleans, 1977.

59. Vallbona, C., et al. Cardiodynamic studies in the newborn II. Regulation of heart rate. *Biologia Neonatorum,* 1963, **5,** 159–199.

60. Werner, E. E. *Cross-cultural child development: A view from the planet Earth.* Monterey, Calif.: Brooks/Cole, 1979.

61. Winick, M. Childhood obesity. *Nutrition Today,* 1974, **9:**3, 9–12.

62. Wolff, P. H. Observations on newborn infants. *Psychosomatic Medicine,* 1959, **21,** 110–118.

63. Wolff, P. H. The development of attention in young infants. *Annals of the New York Academy of Science,* 1965, **118,** 815–830.

64. Wolff, P. H. The causes, controls and organization of behavior in the neonate. *Psychological Issues,* 1966, **5:**1.

65. Yarrow, L. Breast-feeding: The new etiquette. *Parents' Magazine,* 1979, **54:**9, 46–48.

5

Sensori-motor Development

Nowadays child developmentalists marvel at the competence of infants. Only a few decades ago newborn babies were thought to be quite insensitive and to have no capabilities for responding and relating to others. Because their motor abilities are extremely limited and they cannot talk, infants are not very capable of communicating their perceptions, understanding, preferences, and goals. New research methods, however, have shown infants to have remarkable perceptual abilities and to be able to respond and communicate if given the right opportunities. This chapter is concerned with the patterning and sequencing of infant competencies in the ecology in which babies develop.

QUESTIONS TO THINK
ABOUT WHILE READING
THIS CHAPTER

1. How does the world look, sound, and feel to a newborn baby? To an older infant?
2. How can researchers tell what a baby sees and hears?
3. Which sights and sounds have special significance for the young infant?
4. What are the behavioral competencies of the newborn?
5. How do infants and adults communicate with each other?
6. What is sensorimotor intelligence?
7. In which macrosystems do infants show acceleration in sensorimotor development?
8. What are some interactions within the family microsystem that have special significance for sensorimotor development?

Motor Behavior and Development

Motor development means increasing control over the movements of the body and its parts. The infant is born with action patterns, reflexes, that are ready to use. Originating in the subcortical (nonthinking) regions of the brain, the newborn's reflexes are modified by higher brain centers, which both facilitate and inhibit [6]. Reflexes serve the infant until further cortical development makes additional voluntary control possible. The transition from largely reflex to more voluntary behavior takes place at between 2 and 4 months of age. The previous chapter mentioned the age of 3 months, or the age range between 2 and 4 months, as the time when regulation of states and basic processes is normally achieved. All these transitions toward maturity are based upon the development taking place in the nervous system.

Well-integrated behavior patterns that are elicited by a specific stimulus are called *reflexes.* Some of them are protective, such as blinking, withdrawing from painful stimuli, and shivering. Others that may have been protective in the early history of the species include the startle or Moro reflex, the Darwinian or grasp reflex, and the Babkin reflex, in which pressure on the infant's palms causes him to raise his arms, close his eyes, turn his head to the midline, and open his mouth. The baby makes postural adjustments to being held prone and in midair. Sometimes these are called *antigravity reflexes.* If not encumbered by clothing and bedding, a new infant will creep, or at least make progress, when prone. Newborns will walk when supported adequately in upright position, with their feet touching a surface. Whether creeping and walking should be called reflexes is debatable, but they are patterns that are ready to work at birth. If a newborn is lying on his back, and someone presses the legs or the arms down to the bed and suddenly releases them, the limbs quickly assume the flexed position.

The baby is ready at birth to find his food, take it into his mouth, and swallow it. The *rooting reflex* is a response to a touch on the cheek and/or lip. When touched on the cheek, perhaps several times, he opens his mouth and moves his head toward the source of the touch. When touched above the lip, he opens his mouth and moves his head from side to side. These movements are useful for finding the nipple. When touched on the lip, the baby purses his lips or pouts, probably causing erection of the nipple and making it easier to grasp. When the nipple is grasped, it delivers the stimulus to the *sucking* reflex and he sucks, using both *expression* and *suction.* Expression is a lapping movement, whereas suction is a negative pressure, created by increasing the size of the mouth cavity. Even though newborn infants are very skillful in rooting and sucking, sucking behavior is by no means automatic, in the manner of a startle reflex. Sucking is adapted to the pressure of the milk flow [31]. When milk is flowing fast, as it does in the beginning of a breast-feeding or from a bottle whose nipple has big holes, the baby sucks continuously. When the flow is slower, the baby pauses, sucks in a burst of sucks, pauses again, and continues in this pattern. Mothers and caretakers often jiggle the pausing infant, but research shows that it is the milk pressure and not the jiggling that controls the sucking pattern.

Sucking is soothing, and infants will suck on anything in the mouth. Pacifiers are used widely throughout the world, since it is well known that they will help a baby to go to sleep and stay asleep. An experiment on 4-day-old infants demonstrated the power of the pacifier to block responses during sleep [69]. The subjects were tickled with a camel's hair brush during regular sleep while sucking and not sucking. They responded less while sucking. While asleep and not sucking, but with the pacifier in the mouth, the baby was likely to respond to tickling with a new burst of sucking.

Sucking is closely related to *looking.* A film analysis showed 2- and 3-day-old infants frequently alerting before and after their hands contacted their mouths [33]. The authors suggested that this pattern may be the early unified behavior from which eye-hand coordination is later differentiated. At birth, however, and for several days thereafter, the infant sucks with his eyes shut [9, p. 287]. If he looks, he stops sucking. Even by 2 months, when he may appear to be looking and sucking at the same time, recordings show that he is not doing so, but that the two actions are closely coordinated.

Posture

The tonic-neck-reflex position is the usual posture when the newborn lies supine (face up). The head is turned to one side (the right, in about 75 per cent of infants [55]), and the arm on that side is bent up as though the baby were looking at his hand. The other arm is stretched up. The choice of right or left is related to prenatal and birth positions [43]. Mothers are more likely to hold right-turning babies on their left shoulders, and left-turning babies on their right [23].

The three photographs show typical newborn behavior when the baby is prone (on her stomach). She raises her head to free her nose and turns her head to the side. She also makes crawling movements. When held in a sitting position, she pulls her head forward after it has fallen back, as can be seen in the two photographs. Held upright over a shoulder, she usually alerts, becomes quiet, and looks. Customs of child care are different in regard to holding a baby upright. In North America, it is customary to leave babies lying down except when they cry or give other signs of needing attention. When babies are carried on their mothers' backs, without support to the head, they gain control over their heads quickly, as though only a small amount of practice were needed. When babies are swaddled or tied to cradle boards, of course, they cannot hold their heads up. Yet when they are freed at a later age, they are able to do so with a little practice.

Babies act as though urged toward an upright position. Efforts when prone bring the chest and head higher and higher. Efforts when supine include pulling with arm and neck muscles when held by arms or hands, lifting the head, stopping crying when picked up. A supine crying infant will often quiet when picked up and will then maintain the quiet alert state when propped or held in upright positions. An upright position offers much more visual stimulation than does lying on either back or stomach. In the United States the average baby sits with only slight support by 4 months, and unsupported at 6½ [1]. During the time in between, the caregiver determines how much time the baby has to enjoy the advantages of sitting up. The next important postural achievement is standing up, which the average infant can do with a person's help at 8 months, and soon thereafter with the aid of furniture. Pulling to standing is achieved on the average at 8 months, and standing alone at 11. Standing up, of course, gives greater scope for experience than does sitting, and so each step in postural maturity brings more experiences with space, things, and people.

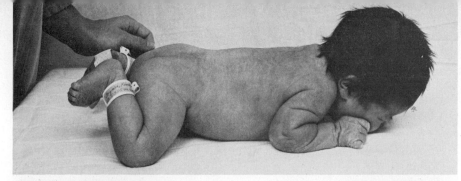

The neurological examiner places the baby prone, with her face on the table. The baby raises her head and turns it to the side.

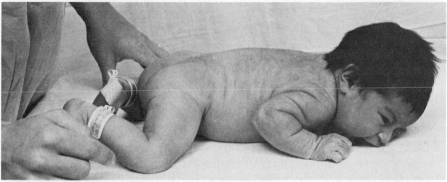

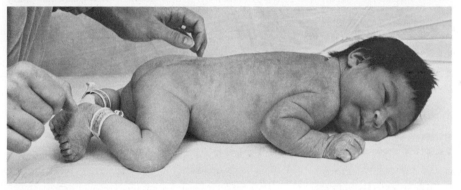

Postural adjustment is shown in the second picture. As the examiner raises the baby to a sitting position, her head falls backward slightly. She then brings her head forward.

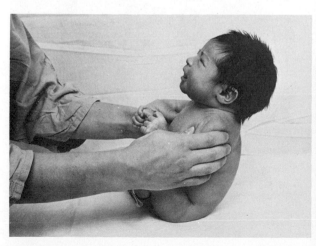

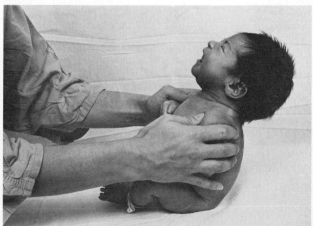

Locomotion

The baby's world expands and stimulation increases greatly when he learns to move from one place to another. Much maturation and learning go on before the infant actually creeps, crawls, or hitches.

Growth of the parts of the brain concerned with locomotion is indicated as the baby progresses through the locomotor sequence. The *cerebellum*, which grows rapidly during the first year, is concerned largely with balance and posture. The sequence of motor development is shown in Figure 5–1. Here is shown progression from fetal position to walking.

The locomotion of the first year is creeping, of the second year, walking. Each of these patterns of moving can be traced from early beginnings. Considering creeping, you can see its beginning in the early attempts of the baby to raise his head when he is in prone position. Most newborn babies do this momentarily. By 2 months they raise themselves on their arms. Although many babies make progress by crawling during their first weeks, this reflexlike movement fades out, leaving infants stationary until they develop the more purposive kind of creeping movements. Although maturation plays a major role in the achievement of creeping, anyone who watches a baby go through the final stages before creeping sees a great deal of effort expended. For instance, the *swimming stage* is one in which the baby perches on his abdomen and pushes. Any

FIGURE 5–1
A baby's progress in locomotion. (After M. M. Shirley. *The first two years: A study of twenty-five babies.* Vol. II. Intellectual development. Copyright 1933 by University of Minnesota, Minneapolis.)

progress at this point is likely to be backward and slight. Shortly afterward comes a stage when babies try out a variety of methods, such as using the stomach as a pivot, hitching by means of head and feet, shoulders and feet, or buttocks and hands, making a bridge by standing on toes and hands and scooting backward. A few infants retain idiosyncratic ways of creeping. Most do it in the usual style, which is shown in Figure 5-1. Babies use creeping movements as their first method of stair climbing.

Basic to walking are holding the head and shoulders erect, sitting, making stepping movements, and standing. Even in the first three months, most infants resist with their feet when held in standing position. Gradually more and more of the baby's weight is borne by the feet. Stepping movements (while held) begin in what looks like dancing, standing on the toes, lifting one foot and then the other and putting both feet down in the same place. Later come putting one foot down ahead of the other and bouncing. Before they can pull themselves up into standing position, most babies can stand holding on to helping hands or to the rail of a playpen. Some children, however, learn to pull up before they can remain standing [22, p. 39].

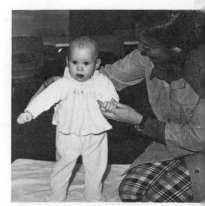

The average age for walking alone is 11.7 months; most children walk by 15 months[1]. Parents often think that their baby really could walk alone because he gets around so easily with one hand held or with just one hand on a piece of furniture. The stage of cruising or walking with help seems to be a period of perfecting walking skills and gaining confidence before setting out independently. Walking is unsteady at first, gradually improving with maturing and practice. Maturation includes a change in proportions and posture, as well as neuromuscular development. The toddler has short legs, a long trunk, large head and abdomen, and consequently a center of gravity high in his trunk. In order to balance himself better, he spreads his feet, walking on a broad base. As his proportions change toward those of childhood, he can afford to place his feet closer together. By the second half of the second year, he can run, covering territory at least twice as fast.

Locomotion includes climbing, too, which looks much like creeping, but begins in the second year, usually in the first three months. Climbing further enlarges the infant's scope of activities, giving him the run of all the floors of his home and access to the sofa, chairs, tabletops, cupboards, drawers.

Because the world expands so enormously with sitting, creeping, walking, running, and climbing, there are a multitude of opportunities for the sense of autonomy to grow. So many choices to make! So many ways in which to test oneself! So many avenues to discovery of powers and limits on powers! It can be very heady or even overwhelming.

Manipulation

If a newborn baby is placed prone on a supporting pillow, with arms free to move, she will move her arms, extending them and pulling them

toward her body. Careful observations of 9 infants found them extending their arms 6 or 7 times per minute [54]. When objects were placed within reach, 36 per cent of the arm movements resulted in contact. The authors thought that the contacts were by chance. It seems likely, however, that these movements would serve as a global activity out of which reaching could be established through learning. Reaching, of course, requires coordination of arm movements with grasping movements.

Gesell's extensive research gave a picture of the newborn as having a reflex grasp but as using eyes more than hands for contacting and exploring [22]. The baby grasps objects that touch his hand. Grasping advances through a regular sequence, from a primitive, palmar grasp, through using thumb and palm at 6 months, thumb and fingers at 8 months, and the forefinger in precise opposition to the thumb at 11 months. Both hands are active in the early stages of reaching and grasping. At 2 to 3 months an infant can reach an object placed in front of his shoulder on the same side. The process of learning to reach across the midline for an object takes another 2 or more months of growth of the neuromuscular system and opportunities for trying out new coordinations (or adapting action schemes). When reaching behavior was studied in 4 age groups, the following age-related behaviors were observed [53]. At 9–11 weeks babies flailed with a loose fist, contacting 33 per cent of objects placed in the midline. At 12–14 weeks the hand was extended with fingers curled inward, direction was better, and 66 per cent of reaches succeeded. At 15–17 weeks, hands were held open and success rate was 93 per cent. At 18–20 weeks, 100 per cent of reaches succeeded, hands were always open with fingers toward the object, and many infants grasped the object, as well as touching it. Being able to reach across the midline makes the infant much more competent in securing and manipulating objects.

Other refinements of reaching and grasping are accommodations to different weights of objects. At 6 or 7 months a baby grips tightly, with no adaptation to weight. At around 9 months she adjusts the grasp to the weight *after* picking up the object. By around a year, grasp is adjusted perfectly on picking up an object for the second time. By about 18 months weight is anticipated by size of object.

Cognition

Cognition comes from a Latin word meaning "to know," "to become acquainted with," "to perceive." Psychologists use the term to refer to the mental activities of attending, perceiving, remembering, problem-solving, and thinking. Sometimes they speak of perception and cognition as different processes, but it is difficult to say where one stops and the other begins. We include all mental or intellectual activities in *cognition*.

Attention

An infant is judged to be attending to a stimulus when he stops any ongoing activity, such as sucking, fussing, or moving, becomes quiet, and orients toward the stimulus, possibly turning eyes or head. From his vast experience with newborns, Brazelton gives examples of the ways in which normal infants control their attention to stimuli immediately after birth [6]. With face alert, the baby turns repeatedly toward a human voice. She attends to a female voice more than a male one, and to human sounds more than to pure tones. After stopping sucking in response to a pure tone, she resumes steady sucking, but after stopping to a human voice, she sucks in a burst-pause pattern. She turns eyes and head to a picture of a human face, but looks without turning to a picture of a scrambled face. She turns to the smell of milk, but not to water or sugar water. With human milk the sucking pattern is different from the mode of sucking cow's milk formula.

Signs of attention: orienting, turning, looking, sucking change, heart rate change

Several criteria in addition to general orienting are available for judging whether an infant is attending to a stimulus. Changes in sucking can be monitored exactly. The object of gaze can be determined by looking directly into the baby's eyes or by a reflected beam. Heart-rate deceleration indicates when a subject focuses attention on the external environment either in attending to a stimulus, anticipating a noxious stimulus, or preparing to make a motor response [51,61].

Perception

Investigators ask three types of questions about perception. First, what can a baby discriminate? This question occupied the early researchers in child psychology. What can a baby see, if anything? Does he hear at birth and can he tell the difference between various sounds? Does he smell, taste, and feel pain? There was a time when psychologists thought that newborns perceived little or nothing. Robert Fantz, in the 1950s, developed methods through which he and many psychologists since then have found that infants make fine perceptual discriminations.

The second question concerning perception is that of selection. To what will infants attend, and under what conditions? Methods of studying stimulus discrimination and perception preference and attention were first developed by Fantz in the visual field. Fantz made two important discoveries: when shown two different stimuli at the same time, an infant usually looks more at one than at the other; infants look less and less at a repeated stimulus and pay more attention to a new stimulus. Preference studies make use of the first finding, habituation studies, of the second.

A third question deals with organization and classification. Human beings perceive the world in organized ways, and they do so from birth or very soon thereafter. They see certain light waves as colors and hear certain sound waves as speech. From each sensory modality they select certain stimuli as special and meaningful [2].

Infants organize stimuli

Vision. Newborns see objects clearly when they are 9 or 10 inches away from their eyes, but see fuzzily as distances increase. Thus new babies are equipped to look at the faces of people holding them in their arms. By

3 months the baby can look around the room and see his parents coming and going.

Acuity has been studied by using Fantz's technique, or an elaboration of it, to see when the infant is fixating. The experimenter looks through a peephole to see what is reflected from the infant's corneas. He records the amount of time that the baby looks at the target. The basic method is to present a plain gray stimulus with a black-and-white striped one. If the baby looks longer at the pattern, she can discriminate it from the plain gray. The stripes are adjusted to the smallest size at which the baby can discriminate them from the gray. This size represents the visual acuity of the infant. Newborn infants can see stripes 1/8 inch wide at a distance of 10 inches. A 6-month-old can see 1/64-inch stripes at the same distance [18]. Newborns see not only with the central part of the retina, but with the peripheral parts, too. Central and peripheral visual systems are quite mature by 6 months [12]. However, further development of the visual system continues throughout early childhood.

Another way of investigating discrimination, or whether an infant is perceiving a stimulus, is through habituation experiments. After a stimulus has been presented several times, the subject habituates, or stops paying attention to it. In common terms, he gets tired of it, or bored. A new stimulus will claim his attention. Therefore an experimenter can present a stimulus that is slightly different from the original and can determine whether the subject perceives it as the same or different. Bornstein used habituation to show that 4-month-old infants saw the same basic colors that adults see [3]. First, the infants discriminated between two wave lengths that came from different hues. Then they were shown two wave lengths separated by the same difference in the spectrum but within one color band. The second pair of waves were not seen as different. For example, they responded differently to blue and green, but not to two blues that were as far from each other in the spectrum as were the blue and green from one another. Color vision represents one way in which human beings organize sensory stimuli into categories [2]. Infants as young as 3 months, and perhaps younger, use the same categories that adults do in organizing visual sensations related to the spectrum of light.

Preference for patterns and forms was first studied by Fantz, who used his peephole equipment to show pairs of stimuli and to measure the length of time that the baby looked at each [18]. Cohen [11] summarizes the findings of a very large number of studies that have been done since then to find out what kinds of displays infants will look at and how they perceive them. Infants in the first one or two months of life can process visual stimuli that have high contrast (differences between light and dark, as in stripes and checkerboards) and low spatial-frequency information (simple figures). When looking at triangles, circles, and squares, infants under one month look at a single edge or angle, but by two months, they scan the figure. At between 2 and 4 or 5 months, simple forms are seen as units. After 5 months, more complex forms and patterns are seen as wholes. As early as 3 months a simple pattern of dots can be discriminated [44].

Perhaps the most interesting of infant visual behaviors are responses to faces. Newborns look longer at a picture of a face than at bulls-eyes or other simple stimuli [19]. Faces have a great deal of light-dark contrast, especially the eyes. As they do in scanning geometric figures, infants of 1 month scan only a small portion of the edge of a face, the hairline or chinline [42]. At 2 months babies looked at the inside of the face, especially at the eyes. When the baby looks into the parents' eyes of course they feel a sense of communication. Several studies indicate that infants younger than 4 months respond to features, usually eyes, rather than to the face as a whole, and that after this age they see the face as a whole, and can judge how closely a stimulus resembles a human face [12]. After 5 months of age facial features have more and more meaning, first in discriminating photos of men and women and next in telling the differences between individuals of the same sex and generalizing between different pictures of the same person. That is, infants recognize the invariant aspects of faces during the first half year of life. By 6 months or before, babies discriminate different facial expressions.

A sex difference has been found in newborn response to faces [26]. With the baby's sex unknown to the experimenter, who nodded and smiled in attempts to elicit and hold eye contact, the occurrence and duration of eye contact was recorded by an electric recorder. No sex differences were found in the number of times eye contact was made, but girls spent more time in eye contact than boys. That is, girls looked longer. The reason for the sex difference is not known. It could be the greater maturity of girls at birth. Or it could be an innate sex difference, not related to maturity. Because the difference in length of time in eye contact has also been found in childhood and adulthood, an innate difference is plausible. On the other hand, the advantage of the girl at birth could be strengthened and maintained by responses from the adults who look at her.

In conclusion, faces make a strong claim on the attention of infants. There is a possibility that infants have a category of *faceness*. Perhaps there is a predisposition to organize certain stimuli into a face category, just as there is a predisposition to organize wave lengths into categories of color. Faces are very important in human interaction throughout life. The visual preferences of the infant affirm that importance.

Hearing. Because fetuses can hear in utero, it is no surprise that infants can hear well at birth. A newborn will turn to the sound of a voice [7] and to the sound of a rattle [45]. The babies who turned to the rattle ". . . displayed lengthy and vigorous responses, suggesting that they were making a deliberate attempt to investigate the locus of the shaking rattle; they hunched their shoulders, actively pulled their heads up, turned to the side of the stimulus, and then seemed to inspect the sound source visually." The experimenters stressed that three conditions facilitated the

Looking behaviors:
Birth—At whole faces
1 mo.—Scans part of
*   perimeter of faces*
2 mo.—Fixates eyes
4 mo.—Responds to
*   features*
5 mo.—Responds
*   to whole face; recog-*
*   nizes invariants*
6 mo.—Discriminates
*   expressions*

infants' searching for the rattle. They were in a quiet, alert state when tested. They were held in such a way that they could turn easily, almost supine, with head and shoulders cupped in the examiner's right hand, and lower back and buttocks supported by the left hand. Third they were given plenty of time to respond. It took an average of 2.5 seconds for the response to begin, and 5.5 seconds to end.

Infants can distinguish one *pitch* from another, as shown by experiments in which a musical note is played while an infant is sucking. The baby stops sucking, but when the note is repeated several times, he habituates (ceases to respond). A new note is sounded. The baby stops sucking. Change in heart rate can be used instead of sucking to demonstrate discrimination between sounds. Low-pitched sounds soothe crying babies and stimulate motor activity in alert, inactive infants, whereas high frequencies tend to promote distress [17]. Pure tones have been found to be ineffective stimuli, but when pure tones are combined they act as stimuli. Different combinations of tones resulted in different responses, measured by heartbeat, eye movements, and finger movements [65].

Newborns react differently to different degrees of *loudness*. When white noise was played at 55, 70, and 80 decibels, heart rates and motor responses increased with the level of the sound [62]. The minimal sound that an infant can hear, 35 or 40 decibels, is equivalent to the minimal levels for children and adults [17].

Changes in sound also produce different responses. *Rise* time is the length of time taken by a sound to reach its highest level of loudness. When newborns in the state of alert inactivity heard sounds with slow rise time, they opened their eyes. Sounds with fast rise times were followed by eye-closing and increased head movements. The author concluded that the slow-rise sounds elicited orienting and the fast-rise sounds elicited defensive movements [32].

Lullabies, songs designed especially for babies, combine low pitch, slow rise time, and rhythm, all of which psychologists have demonstrated to be soothing. Another soothing rhythm is the heartbeat sound, which has been the focus of several studies. In a newborn nursery, a group of babies was exposed continuously to a recorded heartbeat sound and compared for crying with a group that did not hear the heartbeat [56]. The infants who heard the heartbeat cried less. Another study found a metronome and a lullaby sung in a foreign language to be as effective soothers as the heartbeat sound [5]. It is likely that the infant's prenatal experience with heartbeat predisposes him to find comfort in a rhythmic sound. As a fetus, he heard and felt his mother's heartbeat steadily for many months, while he lived in complete comfort and security.

Newborn babies cry to the sound of a newborn baby crying. Tested in cribs with constant temperature and constant visual environment, 100 newborns were divided into groups that were exposed to one of these stimuli: no sound, a synthetic cry, a 5-month-old baby crying, and a new-

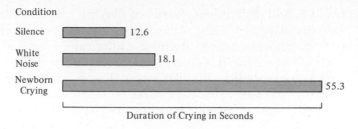

Condition

Silence 12.6

White Noise 18.1

Newborn Crying 55.3

Duration of Crying in Seconds

FIGURE 5-2
Newborn infants cry longer when they hear the crying of another infant than they do under conditions of silence or white noise. (Data from M. L. Simner. Newborn's response to the cry of another infant. *Developmental Psychology*, 1971, **5**, 136–150.)

born cry [59]. Crying and heart rate were recorded. Crying occurred in over twice as many of the newborn-crying-tape group as in the no-sound control group. There was not a statistically significant difference between the no-sound group and the other two groups. When duration of crying time was measured, the babies who heard the newborn-crying tape cried significantly more than the no-sound and synthetic-cry infants. As Figure 5–2 shows, babies cried longest at the newborn cry, next at the older infant's cry, and least during silence. Heart-rate increases in both the white-noise group and the crying-tape group exceeded those in the silent control group. Therefore, both sound conditions promoted greater arousal levels, whereas the crying sound stimulated crying. The experiment shows that the newborn infants responded to the vocal properties of the sound of newborn crying. In subsequent experiment, infants heard recordings of their own crying. Their reactions were compared with those shown when exposed to the crying of another newborn. A baby's own cry was a more powerful stimulus, in terms of heart-rate increases and duration of crying. It seems likely, then, that as the baby hears himself crying, he is stimulated further to crying.

Infants between 7 and 20 days of age quieted sooner to their mothers' voices than to the voice of a stranger [27]. Babies of 2 months have shown, through changes in their looking behavior, that they can discriminate between different voices, different tone qualities of the same voice, and probably between different statements by the same voice [14]. Young infants can perceive small differences between the sounds that make up human language. The difference between *p* and *b* was distinguished by month-old babies, who demonstrated through their sucking behavior that they perceived the sounds as different [16]. Other studies have used heart-rate changes to show that young infants could distinguish between phonemes. *P* and *b* are different in the onset of voicing. When nonspeech sounds were made to differ the same amount, along the same dimension, they were not perceived as different. These findings, and similar ones with other pairs of speech sounds, indicate that infants, as well as older people, perceive speech categorically. Just as they perceive categories in the light spectrum as specific colors, they perceive certain classes of sounds as speech phonemes. Infants also perceive selected musical sounds categorically [30]. Throughout infancy there seems to be some development in discriminating between phonemes [2]. For example, *s* and *z* were discriminated at 8 months, but not at 4. At neither age could babies discriminate between *f* and *th*. Cross-culture studies indicate that varying lengths of exposure are required for learning to discriminate various phonemes. Because adults rarely learn a foreign language without an accent, it is likely that for learning the discriminations, exposure is age-specific. We can attest that in adulthood it can take more than 3 years of exposure to Hindi to be able to hear the difference between aspirated and nonaspirated consonants!

Tactile Senses. Skin, muscular, and vestibular (inner ear) senses are highly developed before birth, having functioned prenatally longer than the other senses. Sensations from lips, mouth, and other orifices are included in tactile sensations. The skin, being the locus where the individual is in physical contact with his environment, is the place where much interaction occurs. To name the sensations heat, cold, pressure, and pain tells a minimum about tactile experience. Experiments and clinical experiences with infants have led to the conclusion that tactile stimulation is essential for normal development. Patting, caressing, cuddling, carrying, rocking, changing position, washing, drying—all these activities seem to be soothing and to promote well-being in babies. There is a connection between the skin and the sympathetic nervous system.

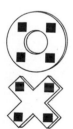

Tactile stimulation from handling objects usually occurs along with visual stimulation, as the baby watches what he is doing with his hands. The two modes of perception were separated in an ingenious experiment [60]. Seated on their mothers' laps at a table in a darkened room, 10-month-old infants played for 2 minutes with a wooden cross or a wooden circle. The object was removed and a new play period begun, with either the same object, or the other one. The two looked alike, because phosphorescent tape was stuck to them in identical patterns. The babies played more with the unfamiliar object, showing that infants can get information from tactile experience alone, and that they prefer novel stimuli in the tactile mode.

Temperature is another dimension of skin sensitivity. Little research has been done on temperature discrimination, but it has been shown that infants respond to cold and warm stimuli applied to their skin [52]. Infants increase their muscular activity when the surrounding temperature drops.

Taste. Taste buds are well developed in fetal life. The newborn has more taste buds and a wider distribution of them than does an adult. Two studies indicate that newborns distinguish between water and a sweet solution, as any baby nurse knows. After adapting to either water or glucose placed in a drop on the tongue, newborns respond to the other liquid, showing that they distinguished between them [67]. Preference during the first feeding was estimated by measuring the amounts taken of various solutions [41]. It was assumed that preference was the result of taste. The babies drank more sugar solution than water, showing different intakes for the four sugars (sucrose, fructose, glucose, and lactose) at

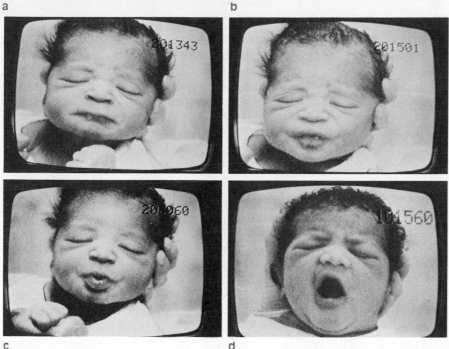

a

b

c

d

different degrees of concentration. Sucrose was the most preferred, and then fructose. As concentrations increased, the infants drank greater quantities. Further indication that babies really do like sugar came from Lipsitt's [39] findings on sucking patterns of newborns who were given sucrose solution. "Getting excited over savory substances" is how he described it. While taking in sugar, infants slowed down the rate of sucking within each burst of sucks, as though they were savoring the sugar in their mouths.

Infants show displeasure at bitter tastes [2]. Taste perception, like seeing and hearing, is categorical, the classifications of taste being sweet, salt, bitter, and sour.

As mentioned earlier, Brazelton reports that the newborn infant can discriminate between human milk and cow's milk that has been altered to resemble human milk as much as possible [6]. It seems likely that this competency has survival value for the young infant, just as does the preference for looking at a human face.

Smell. Newborn babies react to strong and mild odors by turning away, moving, and showing changes in breathing. Because the two nostrils receive stimuli at slightly different times, location of odors is possible. The ability to locate smells is probably innate [4]. During the first few days of life, infants showed discrimination between different odors by habituating to one and then responding to a new one [57]. Some babies were more responsive and more consistent in reactions to odors than were others. For example, oil of lavender elicited a response in one particular infant every day, but no response in two of the other subjects.

Although the olfactory system matures early in life, man does not have as keen a sense of smell as most animals and does not use information from smell as much as from vision and hearing. Perhaps olfaction plays a bigger role in the infant's life than in the adult's, because odors from the mother and other caregivers may be significant. As mentioned earlier, the baby will turn to his mother's breast pad. Her milk is surely very significant.

Sensorimotor Intelligence

Sensorimotor intelligence is active, practical, problem-solving, and present-oriented

Piaget's basic concepts, including the main periods of mental development, are outlined in Chapter 2. We now turn to the details of the sensorimotor period. The first 2 years of life are the sensorimotor period in Piaget's conceptualization of intelligence [50]. The term *sensorimotor* reflects the fact that infant actions are behaviors of a whole organism, difficult to analyze into mental or physical. Incapable of speech and abstract thought, a baby *acts* on objects and persons. As Piaget says, infants have practical intelligence, oriented toward solving problems of action. The sensorimotor period lasts until the child reorganizes his intelligence on the next level, the period of *preoperational thought*. The change-over usually occurs at between 18 months and 2 years and marks the end of infancy, from a cognitive standpoint. Now the child can represent objects and actions in his mind, without acting on objects. He uses symbols and/or words to stand for objects and actions.

Starting with the resources she has for dealing with the world, the baby uses them to develop new patterns of action. For example, she integrates schemes of mouthing, holding, and looking. The result is an examining scheme. Using this method of exploration many times with toys, bottles, clothing, and other objects, the infant makes progress toward the conviction that objects are permanent. Other behavior patterns, involving seeing, smelling, tasting, hearing, touching, and manipulating are used in getting knowledge of the world. Locomotion, moving from place to place, gives the baby chances to map out the space in which she lives, getting to truly cognize it, and herself as an object in space.

As experience with reality shows existing resources to be inadequate or insufficient, the baby develops new schemes through accommodation or improvements in what she has. When the child falls only slightly short of being adequate to cope with an experience, her feeling tone is pleasant and interesting. Growth is stimulated. When she is very inadequate in dealing with the experience, the child is frightened or she may not even perceive the problem.

Substages of Sensorimotor Intelligence. Piaget has described six substages of the period of sensorimotor intelligence, the period during which the infant establishes basic knowledge of the world. He is not concerned with the exact ages at which children reach the successive stage of intelligence. He is interested in *how* rather than *when*, and in which structures are invariably built before certain other structures.

1. The Use of Reflexes. Reflex action patterns such as the sucking reflex, are embedded in the whole spontaneous rhythmic action of the infant. Some of the reflexes develop through use and become differentiated. The reflex actions and perceptual abilities are the schemes of the first stage of sensorimotor intelligence. This stage includes approximately the first month, during which the various abilities improve and consolidate. *Birth to 1 month*

2. The First Habits: Primary Circular Reactions. Neonatal behavior patterns begin to change through maturation and experience. The baby learns to bring his hand to his mouth and to suck on it, most likely his thumb. He touches his hands together and fingers them, looks at his hands and at objects grasped by his hands. Objects grasped by the hands are carried to the mouth. He looks at an object making a noise. He does not know what he can cause and what takes place independently of his own actions. This stage lasts until about 4 months. *1 to 4 months*

3. Secondary Circular Reactions. The baby develops ways of prolonging interesting events. When a change in the environment results from his actions, he is likely to repeat those actions. He reaches for the toy suspended from his crib, hits it, watches it move, and hits it again. *4 to 8 months*

He becomes an active explorer, showing more and more interest in objects, in the outside world, and in his effects on them. He still does not search for an object that has disappeared, suggesting that he still does not conceive of it as existing permanently. However, if all but a small part of an object is covered, as when his bottle sticks out from under his blanket, he recognizes it and can recover it. If an object is made to disappear slowly, he follows it with his eyes and continues the movement of his eyes in the direction in which the object went. If, however, it is jerked away, or quickly screened, he does not look for it. One of Piaget's experiments with his son, Laurent, showed that the baby did not even miss the bottle when it was hidden quickly. Just before a feeding time, when Laurent was hungry, Piaget showed him his bottle, whereupon Laurent cried. Piaget quickly hid the bottle and Laurent stopped crying. This sequence was repeated several times. When Laurent could see a small portion of the bottle, he cried harder than ever [49, p. 30].

Another interesting aspect of substage 3, evident in Laurent's behavior, was failure to realize the existence of the nipple if it did not show. When he saw a small portion of the bottle but not the nipple, he tried to suck the bottle itself, but when the nipple was visible, he turned the bottle around so that he could suck the nipple. Thus, he cognized the bottle as a suckable object, but unless he could see the nipple, he did not deal with the bottle as an object with a specialized suckable portion. Thus, in this stage, objects are becoming endowed with permanence, but the process is not complete. The next stage begins at around 8 months.

4. Coordination of Secondary Schemes. Secondary circular reactions *8 to 12 months*

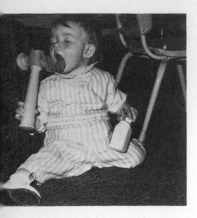

become coordinated with each other to form more complex schemes. The new schemes are used definitely as means to ends. This is the earliest age at which the baby shows intention in a definite and unmistakable way. For example, hitting is not just for the sake of hitting, but in order to grasp a new object. Piaget tells how Laurent, at 9½ months, pushed his father's hand and at the same time pulled on the toy that Piaget was holding.

There is true searching for a vanished object, although still not complete appreciation of the object's permanence. Piaget describes how his daughter Jacqueline searched for a toy parrot. First, Piaget covered it with his hand. Jacqueline raised his hand and grasped the parrot. Piaget slowly took the toy away from her, hid it under a rug, and put his hand on her lap, on the spot where the parrot had first been. Jacqueline raised his hand and looked under it for the parrot. This process was repeated three times [50, p. 51].

In this stage the baby can predict certain events from others. Setting the table may show her that dinner is imminent. Father's putting on his coat may indicate that he is leaving. The stage occurs at about 8 to 12 months.

12 to 18 months

5. *Tertiary Circular Reactions.* Instead of merely prolonging or reproducing interesting events, the baby tries to produce new events. He experiments to see what will happen. He appears definitely curious, looking for new experience.

Now the baby looks for a vanished object in the place where it disappeared instead of in the place where he last found it. He demonstrates increased understanding of movements of objects by following a trajectory and looking at its end and by throwing something in back of himself and turning around in the other direction to look for it.

Throwing and dropping toys are common kinds of play at this age, as the infant examines movements of objects, disappearance, and reappearance, building his understanding of the permanence of objects. Piaget watched Laurent using various methods of letting a tin can fall from his hands and then dropping a chunk of bread first as a whole and then in the form of crumbs. Later Laurent dropped toys from different positions. The usual age for this stage is 12 to 18 months.

18 to 24 months

6. *Invention of New Means Through Mental Combinations.* Instead of having to go through a series of sensorimotor explorations and trials, the child can find solutions mentally. He begins this stage by representing objects and actions to himself. Probably the first kind of representing is to act it out. Piaget's daughter, Lucienne, illustrated this behavior when she was trying to get a little chain out of a match box. She looked at the small opening, not knowing how to open it wider, then opened and shut her mouth several times, each time opening it wider [50, pp. 337–338]. After a few quiet moments, she used a new technique to open the box with her finger. Lucienne's opening of her own mouth was a symbolic act, representing the opening of the box, which she desired. This stage, in coping with problems, is midway between trying out solutions in ac-

tion and thinking them out. When problems are solved by thinking, without any action, the child is representing objects and actions to himself by symbols that are entirely within. He thinks of ways of acting and tries them out by thinking. He can think of objects that are not present, of past events, and of events that might happen.

The toddler shows his new powers by imitation and pretending and by insightful problem solving. When he imitates a past event, he shows that he has a mental image of it. When he pretends, he uses a mental image of a behavior pattern to act out that pattern in a new situation. Feeding a doll, he uses his mental image of his mother's behavior, acting it out at his little table. The achievement of imitation, pretending, and insightful problem solving marks the completion of the stage of sensorimotor development. As with all the stages outlined by Piaget, the average age for beginning and ending a stage is not placed exactly but approximately. The sensorimotor stage, according to Piaget, ends at around 2 years.

Concept of Permanence of Objects. Piaget maintains that the young infant does not know that objects continue to exist when he is not looking at them. "The universe of the young baby is a world without objects, consisting only of shifting and unsubstantial 'tableaux,' which appear and are then totally reabsorbed, either without returning, or reappearing in a modified or analogous form."[50]

Stage 4 has held special interest for psychologists. Many infants have taken part in experiments similar to Piaget's sequence with Jacqueline and the parrot. The experimenter hides the object in front of the watching child, at Point A. The Stage 3 child will not search; the Stage 4 child will look for the object and find it. Then, with the child still watching, the experimenter hides the object at Point B. The child searches at Point A. The Stage 5 child will search at Point B, but if the object has been visibly hidden at B and then *invisibly* moved farther, the child will not continue his search beyond B. It is only at Stage 6 that the child can deal with an invisible displacement, as though he is sure that the object must be hiding somewhere.

Piaget's theory holds that until the end of the sensorimotor period, the child knows objects only in relation to his own actions upon them. That is, he is egocentric in his knowledge of the world, seeing it only in terms of what he does. In that sense, objects cease to exist when the child does not perceive them. Donaldson suggests that failure to search in Stage 3, failure to search in the right place in Stage 4, and failure to persist with searching in Stage 5 do not necessarily show that the child believes that the object no longer exists [15, pp. 20–22]. It could be that the baby simply does not know that objects *move*, and that because they move, an object can appear in different places. Donaldson mentions an experiment by Bower and Wishart, in which objects were made to disappear by turning off the lights. Using infrared film the experimenters found the babies reaching for toys in places where they had previously seen them. They acted as though the toys still existed, even though they could not see them.

There is no doubt that infants have to learn some facts about movement. A child has to find out that when an object is moved, it can be put back again; that when it turns around, it can be turned in the other direction; that when an object is moved away, he can reach it by a path other than the one taken by the object, in fact by many different paths. The sensorimotor child is only starting to develop understanding of the spatial relations *on, in, in front of, behind,* and *under.*

Communication

Language, a special kind of communication, is a cognitive activity that serves both social and cognitive purposes. Communication, a necessarily social activity, might well be placed in the following chapter, which deals with the development of infants' relations with others. The problem of where to consider communication points up the fact that the infant grows as a whole person. Any attempt to separate out different kinds of development involves some difficulties.

Nonverbal Communication

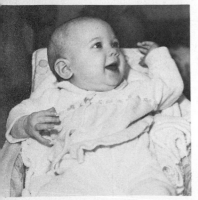

The newborn infant communicates with the people he encounters in that first alert hour, gazing at eyes, turning to the sound of a voice, rooting, sucking, and crying. Brazelton describes the fascination that a newborn infant exerts over the examiner administering an assessment scale. ". . . the neonate not only searches for the observer's face, but, when he finds it, his face and eyes become wide, soft and eager, and he may even crane his neck, lifting his chin gently toward the source of the voice. As he does so, his body tension gradually increases, but he is quietly inactive. A nurturing adult feels impelled to respond to these signals by picking the baby up to cuddle him" [7].

Babies tell caregivers about themselves through state behavior, facial expressions, and gestures. Facial expression and eye contact continue to be avenues of communication between infants and adults, just as they are between other people. The patterning and timing of gazing between preverbal infants and adults is similar to the looking that adults do when they converse with each other [29]. Children in the second year often communicate purposefully with their hands, pulling another person to show him something, pushing him away, putting a hand over a mouth that is saying what the child does not want to hear, and pointing at food, toys, and wet pants. Pointing has been observed in children as young as 10 months, in many year-olds, and in practically all babies at 15 months [35]. Following another person's gaze is usually well developed by 1 year. Pointing by another person is understood as early as 9 months when the finger is near the object pointed to, and when additional cues of movement are given. When the object is not in the same visual field as the pointing finger, comprehension is likely at 12 months or later.

Talking plays a part in communication from the beginning. Caregivers talk and the infant responds; infants vocalize and the caregiver responds.

Entrainment. When sound films of a conversation are microanalyzed, the speaker and the listener are found to move in synchrony with what is said [13]. It is like a dance, with the listener entering into the tempo of the speaker. The taking on of an ongoing rhythm of timing is called *entrainment*. Infants become entrained to speech and other rhythms, too, such as the family rhythms of sleeping and eating. Entrainment to speech has been observed in an infant 20 minutes after birth. Babies thus participate actively in responding to human speech with specific movements. Entrainment may be the first process in learning or acquiring language. Infants are equipped at birth (and before) to perceive human speech as different from all other sounds, and to respond to it in a particularly human way. The responsive movements made by the entrained infant are, no doubt, perceived by the speaker, creating a conviction that the two are communicating.

Prespeech Communication. The kind of speaking known as "baby talk" seems to follow rules of expression and timing, creating short, dramatic episodes with a short succession of climaxes, using repetition and musical, questioning intonation. The mother times her comments, buildup, and pauses to wait for the baby's responses.

Mothers and other people continue to adapt their speech to the maturity of the baby, and indeed, to older children also. For example, utterances to infants of 4 to 6 months were longer and more complex than to 8-months-old babies, indicating that the older babies were probably responding more to simple comments than to complex ones [58]. The 8-months-olds were getting some meaning from their mothers' words.

Pre-speech communication between mothers and young infants was studied by Trevarthen [63] at the University of Edinburgh and by Mundy-Castle [46] at the University of Lagos. Scottish and Nigerian mother-baby pairs were observed by the same technique, photographing by video-recorders that gave a simultaneous split-screen display of mother and baby. Observers could thus watch both the mother and baby as they interacted. Mother-infant pairs in both countries cooperated to build patterns of interaction. During the first two months, babies alternated looking with their mothers, reached, smiled, imitated the mothers' movements of mouth, tongue, arms, and her vocalizations. After two months, infants shared with mothers in acting on objects and in reciprocal actions, including rhythmic singing, clapping, body dance, laughing, game playing, and conversational exchanges. Imitation and the beginnings of speech were observed at much younger ages than those at which other researchers have reported these activities. Mundy-Castle gives the earliest ages at which he found the following behaviors: pointing at, reaching for, and grasping mother's tongue, imitating smiling and tongue protrusion—22 days; imitation of mouth shape into "O"—30 days; pro-

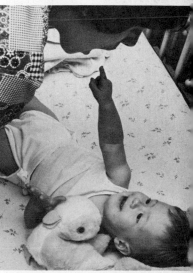

toconversations, using one-syllable vocalizations—40 days; prespeech, imitation of vocalization and mouth movements—42 days.

This cross-cultural study suggests that the mother-infant context of communication is universal. The basis of language development is in rules of interaction learned through joint activities with the mother and other people. The joint activities are emotional as well as motoric and cognitive, creating a bond between the baby and the person who shares the interaction.

Another approach to the study of prespeech was made by a psycholinguist father who recorded and analyzed the meaningful sounds made by his son Nigel before vocalizations were recognizable words [25]. The earliest consistent sounds were not requests, but more like comments on the present moment. Some highlights of Nigel's pre-speech are shown below. Even if you cannot read the linguistic symbols, you can see that Nigel made a variety of sounds, each of which always meant the same thing.

Nigel's prespeech sounds		
6–7 months:	a high-pitched squeak	"what's going on?"
8 months:	[ə̀] mid-low to low	"yes, we're together"
	[ə̀] mid to low	"look, that's interesting"
9½ months:	[nà]	"I want"
	[ɜ̀] or [n̂ŋ],	"do that"
	n[m̂n̂ŋf]	"do that—I insist"
10½ months:	nà . . . mid to low	"give me that"
	bə̀ mid to low	"give me my bird"
	gesture: beating time	"make music"
	ɜ̀, n̂ŋ mid to low	"do that"
	m̂n̂ŋf high to low	"do that—I insist"
	ɛ̀ low	"yes? here I am"
	ʔø, ʔɔ̀, dɔ mid to low	"nice to see you"; and "let's look at this"
	əǹǹf high to low	"nice to see you—at last!"
	gesture: opening and closing fist	"goodbye"
	ə̀, œ̀ mid-low to low	"that's interesting"
	bə̀, d̀ɔ, ə̀ mid-low to low	"look, a commotion"
	à mid-low to low	"that's nice"
	n̂ŋ mid-low to low	"that tastes nice"
	g̊ʷ ɣ ꞁ . . . low	"I'm tired"
12 months:	[ɛ̀ˠa]	"that's what it is (and that's what I wanted)"
	[d̀ɔ] or [dɛ̀ə]	"look"
	[ā̀nnā̀]	"Anna" (a personal name)

First Words. During the first half of the second year the average baby acquires a vocabulary of a few words. Because there is wide variation, the normal vocabulary at 18 months can be said to be more than three and less than 50 [36, p. 128]. As did Nigel's prespeech sounds, first words often stand for statements or phrases. They can be comments, questions, or commands. A word may stand for a whole rush of experiences, as did "car, car, car" said by a toddler as she enjoyed an automobile outing. During the middle part of the second year, combinations of words may be functionally one-word utterances, such as *allgone*. When two words are put together, the child has reached the end of infancy, completing the sensorimotor period of development. He has come to realize that words stand for things and actions. Instead of having to go through sensory and motor acts, words can be manipulated in a twinkling. One doesn't even have to be where the problem is. He can think and talk about things that are remote in time and space.

The ability to communicate with language must surely facilitate the sense of autonomy. For instance, saying "drink" can produce water at one's lips, or "out" can transform the whole environment from indoors to outdoors. The extension of the child's powers and control is enormous. As it dawns upon him that everything has a name, that verbal symbols exist and that he can use them, he must have a surge of satisfaction over his expanded powers. One can imagine next a push to discover just how much he can do with these symbols, words, in both understanding and controlling the world and the people in it, including himself.

In Nelson's longitudinal research on language acquisition between the ages of 10 and 25 months, 18 mother-infant pairs were studied [47]. Instead of trying to determine when the babies said their first words, a difficult thing to do, Nelson used 10 words as an indicator of speech onset. The average age at which the subjects used 10 words was 15.1 months. The range was from 13 to 19 months. Another milestone, the use of 50 words, was achieved at an average age of 19.6 months, with a range of 14 to 24 months. The acquisition rate, or number of words added per month, was 11.1 between the age at 10 words and the age at 50 words. Infants varied in acquisition patterns, some starting early, some late, and some accelerating faster than others. The usual course was an initial period of slow growth in word acquisition followed by an increase and then a period of rapid word acquisition during the 2 months prior to and including the age at which the vocabulary reached 50 words.

Phrase onset was indicated by the child's use of 10 phrases, no matter whether they were used as wholes or constructed from parts. The average age for 10 phrases was 19.8 months, with a range from 16 to 24. Thus the age of phrase onset is almost identical with the age of using 50 words. The average number of words used at 2 years was 185.9, with a range from 28 to 436. Mean length of utterance at age 2 was 1.9, about 2 words per utterance.

When children first put words together, they talk about the sensorimotor world [8, p. 264]. In a large number of languages studied by Brown, the first stage of utterance contains the same sorts of relations and propositions. That is, toddlers everywhere talk about the same subject matter. Examples include *that ball, more ball, all gone ball, Daddy chair, go store, big house,* and *Daddy hit.* Thus, they tell about things existing, disappearing, recurring, being owned or possessed, being located, and being acted upon.

Assessing Infant Development

Evaluations for normalcy can be done shortly after birth. The Apgar Test and the Brazelton Neonatal Assessment Scale have already been mentioned. The former measures functions needed to sustain life. The latter tests neurological adequacy and responses to environmental stimuli that show capacity to adapt to living in the world. Other kinds of neonatal tests measure vision, hearing, learning, and developmental risk [20].

Piaget's concepts of sensorimotor development form the basis for the scales of psychological development constructed by Uzgiris and Hunt [66]. Gesell, who was mentioned as a developmental psychologist in Chapter 1, was the first to standardize an infant developmental test [22]. The items were divided into 4 categories, motor, adaptive, language, and personal-social behavior. The tests were arranged in age-levels according to success of the average child (in his middle-class sample).

The Bayley Scales of Infant Development consist of a motor scale and a mental scale, derived from repeated examinations of 1,409 infants in 12 research centers scattered throughout the United States [1]. Norms are given for each half-month level. The Bayley scales have been used in several different parts of the world, since they provide a method for comparing different populations of infants.

It is not surprising that infant tests do not correlate well with IQ in childhood. Gesell was not trying to measure intelligence, but development as a whole. Although Bayley's test gives a mental quotient, she thinks of intelligence as taking different forms at different periods of development. An analysis of data from Bayley tests has born out Bayley's conception of the changing nature of intelligent behavior [40]. The stages defined bear a resemblance to Piaget's stages. Infant tests are useful for clinically assessing normalcy, diagnosing defects, planning strategies for coping with problems of development. Research studies employ infant tests for investigating differences between populations that have been treated differently by nature or by experimenters.

Ecology of Sensorimotor Development

All levels of the physical and social ecology contribute to motor, cognitive, and language development in infancy. Although more research has been done on the microsystems level than on macrosystems, there is still considerable information about processes of development available from cross-culture research.

Macrosystems vary widely in customs and beliefs concerning infant care, in the physical environment and resources they provide, and in the language spoken. There are also genetic differences between the populations that participate in various macrosystems. Cross-culture researchers try to describe differences between populations of infants and then to find the reasons for those differences. They also look for consistencies across cultures that may throw light on universal processes, as, for example, the finding that the order of first sentences is the same across cultures.

The most striking of cross-culture comparisons was done by Geber, who tested over 300 infants in Uganda in the 1950s [21]. She found an extraordinary acceleration in psychomotor development at birth that disappeared later. The average Uganda newborn held his head steady when drawn to sitting, sat alone at 4 months, stood alone at 8, and walked at 10. Language, problem-solving, and personal-social development were also advanced beyond European standards. Since Geber's studies, many tests of infant development have been given in Africa, Asia, Central America, and Australia. Africans have continued to show the greatest acceleration, followed by Central Americans and then Asians. By age 2, most of these populations of infants were no longer advanced by European and American standards. They fell further behind, and continued to lag below the test norms.

Werner draws the following conclusions from studies done on five continents since the 1950s [68]. There seems to be an interaction between ethnicity, amount and type of caretaker stimulation, and nutritional status. Even in the same ecological setting, Negroid infants showed greatest early acceleration, Central American and Asian next, and Caucasian least. Within ethnic groups, greatest early acceleration occurred in traditional cultures, where infants were treated permissively, fed on demand, carried, dressed in little or nothing, kept close to adults, and cared for by several people. The same groups showed greatest decline after weaning, when they were no longer carried and stimulated. These toddlers had low scores in motor development and lowest scores in adaptive and language development. Nutritional deficits occurred when breast-feeding stopped, adding to (or interacting with) the depressing effects of lowered personal interaction and decreased stimulation.

Psychomotor development is affected by ethnicity, stimulation, nutrition

Social class differences have been found in maternal behavior that has significance for sensorimotor development. Lower-class mothers tended to think that they could have little influence on the development of their infants, that environmental influence was minimal, that babies could not communicate with adults, and that it was silly to talk to babies [64]. Middle-class mothers vocalized more in response to their infant's vocalizations, in contrast to lower-class mothers, who were more likely to touch their babies in response to vocalization [37]. These and other studies fit with the finding that mothers' educational level (an aspect of social class) correlates with infants' scores on developmental tests [28].

Maternal correlates of sensorimotor development: responsive vocalizing, education, belief in own influence

Microsystem Influences

For most infants the home is the most influential of microsystems because home is where they spend most of their time, interacting with their most significant people. Although much research on infancy has focused on maternal behavior, fathers are now receiving a lot of well-deserved attention and siblings are beginning to be noticed as salient. Perhaps the day of grandparents is not far off!

Family interaction is difficult to observe and analyze, but a few studies have already shown what seems intuitively true, that parents affect each other in their interactions with children. For example, when fathers were supportive to mothers and evaluated them positively, mothers were more likely to show competence in breast-feeding their babies, and the babies were more likely to show alertness and motor competency [48]. When fathers share in housework and child care, the mothers have more energy and time for playing with the baby. Fathers contribute their own special kind of play. With two participating adults, a baby has more varied exeriences in all sensorimotor areas. Similarly, siblings, grandparents, relatives, and neighbors can affect the functioning of parents and can also have direct interactions with infants. Although 18-month-old infacts prefer to interact with parents rather than with siblings, they watch and imitate siblings, often trying to act upon the same toy [34].

Positive influences on infant development: safe space, appropriate toys, and responsive people

Sensorimotor development is enhanced by the following conditions or actions in the home setting: a physical environment that permits safe exploration; appropriate play materials; responsive adults available. The adults and older children share experiences, act as consultants, encourage motor activity and problem solving, and talk responsively. Language development is very sensitive to the amount and variety of the mother's speech [10] and to acceptance of what the toddler says [47].

If a day-care center is also one of the infant's microsystems, the same principles hold true: Participants affect each other and all relationships within the system; sensorimotor development is influenced by the conditions and activities mentioned. Social interaction differs in that other infants and children are part of the system. The next chapter will discuss some of these interactions. It will show that some programs for infants and parents have very positive effects on sensorimotor development. Of course the mesosystem, the connections between the infant's microsystems, has important potential for enhancing positive effects.

Summary

Infants are competent in perceiving, but limited in motor control. Reflexes are action patterns that are well formed when the baby is born. Reflex behavior serves the infant in protection, food-getting, posture, locomotion, grasping, orienting to sounds and to visual stimuli. Developmental sequences are traced for posture, locomotion, and manipulation. Trends from global to differentiated movements can be seen.

Cognitive behavior is studied as attention, perception, remembering, problem solving, and thinking. A normal infant is alert immediately after birth, attends to various sensory stimuli, turning to locate sources of stimuli, adjusting sucking movements, and altering heart rate. Visual preference and discrimination can be tested by measuring the time that infants spend looking at one of two simultaneously presented stimuli. Processing ability controls early preferences, which are for simple figures and high contrast. A new stimulus is preferred to a familiar one. Faces, attractive from the beginning, are perceived and understood in greater detail and with more meaning as maturity increases. Infants perceive the same color categories that adults do.

Infants can distinguish between various sounds. They perceive categories in human speech sounds and in some musical sounds. They can discriminate between voices and tones of voices. Other sounds of special significance for infants are babies' crying and the human heartbeat. Stimulation of the skin, muscular, and vestibular senses is important for the infant's physical and emotional health. Tactile stimuli from manipulation, even without accompanying visual information, are significant. Novel tactile stimuli are preferred for manipulation. Preferences for tastes and odors are present. Babies like sweet tastes, human milk, and the smell of their mothers' milk.

Piaget delineates 6 substages of sensorimotor intelligence, representing cognitive development from birth to about 2 years. The sensorimotor child understands the world in terms of his actions in it. The stage ends with achievement of representative thought, language, and a concept of the permanence of objects.

The newborn communicates through gesture and state behavior, and responds to language specifically. Intentional vocalizations produce some consistent and meaningful sounds before the baby speaks real words. Infants begin to put words together at about the time that their vocabularies reach 50 words. They then talk about the sensorimotor world.

Assessments of development of the newborn can test ability to sustain life, neurological integrity, and capacity to adapt. Later, tests can measure progress through Piagetian stages, overall development, motor, and mental development. Infant tests do not predict later IQ, but they are useful for clinical and research purposes.

Sensorimotor development is most accelerated in African infants living in traditional societies. Asians, Central Americans, and aborigine Australians are also accelerated as compared with norms for North American Caucasians and Europeans. After weaning, development slows down to below those norms. Differences are probably due to differences in genetic make-up, caretaker behavior, and nutrition. Social-class differences in maternal behavior and beliefs favor the development of middle-class North American infants.

Family interaction affects infants directly and indirectly, as when the father is supportive of the mother. Richness is added to the baby's life when father and siblings play and share caregiving, because interaction styles differ.

References

1. Bayley, N. *Bayley's scales of infant development.* New York: Psychological Corporation, 1968.
2. Bornstein, M. H. Two kinds of perceptual organization near the beginning of life. *Minnesota Symposium on Child Psychology,* Minneapolis: University of Minnesota Press, 1979.
3. Bornstein, M. H., W. Kessen, and S. Weiskopf. The categories of hue in infancy. *Science,* 1976, **191,** 201–202.
4. Bower, T. G. R. *Development in infancy.* San Francisco: W. H. Freeman and Company, Publishers, 1974.
5. Brackbill, Y., G. Adams, D. H. Crowell, and M. L. Gray. Arousal level in neonates and older infants under continuous auditory stimulation. *Journal of Experimental Child Psychology,* 1966, **4,** 178–188.
6. Brazelton, T. B. Behavioral competence of the newborn. *Seminars in Perinatology,* 1979, **3,** 35–43.
7. Brazelton, T. B. Evidence of communication during neonatal assessment. In M. Bullowa (ed.) *Before speech: The beginning of interpersonal communication.* New York: Cambridge University Press, 1979.
8. Brown, R. Development of the first language in the human species. *American Psychologist,* 1973, **28,** 97–106.
9. Bruner, J. S. *Beyond the information given.* New York: W. W. Norton & Company, Inc., 1973.
10. Clarke-Stewart, K. A. Interactions between mothers and their young children: Characteristics and consequences. *Monographs of the Society for Research in Child Development,* 1973, **38:**6–7.
11. Cohen, L. B. Our developing knowledge of infant perception and cognition. *American Psychologist,* 1979, **34,** 894–899.
12. Cohen, L. B., J. S. DeLoache, and M. S. Strauss. Infant visual perception. In J. D. Osofsky (ed.). *Handbook of infant development.* New York: John Wiley & Sons, Inc., 1979.
13. Condon, W. S. Neonatal entrainment and enculturation. In M. Bullowa (ed.). *Before speech: The beginning of interpersonal communication.* New York: Cambridge University Press, 1979.
14. Culp, R. E. Effect of voice quality and content on the looking behavior of two-month-old infants. Paper presented at meeting of the American Psychological Association, New Orleans, 1974.
15. Donaldson, M. *Children's minds.* New York: W. W. Norton & Company, Inc., 1978.
16. Eimas, P. D., E. R. Siqueland, P. Jusczyk and J. Vigorito. Speech perception in infants. *Science,* 1971, **171,** 303–306.
17. Eisenberg, R. B. The organization of auditory behavior. *Journal of Speech and Hearing Research,* 1970, **13,** 461–464.
18. Fantz, R. L. The origin of form perception. *Scientific American,* 1961, **204,** 66–72.
19. Fantz, R. L. Visual perception from birth as shown by pattern selectivity. In H. E. Whipple (ed.). *New issues in infant development.* Annals of the New York Academy of Sciences, 1965, **118,** 793–814.
20. Field, T. M. (ed.). *Infants born at risk.* New York: SP Medical and Scientific Books, 1979.
21. Geber, M. The psychomotor development of African children in the first year and the influence of maternal behavior. *Journal of Social Psychology,* 1958, **47,** 185–195.
22. Gesell, A., and C. Amatruda. *Developmental diagnosis.* New York: Hoeber, 1951.
23. Ginsburg, H. J., S. Fling, M. L. Hope, D. Musgrove, and C. Andrews. Maternal holding preference: A consequence of newborn head-turning response. Paper

presented at meeting of the American Psychological Association, San Francisco, 1977.

24. Gregg, C., R. Clifton, and M. Haith. Heart rate change as a function of visual stimulation in the newborn. Paper presented at meeting of the Society for Research in Child Development, Philadelphia, 1973.

25. Halliday, M. A. K. One child's protolanguage. In M. Bullowa (ed.). *Before speech: The beginning of interpersonal communication.* New York: Cambridge University Press, 1979.

26. Hittelman, J. H., and R. Dickes. Sex differences in neonatal eye contact time. *Merrill-Palmer Quarterly,* 1979, **25,** 171–184.

27. Hulsebus, R. Latency of crying cessation measuring infants' discrimination of mothers' voices. Paper presented at meeting of the American Psychological Association, Chicago, 1975.

28. Ivanans, T. Effect of maternal education and ethnic background on infant development. *Archives of Disturbed Children,* 1975, **50,** 454–457.

29. Jaffe, J., D. N. Stern, and J. C. Perry. "Conversational" coupling of gaze behavior in prelinguistic human development. *Journal of Psycholinguistic Research,* 1973, **2,** 321–329.

30. Jusczyk, P. W., B. S. Rosner, J. E. Cutting, C. Foard, and L. Smith. Categorical perception of nonspeech sounds in the two-month-old infant. Paper presented at meeting of the Society for Research in Child Development, Denver, 1975.

31. Kaye, K. Milk pressure as a determinant of the burst-pause pattern in neonatal sucking. *Proceedings,* 80th Annual Convention of the American Psychological Association, 1972, 83–84.

32. Kearsley, R. B. The newborn's response to auditory stimulation: A demonstration of orienting and defensive behavior. *Child Development,* 1973, **44,** 582–590.

33. Korner, A. F., and L. M. Beason. The association of two congenitally organized behavior patterns in the newborn: Hand-mouth coordination and looking. *Personality and Motor Skills,* 1972, **35,** 115–118.

34. Lamb, M. E. Interactions between eighteen-month-olds and their preschool-aged siblings. *Child Development,* 1978, **49,** 51–59.

35. Lempers, J. D. Young children's production and comprehension of nonverbal deictic behaviors. *Journal of Genetic Psychology,* 1979, **135,** 93–102.

36. Lenneberg, E. H. *Biological foundations of language.* New York: John Wiley & Sons, Inc., 1967.

37. Lewis, M., and C. D. Wilson. Infant development in lower-class American families. *Human Development,* 1972, **15,** 112–127.

38. Lewis, T. L., and D. Maurer. Newborns' central vision: Whole or hole? Paper presented at meeting of the Society for Research in Child Development, New Orleans, 1977.

39. Lipsitt, L. P. Infant sucking and heart rate: Getting excited over savory substances. Paper presented at meeting of the Society for Research in Child Development, Denver, 1975.

40. McCall, R. B., D. H. Eichorn, and P. S. Hogarty. Transitions in early development. *Monographs of the Society for Research in Child Development,* 1977, **42:**3.

41. Maller, O., and J. A. Desor. Effect of taste on ingestion by human newborns. In J. Bosma (ed.). *Fourth symposium on oral sensation and perception: Development in the fetus and infant.* Washington: U.S. Government Printing Office, 1974, pp. 279–291.

42. Maurer, D., and P. Salapatek. Developmental changes in the scanning of faces by young infants. *Child Development,* 1976, **47,** 523–527.

43. Michel, G. F., and R. Goodwin. Inter-uterine birth position predicts newborn

head position preferences. *Infant Behavior and Development,* 1979, **2,** 29–38.

44. Milewski, A. E. Visual discrimination and detection of configurational invariance in 3-month infants. *Developmental Psychology,* 1979, **15,** 357–363.

45. Muir, D., and J. Field. Newborn infants orient to sounds. *Child Development,* 1979, **50,** 431–436.

46. Mundy-Castle, A. C. Perception and communication in infancy: A cross-cultural study. University of Lagos, Nigeria, 1981. (Mimeograph)

47. Nelson, K. Structure and strategy in learning to talk. *Monographs of the Society for Research in Child Development,* 1973, **38:**1–2.

48. Pedersen, F. A. Mother, father, and infant as an interactive system. Paper presented at meeting of the American Psychological Association, Chicago, 1975.

49. Piaget, J. *The construction of reality in the child.* New York: Basic Books, Inc., Publishers, 1954.

50. Piaget, J., and B. Inhelder. *The psychology of the child.* New York: Basic Books, Inc., Publishers, 1969.

51. Porges, S. W. Heart rate indices of newborn attentional responsivity. *Merrill-Palmer Quarterly,* 1974, **20,** 231–254.

52. Pratt, K. C., A. K. Nelson, and K. H. Sun. *The behavior of the newborn infant.* Ohio State University Studies, Contributions to Psychology, No. 10, 1930.

53. Provine, R. R., and J. A. Westerman. Crossing the midline: Limits of early eye-hand behavior. *Child Development,* 1979, **50,** 437–441.

54. Ruff, H. A., and A. Halton. Is there directed reaching in the human neonate? *Developmental Psychology,* 1978, **14,** 425–426.

55. Saling, M. Lateral differentiation of the neonatal head turning response: A replication. *Journal of Genetic Psychology,* 1979, **135,** 307–308.

56. Salk, L. Mother's heartbeat as an imprinting stimulus. *Transactions of the New York Academy of Science,* Serial II, 1962, **24,** 753–763.

57. Self, P. A., F. D. Horowitz, and L. Y. Paden. Olfaction in newborn infants. *Developmental Psychology,* 1972, **7,** 349–363.

58. Sherrod, K. B., S. Friedman, S. Crawley, D. Drake, and J. Devieux. Maternal language to prelinguistic infants: Syntactic aspects. *Child Development,* 1977, **48,** 1662–1665.

59. Simner, M. L. Newborn's response to the cry of another infant. *Developmental Psychology,* 1971, **5,** 136–150.

60. Soroka, S. M., C. M. Corter, and R. Abramovitch. Infants' tactual discrimination of novel and familiar tactual stimuli. *Child Development,* 1979, **50,** 1251–1253.

61. Sroufe, L. A., and E. Waters. Heart rate as a convergent measure in clinical and developmental research. *Merrill-Palmer Quarterly,* 1977, **23,** 3–27.

62. Steinschneider, A., E. L. Lipton, and B. Richmond. Auditory sensitivity in the infant: Effect of intensity on cardiac and motor activity. *Child Development,* 1966, **37,** 233–252.

63. Trevarthen, C. Communication and cooperation in early infancy: A description of primary intersubjectivity. In M. Bullowa (ed.). *Before speech: The beginning of interpersonal communication.* New York: Cambridge University Press, 1979.

64. Tulkin, S. R., and J. Kagan. Mother-child interaction in the first year of life. *Child Development,* 1972, **43,** 31–41.

65. Turkewitz, G., H. G. Birch, and K. K. Cooper. Patterns of response to different auditory stimuli in the human newborn. *Developmental Medicine and Child Neurology,* 1972, **14,** 487–491.

66. Uzgiris, I. C., and J. McV. Hunt. *Toward ordinal scales of psychological development in infancy.* Champaign, Ill.: University of Illinois, 1972.
67. Weiffenbach, J. M., and B. T. Thach. Taste receptors on the tongue of the newborn human: Behavioral evidence. Paper presented at meeting of the Society for Research in Child Development, Denver, 1975.
68. Werner, E. E. *Cross-cultural child development: A view from the Planet Earth.* Monterey, Calif.: Brooks/Cole, 1979.
69. Wolff, P. H., and M. A. Simmons. Nonnutritive sucking and response thresholds in young infants. *Child Development,* 1967, **38,** 631–638.

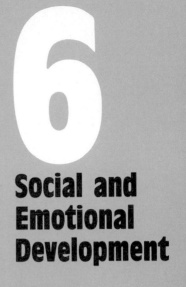

6

Social and Emotional Development

There is a feeling, or affective, side to all action and experience, as well as a thinking or cognitive side. Just as the baby's ways of thinking develop as her body matures, so do her ways of feeling, and ways of relating to people. Social development is closely connected with emotional, because feelings are part of interactions with people.

QUESTIONS TO THINK
ABOUT WHILE READING
THIS CHAPTER

1. How does the infant's self develop?
2. What are the normal crises of psychosocial development in infancy?
3. What are the social-emotional behavioral systems and how are they coordinated with each other?
4. Into which characteristics can temperament be analyzed?
5. How does an infant's temperament affect family interaction?
6. How does a macrosystem affect social-emotional development?
7. How is a family as a microsystem affected by an infant?
8. How do an infant's microsystems contribute to optimal development?

The Developing Self

The newborn is very much influenced by what is going on inside, by state, hunger, pain, and comfort. After physiological equilibrium is established, and the cognitive stage of primary circular reactions completed, the baby turns her attention more to what is going on in the world outside. It may be that at this point, she begins to be aware of a difference between herself and the rest of the world. Now she can have expectations about what will happen, what she, herself, can do, what others will do for her, and how the world will be.

Erik Erikson on Psychosocial Development in Infancy

A healthy person grows through solving a series of crises throughout life, building upon strengths developed in the previous stage. The first crisis of life, the development of a sense of trust, takes place during the first year. If solved successfully, the child has a good base for going on to the next stage of development, and for solving problems of trust that occur through life. The second crisis, the development of a sense of autonomy, is met during the second year of life, and may occupy the child beyond 3 years of age. Erikson's discussion of these stages follows [9a].

The Sense of Trust. Begun with the first experience of securing food and skin stimulation, the growth of trust continues through experiences with things, other people, and the self. The good feelings from tension reduction, repeated consistently in good physical care, make the baby confident that he will be fed when hungry, dried when wet, rocked when restless, and stimulated when bored. He is confident also that he can do something toward initiating these satisfying experiences.

People, primarily mother, are part of the good-feeling experiences and come to stand for the whole. Thus, the 4-month baby, crying from hunger, stops crying and even smiles when he sees his mother or hears her footsteps, trusting that she will feed him.

Appreciation of the permanence of objects is a basic ingredient of the sense of trust. Through his interactions with the world during his first year and a half, the baby comes to know that things exist even when he is not perceiving them. As described in the previous chapter, the first 18 months are the sensorimotor period, in Piaget's series of stages. The two essential achievements of this period are a realization of the permanence of objects and the organization and control of his movements in space. These two achievements go along together. As the baby controls the movements of his body, he deals with the objects of the world, seeing and feeling them, noticing them as they appear and disappear, understanding that events can take place when he is not watching. He comes to trust the world to have certain kinds of order in it, to be dependable. He also comes to know his own powers and how to use them, a beginning of the sense of autonomy.

Establishing trust also involves learning that mother (and others) exists even when she cannot be seen, and that she will come again and again. The game of peekaboo dramatizes mother's disappearance and reappearance. In playing it, the infant lives and relives the frightening situation which has a happy ending, enjoying it throughout the months when trust is growing as he learns that mother continues to exist apart from him. His sense of self begins perhaps from this knowledge and certainly grows as he explores his own body. Fingering his hand and watching it move yield one complex of sensations; fingering the blanket gives another. Reaching, grasping, securing, releasing, touching, mouthing—all tell him what is himself, what are other things and what he can do, or what he can trust his body to do with the world. As a good feeling goes along with the accumulation of knowledge of his body, his power, the objects outside himself, and other people, then the sense of trust grows. Mistrust arises from discomfort; disappointment; anxiety; inability to explore, discriminate, and cope with the world.

The period of development of trust is the *oral stage* in psychoanalytic theory. The mouth is the site of the most important experiences, feeding and the love relationship associated with feeding. Pain from teething is associated with biting and cruel, harsh experiences. In many psychoanalytic writings the skin senses and other senses, too, are greatly overshadowed by the significance of the mouth.

The Sense of Autonomy. The beginnings of autonomy can be seen during the first year, when a baby shows signs of pleasure at being able to control a toy or a person. Because motor coordination is not very effective at this age, an infant may not have many opportunities for control. Infants do give appreciative smiles and gurgles when friendly psychologists rig up motion pictures that they can control by sucking, or mobiles that can be operated by pressing the head on a pillow. However, choice making and control approach crisis dimensions in the second year when the toddler shows more and more concern with doing for herself, choosing, holding on, and letting go.

When the child discovers, through active testing, that there are many situations in which she can choose and live comfortably with her choice, then she feels good about herself. She can decide whether to take a proffered hand or not, whether to play with the truck or the bunny, whether to have a second serving of applesauce or not, whether to sit on grandma's lap or stand on her own feet. Clear and firm restrictions will prevent her from making choices that are beyond her. Frustration and consequent anger are frequent even in older infants who are guided with skill and understanding. Temper outbursts increase in the latter part of infancy, as the child tests herself to find out what she can do and tests her parents and her world to find out what they will let her do. Each successful encounter and choice adds to her sense of autonomy.

Shame and doubt arise when disaster follows choice making and also when the child is not allowed to make enough choices. Shame, doubt, and inadequacy (lack of autonomy) lead to extremes of behavior—rebellion or oversubmissiveness, hurling or hanging on tight.

The period of autonomy is the anal stage in psychoanalytic theory. The central problem is dramatized by the idea of the anal sphincters that open or shut, hanging on or letting go. Depending on the child's experiences with bowel control and control by other people, his personality takes on characteristics like suspicion or confidence, stinginess or generosity, doubt and shame, or autonomy and adequacy.

Social Cognition

In learning about the self, a person learns about others, and in learning about others, a person learns about the self. The relationship between the self and others completes social cognition. Interaction with people provides experience from which the infant acquires knowledge of the self. Observation of other people's interactions gives a baby some information on which to base behavior with those people. Infants' responses to strangers seem to be influenced by previously watched behavior of mother and stranger [20].

It is certain that a baby has some knowledge of self when she uses *me*, *mine*, or her own name, and points to herself and pictures of herself. These achievements are common by or before 2 years. In order to find out more about the self-concept before emergence of language, Michael

Lewis and his associates have done a series of studies that demonstrate the development of self-cognition [20]. Mirrors, videotapes, and pictures were shown to infants between 9 and 24 months in order to see whether they recognized themselves. After showing a mirror, rouge was applied to the baby's face. The mirror was shown again. Body-directed behavior increased, and touching the nose increased with age, suggesting a gradual increase of knowledge of whose image was in the mirror. A mirror image gives an immediate response contingent upon the baby's action, as well as an image. Pictures give only the image. If a picture of the self is to be recognized, the baby must know something about his own features. When viewing colored slides of themselves and peers, babies as young as 9 months smiled more at their own pictures and frowned more at peers! One-quarter of the 18-months-olds labeled their own pictures correctly.

Knowledge of others has been demonstrated with pictures. Between 9 and 12 months, infants could distinguish between photographs of baby and adult faces. They preferred to look and smile at the babies. They could tell the difference between photographs of self and adults before they distinguished between self and other babies. Concepts of self and others can thus be seen to emerge before the end of the first year and to develop throughout infancy.

Emotions

Everyone knows that emotions include joy, fear, and anger, but there are many theories as to just what an emotion is. As a working definition, we shall say that an emotion is a feeling plus a tendency toward a certain kind of action. A stirred-up state of the organism occurs with an emotion. There is also a cognitive side of the experience. The whole person —body, mind, and feelings—is involved in an emotion.

Can newborn babies experience different emotions? Many people think they can, but psychologists tend to say that emotions develop. The first theory of development of emotions, Katherine Bridges' theory, states that the newborn experiences excitement, a global emotion [7]. Differentiation from global to specific occurs. (See "Differentiation and Integration" in Chapter 2.) Out of excitement come distress and delight, at about 3 months. By six months differentiation of distress produces fear, anger, and disgust, while excitement, distress, and delight continue. By 2 years, Bridges said, 11 emotions are distinguishable. Like Bridges, present-day psychologists think that true emotions do not begin until the baby can make some distinction between self and environment [32]. Emotions are traced back to early beginnings in the first month, just as Piaget traces cognitive development from the reflex stage of the first month. Joy, well developed at 7 months, is traced back through active laughter at 4 or 5 months, through pleasure, shown at 3 months, turning-toward at 2 months, and reflex smiling at birth.

Birth —Reflex smile
2 mo. —Turning toward
3 mo. —Pleasure
4 mo. —Active laugh
7 mo. —Joy

Patterns of Relating to People and Things

Emotions develop in contexts of self and others. We shall use some of Bowlby's and Ainsworth's concepts to discuss them as social-emotional systems: attachment-affiliation, fear-wariness, anger-aggression, and curiosity-exploration. (See "Ethology: The Study of Evolutionary Adaptation," in Chapter 1.) These systems are coordinated with each other, to keep the baby comforted, fed, and safe while she is vulnerable, and yet to encourage the independence and exploration essential for growing up.

Attachment-Affiliation

Human beings are drawn together from the moment of birth, when a mother, and a father if he is present, become enchanted with their baby and bonded with a tie of love. It takes a little longer for the baby to build attachments to parents and to make friends, but the newborn has some resources for later loving and liking. Certain behavior patterns of the newborn serve to bring baby and mother into contact. Crying provokes an anxious feeling in the parent. She tries to relieve it and soon finds that close bodily contact soothes crying. The baby clings and nestles, stimulating cuddling. The baby sucks, giving pleasure and relief to the mother. The baby looks, eliciting gazing and talking. The baby builds an attachment to the person who responds to her signals of hunger, satiation, distress, and boredom, to gazes and coos and bids for social response. Baby's attachment grows as the mother feeds promptly, allows the baby to decide how much to eat, picks the baby up and cuddles at signs of distress, and engages in face-to-face interaction. No doubt there

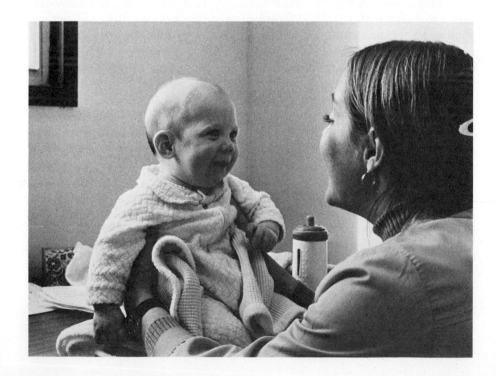

are other activities that contribute to attachment, such as positioning the baby comfortably for play and viewing, making interesting sights and sounds available, and encouraging the use of emerging powers.

The Strange Situation: A Research Instrument.   Mary D. S. Ainsworth and her associates have conducted many experiments on the nature of attachment and its relation to other behavior systems [2].   A sample of a year-old baby's attachment behavior is elicited by a controlled experimental procedure called "the strange situation."   In a room with a supply of toys, the following episodes, each three minutes long, take place:

1. The mother enters with the baby, sits down, puts the baby down, and does nothing unless the baby seeks her attention.
2. A stranger enters, sits quietly, then converses with the mother, then gradually approaches the baby, showing a toy.   The mother leaves.
3. If the baby is not active, the stranger tries to interest him in toys.   If the baby cries, she tries to comfort him.
4. The mother enters and pauses in the doorway.   The stranger leaves. The mother has been told that only after the baby is again settled in play with toys, she should leave.
5. The baby is alone.
6. The stranger enters and behaves as before.
7. The mother returns.   The stranger leaves.

Different patterns of behavior in the strange situation were identified and shown to be related to infant behavior in other situations and to the ways in which mothers interacted with babies.   There were three main patterns, one of which indicated secure attachment, and two, insecure attachment.   The patterns have been labeled A, B, and C.   Description of infant and mother behavior follow.

Group B.   These babies explore the toys and room while their mother is present, show distress and decreased exploration when she leaves, seek closeness and interaction when the mother returns.   They are securely attached.   Home observations during the first year showed the mothers responding sensitively to babies' signals, and babies being more cooperative than other babies with mothers and other people.

Securely attached baby explores when with mother; shows distress when mother leaves; seeks closeness on her return

Group C.   Babies show some anxiety before separation and much anxiety when mothers leave.   When mothers return, babies are ambivalent, seeking contact and yet resisting and rejecting the mothers' advances. Home observations showed these mothers not as appropriately responsive as Group B mothers.   There is, of course, the possibility that Group C babies give signals that are harder to interpret and that they are less easily satisfied.

Group A.   Babies rarely cry upon separation and often avoid and ignore the mother at reunion, sometimes mixing approaching and rejecting. They are negative when held and when put down.   In home observations, Group A mothers showed aversion to physical contact and restriction in expressing affect. The role of physical contact seems to be an important one in soothing anxiety in primate babies, human as well as monkey (See "Comparative Developmental Psychology" in Chapter 1.) Group A babies apparently feel the need to snuggle close to their mothers but fear rejection. In avoiding and ignoring, they are defending themselves from further hurt.

Attachment and the Sense of Trust. Ainsworth's studies have shown that when mothers respond sensitively to babies during the first year, the babies show secure attachment at one year of age [1]. A secure attachment develops as the infant comes to trust the mother or other person. The baby builds expectations that the sensitively responding caregiver will continue to meet her needs. No doubt these experiences contribute to trust in general, the sense of trust. The securely attached, trusting infant is in turn sensitive to the caregiver and tries to cooperate with directions and requests. Attachment is therefore the foundation for moral development. A well-attached baby accepts and absorbs the rules given by the persons of attachment. These rules include the knowledge, beliefs, values, and skills of the culture. They include rules about how to speak, or language.

Attachment is base for social, emotional, and cognitive development

During social interchanges, infants smile and later laugh, showing that they feel pleasure and joy. During play with people, infants cause events to happen.

In perceiving stimuli that he himself has caused, an infant experiences contingent stimulation. One of the earliest and most frequent ways in which a baby gets contingent stimulation is for his family members to play with him. Mother makes a noise when Baby makes a noise. Grandpa lifts him high when he puts his hand on Grandpa's face. Dad puffs out his cheeks when Baby puts his hand in his mouth. These and other similar interactions have been found to elicit vigorous smiling and cooing as the infant enjoys continuing success in eliciting responses [37]. Baby shows joy as he realizes that he can make something happen and that people become important parts of that pleasurable situation as they play with him. The absence of social play with contingent stimulation may constitute serious deprivation to an infant. Such deprivation may contribute to the failure-to-thrive syndrome, shown by neglected infants and infants in institutions.

Attachment Figures: When and Who. An attachment is a bond to a specific person. Therefore, an infant has to be able to tell one person from another in order to become attached. Even in the first month infants show differences in distress and comfort in feeding when changed from one caregiver to another. By 3 to 5 months of age infants show recognition of the mother by excitement and approach movements to her but not to a stranger [39]. At this age most infants show confidence in the mother, as though they expect her to comfort them. Another sign of growing attachment is keeping the mother in view, even while in someone else's arms. Definite indications are crying when the mother leaves, crying when picked up by someone else, and stopping when taken by the mother, clinging, following, and greeting.

We have been referring to the attachment figure as the mother only because the mother is the first attachment figure for the majority of babies. Infants also build attachments to fathers when they have the opportunity. Sometimes fathers are the first and favorite attachment figures. Infants become attached to siblings, grandparents, friends, day-care-givers, in fact to anyone who gives regular, sensitive care and interesting stimulation. Most infants have made one or more attachments by 6 months of age. If a first attachment has not been made by age 2, it is difficult to do so, but it may be done as late as 4 to 6 years [29]. Early attachments are the base from which social behavior is developed. Young children in institutions, lacking attachment figures, are likely to be clinging, attention-seeking, and overly friendly with strangers. When they go to school, they tend to be restless, disobedient, and unpopular, and to fight with other children. Early attachment experiences, then, have a bearing on later social abilities, including affiliation, or making and keeping friends.

Attachment Objects. Security blankets have been made famous by Linus, the comic-strip character who suffers torture when his blue blanket is gone. Many babies use the attachment behavior of sucking and/or clinging with objects, as well as with persons. Pacifiers and thumbs are sucked most often; blankets and fuzzy animals are cuddled. Sucking and cuddling may be combined, as by our grandson,, who sucked his thumb while clinging to a koala bear. (He wore the fur off two koalas.) Attachment objects seem to relieve tension and give security to little primates. We have already mentioned Harlow's well-known monkeys, who clung to cloth mothers when frightened. Sometimes hard objects, such as toys and bottles, also serve as attachment objects.

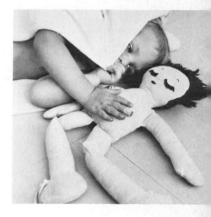

The use of attachment objects by 690 children between 18 and 63 months was analyzed to give the following results [25]. Attachments to objects are normal. Pacifiers, most popular of all, were enjoyed by 66 per cent of infants at 3 months. Blankets, a close second, were fondled by 60 per cent of 18-months-olds. As Figure 6–1 shows, the 3 types of attachment objects varied in popularity from one age to another, pacifiers declining from a high at 3 months to zero at 24. The peak use of blankets was at 18 and 24 months. Attachment objects can help children to face anxiety and difficulties, such as separation from mother and going to the doctor.

Institutional children do not develop object attachments as frequently as do children living in families [25]. Perhaps their lack of human attachments impairs their ability to form bonds.

Affiliation. Friendly interaction is an important part of social life to infants, as well as to people of all ages. Reflex smiling occurs even before

FIGURE 6-1
Use of attachment objects in infancy. (SOURCE: R. H. Passman and J. S. Halonen. A developmental survey of young children's attachments to inanimate objects. *Journal of Genetic Psychology*, 1979, *134*, 165—178.)

Per Cent of Children with Attachments

Pacifier

Blanket

Hard Object

Age in Months

social smiling at around 3 months. From this time on, the baby responds to social approaches and initiates them, using smiling and vocalizing with anyone who will participate. Games evoke joy, shown in smiles and laughter. By 9 months or before, when strangers may provoke anxiety by coming too close, a gentle, patient stranger can still win smiles and be a partner in play. Young infants can tell the difference between adult strangers and baby strangers. They prefer to interact with babies [19]. Infants even prefer to interact with peers rather than their mothers when both are available [21.].

The social behavior of infants varies under different circumstances, including the following: the setting—home, day care, laboratory, or other; the objects present—number, toys or not, large or small; the people present—family members, teacher, stranger, peers; number of peers. Infants as young as 6 months, when placed close to each other, will vocal-

ize, touch, and smile at one another [36]. By 12 months or earlier, they make contact over objects, conflicting over small objects and gradually learning to offer and accept. Children between 12 and 24 months, in pairs of unequal ages, played ball games spontaneously. They alternated behaviors, imitated each other, and signaled intent and awareness of games [12]. A study in a day-care center compared the social behavior of infants between 7 and 14 months with that of a group of toddlers between 15 and 31 months [11]. The toddlers made 3 times as many social contacts with peers as did the infants. Both groups made similar use of objects and touching, but toddlers used a great deal more talking. The most successful behavior for initiating contacts was giving, taking, or showing an object, while touching was least successful. The age difference in contacts, therefore, was due to the toddlers talking more. The children who were more responsive to others received more responsiveness from others, a finding that agrees with other studies on popular and unpopular infants. Responsiveness begins early in life to be a key to being liked.

Babies are like older people in being more responsive to their friends (familiar peers) than to unfamiliar peers, and in their own homes than in laboratories or other settings [21]. They get along better in dyads than in larger groups, perhaps because the dyad is simpler.

Curiosity-Exploration

Infants find nurture for cognitive development through exploration. Curious about the world, they use schemes for locomotion and examining to get information about space and the objects in it. They show pleasure when engaged in exploration. Contingent stimulation occurs in the world of objects, as well as with people. When a baby finds out something works, she shows joy. She puts a clothes pin into a jar, turns a light on, or opens a box to find a toy in it.

Human babies, as well as monkey, use the mother as a base from which to explore. When put down beside the mother, even in a strange room, especially if there are toys and other interesting objects along the way, a baby will creep or toddle around the room, or into an adjoining room. As long as the mother seems to be accessible, the baby is able to make excursions into the unknown, looking back every now and then to make eye contact, or creeping back to touch or embrace. Thus the infant plays a part in keeping safe while getting new experiences, by keeping open the lines of communication with the mother.

When the mother departs or is inaccessible, the baby drops exploration and tries to regain the mother's presence by attachment behavior, following her to the door, crying, calling, searching, and protesting. If play is resumed, exploration is not so vigorous. Frightening events are much more frightening. When the mother returns, attachment behavior is heightened, and play ignored for a while. Securely attached infants are less disrupted than insecurely attached by brief absences of the mother. At home, of course, mothers go to another room for a while, without undue upset, or they leave the baby with other attachment figures. With

Attachment behavior: Trying to contact attachment figure; contacting

a prolonged maternal absence, even a securely attached baby feels distress, even despair, before turning back to play and exploration. The return of the mother then causes intense attachment behavior, with clinging and following blocking out curiosity and interest in play. The baby may also feel angry at the mother, and show it by refusing to look at her, rejecting embraces and yet seeking them, and other negative behavior, all incompatible with exploration. When attachment supports exploration, positive affect and intellectual growth occur; when attachment and exploration are out of balance, emotional problems prevent cognitive efforts.

Fear-Wariness

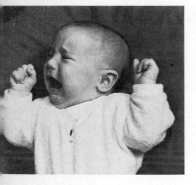

The startle reflex of the newborn may be the behavior pattern from which fear is later differentiated [32]. During the early weeks, infants sometimes cry after prolonged looking at a stimulus, as though they had been unable to look away. The behavior that spells fear to most people is frowning and/or crying, together with avoidance or trying to get away. By around 4 months of age, infants often stare soberly at strange faces and then cry and/or turn away. This reaction, an uneasiness with the unfamiliar, is called wariness [8]. By 9 months, reactions to strangers are more immediate and more intense, and are called *fears*. Between 4 and 9 months, the infant acquires much experience, a more powerful memory, and the ability to move around. Remembered experiences may include trips to the doctor's office, where a stranger in white stung him with a needle, encounters with grown-ups who snatched him up quickly, being knocked over by a dog, or falling down some steps into a dark room. An experience that evokes such memories stimulates fear.

A wary or frightened baby turns to his mother, father, or other figure of attachment, withdrawing from the fear stimulus and using attachment behavior to relieve distress. Bodily contact is especially comforting. Even adults want to cling to a loved person in the face of danger. The baby, whether human, monkey, or chick, keeps the attachment figure within view or earshot. At the emergence of something frightening, or at a call from the mother, the baby is ready to scurry back to safety. The attachment behavior system and the fear-wariness behavior system are thus coordinated to keep a baby safe while allowing a little distance and opportunities for learning and growing up. Mother's or father's presence allows baby to explore not only objects and places, but to become familiar with other people, to develop modes of social interaction, and to make friends. Attachment thus provides the base for affiliation, as fear-provoking strangers are transformed into persons who can be trusted. Adults know something of this experience also, when they are introduced to strangers.

Anger-Aggression

Among the different cries of the newborn, the type that goes with prolonged distress may indicate rage or anger. If Bridges' theory and its modern descendants are right, then anger is not differentiated out of distress until around 3 months of age. At this point, the baby has built some expectations about the world, and when those are severely violated, anger occurs. Violations include restraining, blocking, frustrating, or interrupting progress toward satisfaction. The action tendency that is part of anger is lashing out or attacking.

During the second year, when the desire to establish autonomy is strong, interference with choice making is likely to bring angry resistance, crying, screaming, kicking, perhaps hitting, throwing, and biting. For establishment of a sound sense of autonomy, a baby grows by having many experiences in successful choice making and few in choosing activities in which he cannot succeed.

Goodenough's comprehensive and classic study, *Anger in Young Children*, describes and analyzes 1,878 anger outbursts of children in the first 8 years of life [13]. Because the observations were recorded by parents, the cases were necessarily selected from families where parents were unusually cooperative and intelligent. As can be seen in Figure 6–2 there was a marked peak in anger outbursts during the second year and then a rapid decline. Little sex difference appeared in infancy, but during the preschool period, boys had significantly more outbursts than girls. At all ages, however, differences between individuals were greater than differences between the sexes.

Anger behavior changed with age. Most of the outbursts during the first 3 years involved display or undirected energy. Such behavior included crying, screaming, stiffening the body, throwing self on floor,

Anger: a response to frustration and violation of expectation

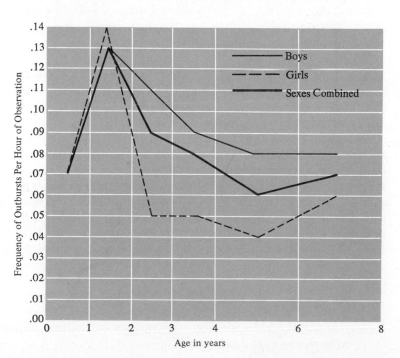

FIGURE 6–2
Number of anger outbursts in 10 hours by age and sex.
(SOURCE: Adapted from F. L. Goodenough. *Anger in young children.* Minneapolis; University of Minnesota Press, 1931.)

stamping, jumping up and down. With age, such primitive bodily responses tended to be replaced with more directed, less violent, more symbolic expressions. The duration of outbursts changed very little, however.

Physical factors were influential. Anger occurred before mealtimes more than at any other times of day. Children were angry more when ill, even with slight colds or constipation. Outbursts were more frequent among those who had recovered from one or more fairly serious illnesses than among children who had not been ill.

Many psychological factors were shown to be significant. Children who were being toilet trained showed more anger on days following bedwetting than on days following dry nights. The more adults in the home, the more likely was a child to become angry. When parents shifted from one method of control to another, the child tended to have more outbursts. "Giving the child his own way" was reported more often for children who had many outbursts than for those who had few.

Roots of Violence. All people experience anger, but some express it violently. When a highly active infant does not receive outside control, but instead is overstimulated, he is likely to break things and hurt people. He feels helpless to control his actions. Especially if other forms of satisfaction are not available, he may come to enjoy being destructive. At the other extreme, if outside controls are very strict, preventing even exploration, inner controls may be stifled. Either situation can lead to violent expression of anger. When the baby is treated violently and cruelly (abused), he is likely to make these forms of behavior part of his own. When given suitable choices within firm limits, and treated with love and respect, even the highly active, aggressive infant can gradually develop his own controls.

Temperament

Any parent of more than one child will notice consistent differences in style of behavior, often from the first days of life. One may be quiet, one active, one very adaptable, one irritable. Such qualities are aspects of behavioral style or temperament. Thomas and Chess conducted longitudinal studies of temperament for over 20 years, beginning with infants at 3 months of age [34]. They have found the same 9 categories of temperament in middle-class American babies, infants in other cultures, and infants with neurological defects. Children are rated according to the following characteristics. For each category we give examples of behavior considered in making the ratings.

THOMAS AND CHESS'S
CATEGORIES OF
TEMPERAMENT

1. *Activity level.* How much does the child move, and what proportion of the time is she active?
2. *Rhythmicity.* How regular are various functions, including sleep-waking, hunger, and elimination?

3. *Approach or withdrawal.* Are first reactions positive or negative to a new person, toy, food, or any other new stimulus?
4. *Adaptability.* How easily are responses modified to new or changed conditions?
5. *Threshold of responsiveness.* How intense a stimulus is required for a response to sensory stimuli, objects, and persons?
6. *Intensity of reaction.* How strong or energetic is a response?
7. *Quality of mood.* What is the proportion of pleasant, joyful, friendly behavior to unpleasant behavior, crying, and unfriendliness?
8. *Distractibility.* How much is ongoing behavior altered to an extraneous stimulus?
9. *Attention span and persistence.* How long is one activity carried on? How much is an activity maintained in the face of obstacles?

Types of Temperament

Each infant, of course, has her own particular combination of temperamental characteristics, but Thomas and Chess identify these three general types.

The Easy Child. A joy to family and friends, the easy child is rhythmic, adaptable, mild, and positive. She accepts schedules, new foods, and strangers, adapts to new places, and accepts frustrations and rules. About 40 per cent of the middle-class sample were easy children.

The Difficult Child. Hard to live with, the difficult child is irregular, negative, withdrawing, slow in adapting, and intense in mood. This child sleeps poorly, cries often and loudly, laughs loudly, has temper tantrums, and takes a long time to adjust to new routines, people, and places. Fortunately for families, only about 10 per cent of children were difficult.

The Slow-to-Warm-Up Child. Easier than the difficult child, the slow-to-warm-up type shows mild negative responses to new experiences and is slow to adapt to change. If given time to accept the new without pressure, she develops positive behavior. The slow-to-warm-up child does well in a patient family. About 15 per cent of the children were of this type.

Stability of Temperament

As children grow up, temperamental characteristics are modified by experience. The difficult child does not always remain difficult, nor is the easy child without problems. Studies of temperament over time are not very conclusive. The one characteristic that seems to be most stable is activity level. It was the only stable characteristic of three (activity level, vigor, and persistence) that were studied over a period of 13 to 44 months of age [10]. No sex differences were found in any of the 3 measures.

Ecology of Social-Emotional Development

Macrosystem Influences

All levels of the social ecology contribute to the social-emotional development of the child. Although face-to-face interactions take place in microsystems, those interactions are affected by the macrosystem and exosystems.

The physical setting of the macrosystem structures some of the infant's experiences. In coastal Brazil, for example, people flock to the beaches, wearing next to nothing. Babies are free of clothing restrictions and enjoy opportunities for skin-to-skin contact. Contrast their daily round with that of infants in northern Russia, swaddled in many layers of warm clothing. Infants are probably affected by the esthetic setting of the macrosystem. The art, music, architecture, and toys must influence the modes of emotional expression that children develop.

A macrosystem also structures values and beliefs as to how to attain goals shaped by the values. For instance, what is an ideal person, and how must babies be reared in order to guide them toward that ideal? If the ideal child is polite, obedient, and neat, then how should parents deal with the baby who is developing a sense of autonomy? The macrosystem of colonial North America supported the belief that the toddler's will should be broken in a vigorous contest between parent and child. A strong belief alive in our present macrosystem is that the sense of autonomy should be nurtured by letting the toddler make decisions within his own capabilities. Peer interaction in infancy may be thought valuable or unnecessary for social-emotional development.

Government policy uses resources according to macrosystem values and beliefs. Infant well-being is enhanced by policies that support responsible parenthood and that make it easier for families to take good care of their babies. Poverty, especially in the inner city, affects social-emotional development by increasing maternal depression and marital discord.

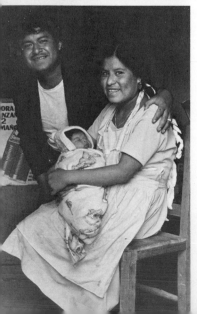

The family system, a part of the macrosystem, structures the social life of the infant by determining who are the caregivers. Fathers in the United States are presently gaining recognition and approval as caregivers. In the extended family system, common in Asia and Africa, grandmothers, sisters, sisters-in-law, and even cousins may help each other in taking care of infants. In communal societies, there is a general conviction that children are everybody's concern, or more simply, most people like children. A review of a large number of anthropological studies indicates that when mothers and young children are at home all day, with no other company, children are more likely to be rejected [27]. Anyone gets tired and irritated by long-lasting, unrelieved responsibility, and mothers are no exception. Children receive more warmth and acceptance when fathers or others participate in their care at home on a day-to-day basis and also when grandparents are there.

As a macrosystem changes, infant social life may change, too. When social change involves a withdrawal of support and/or power from mothers, their roles become extremely difficult. An example is the Akan women of Ghana who have gone from rural matrilineal families to live in cities [23]. As a mother, the Akan woman living with her own mother had the assistance of many of her female relatives. While bringing up her baby, she was also able to work at farming and selling, or in business and thus earned money while rearing children, often many children. Thus, she was independent of her husband. With the move to the city, she lost not only the ready help she had with child rearing but also her financial independence. Newly dependent upon her husband for money and help, shorn of her power, she became a different kind of mother. The shape of family interactions was next modified by the husband's response to the change.

Exosystems

Family members take part in microsystems other than the family, often without the baby. Baby's exosystem may include golf club, school, and church, but most important, it includes the parents' jobs. When father is away working, he is not home playing with baby or giving care. Some fathers' jobs are so demanding that the men have little time and energy left for fathering. If a mother has a job, she, too, is less available to a baby. The resulting relationship with the baby depends, at least in part, upon the mother's beliefs about whether a mother should take exclusive care of her baby [15]. Negative reunion behavior was shown in Ainsworth's Strange Situation by babies whose mothers' work status conflicted with their beliefs. That is, insecure attachment was shown by infants of nonemployed mothers who thought that they should not take exclusive care of their infants, and by infants of working mothers who thought that mothers should be the only caregivers. The study suggests that the mother's dissatisfaction with her employment status affects the quality of the baby's attachment.

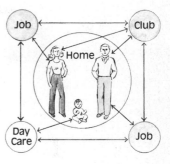

Among mothers of children under 3, living with their husbands, over a third are employed [16]. Mothers from one-parent households are employed at a higher rate. Parental employment, of course, affects the baby by supplying financial support for the microsystem. The amount of money earned largely determines socioeconomic status, which is very low indeed for most mother-headed households. Financial need far outweighs all other reasons for mothers of young children working outside their homes [14].

In the world of work, there are some jobs where the workers' family life is considered important. Family life and jobs are fitted together by flextime, maternity and paternity leave, educational and counseling programs, recreation that includes families, and day care for children of employees.

Microsystems

A baby's entrance into a family makes that family into a different microsystem from what it was before. Everybody's relationships change.

More is known about how the mother-father-baby triad (three persons) interacts than about the interactions in families of four or more, but nobody doubts that a baby's arrival has a big impact on any family system. The wider social network is affected, as well as the household in which the baby lives, because interactions with grandparents, relatives, and friends are changed. Another microsystem that infants enter is the daycare group.

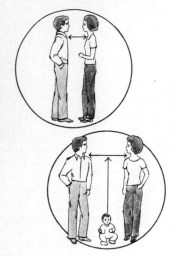

Family Microsystem. A baby's entrance into a family causes changes in the roles that the mother and father play. The first baby, of course, makes a man and a woman into parents. As parents, they are likely to pay more attention to traditional male and female pursuits, the man working harder to earn money and provide a structurally adequate home, the woman giving up her job at least for a while, and working at home-making and child care. They may evaluate each other more along these lines than before, and additionally as parents. The help and support that the father gives the mother will make her feel more or less able to do well, and will affect the amount of time and energy she has to spend with the baby. Similarly, her attitude toward her husband as a father will probably affect his competence and pleasure in fatherhood.

Home observations of middle-class parents and infants, aged 15 months, showed some relationships between husband-wife interactions and parent-infant interactions [5]. Parents were observed in their customary behavior together, together with the baby, and each parent alone with the baby. Results showed that the frequency with which wives talked about the baby was related to the frequency with which husbands played with the baby, talked in stimulating ways to the baby, and made physical contact. The stimulating, playful fathers were rated high in affection. Because this study was correlational, we cannot tell whether the mother's interest in the baby encouraged the father's interest, or whether the especially enchanting babies elicited extra attention from both parents, or whether the father's delight in the baby made the mother focus on the baby. Perhaps some of each process was involved. The study also suggested that attention toward the baby formed the basis for enjoyable interaction between husband and wife. When spouses rated high on spousal harmony, facilitation of three-person interaction, and sharing pleasure, the mothers, and especially the fathers, were actively involved in parenting.

A second or later-born baby affects existing parent-child interaction, as well as husband-wife interaction. Comparisons of mother-toddler interaction were made before and after the birth of a sibling [18]. As might be expected, there was a decrease in the amount of time that the mother and child spent in joint attention and joint play, even when the mother was not with the new baby. Several measures showed a decrease in mothers' playful and attentive interest in the older child. Because she has less time for the older child, the mother may well enlist more help from the father than he has previously given. The older child then has more inter-action with the father than before.

At the birth of the second child, the parents, having developed their philosophy and techniques for child rearing, are not so easily influenced by educational programs as they were after their first baby was born. The records of the Harvard Preschool Project confirm this conclusion [38]. Firstborn children benefited greatly from a comprehensive program to promote competence in parents and infants, but later-born children did not seem to gain from participation.

An older sibling is an important influence on a baby. Young ones watch their brothers and sisters, follow them, imitate them, and pay at-tention to the toys used by the older children. Older sisters often teach younger children. Even in the presence of the mother, babies' explora-tion is enhanced by an older sibling [30]. The babies explore over a larger area, inspect and manipulate objects more, and fret less.

The infant's own characteristics contribute to family interaction. Al-though North Americans are less set in their sex preferences than Asians (who usually want sons more than daughters), most parents want a son if they plan to have only one child and to want a boy and a girl if they are going to have two [22]. As few parents go to the trouble of trying to produce the gender they prefer, a fair number are disappointed in what they get.

The baby's appearance may be more or less pleasing. Not only is the matter of beauty or good looks involved here but of an appearance that suggests something significant to the parents: a family resemblance caus-ing pride or the expectation that the new baby will act like Aunt Rosa or like her big sister; fragility, including delicate handling, or sturdiness, in-citing rough play; a characteristic thought to predict a personality trait, such as a weak chin indicating weak character. Temperament is impor-tant to family functioning. Practically nobody has much trouble with an "easy child," but the slow-to-warm-up child can fit well with gentle, pa-tient, understanding parents, and disastrously with their opposites. With help from friends, relatives, teachers, or counselor, however, par-ents can learn to provide an environment in which the slow-to-warm-up child can thrive. The "difficult child" requires even more from parents, and they require even more from their sources of support. How difficult the child is depends partly on the parents, as a study of mothers' percep-tions of temperament has shown [3]. The mothers rated as difficult the babies who were fussy and hard to soothe. These infants cried at a higher pitch and paused longer between cries than did less difficult babies. The younger the mother, and the fussier the baby during observations, the more difficult the mother rated the baby. The more extraverted (gregari-ous, influential over others, expressive, demonstrative) she rated herself, the less she saw her baby as difficult. Therefore, what makes an infant seem difficult is not only the baby's own behavior, but the experience and personality of the mother. When mothers rated their babies as difficult at 3 months of age, they interacted less and were less responsive than mothers who did not think their infants difficult [9]. When observed again at 8 months, the mothers were still less responsive to difficult babies.

Many abused babies start life as difficult children. As we say elsewhere in this book, child abuse has multiple causes, located in all levels of the ecology, and within the child who is the victim. Crying is an aversive stimulus. Prolonged, loud, shrill crying is an extremely aversive stimulus. The parent who cannot soothe the crying baby is likely to feel a failure, and eventually to stop trying, and to feel angry at the baby. The parent may then abuse or neglect the difficult baby, especially if other stresses leading to abuse are present—poverty, an unwanted pregnancy, too many children to care for, an urban ghetto environment, marital discord, lack of support from relatives and friends, ignorance of child development, extreme youth, and personal experience of violence.

Positive Family Influences on Cognitive Development. Many studies have shown a relationship between the microsystem of the home during infancy and the intelligence and/or competence of the young child. The physical environment that supports all-around development is a safe place in which the child is free to explore a variety of objects that he can manipulate and from which he can get contingent responses. The family members, of course, are the ones who design the space and objects in it, and who make it available to the infant.

Although research on nurturant parent-infant interaction has been done more with mothers than with fathers, siblings, or other relatives, we believe that the findings on mothers apply just as well to the other persons who give care to the baby, who teach, enjoy and play with the baby. The following experiences are conducive to the baby's emotional health, as well as to cognitive development and general competence:

1. *Security.* The parent provides a secure base from which the baby can explore space, objects, and other persons.
2. *Freedom to explore.* The child has freedom to explore the environment of space, objects, and persons, rather than being confined in a small space. Before the baby can move under his own power, freedom includes being moved from place to place and being positioned favorably for having interesting experiences.
3. *People talking.* People talk to the baby about what he is doing and seeing, about objects, activities, persons, feelings, and anything else of interest to both.
4. *Availability* of caregivers for sharing experiences, interpreting, giving help, and starting the baby on new activities when appropriate. The caregiver does not give constant attention, but is there when needed.
5. *Play and enjoyment.* Baby games not only give contingent stimulation and promote the sense of autonomy, but they give mutual pleasure and strengthen bonds of attachment.

Family Influences on Sex Knowledge and Gender Role. By 2 years or earlier, a child knows that he is a boy or she is a girl. This knowledge comes mostly from experiences in the family.

Babies learn the names of eyes, nose, mouth, fingers, toes, and many more parts of the body as parents tell them, often playing games such as "This little piggy went to market." A child's concept of self is built as he learns about his physical self in this way. In a happy, affectionate context, he feels good about himself and his body.

When a baby fingers his genitals, as every infant does, there is probably one chance in ten that the mother who lovingly names his toes, will exclaim happily, "There's your penis." More likely, she will say nothing to him, possibly removing his hands from his penis and distracting him with a toy or something to look at or listen to. Infants are sensitive to sexual stimulation, showing signs of relaxation and pleasure when their genital areas are touched. Newborn boys have erections of the penis. Both boys and girls learn to stimulate their genitals during infancy, through the process of exploring their bodies.

Although some societies permit expression of infant sexuality, North Americans and many Europeans take a stern attitude toward it. However, parent educators have long believed that it was wise to use the names of organs and functions and to permit babies to explore their bodies. Reasons for this point of view include promoting cognition (increased knowledge of the world, a clear body image), building a positive self-concept, and laying a foundation for good sexual adjustment as an adult.

Families tell and show infants how boys and girls are supposed to behave, and also how men and women behave. Even at birth, parents begin to apply their stereotypes about behavior of each sex [28]. Although a group of boy and girl newborns did not differ in length, weight, or Apgar scores, daughters were seen as little, beautiful, cute, fine, and resembling their mothers. Fathers saw greater sex differences than did mothers, in keeping with father behavior throughout childhood. Fathers distinguish more between boys and girls than do mothers, and place more emphasis on boys acting masculine and girls feminine. Older siblings also teach younger ones about masculine and feminine behavior, acting as role models, reinforcing appropriate behavior as they see it, and giving direct instructions.

A series of studies by Parke and others shows fathers treating boys and girls differently from birth onwards [24]. Fathers touched and talked to newborn boys more than to newborn girls. At 3 months, fathers held daughters longer and closer, and looked at sons more. They provided more visual and tactile stimulation for sons. Cross-cultural studies also show fathers interacting more with sons than with daughters. Because fathers and mothers differ in their style of interacting with infants, sons and daughters have quite a different experience. What is more, the babies learn that father, a man, plays a lot, but does not do much feeding, diapering, bathing, and other caregiving, while mother, a woman, does the opposite and also talks more. And boys receive more father-type behavior than do girls. A similar sex difference has been seen in father and mother monkeys [33]. Fathers played with infants far more than did mothers, but fathers showed practically no contact, protection, or grooming behavior. This is not to suggest that human fathers cannot learn to diaper and mothers cannot play, but only that some activities seem to "come naturally." Adults vary in their concepts of appropriate gender-role behavior. They vary all the way from rigid and strict differentiation to androgyny, or believing that both men and women have masculine and feminine characteristics that are quite all right to express. Androgynous parents believe in kissing and hugging their sons and comforting them when they hurt; they believe in giving their daughters toy trucks and engaging them in rough-and-tumble play. Babies, like parents, vary in their understanding of boys, girls, women, and men.

One-Parent Homes. Both parents contribute to infant social and cognitive development, through their own relationship and through interaction with the baby. As we have seen, fathers' special sphere is play, mothers' is verbal interaction. When a parent is absent, either through living elsewhere or through never spending time with the baby, the parental contribution is diminished. Most one-parent homes contain a mother, although more and more fathers are seeking and getting custody of children after divorce. When fathers succeed in getting custody of children, they do so because they want it very much and try very hard. In contrast, many mothers are bringing up children by default.

The great majority of mother-headed families are poor. Many of these mothers are very young. Poverty and youth make up two sources of stress. Unrelieved responsibility is a severe stress. When mothers are so burdened, they are unlikely to be sensitively responsive caregivers, accessible, and interacting verbally. Without the joy, stimulation, contingent responses, and male-role behavior of a playful father the infant is doubly deprived. Evidence of fathers' importance comes from a comparison of father-present and father-absent black infants, 5 to 6 months old, living in an inner city [26]. Number of household members was the same for both groups. Boys who had little or no interaction with fathers were lower in social responsiveness, lower in tests of sensorimotor intelligence, and less interested in novel stimuli. Differences were not found between father-present and father-absent girls.

If the one-parent family lives in a supportive social network, parent and baby will be less deprived than if they live alone. They may live with the mother's parents, who give financial support and share in parenting with her. Perhaps her siblings also help and play with the baby, her father and brothers providing male interaction. A few women who choose single-parenthood deliberately are able to earn enough money to support their families well, and can draw upon adequate social networks.

Microsystems Providing Supplementary Care. Group care of infants has been common for years in the collective societies of Israel, China, and the Soviet Union. Friendship and cooperation between infants is consciously fostered, guided by macrosystem values and directives. Chinese babies, for example, are expected to be loving and helpful to one another [31]. They are taught through example, songs, stories, slides, and direct instruction, such as encouraging one toddler to help another who has fallen down. In many of the Israeli *kibbutzim,* infants spend more time with peers and *metaplot* (caregivers) than they do with parents.

In North America, group care is not yet sufficient to supplement all the homes in which caregivers need assistance. These homes include those where both parents are employed, one-parent families, and overburdened families. Although grandmothers often help, many are also employed, and others live far away. There are two types of professional day care, home care and center care. Home care in their own neighborhood is preferred by a majority of parents.

Home day care, also called family day care, is done by women (and very occasionally by men) in their own homes. Their own children may be included. When home day care is licensed, it is also regulated and supervised, with guidelines as to how many children of which ages may be cared for by one person. Training courses may be given for day care providers, giving both preparation and on-the-job instruction and support. Every home-day-care center is a unique microsystem, built in a particular home from the interaction of a unique caregiver with a small number of unique infants.

Center day care is carried on in a setting designed especially for the pur-

pose, perhaps built for it, or more likely, renovated. A professionally trained person usually directs the center and supervises additional caregivers of varying degrees of expertise. Licensing, regulations, and supervision vary from state to state. A federal publication, *Serving Infants*, gives eighteen principles for creating and maintaining an optimal day-care environment [17]. Some day-care centers are run for profit, some as nonprofit-making services, and some for research, teaching, and demonstration. There are also intervention programs, in which infants at risk are given special nurture.

Although one particular day-care service may fit the needs of a particular parent-infant pair and not another, there are some characteristics of all good day-care arrangements. Safety and good physical care come first, of course, including good food and arrangements for rest and sleep. Next come the experiences summarized under family influences on cognitive development: security, freedom to explore, people talking responsively, availability of caregivers, play, and enjoyment. Attachment to a caregiver is necessary for the baby to have a secure base in the day-care home or center. Therefore it may be helpful for each baby to be assigned to a particular caregiver, even though others assist in care.

Positive effects, including cognitive growth and general competence, have been found when infants in high-quality day-care centers were the subjects of research. No adverse effects on intellectual and social development have been found, and disadvantaged infants have gained considerably [4, 6]. High-quality day care does not disturb the infant's attachment to the mother, and increases interactions with peers [6]. By working with the home microsystem, intervention programs have had excellent results in infant development, including infants at risk. Unfortunately many day-care microsystems are not of the same level of quality as those centers where research has been done.

Some differences in home care and center care were found when toddlers were observed in both settings in two large cities [35]. In homes, children talked more with caregivers, expressed affect more readily, and spent less time in self-consoling activities, such as thumb-sucking. In both settings, boys were aggressive more often than girls, and caregivers picked up girls more frequently. The observers in center care saw very little joy, humor, playfulness, or affectionate physical contact, although neither did they see much anger or punishment. Efficiency seemed to be more important than letting toddlers develop autonomy by doing for themselves and making decisions. Of course there were differences in caregivers. The observers concluded that neither home or center care was providing the toddlers with optimal opportunities for independence and stimulation. Although this study cannot tell us how typical were these day-care settings, it does underline the importance of judging each setting on its own meris. If parents know what to look for, and if they observe before choosing, they can often find more adequate day care than if they are not selective.

Mesosystem

Babies benefit when parents and caregivers communicate with each other

Links between home and day care are very important to the functioning of the child involved, and indeed, to both microsystems. The baby cannot tell the caregiver how mother fixes his bottle or tucks in the blanket, nor can he explain to mother at the end of the day that today he was pushed over by a bigger child, did not feel like eating lunch, and took an extra long nap. The home microsystem can be strengthened by a caregiver who will talk with parents not only about daily happenings, but also about their concerns, hopes, and joys concerning the child. Parents can learn in a parent-child center about how infants grow and what sorts of objects and interactions are conducive to healthy development. Caregivers can learn from parents, each of whom knows a particular baby in depth. Caregivers can bring groups of parents together for mutual learning and also for support of the day care home or center.

Summary

Physiological and sensorimotor development contribute to differentiating the self from the rest of the world. The self becomes known through interactions with people and objects, and through knowledge of other people. A sense of trust develops as needs are met and contingent stimulation is experienced. The sense of autonomy grows through making successful decisions and gaining control of self and environment.

Emotions, which involve body, mind, and feelings, become differentiated in infancy, developing in contexts of self, other people, and objects. Social-emotional behavioral systems are coordinated to protect the infant while stimulating development. The attachment-affiliation system provides for bonds between the baby, family, and others. Attachments to objects offer some security. Individual differences in social skills and popularity with peers are seen during the first year of life.

Serving sensorimotor development, the curiosity-exploration system is coordinated with the attachment system. The infant is thus kept safe while exploring. Also coordinated with attachment, the fear-wariness system keeps the baby away from strange, unknown, and dangerous situations and close to the caregiver. The anger-aggression system provides responses to frustration, protecting the growth of the sense of autonomy.

Social-emotional development is influenced by macrosystem variables of geographic and climatic settings, values and beliefs concerning personality, family life, gender roles, government policies, and economic level. In the baby's exosystem, parents' employment is very significant. An infant affects family interaction, changing this microsystem by entering it and living in it. Assuming new roles, the husband and wife revise their own relationship as well as those with children. Older siblings also move into new roles and behaviors. The baby's temperament interacts with parental characteristics, such as age, and macrosystem variables, such as poverty. Abuse and neglect of infants have roots in all levels of the social ecology, including the infant. Families nurture cognitive development by providing security, freedom, responsive talking, caregiver availability, play, and enjoyment. Knowledge of sex and acquisition of gender-role behavior are acquired in family interaction from birth onward.

Common in collective societies, group care is increasing in North America. Many parents prefer to have their babies cared for in their own homes, homes of relatives, or day-care homes. Others use day-care centers, where a professionally trained person directs the care of a group. High-quality group care has been shown to benefit disadvantaged infants. Some day-care programs are not of high quality. The infant's mesosystem is important to the well-being of baby and family, and to the functioning of the day-care system.

References

1. Ainsworth, M. D. S. Infant-mother attachment. *American Psychologist,* 1979, **34,** 932–937.
2. Ainsworth, M. D. S., and S. M. Bell. Attachment, exploration, and separation: Illustrated by the behavior of one-year-olds in a strange situation. *Child Development,* 1970, **41,** 49–67.
3. Bates, J. E., C. A. B. Freeland, and M. L. Lounsbury. Measurement of infant difficulties. *Child Development,* 1979, **50,** 794–803.
4. Beller, E. K. Early intervention programs. In J. D. Osofsky (ed.). *Handbook of infant development.* New York: John Wiley & Sons, Inc., 1979.
5. Belsky, J. The interrelation of parental and spousal behavior during infancy in traditional nuclear families: An exploratory analysis. *Journal of Marriage and the Family,* 1979, **41,** 749–755.

6. Belsky, J., and L. D. Steinberg. The effects of day care: A critical review. *Child Development,* 1978, **49,** 929–949.
7. Bridges, K. M. B. Emotional development in early infancy. *Child Development,* 1932, **3,** 324–342.
8. Bronson, G. Aversive reactions to strangers: A dual process interpretation. *Child Development,* 1978, **49,** 495–499.
9. Campbell, S. B. Mother-infant interaction as a function of maternal ratings of temperament. *Child Psychiatry and Human Development,* 1979, **10:**2, 67–76.
9a. Erikson, E. H. *Childhood and Society.* New York: W. W. Norton Co., Inc., 1963.
10. Feiring, C., and M. Lewis. Temperament: Sex differences and stability in vigor, activity, and persistence in the first three years of life. *Journal of Genetic Psychology,* 1980, **136,** 65–75.
11. Finkelstein, N. W., C. Dent, K. Gallacher, and C. T. Ramey. Social behavior of infants and toddlers in a day-care environment. *Developmental Psychology,* 1978, **14,** 257–262.
12. Goldman, B. D., and H. S. Ross. Social skills in action: An analysis of early peer games. In J. Glick and K. A. Clarke-Stewart (eds.) *The development of social understanding.* New York: Gardner Press, 1978.
13. Goodenough, F. L. *Anger in young children.* Minneapolis: University of Minnesota Press, 1931.
14. Gordon, H. A., and K. C. W. Kammeyer. The gainful employment of women with small children. *Journal of Marriage and the Family,* 1980, **42,** 327–336.
15. Hock, E. Working and nonworking mothers and their infants: A comparative study of maternal caregiving characteristics and infant social behvior. *Merrill-Palmer Quarterly,* 1980, **26,** 79–101.
16. Hoffman, L. W. Maternal employment: 1979. *American Psychologist,* 1979, **34,** 859–865.
17. Huntington, D. S., S. Provence, and R. K. Parker. *Serving infants.* Child Development/Day Care No. 2. Department of Health, Education, and Welfare. Publication No. (OCD) 73–14. Washington: U.S. Government Printing Office, 1971.
18. Kendrick, C., and J. Dunn. Caring for a second baby: Effects on interaction between mother and firstborn. *Developmental Psychology,* 1980, **16,** 303–311.
19. Lewis, M., and J. Brooks-Gunn. The effects of age and sex on infants' playroom behavior. *Journal of Genetic Psychology,* 1979, **134,** 99–105.
20. Lewis, M., and J. Brooks-Gunn. Toward a theory of social cognition: The development of self. In I. C. Uzgiris (ed.) *Social interaction and communication during infancy.* New Directions for Child Development, No. 4. San Francisco: Jossey-Bass, 1979.
21. Mueller, E., and D. Vandell. Infant-infant interaction. In J. D. Osofsky (ed.). *Handbook of infant development.* New York: John Wiley & Sons, Inc., 1979.
22. Norman, R. D. Sex differences in preference for sex of children: A replication after 20 years. *Journal of Psychology,* 1974, **88,** 229–239.
23. Oppong, C. *Marriage among a matrilineal elite.* Cambridge: Cambridge University Press, 1974.
24. Parke, R. D. Perspectives on father-infant interaction. In J. D. Osofsky (ed.). *Handbook of infant development.* New York: John Wiley & Sons, Inc., 1979.
25. Passman, R. H., and J. S. Halonen. A developmental survey of young children's attachments to inanimate objects. *Journal of Genetic Psychology,* 1979, **134,** 165–178.
26. Pedersen, F. A., J. L. Rubenstein, and L. J. Yarrow. Infant development in father-absent families. *Journal of Genetic Psychology,* 1979, **135,** 51–56.

27. Rohner, R. P. *They love me, they love me not.* New Haven, Conn.: HRAF Press, 1975.
28. Rubin, J. Z., F. J. Provenzano, and Z. Luria. The eye of the beholder: Parents' views on sex of newborns. *American Journal of Orthopsychiatry*, 1974, **43,** 720–731.
29. Rutter, M. Maternal deprivation, 1972–1978: New findings, new concepts, new approaches. *Child Development*, 1979, **50,** 283–305.
30. Samuels, H. R. The effect of an older sibling on infant locomotor exploration of a new environment. *Child Development*, 1980, **51,** 607–609.
31. Sidel, R. *Women and child care in China.* New York: Penguin Books, 1973.
32. Sroufe, L. A. Socioemotional development. In J. D. Osofsky (ed.). *Handbook of infant development.* New York: John Wiley & Sons, Inc., 1979.
33. Suomi, S. J. Adult male-infant interactions among monkeys living in nuclear families. *Child Development*, 1977, **48,** 1255–1270.
34. Thomas, A., and S. Chess. *Temperament and development.* New York: Brunner/Mazel, 1977.
35. Tyler, B., and L. Dittman. Meeting the toddler more than halfway. *Young Children*, 1980, **35:**2, 39–46.
36. Vandell, D. L., K. S. Wilson, and N. R. Buchanan. Peer interaction in the first year of life: An examination of its structure, content, and sensitivity to toys. *Child Development*, 1980, **51,** 481–488.
37. Watson, J. S. Smiling, cooing and "The Game." *Merrill-Palmer Quarterly*, 1972, **18,** 321–339.
38. White, B. L., B. T. Kaban, and J. S. Attanucci. *The origins of human competence.* Lexington, Mass.: D. C. Heath & Company, 1979.
39. Yarrow, L. J. The development of focused relationships in infancy. In B. Staub and J. Hellmuth (eds.). *Exceptional infant.* Vol. 1. Seattle: Special Child Publications, 1967.

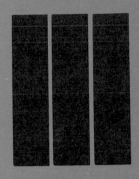

The Young Child

7

Healthy Physical Development and Coordination

Health is an overall condition of well-being and good functioning. A child's health is reflected in his growth, motor and mental competencies, social functioning, and freedom from disease. In this chapter we deal with children's bodily health, as shown by physical development and coordination. We also discuss the relation of health to the ecology of the child.

During the years from 2 to 6, the toddler's body changes into a school-age child's, growing fast, but not so fast as it did in the first two years of life. Increases in height and weight are easily noticed, as are changes in proportions. Growth can be assessed by precise scientific methods. Control and use of the body changes along with physical development.

QUESTIONS TO THINK ABOUT WHILE READING THIS CHAPTER

1. What can height and weight tell you about a child's health?
2. What information in addition to height and weight would help you in assessing health?
3. What can bones reveal about growth and health?
4. In what ways do child populations vary according to macrosystem resources for growth?
5. How do the food needs of a young child differ from those of an adult?
6. What are some ways in which motor development is the same for all children, and some ways in which it varies?

Bodily Growth

"My, how you've grown!" This comment is often made by an adult who sees a child after an interval. The child has, of course, grown taller and heavier. "You look so grown-up" usually refers to a change in shape. Nobody comments on internal changes that are just as important in physical development as are increases in external measurements.

Height and Weight

The growth rates of height and weight decelerate slowly during the preschool period. That is, the rate of increase of height and weight is smaller than it was in infancy, and it becomes smaller as the preschool child grows older. Figure 7–1 shows increases in height and weight. The percentage increase in height or weight is smaller with each additional year of age. In other words, the velocity of growth decreases.

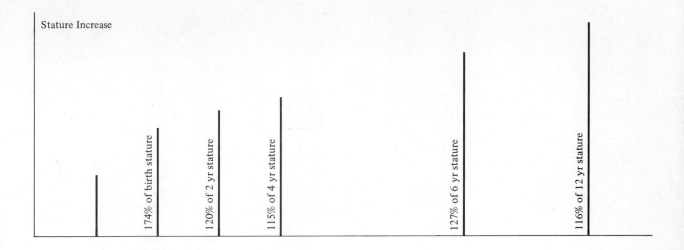

Stature Increase

174% of birth stature

120% of 2 yr stature

115% of 4 yr stature

127% of 6 yr stature

116% of 12 yr stature

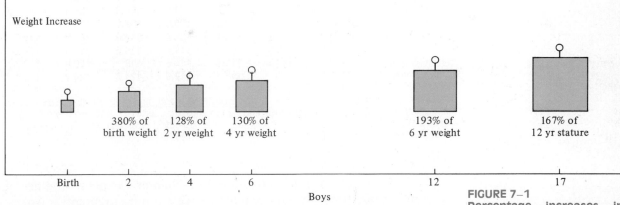

Weight Increase

380% of birth weight

128% of 2 yr weight

130% of 4 yr weight

193% of 6 yr weight

167% of 12 yr stature

Birth 2 4 6 12 17

Boys

FIGURE 7–1
Percentage increases in stature and weight in early childhood.

Assessing Height and Weight. Parents usually weigh their children on the bathroom scale and measure them on a door frame, perhaps on the children's birthdays. If the family does not move or paint the frame, a permanent growth record is built. Growth researchers use carefully defined methods and conditions of weighing and measuring, and precise scales and measuring boards. For instance, a child is weighed and measured within a day or two of his birthday, at a constant time of day, in specified clothing or lack of clothing, with a special technique of measuring that is repeatable within narrow limits. Although a few millimeters or grams make no difference in the home measurements, they do in making growth norms and studying the dynamics of growth. The tables on these pages are the result of controlled measurements on large numbers of children. Differences between black and white children are small enough that these tables can be used for both. Black children are smaller at birth than white, but during the years from 2 to 5, they are slightly taller and heavier than white children [15, 28, 38].

TABLE 7–1
Percentile Distribution of
Stature (in Centimeters) of
Males and Females from
Age 2 Through 6½ Years,
United States.

Sex and age	Percentile						
	5th	10th	25th	50th	75th	90th	95th
Male	Stature in centimeters						
2.0 years	82.5	83.5	85.3	86.8	89.2	92.0	94.4
2.5 years	85.4	86.5	88.5	90.4	92.9	95.6	97.8
3.0 years	89.0	90.3	92.6	94.9	97.5	100.1	102.0
3.5 years	92.5	93.9	96.4	99.1	101.7	104.3	106.1
4.0 years	95.8	97.3	100.0	102.9	105.7	108.2	109.9
4.5 years	98.9	100.6	103.4	106.6	109.4	111.9	113.5
5.0 years	102.0	103.7	106.5	109.9	112.8	115.4	117.0
5.5 years	104.9	106.7	109.6	113.1	116.1	118.7	120.3
6.0 years	107.7	109.6	112.5	116.1	119.2	121.9	123.5
6.5 years	110.4	112.3	115.3	119.0	122.2	124.9	126.6
Female							
2.0 years	81.6	82.1	84.0	86.8	89.3	92.0	93.6
2.5 years	84.6	85.3	87.3	90.0	92.5	95.0	96.6
3.0 years	88.3	89.3	91.4	94.1	96.6	99.0	100.6
3.5 years	91.7	93.0	95.2	97.9	100.5	102.8	104.5
4.0 years	95.0	96.4	98.8	101.6	104.3	106.6	108.3
4.5 years	98.1	99.7	102.2	105.0	107.9	110.2	112.0
5.0 years	101.1	102.7	105.4	108.4	111.4	113.8	115.6
5.5 years	103.9	105.6	108.4	111.6	114.8	117.4	119.2
6.0 years	106.6	108.4	111.3	114.6	118.1	120.8	122.7
6.5 years	109.2	111.0	114.1	117.6	121.3	124.2	126.1

Source: P. V. Hamill, R. A. Drizd, C. L. Johnson, R. B. Reed, and A. F. Roche. *NCHS growth curves for children birth–18 years.* Vital and health statistics: Series 11, Data from the National Health Survey: no. 165. (DHEW publication No. (PHS) 78–1650.) Washington: U.S. Government Printing Office, 1977. Table 13.

The section "Physical Development" in Chapter 4 explains the use of percentile tables in evaluating height and weight measurements. An example to use with the tables for young children is that of David, age 4, who measures 100.3 centimeters and weighs 15.8 kilograms. Table 7–1 shows that David's height is just above the 25th percentile. Table 7–2 shows that his weight is also just above the 25th percentile. Because the measurements are between the 25th and 75th percentiles, David's height and weight are within the range of measurements considered to be average. He is, however, shorter than about 75 boys out of 100 his age, and lighter than about the same number. David probably looks neither fat nor thin, because his height and weight are in harmony with each other.

Another method of assessing a child's height and weight is by using a graph or chart, such as those shown in Appendix A. Such a graph is derived from the same measurements on which the tables are based. The curves on the graph show the selected percentile points at each age level, the 50th percentile indicating the mean or average. The child can be measured and his measurements plotted repeatedly over a period of time. For example, a child may be measured on his birthday every year. The result is a longitudinal record showing the child's growth over time, and

TABLE 7–2
Percentile Distribution of
Weight (in Kilograms) of
Males and Females from
Age 2 Through 6½ Years,
United States.

Sex and age	Smoothed percentile						
	5th	10th	25th	50th	75th	90th	95th
Male	*Weight in kilograms*						
2.0 years	10.49	10.96	11.55	12.34	13.36	14.38	15.50
2.5 years	11.27	11.77	12.55	13.52	14.61	15.71	16.61
3.0 years	12.05	12.58	13.52	14.62	15.78	16.95	17.77
3.5 years	12.84	13.41	14.46	15.68	16.90	18.15	18.98
4.0 years	13.64	14.24	15.39	16.69	17.99	19.32	20.27
4.5 years	14.45	15.10	16.30	17.69	19.06	20.50	21.63
5.0 years	15.27	15.96	17.22	18.67	20.14	21.70	23.09
5.5 years	16.09	16.83	18.14	19.67	21.25	22.96	24.66
6.0 years	16.93	17.72	19.07	20.69	22.40	24.31	26.34
6.5 years	17.78	18.62	20.02	21.74	23.62	25.76	28.16
Female							
2.0 years	9.95	10.32	10.96	11.80	12.73	13.58	14.15
2.5 years	10.80	11.35	12.11	13.03	14.23	15.16	15.76
3.0 years	11.61	12.26	13.11	14.10	15.50	16.54	17.22
3.5 years	12.37	13.08	14.00	15.07	16.59	17.77	18.59
4.0 years	13.11	13.84	14.80	15.96	17.56	18.93	19.91
4.5 years	13.83	14.56	15.55	16.81	18.48	20.06	21.24
5.0 years	14.55	15.26	16.29	17.66	19.39	21.23	22.62
5.5 years	15.29	15.97	17.05	18.56	20.36	22.48	24.11
6.0 years	16.05	16.72	17.86	19.52	21.44	23.89	25.75
6.5 years	16.85	17.51	18.76	20.61	22.68	25.50	27.50

Source. P. V. Hamill, T. A. Drizd, C. L. Johnson, R. B. Reed, and A. F. Roche. *NCHS growth curves for children birth–18 years.* Vital and health statistics: Series 11, Data from the National Health Survey; no. 165. (DHEW publication No. (PHS) 78–1650.) Washington: U.S. Government Printing Office, 1977. Table 14.

showing it in relation to the growth of other children. The graph shows where the child is now, where he has come from, and suggests the direction in which he is heading. The individual curve can be seen to approximate one percentile curve, or to move from one to another. Satisfactory growth is shown when a child's curve is roughly parallel to the printed curves. To be at or above the mean is not appropriate for all children. A child of small parents, for instance, may show satisfactory growth by having height and weight curves that are near the 25th percentile from year to year.

Cross-Culture Comparisons. Body size varies in different parts of the world. Physical measurements on 160 samples of 4-year-old children represent Africa, Asia, Australia, Europe, the Americas, West Indies, and the Malay Archipelago [27]. These samples differed as much as 17 centimeters in average height and 5.9 kilograms in average weight.

The shortest group was from Bihar, India. The sample of over 3,000 children averaged 85.8 centimeters in height. The diet in Bihar is commonly deficient in calories, proteins, calcium, and vitamins. The Bihar children were fifth lightest, at an average weight of 11.8 kilograms. The

FIGURE 7–2
Average weight-for-age of children in four underdeveloped countries, shown in relation to average weight according to the standards of the Institute for Nutrition in Central America and Panama. The median of Iowa curves is also indicated, showing that averages for normal Central American children are very close to those for a sample of North American children. (SOURCE: Data from M. Béhar. Prevalence of malnutrition among preschool children of developing countries. In N. S. Scrimshaw and J. E. Gordon (eds.). *Malnutrition, learning and behavior.* Cambridge: M.I.T. Press, 1968. Also from R. L. Jackson and H. G. Kelly, Growth charts for use in pediatric practice. *Journal of Pediatrics,* 1945, **27**, 215–229.)

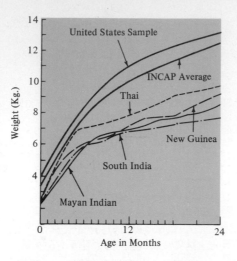

lightest sample was from Bangladesh, another area prone to famine and found by a survey team to be deficient in total calories, protein, vitamin A, riboflavin, and iron. The Bangladesh 4-year-olds were taller than only three other groups: the Indians, Kwango Negroes, and Vietnamese.

The tallest sample was Czech, having an average height of 103.8 centimeters. Next tallest was Dutch, 103.5, and next, United States whites, 102.9. The heaviest children were Lithuanians, at 17.3 kilograms, then Latvian, 17.2, and Czech, 17.1. Norwegian and Dutch were also heavier than United States white children, who averaged 16.7 kilograms. In the middle of the height ranks were Polynesians, at 96.6 centimeters. Children in the West Indies and Jamaica were midway in weight, averaging 6.6 kilograms.

Growth in weight among preschool children from several underdeveloped countries is shown in Figure 7–2. The children are compared with INCAP standards (Institute of Nutrition of Central America and Panama). The children from Thailand and New Guinea followed an almost normal course of growth for the first 3 months, fell farther and farther below normal for the next year, and then maintained a low level of weight growth. The Guatemalan and Indian children showed a pattern similar to those of the other two groups in the first 3 months, but after that diverged farther from the INCAP standard. As far as these graphs show, the children do not seem to be dropping farther below the standard line.

Body Proportions

Shapes of body and face change considerably during the years between 2 and 6, as the toddler loses his cute baby look, stretching up to become more linear, and more easily balanced.

Proportions change because of differential growth rates of various parts of the body. The principle of developmental direction is illustrated here by the growth that takes place in a cephalocaudal (head to tail) direction.

Development is at first more rapid in the head end of the body, with the tail end reaching maturity later. At age 2, the head is still large in relation to the trunk and legs. The abdomen and chest measure about the same but after 2, the chest becomes larger in relation to the abdomen [23, p. 74]. The abdomen sticks out, since a relatively short trunk has to accommodate the internal organs, some of which are closer to adult size than is the trunk. Thus the toddler is top-heavy. The head itself grows according to the same principle, with the upper part closer to completion than the lower part. A large cranium and a small lower jaw give the characteristic baby look to a 2-year-old's face. These proportions, plus fat, result in the diminutive nature of immature creatures that adults find emotionally appealing. Americans call baby humans, puppies, kittens, and other animal infants *cute*. Germans add *chen* to babies' names, and the French add *ette*. As the legs, trunk, and jaw grow in relation to the head, the baby loses his appealing, diminutive look. By the time the child starts to kindergarten or first grade, proportions more nearly resemble those of the children in the rest of the grades than they resemble those of preschool brothers and sisters at home. See the end papers on the inside of the front or back covers for an illustration of the changing proportions of boys and girls between 1½ and 6.

Various tissues and organs change in their growth rates, as do the overall measures of height and weight.

Tissues and Organs

Fat and Muscle. The growth patterns of fat and muscle underlie the change from babylike to childlike appearance. Fat increases rapidly during the first 9 months of life, decreases rapidly in thickness from 9 months to 2½ years, and decreases slowly until 5½. At 5½, it is half as thick as at 9 months. Thus does the chubby baby grow into a slender child. Muscle tissue follows a different pattern, growing at a decelerating rate throughout infancy and childhood, lagging behind other types of tissue growth until the puberal growth spurt. Sex differences show up in tissue growth, too. Boys have more muscle and bone than girls; girls have more fat than boys. Of course, there are individual differences, too, in all aspects of growth. Individual differences in amount of fat are greater than sex differences.

Skeletal System. Bones of young children have their own qualitative as well as proportional characteristics. The younger the child the more cartilage there is in his skeletal system and the less the density of minerals in the bones. The joints are more flexible; the ligaments and muscles are attached more tenuously than in an older child. Thus it is easier to damage young bones, joints, and muscles by pressure and pulling and by infections. The skeletal system is very responsive to changes in environment that produce malnutrition, fatigue, and injury. Bone maturation has been found to be retarded by 2 or 3 years in young children of poor, under-

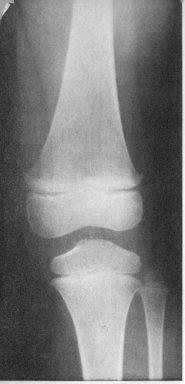

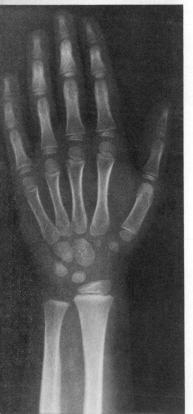

developed countries [31]. Head circumference was found to be smaller in malnourished preschool children as compared with well-nourished children of the same ethnic origin.

In order to understand how bones can be used for assessing growth, a description of bone growth in general is necessary. Early in prenatal life the precursors of most bones appear as cartilage. (The bones of the upper part of the skull develop from membranous tissue.) The cartilage is gradually replaced by bone beginning in the sixth week after fertilization. From this time until the individual is in his twenties, bone is being laid down, starting from centers of ossification that appear in highly uniform places in each cartilage. Ossification takes place in the cells through a process of formation of organic salts of calcium and phosphorus. The centers of ossification appear in a fairly uniform order. Bones grow in width or diameter by the addition of bony material on the outer surface of the bone underneath the *periosteum* (a membrane that surrounds the bone). Long bones grow longer by the addition of ossified materials at their ends. The shape of a bone is developed and maintained by the action of cells that remove calcified material, as well as of those that deposit it.

In long bones another ossification center appears at the end of the cartilage that forms the model of the growing bone. This separate piece of bone is called the *epiphysis*. The cartilage between the epiphysis and the shaft of the bone (the growth plate) becomes thinner and thinner as growth proceeds. Eventually, in normal human beings the epiphysis and bone shaft fuse into one piece of bone, and lengthwise growth in that bone ceases. Just as the timetable of the appearance of centers of ossification is fairly regular for the individual, so the fusion of epiphyses and bone shafts follows a time pattern [29]. As each piece of bone grows, its size and shape changes in a systematic fashion that varies relatively little from one person to another.

All of these changes in body tissue can be followed in X rays of the bones. The cartilaginous material is transparent to X rays; the ossified material, opaque. Most of the studies of skeletal development have been done using X rays of the left hand and wrist. The developed film is compared with standard illustrations in order to match it as closely as possible to one of them. The skeletal status of a child is expressed in terms of skeletal age. The skeletal age is the average number of years at which the same degree of skeletal development was attained by the children on whom the standards were based. Mental age, which is discussed in the next chapter, is a similar derived measure of development and is defined in much the same way as skeletal age.

X rays of the hand yield information about the quality of a child's growth. Lightly mineralized bones may be caused by insufficient intake of calcium, or insufficient metabolism of calcium, or both. An X-ray film may therefore yield supplemental information concerning the nutritional status of a child. Some kinds of illnesses and other traumatic events in the child's life may result in bands of increased density of the bone at the growing end of the long bones [30, p. 19]. If they occur, they become permanent records of disturbances in the body's metabolism during that period of the child's life.

The principle of critical periods (See Chapter 2) is illustrated in the disruption of the orderly sequence of appearance of ossification centers during illness [30]. During a period of illness, calcium metabolism is likely to be disturbed. If a child is ill just when he is due to develop a particular ossification center, that center may be delayed for a time, even until the appearance of an ossification center that normally comes later. If an X ray is taken after these events, even years later, it will show imbalances in the development of individual bones and ossification centers. Because the age of the bones can be estimated from their appearance in the X ray, the timing of the crises can also be estimated. The clinician can then make a judgment as to how severe was the impact of the illness on the skeleton and perhaps on the total organism. Later X-ray examinations can indicate the time at which the child has made a complete recovery.

Teeth. By 2 years, most children have a full set of 20 primary (deciduous) teeth. At between 6 and 7 years, these teeth begin to shed, starting with the lower central incisors. The first permanent teeth, the "6-year" or first molars, erupt. Parents often do not realize the importance of taking good care of the "baby" teeth because they know they will be replaced. Physical examinations of lower-income children in Tennessee revealed 42 per cent of the urban children and 71 per cent of the rural children with teeth that had active caries that were so severe that crowns were broken down, pulp involved, or extraction indicated [8]. One of the rural children had 19 such teeth. Dental care includes much more than attention to cavities, although treatment of caries is very important. A dentist also monitors the development of teeth in order to see whether intervention is needed, and if so, to plan for it at the best time. Dental maturity can be measured by matching X rays with standards [9].

Digestive System. The child's digestive system is different from the adult's in several ways that have implications for child care. At between 4 and 6 years of age, the stomach has less than half of the capacity of the average adult stomach. Calorie needs per unit of body weight, however, are almost twice as great as that of an adult[23]. The shape of the stomach is straighter than in older children and is more directly upright than an infant's or older child's. Thus it empties rather readily in either direction. The lining of the digestive tract is easily irritated by seasonings and roughage.

Respiratory System. During the preschool years the respiratory system matures in function sufficiently to establish the adult mode of breathing. Abdominal and chest movements are combined. Air passages are relatively small. The lymphatic system is prominent, with tonsils and adenoids at maximum size. The respiratory system is very vulnerable to infection in early childhood.

Sense Organs. Eyes, ears, and taste buds are known to have special characteristics in early childhood, and it seems likely that all the sensory apparatus is somewhat different from that of the adult. The macula of the retina is not completely developed until about 6 years, and the eyeball does not reach adult size until 12 or 14 [23]. The young child is farsighted because of the shape of the eyeball. Estimates for visual acuity, taken from several studies [10] are as follows: at two years, 20/100 to 20/40; at three, 20/50 to 20/30; at four, 20/40 to 20/20; at five, 20/35 to 20/25; at six, 20/27. Thus, even at 6 years of age, the estimated acuity is not yet 20/20. Investigations of the ways in which children use their visual mechanism show that they function in immature ways during the preschool years. An analysis of 109 vision-screening projects shows that 6 per cent of the children were referred for professional eye examinations and that 75 per cent of those examined had abnormal eye conditions. One to 3 per cent of preschool children require glasses [35].

Taste buds are more generously distributed in the young child than in the adult, being scattered on the insides of the cheeks and the throat as well as on the tongue. Taste sensitivity is probably high.

The ear, too, is significantly different in the young child because of the Eustachian tube, which connects the middle ear with the throat. The tube is shorter, more horizontal, and wider in the infant and preschool child than in the older child and adult. Invading organisms find an easy entrance route from the young child's throat to her middle ear. Hence she is more susceptible to ear infections than is the older child.

Brain. By the end of infancy the brain has as many nerve cells (neurons) as it will ever have, because increase through cell division is finished. Increases in weight from now on will be due to increases in the size of the neurons and the supporting tissue. Connections between neurons increase and elaborate. Myelin, the fatty insulating material, is laid down. At birth the brain is already 25 per cent of the weight that it will

FIGURE 7–3
Growth of three types of tissue during the preschool years. (SOURCE: Adapted from J. A. Harris, C. M. Jackson, D. G. Paterson, and R. E. Scammon. *The measurement of man.* Minneapolis: University of Minnesota Press, 1930.)

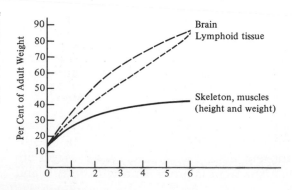

be at maturity.   As Figure 7–3 shows, the brain grows at a faster rate than other types of tissue during infancy and early childhood.   By 3 years the brain has about 75 per cent of its adult weight, and by 6 years, 90 per cent.   At age 5 the total nervous system is 5 per cent of total body weight, whereas in adulthood, it is 2 per cent [23].

The curve of brain growth in Figure 7–3 is somewhat misleading in its smoothness.   There are small spurts of gain in brain weight (of between 5 and 10 per cent) occurring between 2 and 4 years, 6 and 8, 10 and 12, and 14 and 16 [11].   These spurts correspond in time with ages when Piagetian stages of cognitive growth are achieved.   It seems reasonable that the growth and maturation of the brain are intimately connected with the restructuring of the mind.   The spurt of brain growth during the preschool period, between 2 and 4, is the time when the child is achieving and developing representational thought.

Ecology of Healthy Physical Development

All levels of the ecology contribute to children's health and growth.   Although the microsystem of the home is where basic transactions take place, exosystems and macrosystems determine the resources that the home and family have to offer to the child.   We will start with some macrosystem influences on the ways in which families maintain the health and growth of their children.

Macrosystem Influences on Health

The comparisons of growth rates in various cultures earlier in this chapter give some notion of macrosystem differences in resources for growth. Resources include food, sanitation, protection from injury, and medical care.   A comparison of death rates in different countries in Table 7–3 indicates the life-and-death power of macrosystems.

	Annual deaths per 1,000 aged 1–4		Annual deaths per 1,000 aged 1–4
Denmark	0.6	Philippines	7.5
Netherlands	0.7	Brazil	11.5
Greece	0.8	Ecuador	13.7
Czechoslovakia	0.9	Turkey	14.6
Trinidad and Tobago	1.7	Afghanistan	24.1
Portugal	1.9	Egypt	24.9
Thailand	3.7	Congo	30.0
Sri Lanka	3.8	Madagascar	33.3
Venezuela	4.0	Benin	45.0
Mexico	4.6	Togo	45.0

TABLE 7–3
Death Rates of Children Aged 1 to 4 in Selected Countries of the World, 1976–1977.

Source: M. C. McHale, J. McHale, and G. F. Streatfeild. *Children in the World.* Washington: Population Reference Bureau, 1979.

Nutrition. A poor country usually has insufficient food. Extreme malnutrition, suffered by 10 million children, is primarily due to lack of food in the countries in which they live. Another 90 million children suffer from moderate malnutrition [26]. A small proportion of malnourished children live in countries that are not poor, however, such as the United States of America.

The distribution customs of a macrosystem also influence children's food intake. If there is not enough food, women and children, especially girls, may be the last to be fed, as in India. Or, children may be the first to be fed, as in China, and as in many families in the United States. There may be enough food in the country, but poor people do not have enough money to buy it. Among government programs that equalize food distribution are school lunches in the United States, and apples and milk in schools in New Zealand. There may be surpluses in some areas and shortages in others, because of inadequate storage and transportation. Enough food may be grown, but much of it lost to pests and spoilage.

Beliefs and customs may contribute to malnourishment even when adequate food is available. Especially during the period of transition from breast milk to solid foods, which may occur as late as 2 or 3 years, beliefs about what is good and bad for children may be harmful. If meat and fish are thought unsuitable for young children, then protein deficiency is likely, and perhaps calorie deficiency also. If custom dictates that toddlers eat foods as prepared for adults, children may get roughage, spices, and unchewable foods, resulting in irritation to their digestive systems, and insufficient nutrients. If, on the other hand, the macrosystem includes education for mothers in the knowledge and practices of nutrition, young children will be better nourished, even in a poor country. A demonstration of the importance of mothers' knowledge was done among low-income families in Lebanon [4]. Mothers' knowledge and practices of nutrition were highly correlated with the degree of adequate growth achieved by preschool children.

Sleep and Rest. The timing of children's sleep and arrangements for it vary between macrosystems. In one-room dwellings, of course, the whole family sleeps together, or perhaps mother and children do. In countries with warm climates an afternoon nap is often the custom for adults, as well as for children. There is no question of when the child is old enough to stop having a nap or rest, because he will never be too old for a siesta. In very warm climates everyone tends to rise early in the morning. The evening meal may be very late, from the viewpoint of Americans. In traditional societies, children's bedtime is likely to be the same as adults'. In India we often saw young children out in the evening with their parents, falling asleep here and there on a friend's sofa, snuggled up to their mothers, or lying on an extra chair at a concert. Nobody ever seemed to regard young children's sleep as problematic.

Sleep can be quite a problem in the Western World, where everybody runs on schedule, and every child is supposed to have his own bed, and if possible, his own room. Parents, believing that sleep is important for health and growth, would like their children to sleep at least as much as average (12 hours at 2 to 3, 11 hours at 3 to 5), and to conform to the common pattern of an afternoon nap. Parents also value time to themselves, evenings undisturbed by children. The ideology of the macrosystem justifies parents' desire for a quiet evening. Therefore it is considered good for the child and good for the parents to have the child go to bed early and sleep all night. Further justification comes from the fact that busy family schedules do not allow for young children's falling asleep when and where they please. If they do not sleep during the hours planned for them, they become tired. However, when children are not ready for sleep, they resist going to bed or staying in bed, thereby disrupting their parents' free time and causing family conflict. A room of one's own can add to the young child's sleep problems. Dreams may be disturbing because they are not clearly distinguished from reality. A child may waken and want human contact. The Samoan child, sleeping on his mat in the one-room *fale*, will easily find a touch or word of comfort, but the American child may cry in fear and loneliness until a parent wakens and comes to his room.

Disease Control. Climate puts some limits on problems of disease control, making it a more difficult problem in the tropics than in temperate zones. Economic factors are important. Poor countries have less to spend on sanitation, immunization, pest control, health education, and medical treatment.

Beliefs, customs, and rituals are often functional in disease control, as long as stable conditions prevail. In India, a multitude of disease organisms are controlled by Hindu rituals of handwashing before meals, daily baths, and clean clothing, eating of only freshly cooked food, and cleanliness on the part of the cook. An example of changing conditions comes from Western Samoa. The old custom for disposing of human wastes was by using the tides. Privies were built at the ends of catwalks, built

Disease control is affected by climate, economics, ideology

out over the water of estuaries. The tides provided a natural sewer system. By 1970 there was great overcrowding owing to the population explosion. The incidence of water-borne diseases shot up to unprecedented heights. The government outlawed privies built over the water, but customs are slow to change, even when they become nonfunctional or harmful.

Immunization programs are initiated for the common good. Many countries have been aided in such programs by the World Health Organization, which cuts across macrosystems. The World Health Organization also promotes sanitation, medical treatment, nutrition, and pest control, such as *anopheles* mosquito eradication.

Disease patterns of young children vary according to the macrosystems in which they live. Figure 7–4 shows causes of death in selected countries. Causes of acute illness of United States preschool children are shown in Figure 7–5. Respiratory conditions are the most prevalent kinds of illness for these children. Children in tropical climates encounter all the diseases represented in Figure 7–5 and those caused by a host of additional invading organisms. Diarrhea, which can have various causes, is the most frequent cause of death of children in Latin America and in other parts of the world with tropical climate and very low average income. When a malnourished child gets diarrhea, it is much more serious than in a well-nourished child. Appetite is decreased, further dehydration and malnutrition occur, and growth is depressed. The combina-

FIGURE 7–4
Major causes of deaths of children aged 1–4 years in selected countries. (SOURCE: Adapted from M. C. McHale, J. McHale, and G. F. Streatfeild. *Children in the World*. Washington: Population Reference Bureau, 1979.)

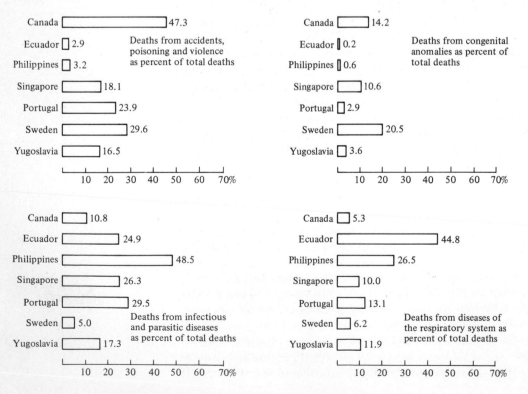

208 The Young Child

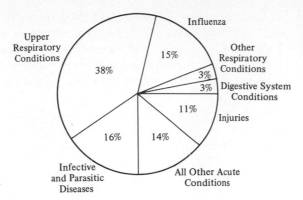

FIGURE 7–5
Incidence of acute conditions as per cent of total number of acute conditions reported for children under six years in the United States. (Source: C. S. Wilder. Acute conditions: incidence and associated disability. National Center for Health Statistics. Series 10, no. 98. D.H.E.W. publication (HRA) 75–1525. Washington: U.S. Government Printing Office, 1975.)

tion of malnutrition, infection, and diarrhea results each year in the death of many young children [36].

Injury Control. As Figure 7–4 shows, accidents, poisoning, and violence rank high as causes of child death in countries where diseases rank low, the prosperous and industrialized nations. This finding does not mean that there are few accidental and violent deaths in poor countries, but only that diseases claim many more lives than they do in prosperous countries. In a given 10-year period in the United States, the rate of accidental child deaths stayed about the same, whereas deaths from other causes decreased by about 30 per cent [1].

Figure 7–6 gives the death rates from all types of accidents combined, and the percentage caused by accidents of all deaths, for boys and girls separately. Accident rates have increased during the past decade largely because of the increase in the number of motor vehicle accidents. The other main types of accidents to young children are the result of traffic, fires, explosions, burns, drowning, poisoning, falls, and inhaling or ingesting food and other objects. Another study [2] showed that about 25 per cent of the annual deaths from accidental poisoning in the United States were deaths of children between 2 and 4 years of age. The agents of death were chiefly aspirin and other salicylates, petroleum products, lead, and household pesticides.

Abuse by parents and other persons is a source of injuries to children, and even a cause of deaths. Many such injuries are reported as accidents. An estimate of numbers of United States children suffering parental violence is between 1.5 and 2.0 million per year [34]. Siblings also injure one another. Violence is very common between young siblings.

Factors within the macrosystem work for or against keeping the young child safe from injuries, both accidental and intentional. These factors include physical conditions, beliefs, customs, laws, and support systems.

Physical conditions include the layout of streets and cities, the type of housing available for families with children, presence or absence of recreation areas, parks, and child care centers, and the equipment used for children, such as cribs, toys, clothes, and seat belts. For example, in the

Child safety is affected by physical arrangements, beliefs, customs, and laws, and support systems

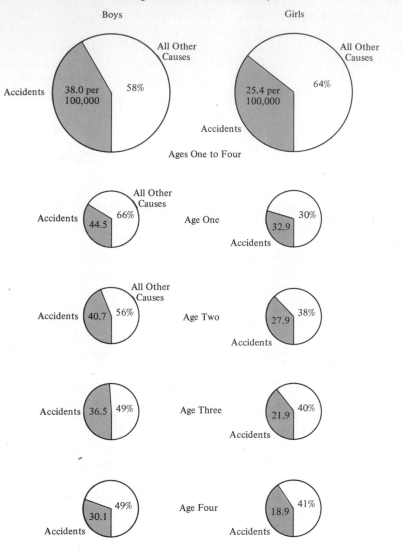

Average Annual Death Rate Per 100,000

Boys | Girls

All Other Causes

Accidents | 38.0 per 100,000 | 58%

All Other Causes

25.4 per 100,000 | 64%

Accidents

Ages One to Four

All Other Causes

Accidents | 44.5 | 66% | Age One | 32.9 | 30%

Accidents

All Other Causes

Accidents | 40.7 | 56% | Age Two | 27.9 | 38%

Accidents

Accidents | 36.5 | 49% | Age Three | 21.9 | 40%

Accidents

Accidents | 30.1 | 49% | Age Four | 18.9 | 41%

Accidents

FIGURE 7–6
Death rates from accidents among boys and girls aged 1–4, and accidental deaths as a percent of all deaths in the United States. (SOURCE: Accident mortality at the preschool age. *Statistical Bulletin*, 1975, 56: 5, 7–9.)

city of Jogjakarta, on the island of Java, the broken sidewalks overflow with pedestrians, while traffic jams the streets. We never saw a park or playground. In Palmerston North, New Zealand, smooth sidewalks (called footpaths) line broad streets. There are big parks and little parks, playgrounds equipped for young children, wading pools, adding up to some play space within walking distance of every home.

Beliefs, customs, and laws determine the incidence of many types of accidents. The enactment and enforcement of traffic and driving laws are especially important, because motor vehicles can rank high as causes of death and injury. In the dangerous physical environments of Asia and Africa, the custom of constant supervision by child nurses keeps young children relatively safe. In India, little children can look and listen as they go everywhere with parents, but the exploration of space and objects is discouraged.

Child abuse is supported by the combination of a belief in violence as a way of solving problems and a belief in the right of parents to do as they wish in the privacy of home. Social support systems can minimize both accidental and intentional injury to young children, by helping parents to maintain the vigilance that safety requires. Macrosystems vary in the structure of families and social networks, and in the availability of education for parenting and assistance in child care.

Medical Care. Availability of professional health care varies from one physician per 334 persons in the U.S.S.R. to one to over 9,000 in Asia and Africa [26]. The figure for Northern America is one to 606. In the poorer areas of the world, less than 15 per cent of people live within walking distance of *any* kind of health facility. Of course, the number of physicians does not tell the whole story as to whether all children have access to medical care when they need it. Throughout most of Western Europe, for example, medical care is paid for by taxes or industry, and a family is not required to pay when they receive care. If payment is required when a child goes to the physician or health facility, then poor families do not receive adequate care for their children. Even families in middle-income brackets are unlikely to buy preventive supervision when they have to pay large fees for it.

An effort to give services to low-income children has been made by the United States government. During one fiscal year, 1,865,000 children attended well-child clinics of the Maternal and Child Health Services program [32]. However, the Harvard Child Health Project Task Force has pointed out serious inequities between poor and well-to-do children [18.] Seven per cent of United States children have no regular source of medical care. Children from low-income families are 8 times more likely to have no regular source of care than are other children. The Task Force made recommendations for increasing affordability and accessibility of care, and improvement in these areas: early recognition of problems, especially those leading to chronic impairments, such as middle-ear infection; better follow-up of acute illnesses in order to prevent permanent disabilities; better care for the special health problems of children, "care, not simply cure, for the high numbers of children and their families."

The microsystems are the settings in which physical care is given and children develop their bodies optimally or poorly. The home is, of course, the most important microsystem in the healthy development of most young children. Medical and health facilities are contributing microsystems. The homes of family and friends may also promote healthy development.

Available medical care is accessible and affordable

Microsystem Influences on Health

Nutrition. The person who feeds the young child—parent, day-care provider, or other caregiver—has three tasks. The first is choosing foods that supply adequate nutrients in sufficient quantities. Next is preparation of foods in ways that make them acceptable and suitable to the child. Then comes the timing and conduct of meals.

Although requirements may vary between groups, and certainly between individuals, all young children are similar in the nutrients they need. For instance, a four-year-old needs 50 per cent more protein per pound of body weight than does his father, because the child is growing. Because of high needs for protein, minerals, and vitamins, along with a small stomach, there is little room in a young child's diet for foods that supply only energy, such as sugar. The following guide for feeding the preschool child is from the United States government [3].

> 3 or more cups of milk and milk products.
> 2 or more servings of meat, poultry, fish, and eggs.
> 4 or more servings of vegetables and fruits, including a citrus fruit or other fruit or vegetable high in vitamin C, and a dark-green or deep-yellow vegetable for vitamin A at least every other day.
> 4 or more servings of bread and cereal of whole grain, enriched or restored variety.
> Plus other foods as needed to provide additional energy and other food values.

Figures are not to be taken completely literally. Individuals vary in the amounts they need and in the amount they eat from one day to another and from one meal to another. If the foods offered are chosen along the lines of this plan, most preschool children will take what they need from it.

Snacks are an important part of young children's nutrient intake. A longitudinal study of a group of middle-class children showed that during the preschool years, 22 per cent of their calories came from snacks [6]. As only 12 per cent of their protein came from snacks, it can be seen that better planning could have resulted in more valuable snacks and a better balancing of nutrients throughout the day. If completely unplanned, snacks are all too likely to be long on carbohydrates and fats and short on proteins, minerals, and vitamins. Having limited capacity for intake and high need for growth-promoting foods, a preschool child cannot afford to eat many empty calories (foods devoid of proteins, minerals, and vitamins).

Little is known of the roles played by trace elements in human growth and health, but many such elements are essential. Fluorine is one element that is well known for its contribution to sound teeth. If a family lives where the water supply is not adequate in fluorine, all members, especially young children, should have fluorine supplements. Parents should get guidance from their dentist on this matter, along with regular attention to the teeth of their preschool children.

Foods suitable for young children are bland, not high in seasonings. Peppers and other spices may damage their gastrointestinal systems. Nor are seasonings, including added salt, needed to make food attractive to the young child, who has abundant taste buds. A few years ago, baby foods were made with excessive salt and other flavorings in order to please mothers who tasted them. This mistake has been corrected, but many mothers flavor young children's food the way they themselves like it instead of realizing that preschool children are satisfied with bland food, and that it is better for them than highly flavored food. Sugar may be an even worse detriment than salt in the diets of many young children. Fruits and simple desserts provide enough sweets, but candy, sugar-coated cereals, sugar-containing beverages, and gum are all devoid of growth-promoting nutrients. These substances displace useful nutrients from the diet and also promote tooth decay.

With fewer teeth than an older child, the preschool child needs to have meat cut into small pieces. The young child can chew raw vegetables, and enjoys them. Cooked vegetables were disliked by over half the preschool children who took part in a study of food attitudes [6]. Probably the flavor of vegetables is the main offender, although the texture may also be unpleasant. (Because many North Americans overcook vegetables, the results are often strong, mushy, and dull-colored.) Young children often prefer raw vegetables to the cooked vegetables typically served to them. Very few, only 1.7 per cent, of the children disliked milk, and only 3.5 per cent disliked fruit. When favorite foods were discussed, meat was at the top, with 38.8 per cent nominating it as best liked.

Touch and texture are also important in eating. A meal is made attractive by a combination of crisp, chewy, and soft foods. Children often want to feel the slipperiness of gelatin and spaghetti, the crinkliness of lettuce, and the cloudlike softness of a soufflé. Bright colors and color contrasts are thought to be effective in making meals attractive to children as well as to adults. Young children prefer lukewarm food to hot food. The sense of smell doubtless plays an important part in the enjoyment of eating.

Emotional Aspects. Emotional surroundings can enhance or depress appetite. Conversely, hunger disposes the child toward anger outbursts. Excitement and upset conditions cause the stomach to stop its movements. To eat with the family may be too stimulating for a young child, or it may add to his happiness and feelings of belonging, depending on what goes on at the family table. He benefits from a structured program, including regular mealtimes. Breakfast may be his best meal. He is most likely to take in adequate nutrients if he comes to his meals hungry, but not famished, and exercised, but not exhausted.

Problems with eating can easily get started at between 2 and 3 years of age. Appetite may decrease, because the rate of growth has slowed down. Parents, remembering the joyous abandon with which their baby waded into his food, may worry when they see that the same child at 2½ toys with his food and fusses over what he will eat and what he will not eat. Urging and forcing at this point often prolong and complicate the problem. Eager to exercise his autonomy, the 2-year-old wants to choose and decide for himself. It is satisfying to decide to eat a small serving and then to ask for more or to refuse it; it can be very annoying to have too large an amount presented, especially if it is poked at you in spoonfuls. If the child can do it himself, his sense of autonomy is enhanced. He can make progress with a spoon and even more with his fingers if given foods that are easy to pick up. Custard and soup are easier to drink than to spoon up. The young child profits from all arrangements that facilitate self-help and from wide limits within which to do it himself. He does need limits, though, for healthy development of the sense of autonomy. The child suffers, as well as the family, when he is allowed to throw his applesauce on the floor or to grab the food from his neighbor's plate. It is important for him to feel that what he does is all right, but for him to have that feeling, his behavior has to be acceptable to the people around him.

Feeding children is an important function of day-care providers. By following the principles just outlined, adequate meals will be offered at appropriate times. Because many young children are hungriest at breakfast, it is especially important to provide a substantial, nutritious meal at that time. Relationships between home and day-care center (the mesosystem of the ecology) are very important in regard to nutrition. Communication from both microsystems will result in parents' knowing what their children are going to eat and have eaten, and in day-care providers' knowing something about the child's way of eating at home. If the child is not hungry or has eaten in an unusual way, the adult who knows about it will tell the other.

Eating in groups makes sociability possible. With either family or peers, conversation can be encouraged. Sometimes education is more possible in one setting that in another. For example, efforts to teach chil-

dren to like vegetables have been carried out in nursery schools. The following two studies illustrate different approaches. In the first program children received stickers for each portion of vegetables they ate [20]. The stickers were exchangeable for a dessert. The subjects duly tasted and ate more vegetables, dropping their intake somewhat after the reinforcements were discontinued. Another approach consisted of demonstration, discussion, games, dramatic play, and pointing out qualities such as color, texture, shape, growth properties, and food value [17]. Beets, Brussels sprouts, cauliflower, and squash, upon which all these activities were focused, were more accepted after the experiment than before. The children ate larger quantities, and more children ate the vegetables. Good nursery schools include nutrition education as part of the program, by planning and serving nutritious, attractive meals, by letting children help with food preparation, and by stimulating interest through art, games, and stories.

Sleep and Rest. The microsystems of home and day-care provider are both responsible for arranging sleep and rest. Because schedules are part of everyday life in North America, child care includes planning for sleep and rest at times when children can best use it, and coordinating schedules if a child receives care in more than one microsystem. Bed-going is usually acceptable after a day that includes outdoor play and satisfying meals, and after a regular series of steps toward bed. First comes cutting down stimulation and minimizing excitement—reading a story or singing rather than chasing or playing horsey. Then comes getting ready for sleep in a familiar routine, such as toileting, washing, tooth-brushing, putting teddy bear into bed, a hug and a kiss. Prompt reassurance will help a child to settle down after a dream or disturbance.

A child may be tired, needing rest, and still not want to go to sleep. Rest will be possible if the daily plan includes quiet times as well as times for vigorous activity. In nursery schools and day care centers, teachers usually alternate quiet and active play, with a quiet period of reading, stories, or music coming before meals. The time before meals is often the busiest time for the parent doing the cooking. The other parent, partner, or an older child can contribute to the health of the young child by sharing a quiet time with him or her.

Training in Self-care. The toddler wants to do things for herself and to make choices as to what, how, and when. In wanting autonomy, the young child makes it both easier and harder for the caregiver to shift some of the responsibility to the child. She will be happy to wash her own hands, but will often want to play in the water. He will be proud when he can go to the toilet by himself, but will not appreciate being taken to the toilet while engaged in interesting play, even though mother or teacher knows it is time to go. As with the management of sleep, it is easiest to teach self-care by making room for it in the plan of the day, leaving time for transitions, and arranging equipment with which the child can cope. He can put on easy clothes that are laid out neatly, in order. She will put away toys if they have their own places, and there are not too many out.

Keeping Children Safe. In all of the child's microsystems, provisions for safety begin with arranging the environment to allow for exploration and play that will not cause harm. Although young children can accept some restrictions, and will often obey rules, there are chances that are too big to take. Such dangers include leaving poisons (cleaning materials and medicines) where children can reach them, leaving an open fire un-guarded, and letting a young child play outdoors unsupervised and unre-stricted. Sometimes toys are dangerous, because of sharp points or edges, breakable parts, portions that can be swallowed.

The prevention of child abuse is necessary if children are to be kept safe at home. Although much is yet to be learned about this problem, it is known that abusing parents need help, and parents need help with feel-ings of frustration and anger before they behave violently toward chil-dren. Also, they often need to learn more facts of child development and what to expect of young children. A parent may be overwhelmed by too great a burden of work and child care, by a particularly difficult child, or by other problems. Help from a social network keeps many mothers from unmanageable feelings, but some parents are quite isolated. Help may be available from another of the child's microsystems, if the meso-system (communications) is strong enough. A day-care provider might give support and information as to where to get professional help. An-other source is the provider of health care.

Care of Ill and Injured Children. The health-care provider is one of the child's microsystems. If a child has received health supervision and im-munizations from a physician or clinic, then he is already familiar with the person who will care for illness and injury. As with the day-care cen-ter, relationships with the home are important in coordinating services to the child.

It is frightening to be hurt or sick—frightening to anyone, but espe-cially to a preschool child. Pain itself can be frightening as well as un-pleasant. Reduced to a lower level of autonomy, the child is disturbed at not being able to control himself and the environment as efficiently as normally. His thinking and his actions are less adequate for coping with the world.

An ill or hurt child is helped by: Parent's pres-ence, realistic reassurance, structured program

Reassurance from parents makes the pain and fright possible to bear, just as Mother's presence in a disturbingly new situation gives a young child courage to explore. The most reassuring parent is one who com-bines sympathy with the calm expectation that balance and normalcy will be restored in due time. The ill or injured child is comforted and strengthened by having the limits of his activity redefined appropriately. For instance, ''You are going to stay in your bed, but you can move around it all you like. I'll give you this box of toys to play with now. After your

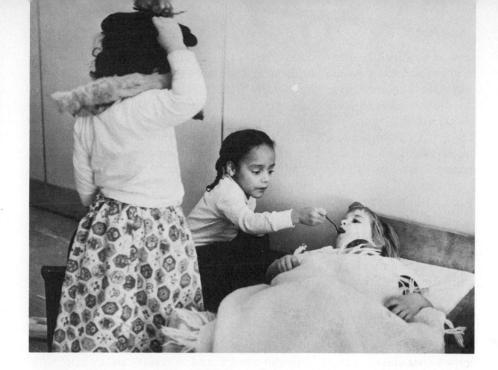

nap, you can choose a story for me to read to you." If toys and activities require less effort than his normal top speed, then he can still feel satisfied with what he achieves.

When children must go from the home microsystem to another (the doctor's office or hospital) for medical care, they are assisted by a well-functioning mesosystem. The family can bridge the distance between home and hospital by becoming familiar with the hospital and by sharing knowledge and experience with the child. They can use books that prepare the child [5], actual visits, playing games that dramatize it, and reassurance that a parent will stay with the child. The doctor or hospital can also contribute to a strong mesosystem. For example, Canadian children living in Calgary have an opportunity to learn about hospitals when they are well [33]. Kindergarten children go in groups of 15 or 20 to one of five participating hospitals for an orientation program that takes 1½ hours. Using a large panda bear that has a rectum, children observe and practice taking temperatures, giving hypodermics, and other nursing and treatment procedures that a child is likely to experience when she becomes a patient in hospital. They see the playroom, kitchen, and other parts of the hospital. Guides encourage questions and discussion. Similar programs, using trained volunteers, have been set up in several communities in the United States. Such programs probably reduce somewhat the child's dread of going to a hospital when hospitalization is necessary.

Hospital care for young children has been slowly undergoing a revolution. Gradually doctors, nurses, and parents are accepting the evidence that it is damaging for children between 6 months and 3 years to be separated from their mothers, and that even after 3 years of age, separation may be harmful. Some hospitals now permit and even encourage parents to stay with their young children so as to give them the emotional support that they need every day but all the more when they are ill. Visiting rules have been liberalized in many places, too. Play programs make hospital living more pleasant and help children to express their feelings. There is still a big educational job to be done in adapting hospitals to children's emotional needs. Unfortunately some medical personnel still interpret a young child's stony silence as good adjustment, and the flood of tears released by his parent's arrival as evidence that parents are bad for him in the hospital.

Motor Development and Activity

The Developmental Sequence

Motor development can be seen in age-related changes in patterns of coordination and in increasing strength. Activity can be considered as proportion of active time to quiet time, or as tempo or speed of action.

The chart of motor behavior, Table 7–4, drawn from several sources, shows that development between ages 2 and 5 results in a child who moves and manipulates more like an adult than he does like the toddler he used to be. Having worked through stages of using a spoon and fork, holding a glass, and pouring from a pitcher, he can feed himself neatly without having to try very hard. He can even carry on a conversation at meals. He can cut and fold paper. From imitating a circular stroke at 2, drawing a vertical line at 3, and copying a square with some accuracy at 5, he is poised on the brink of learning to write. The 2-year-old, to whom walking steadily, running, and climbing are thrilling achievements, advances through walking tiptoe, hopping, jumping, tricycling, agile climbing, and stunting to the graceful age of 5. Skipping, hopping skillfully, running fast, he looks into an exciting future of skating, swimming, and riding a two-wheeler. Balls, the toys beloved by babies, children, and adults, are used with increasing maturity.

Individual Differences. One child differs from another in the speed with which he progresses through a sequence of behavior patterns. We have seen 4-year-olds who could swim and ride bicycles and 6-year-olds who spilled their food consistently. Children differ also in speed, power, and accuracy of their muscular coordinations, as witness the "natural athletes" who throw and catch balls efficiently in the preschool years. They differ, too, in balance and grace. When reading a chart that shows average development for various ages, it is important to keep in mind that this is a summary of a group of children and that it does not picture any one child as he is.

Sex Differences. Girls begin early to show superiority in manual dexterity. Between ages 2 and 6, boys have been found to excel in going up and down ladders and steps, throwing, catching and bouncing balls, and jumping from boxes and ladders [25]. Girls performed better than boys in hopping, skipping, and galloping [13]. The latter can be confirmed by observing a kindergarten in the fall, where there are almost sure to be several little boys who merely run or gallop while the other children skip.

Boys and girls differed in their use of outdoor space in a nursery school where every effort was made to offer freedom of choice to all [16]. The children's parents showed little interest in sex-differentiated behavior. Even so, boys played outdoors more than girls, spending more time in sand, on a tractor, on climbing equipment, and near an equipment shed.

TABLE 7–4
Some Landmarks in Motor Development During the Years from Two to Five, from Basic Normative Studies. The Item Is Placed at the Age Where 50 Per Cent or More of Children Perform the Act. (Initials in parentheses refer to sources. See footnotes.)

	Age two	Age three	Age four	Age five
Eye-Hand	Builds tower of 6 or 7 blocks (KP) Turns book pages singly (KP) Spoon into mouth without turning (KP) Holds glass in one hand (KP) Imitates vertical and circular strokes (KP) Puts on simple garmet (KP)	Builds tower of 9 blocks (KP) Makes bridge of 3 blocks (TM) Catches ball, arms straight (MW) Spills little from spoon (KP) Pours from pitcher (KP) Unbuttons, puts shoes on (KP) Copies circle (TM) Draws straight line (TM)	Cuts on line with scissors (GI) Makes designs and crude letters (GI) Catches small ball, elbows in front of body (MW) Dresses self (GI) Throws ball overhand (KP)	Folds paper into double triangle (TM) Copies square (TM) and triangle (KP) Copies designs, letters, numbers (GI) Catches small ball, elbows at sides (MW) Throws well (G) Fastens buttons he can see (GI)
Locomotion	Wide stance, runs well (KP) Walks up and down stairs alone (KP) Kicks large ball (KP) Descends large ladder marking time (MW) Jumps 12 inches (MW)	Walks tiptoe (KP, B) Jumps from bottom stair (KP, B) Stands on one foot (KP, B) Hops, both feet (MW) Propels wagon, one foot (J) Rides tricycle (KP) Descends long steps, marking time, unsupported (MW) Jumps 18 inches (MW)	Gallops (G) Descends small ladder, alternating feet easily (MW) Stunts on tricycle (G) Descends short steps, alternating feet, unsupported (G) Skips on one foot (KP)	Narrow stance (GI) Skips (G, MW) Hops on one foot, 10 or more steps (MW) Descends large ladder, alternating feet easily (MW) Walks straight line (GI)

Sources:
B—N. Bayley. Development of motor abilities during the first three years. *Monographs of the Society for Research in Child Development*, 1935, 1.
GI—A. Gesell, and F. L. Ilg. *Child development.* New York: Harper & Row, Publishers, Inc., 1949.
G—M. V. Gutteridge. A study of motor achievements of young children. *Archives of Psychology*, 1939, **244.**
J—T. D. Jones. *Development of certain motor skills and play activities in young children,* Child Development Monographs. New York: Teachers College, Columbia University, 1939, No. 26.
KP—H. Knobloch and B. Pasamanick. *Developmental diagnosis*, 3rd ed. New York: Harper & Row, Publishers, Inc., 1974.
MW—C. L. McCaskill and B. L. Wellman. A study of common motor achievements at the preschool ages. *Child Development*, 1939, 9, 141–150.
TM—L. M. Terman and M. A. Merrill. *Stanford-Binet intelligence scale.* Boston: Houghton Mifflin Company, 1960.

Girls spent more time indoors, using the craft tables and kitchen more than boys did. Even in the same environment, small groups of boys spent more time than small groups of girls in rough and tumble play [9a]. Rough and tumble play involves chasing, hitting and wrestling, all in a friendly, playful way, without intent to injure.

Posture

Posture is the way in which the whole body is balanced, not only in sitting and standing but also in play and rest. Posture is neuromuscular behavior, just as surely as bouncing a ball and drawing a circle are. Parents and teachers rarely make great headway when they try to get children to stand up straight or otherwise consciously improve their posture according to standard ideas of what good posture is. The ways in which a child stands, sits, and moves are the results of a dynamic interplay of forces that cannot be controlled by holding his head up or throwing back his shoulders. This is not to say that good posture is unimportant in its influence on health, growth, and efficiency of movement. It is very important indeed, but it is achieved through good muscle tone and healthy skeletal development, as well as through general physical and mental health. Figure 7–7 illustrates good and poor posture in the preschool child.

The child's own personality is expressed in his posture, both his general attitudes toward himself and the world and his specific ups and downs. Sometimes a sagging, slumping body is the first indication that something is wrong. A handicap, such as blindness or deafness, often

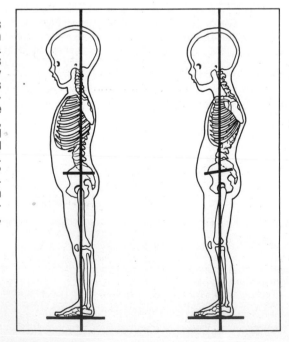

FIGURE 7–7
The child on the left shows good posture, the child on the right poor posture. The first child's body is arranged symmetrically about a line that passes through his center of gravity. The head and chest are high, chin in, abdomen in, shoulder blades in, and curves of back small and knees straight. (SOURCE: Fig. 4.3 on p. 90 of *Good posture and the little child*. Children's Bureau Publication 219. Washington: U.S. Government Printing Office, 1935.)

leads to a characteristic posture. A beautifully balanced body is one indication of a healthy child.

Some children are more active than others, as everyone knows. Extremely high levels of activity, or hyperactivity, are sometimes considered problematic. Activity levels and correlates of high activity were studied in 129 children in an ongoing study by Buss, Block, and Block [7a]. The children were tested at ages 3, 4, 5, and 7, using an actometer, an instrument that records movement when strapped to a child's limbs or back. Trained teachers judged personality characerics. Like previous studies that have shown boys to be more active than girls if any difference was found, this study showed a small difference in favor of boys at age 4, but none at ages 3 and 7. Consistency of activity scores over time was moderate. Many significant differences were found between more and less active children in personality characteristics. Highly active children were judged more energetic, restless, and fidgety, and less inhibited and cautious. These children were seen as less obedient or compliant, less shy and reserved, more self-assertive, more aggressive, more competitive, and more manipulative.

When the children in the Buss, Block, and Block study were 5 years old, they were observed with their parents while the parents taught them specified tasks [7]. Parent-child interaction was significantly affected by child activity level. Parents of the more active girls entered into power struggles with their daughters and showed hostility toward them, whereas parents were more patient and responsive to less active girls. Mothers behaved similarly with active girls and active boys, but fathers enjoyed their active sons in a comradely style, even though they also engaged in power struggles with them.

Although the research by Buss and associates did not find a relation between activity and IQ, another study using an actometer and ratings did show a negative relationship between activity and IQ, and activity and other cognitive tests [14]. The relation of intelligence to motor activity, then, requires further study.

The right and left sides of the brain have specialized functions. The term *laterality* refers to this fact. Preference for the right or left hand is also called laterality, but the hand preference is only one result of the laterality of the brain.

The parts of the brain that control speech and language reception are usually in the left hemisphere. So also is the part that controls the right side of the body. Almost all right-handers are lateralized for speech on the left side, but the converse is not true for left-handers [21]. About two-thirds of left-handers are lateralized for speech on the left, just like right-handers. Most of the remaining left-handers are lateralized for speech on the right, but a few seem to have some language areas in both sides of the brain. Specialization in the brain hemispheres occurs early in life, even prenatally. Infants, like adults, usually give more left-hemisphere response to speech, and right-hemisphere response to music [21]. About 11 per cent of persons are left-handed [39]. The same percentage of left-handers was found in a study of preschool children [19].

The left-handed person incurs many disadvantages. In a world designed for right-handed people, he has to adjust to scissors, classroom chairs, table settings, and countless other arrangements that are awkward for him. There are certain prejudices against left-handers, although feelings against them vary from time to time and from culture to culture. It seems wise for teachers and parents to respect a preference for the left hand and to help the child by giving him left-handed equipment when possible and by showing him how to adapt in places where he has to use right-handed tools and arrangements.

Lefties need left-handed equipment

Perceptual-Motor Learning

Many motor acts, both large and small, are started and guided by a child's perceptions, or interpretations of sensory experience. In catching a ball or coloring a picture, the hands are seen and coordinated in relation to the ball or the crayon and paper. Body awareness is involved in perceptual-motor learning, for a person has to know where the different body parts are in space in order to control what they do. Thus, dance and creative expression contibute to perceptual-motor development through heightening body awareness. Sensory experience is linked to motor in drawing, cutting, painting, clay work, carpentry, playing with balls, blocks, and puzzles, and, in fact, with most nursery school activities.

Finger movement and awareness have been studied for the insight they give into the development of body schemes, body image, and sensory integration [22]. Children from 3 to 5 were given tasks involving their fingers. The easiest task, done by 85 per cent of 3-year-olds and by nearly all 5-year-olds, was to oppose each finger to the thumb, after the examiner had touched the finger while the child was watching. The subject thus had both visual and tactile cues to use in guiding his finger movements. The task of opposing fingers to thumb was much more difficult when only visual cues were given by the examiner demonstrating the action. Three-year-olds apparently did not discriminate fully one finger from the others. The most difficult of all tasks was to point to the fingers of a model after the examiner had touched the corresponding fingers of the child, but with the child's hand shielded so that he could not watch. Only about 10 per cent of 3-year-olds and 50 per cent of 5-year-olds succeeded. This task involved integrating tactile information with visual discrimination, as well as transferring representation from self to model. The tasks thus explored perceptual differentiation, intersensory integration, and symbolic representation, all of which develop rapidly between 3 and 5 years of age. These processes provide a basis for organizing bodily experiences and for building a body image.

Movement Education. For the harmonious development of the person, movement experiences and education are significant during the preschool years. At this time, the brain is immature, with communication between the two hemispheres limited. It is suggested that the child needs experiences that will stimulate even development of both hemispheres, rather than getting a concentration of speech, reading, and counting that involves mostly the left hemisphere. "Perhaps, then, as much emphasis should be given to music, rhythmic exercises, body awareness, graphics, and solid constructions as to speaking, listening, reading and counting" [37].

Movement has many important meanings to the young child [12]. It means life, since she thinks that things that move are alive. Movement helps her to discover her body and to form a body image and concept of self. Through movement, she explores the environment, builds concepts of space, and orients herself in space. Being able to control her movements means being able to control what happens to her and to keep her safe. Communication can take place through movement, the language of behavior. Controlled movement brings pleasure in itself as well as the satisfaction of mastery.

Unfortunately, many people still think of physical education as exercise drills and, therefore, inappropriate for the young child. The old point of view is that because young children are very active, they get all the exercise they need.

Young children will educate themselves to a large degree if they have a physical environment that makes it possible for them to do so. The planning of such an environment is, in itself, teaching. Much of the educating carried on by preschool teachers and parents consists of arranging the environment, or setting the stage, including dressing the child for easy movement. Children will use space and equipment for developing and perfecting the movements of which they are capable, whether they be the basic movements of walking, running, crawling, climbing, jumping, pushing, pulling, and grasping, or the skilled movements of throwing, catching, tricycle riding, swimming, and so on. The designing and equipping of movement centers can be observed in a good nursery school and can be studied through the writings of specialists in movement education for young children, such as Flinchum's book, *Motor Development in Early Childhood* [12].

Teachers teach young children through encouragement and enthusiasm, rather than showing them just how to execute a movement, by asking questions rather than telling them, by setting up situations that encourage exploration and practice [12, pp. 80–92]. For example, children are encouraged to discover different ways of throwing, catching, and carrying a beanbag, or different ways of moving around, into, and out of a circle. Teachers do not suggest that the child may fall by saying, "Be careful, don't fall." If a young child is very limited in his movements, he may need remedial work in terms of a careful program of extra reinforce-

ment, encouragement, and exposure to appropriate materials and situations.

Dance Movement. Music and rhythm provide links between movement, emotional expression, creativity, and self-awareness. With their limited verbal capacities, children can use music and suggestion to move happily and sadly, to express moods and experiences, and to understand relationships with space. From watching other children, a child gets notions of how they are feeling and thinking, perhaps by imitating the motions and savoring his own experience as an elephant or a butterfly.

Summary

During the years from 2 to 6 the child's body changes in shape from chubby to slim. Growth in height and weight becomes slower and slower. Tables of height and weight standards are used for assessing a child's growth, by comparing her with other children and with her own record. Children's height is related to parents' height. Body size and growth patterns vary between macrosystems, as well as between individuals.

Fat thickness decreases. Muscle tissue grows slowly. Skeletal growth can be assessed by the appearance of ossification centers in the wrist and by changes in shape of the individual bones, seen in X rays. Dental care is important for health, even though the 20 primary teeth will be shed, starting at age 6 or 7. The stomach, being relatively small, straight, and upright, empties easily. The respiratory system and middle ear are vulnerable to infection. Taste sensitivity is problably high. The brain makes up a relatively large part of body weight, being closer to its mature weight than is the rest of the body.

Macrosystems differ in their support of life and growth through the quantity and quality of food available to young children, in beliefs and customs regarding food and eating, sleeping, sanitation, and safety. Climate and economic factors also affect disease control. Safety from accidental injury and abuse depends upon physical conditions, space and equipment, as well as customs, beliefs, laws, law enforcement, and social support systems. Medical care differs between macrosystems in quality, availability, and emphasis.

Physical care is given in microsystems, especially the home. Day care is an important microsystem for growing numbers of children in the United States. Nutrition, rest, training in self-care, and safety arrangements are all provided by caregivers, through management of settings and timing, as well as through transactions with children. Other important microsystems are those in which medical care is given. Mcsosystems, or relations and communications between microsystems, play vital roles in the provision of health care and nurture.

Motor development occurs in a regular, age-related sequence. Variations in coordination and selection of motor activities are seen between individuals, sexes, and groups. Posture indicates health and expresses feelings. Motor control includes the ability to move slowly and to be still. Hyperactivity and impulsiveness probably result from a central nervous system condition. Activity level affects parent-child interaction. Lateralization (sidedness) of the brain determines hand preference. The left-handed child can be helped by adaptations in position and by left-handed equipment.

Perceptions guide motor learning. Body schemes and images are developed from sensory-motor experience. Movement education enhances such learning, as well as the learning of motor skills and communication. Self-awareness, creativity, and pleasure are also products of dancing and movement education.

References

1. Accident mortality at the preschool ages. *Statistical Bulletin*, 1975, **56**:5, 7–9.
2. Accidental deaths high at the preschool ages. *Statistical Bulletin*, 1969, **50**:9, 6–8.
3. Agricultural Research Service. *Food for fitness.* Washington: USDA, 1964.
4. Al-ki, I. J., A. A. Kanawati, and D. S. McLaren. Formal education of mothers

and their nutritional behavior. *Journal of Nutrition Education*, 1975, **7**:1, 22–24.

5. Altshuler, A. *Books that help children deal with a hospital experience.* (DHEW Publication No. (HSA) 76-5402.) Washington: U.S. Government Printing Office, 1976.

6. Beyer, N. R., and P. M. Morris. Food attitudes and snacking patterns of young children. *Journal of Nutrition Education*, 1974, **6**:4, 131–134.

7. Buss, D. M. Predicting parent-child interactions from children's activity level. *Developmental Psychology*, 1981, **17,** 59–65.

7a. Buss, D. M., J. H. Block, and J. Block. Preschool activity level: Personality correlates and developmental implications. *Child Development*, 1980, **51,** 401–408.

8. Carter, J., B. Gilmer, R. Vanderzwaag, and K. Massey. Health and nutrition in disadvantaged children and their relationship with intellectual development. Nashville, Tenn.: George Peabody College for Teachers and Vanderbilt University School of Medicine, undated.

9. Demirjian, A., H. Goldstein, and J. M. Tanner. A new system of dental assessment. *Human Biology*, 1973, **45,** 211–227.

9a. DiPietro, J. A. Rough and tumble play: A function of gender. *Developmental Psychology*, 1981, **17,** 50–58.

10. Eichorn, D. H. Biological correlates of behavior. In H. W. Stevenson, J. Kagan, and C. Spiker. *Child psychology.* The Sixty-second Yearbook of the National Society for the Study of Education, Part I. Chicago: University of Chicago Press, 1963, pp. 4–61.

11. Epstein, H. T. Growth spurts during brain development: Implications for educational policy and practice. In J. S. Chall and A. F. Mirsky (eds.). *Education and the brain.* The Seventy-seventh Yearbook of the National Society for the Study of Education, Part II. Chicago: University of Chicago Press, 1978.

12. Flinchum, B. M. *Motor development in early childhood.* St. Louis: The C. V. Mosby Company, 1975.

13. Gutteridge, M. V. A study of motor achievements of young children. *Archives of Psychology*, 1939, **244.**

14. Halverson, C. F., Jr., and M. F. Waldrop. The relations between preschool activity and aspects of intellectual and social behavior at age seven and one-half. *Developmental Psychology*, 1976, **12,** 107–112.

15. Hamill, P. V., F. E. Johnston, and W. Grams. *Height and weight of children: United States.* Public Health Service Publication No. 1000. Series 11, No. 104. Washington: U.S. Government Printing Office, 1970.

16. Harper, L. V., and D. M. Sanders. Preschool children's use of space: Sex differences in outdoor play. In R. C. Smart and M. S. Smart (eds.). *Readings in child development and relationships.* 2nd ed. New York: Macmillan Publishing Co., Inc., 1977.

17. Harrill, I., C. Smith, and J. A. Gangever. Food acceptance and nutritional intake of preschool children. *Journal of Nutrition Education*, 1972, **4,** 103–106.

18. Harvard Child Health Project Task Force. *Toward a primary medical care system responsive to children's needs.* Cambridge, Mass.: Ballinger, 1977.

19. Hildreth, G. Manual dominance in nursery school children. *Journal of Genetic Psychology*, 1948, **72,** 29–45.

20. Ireton, C. L., and H. A. Guthrie. Modification of vegetable-eating behavior in preschool children. *Journal of Nutrition Education*, 1972, **4,** 100–103.

21. Kinsbourne, M., and M. Hiscock. Cerebral lateralization and cognitive development. In J. S. Chall and A. F. Mirsky (eds.). *Education and the brain.* The Seventy-seventh Yearbook of the National Society for the Study of Education, Part II. Chicago: University of Chicago Press, 1978.

22. Lefford, A., H. G. Birch, and G. Green. The perceptual and cognitive bases for finger location and selective movement in preschool children. *Child Development*, 1974, **45**, 335–343.

23. Lowrey, G. H. *Growth and development of children*. 6th ed. Chicago: Year Book Medical Publishers, Inc., 1973.

24. Maccoby, E. E., and C. N. Jacklin. *The psychology of sex differences*. Stanford, Calif.: Stanford University Press, 1974.

25. McCaskill, C. L., and B. L. Wellman. A study of common motor achievements at the preschool ages. *Child Development*, 1938, **9**, 141–150.

26. McHale, M. C., J. McHale, and G. F. Streatfeild. *Children in the world*. Washington: Population Reference Bureau, 1979.

27. Meredith, H. V. Body size of contemporary groups of preschool children studied in different parts of the world. *Child Development*, 1968, **39**, 335–377.

28. Owen, G. M., and H. Lubin. Anthropometric differences between black and white preschool children. *American Journal of Diseases of Children*. 1973, **126**, 168–69.

29. Pyle, S. I., H. C. Stuart, J. Cornoni, and R. Reed. Onsets, completions and spans of the osseous stage of development in representative bone growth centers of the extremities. *Monographs of the Society for Research in Child Development*, 1961, **26**:1.

30. Pyle, S. I., A. M. Waterhouse, and W. W. Greulich. *A radiographic standard of reference for the growing hand and wrist*. Cleveland, Ohio: Press of Case Western Reserve University, 1971.

31. Scrimshaw, N. S. Malnutrition, learning and behavior. *American Journal of Clinical Nutrition*, 1967, **20**, 493–502.

32. Snapper, K. J., and J. S. Ohms. *The status of children, 1977*. (DHEW Publication No. (OHDS) 78-30133.) Office of Human Development Services. Washington: U.S. Government Printing Office, 1978.

33. Stainton, C. Preschoolers' orientation to hospital. *Canadian Nurse*, 1974, **70**:9, 38–41.

34. Steinmetz, S. K. Investigating family violence. *Journal of Home Economics*, 1980, **72**:2, 32–36.

35. U.S. Public Health Service News Release. Cited by A. F. North, Jr. in Research Issues in Child Health I: An Overview. In E. Gotberg (ed.). *Critical issues in research related to disadvantaged children*. Princeton, N.J.: Educational Testing Service, 1969.

36. Werner, E. E. *Cross-cultural child development: A view from the planet Earth*. Monterey, Calif.: Brooks/Cole, 1979.

37. Whitehurst, K. E. The young child: What movement means to him. In *The significance of the young child's motor development*. Washington: National Association for the Education of Young Children, 1971.

38. Wingerd, J., E. J. Schoen, and I. L. Solomon. Growth standards in the first two years of life based on measurements of white and black children in a prepaid health care program. *Pediatrics*, 1971, **47**, 818–825.

39. Wittrock, M. C. Education and the cognitive processes of the brain. In J. S. Chall and A. F. Mirsky (eds.). *Education and the brain*. The Seventy-seventh Yearbook of the National Society for the Study of Education, Part II. Chicago: University of Chicago Press, 1978.

8
Thought, Language, and Imagination

Jennifer is sorting the nails out of her father's toolbox into three glass jars, one for each size of nail. She looks serious as she says, "This is a baby nail and it goes in here. The mommies go in this jar. This big nail is a daddy and it goes in here." Is she working or playing? Is she thinking or imagining? She is doing useful work for her father. She chose to do this work and therefore is probably enjoying it. She is classifying objects according to size, a cognitive activity. At the same time, she pretends that nails are people in a family, who can also be sorted according to size. She is simultaneously carrying on processes of thinking, imagining, and language that we often separate in order to discuss and study. Older children and adults can separate work from play, thinking from talking, and reasoning from pretending, but young children are less differentiated. They react more globally, more as wholes. Their mode of operation has a strong imaginative component that operates in concert with language and controlled thought.

It is easier to explore the mind of the preschool child than that of the infant. The young child can talk. Even so, communication with adults is far from perfect. When differences are understood, the generation gap can be more easily bridged. After North American psychologists' rediscovery of Piaget's work, in the 1960s, many researchers were stimulated to find out why young children's thinking was so different from that of older children, and to define the mental operations of which a young child was capable.

QUESTIONS TO THINK ABOUT WHILE READING THIS CHAPTER

1. What sort of experience does the young child use in developing her mind?
2. What mental processes are employed in making sense out of the world?
3. How do children show that they are using representational thought if they do not yet use words?
4. How can memory and attention be aided?
5. How have researchers recently shown that young children are more competent mentally than some of Piaget's experiments would lead one to believe?
6. How do children form concepts of classes or categories, time, space, and quantity?
7. What are the main functions of play in the life of a child?

8. What are the different ways in which children use symbols in play, art, language, music, dance, and humor?
9. How is play influenced by the ecology in which the child lives?

The toddler is a unique self, emerging from 1½ to 2 years of infancy, with a wealth of experience in interacting with people and objects in the physical settings of home and a few other microsystems. The end of the sensorimotor period is marked by the emerging ability to represent objects and actions. Modes of representation include imitation, language, and imagination, all of which develop rapidly during early childhood.

Sources of Mental Competencies

Young children want to find out and to know all sorts of things about the world and the people in it. While exploring their own microsystem settings and interacting with their comembers, their experiences affect the way they pursue discovery and problem solving. From his study of the origins of competence, Burton White concluded that "a rich social life" was a very significant antecedent of achievement and competence in early childhood [65]. The most important single measure was the amount of live language directed to a child. Features of the rich social life included procuring services and gaining attention from an adult. Through these activities the child could share her interesting experiences, get help when it was needed, and thus enjoy continual successes in finding out how things worked, what was possible and what was not, the names of objects and actions, and generally making sense out of her world.

The following important processes occur within a social context. First, the child keeps and strengthens her natural desire to know, to find out, to understand. Second, she learns language as a result of other people talking to her while they carry on activities with her, talking about what is going on. Third, through social experience she increases understanding of how other people feel and think. Fourth, the child gains more and more control over her world as caregivers arrange a responsive environment, give help when needed, and allow freedom to choose. With all of these increases in competency, especially the ability to decide and control, the child enjoys a feeling of independence, in Erikson's terms, a sense of autonomy [19]. The sense of initiative also grows as the child explores and discoveres in socially approved ways.

Social Interaction: Shaper of Thinking

When the sense organs are stimulated, perceptual processes select, sort, process, organize, and store the products of the senses. Children actively seek sensory experience, feeding the sense of initiative through exploring. The young child touches objects eagerly, grasps them, runs his fingers and palms over them, even scratches them with his fingernails. Al-

Sensory Experience: Raw Material for Thinking and Imagining

though he has learned, to a large extent, to keep objects out of his mouth, such inhibitions are not complete and he may explore an object with his lips and tongue. Color is important, often featured in his comments, and greatly enjoyed in toys, art, clothing, and nature. He experiments with sounds, using his voice, musical instruments, and any casual sound makers that come into his grasp. Stimulation of inner ear senses occurs most deliciously with swinging, rocking, twirling, hanging by the knees, somersaulting, riding fast, and being tossed high by daddy and other strong persons. Kinesthetic stimulation from muscle movements is also enjoyable. Experiences with taste and smell are interesting, especially when adults suggest, share, and talk about them.

A wide range of sensory experiences probably contributes to brain development, particularly during the preschool period. The connection between the two hemispheres of the brain is less complete than it will be after 7 or 8 years of age. In order to develop both sides of the brain fully during the time before much intercommunication occurs, it is recommended that children have abundant music, rhythmic exercises, movement exploration, art materials, and other right-hemisphere-related experiences, as well as those more pertinent to the left hemisphere, such as speaking, listening to speech, reading, and counting [16].

Features of Mental Development

Growing competency in thought, language, and imagination can be seen as the child understands the world better and reaches goals through increased control over body and mind. Margaret Donaldson, in her book *Children's Minds* discusses the following processes as features of mental development in early childhood: making sense out of the world, gaining control, and using language [17].

Children want to know, to find out, and to understand. Realizing that objects have names, children ask "Wazzat?" They find out what objects can do and what can be done with them, using examining schemes developed in infancy, and refined in the preschool years. What can a tricycle do? The wheels can be spun, the bell rung. You can ride on it, bump into things, fall off, give a friend a ride, use it for a truck or a plane, paint it with water, and put in into the garage. Blocks can be stacked, paint spread, and clay rolled. More and more, even endless, discoveries and uses can be found for blocks, paint, and clay. Puzzles pose problems to be solved; solutions represent control. So might washing the lunch dishes and shoveling the snow off the walk. Sometimes tasks are too difficult and problems cannot be solved when the child does not know enough or cannot find the answers. A fair proportion of successes will maintain motivation for exploring and finding answers.

Curiosity is promoted by adults who encourage and approve of exploration, who share the child's enthusiasms, and who are themselves curious. When adults are open and available, children will ask them questions and enlist their aid in making sense out of the world.

A child wants to make sense out of the social world, too. She knows that people are different from objects. Even young infants behave in different ways toward people and things. The child tries to find out how people operate and how to solve problems of interpersonal relationships. Although we discuss person-to-person interaction more fully in the following chapter on social development, we do not mean to imply that social interaction is not cognitive. Of course children think about other people and themselves, and they use cognitive processes in solving social problems.

In a series of studies on children's learning of interpersonal problem-solving, Shure and Spivack [55] have shown that these cognitive skills can be taught by teachers in a nursery school and at home by mothers who have themselves received training. Mothers learned to use games and dialogues that led their children to think about feelings of self and others, to consider effects of their children's actions on others, to think of alternative solutions and outcomes of various solutions. When children increased in cognitive skills, their behavior in school improved. Behavioral changes included these: greater ability to wait for what they wanted; increased sharing and taking turns; being less upset by frustration; more socially outgoing; less fearful of entering social situations; more able to express emotions. These studies illustrate the wholeness of the child, showing that the child uses cognitive processes to make sense out of the world, and in succeeding, develops emotionally and behaviorally.

Reasoning. Wanting to know involves finding out what is possible and what is not. When the child comes to know that something is real or true, he reasons that something conflicting with it is impossible, as in the following examples.

AMY: Is God a boy or a girl?
JOHN: I think God is a girl.
AMY: No, God can't be a girl, because they call him *he*. If God were a girl, they'd call him *she*.

Matthew, aged 4, opened a box and found some ear rings that his father, an art dealer, had just brought home.

FATHER: Be careful with my ear rings, Matthew.
MATTHEW: Those aren't your ear rings.
FATHER: Yes, they are. I just bought them.
MATTHEW: They can't be yours because you don't have any holes in your ears.

Gaining Mental Control

Representation by deferred imitation, pretending, language, and graphic symbols

Throughout childhood, mental development involves strengthening control over the operations or actions of the mind. During the preschool years, important gains are made in the following areas.

Representational Thought. During the latter half of the second year, the toddler can refer to people, objects, and actions that are not present. This he does first by what Piaget calls deferred imitation, reproducing a gesture or action seen previously [47]. Sarah came into the house after "helping" her father feed the pigs. She made a snorting-slurping noise obviously representing piggish behavior. Next the toddler shows by pretending or symbolic play that she is thinking of something not present. A few weeks later Sarah put a bottle cap into a pot, put a cover on the pot, waited for a moment, took off the cover, put the bottle cap in her mouth, spat it out, made the sound that she made when food is hot, and laughed. In this scene Sarah used actions to represent her mother's actions in cooking and her own in eating. In using her sound for *hot* she was also beginning to use words to represent recalled experiences. She used the bottle cap as a symbol for food. Her laugh indicated the play-pretend nature of the episode.

Nobody knows when the *mental image* first appears. Piaget calls it an internalized imitation. Because it is internalized, it cannot be seen by the observer, but presumably children begin thinking with mental images at the end of infancy. As children learn language (which consists of commonly understood symbols), they use it for representational thought, as well as for communicating with others. Another type of representation is drawing, or graphic representation at about 2½ years. Representation in symbolic play will be discussed later.

Attention. A young child has limited ability to keep attention focused on the heart of a problem, ignoring distraction, his own wishes, and other irrelevant features before acting or coming to a conclusion. In other words, it is hard for the young child to stop and think. It is difficult to bring past experience to bear upon a present problem, keeping the present situation in mind while comparing it with stored knowledge. In many of

Piaget's experiments the young child fails to solve a problem because his attention is held by one perceptually salient feature. He does not consider the other features. In one such problem identical amounts of liquid are put into identical glasses. The child agrees that the amounts are the same. The experimenter pours the liquid from one glass into a taller, thinner glass and asks which glass has more liquid. The young child usually says that there is more in the tall glass. He focuses on the greater height of the liquid and does not take into account the change in the width of the glass, nor does he consider the pouring that transformed the appearance of one portion of liquid. Another illustration of the dominance of perception is the ease with which young children can be fooled by a magician. Although the older members of the audience reject the evidences of their senses because they reason on the basis of past experience, the preschool children really believe that the magician found his rabbit in the little boy's coat pocket and that the card flew out of the air into the magician's hand.

Same amount.

Same amount?

To stop and think requires inhibition of thinking and acting. In the previous chapter the problem of hyperactivity was mentioned. Inhibition is one of the normal functions of the nervous system. As the nervous system matures, inhibitory control increases. Throughout early childhood experience builds upon the strengthening physical base for control of thought and action. Children can be helped to develop attentional control. (See "Memory" later in this chapter.)

The child gains the ability to control and direct his thinking as he becomes more aware of himself and his thinking [17, p. 96]. To stop and think, or to think what you are doing, implies choosing what to do next. Awareness, choice, and control are closely related.

Metacognition. Awareness and understanding of thinking is called *metacognition.* Although there is evidence that young children have some notion of mental processes in themselves and others, such knowledge is probably quite limited. Children's metacognition has been studied by exploring their understanding of various words that refer to mental processes, such as *know* and *guess* [42] and *remember* and *forget* [64]. Children as young as 3 may have some notion of the outward or behavioral aspects of these internal processes. In order to test for understanding of "know" and "guess" an object was hidden while the child either watched or covered his eyes. Then he looked in one of the possible hiding places. If he found it, the experimenter asked whether he knew or guessed that the object was there. Four age-related stages in the development of understanding were found in children between 3½ and 7 years. First, a child had no knowledge of the meaning of "know" or "guess." Second, the words were understood in terms of outcome. If the child found the object, he said he knew where it was, whether he had actually seen it hidden, or not. The third stage was a transition from the outcome stage to the adult way of thinking. In the fourth, the adult stage, children showed accurate understanding of the terms. (*Know* required having

Metacognition: Thinking about thinking

seen it hidden.) Although some children were in the transitional stage up to 6½ years of age, most children achieved the adult stage by 5½. Similarly, when children's notions of "forget" and "remember" were explored, 3-year-olds had little or no understanding, 4-year-olds based their answers on outcome ("remember" was seen as successful search behavior), and children between 4 and 7 were closer to adults in understanding.

Development in metacognition, or understanding of mental processes, follows the same pattern as conceptual development in general. Metacognition becomes more and more free from concrete events as mental operations become more flexible and powerful.

Memory: recognition and/or recall

Memory. The processes basic to recognition mature during infancy [20]. Preschool children have excellent recognition memory. They can easily tell whether they have seen an object or person before, or have heard a story. To recall is more difficult than to recognize, as everyone realizes when he says, "Your face is familiar, but I can't recall your name." A stimulus, the face, is present in the case of recognition, but the name is not present, and must be retrieved from storage. Competency in recall develops throughout childhood, influenced by experience and teaching, and is closely related to learning, knowledge, reasoning, and mental control. Young children show that they are recalling events and experiences by acting them out, even before they talk about them, as did Sarah with the cooking pot and bottle cap. A toddler easily recalls that a toy is in a particular cupboard or that mother's jewelry is in a certain drawer. Recall is shown when a child asks, "Is Grandma coming?"

Research on memory in older children has shown the importance of plans they make and the strategies they use for organizing, storing, and retrieving material. Studies of younger children's memory have focused on questions of what actually contributes to improved recall throughout the preschool years, and whether they do any planning about remembering. Children between 2 and 5 took part in a series of experiments to explore strategies for remembering [44]. The first experiment tested recall of related and unrelated items. The items were small, attractive objects that children could readily name. The related items were related in two ways, by category (animals, transportation, and utensils) and by sound of initial letter (*b, c,* and *p*), as shown in Figure 8–1. The unrelated

Figure 8–1
Items used for testing preschool children's recall. SOURCE: M. Perlmutter and N. A. Myers. Development of recall in 2-5 to 4-year-old children. *Developmental Psychology*, 1979, **15**, 73–83.

Related by Sound and Category   Unrelated Items

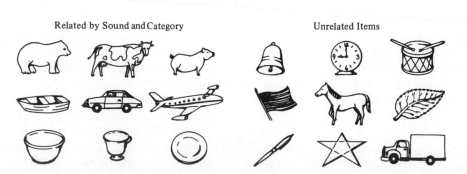

items were different in category and in initial sound. Each group of nine items were in a box. The experimenter opened a box, took out each item in random order, named it, put it back, closed the box, and asked the child what he or she remembered. There were very few wrong responses, indicating that even the youngest children made judgments as to accuracy of their recall. Older children (average age 4) recalled more items than younger (average age 2–11). The difference between the two age levels was greater for related items, suggesting that the older children made more use of categories. In further experiments, help in remembering was provided by presenting the items in categories, and also by asking the child to recall by category. ("Can you remember any more animals?") Both younger and older groups improved when given category cues. Apparently young children do not make category cues for themselves when trying to remember. The assistance given by the experimenter allowed them to gain access to their memory stores. Because the older children did better than the younger on free recall, it seems likely that the older ones had gone further in organizing memory stores semantically (according to meaning). Neither group used verbal rehearsal, a strategy often used by school-age children. From these experiments we can conclude that although young children store memories very well, they are in only the early stages of developing efficient strategies for retrieval.

Planning for remembering can be seen on a simple level in children as young as 3 [62]. Children of 2 and 3 years watched an experimenter hide a toy dog in a box. Half were told to "wait with the dog" and half to "remember where the dog is" while the experimenter went out of the room. The 3-year-olds who were told to remember did more looking at the box and touching it. In addition, some children nodded at it and moved it to a distinctive position. These spontaneous actions indicate that the children did make plans for remembering. This task could be done by using external cues; it did not require an internal memory storage. This is the type of memory task that young children can perform independently. Although they have little or no skill in forming strategies for internal retrieval, such as verbal rehearsal, they are able to devise actions related to external cues.

Even though the preschool child does little planning for remembering, some of his spontaneous activities do aid memorizing. Young children are notorious mimics, often repeating the words and actions of others. Although they are not rehearsing with a purpose in mind, a plan for remembering, they are performing the very actions that older children and adults do when they are trying to memorize. Young children also frequently group objects in play. Even an infant will put a number of clothespins into a milk bottle or blocks into a basket.

Parents aid their children's memories in these ways:

Pointing out relevant stimuli: "This is a daffodil because it has a little cup in the middle and petals around the outside."
Labeling: "This is a screw driver and that's a drill."
Grouping: "Let's put these wooden beads here and these plastic beads there."

Hearing and saying names: Reading a story, then rereading it and letting the child fill in names.
Rhyming: Reading rhyming picture books, making up rhymes.
Playing word games: "The little boy ran and jumped and skipped and......?"

In schools for young children in China, repetition is used in singing, dancing, and going through the same routines. Action and pictorial memories are thus stored along with symbolic memories, with different sensory modalities being thus activated. The Montessori system also uses repetition in routines, as well as the child's own actions in concert with vivid sensory experiences in seeing, hearing, and touching. Different cultures, schools, and families put their own particular emphases on memory aids for children.

Perspective-Taking. Can a young child take the point of view of another person? Common sense would say *yes*. After his mother falls down, 2-year-old Brian pats her leg and say, "Mommy hurt?" It looks as though he has some notion of how she feels. He knows how it feels to fall down. Suppose his mother is crying because she feels fat and dowdy and she suspects that her husband is interested in another woman. Brian understands that Mommy hurts, but he cannot go any further in taking her point of view. Even if she tells him why she is crying, he has no experience to use in interpreting his mother's situation to himself. There are many ways of taking the perspective of another person; it can be in terms of feelings, thoughts, visual experience, language, values, or other areas.

Children as young as 2 showed that they realized that another person has to look at a picture in order to see it [35]. When asked to show a picture, most children turned the picture toward the adult, even though they could not then see it themselves. Language adaptation was demonstrated by 4-year-olds who were asked to explain the workings if a toy to 2-year-olds, 4-year-olds, and adults [24]. They used short, simple sentences to 2-year-olds and longer, more complex statements to peers and adults. The function of speech to the 2-year-olds was to show and tell and to direct attention. With adults, children shared thoughts, sought information and support, and expressed uncertainty. Surely these 4-year-olds took the perspective of persons at three different stages of maturity.

One of Piaget's experiments shows young children to be quite unable to take a spatial perspective other than their own [46]. A child sits facing a 3-dimensional model of 3 mountains, one with snow, one with a house on top, and one with a red cross. A doll is placed in a position other than the child's. The child is given pictures of the mountains from different perspectives and asked to choose the one that the doll sees. Most children under 7 choose the picture that represents their own perspective. Piaget calls this an egocentric response and says that the child thinks that the doll's point of view is the same as his own.

Several psychologists have shown that young children can indeed take another spatial perspective if the task is made easier. For example, Borke used Grover, a character from *Sesame Street*, who drove his car along a road and stopped to look at scenes mounted on a turntable [10]. She asked 3- and 4-year-olds to "move the turntable so that the fire engine looks the way Grover sees it." The scenes that Grover saw varied in difficulty. When scenes contained toy objects, children matched the scene to Grover's perception 80 per cent of the time. In Piaget's terms, they gave decentered, or nonegocentric responses. Children of 3 and 4 achieved an even greater success rate, of 90 per cent, on another spatial perspective task in which a child hid a doll so that a policeman would not be able to see it [31]. Donaldson explains the children's success, in contrast to the failure of children the same age on Piaget's mountain test. The policeman task was easier because the child had only to tell whether the doll could be seen, and not how it would look. More important, though, the policeman task made sense to the child because it was within his experience. Little children play hiding games, starting with peek-a-boo. They also understand the motives and intentions of the characters. They have experienced being naughty and wanting to evade detection. Therefore the child understands what he is supposed to do with the problem. In contrast, the mountains task has nothing to do with anything in the child's experience. There are no motives involved. It is entirely abstract from the human feelings within which the young child operates. Piaget is correct in saying that the young child cannot decenter enough to solve the mountains test, and that older children can do so. But young children can move away from their own perspectives in situations that have real meaning to them.

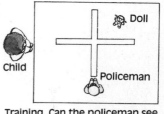

Training. Can the policeman see the doll?

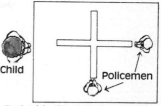

Test. Hide the doll where both policemen can't see him.

Using Language

The year-old baby may say 2 or 3 words: the 6-year-old talks in grammatically correct sentences and comprehends over 14,000 words [13]. (This count includes inflected and derived words. For root words, the number comprehended is about 8,000). Such rapid learning, about 9 new words a day, and such competence are quite amazing. What is more, the 5-year-old who has been exposed to 2 languages is fluent in both. Preschool progress in developing and using language can be considered in the following ways.

Biological Foundations. Language rests upon a bodily base possessed by human beings only. The higher primates share some of this base, as shown by chimpanzees and gorillas that have been taught to communicate with linguistic symbols. Chimpanzee and gorilla brains have a lot of what it takes to learn language, provided that the animals are reared in the social-emotional-linguistic environment that supports language. They do not have the speech organs necessary for producing language as humans know it. Furthermore, no chimpanzee, no gorilla, has ever learned sign language or the use of symbols with the speed and spontaneity that the most ordinary human baby displays in learning to talk. The human brain, hearing system, speech organs, and social organizations are uniquely adequate for understanding and producing language.

The biological nature of language is shown in the universal sequence of language milestones and their relationship to motor development in infancy. All normal children, growing up in a normal social environment, speak words by 2 years, most children by one year [36]. They combine words by 3 years, usually by 22 months. Two-year-olds can be expected to have a vocabulary of at least 50 words [42a]. There *must* be universal human language-learning abilities. The nature of those processes is a challenge to psychologists and linguists. One approach to these processes is through the mother-infant interactions system. In "Language" in Chapter 5, we discussed the mother-infant system as the foundation of language learning. Mother-infant interactions show similar patterns in different cultures, suggesting a basic interpersonal framework that is fundamental to all languages.

Differentiation of Language Out of Experience. Children speak before they know that they are using language, just as they think before they reflect upon themselves as thinkers. One of the achievements of childhood is coming to know that words exist as words, apart from the situation in which they are spoken. In everyday life, speech occurs in a framework of action. Words have meaning as part of a whole experience, not as separate entities. For example, if you are in Malaysia and someone says "Selamit pagi," you will realize that he is greeting you. You are familiar with the situations in which people greet one another, and this fits. You recognize a tone of voice, a look, a hand gesture, or a bow. Soon you will be saying *Selamit pagi* for a greeting. An adult realizes that *Selamit pagi* is a word or words; a two-year-old would not. The child's days are full of words embedded in actions and feelings. Good girl. You ate all your dinner...... Time to go to bed now...... Up you come onto Daddy's lap. A child learns only gradually that all these are words and that they exist apart from people and actions. This piece of learning is essential for learning to read, and some children start to school without it. The child must know that there are words and that words correspond with sounds and also with marks on paper. Such knowledge is gained, of course, from books, having them read and looking at them oneself. Labels and other small pieces of writing also serve this purpose. Another way of learning about words is to tell stories that someone writes down and reads back to you. You thus live each step of the process: saying words, seeing marks made in response to them, and then hearing those words uttered while the reader looks at the marks. Play with words also contributes to differentiating words out of total experience.

Learning Words. Baby biographers and early child psychologists counted the number of words their subjects spoke. (The *adults* knew a word when they heard one, even though the children said them as embedded in experience.) The researchers charted information on average numbers of

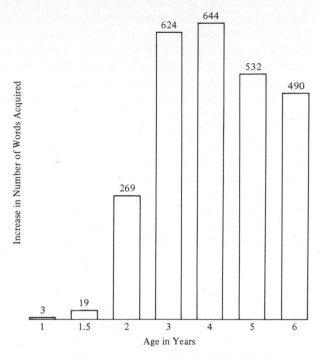

Figure 8–2
Number of spoken words added to vocabulary each year from ages 1–6. Source: M. E. Smith. An investigation of the development of the sentence and the extent of vocabulary in young children. *University of Iowa Studies in Child Welfare,* 1926, 3:5.

words in active (spoken) and passive (understood) vocabularies at each age. They found a dramatic increase during the preschool years, as shown in Figure 8–2, which is based on data published in 1926. In this classic study, pictures and questions were used to elicit spoken words from children. Vocabulary norms were assembled by the makers of intelligence and language tests, who could then judge how a child compared with the average in number of words understood. From the rate of acquiring new words, we can get an impression of the rapidly increasing competence of the child and the extraordinary achievement of learning 2 or more words every day. Word counts and norms for use of parts of speech, type of sentence, and so on are descriptive.

Children's words can also be studied for their meaning and the uses to which the child puts them. This approach tells more about the process of language acquisition, as has been shown in "Language" in Chapter 5, where infant language development was described.

Using Rules. Every language has rules as to sounds permitted, the combining of sounds, and the structure of sentences, or the combining of words. When children talk, they talk according to rules, even though they cannot tell you the rules. Not even educated adults can verbalize all the rules for speaking their own language correctly. Often a person knows that a statement is not exactly right and she can correct it but cannot state the rule that guided her.

The beginning speaker starts with simple rules and adds most but not all of the rules for adult speech before reaching kindergarten. Some of the first rules are not quite the same as those governing adult speech. The child modifies rules to be more like adult rules as she analyzes the language on more complex levels and as she has new experiences that require revision of the rules she already has. One of the early rules seems to be that the subject goes before the verb.

The first sentences have been called *telegraphic speech*, because they include only words carrying essential meaning. In comments such as "See doggie," "Mommy come home," and "Go car," only words carrying necessary information are used. However, these sentences can be understood, because the order of the words is correct. Even though the child reduces sentences to the barest essentials, he usually preserves the word order, an extremely important dimension of English grammar. When passive sentences are first encountered, they are often understood in terms of the order of an active sentence. For instance, 3-year-olds, when asked to show the picture indicating "the cat is chased by the dog," will point to the picture of the cat chasing the dog, indicating that order is more important than form to the young child. This finding is not unexpected for speakers of English, a language in which order is very important. It is surprising, however, that Russian children also order their first two-word sentences strictly, even though Russian is a heavily inflected language, and word order is not so salient as it is in English [57]. In fact, it seems to be universal that the subject precedes the object in the dominant actor-action form of a language.

When a rule is first grasped, it may be applied too widely. "I goed out and bringed my truck in." The rule is to make the past tense by adding *ed*, but there are exceptions! "He fixed it hisself." What could be more logical when all the other reflexive pronouns are made by combining the possessive pronoun with self? Myself. Yourself. Herself. In saying "hisself," the child is applying a rule and does not yet know about the exception. Likewise, the rule for forming plurals, the addition of *s*, is first applied to exceptional words, as well as regular ones, producing *mans*, *mouses*, and *gooses*.

The question of how children form language rules is the subject of theorizing and research. Have they a special "language acquisition device," as proposed by linguist Noam Chomsky [14], or are rules made through the same cognitive processes that children apply to solving nonlinguistic problems? MacWhinney has addressed this question by testing a model of the processes by which children learn to put together morphemes (smallest meaningful sound units) to make words [38]. In order to test general applicability a broad cross-cultural approach used information from Hungarian, Finnish, German, English, French, Latvian, Russian, Spanish, Arabic, and Chinese. In all these language contexts children used 3 central abilities in a preferred order. They learned language forms by rote, if possible, which meant using morphemes in the same combination in which they heard them. Next, they used combination of morphemes, as for example, when required to say a plural that the child had not heard. For two wives, a child might say *wifes*, by combining the

Morpheme is the smallest meaningful unit of speech

morpheme *wife* with the morpheme *s*. In adding *s* to *wife*, the child seems to be realizing that adding *s* makes the word mean more than one. The third method, analogy, involves seeing a similarity between the word to be changed and a word that is known. For example, in Jean Berko's classic study, the child is shown a picture and told that it is a *wug* [7]. He is then shown another picture just like the first. If the child then says that there are two *wugs*, he may be using analogy by comparing *wug* to *bug—bugs*, making the plural of *wug* in the same way that he knows in relation to *bug*. MacWhinney's study dealt with many additional regularities of children's learning to put words together. The "language acquisition device" is becoming more available for analysis. The methods of rote, combination, and analogy are not special to language, but are used in solving other kinds of problems.

Two decades ago psychologist Ruth Weir tape-recorded what her young son Anthony, age 2½, said while alone in his crib, before he went to sleep [61]. Weir's book, *Language in the Crib*, gave psychologists a fascinating view of one little boy's devices for languages acquisition. He practiced sounds, words, and grammar. Some of Anthony's systematic manipulations of language resembled grammars and drills written for the study of a foreign language. Here are some examples.

ANTHONY'S SPONTANEOUS EXERCISES IN GRAMMAR*
Noun substitution:
  What color. What color blanket. What color mop. What color glass.
Noun modifiers:
  There's a hat. There's another. There's a hat. There's another hat. That's a hat.
Verb substitution:
  Go get coffee. Go buy some coffee.
Practice of negatives:
  Like it. Don't like it. Like it daddy.
Question-and-answer dialogue:
  There is the light. Where is the light. Here is the light.
Sound play:
  Train. Anthony can see the plane. Plane. Plane. See bubble. Bubble's here. Bubbles. Flowers. Bed flowers.
Comment on his own achievements:
  One two three four. One two. One two three four. One two three. Anthony counting. Good boy you. One two three.

Communicating with Others. Language involves much more than learning rules, because language is used for communicating meaning to other people. Young children use gestures, such as pointing, for communicating, even when they are also able to use words. Gestures often work quite well when the object of the communication can be seen. Speech is needed when simply pointing to an object is not enough to express the meaning that the child wants to communicate. Speech is often not adequate when children have very small vocabularies. At this point, words

*R. H. Weir. *Language in the crib*. The Hague: Mouton, 1962.

may be *overextended*. *Do* is overextended to take the place of several verbs that refer to a person acting on objects. Other general purpose verbs are *go* and *make*. The child says "Make that," pointing to the hand on a clock, apparently requesting the adult to move the hand on to another place on the dial [15]. A young child must often experience failure in communicating when his language is inadequate and when the other person cannot get enough cues from gestures and/or context. Or the other person may not try very hard to understand.

Until recent years young children were thought to be egocentric or unable to take the hearer's perspective when speaking. Piaget and Inhelder wrote, "The fact is that the speech of subjects between four and six (observed in situations in which children work, play, and speak freely) is not intended to provide information, ask questions, etc. (that is, it is not socialized language), but consists rather of monologues or 'collective monologues' in the course of which everyone talks to himself without listening to the others (that is, egocentric language)." [47, pp. 121–122].

Although children do at times speak for purposes other than communication, this does not mean that they are incapable of taking the other person's perspective when trying to communicate. An impressive demonstration of linguistic perspective-taking occurred in a bilingual kindergarten, where children were found switching languages spontaneously according to the one best understood by the listener [25]. We ourselves have seen the same performance by a 4-year-old boy in India. An example of 4-year-olds adapting their language to the listener was given under the heading "Perspective Taking" in this chapter.

The communicative abilities of 2-year-olds were demonstrated by Wellman and Lempers, who analyzed videotapes of spontaneous behavior of young children in a toddler play group [63]. They looked for incidents when a child tried to show something to another. Communicators' behavior included getting attention by both verbal (Hey; you; child's name) and nonverbal (waving; banging; touching) means, pointing out, showing, taking, or orienting the object to the receiver, taking the receiver to the object, removing an obstacle, making verbal comments, and looking at the receiver. The communicators addressed 80 per cent of their messages to adults and 20 to peers. Most (79 per cent) of the messages received adequate responses. In over half the cases where the message got no response, the communicator made further efforts. In all cases where the receiver indicated nonunderstanding, the communicator tried again. These results show considerable communicative competence in young children. They obviously tried to send meaningful messages to others by engaging them in interacting, formulating messages to fit the recipient, and using feedback to reformulate. In showing an object, the referent is outside the subject, in contrast to an idea, which would be inside. The language and cognitive limitations of 2-year-olds limit their ability to communicate ideas, but they can deal with objects.

As children develop during the years between infancy and school age, the meaning and content of the language change, keeping pace with the children's personal growth and developing knowledge and understanding of the world. The content, meaning, and purposes of spontaneous speech have been traced in 100 children between 2 and 5 in a nursery school setting [54]. Three groups of subjects were studied, advantaged white, advantaged black, and disadvantaged black. Analysis of 2,000 statements yielded nine categories of motives, grouped into personal, social, and other. Two-year-olds used these categories: *Reporting*, "I have new shoes."; "Look at the cement mixer."; *desire*, "Can I have some?"; *possession rights*, "That's my wagon."; "Me too."; "I have new shoes, too."; *learning statements*, "How does this go?"

Several age trends appeared. Younger children directed more comments to adults than did older children; older children directed more comments to other children than did young children. The age trend, therefore, was to talk less to adults and more to other children. Self-differentiation increased with age, showing a marked increase at age 3, the time of onset of the sense of initiative in Erikson's scheme. At this point, children made many more ego-enhancing comments, including boasting, teasing, denigrating others, and assuming the teacher-role. "When I grow up, I'm going to be a pilot." "Look at my big house." Social motives also change with age, with a marked change at 3 or 3½. Two-year-olds made many self-referring statements of an immature category. "Me too." "I listen to Batman, too." Statements of joining and collaborating, showing more maturity, increased with age. "Let's play house." "Give me some more, mommy; stop that, baby." By 4 or 5, children began to adapt their speech much more to the needs of the listener. Thus, the children's spontaneous remarks showed increasing verbal interaction with self-other differentiation.

Private Speech. Some of young children's language is not directed to other people; its purpose is not to communicate with others. It is this type of talking that Piaget called egocentric, meaning centered on the self, or from the point of view of the self. The term *private speech* also refers to language that is not directed to other people, but this term does not imply a cognitive limitation. Rather, it leaves open the possibility tht private speech serves other purposes. Adults, as well as children, sometimes talk to themselves, using words for thinking, problem-solving, guiding their own behavior, and even for pleasure, as in reciting poetry.

Rubin and Dyck investigated the private speech of 20 children, age 41 to 63 months, by recording their behavior during play sessions in a room with attractive toys [50]. A minimally responsive adult was the only person present. Speech not addressed to the adult was considered private speech and was analyzed by type of play and function of the speech. Rubin and Dyck found that the children used speech to direct and comment on their own actions ("Go get that truck now."), to comment on the toys and materials ("Oh look, it's wiggly."), and in pretending to talk for animals and toys, which may be practice for social discourse. Self-directing speech occurred while exploring toys and materials, while playing with them, and while making transitions from one kind of play to another ("Putting horsie in and then be Farmer Jack.").

Private speech may help children to form concepts. Although children and nonhuman primates can form visual concepts without verbal labels, they seem to be unable to form temporal concepts without verbal labels [8]. For example, preschool children, not using labels, easily distinguished between one and two circles or other objects, but not between one and two flashes of light. Poor ability to deal with time sequences has also been found in older children with language deficiencies. Children play with sounds and words, creating beauty and pleasure for themselves and unintentionally delighting adults who overhear them.

Ellen enjoys rhythm and imagery as she chants her moon song.

> Crescent, crescent, crescent, crescent,
> Crescent goes to sleep, crescent wakes up.
> Ballie, ballie, ballie, ballie,
> Ballie goes to sleep, ballie wakes up.

Donald creates fresh images in his fog poem.

> Fog on the hill
> Moving toward morning
> Sliding down the valley
> Rolling like a barrel
> And there's some more
> Covering up the green.

The sound play in Anthony's crib language was prominent. He seemed to be playing with sound when he said, ". . . in a pretty box—and cakes—what a sticks for cakes—for the click." Recently Anthony's sayings have been reanalyzed as poetry [1]. Anthony showed progress as a poet during the two months in which his mother recorded his utterances. He advanced in his use of alliteration, rhyme, meter, and other poetic devices.

Receptive language or hearing what others say, affords similar pleasures in sound play, rhythm, and imagery and equips children with devices to produce more pleasure for themselves. Children enjoy hearing the traditional nursery rhymes and the modern Dr. Seuss. They repeat satisfying passages, lingering over the intriguing bustard who only eats custard with sauce made of mustard. They sing songs and play records that give them pleasure through sound.

Ecology of Language Development. Akbar, the great Mogul emperor of India, had a hypothesis concerning the origins of language.

His Majesty said that speech came to every tribe from hearing, and that each remembered from another from the beginning of existence. If they arrange that human speech did not reach them, they certainly would not have the power of speech. [2, p. 58].

Because some of the wise men in his court were skeptical, Akbar undertook an experiment in child development. He ordered that a group of newborn infants be placed in a community of dumb persons to be raised to age 4 without ever hearing language spoken. When the children reached 4 years, not one of them spoke a word! Akbar had proved what is commonplace knowledge today. An essential condition for learning to talk is to live in a language environment. Language environments differ between macrosystems and between microsystems. The growing child is influenced by both.

The child's primary language, or mother tongue, is the language of his society. If he lives in a society where more than one language is usual, such as in Switzerland, then he learns more than one from an early age.

As previously stated, there are common features of language learning, but there are also some distinctive ones. In MacWhinney's cross-cultural comparisons, he found that certain forms are acquired earlier in some languages than in others [38]. For example, Latvian children learn *is* and *is not* at an earlier age than do German children. The most likely reason is that these words also function as *yes* and *no* in Latvian, but not in German. Another example is the learning of tone, which occupies a minor role in English, but a very important role in Mandarin Chinese. Chinese children make significant errors when first applying tonal patterns to sentences.

Differences in dialect occur on the macrosystem level of social class and ethnic group. Black English, for example, differs from standard English in grammar and vocabulary. Even though a child may speak Black English or another dialect correctly and fluently when he goes to school,

he is at a disadvantage if he does not speak standard English, the language in which the school operates.

Social-class differences are seen in language use and teaching styles of parents. In general, middle-class mothers, in contrast to lower-class, speak in more complex, elaborated language, anticipate errors, give more instruction and less negative feedback.

Conceptual Development

Efforts to make sense out of the world result in the world's becoming more consistent, regular, and predictable to the young child. She sees common features of certain objects, actions, and experiences, and generalizes from them. A concept of birds is built from experiences with a number of flying creatures who possess beaks and feathers. Concepts of *up* and *down* come from one's own bodily movements and from moving objects. Regular development in various types of concepts has been traced through the preschool years, giving some hints as to the underlying processes.

Categories. The tendency to group objects (to place them in categories) can be seen even during the sensorimotor period. For example, when given 2 sets of dissimilar objects, 1-year-olds touched several clay balls in succession, and several yellow cubes [48].

When young children group or classify objects, or otherwise show that they judge objects to be similar, they do it intuitively. Piaget's term for this period, approximately 4 to 7 years, is the period of intuitive thought. In an intuitive judgment of sameness, the person looks at the objects as wholes, instead of analyzing them in terms of color, size, shape, or any other dimension or detail. If two items look the same (or perhaps if they act the same), they are judged to be the same. Development in categorizing follows the developmental principle of differentiation and integration. In the preschool period, children group on overall impressions; in the period of concrete operations, in the school age, they compare on different dimensions and consider more than one aspect of each object when sorting them into groups. The older children *differentiate* the objects into dimensions and then integrate the details of information into a judgment about the object. Smith and Kemler devised an experiment to show that younger children saw things whole whereas older children analyzed and put results together [58]. They used objects that varied in size and brightness, planned that some were very similar on both dimensions (for example, a half-inch, light gray square and a 1-inch, white square) and some identical on one dimension but very different on the other (for example, same-sized white and black squares). When asked to "put together the ones that go together," the young children grouped the white and gray squares, while the older ones grouped by one dimension, either color or form. The intuitive, global approach of young children is consistent with their efforts to make sense out of the world. In their explorations and efforts to understand, it is useful to organize by wholes, to

Categories of young child are global; of older child, differentiated

appreciate similarities in appearances and actions of dogs, cars, and other groups of items that recur in the child's world. Children as young as 3 will group by similarity when tested with categories with which they have had real experiences, such as cats, fish, and airplanes [49]. They will also group by complementarity or relation of function rather than analyzing arrays of objects for details that match. For example, when asked what goes together from a collection of dolls and toy furniture, a 3-year-old would put a doll with a crib, whereas a 6-year-old might group crib, chair, and table.

Researchers have long been intrigued with the question of whether children will group on the basis of color or form. The basic method is to require a choice such as the one shown in the margin. A recent study of Israeli children [41] replicated the results of a study of American children done in 1929 [11]. At ages 2, 4, and 5 children tended to match by form; at age 3 they matched by color. So far, there seems to be no satisfactory explanation of the rise and fall of color preference during the preschool years.

Which of

goes with

Time Concepts. The earliest experiences of time are most likely those of bodily rhythms, states that recur in regular patterns, such as hunger, eating, fullness. Interactions with the environment impose some patterns on bodily rhythms, as the child's rhythms become entrained to the family's rhythms. Other early experiences that form the basis of time perception include dealing with a succession of objects, such as filling a basket with blocks; taking part in an action that continues and then stops, such as pushing or pulling a wheeled toy; hearing sounds of varying lengths. These experiences, each a seriation of events, are one type of operation that is basic to the notion of time, according to Piaget [47, p. 198]. Events such as these constitute the order of temporal succession. A second type of experience basic to time concepts comes from temporal metrics, the repetitions of stimuli in patterns, such as music and dance, or even rhythms of patting that a parent might do to a child in arms.

Understanding of terms of temporal succession was tested in children of ages from 3 to 5 by having them perform actions with toys [21]. The terms were these: before, after, together with, first, last, ahead of, and behind. An example of a temporal task was to "make the doll get up the way I tell you," when dolls named Mary and John were lying in little beds. The examiner would say, "Mary gets up before John." Three-year-olds did better than chance in demonstrating understanding of *before*, *after*, *first*, and *last*. Understanding of temporal terms developed gradually throughout the age period 3 to 5, but was not complete at the end of that time. This method of examining temporal concepts is very precise in comparison to observational studies that record the child's time-related behavior and use of temporal terms. An older study, using observation of middle-class nursery school children, gives a very comprehensive picture of the temporal concepts that the child uses in spontaneous

TABLE 8–1
Temporal Terms and
Behaviors Used by
Members of a Nursery
School Group.

Age in months	Temporal terms and behaviors
24	Going to, in a minute, now, today.
30	Morning, afternoon, some day, one day, tomorrow, last night.
	Uses more future words than past words.
36	All the time, all day, for 2 weeks, what time, it's time, lunch time.
	Pretends to tell time. Tells age.
42	For a long time, for years, a whole week, in the meantime, it's almost time, a nice long time, on Fridays.
	Uses past and future tenses accurately. Some confusion in expressing succession of events.
48	Month, last summer, next summer.
	Understands sequence of daily events.

Source: L. B. Ames. The development of the sense of time in the young child. *Journal of Genetic Psychology,* 1946, **68,** 97–125.

speech. Table 8–1 shows time concepts used in speech at ages between 2 and 4. These concepts include duration, as well as succession.

Experiments on understanding of duration have shown that the young child makes judgments about duration intuitively or globally, just as she does in regard to categories [37]. If a toy car goes faster than another toy car, the child is likely to say that the trip lasted longer, whether it actually does or not, because there was more of a very salient dimension. Taking the experience as a whole, *more* meant *more,* and duration was included. In other words, time-related cues were not differentiated from cues that were unrelated to time.

Space Concepts. By the end of infancy, the child has acquired some concepts of his own body and how it moves, some notions of objects and how they move, and some experience in moving through space and manipulating objects. At this point, Piaget and Inhelder maintain, the child has *topological* knowledge of space [47]. Topological knowledge has to do with spatial relations between objects or details of objects. Piaget illustrated topological knowledge by the way in which a child draws a human figure. The two eyes are always shown side by side, in proximity, separated from each other, and enclosed by the head. There is continuity between legs and body. A second kind of spatial knowledge is *projective*, in which the child sees the placement of objects in relation to her own point of view. If the child is in position 1, object A is in front of B. If the child is in Position 2, object B is in front of A. Terms of projective space are these: in front of, behind, above, below, left, and right. In a third system, *Euclidean* space, an object can be located in reference to other objects, without reference to the person, in terms of coordination of three axes, the vertical from below to above and the two horizontals, from in-front-of to behind, and from left to right. Systems of projective and Euclidean space develop during the preschool years, but not completely.

Spatial knowledge: Topological, projective, Euclidean

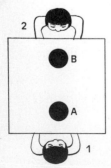

The progression in development of coordinated space concepts was demonstrated in several experiments by Acredolo [3]. She was interested in how a child came to know the spatial environment surrounding him. She tested children between 3 and 5 years in a room laid out as in the diagram. From Position 1 the child was trained to turn either right or left to find a trinket in one of the cups. The child was then changed to Position 2 and asked to find the trinket, which had been placed in the same cup in which it had previously been found. If the child went to the correct cup, she was coordinating projective and Euclidean space. All the 5-year-olds adjusted to the change in point of view, turning in the opposite direction from which they had been trained, and choosing the correct cup. Sixty per cent of 4-year-olds succeeded, and 50 per cent of 3-year-olds. When landmarks were added, the younger children improved their performances, apparently aided by topological cues. Acredolo points out that when space concepts are tested with a small model, the child still has topological cues in the larger environment of the room in which he is. Only when the whole surrounding space forms the experimental environment, is it possible to test the use of projective and Euclidean space without the child's getting assistance from topological space. In further study of how the child becomes familiar with his surrounding space, children explored unfamiliar territory [4]. Half of them went alone, and half held an adult's hand. Active exploration improved spatial memory for 3- and 4-year-olds. The older children apparently had an effective, flexible method of encoding spatial information, but the younger ones' attention to relevant cues was aided by self-directed activity.

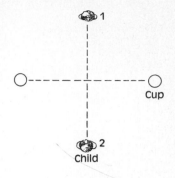

A sex difference was found in one study of the ways in which 5- and 6-year-olds remember and represent their large-scale environment [56]. Boys did better than girls in remembering and constructing a model of their kindergarten classroom, including a detailed arrangement of furniture and equipment. Although a sex difference in spatial ability is established for adolescents, and possibly for older children, it has rarely been demonstrated in young children. The authors suggest that the difficulty of the spatial task overloaded the relatively less powerful spatial systems of the girls.

Quantity Concepts. Concepts of quantity may be numerical, but not necessarily so. *More or less* and *all, some,* or *none* refer to quantity, but not to numbers. A child can choose the dish with more ice cream in it, rather than the dish with less, even before she can respond differentially to the words *more* and *less*. *More* is understood earlier than *less*.

A concept of *another* is built during the preschool years. The young child does not know whether a succession of objects that look alike are one and the same object or a series of objects. Jacqueline, age 2½, walking in the woods with her father, was looking for slugs (snails). Catching sight of one she commented, "There it is." Seeing another, several yards away, she cried, "There's the slug again." Piaget took her back to see the first one again and asked if the second was the same or another. She answered "yes" to both questions. Jacqueline had no concept of a class of slugs [45, p. 225]. A 2-year-old ordinarily has the concept of "another" when it is a case of wanting a cookie for each hand, or asking for more. The difference between cookies in the hands and slugs on Jacqueline's walk is that the two cookies are present at the same time, whereas the slugs were seen in succession.

Young children are interested in counting and do so spontaneously. Anthony's bed-time talk, described in the section on Language, included counting, and praise of himself for counting. Two-year-olds are known to count 2 objects, and 4-year-olds, 4. When young children count large numbers of objects, they are not always accurate. From extensive studies of children's behavior with numbers, Gelman and her associates have shown that children as young as 2½ follow 5 principles of counting, even though they may not have developed all the strategies needed to apply the principles correctly [22, 23]. The principles are these:

1. One-to-one correspondence. Each item must be given one unique tag.
2. Stable order. The tags given must be from a stably ordered list.
3. Cardinal principle. The last tag given designates the number of items in the array counted.
4. Abstraction. Any set of items can be counted.
5. Order-irrelevance. The items to be counted can be tagged in any order, as long as each is tagged once and only once.

The first principle is usually applied by pointing to each item as it is counted. Almost all 3- and 4-year-olds point as they count, but only 16 per cent of 3-year-olds and 63 per cent of 4-year-olds counted accurately arrays up to 13 items [52]. The child may know that a stably ordered list should be used in counting, but make mistakes in producing the conventional list of numbers. Or she may invent her own list and apply it properly, but a list such as 2, 7, 11, or A, B, C does not give the right answer. Inventing one's own rules in counting has parallels in language, in that children for a time apply their own modifications of rules for making plurals and tenses [22].

How-to-count principles form a scheme

Gelman suggests that the how-to-count principles form a scheme that serves as a guide and motivation to counting behavior. The child uses the scheme to evaluate and eventually correct her own counting. She counts, and searches for more things to count. Children apply the rules of counting before they are aware of them. Application is made by 2-year-olds, but children are 4 or 5 before they can use the principles to justify their actions. Again, this progression reminds us of language development, in which rules are applied from the moment of first combining words, but in which understanding of the guiding rules comes much later.

Causality Concepts. Young children express knowledge of cause and effect in their spontaneous statements and questions, and in their replies to questions. In order to chart the development of verbal expressions of knowledge of causality, Bloom and Hood followed the spontaneous speech of 8 children from about 24 to 41 months [9]. They analyzed recorded samples, beginning when causal utterances were first made. Most of the children started to make causal statements at 25 months of age, one at 24, and one at 29 months. Examples of causal statements are these:

PETER, at 25 months (*putting pen away and looking for another*): Get another one. It dirty.
ERIC, at 31 months (*pretending*): I'm putting medicine on the lamb's leg 'cause he had a booboo. [9, p. 5]

The adults in the children's lives began to ask *why* questions as soon as the children began to make causal statements. All but one child began to answer *why* questions in terms of cause and effect at least 2 months after the adults began to ask *why* questions, at about 30 months of age.

ERIC, at 28 months: There's no more juice for you.
L.: Why?
ERIC: 'Cause I drink it all. [9, p. 6]

With one exception, the children asked *why* questions only after they could give well-formed answers to adults *why's*.

DAVID, at 39 months, wants 2 pieces of bread.
M.: I'll cut it for you, so you'll have two.
DAVID: No, don't cut them. Why you go and cut them? [9, p.7]

The children varied in the form and use of their statements and questions. They first focused on their own intentions and gradually progressed toward taking the listener's intentions into account. They anticipated imminent events before they reflected on immediate past events.

Young children realize that a cause precedes an effect, but they often are not able to verbalize their understanding, and they may have little knowledge of the situation referred to. When experiments are designed to make it easy for children to reason about events that are meaningful to them, they show that they consider temporal order in assigning causality [12, 34]. For example, Kun put a picture of each event of three-term causal sequences on a card. One such sequence was this: Scott pulled the dog's tail; the dog bit Scott; Scott cried. The child pointed to a card when asked these questions: Why did . . . happen? What happened next? Gallukadi prond (a nonsense question)? Children as young as 2 were likely to choose the antecedent event as the cause. By 3, children comprehended clearly.

Play

The subject of play intrigues philosophers, ethologists, and anthropologists, as well as child psychologists and teachers. Play is usually a freely chosen activity, carried on for its own sake, not for products or results. The problem of defining play is almost insuperable, because it varies greatly in form and function, and we have to consider not only the player's actions, but his interactions, intentions, and feelings. Compare blowing bubbles with playing chess! We know that higher animals play more than lower animals, and children more than adults. Play serves the development of creatures who have a lot to learn and who benefit from flexible, innovative behavior. At the same time, the play of the young contributes to adults, giving joy and introducing their elders to new territory and new ideas. In playing together, the partners cooperate to create new patterns. Our special interest at this point is in the function of play and types of play in the mental development of the young child. In the next chapter we shall be concerned with the role of play in social development. The two areas, of course, are not separated in real life. The whole child plays, and through play, integrates her whole life.

Functions

The following list may not be complete, but it covers many functions of play that contribute to the well-being and development of the child.

Enjoyment. Play is fun. There is no doubt that play brings pleasure. Pleasure comes from doing what one wishes to do, and freedom to choose is part of play. Enjoyment is easy to see in the simplest and most univer-

sal type of play, self-motion. Young children love to swing and slide; old people rock and drum their fingers; dolphins and whales leap from the sea into the air; lambs and goats jump over hummocks and one another. We laugh and smile as we see all these actions, knowing that they are fun.

Exploration. Play is a way of getting information about new environments, objects, and people. With their limited experience, young children encounter many new situations. Their curiosity, or desire to explore and discover, is fitting at a time when the world is so full of unknowns. The preschool stage of personality development, in Erikson's theory [19], is the development of the sense of initiative. To this end, the young child explores by moving through space, acting upon the world, experiencing it through his senses, thinking and reasoning about his experiences, and extending both experience and understanding through symbolic play. Types of symbolic play will be discussed later.

Consolidating New Skills. Through practice during play, children improve developing skills and weave them into larger units. A child will ride his tricycle round and round until he controls it well enough to carry a passenger on the back, and he pretends as a member of a socially interacting pair, engaged in dramatic play. A young child will practice to attain a level of mastery appropriate for the ways in which he wants to use a particular skill. Counting is a skill that seems to be especially desired. Children practice it often.

Problem Solving. Puzzles and games pose problems to be solved, but in a nonthreatening context. Children choose to engage in problem solving, regarding it as play. A playful, exploratory attitude makes it possible to think flexibly; play contributes to later problem solving that is required as a task, as shown by the following experiment. Four-year-olds were given a task of getting a marble out of a box [60]. To solve it, they would have to join 3 sticks by fitting them into blocks, making a tool long enough to open the box that contained the marble. One group was allowed to play with the materials before trying to get the marble. The other group was given instructions on placing the sticks in order of length. The children who played solved the problem more quickly and with fewer hints from the experimenter. The children who played had the advantage of more flexible behavior, and probably were also more motivated.

Symbolic play, in the form of fantasy and artistic expression, is used to solve problems of feelings and relationships that cannot be addressed through direct reasoning. A child (or adult) may be unable to verbalize a problem or to see it in steps, and yet be able to express it and gain insight through a dream, drama, or dance.

Creative Use of Symbols. The use of symbols in play is also called imaginative behavior, or creativity. Teachers of young children have long had a sense of the centrality of imaginative play in the life of the child, realizing that spontaneity and freedom of choice facilitate growth through play. Although there has been little corroborating research until recently, traditional nursery school teachers have maintained that play is the mode in which young children learn best. Presently, theorists are seeing symbolic play as an essential psychological function that integrates thinking and feeling.

The sensorimotor stage ends with the toddler using symbols, the words learned from his family, the sounds that he himself makes stand for actions and objects, the play materials he uses to represent objects in his play. From this time on, the child uses symbols in almost everything he does. Any stimulus can serve as a symbol. The essence of a symbol is that it communicate something of the nature of the entity to which it refers [59]. A symbol has two parts, the vehicle and the referent. For example, a child paints a picture of a house. The pattern made by paint on paper is the *vehicle* by which the child *refers* to his experience of a house or houses. Through his painting, he communicates his concept of house to others who look at the painting. He might have used blocks or clay for the vehicle. Among the media used for vehicles are language, movement, music, dance, graphic materials, sand, and water.

Symbol: Vehicle and referent

In making a symbol out of paint, paper, and his experience of house, a child performs a creative act. Having done so, his concepts of house and of painting are enriched. Symbolic activity is an important mode of expression, understanding, and intellectual development for everyone, but especially for young children, who are not able to use forms of logic and abstraction that are available to their elders.

Types of Symbolic Play

In using a particular medium, the child makes and perceives symbols that belong to a particular symbol system—graphic, musical, numerical, gestural, linguistic, sculptural, and so on. Different media are suited to communicating different messages. If a variety of media are available, the child can be expected to use them freely in working out conflicts and tensions, in trying to understand puzzling experiences, in expressing feelings, and finding pleasure and comfort.

Creating with Art Materials. When a child first encounters paint, clay, or any new material, he explores it to find out what it is like, and what he can do with it. (Not only children. Watch an African student in the first snowfall of a North American winter!) After learning something about how to control the medium, the child begins to use it symbolically. A series of stages can be identified in children's painting, sculpture, carpentry, and block building. Stages for the graphic arts follow:

1. SCRIBBLING, FROM 1 TO 3 YEARS. During the first quarter of the second year, a baby will make marks with a crayon on a paper, after a demonstration or encouragement to do so. By 18 months, he will scribble spon-

Scribbling

taneously. Even if paper and crayons are not given, 2-year-olds will make marks in the sand, on a sidewalk or wall. The young child shows great interest in what he has made. He tries out different types of strokes and placements [32]. The two-year-old makes 20 basic scribbles.

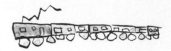

2. SHAPE AND DESIGN. From 2 to 5 years. The child uses the lines that he has developed through his scribbling and makes shapes and designs from them. Even though he cannot write, the average kindergartner can tell printed characters from scribbling [26]. In a kindergarten of high socioeconomic status, 75 per cent of the children could distinguish cursive writing from scribbling. When children are making shapes and designs, they do so for the pleasure of making them and not to represent something. A child develops his own style and preferences while discovering how to make more complex designs.

3. PICTORIAL, FROM AGE 4 ONWARD. Now the child uses his lines, shapes, and designs to represent reality. Drawings of people are usually the first recognizable pictures. All over the world, children make their early drawings in the same ways. Their pictures of people, houses, trees, suns, boats, trains, and cars give little hint as to whether the young artists were American, Scottish, or Indonesian.

Pretending. In make-believe or fantasy play, children transform people and things by way of gestures and speech, producing an action or an interaction between symbolic characters within symbolic environments. The earliest kind of pretending occurs at the end of the sensorimotor stage, when the child imitates his own past actions in very simple, concrete ways. Thus, he shows that he has mental images of these actions. For instance, he pretends to go to sleep, curling up in the doll bed or on a pillow, shutting his eyes momentarily. He pretends to drink out of a cup and to eat from a plate. Thus, the first objects used for pretending are real pillows or cups. The next step in pretending is to play that another object is a pillow or a cup while pretending to sleep or drink. In so doing, the child is using an action symbolically at the same time that he is transforming an object into a symbol. In choosing objects to use for symbols in pretend play, children take the most appropriate item available [27]. If the play calls for a cat, then a real cat or a toy cat would be preferred to a doll. The object is not chosen at random, as though any old thing would do.

Between 2 and 4 years, simple imitation and object transformation give way to elaborate role play. Transformations made by 4-year-olds were observed during free play in the absence of an adult, for 3 consecutive days [40]. Play partners were strangers at first. Transformations were performed on materials and on ideas, the latter increasing as play partners became more familiar with each other. Examples of transforming a material are these: Making a cupboard into an oven, pretending a toy camera would take pictures, and pretending that a block was Charlie Brown. An ideational transformation is shown in the following scene: "Pretend I'm a lady, okay? Pretend I'm the lady who serves you," says Susan as she and

Nancy embark on a restaurant fantasy in which Susan is the waitress and Nancy the customer [40].

When pretending with one another, children cooperate, communicate, each taking the perspective of the other and simultaneously taking perspectives of the roles they are playing. Children know when they are pretending, and the difference between real and make-believe. A child can step out of a role to speak to the teacher and go back into it smoothly. Pretend play is a situation in which the preschool child can think an action and think it undone. That is, the child's thoughts are reversible. Reversibility of thought in reasoning and problem solving is not attained until the Piagetian stage of concrete operations. Hypothesizing that reversibility of thinking in make-believe play is the precursor of operational reversibility, Golomb and Cornelius asked children questions about their symbolic play, making them aware of their mental operations while pretending [28]. The children made immediate improvement on tests of conservation, such as the test with the glasses of liquid, mentioned in "Attention" earlier in this chapter. Having been made aware of their own reversible transformations on ideas and materials, they became more able to see that the transformation in the water (and other test materials) was also reversible. The experiment documents the cognitive benefits of pretend play, making them as clear as the social and emotional benefits.

Reversible thought appears first in pretending

Imaginary Companions. An imaginary playmate is a special kind of pretend play, in which a child symbolizes a person, or perhaps an animal who provides companionship. Because firstborns and children with younger siblings more often create imaginary playmates than do children with older siblings, it seems likely that loneliness prompts the creation [39]. An imaginary friend could be a partner in play, a sympathetic listening ear, and a target for the expression of otherwise unmanageable feelings.

Questionnaires answered by parents of preschool children indicated that equal percentages of boys and girls, 28 per cent of the total group, had one or more imaginary playmates [39]. The children rarely played with imaginary companions when they had opportunities to play with real children. Outstanding characteristics of children with imaginary playmates were: they initiated more play on their own and engrossed themselves in it; they engaged in more different activities with household members; boys were more capable (than boys without imaginary playmates) of talking and interacting with adults. Half of the children had just one imaginary playmate; a quarter had two. Boys created companions in the ratio 3.5 boys to one girl; girls created 1.3 girls to one boy. Most of the parents (62 per cent) thought that the imaginary playmate was good for their child. Only 4 per cent of the parents thought that the playmate had a harmful effect.

Stories and Poems. In discussing language development, we have already mentioned that language is a symbolic system, and that poetic devices can be noticed early in the sound play of young children. Symbolism is used in the stories and poems that children create, serving the expression of problems and feelings, and working toward solutions.

At the end of the sensorimotor period the child reconstructs past events by deferred imitation. When she pretends, she is considering what *might* happen rather than what *did* happen. A young child tells stories through props that she endows with qualities of live participants, while she herself becomes not an actor, but a narrator [51]. There is a difference between pretending in symbolic play and telling a story [53]. In pretend play the child moves in and out of roles in the story and roles of narrator and stage manager; in telling a story the child must keep within the role of narrator. Development as a narrator moves from using material props to acting out the story, to using ideas expressed in language. In other words, the symbols of the youngest story tellers are tangible, outside the child. These symbols are gradually replaced with intangible symbols, from within. Even older preschool children need a few props for a story. As the child gains control of the narrator role, she also uses metanarrative, making comments about the story to the audience, such as "Let's pretend," or "These are the princess' jewels."

Deferred imitation: What did happen
Pretend play: What might happen

Music and Dance. The baby encounters a symbol system in the music of the family's singing, playing instruments, or playing the television and radio. The family's music comes from its macrosystem. Eastern and Western music differ considerably. From infancy, the child listens and responds with gesture and voice. A Balinese baby participates in symbolic gestures as his parents guide his body through stylized motions. American parents also teach gestural symbols as they play pat-a-cake and later take part in action songs with their toddlers. In Bali children go to the traditional dance dramas, along with everyone else in the village. In India all ages turn out for the annual performance of the Ram Lila, a religious song and dance drama. Children and adults experience their religious heritage through the symbols of music, dance, and drama.

Music and dance are important in the programs of preschools and kindergartens. Children are offered varieties of experiences with listening, group singing, action songs, making and playing simple instruments, exploring bodily movement, and making songs out of bodily rhythms and dances out of small and large events. Children use music and dance symbolically to express their feelings and to experience a variety of feelings. Sylvia Ashton-Warner, a great teacher, says, "More than any other medium, dance is the one complete surfacing of all that we are, and is often the most healing of media." [6].

Children gain in ability to use music and dance symbolically when they learn skills of music and gesture. Teachers also use singing and movement to teach cognitive skills. For example, songs are built from the colors children are wearing, numbers are chanted, right is discriminated from left in Looby Lou.

Humor. Humor reduces anxiety and tension, transforming unpleasant feelings into more pleasant ones. The subject matter of young children's jokes reflects their concerns because they, like older people, create symbols out of words and actions that represent life's problems. Young children laugh about falling down, falling apart and growing together, getting lost and found, being hurt and getting well, toilet accidents or deliberate excretions, using inappropriate names, and saying forbidden words. Underlying such humor are children's envy of adult size, power, and privileges; worry over the wholeness and safety of their bodies; frightening aggressive impulses, and resentment of adult control in the face of their own striving for autonomy.

Three main types of humor were derived from observations of nursery school children's participation in humorous events [29]. The definition of humor events included surprising or unexpected events at which children smiled or laughed, and incongruous or inappropriate behavior that seemed to be intentional. The three main types of humor were *responsive, productive,* and *hostile.* Responsive humor included responses to events, people, statements, stories, songs, and animals. Examples were finding a "baby peanut" in a shell, someone's falling over a chair, and a funny story. Productive humor included silliness and clowning, teasing, word play, absurd creations, and displacement of injury to self-esteem. Hostile humor included humorous threats or attacks, making fun of someone else, and rebellion against authority. Productive humor was most common. Boys displayed more productive and hostile humor than girls; girls showed more responsive humor than boys. The most frequent type of responsive humor was response to events; the most frequent types of productive humor were silliness and absurdity. There was no evidence for a generalized trait that could be called sense of humor. In the nursery school, situations that elicited most productive humor were unstructured, such as free play and playing with blocks. Responsive humor occurred more often when the situation allowed for unexpected events.

Ecology

Ideology affects children's play. If the play is believed to be a valuable contributor to children's happiness, health, and growth, then school systems will make provision for play and community planning will take account of play space in neighborhoods. Beliefs about gender-appropriate behavior determine restrictions placed on the play of boys and girls. Degree of prosperity and of industrialization will affect play space, play materials, and subject matter for symbolic activities.

On the microsystem level, play is affected by settings and persons. In order to facilitate play, parents and teachers set the stage, making a safe place in which the child can explore, pretend, create with toys, materials, and playmates. Adults can be playmates, as well as other children. In promoting play, a certain amount of order is helpful, but not too much. The art of teaching young children includes giving freedom to create, along with props and equipment.

The ecology of play can be studied from the standpoint of physical settings, types of environment, and their arrangement in a nursery school. It can also be viewed in terms of the persons interacting within the setting, their ages, sex, number, and personal characteristics. Several studies of parent-child interactions consider children's willingness to spend time and effort in an unstructured situation. Children are more likely to be curious, exploratory, and competent when parents are supportive, warm, nonintrusive, and encouraging of children's exploration and autonomy [18, 30]. Curiosity and exploration are strongly related to play.

Summary

Young children are eager to explore the world of people, objects, and space, to make sense out of it, and to control it. They reason about the information gained from social and sensory experience.

Mental operations come under increasing control, gaining in power and flexibility. Representational thought elaborates as symbols are used in the places of people, objects, and actions. Symbols take the form of actions, verbalizations, writing, and expression in various media. Control of attention and thinking develops as children gain ability to inhibit action and to wait before choosing and deciding. Metacognition, the awareness and understanding of mental processes in self and others, increases with age and experience. Already competent in storing memories, young children develop strategies for recall. They can be helped to acquire and improve the strategies of planning, categorizing, and searching. Young children can take the perspective of another person in situations that have real meaning for them, but they cannot do so in abstract situations that do not make sense to them.

Young children learn language rapidly, becoming fluent by 5 in the languages to which they have been exposed. The biological base for language is uniquely human. Language is first embedded in experience, and must be abstracted out of it to be recognized as separate. A child must discover that a word is a word, and next that words can be written, and written words read. Children use rules for generating language long before they are aware of rules. Early language-learning strategies are the same across cultures. Language is used not only in communicating with others, but also in private speech. Language serves in self-direction, thinking, remembering, concept formation, play, and pleasure. Language development occurs only in a language environment, the language of the macrosystem and of the child's microsystems. Social class and ethnic group modify the language of the society.

A child builds concepts by generalizing from experiences that seem regular and predictable. Objects are grouped into categories, at first globally, in terms of wholes, but later more analytically in terms of dimensions. Some dimensions are more salient than others, depending somewhat on age. Time concepts come from repetitions and rhythms becoming associated with labels. Space concepts come from moving through space and manipulating and watching objects moving. Three spatial reference systems are topological or details of objects, projective or in terms of where the person is, and Euclidean, in which objects can be located on axes. Quantity concepts include the meanings of words that are not numerical, such as *more* and *another*. Young children often count, applying the 5 rules of counting before they can apply them correctly. Young children realize early that cause precedes effect.

Play performs many functions in the life of the child, the overall one being integration of life. Functions include enjoyment, exploration, consolidating new skills, problem solving, and creativity. In symbolic play, children use all sorts of media as vehicles to refer to their experiences. In using the symbol systems of art, children first explore the material, then develop some techniques of control, and then create symbols. Pretending or fantasy transforms people and objects into symbols by way of speech and gestures. Stories and poems are also used symbolically. Music and dance provide symbolic communication from the wider society as well as a mode of expression for the child, and communication for the child in her microsystems. Humor often transforms anxieties into symbolic form, where they can be handled with pleasure. The ecology of play is significant on all levels.

References

1. Abrams, D. M. The poetry of early word play: A reanalysis of Ruth Weir's *Language in the Crib*. Paper presented at meeting of the Society for Research in Child Development, New Orleans, 1977.
2. Abu-l-Fazl. *The Akbar Nāma*. Vol. III. Translated from the Persian by H. Beveridge. Delhi: Rare Books, 1973.
3. Acredolo, L. P. Developmental changes in the ability to coordinate perspectives of a large-scale space. *Developmental Psychology.* 1977, **13**, 1–8.
4. Acredolo, L. P., and A. L. Feldman. The effect of active versus passive exploration on memory for spatial location in children. *Child Development,* 1979, **50**, 698–704.
5. Ames, L. B. The development of the sense of time in the young child. *Journal of Genetic Psychology,* 1946, **68**, 97–125.
6. Ashton-Warner, S. *O children of the world.* Vancouver, British Columbia: First Person Press, 1974.
7. Berko, J. The child's learning in English morphology. *Word,* 1958, **14**, 150–177.
8. Blank, M. Cognitive functions of language in the preschool years. *Developmental Psychology,* 1974, **10**, 229–245.
9. Bloom, L., and L. Hood. What, when, and how about why: A longitudinal study of early expressions of causality. *Monographs of the Society for Research in Child Development,* 1979, **44:**6.
10. Borke, H. Piaget's mountains revisited: Changes in the egocentric landscape. *Developmental Psychology,* 1975, **11**, 240–243.
11. Brian, C. R., and F. L. Goodenough. The relative potency of color and form perception at various ages. *Journal of Experimental Psychology,* 1929, **12**, 197–213.
12. Bullock, M., and R. Gelman. Preschool children's assumptions about cause and effect: Temporal ordering. *Child Development,* 1979, **50**, 89–96.
13. Carey, S. The child as word learner. In M. Halle, J. Bresnan, and G. A. Miller

(eds.). *Linguistic theory and psychological reality.* Cambridge, Mass.: The M.I.T. Press, 1978.

14. Chomsky, N. *Language and mind.* New York: Harcourt Brace Jovanovich, Inc., 1968.

15. Clark, E. V. Strategies for communicating. *Child Development,* 1978, **49,** 953–959.

16. Crinella, F. M., F. W. Beck, and J. W. Robinson. Unilateral dominance is not related to neuropsychological integrity. *Child Development,* 1971, **42,** 2033–2054.

17. Donaldson, M. *Children's minds.* New York: W. W. Norton & Company, Inc., 1979.

18. Endsley, R. C., M. A. Hutcherson, A. P. Garner, and M. J. Martin. Interrelationships among selected maternal behaviors, authoritarianism, and preschool children's verbal and nonverbal curiosity. *Child Development,* 1979, **50,** 331–339.

19. Erikson, E. H. *Childhood and society.* New York: W. W. Norton & Company, Inc., 1963.

20. Flavell, J. H. *Cognitive development.* Englewood Cliffs, N.J.: Prentice-Hall, Inc., 1977.

21. Friedman, W. J., and P. B. Seely. The child's acquisition of spatial and temporal word meaning. *Child Development,* 1976, **47,** 1103–1108.

22. Gelman, R. Preschool thought. *American Psychologist,* 1979, **34,** 900–905.

23. Gelman, R. and C. R. Gallistel. *The child's understanding of number.* Cambridge, Mass.: Harvard University Press, 1978.

24. Gelman, R., and M. Shatz. Appropriate speech adjustments: The operation of conversational constraints on talk to two-year-olds. In M. Lewis and L. A. Rosenblum (eds.). *Interaction, conversation, and the development of language.* New York: John Wiley & Sons, Inc., 1977.

25. Genishi, C. Code switching in four Spanish-English bilingual kindergarteners. Paper presented at meeting of the Society for Research in Child Development, New Orleans, 1977.

26. Gibson, E. J. The ontogeny of reading. *American Psychologist,* 1970, **25,** 136–143.

27. Golomb, C. Pretense play: A cognitive perspective. In N. R. Smith and M. B. Franklin (eds.). *Symbolic functioning in childhood.* Hillsdale, N.J.: Lawrence Erlbaum Associates, 1979.

28. Golomb, C., and C. B. Cornelius. Symbolic play and its cognitive significance. *Developmental Psychology,* 1977, **13,** 246–252.

29. Groch, A. S. Joking and appreciation of humor in nursery school children. *Child Development,* 1974, **45,** 1098–1102.

30. Harrison, D. M., J. H. Block, and J. Block. Intolerance of ambiguity in preschool children: Psychometric considerations, behavioral manifestations and parental correlates. *Developmental Psychology,* 1978, **14,** 242–256.

31. Hughes, M. Egocentrism in preschool children. University of Edinburgh: Unpublished doctoral dissertation, 1975. Cited in M. Donaldson. *Children's minds.* New York: W. W. Norton & Company, Inc., 1979.

32. Kellogg, R., and S. O'Dell. *The psychology of children's art.* New York: CRM-Random House, Inc., 1967.

33. Kessen, W., et al. Children of China: Report of a visit. Paper presented at meeting of the American Psychological Association, New Orleans, 1974.

34. Kun, A. Evidence for preschoolers' understanding of causal direction in extended causal sequences. *Child Development,* 1978, **49,** 218–222.

35. Lempers, J. D., E. R. Flavell, and J. H. Flavell. The development in very young children of tacit knowledge concerning visual perception. *Genetic Psychology Monographs,* 1977, **95,** 3–53.

36. Lenneberg, E. H. *Biological foundations of language.* New York: John Wiley & Sons, Inc., 1967.

37. Levin, I. Interference of time-related and unrelated cues with duration comparisons of young children: Analysis of Piaget's formulations of the relation of time and speed. *Child Development*, 1979, **50**, 469–477.

38. MacWhinney, B. The acquisition of morphophonology. *Monographs of the Society for Research in Child Development*, 1978, **43:**1 & 2.

39. Manosevitz, M., N. Prentice, and F. Wilson. Individual and family correlates of imaginary companions in preschool children. *Developmental Psychology*, 1973, **8**, 72–79.

40. Matthews, W. S. Modes of transformation in the initiation of fantasy play. *Developmental Psychology*, 1977, **13**, 212–216.

41. Melkman, R., A. Koriat, and L. Pardo. Preference for color and form in preschoolers as related to color and form differentiation. *Child Development*, 1976, **47**, 1045–1050.

42. Miscione, J. L., R. S. Marvin, R. G. O'Brien, and M. T. Greenberg. A developmental study of preschool children's understanding of the words "know" and "guess." *Child Development*, 1978, **49**, 1107–1113.

42a. Nelson, K. E. Structure and strategy in learning to talk. *Monographs of the Society for Research in Child Development*, 1973, **38:**1–2.

43. Nelson, K. E., and N. Earl. Information search by preschool children: Induced use of categories and category hierarchies. *Child Development*, 1973, **44**, 682–685.

44. Perlmutter, M., and N. A. Myers. Development of recall in 2- to 4-year-old children. *Developmental Psychology*, 1979, **15**, 73–83.

45. Piaget, J. *Play, dreams and imitation in childhood.* London: Wm. Heinemann Ltd., 1951.

46. Piaget, J., and B. Inhelder. *The child's conception of space.* London: Routledge & Kegan Paul, 1958.

47. Piaget, J., and B. Inhelder. *The psychology of the child.* New York: Basic Books, Inc., Publishers, 1969.

48. Ricciuti, H. N. Objects grouping and selective ordering behavior in infants 12 to 24 months old. *Merrill-Palmer Quarterly*, 1965, **11**, 129–148.

49. Rosch, E., and C. B. Mervis. Children's sorting: A reinterpretation based on the nature of abstraction in natural categories. In R. C. Smart and M. S. Smart (eds.) *Readings in child development and relationships.* 2nd ed. New York: Macmillan Publishing Co., Inc., 1977.

50. Rubin, K. H., and L. Dyck. Preschoolers' private speech in a play setting. *Merrill-Palmer Quarterly*, 1980, **26**, 219–229.

51. Rubin, S., and D. Wolf. The development of maybe: The evolution of social roles into narrative roles. In E. Winner and H. Gardner (eds.). *Fact, fiction and fantasy in childhood.* San Francisco: Jossey-Bass, 1979.

52. Saxe, G. B. A developmental analysis of notational counting. *Child Development*, 1977, **48**, 1512–1520.

53. Scarlett, W. G., and D. Wolf. When it's only make-believe: The construction of a boundary between fantasy and reality in storytelling. In E. Winner and H. Gardner (eds.). *Fact, fiction and fantasy in childhood.* San Francisco: Jossey-Bass, 1979.

54. Schacter, F. F., K. Kishner, B. Klips, M. Friedrichs, and K. Saunders. Everyday preschool interpersonal speech usage: Methodological, developmental, and sociolinguistic studies. *Monographs of the Society for Research in Child Development*, 1974, **39:**3.

55. Shure, M. B., and G. Spivak. Interpersonal problem solving, thinking and adjustment in the mother-child dyad. In M. W. Kent and J. E. Rolf (eds.) *Primary prevention of psychopathology.* Vol. III. *Social competence in children.* Hanover, N.H.: University Press of New England, 1979.

56. Siegel, A. W., and M. Schadler. The development of young children's spatial representations of their classrooms. *Child Development*, 1977, **48**, 388–394.

57. Slobin, D. I. The acquisition of Russian as a native language. In F. Smith and G. A. Miller (eds.). *The genesis of language.* Cambridge, Mass.: The M.I.T. Press, 1966.

58. Smith, L. B., and D. G. Kemler. Developmental trends in free classification: Evidence for a new conceptualization of perceptual development. *Journal of Experimental Child Psychology,* 1977, **24,** 279–298.

59. Smith, N. R. Developmental origins of structural variation in symbolic form. In N. R. Smith and M. B. Franklin (eds.). *Symbolic functioning in childhood.* Hillsdale, N.J.: Lawrence Erlbaum Associates, 1979.

60. Smith, P. K., and S. Dutton. Play and training in direct and innovative problem solving. *Child Development,* 1979, **50,** 830–836.

61. Weir, R. H. *Language in the crib.* The Hague: Mouton, 1962.

62. Wellman, H. M. The early development of intentional memory behavior. *Human Development,* 1977, **20,** 86–101.

63. Wellman, H. M., and J. Lempers. The naturalistic communicative abilities of two-year-olds. *Child Development,* 1977, **48,** 1052–1057.

64. Wellman, J. L., and C. N. Johnson. Understanding of mental processes: A developmental study of "remember" and "forget." *Child Development,* 1979, **50,** 79–88.

65. White, B. L., B. T. Kaban, and J. S. Attanucci. *The origins of human competence.* Lexington, Mass.: D. C. Heath & Company, 1979.

9
People and Feelings

Sarah, our 2-year-old granddaughter, had been going by herself to her own little toilet chair in the family bathroom. One day her mother found her with one foot on the big toilet seat and the other on the water tank of the toilet. With great care Sarah turned around, sat on the big seat, urinated, let herself down to the floor, looked into the toilet and announced, "A big, big hole. Sarah not fall in."

This incident illustrates several points to be made in this chapter. Sarah's developing sense of autonomy led her to decide for herself when to go to the toilet, and to take care of herself. Using her curiosity-exploratory behavior system, she tried new approaches and methods of going to the toilet. She recognized that she had felt some fear of the big hole, but that all had turned out well. She had not fallen in. Why was the big toilet worth the risk? Because the other family members used it, Sarah could see that the big toilet was the way to go. She was becoming socialized, learning and living according to the rules and customs of her family microsystem. And in this incident the rules and customs were also those of her macrosystem. This chapter deals with changes in children as they interact with other people to function as members of microsystems within a particular macrosystem.

QUESTIONS TO THINK
ABOUT WHILE READING
THIS CHAPTER

1. Of what significance are the sense of autonomy and the sense of initiative to the social and emotional development of the young child?
2. What are the implications of Hogan's theory of moral development for the care and education of young children?
3. What do children learn from play with peers?
4. How do children act with older and younger children?
5. Why do girls and boys behave differently?
6. What can be learned from cross-culture comparisons of parent-child interaction?
7. How are young children affected by the transitions of sibling birth and divorce?
8. What resources exist for helping parents in the United States with child rearing? What other resources are there in other macrosystems?

Erikson gives a broad picture of what happens to the child as a person. With his background in European psychoanalysis and his experience in the United States, Erikson's theory applies to children in the macrosystem to which we and most of our readers belong [5].

The first normal crisis, that of developing a sense of trust, is fairly well solved in infancy through building secure attachments and sensorimotor competencies. The second normal crisis begins in the second year and reaches some resolution at around 3 years of age. The third normal crisis begins during the preschool years and ordinarily ends at around 7. No crisis is ever fully resolved, but only partially during its period of dominance. There is always some backing up and reworking of old problems. Even with a firm sense of trust, there are frights over Mother's being away too long or strangers threatening. Even with a strong sense of autonomy, a child occasionally asserts it in a temper tantrum, a refusal to eat, or a toilet "accident." Little threads of problems run through life as imperfections in trust and autonomy, demanding attention and solutions.

The sense of autonomy blossoms as the child of 2 or thereabouts experiences the power of doing and deciding that comes with his wealth of budding abilities. Walking freely, although in a jerky trudging style, running a bit stiffly, climbing, bear-walking, knee-walking, galloping, riding a kiddy car, there are many independent modes of locomotion to exploit and choose from. The house and yard are for exploring. The child's hands are competent in reaching, grasping, letting go, throwing, turning, pulling, pushing. Toys to manipulate, tools that extend the powers of his hands, milk bottles with clothespins, puzzles, peg boards, crayons and paper, sand and water, mud—all give choices and successes. "Shall I play with it or not? . . . I'll do what I want with it. . . . What I do is all right."

Talking brings control over both the self and others and a corresponding strengthening of the sense of autonomy. Even headier is the power to cooperate with people or not. If you ask a 2-year-old, "Do you want to go outdoors?" the chances are that he'll say *no*. Even though he really would like to go out, he gets tremendous momentary satisfaction out of deciding thus. If you say, "We're going out now," he'll most likely trot along happily, the decision having been kept out of his hands. Similarly, with helping him finish a job that is too hard, like putting on boots, it is better to do it than to ask, "Shall I help you?" There are many opportunities for choosing and deciding, even when adults limit them. The child decides whether to kiss, hug, and give other endearments, whether to finish dinner, and whether to urinate on the toilet or elsewhere. The last decision mentioned, the question of toileting, is the one which, to the psychoanalysts, symbolizes the whole stage of developing autonomy. It is indeed an area where the sternest of parents has a hard time forcing the child and where the child can retain autonomy under severe pressure.

Psychosocial Development According to Erikson

The Sense of Autonomy

The Sense of Initiative

At around 4 years, the sense of initiative claims the center of the stage. The preschool child is an explorer, curious and active. He seeks new experiences for their own sake, the sheer pleasure of sensing and knowing. He also seeks experience in order to fit it in with something already known and to make it more understandable. He pushes vigorously out into the world, seeking a wide range of information about it, about people, and what they do, about what he himself can do. Grasping a piece of reality, like Mother's high heels and handbag, Daddy's briefcase, or a doctor's kit, he creates the experience he wants, trying on the role of a mother or father or doctor, contemplating what these adults do, imagining how it would be if he himself were doing it. Building a store with cartons, he becomes a storekeeper. He paints a picture. He creates a new world in a stream bed. It is at this stage that children put beans in their ears and stir eye shadow into cold cream. If the child's seeking is successful, then he finds a wide variety of things he can do, make, and create, with the approval of his family and other adults. If he succeeds, he continues as an older child and adult to look for new ideas, solutions, answers, reasons, creative experiences. Imagination has already been discussed in greater detail in Chapter 8, where its development is related to cognitive growth and where both these functions are seen as integrated in play, which is the business of the young child.

Moral Development

In order to live with family, peers, and community, a child must acquire the values and behavior patterns of his macrosystem and his microsystems. Moral development includes learning these patterns and making them part of the self. Moral development begins in infancy, when the baby accepts the rules of culture and family from the persons to whom he is attached. Among the various theories of moral development proposed by psychologists, we use those of Hoffman [12] and of Hogan and his associates [13] for discussing children's development of moral thought and action. In Chapter 14 we shall also describe Kohlberg's theory of moral reasoning and judgment.

Hogan's socioanalytic theory of moral development is based on ethology, or evolutionary adaptation (see "Ethology" in Chapter 1.) From this point of view, moral behavior has evolved as a means of human survival. Early man could neither run very fast nor fight well alone; cooperation, group organization, and primitive technology provided for defense and for hunting. Groups survived when they were well organized, when their rules and technology were adapted to the physical and social ecology. Socioanalytic theory assumes that the child's natural tendencies are compatible with the demands of adult society. (An example is Ainsworth's finding that securely attached infants cooperate with their mothers. See "Attachment-Affiliation" in Chapter 6.) The theory also assumes 3 human motives or needs for: social attention and approval; structure and order; and aggressive self-expression. The need for structure is basic to rules, rituals, and organization. The needs for approval and aggressive self-expression result in conflict and in pecking orders, followers, and leaders.

According to Hogan there are three phases of moral development. The first, *rule attunement*, takes place in infancy and early childhood. The second, *social sensitivity*, occurs in the age range from about 4 to 16. The third phase, moral autonomy, takes place in adolescence. The first phase involves living with authority, the second, living with others, and the third, living with oneself.

1. Rule attunement— authority
2. Social sensitivity— others
3. Autonomy—self

Rule Attunement

Sarah has just visited us. Before she came, we worried that she would climb onto the wide railing that goes around our deck, above a 12-foot drop. Sarah did indeed try to climb up. Susan, her mother, said, "No, Sarah, no climbing on the railing." Sarah never again tried to get up. When I, her grandmother, took her to the beach, it was a different story. She started to climb the rocks at the end of the beach. I said, "Just this far, Sarah. Stay on these little rocks. No farther." She kept trying to climb farther, and protesting when I lifted her back to the sand. What was the difference? Perhaps she was more inclined to obey Susan because she is securely attached to her. But there was a difference in the way that the rule was presented. Susan gave a very clear command that put the railing out of bounds. The boundary I gave Sarah was fuzzy. How was she to know which rocks were big and which were little?

Rules and restrictions are accepted by young children when they are given clearly and authoritatively by warm persons to whom they are attached. The phase of rule attunement does not proceed so smoothly when parents are cold and/or permissive. When parents are warm but not authoritative, children tend to be self-confident and assured, but to disobey rules when they feel like it. They know that parents will overlook much disobedience. Children of cold, restrictive parents usually obey, but they are often sullen, angry, and anxious. Cold, permissive parents are likely to have hostile, rule-defying children. The parents of delinquent children are usually cold and permissive. Table 9–1 shows relationships between parental behavior and child behavior.

It is unlikely that any living person is a parent of pure type, entirely warm and authoritative, entirely cold and permissive, and so on. An individual is more or less warm and more or less permissive than others. A parent varies from time to time, situation to situation, child to child. Recalling types of temperament, described in "Temperament" in Chapter 6, it is seen that an easy child may stimulate more warmth in a parent than will a difficult child. No child will be blessed with two perfect parents; no child accepts and obeys all rules with ease. Some temperamental characteristics make certain children especially resistant to following rules.

Parent	Child
Warm and authoritative	Obeys rules easily
Warm and permissive	Self-confident and disobedient
Cold and authoritative	Obeys sullenly, anxious, angry
Cold and permissive	Defiant, hostile, delinquent

Source: R. Hogan, J. A. Johnson, and N. P. Emler. A socioanalytic
theory of moral development. In W. Damon (ed.). Moral development. *New Directions for Child Development,* 1978, No. 2.

Rule Attunement and the Sense of Autonomy. Some rules are easier to
accept than others. For example, when told the name of an object, it is a
rare child who refuses to call it by the name. When Sarah helped me to
wash potatoes in the sink, she was delighted to follow my directions with
the vegetable brush. The difficult times are when the rule conflicts with
a decision that the child wants to make for herself. The developing sense
of autonomy requires many experiences with successful decision making. How can a young child obediently follow the rules and at the same
time develop the sense of autonomy? The art of parenting includes setting up a physical environment and situations in which a child can easily
choose to do right and where temptations to do wrong are few or absent.
The tape recorder is not left on a low shelf; the puzzles are there. The
child decides which of several appropriate dresses or shirts to wear.
Mother offers a choice between two wholesome foods. Preparation for
bed is calm and orderly, with a choice of stories and of cuddly toys. Parental warmth includes approval, praise, hugs, kisses, rewards, and
presents, not only for doing right, but for being the one he is—a particular
child of this parent. Parental authoritativeness includes drawing boundaries, giving clear directions as to what to do and what not to do, and insisting upon compliance.

*Parenting skills: Arranging
space, planning time, giving choices, drawing
boundaries*

Ellen, just under 3, was fascinated by Lucy, a doll that belonged to
Susan, age 5. Susan, knowing Ellen's passion for poking Lucy's blue glass
eyes fringed with long black lashes, made a strict rule that Ellen was
never to touch Lucy. One day Ellen came home from nursery school to
behold Lucy sitting on the sofa. She fell on the doll with cries of joy,
began to poke Lucy's eyes, and paused when her mother chided her,
"Ellen, you know Susie doesn't want you to touch Lucy."

"But Mummy," Ellen said in hurt surprise, "Susie isn't here!"

The voice that commanded Ellen to inhibit her impulses toward Lucy
was entirely external. When the voice was away at kindergarten, it simply wasn't there, and Ellen felt no restraint. She had not internalized the
rule about not touching Lucy.

Internalization of Rules. Rules are internalized, or taken into the self,
during early childhood especially during the time from 3 to 6. The child
shows internalized morality by resisting temptation when nobody is
watching, and by signs of guilt after transgressions. In this stage of devel-

opment of the sense of initiative, many explorations and new activities are undertaken and even more are contemplated. Healthy growth requires a balance between initiative and restraint, strong enough internalized controls to regulate action but not too strong, so as to produce excess guilt and restriction.

From a large body of research, Hoffman concludes that children who control themselves through internalized means and who are independent of external punishment and rewards are likely to have mothers who use inductive discipline [12]. By *inductive discipline*, he means explaining and drawing the child's attention to the consequences of his actions for other people. When children's moral orientation is based on fear of detection and punishment, they are more likely to have been disciplined by adults who asserted their power through physical force, material deprivation, or the threat of these.

Inductive discipline facilitates self-control

Another factor is involved in achieving the balance between too much and too little internalized control. Parental warmth and confidence in the child influence her feelings about her parents and herself. She wants to please her parents and to be like them. If they believe that she can be good, do better next time, live up to their standards and improve as she grows, then the child can believe all this about herself. Parental authoritativeness and consistency also contribute to the child's confidence and balance in the development of inner controls.

Social Sensitivity

Although young children talk to each other, they do not give clear instructions and requests in the ways that parents do. Therefore, they must become sensitive to the expectations, feelings, needs, and intentions of others. Empathy, or imagining oneself into the role of the other, is a process that makes a person socially sensitive.

During the first phase of moral development, rule attunement, family living prepares the child to begin the second phase, the development of social sensitivity. Both phases have roots in the attachment of the baby to parents. When securely attached to the mother, a young child is likely to get along better with peers by doing more sharing, giving, and showing, and by less aggression, crying, and leaving the room [17].

Secure attachment facilitates rule attunement and social sensitivity

In addition to the foundation for social sensitivity in attachment, parents teach empathy when they turn their children's attention to the feelings of other people, particularly when those feelings result from something that their children have done. Zahn-Waxler and her associates examined the ways in which mothers dealt with their toddlers (ages 1½ to 2½) when the children saw others in distress. They trained mothers to observe and make reports on tape recorders of their own behavior and their children's reparation and sympathy [29]. Children's scores were based on these sorts of behaviors: Physical sympathy (hugs victim), verbal sympathy ("all better now?"), giving objects such as food, toys, and bandaids, finding someone to help, and giving protection and physical help. When a child caused distress to another, he was likely to score high in reparation if his mother frequently explained the consequences of his behavior for other people, along with conveying intense feelings. "I'm really disppointed that you ran your truck through Amy's block building. You spoiled her play. She'll think you don't like her to come here." This sort of maternal behavior is like Hoffman's _inductive discipline_, which inclines children to obey rules of their own. The present study shows that inductive discipline also helps children to try to make amends for the distress that they cause to others. In "Making Sense Out of the World" in Chapter 8, we reported that cognitive skill for social problem solving can be taught to mothers and by mothers to their young children.

Moral development is an important part of the curriculum in Chinese nursery schools and kindergartens. Teachers encourage empathy and helping behavior by telling a child to help another who has fallen down, to wipe the tears of someone who is crying, and to apologize for hurting another child. They teach children to say "good morning" and "good bye" as ways of recognizing and considering other persons. Songs, dramatic play, and art work are sometimes used to teach helping behavior. Yao Qiang, who drew the picture on this page when he was 5 years old, shows us a scene when his kindergarten class presented toys that they had made to a class of younger children.

In addition to learning empathy and how to interact with peers, the stage of developing social sensitivity also includes learning principles of social interaction. Through taking turns, sharing, and fair play, a child lays the foundation for understanding and accepting principles of reci-

procity and justice. Abstract principles, of course, are not understood in
early childhood, but the behavior basic to them can be learned, and specific rules internalized. Hogan says that experience and concepts of justice arise in peer group experience that is supervised by fair adults, not
through peer interaction alone [13]. He suggests (and we agree) that turn-
taking and cooperation may occur because adults insist upon them, and
that when groups are unsupervised, bullying, exploitation, and persecu-
tion often take place.

Is the child a boy or a girl? How old is he or she? The answers to these
questions immediately put the child into social categories. Each category carries rules, expectations, and beliefs as to how a child within it
will interact with others. Age and sex classifications shape not only the
attitudes of other people, but the behavior of the child, and the child's
concepts and feelings about himself or herself.

Age and Sex: Regulators of Social Behavior and Self-concepts

Age and Social Interaction

A child interacts with adults, who are much older, and with other children, who can be older, younger, or the same age. Unless a child is a twin, relationships at home are with people of different ages. In traditional societies young children are not placed in groups of children their own age. Only in highly developed societies are there nursery schools, day care centers, and even 24-hour care centers. In the United States the early research on social interaction was done in nursery schools, where same-age groups were available. Only in recent years has research been focused on how children behave with older and younger ones.

Social Behavior with Adults. When Whiting and Edwards studied the social behavior of 3 to 11 years in 6 different cultures, they found some constancies in the acts that children most often direct toward adults. The behaviors are these: seeking help; seeking or offering physical contact; seeking attention; and sociability, or friendly interaction [28].

Social Behavior with Peers. One of the reasons why parents send their children to preschool groups is to have them "learn to get along together." This goal expresses what research confirms, that in playing with peers, or equals, children have experiences that do not occur when playmates are of different levels of development. When they play together, peers contribute, cooperate, and compete as equals. Children learn essential social skills through playing together cooperatively, through aggressive play, and by observing one another. Half a century ago Parten showed age-related types of social play in nursery-school children [22]. She found a sequence of play types, from simple to complex: solitary play, onlooker behavior, parallel play, associative play, and cooperative play. Complexity and amount of interaction increased with age and over time. The most mature level of social play, cooperative play, was carried on in an organized group. Parten found the type of play most frequent at each of the following age levels:

2–2½ years	*Solitary play:* The child is playing alone.
2½–3½ years	*Parallel play:* Children play next to one another, using similar toys performing similar actions.
3½–4½ years	*Associative play:* Children play with one another, talking, replying, and giving playthings back and forth.

Similar but not identical results are found in modern studies using Parten's concepts. Social class seems to make a difference, with middle-class children showing more associative and cooperative play than lower-class children [23]. There is some indication of a secular shift toward less social participation. In a careful replication of Parten's study, done in 1979, 2-year-olds spent more time in unoccupied behavior, solitary play, and onlooker behavior, and less time in parallel and associative play [6].

The most mature level of play, cooperative play, usually involves pretending. In the previous chapter we discussed the importance of pretend play in cognitive development. Now we want to show that pretend play is also a means of social growth, perhaps an essential one. When carrying on dramatic (pretend) play, children cooperate to create and maintain a theme. Each player waits and listens while one performs and then fits a response to the previous action. Each elicits and maintains response from the other or others. Each has the experience of controlling and being controlled, giving and taking, taking turns. They thus experience the alternating behavior typical of basic social interaction patterns. In dramatic play, children also obey rules. The fact that an interchange is play and not literal may be indicated by chanting or using a special voice, but often there are asides, such as "Let's pretend" or "I'll be the mommy and you be the baby." Players show that they recognize that a state of play is in force, that rules are mutually binding, and that both players can modify the theme of the play.

Dramatic play involves trying on of roles in a double sense. A player pretends to be a mother, postman, or doctor, thus exploring various social roles. The players also imagine themselves into each other's roles when they elicit responses and fit their own to the previous actions. Therefore cooperative pretend play contributes to empathy, a necessary ability for moral development in the phase of social sensitivity.

Children learn to use and control aggression in rough-and-tumble play with peers [10]. They learn how to strike out, how to make others angry, how to defend themselves, and how to turn off angry feelings and actions. Fathers and children, usually fathers and sons, engage in rough-and-tumble play, but playing with father is quite different from playing with a peer. Fathers *could* always win. Therefore the father controls the interaction, deciding how far it should go and when it should end. With peers, the control is mutual. The relationship is democratic.

Another frequent form of peer social interaction is observing, imitating, and being imitated. Observed during free play in nursery schools, 4-year-old boys were found imitating one another on an average of 19 times per hour [2]. Girls did less imitating, only about 7 times in one hour. Imitating a peer was closely related to paying attention to what the child was doing. Imitations were verbal and motor, and sometimes a combination of both. Examples of imitated behavior were these: "I've got more cars than you do;" jabbing a paint brush up and down on paper; jumping and peering over a book case; making train noises. It seems likely that the children who received much attention were regarded as sources of information and interesting behavior, and therefore worth imitating. Imitation may also be a friendly gesture, an invitation to interaction.

Social Behavior with Younger and Older Children. Whiting and Edwards, generalizing about children's behavior in six cultures, say that

when interacting with infants, children most often give help, support, and sociability [28]. The six communities studied were in India, Kenya, Mexico, Okinawa, the Philippines, and the United States. An older playmate is likely to dominate a younger one and also to give care and instruction; a younger playmate is likely to show dependence. Further study in six other communities showed children most often giving nurturance to infants and children younger than themselves [4]. Nurturance included offering material goods, physical care, help, comfort, and attention. Opportunities for giving nurture differed from one community to another, because the amount of time spent with young children varied. In the United States community studied, children's interactions with infants were only 3.5 per cent of the interactions recorded, whereas in Kenya and Mexico, 25 per cent of their actions were toward infants.

The setting in which children most often encounter younger and older companions is the home. Brothers and sisters are the usual playmates of a different age, whereas school friends are most often peers. When Abramovitch and her associates made observations of sibling pairs interacting at home, they saw the young children as having a great deal going on between them [1]. The subjects were like-sex pairs, the younger one being 20 months old and the older ones 1 to 2 years older or 2½ to 4 years older, making pairs that were spaced close together or far apart. Although free to leave one another, the pairs tended to stay together and to interact. The average number of acts initiated per pair was 40 per hour, and half of these received responses. The younger children's actions were mostly imitation or prosocial behavior. The latter included giving, cooperating, asking, praise, comfort, hugging, kissing, laughing, and approaching. The older children sometimes imitated the younger in a playful way and often behaved prosocially. Older siblings' aggressive behavior was somewhat more frequent than prosocial. Aggression was both physical and verbal, including hitting, kicking, biting, fighting over an object, commanding, insulting, threatening, and tattling. Siblings spaced far apart did not differ in interaction patterns from those spaced close together. Older girls were most often nurturant, acting like mothers to their little sisters. Older boys were more physically aggressive (as research and common observation almost always find them) but there was no sex difference in verbal aggression. Older brothers were more aggressive than prosocial; older sisters were more prosocial than aggressive.

Because siblings have so many and such varied interactions, it seems likely that interaction patterns learned at home are later used with peers. One piece of evidence comes from the studies that found children in the 1970s less advanced in social participation than in Parten's classic study. Parten's subjects had more siblings than did those in the later studies [6]. More siblings would offer more experience in social participation and more opportunity for rapid development in Parten's sequence of stages of social play.

The young child grows rapidly in knowledge about girls and boys, women and men. She fits her concept of herself to the way in which she finds the social world divided into male and female, and her behavior into what she is told, what she sees, and what she can do. There are age-related sequences in salience of gender, knowledge about gender, and behavior related to gender.

Gender-Related Differences in Behavior. Comparisons often show boys to be more physically active and aggressive and girls more nurturant. Fagot's observations on preferred activities of boys and girls show how boys and girls differ in the patterning of their play. Fagot studied toddlers between 20 and 24 months of age in their homes with their parents [8]. Children between 37 and 54 months of age were observed in nursery schools, interacting with peers and teachers [7]. Table 9–2 shows preferred play behaviors according to whether girls or boys played significantly more of each type of activity.

Concepts of Gender. Like other concepts, ideas about maleness and femaleness develop as the child grows up. Part of self-development is the relating of knowledge about gender to the self, coming to know the self as male or female. *Gender identity* is a conviction of being either a male or a female. Clinical studies indicate that by 18 months a child feels that he is a boy or she is a girl [21]. However, many or most children this age cannot answer the question, "Are you a boy or a girl?" When children's gender concepts are explored by asking them a number of questions, stages of comprehension can be seen. Children are 3 or 4 years old before they can consistently state which is male and which is female of pairs of boy and girl dolls, man and woman dolls, photographs, and the child's own self [26]. Only after children can identify gender accurately do they become certain that gender remains *stable over time*, that a boy has always been a boy and will become a man, and similarly for girls.

An even more mature concept is *gender consistency* across situations,

Sequence of gender concepts: Identity, stability, consistency, genital base

Age level	Girls spend more time in	Boys spend more time in
20–24 months	Play with dolls and soft toys Dancing Asking for help Dressing up	Play with blocks Manipulating objects Play with transportation toys
37–54 months	Cutting, drawing, pasting Play in kitchen Play with dolls Dressing up	Building with blocks Carpentry Play with transportation toys Riding tricycles Outdoor play in sand and mud

TABLE 9–2
Preferred Play Activities of Preschool Girls and Boys at Two Age Levels

Sources: B. I. Fagot. Consequences of moderate cross-gender behavior in preschool children. *Child Development*, 1977, **48**, 902–907; B. I. Fagot. The influence of sex of child on parental reactions to toddler children. *Child Development*, 1978, **49**, 459–465.

which is determined by asking (of a girl) "If you wore boys' clothes, would you be a boy?" and (of a boy) "If you played girls' games, would you be a girl?"

Studies of American children have not come to grips with the question of how gender is assigned. Investigators have not asked children whether they knew that a girl is a girl because she possesses one type of genital organs, and a boy is a boy because he possesses another kind of genitals. A study done on Swedish children did look into this question by using dolls with realistic genitals [19]. The investigators found that young children understood gender consistency before they understood the genital basis of gender. That is, the children knew that gender is constant, permanent, and unchanging before they knew exactly what determines whether a child is a boy or a girl. If their subjects had been American children, it would have been reasonable to think that the children had never been informed about genital differences. However, in Sweden, almost all preschool children receive sex education from parents and teachers [20]. Their education includes information about genital differences. The study indicates that there are two distinct concepts, gender permanence, and the genital nature of gender. The second requires more cognitive maturity than the first.

Shaping of Feminine and Masculine Behavior. There are several sources of influence on a child's development of gender-appropriate actions and feelings. Some influences are within the child, in both mind and body, some in interactions with parents and siblings, and others in interactions with teachers and playmates. Different theories hold one or another of these influences to be most important, but we believe that all are at work in producing gender-typed behavior.

1. COGNITIVE PROCESSES. Behavior is influenced by what the child knows and thinks. As understanding of gender changes, so does gender-related behavior change. Serbin has observed that 4-year-olds are much more concerned over playing with gender-appropriate toys than are 3- and 5-year-olds [24a]. She suggests that *gender salience,* or the significance to the child of gender, is great at age 4 when children are consolidating their new findings and knowledge about proper behavior for males and females and for themselves as members of one sex or the other. As Table 9–3 shows, 4-year-olds are in the process of learning that gender is stable over time and that they are not yet sure that gender is stable across situa-

TABLE 9–3
Development of Gender Concepts and Related Behavior

Age range	Gender concepts and related behavior
2–3 years	Gender identity; knows if it is a boy or a girl.
3–5 years	Identifies gender of self and others; knows gender-appropriate toys and play; plays more with same-sex peers; knows gender is stable over time.
5–7 years	Knows gender is consistent across situations; gender permanence; understands that gender is assigned on basis of genitals; some notions of personality correlates of gender.

tions, that it cannot be changed by dressing or playing like a child of the opposite sex. Boys seem to be more cautious in this respect than girls, for reasons that will be made clear by the fourth influence on feminine and masculine behavior, social pressures and demands.

The child gets knowledge of gender-appropriate behavior from friends and family. Able to identify everybody as male or female, children watch what boys and men do, especially Daddy, and what girls and women do, especially Mother. He tries to behave like boys, men, and Daddy; she, like girls, women, and Mother. Children also hear comments and receive instructions on gender behavior, and they think about what they hear, as well as what they see.

When a concept of gender permanence or constancy is achieved, at between 5 and 7 years, children know that nobody can change gender by acting like a person of the opposite sex. This knowledge must bring a feeling of security as a boy or a girl, and a relaxation in choice of actions. Gender becomes less salient. A boy might be more willing to wear his sister's sweater and to set the table. He knows that he will always be a boy until he becomes a man.

2. BODILY PROCESSES. Sex differences in brain, body, and hormones are fundamental to some behavior differences, especially girls' greater verbal facility and boys' spatial abilities, physical aggression, and greater engagement in vigorous outdoor play. We suspect that some action modes feel more comfortable to girls, others to boys. However, even though we may feel sure that there is a biological base for sex differences in behavior, any pattern of action is the product of both biology and experience. One way of testing whether a strong biological influence is at work is to look for behaviors that occur in many different societies. Even when constant cross-culture sex differences are seen, however, they suggest but do not prove a biological base. Whiting and Edwards studied not only the actual behavior differences between girls and boys, but considered the behaviors in relation to the settings in which they occurred.

3. SETTINGS AND OPPORTUNITIES FOR INTERACTION. Both physical and social settings can contribute to sex differences in behavior. Physical settings have been studied in nursery schools in the United States. Social settings have been compared cross-culturally.

The physical setting determines much of how children play, in both obvious and subtle ways. Arrangements of space and toys may or may not offer opportunities for pretend play, cooperative block building, and moving freely. The effect of density on a group was explored by observing the same groups of six children each, in a large (265 square feet) and small (90 square feet) room [18]. In the high-density room, children spent more time in solitary play and less in interaction with each other. Boys showed more aggression than girls throughout, but were less aggressive in the small room than in the large one. It seemed as though children adjusted to overstimulation and likelihood of intrusion by cutting down on social interaction.

Sex differences in activity have often been noted, with boys playing more actively than girls. Differential activity level of boys and girls may be a result of social factors as well as of indoor-outdoor influences. When preschool children played alone, there were no differences in activity level between girls and boys, but when they played in groups, boys were much more active than girls [9]. Outdoors, boys were more active than girls. Since group play occurs more frequently outdoors, the excitement of the group is often or even usually added to the freedom of the outdoors.

In some macrosystems the settings for social interaction are similar for girls and boys; in others they are quite different. At older ages these differences are well known. For instance, separate schools for girls and boys are common in England but not in the United States. For young children, however, sex differences in settings are not so obvious, but they do exist. Edwards and Whiting point out that in many cultures girls spend more time in the company of younger children and infants [4]. As we mentioned earlier in this chapter, a younger child elicits nurturant behavior from an older child, in the form of giving goods, care, and attention. Many United States studies have found girls showing more interest than boys in babies. Edwards and Whiting reason that, although young children do not differ in nurturant behavior, young girls, being more interested in babies, are more willing than boys to take responsibility for younger children. Mothers may not assign more child care duties to girls, but when they do, girls comply more often than boys. Therefore, girls spend more time than boys in giving nurturance. Because they spend more of their preschool hours in situations that elicit nurturant behavior, girls become more nurturant than boys by the beginning of middle childhood.

Edwards and Whiting note that sex differences in nurturance are greatest in cultures where infants and younger children are most available to children, as in their Kenyan and Mexican communities. Sex differences in nurturance are minimal in cultures where children have little experience with younger ones, as in the community that they studied in the United States. Edwards and Whiting suggest that other differences between girls and boys could also be explained by cross-cultural comparisons of settings. They note that United States children tend to show smaller sex differences than children of other cultures in aggression, responsibility, help-seeking, and attention-seeking, as well as in nurturance.

4. DEMANDS AND PRESSURES ON GIRLS AND BOYS. Within a child's microsystems parents, siblings, teachers, playmates, and others try to elicit the behavior expected of that child as a girl or boy. Parents and teachers arrange surroundings, plan where children play and with whom, give out tasks, tell children what to do, reward and punish behavior, and serve as female and male models. In their efforts, intentional and unintentional, to socialize the child according to gender, all these people act in terms of what they believe to be masculine and feminine behavior. These beliefs are called gender-role stereotypes. Everybody has gender-role stereotypes. At one extreme, male and female persons are thought to be very

different. Each gender has strictly defined ways of dressing, working, talking, thinking, and relating to other people. At the other extreme, male and female are thought to be very much alike, with reproductive functions being the only significant difference; little or no definition of clothing and behaving is made on the basis of being female or male. All societies are organized with some regard for their members being of two genders. The customs, values, and laws of a macrosystem take account of the gender-role stereotypes. Adults and older children interact with younger children in accordance with those stereotypes.

In several studies, Fagot found children, parents, and teachers reacting differentially to boys and girls. A certain behavior pattern drew positive

reactions when shown by a child of one gender, but negative or neutral responses when shown by a child of the opposite gender.

Observations of parents and 2-year-olds showed that boys were more likely than girls to be left alone to play, but that parents more often joined in boys' play than in girls' [8]. Girls received more praise and more criticism from both parents. Mothers criticised more than fathers. Table 9–4 shows positive and negative reactions of parents, peers, and teachers to children's play behaviors. This table combines information from Fagot's study of toddlers at home and her study of 3- and 4-year-olds in nursery school [7]. With each of the play activities occurring in both places, there is a possibility of approval or disapproval from parents, teachers, and peers. For example, when playing with dolls, a boy receives more negative reaction from parents than does a girl. On going to school at 3 or 4, he is likely to find peers also reacting negatively to doll play. As for dressing up, girls are approved at home by parents and at school by peers, whereas boys rarely, if ever, dress up at home, and receive negative responses from teachers when they do so at school. Table 9–2 shows that children prefer the activities approved by parents, peers, and teachers, or that parents, teachers, and peers react positively to sex-preferred behaviors.

Fagot also looked at the responses received by nursery school children whose play preferences were those generally preferred by the opposite sex [7]. She called these children *cross-gender girls* and *cross-gender boys*. Teachers did not react differently to cross-gender children. Cross-gender girls received little or no more negative reaction than other girls, but cross-gender boys got less positive and more negative responses from peers than did other boys. Boys tended to ignore a cross-gender boy when he attempted male-preferred play, but girls interacted with him in female-preferred play. Girls were often negative to him, but sometimes positive, when including him in kitchen play. Cross-gender boys played alone 3 times as often as other children. They were criticised 5 or 6 times as often, and given one quarter as much positive response as other children.

Not only do boys receive more negative feedback for cross-gender behavior at school, but the same feedback occurs at home. In both places the criticism comes mainly from their own sex, boy peers at school and fathers at home. Fagot, as well as others, found that fathers were more concerned about gender-appropriate behavior than mothers [8].

In another study of preschool peer reinforcement of gender-preferred behavior, boys were found giving more reinforcement than girls to *both* sexes [15]. Apparently, boys' interest in appropriate gender behavior begins early in life! Little boys' interventions in peers' gender-related behavior may be the result of their very early experience of having gender-role stereotypes applied to themselves. Boys are taught gender-role behavior more strictly than girls, and allowed less leeway in choosing activities and behavior patterns.

TABLE 9–4
Positive and Negative Reactions by Others to Behaviors of Young Children, by Preference of Males, of Females, or of Neither

Behaviors	More positive	More negative
Preferred by Females:		
Doll Play		
When shown by girls	Mother, father, peers	
When shown by boys		Mother, father, peers
Dance		
When shown by girls	Mother, father	
When shown by boys		
Dress Up		
When shown by girls	Mother, father, peers	
When shown by boys		Teacher, peers
Ask for Help		
When shown by girls	Mother, father	
When shown by boys		Mother , father
Art Activities		
When shown by girls		
When shown by boys	Teacher	
Kitchen Play		
When shown by girls	Peers	
When shown by boys		
Preferred by Males:		
Block Play		
When shown by girls		
When shown by boys	Mother, father, teacher	
Manipulate Objects		
When shown by girls		Mother, father
When shown by boys		
Sandbox		
When shown by girls		Teacher
When shown by boys	Peers	
Carpentry		
When shown by girls		
When shown by boys	Teacher, peers	
Preferred by Neither Males nor Females:		
Help Adult with Tasks		
When shown by girls	Mother, father	
When shown by boys		Mother, father
Be Near Parent		
When shown by girls	Father	
When shown by boys		
Large Motor		
When shown by girls		Mother, father
When shown by boys		

Sources: B. I. Fagot. Consequences of moderate cross-gender behavior in preschool children. *Child Development,* 1977, **48,** 902–907; and B. I. Fagot. The influence of sex of child on parental reactions to toddler children. *Child Development,* 1978, **49,** 459–465.

Sexuality. Young children masturbate and show pleasure in the sensory experience that accompanies stimulation of the genital organs. They are interested in exploring their own genitals and those of other girls and boys. Perhaps pleasurable sensations are enough to make children aware

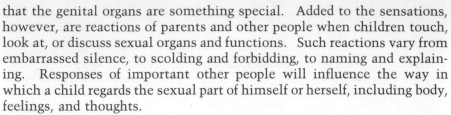

that the genital organs are something special. Added to the sensations, however, are reactions of parents and other people when children touch, look at, or discuss sexual organs and functions. Such reactions vary from embarrassed silence, to scolding and forbidding, to naming and explaining. Responses of important other people will influence the way in which a child regards the sexual part of himself or herself, including body, feelings, and thoughts.

Freud built a theory of personality development based on sexuality, as mentioned briefly in "Psychoanalysis" in Chapter 1. We believe that it supplements the account that we have just given of the development of gender concepts and the shaping of masculine and feminine behavior. Freud's theory pays much more attention to feelings and emotions than the previously mentioned ones. He maintains that the young child is in love with the parent of the opposite sex, wants to be best loved by that parent, and therefore feels hostile to the parent of the same sex. The little girl typically chooses her father to be the father of her future children; the little boy says, "Mommy, when I grow up, I'm going to marry you." She is said to have an Electra complex, he, an Oedipus complex. At the same time, the child feels anxious about rivaling the powerful same-sex parent and worries about being punished. If parents have reacted negatively to the child's masturbating and genital explorations, the child may be concerned about the safety of his/her genital organs. Some parents actually threaten to cut off a boy's penis and he quite reasonably fears that he might lose it. A girl may think that she has lost a penis that she used to possess. (Remember, gender concepts are not entirely stable or consistent.) In order to deal with these threats and fears, the child gives up the ambition to be first with the opposite-sex parent and *identifies* with the same-sex parent.

In identifying with the parent, the child observes the parent carefully and tries to be like the parent in as many ways as possible. The boy may walk like his father, pretend to shave the way he does, and speak in the same manner. Similarly, the girl imitates her mother and tries to help her and share in her mother's typical activities. The same-sex parent is then a model of gender-appropriate behavior, including behavior toward the opposite sex.

Ecology of Social and Emotional Development

The child learns patterns of acting and feeling within a social world. That world can be considered from the various levels of macrosystems, microsystems, and mesosystems. We shall comment on all three, but shall emphasize the family, the setting in which young children's most significant interactions take place.

Macrosystems

Just as macrosystems structure gender-role stereotypes and age-related behavior patterns, so do they have other values and role patterns that influence children's development. Even the definition of what is a child varies from one macrosystem to another. Parental behavior is also defined, along with the sort of child that parental behavior is designed to produce. As long as a student of human development stays within his own macrosystem, he is likely to think that his own society's child-rearing goals and methods are normal, and others deviant. Only through cross-culture comparisons does one come to see that parents tend to bring up the kind of children they want, but that what parents want differs from one society to another. The following discussion of macrosystems compares American child rearing with that of other societies.

Attention-Seeking: An Example of Differences in Macrosystems. When we lived in India, we noticed that children rarely interrupted adults' conversations, nor did they initiate conversations with them. Children often went calling and to parties with parents, but young ones sat quietly beside their parents and older ones might play quietly with each other. The other adults paid little or no attention to the children. In contrast, American children were active, noisy, and demanding of adult attention.

An article by Robert LeVine, one of the investigators in the study of six cultures mentioned earlier in this chapter, helps us to see our Indian observations in perspective [16]. Our society, LeVine points out, believes in encouragement, praise, and reinforcement as methods of teaching children desirable behavior. Psychological research has indeed shown that these methods work. Children learn behaviors for which they are praised and otherwise rewarded. In addition to learning the specific behaviors, however, they also learn to show their socially approved behaviors to the persons giving out praise and encouragement. That is, they seek attention. American parents, along with teachers and psychologists, see attention-seeking as indicating self-confidence, a trait they desire. Psychologist Burton White, for example, lists as a social competency, *getting and keeping adults' attention in socially acceptable ways* [27]. Even though attention-seeking interrupts parents in what they are doing and may be quite irritating, adults generally accept it because attention-seeking and its underlying self-confidence are valued. In the study of six cultures, American children showed over twice the proportion of attention-seeking as children next highest in this characteristic.

In certain African societies, according to LeVine, children learn without praise or explicit approval. They learn by observing and imitating, getting correction if they do wrong, but no comment if they do right. They apparently learn desired skills quickly and easily. Our Indian observations fit with LeVine's report. We recall children watching and listening a great deal. We also remember that Indian adults disliked the intrusive behavior of American children.

Family

Like all microsystems, the family provides a physical setting and persons in face-to-face interaction. Much of this chapter has involved family interaction. The family is the primary setting for emotional and social development. Home is where the child experiences emotional satisfaction, where secure attachment provides a base for exploring the world and reaching out to other people. Within the home, children are prepared for the future as parents understand it, and launched into other microsystems. From the home base, they venture into neighborhood, day care center, school, hospital, library, and other places chosen and arranged by parents, and perhaps assisted by siblings and grandparents.

Parents are guided by their own values and beliefs. Values come from the macrosystem to some extent, but they are also personal and special to the particular family. Beliefs come from education and experience, both of which have macrosystem sources. As we have just shown, the psychology practiced by professionals within a society influences the beliefs and practices of parents.

A family changes through time as its members grow up and grow older. Ecological transitions occur when roles and positions in the family are greatly changed, as with a birth, a death, a divorce, school entrance, and so on. (See "Human Ecology" in Chapter 2.) We shall discuss two of the ecological transitions that most commonly affect preschool children, birth of a sibling and divorce of parents.

Birth of a Sibling. A young child's life changes when the mother becomes pregnant, especially if the child is the firstborn. As the family prepares for a birth, the physical setting will be adjusted to make space for the baby. Parents may or may not include the child in planning for the baby, but even if they do not do so, the child most likely gets an uneasy feeling that something unusual is going on. When questioned, almost all parents will agree that sex education should take place in the home. However, not all take the opportunity provided by a pregnancy, while some do tell the young child that there is a fetus (or baby) inside the mother and that it will come out through her vagina when it is old enough to live outside. Parents may also help the young child to anticipate what the new baby will be like by visiting young infants, preparing clothing and equipment, reading stories, and doll play.

The conduct of birth, of course, affects the young child as well as the rest of the family. In North America the child is usually excluded from the birth and may be separated from the mother for several days while she stays in a hospital with the new baby. A few families conduct births at home or in birth centers, where children can be included. In some societies, however, birth is a community affair, as it is among the Zinacanteco Indians in Mexico. If the birth of a sibling separates the child from the mother, it may or may not be disturbing, depending on whether the caregiver is a familiar person, and whether the child can understand that the separation is temporary.

Research and common experience show that when a mother has a new baby, she pays less attention to and plays less with the older child than she did before the baby was born. (See "Family Microsystem" in Chapter

6.) When behavior and experiences of the older sibling were analyzed according to age, the younger children, around 2, were different from the older ones, between 3 and 4 [14]. Younger children were more likely to stay close to the mother, to ask to be held, to do more aimless wandering, and to spend more time watching and looking with the mother when she was feeding the baby. Also at this time the mothers were more likely to prohibit the children and to have confrontations with them. A comparison between breast-feeding and bottle-feeding mother-child pairs showed more conflict and less play between child and mother if the mother was bottle-feeding.

The birth of a sibling brings quite a few changes to the life of a young child in North America. The changes are even greater in parts of Asia and Africa, where the baby sleeps with the mother until another baby is born, at which time the first one must begin to sleep alone or with older siblings. In Bali, mothers deliberately tease and frustrate the older child, apparently trying to arouse jealousy of the new baby. Such tactics probably promote some independent behavior and propel the child into the society of other children.

We have already discussed behavior of younger and older siblings earlier in this chapter, in connection with social behavior with older and younger children. We showed that a great amount and variety of interaction occurs between siblings, more of it imitative and prosocial on the part of younger siblings, and somewhat more of it aggressive than prosocial on the part of older ones. In summary, having a new sibling brings a wealth of social and emotional experiences to a young child. The experiences include feeling left out, being puzzled, sharing new interests, acquiring information, feeling angry, seeking attention, expressing aggression and nurturance, and being imitated. The ecological transition brings changes in family interaction. The young child builds new relationships not only with the new baby, but with mother, father, and perhaps older siblings and grandparents.

Divorce. Every year, over a million children experience the divorce of their parents. Because a period of disturbed family interaction leads up to divorce and another follows it, we can be sure that at any given time, 3 or 4 million children are feeling the effects of disrupted relationships between their parents. In this chapter, we are concerned with what divorce means in a young child's life.

By the time the transition is made from two-parent to one-parent living arrangements, the child is probably quite confused about the parents' motives, feelings, and intentions toward each other and toward him. Because of limited cognitive ability and experience, the child cannot accurately imagine himself into adult roles. He may think that he caused the separation through being naughty. Feeling guilt and confusion, the child is likely to show behavior disturbances in sleeping, eating, thumb-sucking, and so on. The parent then feels extra stress from the child's behavior.

The separating of warring parents cuts down on the child's stress from their conflict, but makes major changes in the microsystem of the family. One out of 5 families with dependent children is headed by only one parent. At present, mothers head 5.3 million one-parent families with dependent children and 569,000 such families are headed by fathers [25]. Not only do mothers far outnumber fathers as heads of one-parent families, but mothers are much more likely than fathers to have custody of preschool children. The most outstanding changes brought by divorce are, therefore, father absence and economic deprivation. Hetherington and her associates have studied extensively the effects of divorce on young children and their parents. The following information is from a review by Hetherington [11].

After divorce, it is a rare father who contributes enough support to keep the children on the standard of living that they enjoyed before. Many contribute nothing. Few mothers are prepared to earn enough money to maintain their former standard. They may have to move to poorer housing in a poorer neighborhood. If they do take jobs, the children are then deprived of the mother's continued presence, as well as the father's. The mother is often overwhelmed by having to do all the work of keeping up the home, as well as unrelieved child care. The child may then live in chaotic conditions.

The young child is affected in two ways by the father's absence from the home, through the mother, and directly. The mother is affected not only by lack of economic support and help with homemaking and child rearing, but by lack of emotional support, appreciation, and affirmation. When emotionally depleted, a person is less likely to be warmly responsive to young children.

Direct influence of father absence has been shown in infants under 6 months of age. (See "One-Parent Homes" in Chapter 6.) Father absence throughout the preschool years deprives the child of the father's teaching, stimulation, playful companionship, discipline, and serving as a model, affecting the child's cognitive and social development. Boys may have problems in gender-role development. (Girls' disruptions in social-sex development do not usually show up until adolescence.) After divorce, children's play becomes less mature, in terms of Parten's stages. Boys' play disruption lasts longer than girls.

In two-parent families, a good relationship with one parent may be enough to assure good development in a child living in an unhappy family [24]. The father-absent child is not protected by the father as buffer when the mother is depressed, unstable, or incompetent.

Hetherington's studies have shown that family disorganization develops during the first year after divorce, with reorganization taking place in the third year after the parents separated (the second year after legal divorce). At first, the mother is more restrictive, giving more commands, the child ignoring and resisting her. She becomes more effective and less authoritarian over the following two years. When visiting the children, or taking them out, the father is at first very indulgent and permissive and becomes more restrictive. The mother was able to function more positively with the children when the father had a positive relationship with the family and when other support systems interacted with the family, such as grandparents, siblings, friends, and/or a housekeeper.

North Americans often begin parenthood with little or no experience in caring for infants, and little or no help from relatives around the time of childbirth and when their children are young, or, indeed, at any time. Even if grandmothers and older relatives offer advice, the young parents usually do not trust it to be up to date. In contrast, the extended families of Asia and Africa provide assistance and instruction in the management of pregnancy, birth, and child care. What is more, the young mother has already had experience in child care as a preadolescent, when she helped the women in her family who were then mothers of young children. In many African societies, mothers of young children work to produce income for the family. Their relatives share the care of the children. Employment along with child rearing is a normal way of life.

How do North American parents learn to take care of their children? Some instructions are given by hospital and medical personnel. Friends discuss child rearing. Books, magazines, and newspapers give information and advice, based somewhat on research but also on the ideology current in the macrosystem. From the 1940s until the 1970s, most child-rearing books and a number of articles insisted that young children needed the mother's presence almost continually, and some claimed that in working outside the home, mothers harmed their infants and themselves. In the 1970s, the United States Children's Bureau publications and Dr. Spock's book took a more positive attitude toward working mothers. Child-rearing specialists began to acknowledge a mother's need for relief from continual child care, to recognize fathers as caregivers, and to see day care and other aids to the mother as legitimate. We shall discuss several types of groups that give care and education to children and families.

Day Care. Types and functions of day care programs have already been described in "Microsystems Providing Supplementary Care" in Chapter 6. Research in high-quality day care centers has shown no harmful effects on preschool children's attachment to their mothers, intellectual development, social-emotional behavior, or physical health. Few studies have focused upon benefits to the mother, child, and family when good day care permits the mother to earn money and/or to use her abilities in an area additional to child care. An exception is Hetherington, who found that when a divorced mother wished to work and was able to make good provisions for her child and home, her job was likely to have good effects on her, and to do the children no harm [11].

Nursery School or Play Program. Reasons for sending a child to nursery school or a play program may be two-fold: The child's social-emotional development and/or cognitive development are stimulated; the mother has a few hours free from child care, when she can work at a part-time job or do what she wishes. Now that macrosystem ideology has changed to allow mothers some relief from child care, the second reason is more acceptable than it used to be.

Nursery school programs are based on certain philosophies, theories of learning, and values. University nursery schools, used as laboratories for students in child development and early childhood education, often lean heavily on Erikson's theory. The development of the senses of autonomy and initiative are basic concepts in their program planning. Some laboratory schools are organized for special emphasis on cognitive development, some for mental health, others for language. There are programs with special materials and directions for using them, such as the Montessori program. Behavior modification programs, based on learning theory, use positive and negative reinforcement to eliminate undesirable behavior and to establish desirable behavior. Some programs are designed for children with particular handicaps or deficits.

If a nursery school or educational program is to be a supplement to the family, it must fit with the particular needs of the child and with the family's goals and values. Although a great variety of programs exists, it is not always easy for parents to find just the right one. Observation of the program and communication between parents and teachers are needed before the child enters the program, in order to determine whether it will be a good fit.

Parent Education and Support Programs. Nursery schools usually have a policy of trying to involve parents. Some have even gone so far as to require parents to come to regular meetings if their children are to come to school. More frequently, there are occasional meetings that parents attend if they wish. They may discuss their child, view the toys, equipment, and children's art, socialize with one another and the teachers, and have lectures, films, and discussions on child development.

In cooperative nursery schools, parents act as teachers, policy-makers and fund-raisers. In order to prepare for these roles, they learn from teachers, courses, and one another. Groups for parent education and support may also be held apart from children's programs. The New Zealand Parent Centres are operated by parents for parents, with a minimum of professional assistance. In times past in the United States, parent discussion groups were conducted by parents with some guidance from the National Congress of Parents and Teachers, *Parents' Magazine,* and the Cooperative Extension services from state universities.

A Comprehensive Program: Head Start. In 1965 the United States Government and child developmentalists from many fields (See Chapter 1) designed and started a program for poor preschool children that has been incredibly successful. In Sargent Shriver's words, "So, we figured, we'll get these kids into school ahead of time; we'll give them food; we'll give them medical exams; we'll give them the shots or the glasses they need; we'll give them acculturation to academic work—we'll give them a *head start."* [30, p. 52.]

Parents and people from the neighborhood were included in the planning and running of the program. Communities contributed what they could in the way of space, materials, and services. Head Start involved people from different socioeconomic levels and got them working together for the benefit of the children and poor families in the community. The parents who worked in the programs learned about child development and education. Some of them went on to get university degrees and good jobs. Research was done on different types of programs and yielded knowledge of how children learn and teachers teach. About 8 million children and their families benefited from Head Start. At present, budgetary restraints keep registration to about 400,000 children, instead of the 2 million originally planned [3].

The success of Head Start suggested to planners that more children should be reached, and that older and younger children also needed the physical, mental, and social-emotional growth opportunities that Head Start children enjoyed. The program Follow Through was started in order to help Head Start children to maintain their gains throughout the early grades in school, and to develop academic skills. Parent and Child Centers were started in order to reach families of children under 3 years. The program Home Start was established to give children and parents a Head Start-type program at home. At present, home visitors carry on this program with about 20,000 children.

Summary

The normal crises of preschool psychosocial development are, in Erikson's theory, the development of the sense of autonomy and the sense of initiative. Autonomy is enhanced by making decisions that turn out well, initiative by exploring, creating, and playing.

Rule attunement and social sensitivity are the two phases of moral development in which the young child is involved. Warm, authoritative parents promote rule attunement. Secure attachment to parents provides a base for both rule attunement and social sensitivity. Mothers teach empathy by focusing children's attention on results of their actions on other people's feelings, and on ways of making reparation. Principles and patterns of social interactions are learned in supervised play with other children.

Different interaction patterns are learned from experiences with persons of different ages. Children seek contact, attention, and sociability from adults. With peers, type of play varies with age. The age-related sequence of types of play is this: solitary, onlooker, parallel, associative, and cooperative. Cooperative peer play affords experience in alternating behavior, obeying rules, and developing social sensitivity. Rough-and-tumble play with peers teaches use and control of aggression. Children are usually nurturant toward infants. With younger children, nurturance and prosocial behavior are frequent, but in an American study of siblings, older ones were more often aggressive than prosocial. Younger ones were more prosocial than aggressive, and imitated often.

Gender-preferred play behavior is reinforced by playmates, parents, and peers, more by males to males than by or to females. Gender constancy comes through convictions of being a boy or a girl, and realization that everyone always has been and always will be of a particular gender. These convictions, along with biological influences and social interaction, influence children to feel and behave as a member of one sex or the other. Both macrosystem and microsystem influences are at work in developing gender roles and shaping children's behavior in accordance with gender-role ideology. Social ecologies differ in goals for children and related child-rearing methods. Attention-seeking and self-confidence are encouraged in United States children, but not in many other societies.

The child is affected by ecological transitions within the family. The birth of a sibling is a common transition. The experience can be made easier for the young child by preparation during the mother's pregnancy, and giving the child security if separated from the mother at the time of the sibling's birth. Mothers are likely to pay less attention to the older child when a new baby is added to the family. The child has new emotional and social experiences that can promote development. Divorce is another type of ecological transition, involving exit of a family member. The child is affected by economic and homemaking disruptions as well as by parental conflict and deprivation of parental nurturance and stimulation. Divorce is least disruptive when parents cooperate in regard to the children, and when family and friends are supportive.

United States children receive little preparation for parenthood in terms of experience or instruction. New parents use little help and instruction from their families. Parents get advice from medical personnel, books, magazines, friends, and from teachers if the children attend group programs. Help with child care is available from day care programs, nursery schools, play groups, and programs for children and families conducted under government and community auspices.

References

1. Abramovitch, R., C. Corter, and B. Lando. Sibling interaction in the home. *Child Development,* 1979, **50,** 997–1003.
2. Abramovitch, R., and J. E. Grusec. Peer imitation in a natural setting. *Child Development,* 1978, **49,** 60–65.
3. Dittman, L. L. Project Head Start becomes a long-distance runner. *Young Children,* 1980, **35:**6, 2–9.
4. Edwards, C. P., and B. B. Whiting. Differential socialization of girls and boys in light of cross-cultural research. In C. M. Super and S. Harkness (eds.). Anthropological perspectives on child development. *New Directions for Child Development,* 1980, No. 8.
5. Erikson, E. H. *Childhood in Society.* New York: W. W. Norton and Company, Inc. 1963.
6. Etaugh, C., G. Collins, and V. H. Staulcup. Social participation in two-year-old children. *Journal of Genetic Psychology,* 1979, **134,** 159–160.
7. Fagot, B. I. Consequences of moderate cross-gender behavior in preschool children. *Child Development,* 1977, **48,** 902–907.
8. Fagot, B. I. The influence of sex of child on parental reactions to toddler children. *Child Development,* 1978, **49,** 459–465.
9. Halverson, C. F., and M. F. Waldrop. The relations of mechanically recorded activity level to varieties of preschool play behavior. *Child Development,* 1973, **44,** 678–681.

10. Hartup, W. W. Peer relations: Developmental implications and interaction in same- and mixed-age situations. *Young Children*, 1977, **32:**3, 4–13.
11. Hetherington, E. M. Divorce: A child's perspective. *American Psychologist*, 1979, **34,** 851–858.
12. Hoffman, M. L. Development of moral thought, feeling and behavior. *American Psychologist*, 1979, **34,** 958–966.
13. Hogan, R., J. A. Johnson, and N. P. Emler. A socioanalytic theory of moral development. In W. Damon (ed.). Moral Development. *New Directions for Child Development*, 1978, No. 2.
14. Kendrick, C., and J. Dunn. Caring for a second baby: Effects on interaction between mother and firstborn. *Developmental Psychology*, 1980, **16,** 303–311.
15. Lamb, M. E., and J. L. Roopnarine. Peer influences on sex-role development in preschoolers. *Child Development*, 1979, **50,** 1219–1222.
16. LeVine, R. A. Anthropology and child development. In C. M. Super and S. Harkness (eds.). Anthropological perspectives on child development. *New Directions for Child Development*, 1980, No. 8.
17. Lieberman, A. F. Preschoolers' competence with a peer: Relations with attachment and peer experience. *Child Development*, 1977, **48,** 1277–1287.
18. Loo, C. M. Effects of spatial density on social behavior of children. Proceedings, 80th Annual Convention of the American Psychological Association, 1972, 101–102.
19. McConaghy, M. J. Gender preference and the genital basis of gender: Stages in the development of constancy of gender identity. *Child Development*, 1979, **50,** 1223–1226.
20. McConaghy, M. J. Sex-role contravention and sex education directed toward young children in Sweden. *Journal of Marriage and the Family*, 1979, **41,** 893–904.
21. Money, J., and A. A. Ehrhardt. *Man & woman, boy & girl.* Baltimore: The Johns Hopkins University Press, 1972.
22. Parten, M. B. Social participation among pre-school children. *Journal of Abnormal and Social Psychology*, 1932, **27,** 243–269.
23. Rubin, K., T. L. Maioni, and M. Hornung. Free play behaviors in middle- and lower-class preschoolers: Parten and Piaget revisited. *Child Development*, 1976, **47,** 414–419.
24. Rutter, M. Maternal deprivation, 1972–1978: New findings, new concepts, new approaches. *Child Development*, 1979, **50,** 283–305.
24a. Serbin, L. Personal communication, April 1981.
25. Single-parent families in U.S. rose in a decade. *Wall Street Journal*, August 18, 1980.
26. Slaby, R. G., and K. S. Frey. Development of gender constancy and selective attention to same-sex models. *Child Development*, 1975, **46,** 849–856.
27. White, B. L., and J. C. Watts. *Experience and environment. Vol. 1. Major influences on the development of the young child.* Englewood Cliffs, N.J.: Prentice-Hall, Inc., 1973.
28. Whiting, B., and C. P. Edwards. A cross-cultural analysis of sex differences in the behavior of children aged three through 11. *Journal of Social Psychology*, 1973, **91,** 171–188.
29. Zahn-Waxler, C. M., M. Radke-Yarrow, and R. A. King. Child rearing and children's prosocial initiations toward victims of distress. *Child Development*, 1979, **50,** 319–330.
30. Zigler, E., and J. Valentine. *Project Head Start: A legacy of the war on poverty.* New York: The Free Press, 1979.

IV

The School-Age Child

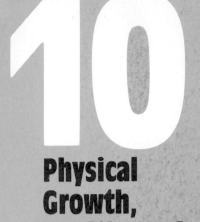

10

Physical Growth, Health, and Motor Development

Slow growth is typical of the period of middle childhood. In both size and proportions, these children change relatively little from year to year. The period of slow growth ends several months before menarche in the girl and a corresponding point of sexual maturity in the boy. Although the period of rapid growth, known as the *puberal growth spurt*, is discussed in Chapter 13, in regard to adolescence, it is important to realize that some children in the elementary school are already in the puberal growth spurt. Growth in height begins to pick up speed, on the average, at about age 9 in girls and 11 in boys. A few girls, however, begin the spurt as early as age 8 and boys at 10. Most girls grow at top speed during their twelfth or thirteenth year, boys during their fourteenth or fifteenth year. A fifth-grade class, like the one in this picture, includes a wide variety of sizes and stages of maturity. We can say that on the average children grow slowly during the early elementary school years.

The middle years are healthier than the preschool period. With growth needs and the burdens of illness claiming less of his energy than they did in an earlier stage of life, the school child has more of himself to invest in

relationships, problem solving, and acquiring of skills and knowledge. Now he works to develop and perfect many motor coordinations, enjoying the sense of adequacy that grows from successful performance. His concepts of himself and his body reflect the interactions of his body with the world and also reflect his perceptions of people's reactions to him.

QUESTIONS TO THINK ABOUT WHILE READING THIS CHAPTER

1. How can height-weight tables be used to evaluate a child's growth?
2. How does the body of a school-age child differ from that of a younger child?
3. How does brain maturation differ between girls and boys?
4. How do children's health problems differ in different parts of the world?
5. How is growth related to macrosystem influences?
6. What is a secular shift in growth?
7. How can schools facilitate children's growth and health?

Physical Growth

Growth can be described in terms of the large, general measurements of height and weight and also in terms of various parts of the body. A third way of considering it has to do with the interrelationships of various aspects of growth.

Growth in Height and Weight

Height increases more steadily than weight, because it is influenced less by environmental changes. Both measurements are, of course, products of the organism's interaction with the environment. However, height depends almost entirely on the linear measure of skeletal growth, and length of the skeletal parts is relatively resistant to short-term environmental pressures. Therefore progress in height is quite regular. As was mentioned in "Skeletal System" in Chapter 7, the bones record such traumas as illnesses and malnutrition, but they do it in terms of bone scars, which can be detected only by X ray. Retarded growth and resulting small stature represent a general result of malnutrition, infections, and stress. Weight, in contrast to height, is a sensitive indicator of malnutrition or overnutrition. Weight is related to volume, which is the product of three linear measures. All types of body tissue, skeleton, muscles, fat, blood, and all the rest, contribute to weight. Thus, although the skeleton is not shortened by an illness or by temporary malnutrition, the soft tissues of the body may be reduced.

Malnutrition + infections + stress → Retarded growth and small stature

Evaluating a Child's Growth. A child's height and weight can be assessed by comparing them with a standard. Either tables or charts can be used. Percentile tables for children from 5 to 12 are given here, in Tables 10–1 and 10–2. The use of these tables is explained in "Proportions and Measurements" in Chapter 4. Charts are given in Appendix B, and their use described there. Both the tables and the charts are from the National

TABLE 10–1
Percentile Distribution of Stature (in Centimeters) of Males and Females from Age 5½ Through 12½ Years, United States

Sex and age	Stature in centimeters, percentiles						
	5th	10th	25th	50th	75th	90th	95th
Male							
5.5 years	104.9	106.7	109.6	113.1	116.1	118.7	120.3
6.0 years	107.7	109.6	112.5	116.1	119.2	121.9	123.5
6.5 years	110.4	112.3	115.3	119.0	122.2	124.9	126.6
7.0 years	113.0	115.0	118.0	121.7	125.0	127.9	129.7
7.5 years	115.6	117.6	120.6	124.4	127.8	130.8	132.7
8.0 years	118.1	120.2	123.2	127.0	130.5	133.6	135.7
8.5 years	120.5	122.7	125.7	129.6	133.2	136.5	138.8
9.0 years	122.9	125.2	128.2	132.2	136.0	139.4	141.8
9.5 years	125.3	127.6	130.8	134.8	138.8	142.4	144.9
10.0 years	127.7	130.1	133.4	137.5	141.6	145.5	148.1
10.5 years	130.1	132.6	136.0	140.3	144.6	148.7	151.5
11.0 years	132.6	135.1	138.7	143.3	147.8	152.1	154.9
11.5 years	135.0	137.7	141.5	146.4	151.1	155.6	158.5
12.0 years	137.6	140.3	144.4	149.7	154.6	159.4	162.3
12.5 years	140.2	143.0	147.4	153.0	158.2	163.2	166.1
Female							
5.5 years	103.9	105.6	108.4	111.6	114.8	117.4	119.2
6.0 years	106.6	108.4	111.3	114.6	118.1	120.8	122.7
6.5 years	109.2	111.0	114.1	117.6	121.3	124.2	126.1
7.0 years	111.8	113.6	116.8	120.6	124.4	127.6	129.5
7.5 years	114.4	116.2	119.5	123.5	127.5	130.9	132.9
8.0 years	116.9	118.7	122.2	126.4	130.6	134.2	136.2
8.5 years	119.5	121.3	124.9	129.3	133.6	137.4	139.6
9.0 years	122.1	123.9	127.7	132.2	136.7	140.7	142.9
9.5 years	124.8	126.6	130.6	135.2	139.8	143.9	146.2
10.0 years	127.5	129.5	133.6	138.3	142.9	147.2	149.5
10.5 years	130.4	132.5	136.7	141.5	146.1	150.4	152.8
11.0 years	133.5	135.6	140.0	144.8	149.3	153.7	156.2
11.5 years	136.6	139.0	143.5	148.2	152.6	156.9	159.5
12.0 years	139.8	142.3	147.0	151.5	155.8	160.0	162.7
12.5 years	142.7	145.4	150.1	154.6	158.8	162.9	165.6

Source: P. V. V. Hamill, R. A. Drizd, C. L. Johnson, R. B. Reed, and A. F. Roche. *NCHS growth curves for children birth–18 years.* Vital and health statistics: Series 11, Data from the National Health Survey; No. 165. (DHEW publication No. (PHS) 78-1650.) Washington: U.S. Government Printing Office, 1977. Table 13.

Center for Health Statistics [19]. They are derived from data from a careful study of a group of children selected to be representative of all children of these ages in the United States. When weighed and measured, the children were wearing a light, standardized clothing that weighed about .25 kilograms.

Predicting Adult Height. As we shall see in Chapter 13, final stature can be predicted fairly well from measurements in childhood. The accuracy increases as the child gets older. If, in addition to measurement of height, one also knows the level of skeletal maturity, the prediction can be accurate to less than an inch, after the age of 7. Because skeletal maturity may not be known, it is possible to use the multipliers given in

TABLE 10–2
Percentile Distribution of
Weight (in Kilograms) of
Males and Females from
Age 5½ Through 12½ Years,
United States.

Sex and age	Weight in kilograms, percentiles						
	5th	10th	25th	50th	75th	90th	95th
Male							
5.5 years	16.09	16.83	18.14	19.67	21.25	22.96	24.66
6.0 years	16.93	17.72	19.07	20.69	22.40	24.31	26.34
6.5 years	17.78	18.62	20.02	21.74	23.62	25.76	28.16
7.0 years	18.64	19.53	21.00	22.85	24.94	27.36	30.12
7.5 years	19.52	20.45	22.02	24.03	26.36	29.11	32.73
8.0 years	20.40	21.39	23.09	25.30	27.91	31.06	34.51
8.5 years	21.31	22.34	24.21	26.66	29.61	33.22	36.96
9.0 years	22.25	23.33	25.40	28.13	31.46	35.57	39.58
9.5 years	23.25	24.38	26.68	29.73	33.46	38.11	42.35
10.0 years	24.33	25.52	28.07	31.44	35.61	40.80	45.27
10.5 years	25.51	26.78	29.59	33.30	37.92	43.63	48.31
11.0 years	26.80	28.17	31.25	35.30	40.38	46.57	51.47
11.5 years	28.24	29.72	33.08	37.46	43.00	49.61	54.73
12.0 years	29.85	31.46	35.09	39.78	45.77	52.73	58.09
12.5 years	31.64	33.41	37.31	42.27	48.70	55.91	61.52
Female							
5.5 years	15.29	15.97	17.05	18.56	20.36	22.48	24.11
6.0 years	16.05	16.72	17.86	19.52	21.44	23.89	25.75
6.5 years	16.85	17.51	18.76	20.61	22.68	25.50	27.59
7.0 years	17.71	18.39	19.78	21.84	24.16	27.39	29.68
7.5 years	18.62	19.37	20.95	23.26	25.90	29.57	32.07
8.0 years	19.62	20.45	22.26	24.84	27.88	32.04	34.71
8.5 years	20.68	21.64	23.70	26.58	30.08	34.73	37.58
9.0 years	21.82	22.92	25.27	28.46	32.44	37.60	40.64
9.5 years	23.05	24.29	26.94	30.45	34.94	40.61	43.85
10.0 years	24.36	25.76	28.71	32.55	37.53	43.70	47.17
10.5 years	25.75	27.32	30.57	34.72	40.17	46.84	50.57
11.0 years	27.24	28.97	32.49	36.95	42.84	49.96	54.00
11.5 years	28.83	30.71	34.48	39.23	45.48	53.03	57.42
12.0 years	30.52	32.53	36.52	41.53	48.07	55.99	60.81
12.5 years	32.30	34.42	38.59	43.84	50.56	58.81	64.12

Source: P. V. V. Hamill, R. A. Drizd, C. L. Johnson, R. B. Reed, and A. F. Roche. *NCHS growth curves for children birth–18 years.* Vital and health statistics: Series 11, Data from the National Health Survey; No. 165. (DHEW publication No. (PHS) 78-1650.) Washington: U.S. Government Printing Office, 1977. Table 14.

Table 10–3 to get a rough estimate for boys and girls whose mid-parent height is average or slightly above average, or close to 169 to 172 centimeters.

Sex Differences. Using the tables for boys and girls, compare the average heights (50th percentile) at each year. Boys are ahead in height from ages 6 through 8. The sexes are equal at 9. From 10 through 12, girls are taller than boys. More accurately, the average girl is taller than the average boy. The difference is small, only 1.8 centimeters at age 12. Next, compare extremes. A girl in the 95th percentile at 12 will be 25.1 centimeters, or about 10 inches taller than a boy in the 5th percentile. If Lanky Linda and Short Shawn are paired for dancing, they will probably

	Multipliers at age					
	7	8	9	10	11	12
For Girls	1.35	1.29	1.23	1.17	1.12	1.07
For Boys	1.47	1.40	1.35	1.29	1.24	1.19

To predict the adult height of a United States child whose parents are of average stature, multiply the child's present height by the appropriate number.

Source: S. M. Garn. Body size and its implications. In L. W. Hoffman and M. L. Hoffman (eds.). *Review of child development research.* Vol. II. New York: Russell Sage Foundation, 1966.

both be embarrassed, because sex stereotypes say that a male should be taller than a female. However, their plight is statistically unlikely, and unlikely also because they will not be interested in the same sorts of social activities. No doubt, Linda is well advanced into her puberal growth spurt, while Shawn has not yet begun to spurt in growth.

The average girl overtakes and passes the average boy in height because she has begun the puberal growth spurt and he has not. Girls enter puberty about 2 years earlier than boys. As the chapter on adolescent growth will show (and as everybody knows), boys overtake girls in height, and the average man is taller than the average woman. Girls' earlier puberty is only one dramatic aspect of a larger sex difference in development. At any given age, a girl is closer to maturity or completed growth than is a boy. For example, 75 per cent of adult height is attained by the average 7-year-old girl and by the average 9-year-old boy. Physiological maturity can be estimated by bone development. At birth, the girl's bones show development 4 to 6 weeks in advance of the boy's [44]. At 11 or 12, she is 2 or 3 years ahead. If female and male heights are compared at the same level of physiological development as shown by bone maturity, the average male is considerably taller than the average female throughout the life span [12].

Proportions

School-age children look different from younger children in face and body, because of changes in rates of growth. The brain case, relatively large at birth, is still large at 5 years. Then the size of the face begins to catch up with the top part of the head. The body looks thinner and more graceful than a young child's body. Fat decreases in thickness and changes in distribution patterns. Increasing grace comes from longer legs, a slimmer body, and a relatively lower center of gravity. These changes make climbing and bicycling easier, because a lower center of gravity is steadying, and long limbs can reach farther. Proportions and center of gravity at different age levels are shown in Figure 10–1.

Sex Differences. Girls have more fat, especially right under the skin. Consequently, girls' contours are softer than boys'. Owing to the earlier eruption of permanent teeth, girls' faces may acquire a mature appearance earlier than boys'. Although differences in skeletal proportions are

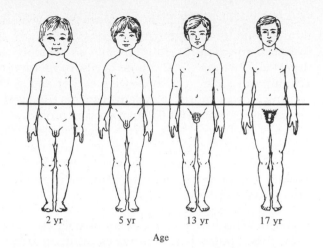

FIGURE 10–1.
Changes in proportions during the school age are seen by comparing a 5-year old with a 13-year-old. Contrasts are also seen between 5 and 3, and 13 and 17. Note the lowering of the center of gravity in the trunk. (SOURCE: Adapted from Carroll E. Palmer. Studies of the center of gravity in the human body. *Child Development* 1944, 15, 99–108.)

much more apparent after puberty, there are some such differences throughout childhood. For example, the average boy exceeds the average girl in length of forearm relative to upper arm and relative to total body height. Sex differences can be seen in hands, also. Girls are more likely than boys to have an index finger longer than a fourth finger [44].

Race Differences. Black and white children, on the average, differ in certain bodily proportions, as shown in ratios of certain dimensions [27]. For blacks, the length of the legs contributes on the average a greater proportion to total stature than it does for whites; or, conversely, whites' trunks are a larger part of their total stature. Not only are blacks' legs (and arms) longer but their feet and hands are also. Similarly, blacks' chests and hips are more slender. One of the conclusions from these comparisons is "This implies that genetic factors affect skeletal dimensions: one's racial background predisposes the skeleton to certain proportions" [27, p. 15].

Certain physiological and anatomical characteristics are especially typical of middle childhood. Appearance changes not only because of new proportions, but because of changes in skin and hair. Both grow less delicate. Hair may darken. The following changes and conditions are important for understanding and supervising the health and growth of children of school age.

Tissues and Organs

Muscles. The muscular system grows bigger and stronger, but it is still immature in function. Children's muscles are more easily injured by strain than are adolescents'. For example, Little League pitchers are prone to "Little League elbow," a muscular injury caused by overuse. Children, especially boys, find it difficult to sit still. Motor inhibition, or immobilizing the muscles, requires more maturity than many first-graders have.

Digestive System. Increasing maturity shows in fewer upsets and by retaining food for a longer time. Thus, the school-age child does not have to be fed so carefully, so often, and so promptly as the preschool child. Because growth is slow, calorie needs, in relation to the size of the stomach, are not so great as they were earlier and as they will be during the coming growth spurt. The danger at this time is that the child will fill up on empty calories, foods that do not promote growth, such as sugar, starches, and excess fats. With relatively low calorie needs, it is important to eat foods that are high in proteins, minerals, and vitamins. The combination of freedom to move out from his mother's supervision, plus a bit of money in his pockets, may result in an excessive intake of soft drinks and candy.

Bladder. Children vary widely in bladder capacity, with boys having less than girls. Individual differences occur in frequency of urination, and difference in one individual from one time to another, because of variations in temperature, humidity, time of day, emotional state, fluids ingested, and so on.

Respiratory System. Breathing becomes slower, deeper, and more regular, changing from 20 to 30 inhalations per minute in the preschool period to 17 to 25 in the school-age period [24]. Infections and disturbances of the respiratory system are fewer and milder than in the early years.

Heart. Slow growth takes place between 4 and 10 years. As the child grows toward maturity, his heartbeat slows down and his blood pressure goes up. Between 6 and 12, he reaches the average adult heart rate of 70–100 per minute. Systolic blood pressure, at an average of 110 millimeters, is still below the adult norm [24].

Ears. Infections are less likely than they were during the preschool years. With the growth of the lower part of the face, the Eustachian tube, leading from the throat into the middle ear, grows longer, relatively narrower, and slanted. Thus, it is harder for disease organisms to invade. With fewer respiratory infections too, there are fewer invading organisms in the child. Although studies on children's hearing have yielded a variety of results, they usually show increasing acuity with age. There is some indication that the average child has greater acuity in the right ear than in the left.

Eyes. The farsighted eyes of the young child change to the more mature shape of eyeball by 6 or 7 years, and grow to adult size by 12 or 14. In the National Health Examination survey, 51 per cent of 6-year-olds had 20/20 distance binocular vision or better; by age 11 the percentage was 56. However, the incidence of distance binocular acuity of 20/70 or less increased steadily from about 1 per cent at 6 to about 11 per cent at age 11. There was no marked age trend for proportion of children with similarly poor near visual acuity; 1.5 per cent of children at age 6, to 3.5 per cent at age 11. In this survey the average boy had consistently better binocular vision, both distance and near, than the average girl [36]. The same was true of monocular vision [34]. In color vision, however, boys were consistently poorer than girls. Seven per cent of boys had color vision deficiencies, as compared with half of 1 per cent of girls. Most of the boys' defects were in red-green types of defects; about two-thirds of the girls' defects were of the red-green type. Black boys had a higher incidence of color deficiencies than white boys [41].

Bones. The skeleton continues to ossify, replacing cartilage with bone. Since mineralization is not complete, the bones resist pressure and muscle pull less than more mature bones do. Good hygiene includes chairs, desks, and shoes that fit, frequent moving around, and caution in carrying heavy loads. For example, if a pack of newspapers is to be slung from one shoulder, it should be changed often from one shoulder to the other.

The skeleton is a useful maturity indicator, because its level of development is closely tied to progress toward sexual maturity. A child who is advanced in bone development will reach puberty at an earlier age than the average child. Black children between 6 and 11 are about 3 months ahead of white children the same age. Differences between the two groups of boys are similar to those between the two groups of girls [38].

Teeth. These are important years for teething, because it is during this period that most of the changes from deciduous to permanent teeth take place. At almost any time, a child has a gap or two in his jaw, a loose tooth, or one just popping through the gum. Nutrition, including sufficient fluorides, oral hygiene, and dental care are very important in assuring healthy teeth. Speech, nutrition, appearance, and body image are all affected by the soundness of teeth. Figure 10–2 shows the jaws with both sets of teeth in place, the deciduous ones in the process of losing their roots through resorption, which prepares them to shed, leaving room for permanent teeth, which will exceed the number of baby teeth. Figures 10–3, a and b show the complete set of 20 baby teeth and the

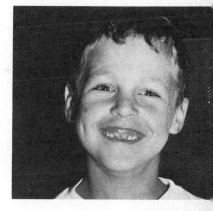

FIGURE 10–2
Dentition of the 6-year-old child. (Source: From "Dental Health Factors for Teachers." Copyright 1966 by the American Dental Association. Reprinted by permission.)

Second Permanent Molars

First Permanent Molars

Second Permanent Molars

Permanent Teeth

Deciduous Teeth

Permanent Teeth

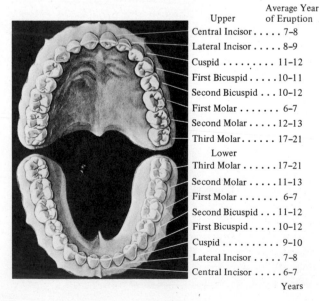

Upper	Average Month of Eruption	Average Year of Shedding
Central Incisor	7.5	7.5
Lateral Incisor	9	8
Cuspid	18	11.5
First Molar	14	10.5
Second Molar	24	10.5
Lower		
Second Molar	20	11
First Molar	12	10
Cuspid	16	9.5
Lateral Incisor	7	7
Central Incisor	6	6

FIGURE 10–3a.
The primary (deciduous) teeth. (SOURCE: From "Dental Health Factors for Teachers." Copyright 1966 by the American Dental Association. Reprinted by permission.)

complete set of 32 adult teeth, indicating the replacements and additions that transform a young child's jaws into mature jaws.

Because the first permanent teeth to erupt in most children do not replace deciduous teeth, they are likely not to be recognized as permanent teeth. These teeth are the first molars, which appear just behind the second deciduous molars. As is the case with the deciduous teeth, there are

FIGURE 10–3b.
The permanent teeth. (SOURCE: From "Dental Health Factors for Teachers." Copyright 1966 by the American Dental Association. Reprinted by permission.)

Upper	Average Year of Eruption
Central Incisor	7–8
Lateral Incisor	8–9
Cuspid	11–12
First Bicuspid	10–11
Second Bicuspid	10–12
First Molar	6–7
Second Molar	12–13
Third Molar	17–21
Lower	
Third Molar	17–21
Second Molar	11–13
First Molar	6–7
Second Bicuspid	11–12
First Bicuspid	10–12
Cuspid	9–10
Lateral Incisor	7–8
Central Incisor	6–7
	Years

some differences in the times of eruption when corresponding teeth in the two jaws are compared. There are also sex differences. The times of eruption of girls' permanent teeth are earlier than those of boys'. This is in line with the faster rate of maturation of girls, but, comparing tooth for tooth, girls are further ahead in the eruption of some teeth than they are for others [44]. There is also a consistent difference between black and white Americans in the time of emergence of the permanent teeth, with blacks being ahead of whites of the same sex [13].

Brain. At between 6 and 8 years, the brain shows a spurt in weight gain and the head circumference a corresponding increase [9]. At the same time the corpus callosum, the main connecting link between the hemispheres, becomes much more mature in structure and function [7]. The period from 6 to 8 is the time when children change from one Piagetian stage to the next. As the next chapter will show, the typical child restructures his mind to achieve concrete operations at the same time that the brain increases rapidly in substance and connections.

The right and left hemispheres of the brain are specialized for various functions. Lateral differences can be shown at birth. During childhood the brain becomes more complex in its organization. The left hemisphere, in about 94 per cent of people, deals with information in an analytic, sequential, time-oriented style. The style of the right hemisphere is global and synthetic, adapted to understanding a situation as a whole. The left, then, is good at organizing, encoding, interpreting and producing language, which occurs in a time sequence; the right is good at perceiving and interpreting pictures and nonlanguage sounds, and solving spatial problems [49]. Girls tend to do better in the skills dependent more on the left hemisphere, while boys are more likely to excel in skills mediated by the right hemisphere [23].

Left hemisphere: Analytical, sequential, time-oriented, language, reasoning

Right hemisphere: Global, synthetic, space, music

Furthermore, a boy's brain is more likely to be more lateralized for spatial ability than is a girl's. Electrical activity in the brain is measured by an electroencephalogram (EEG), which shows where the action is taking place. When boys work on a spatial problem, the EEG shows mostly right hemisphere activity; girls, working on the same problem, are more likely to show activity in both hemispheres [33]. Girls often use some verbal reasoning on spatial problems, whereas boys use more spatial imagery.

Brain organization is different among left-handed people. A review of research concludes that in left-handers the following types of speech-function location are likely: in the left hemisphere, 40 per cent; in the right hemisphere, 20 per cent; in both hemispheres, 40 per cent [40]. Among a group of 5- to 8-year-olds, who were judged to have their primary speech functions located on the right, sex differences in performance were reversed [15]. Girls did better on spatial tasks, boys on verbal, indicating faster maturation in the left hemispheres of girls and in the right hemispheres of boys. Thus the sex difference in hemisphere maturation rates remained stable, even when functional organization changed.

Health and Safety

Not only is middle childhood relatively safe, in terms of death rates. It has become safer. Fewer children die in the United States and in other parts of the world, as can be seen in Figure 10–4. The graph also shows that death rates have gone down more in countries where they used to be very high than in the United States and Denmark where they were relatively low. Even so, most childhood deaths could be prevented. Much remains to be done in reducing deaths from violence (accidents and homicide), the leading cause of death in the United States children, and deaths from disease and malnutrition.

Illness

School-age children have fewer illnesses than preschool children do [48]. The rates for respiratory and gastrointestinal upsets decrease considerably although they continue to be the most frequent types of illness, with respiratory infections the leading cause of illness. Figure 10–5 shows the percentages of various categories of acute conditions reported for a selected year during the National Health Survey. The data were collected from a nationwide sample of families about members of the families who had seen a doctor or been confined to bed because of the condition during any part of the two weeks previous to the interview.

The communicable diseases (including measles, chicken pox, mumps, whooping cough, and scarlet fever) are much less threatening to American children than they were in former years. Table 10–4 shows diseases that are controllable in the United States by routine immunizations. In addition, immunizations for influenza and pneumonia may be given to children at risk. The disease situation varies in different parts of

FIGURE 10–4.
Death rates at ages 5–14 in selected countries. (Source: M. C. McHale, J. McHale, and G. F. Streatfeild. *Children in the world.* Washington: Population Reference Bureau, 1979.)

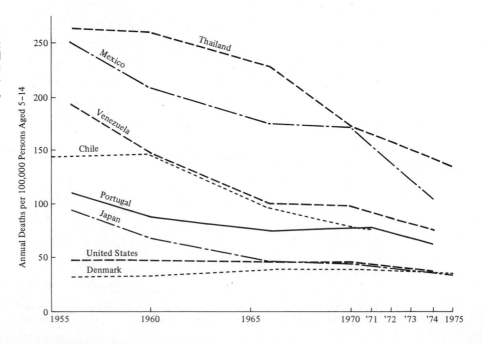

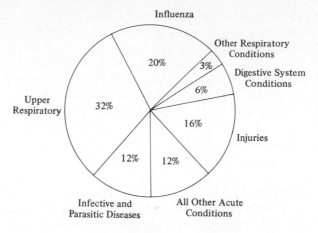

FIGURE 10–5.
Incidence of acute conditions as per cent of total number of acute conditions reported for children 6–16 years in the United States. (SOURCE: C. S. Wilder. Acute conditions, incidence and associated disability. National Center for Health Statistics. Series 10, no. 98. D.H.E.W. publication no. (HRA) 75–1524. Washington: U.S. Government Printing Office, 1975.)

the world. Increasing travel and communication in the world mean that almost any disease might appear in a new location. Therefore, anyone who works with children needs a comprehensive handbook on communicable diseases, not in order to replace the physician who must diagnose and treat but to be able to observe, refer, and cooperate with medical personnel. Such a handbook [3] is available free from many state health departments. See Appendix C for the vaccination schedule recommended by the American Medical Association and the American Academy of Pediatrics, and for a summary of facts about the communicable diseases of childhood, see Appendix B.

Although certain physical conditions are not considered illness, they have harmful long-range effects upon children's health.

Special Health Problems

Dental. Dental caries is a disease even though it is not incapacitating. If untreated, it only becomes more serious and results in loss of teeth. Dental examinations done in the National Health Survey showed an average of 4.4 filled, decayed, or missing permanent teeth in children from 6 to 11 [21]. This figure rose steadily with age, being 6.3 for the age group 12–17 years.

Occlusion of the teeth, the way in which the upper and lower teeth meet and overlap, is also related to health because only when they meet is food chewed adequately, the first step in the process of digestion. Mal-

Smallpox	1796	Polio (Sabin)	1962
Diphtheria	1923	Measles	1964
Whooping cough	1933	Mumps	1968
Tetanus	1936	German measles	1969
Polio (Salk)	1954		

TABLE 10–4
Diseases Controlled in the United States by Routine Immunizations, in Order of Initial Usage of Immunization.

Prepared by Lucile Votta, R. N.

occlusion occurs when the upper and lower teeth do not meet adequately. The lower edges of the upper teeth normally rest in front of the upper edges of the lower teeth. Crooked teeth also are included under malocclusion because they impair biting and chewing. In the National Health Examination Survey of children between the ages of 6 and 11, about two-thirds of children were classified as having normal occlusion, or only minor signs of malocclusion. The remaining third, in the judgment of the dental examiners, had malocclusion that needed attention; of these 14 per cent had malocclusion that was interfering with their appearance, their chewing, or their speech [22].

Nutritional. Long-range problems also include nutrition and fitness. A Canadian dietary survey found that among children 5 to 9 years old, 4.7 per cent of the general population was at risk in regard to protein-calorie malnutrition, whereas 7.7 per cent of Indian and 6.1 per cent of Eskimo were so [39]. Although a United States survey found children age 6 to 11 to be in better nutritional condition than older and younger groups, some deficiencies were found, especially in iron. Low iron values were found in 2.59 per cent of all children and in 9.39 per cent of black children in the 6 to 11 group [1].

Obesity is becoming more frequent among children in the United States. Obese children are likely to be overweight as adults. Although some children are eating too many calories, others are not getting enough. And even more widespread than the problem of insufficient calories is the poor quality of diet. Some children are thin and short because of eating poor quality food and some are obese because of eating poor quality food while at the same time having too many calories.

Chronic Illnesses and Impairments. It is estimated that 15 to 20 per cent of the world's children are handicapped by conditions ranging from minor mental disturbances to major physical disabilities [26]. Five per cent have severe handicaps. The poorer regions of the world have greater proportions of handicapped children. For example, 50,000 blind children in Bangladesh need surgery. Table 10–5 shows numbers of children in the

TABLE 10–5
Number of Children Aged 6–17 with Selected Handicaps, United States.

Type of handicap	Number
Blind and visually impaired	42,800
Deaf and hard of hearing	246,000
Crippled	213,900
Speech-impaired	1,497,100
Emotionally disturbed	855,500
Mentally retarded	983,800
Learning disabled	1,283,200
Multihandicapped	25,700

Source: M. C. McHale, J. McHale, and G. F. Streatfeild. *Children in the world.* Washington: Population Reference Bureau, 1979.

United States with various handicapping conditions. Of 48.5 million children between 6 and 17, 12 per cent are rated as handicapped. Chronic diseases and long-term disabilities may affect growth adversely. They certainly limit some of the child's activities. Conditions likely to retard growth include chronically infected tonsils and adenoids, intestinal parasites, rheumatic fever, and diabetes. Good physical care can alleviate some of these conditions and even in cases where the condition cannot be cured, good care may result in normal growth.

The disabled child suffers not only the discomfort of diagnostic and treatment procedures. He also misses out on some of the activities that normal children have as part of everyday life. Requiring more physical care, he actually receives more nurturance from his mother and often from the whole family. He has a narrower social and interpersonal experience. Parents and often teachers give him less work to do, less responsibility to carry. The specific restrictions required by various handicaps differ from one to another. For example, dietary requirements for diabetics are very embarrassing to some children, who often try to hide their condition from other children.

Accidents

Deaths from accidents are over twice as frequent for boys as for girls between 5 and 14 years of age [29]. Accidents cause 55 per cent of boys' deaths and 40 per cent of girls'. Table 10–6 shows death rates from the leading types of accidents. Motor vehicles are the leading cause of accidental death. The number of children injured is many times more than the number killed.

In an effort to find out personal characteristics of children likely to be injured as pedestrians in traffic, British children between 5 and 10 years old were filmed crossing a street on the way home from school. Their

Type of accident	Death rate per 100,000	
	Boys	Girls
Accidents—all types	23.9	10.9
Motor vehicle	11.0	6.2
Traffic	10.6	6.1
Pedestrian	4.2	2.5
Nontraffic	.4	.1
Falls	.5	.2
Drowning	4.6	1.1
Fires and flames	1.7	1.4
Poisoning by solids and liquids	.2	.1
Firearms	1.7	
Inhalation and ingestion of food or other object		.2

TABLE 10–6
Mortality from Leading Types of Accidents in United States for Boys and Girls Aged 5–14.

Source: Mortality from leading types of accidents. *Statistical Bulletin,* 1978, **59**:3, 10–12.

behavior was analyzed and rated as safe, careless, and unsafe. The unsafe children ran out into the street without looking either way and then ran about unpredictably, whereas the careless children did not look, but walked straight across the street. There were equal numbers of "safe" boys and girls who looked and walked straight across the street. The careless group consisted of 28 boys and 35 girls. The unsafe group was made up of 23 boys and 9 girls. Personality tests showed the careless and unsafe children to be significantly more excitable and tense than the safe ones. Careless children were overconfident, whereas unsafe children were submissive and obedient, but expedient [11].

Ecology of Growth and Health

When an environment offers abundant nutrients, hygienic conditions, and protection from injury, the children in it are likely to maintain health and to grow toward full potential. Differences in children's growth and health, through time and space, can often be traced to ecological differences.

Macrosystem Influences

Geography and Climate. Every macrosystem has a physical setting, in a geographic location in the world. The setting affects agricultural productivity and hence the food supply. Prevailing winds and ocean currents may bring pollution. The setting has a particular climate, which seems to have a direct effect on children's growth. For example, Peruvian children living at a high altitude have larger chests and lungs than children of the same ethnic group living at sea level [44]. It may be that the long limbs and trunks of Africans and the short limbs and trunks of Eskimo represent genetic adaptations to hot and cold climates. A long, slim body loses heat more rapidly than a short, thick one.

Seasonal variation in growth has been found in West European children [44]. They grew faster in height during spring and summer than in fall and winter. During the 3 months of fastest growth, children between 7 and 10 years grew three times as fast as they did during the period of slowest growth. Because blind children did not show the same variation, it is thought that seasonal growth is mediated by light on the eyes.

Cross-Culture Comparisons. Physical measurements of children have been assembled for 8-year-olds, using 300 samples [28]. Mean heights of the various groups varied from 106 centimeters in Bihar, India, to 129 centimeters in Norway, a range of about nine inches. The shortest groups were mainly in Southeast Asia, Oceania, and South America, the tallest mainly in northern and central Europe, eastern Australia, and the United States. Five samples were taller than the United States white group, whereas only the Norwegian average was greater than that of the black sample from the United States. Weight averages varied from 17 kilograms to 27 kilograms, a range of about 25 pounds. The average child in Norway weighed 50 per cent more than the average child in Bangla-

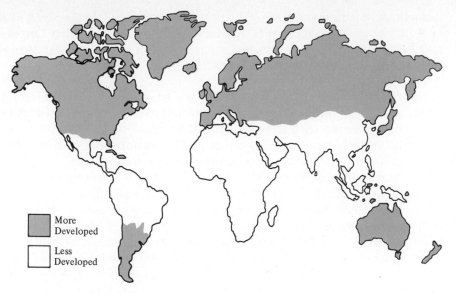

FIGURE 10–6.
More and less developed, or richer and poorer, regions of the world. (SOURCE: M. C. McHale, J. McHale, and G. F. Streatfeild. *Children in the world.* Washington: Population Reference Bureau, 1979.)

desh.   The largest children live in parts of the world where nutritious food is abundant and where the infectious diseases are well controlled or largely eliminated.   The same is true when comparisons are made between head circumferences, or between skeletal maturation, or in time of onset of the puberal growth spurt [47].

Figure 10–6 divides the world into "more developed" and "less developed" parts of the world, or into richer and poorer.   Four out of five children live in the poorer regions, where food, housing, and health protection are not even minimally adequate [26].

When death rates and illness rates are considered, those of children from poor countries greatly exceed those of children from richer countries.   Patterning of causes of death is different between rich and poor.   Where disease control is good, in the more prosperous countries, the proportion of deaths from injuries is greater.   In Canada, for example, where food is plentiful and hygiene good, accidents and violence account for 61 per cent of deaths of children between 5 and 14 [26].

When violence ranks high as a cause of death and injury, as it does in the United States and Canada, reasons must be sought on all levels of the ecology.   Motor vehicle accidents can be analyzed in terms of design of cars, lay-out of streets and towns, laws and law enforcement, and values involving autonomy, speed, and safety.   Child abuse, a growing problem in North America, has roots in macrosystems as well as on other levels. Ideology upholds the privacy of the family, parents' rights, and permission for physical punishment.

Oriental (Chinese and Japanese) children in California are injured less frequently than other Americans and their death rates are markedly lower both in California and Hawaii [29].   In traditional Oriental families, children are carefully supervised and sheltered and discouraged from exploration and initiation of activities. It follows logically that Oriental children would be exposed to fewer hazards than would average Americans in the same physical environment.

Socioeconomic Comparisons. Children from upper socioeconomic levels are larger and grow faster than children in lower levels in every society studied so far, with the exception of Sweden [44, pp 146–149]. Apparently Sweden has extended equal growth opportunities to all of its children. Growth patterns are similar in children of upper socioeconomic status all over the world. Differences due to ethnicity are about 3 per cent for height and 6 per cent for weight, whereas differences between poor and well-off children of the same ethnic group are around 12 per cent in height and 30 per cent in weight [47].

In low socioeconomic levels, growth and health are depressed by inadequate nutrients, physical care, and protection, and by high levels of stress. Growth is affected by the child's own experience of stress in one or more of his microsystems. Parents are stressed by low socioeconomic conditions, and thereby less able to provide care and protection. Although child abuse occurs at all socioeconomic levels, it is more frequent at lower levels, as is violence in general [31].

Secular Shifts. Within a macrosystem changes in growth patterns occur over time. Although comparisons are most often made in terms of height, changes have been noted in weight, chest circumference, head length and breadth, timing of sexual maturity, and strength [37]. Reasons for secular shifts are many, and some are unknown, but dietary changes are surely important. Other macrosystem variables include changes in health practices, living conditions, and social organization.

Increases in height and weight over time have been observed in nearly all the European countries and in Canada, Japan, and the United States. Differences over time are greater than present-day socioeconomic differences in height and weight in Europe, North America, and Japan [44]. In Sweden differences in children's heights between 1883 and 1938 were nearly equal to 1½ years of growth. The secular shift is not always toward greater size. Sometimes the shift is to smaller, as it probably was during the Industrial Revolution, and may be today in India. The secular increase has probably stopped in England, Japan, Norway, and the United States [37]. Although these countries may have come close to providing optimal growth environments for most children, there is no proof that they have done so. Perhaps further ecological improvements would result in additional secular increase.

Microsystem Influences

As children grow older, the home continues to be the most important microsystem in promoting growth and maintaining life and health. The microsystem of the school is second to the home in its influence on growth and health.   Other important influences include the neighborhood, clubs, and the network of relatives and friends.

Home.   The home setting and the family, of course, provide the physical underpinnings of growth and health—food, clothing, bed, baths, protection, and access to medical care.   The family's management of television-viewing is salient to health.   When children are permitted to watch for long periods, they are sedentary, instead of being active outdoors.   The family also contributes to the level of stress encountered by the child, and to the child's progress in taking responsibility for his own health care.

Some children fail to grow normally because of psychological stress in the home.   In such cases, secretion of growth hormone is inhibited [44].   When stress is alleviated, growth hormone secretion resumes and the child catches up in height.   Many children, however, continue to grow normally under family stress.   It is not known why some turn off growth hormone whereas others secrete normally even under very disturbing circumstances.

Another result of family or parental stress is child abuse.   Parents may suffer from problems in marital, occupational, or network relationships, or from ill health or economic pressures.   Family interaction may result in hostility.   One child may be chosen as scapegoat and bear the brunt of abuse.   The whole family then needs help from outside the microsystem of the home.   The mesosystem, the connections with other microsystems, will be critical in leading to assistance.

The family influences health through protection, nutrition, sanitation, activity, rest, stress, teaching, and treatment

Families share macrosystem beliefs and customs in health care; they also have some private beliefs and customs.   Whatever the parents think and do about health care, they pass it on to their children.   All parents make some effort to have children take responsibility for self-care.   School-age children, wanting some independence and privacy, cooperate more or less.   They brush teeth, take baths, hang up clothing, and sneeze into tissues or handkerchiefs in the ways modeled, requested, and demanded by parents.   Parents, most often mothers, manage and arrange the home setting and activities so as to make it easy or difficult to do these tasks.   Parents hope that health practices will carry over into other microsystems, and probably many of them do.

The family of a handicapped child makes special adaptations according to the needs of the child.   More than average time and effort are required when a child needs a special diet, when locomotion and coordination are impaired, when a child is deaf or blind or mentally handicapped.

Neighborhood.   With some freedom from adult supervision, children can make some choices for themselves.   Together with peers, they may take all sorts of health and safety risks that would not be permitted at home, such as playing ball in the street, poking in drains and gutters, stepping onto an ice floe, climbing over a fence into a construction area, chewing a friend's gum, sniffing glue, and filling up on sugary, fatty foods.   Anyone who recalls being a child can add to the list.

Accidents are less likely when neighborhoods afford parks and playgrounds equipped for interesting activity. Some adult supervision is desirable, carried out so as to keep chldren safe and yet preserve their freedom of choice and feeling of privacy.

Homes of Relatives and Friends. In the microsystems of other peoples' homes, children learn alternative kinds of health care. A sick friend is up, running around with a fever, instead of staying in bed drinking fluids. An aunt serves a vegetarian meal, instead of one built around meat. Grandmother's house is very hot. From such experiences children find out what they like, and make plans for themselves.

The school influences health through education, physical setting, nutrition, treatment, activity, and stress

School. Two contributions are made by the school, actual health care and education as to self-health care. Feeding programs are tremendously important in the growth and well-being of children who do not get enough nutrients at home. School lunch programs supply much-needed food to such children. During a recent year, over 11 million United States children received free or reduced-price lunches in school [43]. School lunch programs also upgrade the intake of children who cannot go home for lunch and who might bring or buy a meal of poor nutritional quality. Breakfast programs have made great improvements in the health and learning of children who come to school without breakfast. A school may serve as the location of immunization clinics or for other well-child care. As already mentioned, dental clinics in New Zealand schools give complete care for children's teeth.

Health education in school extends what the child learns at home and, like network homes, gives more alternatives for self-care. At school,

however, the child learns basic information about growth and physiological processes, and reasons are given for recommended practices. Topics include nutrition and hygiene, and perhaps education about reproduction and drugs. Ideally, nutrition education is combined with nutrition programs, allowing the child to learn through eating, cooking, and even growing food, as well as through listening.

Children's growth and health are affected by the physical setting and program. Positive effects come from adequate air and light, comfortable temperature, seats that fit, opportunities for frequent exercise, available drinking water, ready access to clean bathrooms, lack of interpersonal tensions, and education procedures that promote comfortable feelings. Unfortunately we also have to add lack of physical punishment, because in some schools physical punishment is still used.

As part of a program recommended for child health, schools are suggested as centers [42]. A specially trained nurse, with adequate backup, would conduct examinations and referrals and arrange follow-up and communication between teacher and home. All children would receive needed treatment and prostheses, such as glasses and hearing aids. A legal system would support the medical system for children. These recommendations are based on observations of the care that Europeans provide for all children. This care includes money (family support) to ensure enough food, clothing, and shelter for children; nurses who work in clinics, visit homes, and, with other agencies, provide prevention, examinations, treatment, and guidance.

Medical Caregiver. If medical care were given in the schools, as here suggested, then it would be part of a known microsystem. If a physician is the main caregiver, the child will know his office as a microsystem. A clinic may be the health microsystem. Perhaps the child will go to a hospital for diagnosis and treatment, even surgery. All such arrangements have the potential for educating, as well as treating, and for making progress in self-care rewarding. In "Care of Ill and Injured Children" in Chapter 7 we discussed ways of preparing children for hospital experiences and ways of supporting them during such times. Although older children can manage better on their own than younger ones, a sick person of any age needs emotional support, even a family member to stay with the patient.

To keep the child a whole and healthy person, all parts of her life must be held together through communication and relationships. Her microsystems of home and school are integrated when parents and teachers know each other and talk to each other about their mutual interest, this child. Parents may go further and contribute their time and efforts to classroom activities or improving the physical setting of the school. Principals and teachers can create a welcoming climate and start interactions with parents.

Mesosystem Influences

Children, as well as parents, can build and strengthen the mesosystem that links homes. Children's friendships, begun in school and neighborhood, can open ways for their families to relate to one another. Adults' friendships can be broadened to include their children in recreation and mutual assistance.

When the child is ill, the mesosystem between home and medical caregiver can be crucial in recovery and in preventing emotional scars. Although parents can try their best to communicate and to follow directions, much depends upon the doctor, nurse, and hospital administrator. Ideally, they welcome parents, include them in planning, and make partners of them in giving care and treatment. When children are chronically ill or handicapped, educational and medical microsystems are more elaborate, and mesosystems will also be more involved.

Motor Development

In acquiring a motor skill, a child executes an ordered series of movements, directing them toward an end. Usually repetition is required, with adjustment of response to feedback. Some motor skills are learned by imitating others, some through direct instruction; still others are acquired as by-products of activities.

The retention of motor skills may be of very long duration, even without practice. One does not forget how to ride a bicycle or how to swim! The rapid movements of intricate motor skills, such as piano playing, do not seem to require conscious direction [45]. Nor do they depend upon the part of the brain (hippocampus) essential to long-term memory. Motor skills are highly age-related, suggesting the important influence of maturation. The ecology of the child will determine the patterning of skills and the levels to which they can be developed.

Motor Skills of Childhood

By the time they begin elementary school, most children have acquired some skill in the basic motor tasks of running, jumping, throwing, catching, sequencing foot movements, and balancing. Willing to practice in order to achieve competence, children improve through their own efforts. They use the basic skills in games and coordinate them into more complex movements. Between the ages of 6 and 12, boys and girls run about one foot per second faster each year [6, p. 200]. Running is used in playing tag, hide-and-seek, Red Rover, and so on. Jumping forms the base of games such as leap frog and jump rope. Hurdle jumping, on the average, increases at the rate of about 32 millimeters per year except for an increase of 95 millimeters during the eighth to the ninth year [6, p. 193]. Many games use balls and other objects for throwing, pushing, catching, hitting, bouncing, and carrying. Footwork and balancing are important in hopscotch, gymnastics, jump rope, skipping, ladder climbing, bicycling, skating, and statues.

Although children learn much through imitation and practice, they also gain from a good program of physical education, including teaching for bodily awareness, variety and flexibility of movement, and also for skills. For example, a teacher can help a child to jump high by asking him to get the ball suspended over him rather than by saying "Jump as high as you can" [18]. Although most boys learn on their own to throw in a mature pattern, some boys and many girls retain immature patterns continuing to throw underhand [10]. A sex difference is often apparent by age 6. The overhand throw, with accompanying footwork, can be taught. Handwriting, required by the school, is an important small muscle coordination. It is quite a handicap to be poor in writing, the fate of more boys than girls. A slow and poor writer finds it extra hard to express himself and to get his work finished.

Motor tests assess various dimensions of performance. The following are the chief ways in which motor performance is assessed.

Quality of Motor Performance

Strength. The amount of force a person can exert (strength) can be considered in three ways [6, p. 179]. *Static strength* is pressure exerted against an immobile object. *Dynamic strength* is force controlled through a range of motion. *Explosive strength* is the ability to propel an object, such as a ball. Many studies have been concerned with static strength in the hand, which is measured by gripping a dynamometer. Measurements of grip strength show a steady increase throughout the school years, boys showing greater strength than girls at each grade level measured (third, sixth, ninth, and twelfth), and Latin American groups being consistently weaker than Anglo-American and Afro-American. Afro-American girls were significantly stronger than Latin or Anglo girls at all grade levels [17]. Trunk strength is measured by the performance of such exercises as the abdominal pivot (pushing the body around with hands on floor and back arched), push-ups, and leg raising while in sitting position. Limb strength is estimated by dips (squatting and rising), chinning, rope climbing, and push-ups.

Impulsion. *Reaction time,* or time required to respond to a stimulus, is one measure of impulsion. Reaction time may also be considered a measure of speed. Speed of reaction time increases steadily throughout the school age, with boys reacting slightly faster than girls [16]. Other measures include limb thrust, as shown in jumping, shot-put, short dash, and bar vault. A third measure is tapping, turning small objects, removing, and placing pegs. Girls tend to excel in measures of this type, as shown in a test of making dots alternately in two small circles [4]. Children's speed improved with age between 6 and 9, and at each level, girls were faster than boys. Maturation plays a large part, learning a small part, in this age-related reduction in reaction time [8].

Speed. Speed of movement can be measured for the whole body or for various parts, such as arms, hands, and fingers. Such skills as running and hopping show a steady increase in speed throughout the elementary school years. The gap between the sexes begins to widen at 11 or 12 years of age, after which time boys continue to gain while girls tend to taper off [10, pp. 157–158].

Precision. Balance, steadiness, and aiming are all aspects of precision. They are tested by such feats as standing on one foot, walking a line, tracing, threading, jumping and balancing, pursuit aiming, and placing dots in circles. Coordination of the whole body and dexterity of hand and fingers can also be considered as precision. By 12 years of age, children balance in quite mature style [6, p. 212]. Girls tend to do better than boys in accuracy, agility, and rhythmic activities.

Flexibility. Ease of moving, bending, and stretching contributes to most motor skills. Flexibility is extremely important in dancing and in most sports. Flexibility depends largely on the looseness of the joints and also upon the ease with which the muscles stretch and relax. Between 6 and 12 years, a child is likely to grow more flexible in some body regions and less so in others.

Fitness

Fitness includes flexibility and endurance as well as adequate ability to perform in the various skills and dimensions of performance. Fitness is also defined as the ability to supply oxygen to the muscles and the ability of the muscles to use oxygen for work [5, p. 83]. One indicator of fitness is forced vital capacity, the amount of air a child can take in after expelling as much as he can. This measure was used on children between 6 and 11 years in the National Health Examination Survey [20]. Figure 10–7 shows some results of this study. Forced vital capacity increased steadily with age, being larger in boys than in girls, and in whites than in blacks.

Fitness, of course, is an indication of the total health of the child. Exercise, especially outdoor exercise, contributes to the development and maintenance of fitness. Children feel better about themselves, and work better when they are fit. When seventh-grade boys with low self-concepts were given an endurance training program, their self-concepts improved as their physical fitness increased [25].

Laterality

The brain hemispheres become specialized in prenatal life, each one in large part controlling the opposite side of the body. Specialization becomes stronger as the child matures. Specialization includes preference for using the right or left part of the body for certain actions. Awareness of laterality also develops throughout childhood.

Lateral Preference. As mentioned in Chapter 7, about 11 per cent of people prefer the left hand for fine manipulation and the right hand for

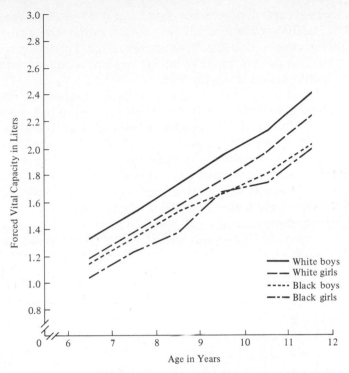

FIGURE 10–7.
Mean forced vital capacity for children aged 6–11 years by age, race, and sex. (SOURCE: P. V. V. Hamill, A. Palmer, and T. A. Drizd. *Forced vital capacity of children 6–11 years.* Vital and health statistics: Series 11, Data from the National Health Survey; no. 154. D.H.E.W. publication; no. (PHS) 78–1651. Washington: U.S. Government Printing Office, 1978.)

grasping and holding, assisting the left hand. Although studies on incidence of left-handedness vary in results, a recent one found 15 per cent of first-grade children using their left hands for picking up an instrument and for drawing. In an older but more comprehensive study, lateral preferences were tested for hands, feet, and eyes [2]. Hand preference was investigated by asking the child to show how he would throw a ball, turn a doorknob, cut with scissors, and write with a pencil. Eye preference was tested by asking the child to look through a kaleidoscope, sight a rifle, and look at the examiner through a hole in a paper. Foot preference was determined by noting which foot was used for kicking, estimating which foot kicked more skillfully. In each area, some children made mixed choices, indicating that preference was not definitely established. Mixed preferences occurred more often at the younger ages, showing that a developmental trend toward laterality continues through the elementary school years. The lateral preference was stronger for feet than for hands and weakest for eyes. Twenty-six per cent of the children showed no clear-cut preference for eyes, whereas 14 per cent showed none for hands, and only 4 per cent for feet. About half the children were consistent in lateral preferences, and the others showed either crossed or mixed preferences. With increasing age, there was increasing use of the hand and eye on the same side.

Lateral Awareness. The same children were tested to see when they knew right and left on their own body parts. All questions were an-

swered correctly by 68 per cent at age 6, 89 per cent at age 7, 95 per cent at 8, and 100 per cent at 11. Right—left awareness of own body is achieved about two years before consistency in hand preference. The authors suggest that the functions of lateral awareness and lateral preference are not closely related to each other.

The ability to make right—left discriminations in regard to the self develops before the ability to do so in regard to other persons and objects. The ability to imitate a model while facing him is more complicated than merely telling right from left, although it includes right—left discrimination. It also involves transposing both the hand and the object acted upon. Success in such a test probably requires taking the other person's point of view and representing to oneself the way objects look and the way the body feels from within the other person. This ability has been found, through a series of tests, to increase with age from 8 to 18 years. Transposition responses increased most markedly between 12 and 14 years of age [46].

Problems of Motor Control

The most extreme problems of motor control are those of spastic and otherwise crippled children, who of course need expert and continuous care. There are also motor problems of less severity that still cause considerable difficulty. Left-handedness can be a problem, because most environments are arranged for right-handed people. Much can be done to ease such difficulties by making convenient arrangements and showing the child how to do it for himself. The left-hander can sit on the left corner of the table. Left-handed scissors and other tools are available.

Mixed cortical control of vision and speech may present problems that need expert help. Although such problems are expressed partly as motor difficulties, they may also be perceptual and cognitive.

Hyperactivity. A hyperactive child, one who cannot keep still as long as others, is often a problem to his parents and his teachers. In a national survey, teachers reported that 12.4 per cent of boys and 3.9 per cent of girls between 6 and 11 were constantly moving [35]. Hyperactive (hyperkinetic) children usually also show inability to maintain attention and effort, and impulsivity, or inability to delay response. Childhood hyperkinesis may have lifelong effects. Many hyperactive children behave more normally when medicated with amphetamines. Obviously, something in their brains is different from those of normal children. A reasonable theory holds that the symptoms indicate a disorder of motivation, owing to inability to see causal relationships between the child's own behavior and the results of those actions [14]. The short attention span and insensitivity to reinforcement may be the result of genetically given factors within the transmitting mechanism of the brain. The next step in development of hyperkinesis would occur in infancy when the baby did not make connections between his actions and their results. If, as he grew up, he became convinced that his efforts made no difference, especially no long-time difference, then he would live for the pleasures of the moment. Treatment involves teaching the child to see behavior outcomes, and to be and feel effective. The methods of behavior modification are well suited to teaching this lesson, in that immediate feedback is given. Gradually the child is taught to monitor his own performance and to rely on naturally occurring feedback instead of immediate artificial reinforcement. Then he is taught to evaluate what he did and to make plans. Another part of treatment is a program with frequent changes of activity and opportunities for movement.

Sex-Inappropriate Gestures. Some gestures are typical of girls and others of boys. Among a group of normal 11-year-olds, girls, not boys, showed the following: limp wrist—bending the wrist toward the palmar surface of the forearm; flutters—rapid up and down movements of the arm, with wrist relaxed; arm fold—hand on opposite arm above the elbow [32]. Studies of gender-disturbed boys have found them displaying these gestures. Such mannerisms probably suggest to peers, as well as to adults, that the child is different, perhaps provoking ridicule or avoidance. Although a direct approach in changing gesture behavior might be of help to the child socially, the underlying cause also needs attention.

Ecology of Motor Development
Macrosystems

Opportunities for motor learning and practice vary between macrosystems and between microsystems. Cultural values play a part, and so do values of home, school, and neighborhood.

Motor development is influenced by climate, terrain, and cultural adaptations to them. In much of New Zealand, the temperature is usually cool but not freezing. In schools and homes, the indoor temperature is about the same as the outdoor temperature. Most houses and yards in New Zealand are small. Families are larger than in North America. Children play vigorously outdoors, in yards, streets, schoolyards, and in the many parks. "What is your sport?" the visitor is asked upon arrival in New Zealand, no matter what his age. Everyone is expected to enjoy outdoor activity, and so he does, using the neighborhood facilities from day to day and the mountains, seacoast, and wilderness areas for weekend and vacation pursuits.

In rural and small-town environments, many different coordinations occur spontaneously, through climbing trees; playing games in vacant lots, fields, or woods; jumping over streams and into leaf piles; crawling under fences and into caves; throwing stones and snowballs; building snowmen, sliding on the ice; sledding; flying kites; bouncing balls; skipping; jumping rope; digging holes; and building huts. Ponds and streams may provide places to swim and skate instead of arenas and swimming pools. The majority of North American children now live in urban en-

vironments, where apartment-dwelling, paved streets, and traffic restrict their spontaneous movement. The affluent suburban child has more freedom of movement than the city child, but his options are pale in comparison with those listed for the child growing up in a rural environment. Rich or poor, the modern child sits for many hours in front of a television set. In order to move freely, developing greater and greater bodily competency, he needs guidance and teaching, some planned space and equipment, and time set aside for motor play.

Exosystems

The playground or facility for children's activities is often the result of community planning, or even planning on a statewide or national level. The child does not interact directly with the town council, recreation commission, or agency board, but their actions determine children's opportunities for vigorous play and games. Sometimes a community, with all good intentions, promotes the development of specialized skills in a few children to the exclusion of all-around motor development in all children. Little League baseball and hockey may be constructive or destructive for average children. If everyone gets a chance to play and the emphasis is on sportsmanship and fun, then the games are healthful. If competition is severe and the best athletes are featured, then the majority of children are restricted in movement and diminished in self-concept. Evidence of child-centered planning occurred in the Province of Saskatchewan, when authorities decided to build enough ice rinks to give every child generous opportunities for skating and playing hockey. Formerly, only the best hockey players were given time in the rinks.

Microsystems

Parents are the first and continuing influences on a child's motor coordination. A freely moving, well-coordinated adult will dance, backpack, bicycle, and swim with a baby or young child. By the time the child reaches school age, he has experienced many movements through his agile parent, has imitated other movements, and has been encouraged in motor exploration. Along with enjoying motor play, he has good feelings (a positive self-concept) about his body and motor abilities. Through varied motor experience, he has developed a body image that is clear for his age. He is ready to develop new skills and polish old ones, because the years from 6 to 12 are a time of life when children want to be good at what they do. Parents can help by encouraging, appreciating, teaching, and giving opportunities for learning many skills, such as throwing, catching, batting, swimming, and skating, dancing, and gymnastics. If such shared activities are fun for both parent and child, then the child gets the general attitude that motor skills make a pleasant and important contribution to life. Most likely it will be fun if the parent sets standards that the child can meet with some effort but not too much strain.

Siblings teach each other many skills. The older one may perfect her own skills while teaching the younger one, and the younger one benefits from an enthusiastic, ever-present teacher who can clearly recall how it feels in the early stages of learning a particular coordination. Grandparents, aunts, and uncles may also promote motor skills. I (MSS) often teach swimming to my granddaughter, who shares my enthusiasm for the water.

Like parents, teachers vary in their own motor development and in their understanding of children's movement. A youth leader, such as a Scout leader, may have a tremendous influence on the children under her care. Many children have had new worlds of bodily experience opened to them through playing games, camping, hiking, and going on trips.

Summary

Growth is slow during middle childhood, picking up in speed as children enter the puberal growth spurt. Height increases are steadier than those in weight, because height is less affected by environmental changes. Tables and charts can be used to assess the growth of a child in relation to other children's growth, and in relation to the child's own growth over time. Predictions of adult height can be made with fair accuracy from childhood measurements.

Girls overtake boys in height because of girls' earlier puberal growth spurt. Girls reach maturity earlier than boys. At any given age, the average girl has achieved a greater proportion of her physiological development than has the average boy.

Differences in proportions between older and younger children can be seen in the ratio of the face to the brain case, in fat thickness and distribution, and in length of legs in proportion to the trunk. Signs of increasing maturity can be noted in all bodily systems, resulting in greater muscular strength, toleration of longer intervals between meals, fewer digestive upsets, greater bladder capacity, more stabilized respiration, slower heartbeat, higher blood pressure, fewer ear infections, eyeballs of mature shape and size, a more ossified skeleton, and progress toward a set of permanent teeth. The brain shows a small growth spurt between 6 and 8, and increasing lateral specialization, in which sex differences occur. Brain organization is different in males and females, and differs in left-handed and right-handed people.

Middle childhood is relatively safe in terms of life and health, and safer in the United States than in many nations in the world. Most of the childhood diseases are controlled by immunization. Health problems include dental caries, malocclusion, nutritional deprivation, obesity, physical and mental disabilities, chronic illnesses, and accidents. Family interaction is changed by having a handicapped child. Boys incur more accidental injuries and deaths than do girls.

Children's growth, health, and survival are strongly influenced by physical settings and climates of macrosystems, through nutrition, infection, altitude, temperature, and seasons. Economic factors influence

children through nutrition, housing, hygiene, education of parents, and stress.

Regular changes in growth patterns, over time, are called secular shifts. A secular shift to increasing height and weight has occurred during past decades in the industrialized nations of Europe, North America, and Japan. The increase is coming to a halt in these nations, and has already done so in the most prosperous groups of children.

Home, school, neighborhood, and social network are influential in a child's growth and health. Families are providers of nutrients, protection, hygiene, nursing care, education for self-care, and access to medical care. Severe stress from outside or within the microsystem may lead to malfunctions in family interaction, resulting in growth failure or violence. School-age children enjoy considerable autonomy in making health-related choices when they are unsupervised and with peers. Networks broaden a child's experiences and choices. Schools may supply nutrients and health care, as well as education in these areas. Delivery of medical services varies between macrosystems, some having stronger mesosystems and government financing than others.

School-age children work at learning motor skills, having achieved the physiological maturity required, and being motivated by a developing sense of industry. Opportunities for learning skills include space in which to move, the required equipment, models to observe, playmates, and sometimes teachers. Motor performances can be assessed along the dimensions of strength, impulsion, speed, precision, flexibility, and fitness. Laterality, or specialization of sides of the body, and awareness of it, increase during childhood. Problems of motor control are varied in type and severity. Such problems can usually be helped by expert teaching and treatment. Ecological influences on motor development include climate and terrain, values, provisions of space, equipment and instruction made possible by communities, parents' abilities, interests, and participation with their children, sibling interaction, provisions in school, and neighborhood networks and organizations.

References

1. Abraham, S., F. W. Lowenstein, and C. L. Johnson. *Preliminary findings of the first health and nutrition examination survey, United States, 1971–1972: Dietary intake and biochemical findings.* (DHEW Publication No. (HRA) 74-1219-1.) Washington: U.S. Government Printing Office, 1974.
2. Belmont, L., and H. G. Birch. Lateral dominance and right–left awareness in normal children. *Child Development,* 1963, **34,** 257–270.
3. Benenson, A. S. (ed.). *Control of communicable diseases in man.* 12th ed. New York: American Public Health Association, 1975.
4. Connolly, K., K. Brown, and E. Bassett. Developmental changes in some components of a motor skill. *British Journal of Psychology,* 1968, **59,** 305–314.
5. Corbin, C. B. Physical fitness of children. In C. B. Corbin (ed.). *A textbook of motor development.* Dubuque, Iowa: William C. Brown Company, Publishers, 1973.

6. Cratty, B. J. *Perceptual and motor development in infants and children.* New York: Macmillan Publishing Co., Inc., 1970.

7. Crinella, F. M., F. W. Beck, and J. W. Robinson. Unilateral dominance is not related to neuropsychological integrity. *Child Development,* 1971, **42,** 2033–2045.

8. Eckert, H. M., and D. H. Eichorn. Developmental variability in reaction time. *Child Development,* 1977, **48,** 452–458.

9. Epstein, H. T. Growth spurts during brain development: Implications for educational policy and practice. In J. S. Chall and A. F. Mirsky (eds.). *Education and the brain.* The 77th Yearbook of the National Society for the Study of Education. Chicago: University of Chicago Press, 1978.

10. Espenschade, A. S., and H. M. Eckert. *Motor development.* Columbus, Ohio: Charles E. Merrill Publishing Company, 1967.

11. Finlayson, H. Children's road behavior and personality. *British Journal of Educational Psychology,* 1972, **42,** 225–232.

12. Garn, S. M. Body size and its implications. In L. W. Hoffman and M. L. Hoffman (eds.). *Review of child development research.* Vol. 2. New York: Russell Sage Foundation, 1966.

13. Garn, S. M., S. T. Sandusky, J. M. Nagy, and F. L. Trowbridge. Negro-caucasoid differences in permanent tooth emergence at a constant income level. *Archives of Oral Biology,* 1973, **18,** 609–615.

14. Glow, P. H., and R. A. Glow. Hyperkinetic impulse disorder: A developmental defect of motivation. *Genetic Psychology Monographs,* 1979, **100,** 159–231.

15. Goleman, D. Special abilities of the sexes: Do they begin in the brain? *Psychology Today,* 1978, **12:**8, 6, 48ff.

16. Goodenough, F. L. The development of the reactive process from early childhood to maturity. *Journal of Experimental Psychology,* 1935, **18,** 431–450.

17. Goss, A. M. Estimated versus actual physical strength in three ethnic groups. *Child Development,* 1968, **39,** 283–291.

18. Halverson, L. E. The young child: The significance of motor development. In *The significance of the young child's motor development.* Washington: National Association for the Education of Young Children, 1971.

19. Hamill, P. V. V., R. A. Drizd, C. L. Johnson, R. B. Reed, and A. F. Roche. *NCHS growth curves for children birth–18 years.* Vital and health statistics: Series 11, Data from the National Health Survey; no. 165. (DHEW publication No. (PHS) 78–1650.) Washington: U.S. Government Printing Office, 1977.

20. Hamill, P. V. V., A. Palmer, and T. A. Drizd. *Forced vital capacity of children 6–11 years.* Vital and health statistics: Series 11, Data from the National Health Survey; no. 164. (DHEW publication No. (PHS) 78–1651.) Washington: U.S. Government Printing Office, 1977.

21. Kelly, J. E., and C. R. Harvey. *Basic dental examination findings of persons 1–74 years.* Vital and health statistics: Series 11, Data from the National Health Survey; No. 214. (DHEW publication No. (PHS) 79–1662.) Washington: U.S. Government Printing Office, 1979.

22. Kelly, J. E., M. Sanches, and L. E. Van Kirk. *An assessment of the occlusion of the teeth of children.* Vital and health statistics: Series 11, Data from the National Health Survey; No. 130. (DHEW publication No. (HRA) 74–1612.) Washington: U.S. Government Printing Office, 1973.

23. Kimura, D. The asymmetry of the human brain. *Scientific American,* 1973, **228:**3, 70–78.

24. Lowrey, G. H. *Growth and development of children.* 6th ed. Chicago: Year Book Medical Publishers, Inc., 1973.

25. McGowan, R. W., B. O. Jarman, and D. M. Pedersen. Effects of a competitive

endurance training program on self-concept and peer approval. *Journal of Psychology*, 1974, **86**, 57–60.

26. McHale, M. C., J. McHale, and G. F. Streatfeild. *Children in the world.* Washington: Population Reference Bureau, 1979.

27. Malina, R. M., P. V. V. Hamill, and S. Lemeshow. *Body dimensions and proportions, white and negro children 6–11 years.* Vital and health statistics: Series 11, Data from the National Health Survey; no. 143. (DHEW publication No. (HRA) 75–1625.) Washington: U.S. Government Printing Office, 1974.

28. Meredith, H. V. Body size of contemporary groups of eight-year-old children studied in different parts of the world. *Monographs of the Society for Research in Child Development*, 1969, **34**:1.

29. Mortality differentials among non-white groups. *Statistical Bulletin*, 1974, **55**:7, 5–8.

30. Mortality from leading types of accidents in United States boys and girls ages 5–14. *Statistical Bulletin*, 1978, **59**:3, 10–12.

31. Pelton, L. H. Child abuse and neglect: The myth of classlessness. *American Journal of Orthopsychiatry*, 1978, **48**, 608–617.

32. Rekers, G. A., H. D. Amaro-Plotkin, and B. P. Low. Sex-typed mannerisms in normal boys and girls as a function of sex and age. *Child Development*, 1977, **48**, 275–278.

33. Restak, R. M. *The brain: The last frontier.* New York: Doubleday & Company, Inc., 1979.

34. Roberts, J. *Monocular visual acuity of persons 4–74 years, United States, 1971–1972.* Vital and health statistics: Series 11, Data from the National Health Survey; No. 210. (DHEW publication No. (HRA) 77–1646.) Washington: U.S. Government Printing Office, 1977.

35. Roberts, J., and J. T. Baird, Jr. *Behavior patterns of children in school, United States.* Vital and health statistics: Series 11, Data from the National Health Survey; no. 113. (DHEW publication No. (HSM) 72–1042.) Washington: U.S. Government Printing Office, 1972.

36. Roberts, J., and K. R. Duyan. *Visual acuity of children.* Vital and Health Statistics: Series 11, Data from the National Health Survey; No. 101. Public Health Service Publication No. 1000. Washington: U.S. Government Printing Office, 1970.

37. Roche, A. F. (ed.). Secular trends in human growth, maturation, and development. *Monographs of the Society for Research in Child Development*, 1979, **44**: 3–4.

38. Roche, A. F. *Skeletal maturity of children 6–11 years: Socioeconomic differentials.* Vital and health statistics: Series 11, Data from the National Health Survey; No. 149. (DHEW publication No. (HRA) 76–1631.) Washington: U.S. Government Printing Office, 1975.

39. Sabry, Z. I., J. A. Campbell, M. E. Campbell, and A. L. Forbes. Nutrition Canada. *Nutrition Today*, 1974, **9**:1, 5–13.

40. Satz, P. Incidence of aphasia in left-handers: A test of some hypothetical models of cerebral speech organization. Gainesville: University of Florida. Mimeo, 1979.

41. Scanlon, J., and J. Roberts. *Color vision deficiencies in children.* Vital and health statistics: Series 11, Data from the National Health Survey; no. 118. (DHEW publication No. (HSM) 73–1600.) Washington: U.S. Government Printing Office, 1972.

42. Silver, G. A. *Child health: America's future.* Germantown, Md.: Aspen Systems Corporation, 1978.

43. Snapper, K. J., and J. S. Ohms. *The status of children 1977.* (DHEW publication No. (OHDS) 78–30133.) Washington: U.S. Government Printing Office, 1978.

44. Tanner, J. M. *Fetus into man.* Cambridge, Mass.: Harvard University Press, 1978.
45. Teyler, T. J. The brain sciences: An introduction. In J. S. Chall and A. F. Mirsky (eds.). *Education and the brain.* The 77th Yearbook of the National Society for the Study of Education. Chicago: University of Chicago Press, 1978.
46. Wapner, S., and L. Cirillo. Imitation of a model's hand movements: Age changes in transposition of left—right relations. *Child Development,* 1968, **39,** 887–894.
47. Werner, E. E. *Cross-cultural child development: A view from the Planet Earth.* Monterey, Calif.: Brooks/Cole, 1979.
48. Wilder, C. S. Acute conditions: *Incidence and associated disability.* Vital and health statistics: Series 10, Data from the National Health Survey, no. 98. (DHEW publication No. (HRA) 75–1525.) Washington: U.S. Government Printing Office, 1975.
49. Wittrock, M. C. Education and the cognitive processes of the brain. In J. S. Chall and A. F. Mirsky (eds.). *Education and the brain.* The 77th Yearbook of the National Society for the Study of Education. Chicago: University of Chicago Press, 1978.

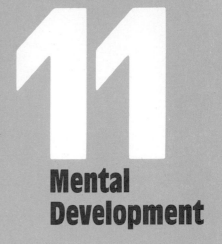

11
Mental Development

One evening when our grandchildren were visiting us, I suggested playing Coffee Pot, a game that I remembered playing when their mother was a child. We explained to Becky and Nathan, "*It* goes out of the room. The rest of us think of an action word. We all know the word, and *It* doesn't. *It* comes in and asks questions to find out what the word is, but because he doesn't know the word, he has to say *Coffee Pot* in its place."

Becky, age 10, caught on after a couple of tries, and fell in love with the game. Nathan, 8 years, was completely mystified. We all took turns explaining and demonstrating, and he tried being *It*, but he never understood that Coffee Pot stood for any word that the group decided on. We shall return to the subject of Coffee Pot when we discuss *metalanguage*, or children's knowledge of the nature of langue.

QUESTIONS TO THINK ABOUT WHILE READING THIS CHAPTER

1. In what ways does the school-age child differ from the young child in intellectual functioning?
2. Why do sensory modalities vary in importance between different cultures?
3. What is field dependence-independence?
4. How does the school child apply reversibility to thinking?
5. What skills are involved in dealing with numbers?
6. Which parental behaviors encourage rapid intellectual development?
7. In what ways does remembering improve during the school years?
8. In what ways does the child's language become more complex?
9. What is the culture of childhood?
10. How does the IQ differ from some other notions of intelligence?
11. How can creativity in childhood be judged?
12. How does schooling transform a child's mind?

Cognitive Development

In getting to know and understand the world, a person explores it through the senses and acts upon the experiences mentally, storing them in memory in retrieval form, reasoning, and thinking. Language is largely cognitive, but involves other processes, too.

The infant's cognitive behavior is sensorimotor, concerned with simple adjustments to the immediate present, symbolic behavior being completely absent. The preschool child uses symbols in representational thought. Beginning at around 7 years, children can use symbols consistently to perform acts of cognition that are abstracted and freed from dependence on sensory stimulation. In this stage of concrete operations, the child mentally performs acts that he formerly really carried out physically. The outstanding cognitive developments during this period are increased freedom and control in thinking and increased understanding of relationships between events and/or symbols. The child takes satisfaction in his feeling that there exists a systematic, productive way of thinking about experience and in his conviction that he can think this way [37, p. 139]. He has a *quantitative* attitude. In becoming aware of systematic thinking, the child lays a basis for the next stage of thinking, in which the scientific method can be used. During the period of concrete operations, however, the child often confuses hypotheses with factual evidence. He thinks of an explanation, looks for evidence to support it, and ignores evidence that contradicts it. Although this way of thinking has been called the egocentrism of school age, it is not confined entirely to children!

Using Sensory Information

Visual perception is very important in Western culture, where children get a great deal of their information from reading and television, and where they must learn to deal with machinery and other fruits of technology. Vision is also primary in hunting societies, such as Eskimo. Hearing may be more important to forest dwellers and to people with an oral tradition, such as the Maori. Kinesthetic perception may be especially meaningful in Bali and in African societies where dancing carries much significance. Within a culture, children vary as to preferences for perceptual modes and as to demands placed upon them.

Intersensory Integration. As the child makes use of his different senses for perceiving, he has the task of putting together the various kinds of information into useful form. He develops more and more effective ways of exploring his environment and of integrating what he finds out about it.

Age-related changes have been shown in the ways in which children examine objects with both eyes and hands [1]. With the task of matching through touching and looking, 3-year-olds made clutching and catching-like movements, using their palms considerably on the objects they were examining. Five-year-olds used their hands more cooperatively, but not until the age of 6 years did children systematically trace the shape of the figure. By about 9, fingertips were used almost exclusively for exploration, but between 6 and 9, palms and fingertips both were used. Eye movements underwent similar refinement, increasing with age in number and in tendency to sweep across the figure and trace its outlines. Accuracy in matching shapes presented in one modality, such as vision, increases throughout the preschool and school years.

The patterning of intersensory integration can be studied by having children match a pattern of events in one modality with a pattern of events in another. Matching through vision and touch, as described, is one such type of task. Matching information from listening and looking is another, a type of task that has implications for learning to read. Good readers usually perform better than poor readers in matching auditory and visual patterns [41]. A comparison of normal and learning-disordered children, 8 to 15 years of age, demonstrated a difference in the processes used by the two groups in dealing with auditory and visual material [45]. Stimuli from both modalities were presented simultaneously in the form of a spoken digit and a digit on a card. Three such presentations were made and the subjects asked to report them. Children in the normal group were more likely than the other group to recall the digits in pairs, one seen and one heard, whereas the learning-disordered children more often recalled just one modality. Older children recalled in pairs more than younger. Thus, the ability to integrate the auditory and visual material was greater in normal children than in learning-disordered, and in older children rather than younger.

Perceptual-Cognitive Style. Individuals differ in the ways in which they extract information from sensory experience. Research has been mainly concerned with visual perception, and the degree to which a person can extract details out of a visual field. For example, in some children's puzzles, a busy scene includes items that are to be found. A jungle contains hiding animals. How many can you find? The Embedded Figures Test presents geometric forms that include simple figures that the person is to identify. This test, and others, have been used by Witkin and his associates in their studies of field dependence [64]. The child who does well at picking out or differentiating the simple forms from the complex forms is *field independent* in cognitive style. Field independence increases as children grow from early childhood to adolescence, but there are stable differences between children. It is useful to be able to differentiate details out of a visual display if you are reading, fixing an engine, hunting, or doing a puzzle; it may be better to see things whole when recognizing faces and operating in a social situation. Actually, both styles of perception are needed. Field dependence-independence seems to be an aspect of personality. Field-dependent children are more sensitive than field-independent children to social cues, both positive and negative; field-independent children seem to be more autonomous [59]. Field independence is related to mathematical achievement [56a].

Find this

In this

Flexibility and Control of Thinking

Although the young child reacts rather promptly to his perceptions of the moment, the school-age child can delay his response while he takes several aspects of the situation into account. His thoughts range back and forth in various directions, dealing with more than one perception at a time, comparing them, considering them in relation to past experience and knowledge. Thus, he shows more control, as well as flexibility.

With his increasing store of memories, his past becomes more and more useful for evaluating and interpreting the present. With increasing age, strategies for memory use improve, enabling the child to see alternative courses of action or alternative reasons, and to delay coming to a conclusion without sufficient evidence [66].

The older child is not easily fooled by the way things look, but considers how they really are, and what they *must* be. With his growing flexibility of thought the child can more easily look at situations from the points of view of other people. The child's increasing mobility of thought enters into everything that he does: his classifying, ordering, and dealing with numbers, his language, his social relationships, and self-concepts. His thinking is limited in flexibility, however. He tends to think about concrete things rather than about abstractions.

Reversibility is one aspect of the flexible and controlled thinking that emerges during middle childhood. Reversibility has two meanings, both of which apply. First, the child can think an act and then think it undone. He can think himself partway through a sequence of action, return to the first of it, and then start out in another direction. In contrast to thoughts, motor acts including spoken words, and perceptions are irreversible; they cannot be undone. Reversibility is one of the most important differences between thought and action. When the child can try out different courses of action mentally, instead of having to touch and see in order to believe, he has the advantage of a quicker and more powerful control over his environment and himself.

The first experience with reversibility is in make-believe play, in which the preschool child can pretend an event and then cancel it by pretending it undone or by switching back into her real self. Or as a storyteller, she can maintain a boundary between herself and the story, switching from speaking for herself to speaking for the characters, and back again. With the reorganization of thinking into concrete operations, the child can use reversible thoughts in planning and problem solving. The second meaning of reversibility is that any operation can be canceled by an opposite operation. For example, the operation of subtracting is canceled by the operation of adding. All children minus all girls equals all boys; all boys plus all girls equals all children.

Reversibility: Pretending —thinking it or thinking it undone; and Canceling operation: $5 - 3 = 2$ or $2 + 3 = 5$

Concrete Operational Skills

Piaget has described the mental operations that typify the thinking of the school-age child. Operations are rule-governed actions, carried out in the mind. Concrete operations represent a transformation in cognition, making the school child a different kind of thinker from the preschool child. This transformation, according to Piaget, is made by the child's own efforts.

Understanding and using certain principles of relationships between things and ideas, the child manipulates or operates on objects, ideas, and symbols. As was true in infancy, "to know an object is to act on it" [38, p. 8]. But now some of the action is interiorized. The child adds and subtracts. He classifies and orders. He applies rules to social situations. Each operation fits into a system, and the systems fit together. The operation two-plus-two-equals-four fits into a system of addition, which is part of a system of arithmetic.

Conservation. As cognitive structures develop, the child builds a more and more permanent, stable, and inclusive picture of the world, the people in it, himself, and their interrelationships. He realizes that certain properties are invariant (remain the same) in spite of transformations (changes) in other properties. Substance, quantity, and number are seen as permanent. Conservation of number, for example, means that the child realizes that 7 is always 7, whether it consists of 3 + 4, 5 + 2, :::., ..:.:, ***, or any other arrangement.

Conservation of substance means that the amount of material stays the same if nothing is added or taken away, even though the shape and/or position of the material change. One of Piaget's methods of exploring a child's conservation of substance is with two equal balls of clay. After the child has agreed that they contain equal amounts, the examiner rolls one ball into a sausage and asks, "Which has more clay?" The child in the stage of concrete operations will say that they are the same, whereas the child who has not achieved conservation of substance will reply either that the ball is larger (because it is fatter) or the sausage is larger (because it is longer). A variation on this test is to break one ball into little bits and ask whether the ball or the heap of bits contains more clay. If the child cannot conserve, he will say that the bits contain less (because they are smaller) or that they contain more (because there are more pieces). Conservation of substance can be demonstrated with liquid, starting with the same amounts of lemonade in two identical glasses and then pouring the contents of one glass into a thinner or a fatter glass. Or liquid from one glass can be poured into two and questions asked about whether the amount of liquid is the same.

Conservation develops throughout the school-age period at different times for different dimensions, varying with substance and situation. Amount and weight are conserved before volume. Although the acquisition of conservation is related to age, it is also related to familiarity, as shown by children conserving earlier when the substance was butter or an elastic band than when it was clay. A liquid was conserved more readily when it was something that children liked to drink and they were told that they could drink it [5]. Conservation tasks can be made easier by allowing nonverbal answers and giving tasks that have meaning in the child's life. Children conserved numbers of candies more readily when they were allowed to place a row of candies in the mouth of Cookie Monster, a Sesame Street puppet [29].

Cross-cultural research on conservation shows the influence of experience on the age at which children acquire conservation skills, and indeed on whether they ever acquire them. Werner identified four patterns of conservation acquisition throughout the world. Children of the urbanized, industrialized world, typified by the United States, conserve numbers, liquid, and substance at age 6 or 7. Oriental children do so earlier. Children in "developing" or less industrialized countries are 2 to 6 years later in conservation. In some remote, isolated societies conservation is not achieved by even 12 to 18 years of age [59].

Relations. From the experience of arranging things in order, the child internalizes concepts of relations. A little girl arranges her dolls so that they can watch her dance for them, the tallest doll on the bottom step, the next tallest on the second step, and so on up to the shortest doll on top. The child's activities are preparing her to have concepts of decreasing and increasing size, concepts of relations. She comes to realize that Lizzie doll is tall in relation to Kimmie, but short in relation to Kelly. (Tall and short, light and dark, new and old, are relational terms, not absolute terms.)

Ordering activities occur often in children's play. Objects collected can be ordered inside their classes—all the coins arranged in order of their minting dates, the evergreen cones according to length. Children may line each other up, using height as a criterion, for the purpose of taking turns. Just as they enjoy using their newly developed ability to classify, so do they enjoy ordering the world in terms of various relations.

Children find the world ordered for them, too. The kindergarten teacher lines them up for going to the bathroom and getting morning milk. Perhaps she helps them to order sounds in terms of high to low or colors from light to dark. Early in the school career, the child meets that remarkable ordering device, the alphabet. An ever widening collection of symbols called words, he finds, can be ordered in terms of their structure and its relation to the alphabet. He learns that many other kinds of relations and orders exist and that it is his job to learn them. Relations of events in time are called *history*. Relations of places in space are called *geography*. (Relate time relations and space relations and you get *geology* and *astronomy*, but these come later in school.)

Numeration. Numbers are concepts derived from the operations of classifying and ordering. A cardinal number is a *class*. *Four* means a group of four apples or four automobiles or four abracadabras. An ordinal number is a *relation*. Fourth is related to third and fifth in size and position. A real understanding of *four* requires an understanding of *fourth*, and vice versa. Thus, Piaget maintains, classifying and ordering are interlocking and essential processes in the development of number concepts. Piaget also points out that an understanding of the principle of *conservation of quantity* is basic to development of the concept of *number* [39].

Flavell has summarized the school child's abilities in dealing with numbers [16]. The role of concrete operational skills can be seen in the following abilities.

1. The child can count. The school child not only recites numbers, but counts sets of objects accurately, using some systematic way of counting each item once and only once. She can count to find out how many items there are; she can follow directions to count exactly 10 objects.
2. Cardinal and ordinal aspects of number are understood. The child knows that when he has counted 10 objects, the last one is the tenth, and that the tenth is higher than the ninth.
3. The child understands written and spoken numbers, can read them and say them, and understands transformations between reading and saying.
4. The child can assemble a set of objects that corresponds in number to another set, or to a cardinal number value. She knows that when she assembles a set to correspond to another set, the two are numerically equal. She also recognizes some relations between sets and uses them to perform simple multiplication and division.
5. Sets are compared accurately in terms of "more than," "less than," and "equal." The child understands the effects of adding and subtracting from equal sets.
6. Number is conserved. The child realizes that a set does not become more or less numerous if its elements are spread out or condensed.
7. The child has some recognition of a set of whole numbers as an ordered series that can be added to repeatedly. She conserves large number as well as small ones.

Transitivity. The child realizes that if A > B and B > C, then A > C, when she can visually compare A with B and B with C, but not A with C. Or, to return to the girl with the dolls, she would be able to compare Lizzie with Kimmie, and Lizzie with Kelly, and then to deduce, without comparing Kelly and Kimmie, that Kelly is taller than Kimmie. Transitivity comes from understanding the relations between ordered items.

Class Inclusion. The child can compare a class of items with one of its subclasses. Piaget's best-known class inclusion test is done with flowers, for example 6 red and 2 white flowers. "Are there more flowers or more red flowers?" The young child answers "More red flowers," because he compares the 2 subclasses. The older child answers, "More flowers." Although the young child can be helped to succeed on similar but easier problems, he cannot do it in this form. A child between 5 and 7, on the brink of concrete operations, can do the problem of class inclusion if he is given a little help in suppressing his perceptions. He can be aided by first comparing the 2 subclasses before being asked the class inclusion question [61], or by being asked the question verbally, without demonstration with objects [65].

Although most of the world's children achieve concrete operations, the beginning of the emergence of concrete operations varies from age 6 or 7 to age 12 or 13. There is little evidence on genetic differences or nutritional factors, but ecological influences have been summarized by Werner [59].

Macrosystem Influences. Concrete operations emerge earlier in children growing up in Western culture than in those living in traditional societies. This conclusion comes from several African and Australian studies that compared children who had been in contact with Western culture and those who had not. Western-type schooling is one type of experience that promotes concrete operations. Another influence is from socialization values. Does the value system stress independence, self-reliance, exploratory play, and gender-role equality, or does it demand obedience, patience, and submission to authority? The former value system enhances early development of operational skills, as well as field independence.

Schooling, socialization values, life style

A third type of influence is the demands of the life style. For example, African children whose mothers made pottery conserved weight earlier than children whose mothers were farmers and merchants. Chinese boys who carried loads of rice conserved weight earlier than their peers who did not carry rice. Field independence and autonomous personal functioning are found more often in hunting and fishing societies than in agricultural [59]. Successful hunters and fishermen differentiate small visual and auditory cues out of the global environment. They see a moving leaf or a ripple and hear a crackle or a splash. The child-rearing practices of those societies tend to be the kind that promote field independence.

Microsystem Influences. A number of studies have shown operational development to be related to the following maternal behaviors: explaining actions, using specific referents in speaking of relationships, specificity in nonverbal communication, social reinforcement rather than direct interference [59, pp. 221–22]. In other words, when mothers teach clearly and nonrestrictively, children's mental development is enhanced.

Parents' teaching style

Reports on parental behavior with field-independent children have been obtained in many parts of the world. It seems that parents enhance field independence by the following practices: high level of companionship, equalitarian relationships, moderate discipline, little directing by the mother, low level of physical punishment by the father [59].

Conceptual Style

Children differ in the types of concepts they form most often and in the speed with which they solve conceptual problems.

Reflective or Impulsive. Reflectivity means delaying reponse while thinking about the problem, considering information and solutions. Impulsivity means responding quickly, without thinking it over. These behaviors were illustrated by 9-year-old boys, when given a test in which the subject is required to pick a figure identical to a model out of six similar pictures [48]. For example, a teddy bear sitting on a chair must be matched. The five wrong choices include a chair that sticks up too far, a bow on the other side of the teddy's neck, and a head tilted upward. The two groups of boys were found to differ not only in the greater length of time spent by reflectives before responding but in the way they went about solving the problem. The reflective children spent less time looking at the standard and more time looking at the alternatives. They appeared to compare alternatives and then to consult the standard for verification, selection, or rejection. The impulsive children apparently compared the standard with one alternative at a time, thus making six decisions in terms of *the same* or *different*. Details were likely to escape them, and although their response was quicker, it was less accurate.

The control systems that guide attention, timing, and organizing are located in the brain. If a child is impulsive it is most likely that he has difficulty in controlling his attentional processes and that the underlying problem is neurological. Often such children are called hyperactive, because their lack of attentional control results in frequent changes of activities. They need help in organizing themselves and in keeping attention focused. They need warm, supportive direction from parents in performing tasks at home, and from teachers in specific techniques of focusing and sustaining attention.

Analytic or Relational. Does a child take things apart mentally to classify them, or does he put them together (relate them)? Give him a basketful of plates, cups, and saucers and ask him to sort them. An analytic response would be to place the plates in one pile, saucers in another, and cups in a group. A relational response would be to put them in sets of plate, saucer, and cup on the saucer.

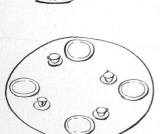

Analytic or Global. Does the child sort by specific features, or does he categorize by impressions of items as wholes? If the basketful of plates is given on a table, with the same directions, a global response may also occur along with a relational one. The child makes place settings around the table, as shown in the margin. Analytic responses are typical of left-brain hemisphere responses, global and relational of the right brain.

Many school tasks and intelligence tests require an analytic style of problem-solving and learning. Analytic children, of course, do better than children with relational and global styles. A global style, however, is better for remembering faces and for appreciating (and perhaps producing) works of art. If a child can use analytic, global, and relational styles as the situation demands, then he is a richer person.

As school-age children grow older, they tend to remember better, as shown by both short-term and long-term *recall*. Improvement may stem from developments in the sensory register, short-term storage, long-term storage, and the control processes of attention, encoding, rehearsing, searching, and enriching with meaning. The organizing and interpreting of experiencing is done, of course, through concrete operations. This fact may account for adults' scanty memories of their preschool days and practically no memories of their infancy. Since operational thinking is the mode in which adults perform, memories organized differently may not be available for recall. Piaget has found, however, that a child may recall an experience in terms of operations that are more mature than those he was able to use at the time of the original experience [40, pp. 82–83]. Children recalled meanings of sentences better than the exact wording [35].

Although recognition memory, especially for pictures, is efficient during the preschool period, it continues to improve through the school years. Adults excel children in recognizing complex pictures [31].

Short-term memory, as shown by recalling lists of words, increased with age between the years of 7 and 17. The adolescents (ages 14 and 17) used superior strategies for recall, as compared with the children ages 7 and 10. However, regardless of strategies used, the older subjects recalled more words, suggesting a greater short-term storage capacity [19].

Long-term memory holds an infinite number of bits of information of enormous variety. Not only does long-term memory hang onto words and images or representations of objects and actions, it also contains rules and procedures for all sorts of actions, both mental and physical. There is little doubt that anything and everything can be stored, if it is properly processed. The problems for researchers are to discover and describe all the processes of storing and retrieving.

The control processes seem to be more modifiable than the sensory register and memory stores. Not only do control processes change as the child grows older but they also respond to teaching and different methods of presenting material. The child can be helped to acquire some of the strategies that he would, in the course of a longer time, work out and adopt for himself.

Attention. As the child gains more and more control over cognitive processes, she becomes better at attending to relevant stimuli and ignoring irrelevant ones. In controlling attention to fit the demands of the task, the child remembers better. During the years between 8 and 14, children show increases in attention to stimuli that they know they are to recall, along with less attention to others [21]. Between the ages of 5 and 9, children develop the control that allows them to direct attention away from an attractive stimulus and to focus attention upon another feature when it is advantageous to do so [22].

Children learn many actions by observing other people and then imi-

tating parts of the behavior. When children were told to watch what a model was choosing, they remembered better than children who had not been told what to watch, and second-graders remembered more than preschoolers [67]. When the children received no instructions as to what to watch, they focused attention more readily on models who were punished and rewarded than on nonreinforced models.

Organizing and Labeling. Organized material is remembered better than nonorganized. The ability to classify is related to success in remembering [56]. Throughout the elementary-school years, there is a continual increase in organizing, labeling, and evaluating, and a consequent improvement in remembering [7, 30]. A spontaneous and effective way of organizing material is to ask questions about it. Children remember the answers to their own questions better than they remember the answers to another person's questions [44]. This finding says something about the roles of curiosity and exploration in children's learning.

Rehearsal. A useful strategy for memorizing is to repeat the item to be learned. Children rehearse spontaneously, increasingly with age, as they become aware that rehearsal works and as they make plans for learning. When short-term memory for word lists was examined in children in grades from 1 through 7, spontaneous rehearsal was found operating by grade 3 [17].

First-graders were able to use rehearsal effectively if they were shown how to do it by a model, whereas third-graders could adopt the technique from verbal instructions [6]. Thus, rehearsal is a technique that the child *can* apply long before he actually *does* use it for remembering. When aided by a method appropriate to his age, the child can improve his memory performance. The same principle holds true for retrieval. First- and third-graders did as well as college students in retrieving stored items from memory when given help with using the alphabet in recalling [24].

Elaboration and Enrichment. There is evidence that children recall both visual and verbal material better when it is presented in context, rather than as single items. Because younger children benefit more than older ones from presentation in context, it seems likely that older ones are more able to make elaborations for themselves, putting isolated items into contexts [27]. Putting words into a story enriches the words, giving them more meaning, and connecting them with other meanings and ideas. The object is enriched with touch experiences as well as ideas when a child handles a toy truck, uses a hammer, pets a kitten, or peels a banana. Singing or dancing to music enriches the music, adding motor and speech actions to listening. Children remember spoken sentences better when they are said with intonation or cadence, another example of enrichment of stimuli by adding another kind of sensory stimulation [47].

An investigation of rehearsal in third-, sixth-, and eighth-grade children showed the enriching function of rehearsing items in different contexts. Subjects were asked to rehearse aloud in preparation for recall of nouns presented in a list of 18. With increasing age, the children recalled more items and they also rehearsed them more actively in a variety of combinations. The authors suggest that although repetition may be sufficient for short-term remembering, long-term memory requires active rehearsal in a number of different sets [34].

Metamemory. As understanding of all cognitive processes increases, the child becomes more and more aware of his own remembering and of other people's memory activities and capacities. As children grow through the elementary school years, they see paying attention as influenced more and more by psychological factors such as motivation, rather than upon external factors, such as noise [28]. Because the school child realizes that he can influence his own processes of remembering, he makes plans and chooses strategies for focusing attention, organizing, rehearsing, and other methods for remembering that he has at his command.

Language

Closely related to both intellectual and social development, language can be considered from many angles. Language is receptive (understanding, listening), and productive (saying, speaking), semantic (with meaning), syntactic (structural), and phonological (sound-making). Communication will be discussed in Chapter 12 *Social Sensitivity*.

Semantics and Syntax

Development can be seen through middle childhood in both semantics and syntax. The number of words used and understood grows steadily. Complex and compound sentences are used increasingly. Acquisition of syntactic structures continues through middle childhood. The following are examples of structures learned between ages 5½ and 9 [8]. *John is easy to see. John promised Bill to go.* The next example is of a structure that some children have not learned by age 10. *John asked Bill what to do.* Most children of 5½ have acquired the structure represented by the following. *He knew that John was going to win the race.*

The use of syntax has been studied by asking children to repeat strings of words with three types of syntax; meaningful, anomalous, and random. Examples of the three are these: Red flowers fill small pots.; Young clothes fill red girls.; Red young clothes girls fill. In the first sentence, syntax and semantics are correct. In the anomalous sentence, the syntax is correct, but the semantics are not. If a child can recall the meaningful and/or anomalous sentences better than the random strings, then he must know something about structure and acceptable word combinations. These three types of strings were used with middle- and lower-class white children and lower-class black children from kindergarten, first,

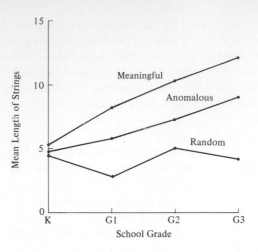

FIGURE 11–1.
Average number of words recalled from three types of word strings at four grade levels. (SOURCE: Data from D. R. Entwisle and H. E. Frasure. A contradiction resolved: children's processing of syntactic cues. *Developmental Psychology,* 1974, **10**, 852—857, Table 2.)

and second grades [15]. Figure 11–1 shows the number of words recalled under each condition at each grade level. Both the meaningful and anomalous sentences were used more successfully as grade level advanced, showing the increasing significance of both syntax and semantics.

The same method was used to compare black and white lower-class children, and lower- and middle-class white children [18]. Yearly growth rate was calculated for performance based on semantic content (by subtracting anomalous scores from meaningful scores) and syntactic content (by subtracting random scores from anomalous scores). Results showed semantic development in all groups during the years from 5 to 8, but there were differences in timing of gains. The white, middle-class children made their greatest gains between kindergarten and first grade; the lower-class black children increased most between first and third grade; the lower-class white children gained more steadily than did either of the other two groups. The group differences suggest that the school made a bigger impact on the black disadvantaged children than on the white middle class, with the white lower-class falling in between as to importance of school to semantic development. The middle-class children had apparently been stimulated earlier, probably at home, perhaps at nursery school as well.

At around the age of 7, when concrete operations begin to be established, a change in semantic development also takes place [2]. From experiments on sorting words into groups, and from association tests (wherein the person responds to a word with the first word that comes into her mind), the connections made between words are different before and after about age 7. The young child usually gives a relational response, whereas the older child and adult respond with a word that is the same part of speech. For example, to the stimulus word *table,* the young child is most likely to say *eat,* but the older child will say *chair.* Other evidence of semantic change is the older child's tendency to group under more hierarchies of abstraction. The same trend can be seen from middle childhood to adulthood. For example, children from grades 3 and 4 grouped *quickly, slowly,* and *very,* but adults added *now* and *again* to the three modifiers grouped by the children.

Children and adults continue to add meaningful words and meanings to words as they learn through reading, talking, and listening. They extract meaning out of sentences containing unfamiliar words, particularly when the new words are heard in several different contexts. Again, the importance of experience is obvious, with school the place where every child may have opportunities for learning new words, meanings, and structure.

Children's understanding of metaphors increases during the elementary school years, especially during the time from 8 to 10 [63]. A training program was effective in increasing understanding and production of figurative language by fifth-graders [62].

Articulation

Normative studies show that most 7-year-olds can articulate all English phonemes satisfactorily. At 5, however, some children do not produce all English sounds adequately. About 75 per cent of 1,500 children tested after entering kindergarten had at least one misarticulation [53]. Articulation tests and others were given to nearly 500 children in the kindergarten, and the tests were repeated at six-month intervals for four years [53]. The children with the lowest scores in the kindergarten were also the poorest articulators when they reached second grade. By fourth grade, they still had a number of articulation problems.

Several practical findings resulted from this study. Kindergarten teachers, without using tests, identified the children with the lowest articulation scores, an indication that teachers' reports would be very helpful in identifying the children who will need speech therapy. The most common misarticulations are with *s, l,* and *r,* but patterns vary from one child to another.

Well-developed articulation is correlated with ability to apply the rules of morphological change [54]. In addition to articulation tests, the children in kindergarten, first, and second grades were also tested for morphology, or ability to change words into plurals, possessives, different tenses, and so on. At each age level, children who made the largest number of errors in articulation were also the children who performed poorly on the morphology test, whereas the best articulators were also superior in morphology. Similar results were obtained in a European study that concluded that if speech problems are treated in the kindergarten, then children are less likely to have reading problems in the first grade [25].

Metalanguage

What do children know and think about the nature of language? Piaget noted long ago that young children think that the name of an object is part of it. A 5- or 6-year-old thinks that the name of the sun is in the sun "because the sun is bright" [36]. By 7 or 8, the child thinks that names were given when the objects were made, by God or by people. It is not until 10 to 12 that the arbitrary nature of names is appreciated, that names are seen as changeable. Several studies have shown that when children speak more than one language, they are more aware than monolinguals of the nature of language, especially that names are arbitrary [4, 10]. Bilinguals are also more analytical and think more flexibly about rules [4] and are more sensitive to feedback cues as to whether they have made a correct linguistic choice [11].

Children from first through fifth grade made gains in understanding arbitrariness of names through a task of renaming the pieces in a game [3]. They were told that they were going to make a new game by changing the way to play Monopoly. We believe that game Coffee Pot performs the same function, although to our knowledge, nobody has tested it.

The Culture of Childhood

The language of childhood has a very distinctive flavor. In fact, it has been said that childhood has its own culture, consisting of behavior patterns that are passed from one generation of children to the next, without benefit (or contamination) of adult intervention. An extensive collection [33] of English children's language humor traces jokes and stories historically and geographically, revealing some connections with European and Middle Eastern children's language productions. Children's humor is shown to have broad, deep, and ancient sources, connecting each generation of children with the past. Children apparently teach their rhymes and riddles to one another, initiating the younger ones, leaving the treasure with them, and then almost forgetting it.

Word Magic. Words give power over reality. The chants of childhood combine names with other magic-making words in order to induce certain feelings or behavior in playmates. For example: Cry, Billy, cry / Stick your finger in your eye / And tell your mother it wasn't I. The name-calling of childhood is half in earnest, half in play. Sometimes it is an imaginative attempt to produce a new verbal pattern, sometimes an effort to control or change reality. Mike, in a burst of annoyance at Chris, shouted "You're a cringing crustacean." The result, a cowed and silent Chris, strengthened Mike's belief in word magic, for had not his words changed his friend?

Word magic, the power of words to change reality, is used more by children than adults, but it is not the exclusive property of children.

Star light, star bright
First star I've seen tonight
I wish I may, I wish I might
Have the wish I wish tonight.

What goes up the chimney?
Smoke.
May your wish and my wish
Never be broke.

If you say RABBITS for your first word on the first morning of the month, you'll have good luck all month. If two people say the same word together spontaneously, each will get a wish if he keeps quiet until asked a question. This is the simple word magic of childhood, so appealing that adults often engage in it "just for fun." (Our family says RABBITS.) Having only recently discovered the very real power of words, it is understandable that children attribute even more power to them than they actually have. It is hard to check reality in this respect. How can we possibly know that it did no good to say RABBITS this month? We have had pretty good luck. It surely did no harm. It was no trouble to say. We'll continue to say RABBITS when we remember. Eventually, of course, the educated person develops intellectually to the point where he rejects word magic from most of his life. Not in his grade-school years, however. The less sophisticated person may continue to use word magic. The highly creative person may continue to play with magic.

Humor. Much of childhood humor is language, but not all of it. Jokes and funny experiences can also be motor, gestural, or in various art forms. Fun making is creative. Lacking space for a thorough discussion of humor in all its forms, we deal here only with humor in language.

Jokes, riddles, and all sorts of fun-making fit the particular needs and abilities of the participants. As in so many areas of development, there is a marked change from early to middle childhood in the type of experience that makes people laugh and smile. The simple incongruities that tickle preschool children are not very funny to the 7- or 8-year-old. There must be surprise and resolution of the incongruity. Schoolchildren, being concerned with industry, duty, accomplishment, achievement, and adequacy, and often feeling otherwise in comparison with adults, enjoy humor that reverses this situation. Sutton-Smith suggests that riddles model the child's experiences in school, when teachers speak incomprehensibly and ask difficult questions. In asking a riddle, the child plays the role of authority and wields power. When jokes and riddles disparage adults, they enable children to release, through laughter, the tensions they feel over their own inadequacies and their relationships with adults.

Sutton-Smith collected and classified jokes and riddles from 623 children in the first eight grades [52]. Children in the first three grades gave mostly riddles. Eighth-graders contributed mostly jokes. Over 60 per cent of the riddles involved implicit classification, as, for example: Q. Why did the dog go out into the sun? A. He wanted to be a hot dog. (Here, the word *dog* must be reclassified.) About 12 per cent were riddle parodies, in which an expectation is upset by a straightforward answer, as in: Q. Why did the chicken cross the road? A. To get to the other side. Patterns between relationships are reversed in 10 per cent of the riddles, such as this: Q. What does one flea say to another as they go strolling? A. Shall we walk or take a dog?

Measuring Intelligence

Everyone has some notion of what is intelligent behavior, but there is no generally agreed-upon definition of it. *Intelligence*, the capacity for intelligent behavior, has been defined by many psychologists who have constructed tests based on their definitions. (*See* "Intelligence Testers" in Chapter 1.) Piaget is interested in how intelligence develops, how the mind operates during the various stages and how all children change the structures of their minds as they mature. The tradition of intelligence testing is very different. By using the Intelligence Quotient (IQ) or other methods of numerical scoring, psychologists focus on differences between children, rather than upon the intelligence that all possess. By testing a classroom, children can be ranked according to their IQs or other scores, but the numerical differences between children may have no practical meaning. A very high score tells that the child has high chances of academic achievement and success, whereas a very low score tells the opposite, but for the majority of scores, those in the middle, the IQ tells very little. It tells nothing about special talents, about motivation, persistence, self-confidence, or many other strengths that influence satisfaction and success. Furthermore, IQ's change. Even if they *were* a valid means of sorting children into groups or classes, this term's grouping would not be the same as next term's. The IQ is, however, useful in research.

Different ecologies require different uses of intelligent behavior for success; parents teach their children the skills that they see children as needing for survival and competence. Native Canadian children learn to cooperate with one another to the extent that they will not answer questions as individuals, but only as groups. Think of what such behavior would to do an IQ score! Many black American mothers teach their children to be obedient to them and to keep quiet in school. When given intelligence tests, these children are likely to be uncommunicative and to refuse to take chances on being wrong. What is adequate behavior in ghetto culture may not succeed with problems posed in the school, or later in a well-paying job. Although entrance into the mainstream of American life does require the learning of certain intellectual skills, an IQ test does little to open the door. Most minority parents want their children to have the advantages enjoyed by the majority, and they know that education offers hope. They therefore reject the tests that have been used as a way of segregating their children from mainstream education.

Imagination and Creativity

Thinking and language are more powerful means of problem solving than they were during the preschool years. Even so, the school child uses all the modes of imaginative expression used by younger children—fantasy, dreams, dramatic play, storytelling, and the various artistic media.

The change-over from young child to school child calls for drawing a clearer line between imagination and reality. Parents and teachers usually think that it is all right for a little child to mix fantasy and truth, but not for an older child to tell imaginary stories as though they were true. The latter may be called lying. Because older children go alone into the world beyond home, their parents want and need to get accurate reports from them. Likewise, teachers require dependable information. Therefore, adults make efforts to teach children from age 7 onwards to tell the truth.

Art in the Early School Age

The years from 5 to 8 seem to be a golden age of creativity in art. Children paint and draw pictures that are appealing and intcresting to adults, the kind of pictures that parents and grandparents like to hang and keep. Then, as this age draws to a close, the child's paintings become less lively, less expressive, and less like those of a "real artist." One of our children commented at age 9 or 10 that she could not draw as well as she used to do, no matter how hard she tried. Howard Gardner, in his book, *Artful Scribbles,* follows his children's progress through the golden age of art and explains what happens [20]. Having learned to handle various media, to make basic lines, shapes, and movements, a child can express ideas and feelings. Children combine different forms of art to sort out their experiences and feelings. The decline in lively, spontaneous paintings and drawings comes at the time when verbal power and logical reasoning ability are increasing rapidly. Brain development probably underlies these changes. The time from 5 to 8 is marked by incrcasing specialization of the brain. As mentioned earlier, the right side of the brain is the main seat of artistic and emotional activity, whereas verbal and logical behavior stems largely from the left.

Gardner goes on to say that the age-related decline in drawing ability is also due to lack of instruction. In China, where drawing and other art

by Tıshy Kirkland, age 6 years

Drawing on the occasion of the author's departure from Nanjing, China by 9-year-old Woo Wing.

forms are taught throughout childhood, children gain skill instead of losing it. (See the drawing above by Woo Ming.)

Measuring Creativity

Some individuals are more creative than others. It is not difficult to pick out some very creative adults, because they are known, or can be rated and chosen on the basis of original work they have done. Because few children ever produce things or ideas than can be rated in the work world, their creativity has to be assessed in other ways if it is to be studied. Observation suggests that children vary widely in creativity. Many investigators have tried to distinguish between creativity and intelligence as measured by standardized tests. Success in separating the two processes came through assuming that creativity includes these two elements: abundant production of unique associations; a playful, permissive attitude [58]. Children were tested individually for amount and uniqueness of production in a relaxed atmosphere of playing games, with no pressures of time and few restrictions. Number of unique responses and total number of responses were measured in verbal and visual situations. The three verbal "games" were instances, alternate uses, and similarities. *Instances* included naming all the round things the child could think of, all the things that make a noise, all the square things, and all the things that move on wheels. *Alternate uses* involved telling all the different ways one could use a newspaper, knife, automobile tire, cork, shoe, key, and chair. *Similarities* consisted of telling all the ways in which a potato and a carrot are alike, a cat and a mouse, a train and a tractor, and several other such pairs. Visual tests were giving meanings or interpretations for a number of abstract patterns and lines. To the left are examples of the drawings used.

All the children in a fifth-grade class were given the creativity tests and the Wechsler Intelligence Scale for Children, as well as ability tests and achievement tests. Behavior ratings were made. As creativity and intelligence varied independently, subjects could be placed above or below the mean for each. The investigators were able to divide the subjects into four groups for each sex: high IQ with high creativity, low IQ with high creativity, high IQ with low creativity, and low IQ with low creativity. Many significant differences between various groups were seen.

Girls high in both dimensions were highly self-confident, interested in academic work, and able to concentrate well. Sought after by peers, they also sought and enjoyed companionship. They were also disruptive in the classroom, seeking attention and possibly eager to propose new ideas and activities in order to relieve boredom. Girls high in creativity but low in intelligence were at the greatest disadvantage of all groups. Cautius, hesitant, lacking in self-confidence, they deprecated their own work, had a hard time concentrating, and disrupted classroom procedures in a protesting fashion. Other girls avoided them and they avoided others. Girls low in both dimensions apparently compensated for poor academic performance by social activity. Compared with the high creative, low IQ girls, the low-low girls were more self-confident, less subdued, and more outgoing. The high IQ, low creative girls were self-confident and assured, able to concentrate, fairly hesitant about expressing opinions, and unlikely to be disruptive. Although other girls sought her companionship, this type of girl was aloof socially, hesitant to overextend herself or to commit herself.

The intelligence score, but not creativity, was related to the behavior ratings for boys in the classroom. The highly intelligent boy was self-confident, interested, and able to cope and to concentrate. The low IQ boys were more likely to be withdrawn, self-deprecating, and self-punishing.

Concept formation in boys was related to both creativity and IQ. High IQ, low creativity boys were least likely of all groups to use themes when asked to group objects together and tell why they grouped as they did. An example of a theme was "getting ready to go out," given by a child who put together a comb, lipstick, watch, pocketbook, and door. Boys high in creativity switched flexibly between two styles of organizing. Further testing showed that the high IQ, low creative boys could use themes if they were asked to do so. When they were given free choice, however, they did not use themes. These results, along with further evidence on girls' acceptance or rejection of unconventional picture labels, leads to this conclusion: the high IQ, low creativity child is likely to be intolerant of unlikely hypotheses about the world, reluctant to "stick his neck out," afraid of being wrong. Anxiety level is low in this group. It looks as though this type of child is attuned to what succeeds in the ordinary classroom.

Creativity seems to be associated with moderate levels of anxiety. The most creative child is not necessarily the happiest. He may well be sensitive to sadness and pain. High creativity involves not only a playful contemplation of the possible but most likely also requires high persistence and concentration, "an obsessive, task-centered reluctance to put a problem aside" [58].

Group Differences in Mental Development

Every child is unique in mind as well as in body. There are, however, some patterns that are typical of certain groups, such as boys and girls, children with high or low IQs, children with special talents, and children with learning disabilities.

Sex Differences

Sex differences in brain lateralization, as mentioned in the previous chapter, are indicated by girls' superiority in language and boys' in spatial performance. The interaction of experience with brain structure is discussed in a review of sex differences in performance [23]. Boys, on the average, do better than girls in tasks requiring mechanical and geometric skill and visual-spatial imagery. Differences show up in advanced math-

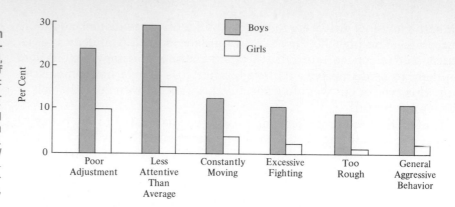

FIGURE 11–2.
Proportions of children consistently showing problem behavior at school, boys and girls 6–11 years of age, United States. (SOURCE: J. Roberts and J. T. Baird, Jr. *Behavior patterns of children in school.* Vital and Health Statistics. Data from the National Health Survey. Series 11. No. 113. DHEW Publication No. (HSM) 72–1042. Washington: U.S. Government Printing Office, 1972.)

ematics but not in simple arithmetic. Boys excel when the sense of direction is important, as in maze problems, map reading, left-right discrimination, rod-and-frame test, geographic knowledge, and various Piagetian spatial tasks. Girls, on the average, have earlier language development than boys. Girls articulate better and can be more easily understood. Girls are more fluent and read better during the school years. Girls' language ability is more closely related to general intellectual performance than is boys', suggesting that girls make more use of verbal means in developing intellectually. It may be that each sex capitalizes on the particular advantage it has, a greater specialization of the right hemispheres for boys and earlier and superior language development for girls. In sex differences, as in all group differences, the difference applies to averages and not to individuals. Some boys excel in language, some girls do superior work in spatial problems.

More boys than girls are problems at school, according to their teachers. Figure 11–2 shows proportions of boys and girls displaying various kinds of problem behavior. Some of these behaviors are social and emotional as well as intellectual. Sex differences in patterning of intellect are greater when boys and girls are treated very differently. We shall return to this topic in the next chapter.

The Gifted

Some children are more competent, more talented, more creative and/or brighter than others. The term *gifted* is applied to those who excel others in some defined way. The definition has to be made by a person or a group. A school committee or department of education decides that children with IQs over 140 are gifted. A ballet mistress declares Tanya a gifted child because she dances better than most of the children Mlle Tiptoe has taught. The judges at the Science Fair say that the creativity shown in Brian's aerodynamics experiment proves him to be a gifted child. In general, children are considered to be gifted when they have high IQs and/or one or more special talents [57]. In defining the IQ point at which children are considered to be gifted, 130 is often chosen. About 2½ per cent of children have Stanford-Binet IQ's of 130 or more. One in

1,000 has an IQ of 150 or more [57]. Terman followed the development of 1,500 children whose IQs averged 150 [55]. Not only were they advanced in grade placement and doing excellent work, they were taller, healthier, and superior socially and morally.

The Mentally Retarded

Like the term *gifted, mentally retarded* is a social definition. When a person's intellectual functioning is inadequate for him to cope with life's demands, he is likely to be considered mentally retarded. An IQ between 50 and 70 is generally taken to indicate an educable mentally retarded child, one who can learn basic skills for self-care and earning a living. These children learn slowly, have difficulty generalizing, and may have poor control over attention. Because they often experience failure, they are likely to have low self-esteem. Special teaching methods take these characteristics into account, arranging tasks in small steps at levels where success is likely, giving prompt feedback and reinforcement, spacing repetitions, and including motor experiences and opportunities for experience with the arts.

The Learning Disabled

This term is applied to children of average or above average intelligence who cannot learn one or more school subjects. Flexibility and control of cognition are basic to learning. As mentioned in the discussion of memory earlier in this chapter, children make plans for learning and memorizing. They develop strategies for scanning and selecting cues. When control processes are inadequate, learning disabilities result. For example, learning disabled boys were less able than normal boys to delay motor behavior [60]. In other words, the learning disabled were more impulsive. Unable to pause long enough to consider alternatives and to make plans, a child with weak cognitive controls has trouble in focusing attention, selecting relevant features and ignoring incidental ones. Flexibility in switching strategies of visual selection ordinarily increases with age [42], but learning disabled children may resemble younger children in having less control over this cognitive process.

Cognitive controls are related to affect, or emotional states. When anxious over being evaluated, children showed deficits in attention [14]. Many college students have had the experience of forgetting what they knew when afraid of failing a particular examination!

Learning deficits have been found to be associated with brain dysfunction [44a]. The nature and patterning of a particular learning disability can often be linked to a certain kind of brain impairment. Dyslexia (reading disability) has been traced to a variety of brain disorders.

Children can often be helped to compensate for learning disabilities. First, the specialist tries to find out just what strategies and control processes the child is using. Then he tries to help the child to develop more successful cognitive methods.

Ecology of Mental Development

Children in different macrosystems differ in cognitive skills, language, symbolic expression, and speed of development. Some of these differences can be traced to physical settings, in which food and health care are more or less adequate. Physical appearance of environments may influence visual perception. Perceptual differences occur between children growing up amid the many straight lines and angles of engineered and carpentered structures, and children who live in round huts amid soft contours of vines and trees, or sand dunes [59]. Values are another source of influence at all levels of the social ecology. The language environment can be considered from the standpoint of the whole culture, or of home, school, and neighborhood. Concepts of time differ from one culture to another. We have already discussed variations in achievement of conservation and other concrete operational skills as related to cultural and family differences. Cognitive style has been shown to vary with child-rearing practices. In the following chapter, family influences will be discussed further. In this section, we discuss the microsystems of school and neighborhood, in which the child develops as a thinking, speaking, creating person.

The School

Schools and the sense of industry are made for each other. It is no accident that children are sent to a special institution that imparts the wisdom of the culture at just the age when they become interested in learning it and in becoming producing members of society. In this section we discuss what schooling does and how it affects children.

Effects of Schooling. In thinking about how schools affect children, Americans are likely to consider different types of schooling. The difference between schooling and *no* schooling has not come into question until recently because it is almost impossible to find a group of European

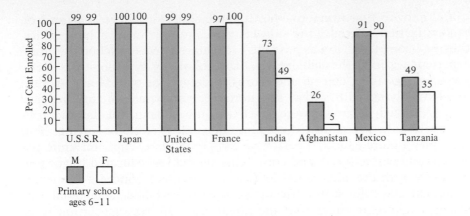

FIGURE 11-3.
Per cent of boys and girls age 6–11 enrolled in school, selected countries. (SOURCE: M. C. McHale, J. McHale, and G. F. Streatfeild. *Children in the World*. Washington: Population Reference Bureau, 1979.)

or United States children untouched by a school. There are, however, millions of children in poor and undeveloped parts of the world who have never been to school. Figure 11–3 shows the percentage of boys and girls in school in selected countries. By comparing groups of these children with their own peers who do not attend school, researchers have been able to disentangle effects of schooling from ethnicity, maturation, and social class.

Two recent studies will serve as examples. Stevenson and his associates gave 15 memory and cognitive tasks to more than 800 5- and 6-year-old children in Peru and Detroit [50]. The Detroit children were Chicano, living in the inner city. The Peruvian groups were from the jungle and the city, from poor and middle-class families, and were divided between those who attended school and those who did not. A sample of parents and children were interviewed in each location. The children who attended school did better in all the tasks than did those who did not go to school. There were very small differences between the 5- and 6-year-olds who did not go to school, indicating that maturation and experience had little effect on the skills measured. Although middle-class children did better than lower-class on several tasks, both social groups benefited from school attendance. That is, schooling improved the performance of both, but did not make them equal. Poor children improved neither more nor less than affluent children. Overall, verbal stimulation by parents was related to higher verbal performance by children. Some differences were found between locations. City children were higher in verbal skills than jungle children, but jungle children did better in perceptual learning. Stevenson and his associates thus showed that school makes an important impact on mental development during the child's first year or months of attending, but that school does not wipe out the contributions of social class, parental stimulation, and location.

Sharp, Cole, and Lave studied the effects of schooling on subjects at the other end of the age scale from those of Stevenson's study [46]. The Sharp team worked in Yucatan, Mexico, with subjects between 10 and 56 from 37 towns that varied in educational facilities and several criteria of modernization. Because the subjects varied in how many school grades they had completed, it was possible to separate effects of schooling from experience gained through living. The following types of tests were given: categorizing objects and words; memory for objects and words; problem-solving with verbal and nonverbal materials; an intelligence test. Although all groups were able to sort into meaningful classes (taxonomically), the less-educated used functions more often for sorting. For example, a more educated person would group plate, cup, and knife together, and onion, bread, and corn, whereas the less educated might put the knife with the onion and the bread on the plate. Success in sorting geometric and color stimuli (triangles, squares, red, blue, and so on) was strongly related to education, and not to age. In free association tests (giving a word in response to a word stimulus), more highly educated groups gave more words that matched stimulus words in terms of parts of speech (an adjective as response to an adjective, an adverb to an adverb). Free recall varied with level of education. The high school students grouped the recalled words by meaning. Short-term recall varied with grade level; the more successful subjects used active rehearsal. The better educated solved logical problems more easily, treating them as puzzles to be solved on their own terms. Less educated subjects stuck less to the conditions of the problems, bringing in personal experience and knowledge. Measured intelligence varied with grade of schooling reached. In summary, going to school longer increased performance on tests of cognitive development and intelligence.

In light of these two extensive investigations, and of several that preceded them, there are some generalizations we can make about what happens to children when they go to school.

1. Language becomes separated out of experience, and impersonal.
2. Rules are used to guide behavior. Rules are expressed verbally, and perhaps written down for permanence, making them impersonal and abstract from a particular experience.
3. Information is classified, organized, and manipulated. The child learns to operate mentally on numbers and words, as activities in themselves.
4. Classifying skills are used in remembering more successfully. Aids to remembering may be given, enabling the child to store and retrieve experiences more efficiently than she would do spontaneously.
5. Metacognition develops as children are encouraged to reflect on the language, thinking, remembering, planning, and choosing that they and others do.

Basic Functions of Schools.   How does a school transform the minds of a child? Even though whole books are written on educational psychology, and much is known about just how schools operate, we believe that the essential transformation occurs when the child learns the basics—reading, writing, and arithmetic. Of course we believe that the additional functions of the school are extremely worthwhile and necessary for children growing up in industrialized societies. Literacy, however, is the primary distinction between an educated person and an uneducated one. (There are over 800 million illiterate adults in the world, two-thirds of them women [26].) The ability to read and write is a powerful tool in everyday life. In India, for example, an illiterate villager must pay a scribe to read and write letters or documents for him, and the risk of being cheated is something he has to accept. Besides the convenience and financial advantages of knowing how to read and write, literacy transforms the mind of the person who achieves it.

Early steps in learning to read are to become aware of language as separate from the rest of experience, and then to realize that language consists of words. Some 5-year-olds come to school without knowing what *word* means [13, p. 93]. Children learn about words as part of language when they have books read to them and when they play word games. Most middle-class parents provide these experiences before children enter school; many lower-class parents do not.

A second big step in learning to read is coming to realize that marks on paper correspond to or stand for spoken words. Even after going to school for 4 months, some children cannot tell how the postman knows which house to bring a letter to or how their mothers know which bus to take [13, p. 99]. If parents have not told their children what grocery lists are for, how Grandma has sent news in her letter, or what street signs say, then teachers have to help children to lay these foundations for matching spoken and written words. Matching sounds to individual strokes, dots, and squiggles comes later. At that point, it is important to let the English-speaking child know that there is not a one-to-one correspondence between sound and letter (in a non-phonetic language like English), and that it will be a gradual process to learn all the variations.

When a child can read a few words, she can discover that written words are enduring, that they can be carried home and read there, they can be used to convey messages, and to remind oneself. Language is becoming further abstracted out of experience as reading and writing. It can be used without gesture, without tone of voice, without anything added to itself, to convey information precisely. Reading and writing show that language is governed by rules, and that the rules can be clearly stated. Arithmetic also gives the notion that there are rules, and that information can be manipulated without any reference to a practical situation or to feeling.

In school, children are taught in groups, by a teacher who verbalizes rules about how they are to proceed with their work. Some rules are general, covering a variety of situations. In contrast, the child apprentice, learning from a parent or a master craftsman, learns specific procedures by watching, helping, and doing them under supervision. Rules are rarely verbalized. For example, the Indian boys who become bone and ivory carvers begin by cutting out the shapes of small pieces of elephant bone that a more experienced, older boy will carve into inexpensive earrings and pins. Each worker can see what the next level of skill looks like, in operation and in products. A child does not make many mistakes, because the master tells him when he may advance to the next operation. If the child develops high skill as he grows up, he may eventually carve ivory goddesses of great intricacy.

Values. The values operating in a particular school come from many sources. The whole macrosystem has educational values. A school system's board of education expresses values in the policies it makes for its schools. (The board of education is an exosystem of the pupil, because it influences his microsystem, the school.) The principal and teachers express their own values, along with those of the board of education (exosystem) and society (macrosystem). Because the United States is a multicultural, rapidly changing society, conflicting values are often problematic. The following list shows some of those conflicts. The reader may wish to add others. We urge students of child development to discuss these questions with people who have a variety of viewpoints, to choose such topics for writing papers, and to clarify their own educational values. We cannot treat all these questions in this book, but we shall comment briefly on one of them.

SOME QUESTIONS OF
VALUES

Excellence for a few or moderate achievement for most?
Sink or swim or special help for the disadvantaged?
Competition or cooperation?
One language or several?
Learning through discovery, or behavior modification?
Conformity or creativity?
Enrichment or back to basics?
Obedience or initiative?
Separation of church and state or religion in school?
Breakfast and lunch at school or only at home?
Sex education in school for all or at home for some?
Shop for boys and cooking for girls or both (or neither) for all?

Gifted children are given special attention in a minority of schools. Programs for the gifted are opposed by people who think them undemocratic. Such people say that the very bright or talented child is luckier than most children without being given extra opportunities; equal opportunities should be available to all. Or they may think that the least able or the disadvantaged children should receive any extra effort to be put forth by the school. Those who support programs for the gifted believe that such children, as well as others, have a right to full development, and that superior human talents are of benefit to the community, nation, and world, as well as to individuals.

There are three main ways of providing for the education of gifted children: acceleration, segregation, and enrichment. All, one, or two may be used with a given child, depending on what is available and what suits the particular individual. *Acceleration* by one or two grades is often satisfactory, because many gifted children are mature physically and socially, as well as mentally. A small school system rarely has sufficient resources and perhaps not enough gifted children to make *segregation* feasible; a larger school system may run part-time classes for the gifted, providing both the methods and subject matter that will challenge them adequately. The drawbacks of segregation are that the gifted may become conceited and unable to get along with average children. Segregation is often satisfactory when done in special talent groups, such as music camps or Saturday science clubs. *Enrichment* may be provided for an individual or small group, either at home, at school, or in the community. It takes a creative and dedicated teacher to devise and provide for special activities in a classroom.

The Family

In "Microsystem Influences," earlier in this chapter, we discussed parental teaching styles and types of parent-child interactions that enhance cognitive development. In this section we consider ways in which families make learning opportunities available to their children. A most comprehensive study on this topic was done in England by the Newsons [32]. Parents were interviewed about their interactions with their 7-year-old children, and the children's achievement in school was related to their experiences in their families. The higher the social class of the family, that is, the higher the income and educational level, the more the parents take the children to cultural places and events, and the more the parents read and make books available.

In addition to finding that the range of cultural opportunities narrowed as socioeconomic status went down, results also showed that school-related topics were carried less into the home, parents tended less to expand children's questions, children received less help and encouragement with school work, and parents tried to conceal their own ignorance. The number of children in the family was related to children's verbal reasoning scores. In the higher classes, as well as the lower, children from families of one to three children did better than children from families with four or more. This finding is consistent with a number of studies that have shown negative relationships between number of siblings and IQ, achievement, and income.

Families treat boys and girls differently in the learning opportunities that they provide. Sex differences in language and other abilities are due, at least in part, to the different experiences that boys and girls have at home. The Newson study showed that these differences were greater in families of lower socioeconomic status. Lower-class boys were the most disadvantaged group, and middle-class girls the most advantaged in terms of family support for activities correlated with school success.

Most parents do the best that they can do for their children. If they do not take them to concerts and libraries, it is probably because they lack the necessary time, money, and transportation facilities and/or knowledge of opportunities. If they do not converse about school-related topics, it is because they do not know much about them. If they have to divide their resources, including attention, too thinly between children, it is not that they want to short-change anyone, but that they do not have enough to go around. We have seen that parents' resources for their children vary with the parents' income and education. Our discussion of family influences on mental development is thus led into the child's exosystem, especially the parents' source of income. But the economic system is beyond the scope of this book, and we shall have merely to point out that income has a profound effect upon the child's development, acting through the parents.

Recreational Settings

Home and school are not the only microsystems for learning and intellectual development. Even though work and play are separated more for the school-age child than they are for preschoolers, play is still an important avenue of mental development.

Neighborhood. From one another, children learn the culture of childhood, the chants and riddles that we have already mentioned in this chapter. They also play remembering games, games of discovery, and games of strategy, all of which require vigorous intellectual effort. The following are first-rate examples.

COGNITIVE GAMES

I Packed My Grandmother's Trunk	Remembering
Coffee Pot	Discovery
Twenty Questions	Discovery
Checkers	Strategy
Chess	Strategy
Monopoly	Strategy
Rummy	Strategy

Neighborhood organizations contribute to the mental development of the children they serve. A community house or an after-school day care center is an important part of some children's lives. Under adult leadership, or at least supervision, children have access to games, puzzles, books, art materials, and all such food for the mind. Girl Scouts, Boy Scouts, and other children's organizations offer programs that promote mental development, along with growth of the whole person. In Scouting, children learn on their own, as well as in the group, through a badge program. About 30 per cent of United States children take part in these activities [43].

Camps. Living at camp can promote mental growth, as well as physical and social. Camps usually offer guided discovery in nature and music, as well as chances to play stimulating games, to hear stories, and even to read books. Private camps are usually affordable only to the affluent, but free camping is offered to some poor urban children. In the middle, there are the camps of churches, Scouts, 4H, and other children's organizations. In the camps for rich and poor, a first-time camper may feel very isolated from home, and suffer home-sickness. In organization camps, especially when a whole troop or club camps together with their regular leader, the child feels comfortable with established links. The same ease in camping occurs in New Zealand, where teachers take their classes camping for several days each year.

Television. Because children spend many inactive hours sitting in front of television sets, there is just cause for concern about the results. Time spent with television is time taken away from other pursuits, such as reading, playing games, practicing motor skills, artistic creativity, listening to music, work, study, taking trips, watching adults, and talking with people.

Children have learned significantly from television programs designed especially to help them with basic academic work [12]. "Sesame Street" and "The Electric Company" have been and are being important aids to the learning of reading and arithmetic. Children's understanding of dramatic programs is often strained, especially in the case of younger children. Second-graders, in contrast to eighth-graders, could give an account of aggressive scenes they saw, but could not understand the motives or consequences of what they had seen [9]. When asked whether television was real or pretend, 6- to 8-year-olds usually said they did not know, but most 9- to 11-year-olds said that "some of the things seen on television are pretend" [51].

Cultural Institutions and Events. Libraries open the world of reading to children after the schools have unlocked the door. Children find appropriate books in chldren's sections with the help of children's librarians. Exhibits, story hours, and programs fill out the offerings. Although most communities have libraries, some children do not live within walking distance. Their access to a library may depend upon having parents who are willing and able to take them to it. The more educated the parents, the more likely they are to provide that access. An English study of 7-year-olds considered library membership according to 5 social classes [32]. In the top class, 72 per cent of children belonged, whereas only 20 per cent of the lowest class belonged to a library.

Some museums are designed especially for children, complete with guides and programs suited to discovery, learning, and enjoyment. Most museums, whether of art or science, usually have an education department, in which children's programs are designed and administered. Although museums are not quite as widespread as libraries, parents are not the only route through which a child may enter. Schools often send classes to museums, where museum personnel conduct tours and give lessons. In at least one big-city museum, the exhibibtion on human reproduction is so excellent that family-life teachers use it consistently in their courses.

Children's theater and concerts are available in many cities. In Rhode Island the Looking Glass Theater travels on request, playing for rural children as well as urban. A state symphony orchestra sometimes performs in schools. Availability of children's art and music programs depends upon adults in the community who work to give children growth opportunities. Some parents take children to theaters and concert halls with them, and also to zoos, circuses, aquariums, and sporting events. All of these experiences add richness to life and act as stimulants to mental growth.

Religious Institutions

Although fewer children take part in religious activities than in groups such as Scouts, religious teaching has much to offer to the mental growth of those who do. A nation-wide United States survey found 10 per cent of children between 6 and 11 involved in Bible school or other religious training or activities [43]. When we asked New Zealand fifth-grade children whether they had been to church or Sunday school during the previous week, 11 per cent said "yes."[49]. The quality of mental stimulation no doubt varies with the type of institution and program. Fundamentalist churches value obedience to church law, memorization, and uncritical acceptance of the Bible; liberal churches promote discovery and criticism. A religious institution may teach culture as well as religion, as do the Hebrew language schools of temples and synagogues.

Mesosystems

A link between two microsystems, the mesosystem holds the child's world together. Because home and school are a child's most important microsystems, the mesosystem between them is especially crucial. A first concern upon entering school is to establish connections between home and school. Otherwise, the young child feels isolated and anxious, uses his energy in self-defense, and has none left for mental development. The mesosystem is built through communication between parents and teachers, sometimes through the child, sometimes directly. Mother or father takes the child to school for the first few times and talks briefly with the teacher. The child may take a favorite toy from home to school, to make a tangible link. The teacher sends notes home and holds an open house and parent conferences. When Johnny can read a little, he takes home books to read at home with his family, and messages he has written. Learning to read and write makes the mesosystem stronger, if teachers and parents make use of it. Siblings enlarge the home-school

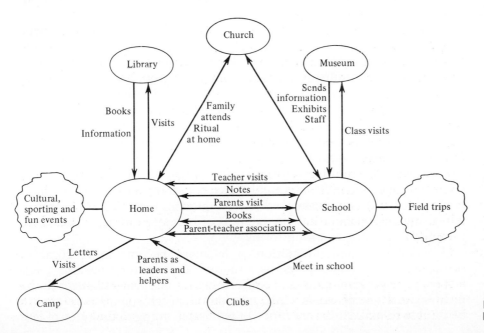

FIGURE 11–4.
Mesosystems in childhood.

mesosystem. Older siblings establish the connection before younger ones go, not always advantageously for those who come after a sibling with a reputation as a trouble-maker. On the whole, though, it is a help and comfort to a young child to have an older sibling in the school system, for protection and guidance while walking to school and playing in the schoolyard, and for giving information about rules and procedures that may be puzzling to the younger one.

Figure 11–4 pictures a child's mesosystems, indicating the nature of some of the connections between microsystems. Each child's mesosystem is unique in its details. Figure 11–4 shows that this child has connections through school to museum, but not through home, and to camp through home, but not through school. Parents are club leaders, but the club meets at school, and so the club is linked with both microsystems. The student of child development can gain insight into a child's life by mapping out his microsystems and mesosystems in detail.

Summary

Between 5 and 7 years, the typical American child acquires the ability to act upon symbols mentally, trying out courses of action in his mind instead of physically. He realizes that there are rules for thinking and that his conclusions can be checked with other people's. Sensory information, the raw material for thinking, is obtained and used differently in different cultures and by individuals who differ in cognitive style and in conceptual style. Increased flexibility, reversibility, and control of thought, along with an increasing accumulation of memories, enable the child to weigh alternatives, to plan, and to take another person's point of view.

The period of concrete operations is Piaget's term for school-age intellectual development. Carrying out rule-governed mental actions, the child manipulates objects and symbols. He achieves conservation in regard to substance, number, quantity, and other properties, realizing that they remain the same through certain changes. Further understanding includes relations, ordering, numeration, transitivity, and class inclusion. Age of achieving concrete operations is influenced by macrosystem values, schooling, life style, maternal teaching style, and parental discipline and companionship.

Remembering improves during the school years. Increasing mental control brings more effective employment of attention. Children think of more strategies for storing and retrieving memories, such as observing, rehearsing, and elaborating. Awareness of memory processes increases, leading to planning and monitoring.

Understanding and production of language become more complex throughout the middle years, as structure and meaning become more elaborate. The development of concrete operations brings changes in the meaning and use of words. Articulation of speech sounds is related to being able to make different forms of words according to the rules of language. The arbitrariness of names is increasingly appreciated. Children learn language and games from older children. The culture of childhood has ancient and broad roots. Appreciation of humor changes as children become more intellectually mature.

The Piagetian approach to intelligence deals with processes and stages of mental maturation; the use of IQ focuses on differences between children, comparing them by scores. Tests developed in one culture may not test the intelligent behavior that is required by a different macrosystem, or by a minority group within a society.

During the early school years, children often make paintings and other works of art that seem like the work of artists. As they grow older, such creativity declines, probably because of increasing verbal and logical abilities, along with lack of instruction in art. Tests for verbal creativity in children use amount and uniqueness of production for criteria.

Cognitive sex differences come, at least in part, from different patterns of brain maturation. Giftedness is a social definition, sometimes made in terms of IQ, sometimes related to creative performance, and often to both. Mental retardation is also socially defined, usually meaning that an individual cannot meet life's demands. Learning disability is an inability to learn a certain subject although still having at least average IQ. Special programs can aid the functioning of the gifted, retarded, and learning disabled.

Cognitive skills develop in response to physical settings and social demands. Values, language, and educational opportunities shape children's minds. Schooling transforms a child's mind by teaching reading, and also through teaching rules, arithmetic, and classifying. Learning to read requires that words be abstracted out of experience and then the realization that marks on paper stand for words. Special contributions to intellectual development are made not only by home and school, but also by neighborhood, camps, libraries, museums, religious institutions, and cultural and sporting events. Learning and development are supported by a strong mesosystem, connecting all parts of a child's life.

References

1. Abravanel, E. The development of intersensory patterning with regard to selected spatial dimensions. *Monographs of the Society for Research in Child Development*, 1968, **33:**2.
2. Anglin, J. M. *The growth of word meaning.* Cambridge, Mass.: The M.I.T. Press, 1970.
3. Ball, S. E., and R. A. Simpson. Shifts from nominal realism in grade-school children as a function of participating in a naming task. *Journal of Psychology*, 1977, **96,** 217–221.
4. Ben-Zeev, S. The influence of bilingualism on cognitive strategy and cognitive development. *Child Development*, 1977, **48,** 1009–1018.
5. Bermudez, J. H., D. C. Prather, G. A. Berry, and R. B. Tebbs. Effect of valence on conservation. *Journal of Psychology*, 1974, **87,** 83–88.
6. Bray, N. W., E. M. Justice, R. P. Ferguson, and D. L. Simon. Developmental changes in the effects of instructions on production-deficient children. *Child Development*, 1977, **48,** 1019–1026.

7. Cermak, L. S., et al. Development of the ability to encode within evaluation dimensions. *Journal of Experimental Child Psychology,* 1972, **13,** 210–219.

8. Chomsky, C. *The acquisition of syntax in children from five to ten.* Cambridge, Mass.: The M.I.T. Press, 1969.

9. Collins, W. A., and S. D. Westby. Children's processing of social information from televised dramatic programs. Paper presented at meeting of the Society for Research in Child Development, Denver, 1975.

10. Cummins, J. Bilingualism and the development of metalinguistic awareness. *Journal of Cross-Cultural Psychology,* 1978, **9,** 131–149.

11. Cummins, J., and R. Mulcahy. Orientation to language in Ukranian-English bilingual children. *Child Development,* 1978, **49,** 1239–1242.

12. Distinguished contribution for applications in psychology award for 1974. *American Psychologist,* 1975, **30,** 65–68.

13. Donaldson, M. *Children's minds.* New York: W. W. Norton & Company, Inc., 1978.

14. Dusek, J. B., N. L. Mergler, and M. D. Kermis. Attention, encoding, and information processing in low- and high-test-anxious children. *Child Development,* 1976, **47,** 201–207.

15. Entwisle, D. R., and N. E. Frasure. A contradiction resolved: Children's processing of syntactic cues. *Developmental Psychology,* 1974, **10,** 852–857.

16. Flavell, J. H. *Cognitive development.* Englewood Cliffs, N.J.: Prentice-Hall, Inc., 1977.

17. Frank, H. S., and M. S. Rabinovitch. Auditory short-term memory: Developmental changes in rehearsal. *Child Development,* 1974, **45,** 397–407.

18. Frasure, N. E., and D. R. Entwisle. Semantic and syntactic development in children. *Developmental Psychology,* 1973, **9,** 236–245.

19. Friedrich, D. Developmental analysis of memory capacity and information-encoding strategy. *Developmental Psychology,* 1974, **10,** 559–563.

20. Gardner, H. *Artful scribbles: The significance of children's art.* New York: Basic Books, Inc., Publishers, 1980.

21. Hagen, J. W. Strategies for remembering. In S. Farnham-Diggory (ed.) *Information processing in children.* New York: Academic Press, Inc., 1972, pp. 65–79.

22. Hale, G. A., S. S. Taweel, R. Z. Green, and J. Flaugher. Effects on children's attention to stimulus components. *Developmental Psychology,* 1978, **14,** 499–506.

23. Harris, L. J. Interaction of experiential and neurological factors in the patterning of human abilities: The question of sex differences in "right hemisphere" skills. Paper presented at meeting of the Society for Research in Child Development, Denver, 1975.

24. Keniston, A. H., and J. H. Flavell. A developmental study of intelligent retrieval. *Child Development,* 1979, **50,** 1144–1152.

25. Maire-Declusy, L., L. Gaches, and N. Colas. Results of a systematic survey and early treatment in kindergarten. *Early Child Development & Care,* 1973, **13,** 413–421.

26. McHale, M. C., J. McHale, and G. F. Streatfeild. *Children in the world.* Washington: Population Reference Bureau, 1979.

27. Meacham, J. A. The development of memory in the individual and society. *Human Development,* 1972, **15,** 205–228.

28. Miller, P. H., and L. Bigi. The development of children's understanding of attention. *Merrill-Palmer Quarterly,* 1979, **25,** 235–250.

29. Miller, S. A. Candy is dandy and also quicker: A further nonverbal study of conservation of number. *Journal of Genetic Psychology,* 1979, **134,** 15–21.

30. Mowbray, C., and C. Luria. Effects of labeling on children's visual imagery. *Developmental Psychology,* 1973, **9,** 1–8.

31. Newcombe, N., B. Rogoff, and J. Kagan. Developmental changes in recogni-

tion memory for pictures of objects and scenes. *Developmental Psychology*, 1977, **13**, 337–341.

32. Newson, J., E. Newson, and P. Barnes. *Perspective on school at seven years old.* London: George Allen & Unwin, Ltd., 1977.

33. Opie, I., and P. Opie. *The lore and language of school children.* Oxford: Clarendon Press, 1959.

34. Ornstein, P. A., M. J. Naus, and C. Liberty. Rehearsal processes in children's memory. *Child Development*, 1975, **46**, 818–830.

35. Paris, S. G., and A. Y. Carter. Semantic and constructive aspects of sentence memory in children. *Developmental Psychology*, 1973, **9**, 109–113.

36. Piaget, J. Children's philosophies. In C. Murchison (ed.) *A handbook of child psychology* (2nd ed.). Worcester, Mass.: Clark University Press, 1933.

37. Piaget, J. *The psychology of intelligence.* London: Routledge & Kegan Paul, 1950.

38. Piaget, J. Cognitive development in children: The Piaget papers. In R. E. Ripple and V. N. Rockcastle (eds.). *Piaget rediscovered.* Ithaca, N.Y.: School of Education, Cornell University, 1964, pp. 6–48.

39. Piaget, J. *The child's conception of number.* New York: W. W. Norton and Company, Inc., 1965.

40. Piaget, J., and B. Inhelder. *The psychology of the child.* New York: Basic Books, Inc., Publishers, 1969.

41. Pick, A. D. Some basic perceptual processes in reading. *Young Children*, 1970, **15**, 162–181.

42. Pick, A. D., and G. W. Frankel. A developmental study of strategies of visual selectivity. *Child Development*, 1974, **45**, 1162–1165.

43. Roberts, J., and J. T. Baird, Jr. *Parent ratings of behavioral patterns of children.* Vital and health statistics: Series 11, Data from the National Health Survey, No. 108. DHEW Publication No. (HSM) 73–1010. Washington: U.S. Government Printing Office, 1971.

44. Ross, H. S., and J. C. Killey. The effect of questioning on retention. *Child Development*, 1977, **48**, 312–314.

44a. Rourke, B. P. Brain–behavior relationships with learning disabilities. *American Psychologist*, 1975, **30**, 911–920.

45. Senf, G. M. Development of immediate memory for bisensory stimuli in normal children and children with learning disorders. *Developmental Psychology Monographs*, 1969, **1**:6, Part 2.

46. Sharp, D., M. Cole, and C. Lave. Education and cognitive development: The evidence from experimental research. *Monographs of the Society for Research in Child Development*, 1979, **44**: 1–2.

47. Shephard, W., and L. M. Ascher. Effect of linguistic rule conformity on free recall in children and adults. *Developmental Psychology*, 1973, **8**, 139.

48. Siegelman, E. Reflective and impulsive observing behavior. *Child Development*, 1969, **40**, 1213–1222.

49. Smart, R. C., and M. S. Smart. Complexity of pre-adolescents' social play and games. *New Zealand Journal of Educational Studies*, 1980, **15**, 81–92.

50. Stevenson, H. W., T. Parker, A. Wilkinson, B. Bonnevaux, and M. Gonsalez. Schooling, environment, and cognitive development: A cross-cultural study. *Monographs of the Society for Research in Child Development*, 1978, **43**:3.

51. Surbeck, E., and R. C. Endsley. Children's emotional and cognitive reactions to television violence: Effects of film character, reassurance, age, and sex. Paper presented at meeting of the Society for Research in Child Development, Denver, 1975.

52. Sutton-Smith, B. A developmental structural account of riddles. In B. Kirschenblatt-Gimblett (ed.). *Speech, play and display.* Phildelaphia: University of Pennsylvania Press, 1975.

53. Templin, M. C. The study of articulation and language development during the early school years. In F. Smith and G. A. Miller (eds.). *The genesis of language.* Cambridge, Mass.: M.I.T. Press, 1966, pp. 173–186.

54. Templin, M. C. Longitudinal study of English morphology in children with varying articulation in kindergarten. Paper presented at meeting of the Society for Research in Child Development, Santa Monica, Calif., 1969.

55. Terman, L. M. Genetic studies of genius: Mental and physical traits of a thousand gifted children. Vol. 1. Stanford, Calif.: Stanford University Press, 1925.

56. Tomlinson-Keasey, C., D. G. Crawford, and A. L. Miser. Classification: An organizing operation for memory. *Developmental Psychology,* 1975, **11,** 409–410.

56a. Vaidya, S. and N. Chansky. Cognitive development and cognitive style as factors in mathematics achievement. *Journal of Educational Psychology,* 1980, **72,** 326–330.

57. Vernon, P. E., G. Adams, and D. F. Vernon. *Gifted children.* London: Methuen and Co., Ltd., 1977.

58. Wallach, M. A., and N. Kogan. *Modes of thinking in young children: A study of the creativity-intelligence distinction.* New York: Holt, Rinehart and Winston, 1965.

59. Werner, E. E. *Cross-cultural development: A view from the planet Earth.* Monterey, Calif.: Brooks/Cole, 1979.

60. Wertlieb, D. Cognitive-affective development and learning disabilities. Paper presented at meeting of the American Psychological Association, Toronto, 1978.

61. Winer, G. A. Enhancement of class-inclusion reasoning through verbal context. *Journal of Genetic Psychology,* 1978, **132,** 299–306.

62. Winner, E. Can preadolescents produce metaphoric figures? A training study. Paper presented at meeting of the Society for Research in Child Development, Denver, 1975.

63. Winner, E., A. K. Rosenstiel, and H. Gardner. The development of metaphoric understanding. *Developmental Psychology,* 1976, **12,** 289–297.

64. Witkin, H. S., R. B. Dyke, H. F. Faterson, D. R. Goodenough, and S. A. Karp. *Psychological differentiation.* New York, John Wiley and Sons, Inc., 1962.

65. Wohlwill, J. F. Responses to class-inclusion questions for verbally and pictorially presented items. *Child Development,* 1968, **39,** 449–465.

66. Wollman, W., B. Eylon, and A. Lawson. Acceptance of lack of closure: Is it an index of advanced reasoning? *Child Development,* 1979, **50,** 656–665.

67. Yussen, S. R. Determinants of visual attention and recall in observational learning by preschoolers and second graders. *Developmental Psychology,* 1974, **10,** 93–100.

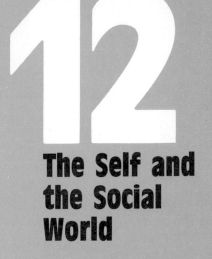

12

The Self and the Social World

Upon reaching the middle years of childhood, the child turns his energies and attention toward a newly expanded world. Reaching the age for school entrance brings freedom to move into new microsystems and to expand a network of social relations. In this chapter we consider children's interactions and relationships with the people in their worlds, and their feelings and thoughts about self and others.

QUESTIONS TO THINK ABOUT WHILE READING THIS CHAPTER

1. How is the sense of industry related to learning at school and playing in the neighborhood?
2. What are some of the influences on the development of self-concepts?
3. What do children learn about rules from other children and from adults?
4. How do interactions differ with children who are younger, older, or the same age?
5. What do children consider in making moral judgments?
6. How can children be influenced to be more generous and helpful?
7. How is social-emotional development affected by the macrosystem?
8. What is a friend, according to children of different ages?
9. How does family interaction differ from parent-child interaction?
10. Why is family reconstitution a complex process?
11. How does a child benefit from the social network?

Directions in Self-development

Self-development continues through the use of physical, mental, and emotional powers in interaction within the home, school, neighborhood, and community.

The Sense of Industry

Sense of industry: Success ——→pride and satisfaction; Failure——→sense of inadequacy

The fourth in Erikson's series of life crises is the development of the sense of industry, or, as he also calls it, the sense of duty and accomplishment [19]. This crisis dominates middle childhood, the elementary school years. With the establishment of a sense of industry, the child takes pride in doing tasks well and in finishing them. During the previous stage, development of the sense of initiative, the child was good at starting, but not at finishing, in exploring, but not in following through. As the sense of duty and accomplishment grows, the child becomes in-

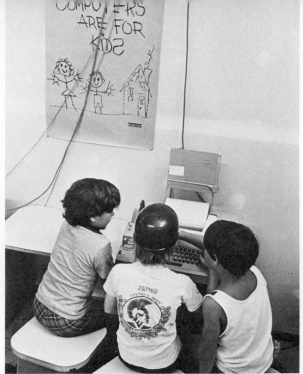

volved in the technology of his culture, whether it stresses fishing and making canoes, or reading, writing, and electronics. Withdrawing from home, mother, and the emotional situations involved in them, he turns to the objects, tools, and techniques of the society in which he lives. Most cultures make provisions for this changeover. Literate societies provide schools where teachers begin the long process of teaching reading and writing. Even in simpler cultures, teachers usually help the children learn the appropriate aspects of technology. Often boys learn farming from their fathers and girls, homemaking from their mothers. In the United States specialists teach such extracurricular subjects as music, dancing, painting, bird watching, star gazing, first aid, camping, and skiing. Recreation workers and youth leaders not only teach such skills but also concern themselves with group dynamics, character, values, leadership, community service, and so on.

There are aspects of industry and duty that are better accomplished with other children (in the peer group) and alone, however, than in an onslaught of lessons. Take baseball, for instance. To be a real American boy or girl, you practically have to know how to play it. It takes thousands of practice throws to get to be a good pitcher and as many catches to be a good fielder. Where could one do all this except in the neighborhood with friends? There are many more games whose rules and coordinations must be learned. During the school years children are willing, even eager, to practice and practice and practice—batting a ball, jumping, skating, jumping rope, singing and chanting the ditties of childhood, sewing doll clothes, cutting out cookies, playing cards and other games, identifying specimens, and arranging collections. There are social skills to develop too, making and keeping close friendships and being a club member.

Success in the stage of industry results in the child's knowing the pleasure and satisfaction of a job well done. She enjoys being a part of a productive situation. She knows that she can produce, achieve, and accomplish in certain areas, and in those situations, she feels adequate. There are enough of them that she has a general feeling of being an adequate person. There are some places where she does particularly well and others where she just gets by. This knowledge is incorporated into her picture of herself.

A sense of *inferiority and inadequacy* is the result when development does not go well at this time of life. As time of entrance to school is usually fixed rigidly, the child who is not ready to enter into the stage of industry is at a disadvantage. Failure in the beginning work is disastrous to her concept of herself as an adequate person.

Self-concepts

With increasing cognitive powers, the child builds more complex concepts of himself, as a thinking and doing person, a child, a boy or girl, a friend, a pupil, and so on. Self-concepts are built from all sorts of experiences with objects and people, alone and in social interaction.

Self-esteem. A child with high self-esteem thinks that she is worthwhile, adequate, and good. She has self-confidence. Examples of test items showing high and low self-esteem are "I'm a lot of fun to be with." "I often wish I were someone else." [12].

Parental warmth, support, authoritativeness, harmony foster high self-esteem in children

The child builds models of self and others from interactions within the family, as well as from experiences in school and community. Self esteem is influenced by what parents tell the child about himself or herself. Coopersmith's original study on self-esteem showed that boys with high self-esteem had parents who were warm, supportive, and authoritative with their sons and who got along well with each other. As we have already shown in earlier parts of this book, prosocial behavior and positive feelings in boys and girls are generally associated with parental warmth, nurturance, and reasonable, firm discipline.

Self-esteem comes from development of the sense of industry, when the child feels successful in learning the knowledge, tasks, and technology of his society. The negative side of the sense of industry, the sense of inferiority and inadequacy, results in anxiety and low self-esteem. How is the child to know whether he is doing well or poorly, and whether to esteem himself highly or not? Some children seek approval from adults or peers. For others, lack of disapproval may indicate success. Still others will think that they must compete and win. If the child believes that the most successful person is the one who scores highest, runs fastest, or makes the most money, she will think that in order to be successful, she must do better than all the others in her class. If competi-

tions were minimized, she might feel successful if she learned to read several new words, or solved the arithmetic problems, or tried a new kind of dive. If only one person can win, and therefore only one succeed, many children will suffer in self-esteem; if everyone can succeed by doing his best, high self-esteem is possible for many. Another way of defining success is through cooperation with others: The child succeeds by being a contributing member of a group or team, or by helping another person.

Self-esteem is also derived from group membership, as well as from personal characteristics and achievements. A child's self-esteem can be affected by shame or pride in his family, ethnic group, or income group (as represented by neighborhood or social network).

Locus of Control. An expression of the sense of autonomy is the extent to which the child feels in charge of what happens to him. If he thinks that he can decide and carry out actions, that he is responsible for much of what he experiences, then he perceives control as inside himself. He has an internal locus of control. If the child thinks that other people, luck, chance, the stars, or fate determine what happens to him, then he has an external locus of control. Locus of control is tested by 40 questions that make up a scorable scale [37]. Examples of questions follow:

Internal locus of control: I determine what happens to me;

External locus of control: Outside forces determine what happens to me

> Do you believe that whether or not people like you depends on how you act?
> Do you believe that most problems will solve themselves if you just don't fool with them?

Locus of control became more internalized as grade level increased, when children were tested in all grades from 3 through 12 [40]. Girls were more internalized than boys in locus of control. When comparisons were made between American children and children from several *kibbutzim*, the same age trend was seen, but Americans became internalized earlier than Israelis [35]. At age 9, the American children were much more internalized than the kibbutz children, but by age 14, they were about the same. The kibbutz groups differed from each other at ages 9 and 10, the greatest internalization being in children from the kibbutz that gave children the most freedom to organize their affairs, promoting trust and group decisions. The early internalizers had been given opportunities for autonomous behavior and had been reinforced for taking responsibility, organizing themselves, and making decisions. These conclusions are strengthened by a study showing perception of parental acceptance related to internal locus of control [41]. We would expect children to think their parents accepted them when the parents trusted them to make decisions and gave them freedom to actually control their own affairs.

When people believe themselves in control of what happens, they try harder to achieve. At all grade levels of the study of children from grade 3 to grade 12, achievement behavior was correlated with internal locus of control [40]. It makes sense to work and to try hard if you believe that you can get results, but to do little if you think that outside forces, and not your own efforts, determine what will happen.

Gender. In Chapter 9 we discussed the young child's gender concepts, gender differences in behavior, influences on gender concept development, and the Freudian view of sexual development. The child enters the school years with a recently established concept of gender constancy, knowledge of gender-appropriate behavior, and an identification with the same-sex parent. How do school-age children develop in regard to gender concepts, characteristics, and behavior?

Freud and his followers call the middle childhood years the *latency period.* The term means that sexual feelings and interest in the opposite sex are repressed or made unconscious. The feelings are latent because they have disappeared only temporarily. The latency period is a time of consolidation with one's own sex. The child is now firmly identified with the parent of the same sex, using this parent as a model of gender-appropriate behavior. Like-sex playmates are preferred. Girls may say that they hate boys, and boys say the same of girls. The self-concept as girl or boy is strengthened by learning and using the *gender-role stereotypes* of the macrosystem. These stereotypes are simply the generally accepted beliefs as to the characteristics of females and males and the behavior appropriate to each sex.

During middle childhood, children realize that gender is expressed not only through choosing toys and clothing, but also in enduring behavior patterns, or personality characteristics. The following study shows what children understood about some common gender-role stereotypes that deal with personality characteristics.

Interviews with children in kindergarten, second, and fourth grades were based on descriptions of behavior that adults had rated as applying to either males or females [55]. Each behavior pattern was put into a story and the child was asked to select the performer from pictures of a male and a female. For example, "One of these people is a bully . . . Which person gets into fights?" Boys and girls showed similar knowledge as assessed by the questions. Kindergarten children had already acquired considerable knowledge, 94 per cent of them indicating that aggressive behavior belonged with the male picture. Second-graders knew more than kindergartners, but fourth-graders' scores were about the same as those of second-graders. Knowledge of expected male behavior (aggressive, strong, adventurous, coarse, independent), was acquired earlier than knowledge of the stereotyped female role (appreciative, emotional, softhearted, dreamy, whiny, fussy). This finding is consistent with results of earlier studies that have suggested greater pressure on boys to learn the masculine role than upon females to learn the feminine role. Another result of the present study was that the older children showed increased knowledge of stereotypes when the examiner was a man, but not when she was a woman. This finding fits with studies that have shown fathers exerting greater pressure than mothers for gender-typed behavior.

Another area of gender-role stereotypes is occupational roles. Children's preferences for occupations show what they think appropriate for themselves: "What do you want to be when you grow up?" Stereotypes for the opposite sex can be explored by asking "If you were a boy (or a girl) what would you like to be when you grew up?" Questions of this sort were asked of children in grades 1, 5, 8, and 11 in public schools in Maine [53]. Answers were classified as traditional or not. For example, traditional male occupations were doctor and truck driver, female were nurse and housekeeper. All of the first-, fifth-, and eighth-grade boys, and most of the older ones chose traditional male occupational roles for themselves; only three-quarters of the first- and fifth-grade girls, and half of the older girls chose traditional feminine occupations for themselves. When choosing for the opposite sex, most girls chose traditional jobs for boys, although not as consistently as did the boys for themselves. Boys chose about as many nontraditional occupations for girls as the girls did for themselves. Boys and girls therefore agreed that traditional occupations are suitable for boys and that girls might have more flexibility in choosing. This study, published in 1980, contrasts with several earlier studies in which girls' vocational opportunities were seen as much more restricted according to tradition or stereotypes. The authors think that the feminist movement has resulted in greater occupational freedom for girls. The study points up the fact that gender-role stereotypes change over time in one macrosystem. Of course, they differ between macrosystems. A decade ago, the development of a feminine self-concept might require a vocational choice such as nurse, teacher, or librarian; today a feminine self-concept may include becoming a carpenter, policewoman, or lawyer.

Gender role stereotypes change over time and differ between macrosystems

Moral
Development

The school child continues to progress in the two phases of moral development that were salient in early childhood, rule attunement and social sensitivity. (See "Moral Development" in Chapter 9). The first phase is closer to completion, while the second occupies the center of the stage.

Rule Attunement. The child has largely internalized the basic rules of his culture and family, the rules that govern talking, eating, personal care, and gender-based behavior. There are many more rules yet to be learned and accepted, but they are not so fundamental, and they may not be internalized so deeply. The child must learn the rules of his second microsystem, the school. These rules can be very difficult to learn when the home-school mesosystem is weak, but if home and school have good communications, the scene is set for learning what the kindergarten teacher tries to teach, and so on through the grades. Variations of rules are encountered through members of the child's social network, who include relatives, family friends, and neighbors. Rules for peer interactions are developed cooperatively in play with other children.

CORRELATES OF FOLLOWING THE RULES. As mentioned in Chapter 9, children are most likely to obey and internalize rules when parents are warm and authoritative. Many laboratory experiments have been used to study children's resistance to temptation, assuming or hoping that a small sample of behavior would represent what really happens when the child is interacting in a microsystem. The typical laboratory situation goes like this: The child is shown several toys; when she handles one, she is punished, usually by a noise; the intensity and timing of the punishment are varied; the child is left alone but observed to see how soon and for how long she plays with the toy that has been accompanied by punishment [30]. Such experiments show that children's behavior is similar to animals' in the same situation. Resistance to temptation is increased with intensity of punishment and with timing of the punishment at the beginning of the act. When a verbal component is added, results are different. With either a simple prohibition or a reason, mild punishment is more effective than severe punishment. Although laboratory experiments give some indications of how punishment and verbalization work, they are not lifelike. In a real microsystem, situations are more complex, and may take place over a longer period of time. Sometimes punishments are, unfortunately, much harsher than a loud noise.

Reason + mild punishment works better than harsh punishment

Laboratory experiments also show that a child is affected by seeing what happens to someone else who does or does not follow the rules. If the model gets punished for a transgression, then the child is less likely to imitate the model. Hoffman suggests that the same is true in real life, that a child is likely to imitate a peer when he sees that peer breaking a rule and receiving no punishment in consequence [30]. In unsupervised peer groups, children may therefore encourage one another to deviate from rules for good behavior.

Rewarded model imitated more than punished model

COGNITIVE DEVELOPMENT AND UNDERSTANDING OF RULES. Piaget has said that young children tend to think that rules are unchangeable and to be followed literally [39]. Following a rule is good; not following it is bad. During the stage of concrete operations, children come to realize that game rules and social conventions are made by persons and that persons can therefore change rules. We remember an incident at a camp when 8-year-old Jill and 9-year-old Kate demonstrated their understanding of rule-making during a game of checkers. After some moments of orderly play, Jill made an extremely irregular move. Kate, watching intently, said nothing. A little later, when Kate broke the rules flagrantly, Jill was silent. "Don't you know you can't do that, Kate?" the counselor broke in. "And, Jill, you made a mistake, too."

"That was no mistake," Jill explained. "We made a rule that each person can cheat once during each game. I cheated and Kate cheated. Now we have to finish without cheating."

In cooperative play, Kate and Jill found that children could make rules. They found that they could come to an agreement and that they could play a satisfactory game within the limits that they created. Children do not always agree on rule-changing as readily as did Kate and Jill. In playing group games, one or more children may know different rules as to who is It or how to free prisoners from a base. Arguments and negotiations ensue, but agreements have to be reached if the game is to continue. Such experiences make it clear to children that a rule is made for a purpose, and that it can be remade. Other experiences that demonstrate rule changeability are visiting in other families, and traveling in foreign countries.

Children can tell the difference between rules-of-the-game, conventions or etiquette, and moral rules. When interviewed about a story of a child hitting another child, almost all 5-to-11-year-olds gave negative responses [52]. Thus they were almost unanimous in upholding a moral rule about not hurting others. Next, the children were asked what they thought of hitting another child when the school rules permitted it. The majority of 5-year-olds thought it was all right; almost all 11-year-olds

thought hitting wrong even if the school did allow it. There was a steady age-related increase in seeing hitting as governed by a moral rule that was unchangeable. The other rules explored with these children had to do with undressing on the school yard, leaving toys out, and refusing to share a snack with another child. Although these actions were judged negatively by themselves, school policies permitting them were accepted by the majority of children, and so were the acts when carried out in a school that allowed them. The study shows that children made judgments about the meaning of the different actions and their relation to the rules governing them. Games rules and manners are changeable; moral rules are not.

Social Sensitivity. We have seen in earlier chapters that in infancy and early childhood social sensitivity grows out of biologically based behavior and attachment between mother and child or caregiver and child. Biological bases of social sensitivity are less understood in middle childhood, and more is known about learning through social interaction. However, we shall begin with a study of a behavior mechanism that is probably the result of evolutionary adaptation. (Ethology, the study of evolutionary adaptation, is discussed in "Behavioral Biology" in Chapter 1.)

Elementary school children were observed on a playground, and incidents of aggression analysed. In 12 per cent of aggressive attacks, another child came to the aid of the victim. A victim was more likely to receive aid from another child if he had signaled submission, by bowing or kneeling, and the aggressor had continued the attack. Thinking of the behavior in terms of group living, it seems that the whole interaction has group survival value. Submission or appeasement signals prevent one individual from killing another, and when the aggressor ignores those signals, other members of the group are motivated to enforce the biological rule. The study indicates that a biologically based behavioral mechanism is at work in the development of altruistic behavior during middle childhood. An ethological interpretation of morality holds that moral behavior evolved to solve early man's problems of survival [31]. Group living and cooperation were necessary for individuals living among predators and lacking fighting teeth, horns, and nails. Early human beings developed culture—language, technology, family structure, rules for authority, and division of labor. Culture is transmitted across generations by teaching and learning, but the biological base for learning and for certain behavior patterns is inherited. The tendency to aid a submitting victim against further attack is probably one of those patterns.

The perception of social cues may be biologically based, with experience adding to skill in inferring thoughts and feelings from another person's behavior. Facial expression, movement patterns, and voice intonation are social cues that carry such information. When films were used to study the perception of these social cues by children from 5 to 10, age was found related to success [25]. Vocal intonations were easiest to distinguish, followed by movement patterns. Facial expressions were most difficult to distinguish.

ROLE-TAKING. Social sensitivity also grows through role-taking, taking the point of view of the other person, or trying to see, hear, feel, and think the way the other person does. We have already discussed how mothers can focus the attention of their young children upon the feelings of others, and how preschool children take on the roles of others in dramatic play. School-age children also use dramatic play. Role-taking skills increase with cognitive development, correlating with age and IQ [48]. When children try to take the point of view of another person looking at an object in a different location, they seem to be asking themselves these questions [44]:

1. Does the other person see something?
2. Does he see what I see or something different? ⎫ What the other sees.
3. Exactly what does he see? ⎭
4. How does it look to him?   What the other experiences.

Age-level differences in social role-taking show an increasing appreciation of the other person as an individual with whom exchange of viewpoints, or mutuality, is possible [43]. An analysis of behavior indicated that at 6, the child typically saw that other people felt and thought differently because they had different information and experience. At 8 the most frequent level of understanding was that people think and feel differently because each person has his own particular aims and values. By 10, the level most often attained was one where the self's perspective was differentiated from the viewpoint of some average person.

VERBAL COMMUNICATION. Verbal communication is a direct way of finding out what another person thinks and feels, and of letting one's own experience be known. Role-taking aids in verbal communication because verbal utterances can be fitted to the other person's understanding as the speaker takes the other point of view. Verbal communication skills have been studied by using games that require appreciation of another person's role and capacities, and communication by words only [20]. Adult A taught the child to play a parchesi-like game. Then the child was asked to teach the game to blindfolded Adult B. As might be expected, children increased in communicating ability as they increased in age from grade 2 through grade 12. Some of the youngest children were almost entirely indifferent to the blindfold, making comments such as "Pick up this and put it in there." None of the oldest group failed to take some account of the blindfold. This experiment illustrates the child's gradually increasing capacity to put himself in the place of the other person and to use his mobility of thought for improved interpersonal communication, sending messages that are meaningful to the other person. Maturity of the listener plays a complementary part in communication. When children from kindergarten through eighth grade were given a task of verbally communicating graphic designs, success was seen to hinge upon the age of the listener as well as the age of the speaker [33]. Such tasks depend upon at least two abilities in the speaker: his ability to use language and concepts that describe the object or action, and his ability to judge what would be meaningful to the other person. The latter involves role-taking.

Children take the roles of others in any or all social interactions—playing with peers, relating to older children, taking care of younger children, interacting with parents and other adults. Parents aid children in role-taking when they do it themselves, taking account of the child's point of view. Communication style was studied in 6-year-olds from two types of home, classified according to the ways in which parents communicated with children [2]. In the first type parents were *position-oriented*, which means that they tried to regulate their children's behavior in terms of socially defined roles. For instance, such a mother would say, "Do it because I tell you to," and "Children are supposed to obey their mothers" or "Act like a nice little girl. Good girls keep their rooms neat." Parents who were *person-oriented* based their regulations upon the individual characteristics, needs, abilities, and motives of the persons involved. Such a father, upon finding out that his son had skipped school would first try to find out why the boy did it, what meaning it had to him, and how he felt about it. Then he would deal with the act on the basis of the reasons for it and its significance to the boy and to the teacher. Children who came from person-oriented families were able to communicate more effectively, taking more account of a listener's perspective.

Moral Knowledge and Judgment: Integration of Phases 1 and 2. Social sensitivity enables the child to think about actions in terms of people's feelings, intention, reasons, and points of view. At the same time, cognitive development and social experience have shown game rules, conventions, and procedures to be made by persons and to be changeable by persons. Other rules are judged to be not changeable, particularly rules that prohibit harming other people. Children make judgments about *how* bad an action is, not merely whether it is good or bad. They are concerned with what is right and what is fair.

Outcomes and intentions influence judgment of goodness or badness

Young children, like older people, take account of the outcome of an act in judging its badness or goodness. If a preschool peer tries but fails to take away a tricycle, he is not considered as bad as though he had succeeded. Parents rarely punish a child for *almost* hitting another child. Attempted robbery and rape get lighter punishments than completed ones. Adults and older children also consider a child or adult robber less wicked if he had good intentions. The child is not very bad when he takes the tricycle from a boy who has had it all morning to give to another who has not yet had a turn. In 1932 Piaget said that young children judge acts by consequences but not by intentions [38]. Ever since that time, psychologists have been doing experiments to see if children could and would take account of intentions. Now it seems quite clear that they can and do by at least 5 years of age, provided that the information about intentionality is given clearly in ways that they can understand and re-member. Darley and his associates found first-graders just as likely as fourth-graders and adults to reduce punishments they had chosen for wrong-doers when they were given reasons that made the actions more legitimate [14]. They first trained the subjects to use a scale of punish-ment, having a big punishment represented by a big rectangle, and using decreasing sizes to stand for medium, small, and no punishment. A story was told and depicted on slides. For example, one child threw a bucket of water on another. The subject then chose the size punishment that the child throwing the water should receive. Next, the subject was told that the child threw the water on a child who was playing dangerously with matches. The subject then chose a punishment and told why it was dif-ferent from the one he gave first. This experimental method made it easy for even the youngest subjects to understand and remember the story while judging the actions and it gave them a method of responding that was also easy.

The finding of Darley reminds us of research we have mentioned pre-viously, such as studies finding that children can reason, count, and con-serve quantity earlier than Piaget has reported. The findings on inten-tionality, like the others, were possible because experimenters simplified procedures so as to make the problems clear to the subjects. Piaget's original hypotheses, experiments, and findings have stimulated others to discover more about how children think.

Information about intentions is often complicated. It must be consid-ered along with the extent and type of damage. Other circumstances may also be salient, such as whether the perpetrator was provoked. In real life, the older child is more able than the younger to collect the infor-mation, hold it in mind, and weigh the various bits of evidence in the light of what he already knows and remembers.

Punishment as a method of attaining justice has been studied in most of the experiments on moral judgment, but punishment is not the only way of dealing with transgressions. In some socially advanced societies, restitution is required instead of punishment. We doubt if restitution is a more cognitively advanced idea. Toddlers can understand the notion of helping a person in distress to feel better, and they spontaneously offer a toy or a pat. It seems to us that restitution could be a much more preva-lent part of moral judgment and action if parents and teachers built upon children's early social sensitivity and showed them how to repair or make up for the damage they do.

Prosocial Behavior. Like all human beings, children are sometimes kind, helpful, generous, and altruistic, putting the feelings and wishes of others before their own. Both giving and helping have been examined in labora-tory experiments. The following influences on generosity have been found:

1. Happy children give more. [49]

2. Modeling. Children give more when they see others giving. [42] Effects persist. [32]
3. Presence of model. Children give more in the presence of a generous model than they do when alone. [42]
4. Preaching. Direct instructions increase generosity in younger (age 6 to 7 in contrast to 9 to 10) children and in girls. [32]
5. Discipline. When children say their parents use high inductive discipline and low-power assertion, those children are more generous, kind, and considerate [15]. Girls ordinarily receive more induction and less power assertion than boys.

A number of experiments have been used to study children's helping behavior. One naturalistic study has been reported earlier in this chapter, the one in which children helped victims whose appeasement signals did not stop their aggressors' attacks. We also mentioned in "Moral Development" in Chapter 9 the spontaneous efforts of toddlers to comfort peers and parents in distress.

Experiments on helping usually take this form: A child plays in a laboratory room; the experimenter gives instructions about staying in the room, or gives a flexible rule as to when leaving is permitted; the experimenter leaves the child alone or with another child; the child hears sounds of another child crying or otherwise expressing distress in the next room. Does the child go to help the other child? If so, when, and under what circumstances? Such experiments have yielded these conclusions:

1. Children help more under rules that are permissive rather than restrictive [46].
2. Boys are more affected than girls by strictness and permissiveness of rules [51].
3. Pairs of children respond more to a child in distress than do single children [46].
4. Girls give more help more promptly when the experimenter behaves warmly; boys are not affected by experimenter warmth [51].

The experiments on prosocial behavior show children trying to make sense out of what they have learned in rule attunement and social sensitivity and to integrate those types of knowledge with biologically based action tendencies. The results portray children as having made progress since their early years in moral judgment and moral behavior.

Living in a Social Ecology

The child's social-emotional environment can be considered at all levels of the ecology. After discussing several significant macrosystem influences, we shall go on to the child's most important microsystems.

Values, beliefs, and organization of the macrosystem are all relevant to social-emotional development. So are the means of transmitting values and beliefs. Organization can be considered as political, socioeconomic, or ethnic. Organization could also refer to the way in which child care and education are shared between various microsystems.

Political Structure. We have already given many illustrations of children receiving different care and education in different societies. The political ideology of a nation or group is reflected in the ways in which children are regarded and treated. In North America, where individual uniqueness, identity, rights, and privacy are highly valued, adults try to rear strong, autonomous, competitive individuals. In India, children are taught to place family welfare above individual desires. Chinese education relates the child to the whole society. Adults take responsibility for children beyond their own families, and children feel affection and respect for adults in addition to their parents and grandparents. Itty Chan, a Chinese-American psychologist describes the Chinese way [6]:

> From what I've seen and learned, children in China are taught "selfish-less-ness" but not "self-less-ness." While Chinese education emphasizes the individual's relationship to society, the sense of self is not lost but is integrated into the group of which the individual is an integral, intimate part, an "insider." In fact, the sense of self is highly valued and respected in the context of relations with other people and is made richer by being a part of the group.
> In China today, children are growing up in a human environment in which there is not only a sense of togetherness and purposefulness, but also an emphasis on people and participation, leadership from within (not above), and a collective creativity. Their sense of social self is accompanied by a sense of being the creator and master of their lives.

Socioeconomic Organization. A nation may be poor, rich, or in-between. We have already discussed economic influences on children's physical development and health and on their opportunities for education.

The organization within a society also divides people on social and economic lines, and affects children's self-concepts along with their opportunities for healthy development. In the United Kingdom, social class divisions are quite complex and rigid. In New Zealand there are few very poor and few very rich; social class distinctions are minimal. The United States is probably in between, with its belief in equality but its actuality of a large number of poor people, and 4, 5, or 6 social classes, depending on how they are defined. The wealth held by the richest 20 per cent of families is about 3 times that of the other 80 per cent [11, p. 49].

The term *class*, or *social class*, refers to the source of the family's income. In the United States, families at the top live on inherited wealth; the upper class earn large amounts as executives and professionals; the middle class earns as professionals, managers, and business people; the working class (sometimes called lower-middle or upper-lower) earn by skilled labor and trades; and the lower perform unskilled labor and are often supported by public assistance. When estimating social-class level, years of education and type of housing and neighborhood may also be used as criteria.

Realities of power and privilege are reflected in the values and behavior typical of people in each social class. Traditional *middle-class* values include morality, respectability, property, work, achievement, getting ahead economically and socially, supporting civic and religious organizations, and education. Democracy in family life has been more typical of the middle class than of others. Now some middle-class families are trying to minimize restrictions of gender role. Husbands, wives, sons, and daughters all work and play according to their talents and interests and as a result of democratic family decision making. A life style that recently challenged traditional middle-class values is the hippie or counterculture style. Instead of striving for achievement, improvement, and status, these people are present-oriented, concerned with love, self-expression, and respect for nature. *Working-class* values and behavior include clearly differentiated gender roles, traditional education, anti-intellectualism, gadgets, sports, physical expression, and physical power. Parents are less likely to discuss things with their children than are middle-class parents, and more likely to tell them what to do. Among the *very poor*, behavior patterns include present-orientation, fatalistic thinking, limited verbal communication, low self-esteem, strict gender roles, exploitation and mistrust of the opposite sex, marital conflict, inconsistency in nurture and discipline and harsh physical punishment.

Very rich children's experience of values and upper-class behavioral demands have been described by psychiatrist Robert Coles in his book, *Privileged Ones: The Well-Off and the Rich in America* [11]. Although rich

children live in "comfortable, comfortable places," with every sort of physical care and educational opportunity, their self-confident parents impose a strict discipline and a set of tough requirements. The children must learn patterns of acting, thinking, and feeling that will fit them to command economic empires, to conduct the family's social life in well-run homes, to assure the continuity of the family, and to be community leaders. During middle childhood rich children become aware that inequalities exist and that they and their families are more privileged than other children and their families. Veronica wonders why their cook has to keep working even when she is ill, and why her children eat food different from Veronica's. Marjorie asks why her father, who tithes to his church, will not give money to the families of miners killed in her grandfather's mine. Larry wants to build new houses with running water and television for his father's migrant workers. These children must learn to stop asking questions about social justice and to accept the facts of inequality. They eventually develop a sense of "entitlement," of being entitled to money, power, and the privileges that go with them [11, p. 363].

These sketches of social-class behavior suggest that children's self-concepts are profoundly affected by membership in a social class. Parents and teachers try to prepare children for life as they see it, and what they see is the view from their own social positions. People of low socioeconomic status actually do have less control over what happens to them than do more affluent people. Poor people therefore tend to be more externalized in locus of control, to think that luck, chance, the government, rich people, or other forces exert more influence than they themselves are able to do. Middle-class children usually show greater internalization than lower-class children. Class differences may be smaller in poor countries, where an external locus of control fits the experience of the majority of people. In India, for example, we often heard middle-class people, as well as poor people, attribute loss, suffering, and failure to fate. Religion and philosophy may support externality, as does astrology.

In addition to locus of control, other parts of the self-concept are influenced by class membership. The lower self-esteem of children of low socioeconomic level reflects the level of power and prestige of their families. Gender concepts related to gender stereotypes are learned from family, relatives and friends, most of whom are members of the child's social network.

Ethnic Group. Certain individuals and their families, grouped in neighborhoods and communities, have social and emotional ties to one another that are based on sharing a heritage and culture. The heritage includes some physical characteristics and a social history. The culture includes a language or ways of speaking, food preferences and ways of cooking, perhaps modes of dress, and probably ways of thinking and feeling. When an ethnic membership defines and organizes a very large portion of a person's life, it could be considered a macrosystem. In the United States, ethnic groups are usually named so as to indicate the for-

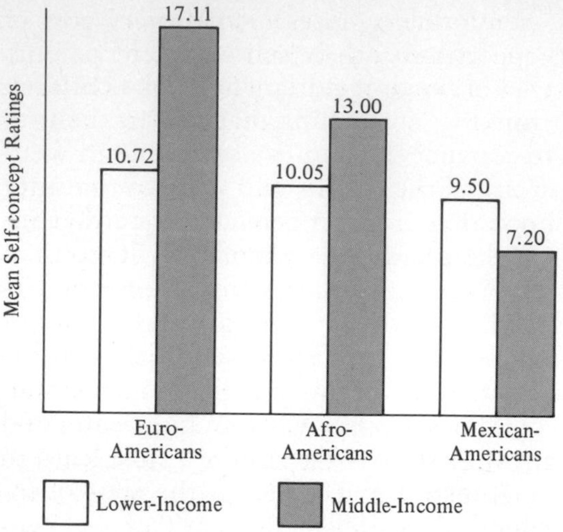

FIGURE 12–1.
Self-esteem of middle- and lower-income American girls in three ethnic groups. (Source: V. R. Fu, M. K. Korslund, and D. E. Hinkle. Ethnic self-concept during middle childhood. *Journal of Psychology*, 1980, 105, 99–105.)

mer geographic or national location of the members, such as Anglo–American, Afro–American, Polish–American, and Hispanic–American. The ethnic groups who lived in the territory before European and other immigrants arrived are native Americans. Everyone belongs to an ethnic group, although ethnicity is more salient to some than to others. Anglo-Americans, who have been here for a long time and have been a majority, often do not think of themselves as ethnic. When an ethnic group has low status, power, and income, its members naturally resent it. Antagonisms and rivalries between ethnic groups are not unusual.

Part of a child's self-concept comes from membership in an ethnic group. The child learns from family members, peers, and teachers whether to feel proud or ashamed, angry or comfortable, competent or incapable because of ethnic membership. As feelings in the group change, so do the feelings absorbed by its children. For example, as black people achieved more civil rights and more opportunities for education and employment, black children's self-concepts became more positive. Studies done over the past 4 decades have shown black children increasing in preference for children of their own ethnicity [56]. A recent study compared self-esteem in 10-year-old girls in 2 income groups in each of 3 ethnic groups [22]. Figure 12–1 shows self-esteem scores of the 6 groups. Among the middle-income groups, ethnic differences in self-esteem were significant, but not in the lower-income groups. Comparing income groups, the middle group had higher self-esteem than the lower.

Television, Transmitter of Values and Beliefs. Television gives children access to macrosystem values and beliefs, even while they sit in the microsystem of the home. As we said in the previous chapter, television does teach and entertain in positive ways, but here we are interested in its impact on social and emotional development.

Advertising is beamed at the child as consumer, trying to influence choices of cereal, candies and other sweets, toys, and eating places. It seems to us that this treatment is exploitation of children for commercial gain, indicating a high valuing of economic gain and a low valuing of child health and contentment, to say nothing of parental discomfort at being pressured.

A survey of weekend and afternoon programs in Boston showed the main subject matter areas to be domestic, interpersonal rivalry, the entertainment world, crime, and the supernatural [1]. About three-quarters of the programs contained violence. The most frequent form of violence involved weapons.

Experimental studies and field surveys have shown a causal link between children's watching violence on television and their later aggressive behavior, according to a report by psychologists to a United States Senate subcommittee [7]. The children most affected by television violence are those predisposed to aggression by other influences in addition to television. There is also experimental evidence that children who watch television a great deal may become habituated or desensitized to violence. While watching violent films, heavy television watchers showed less emotional arousal (measured by galvanic skin response) than infrequent television watchers [9]. Children exposed to filmed violence were more tolerant than a control group of physical aggression and destruction before seeking help[16].

Human violence was rated "more scary" than violence among puppets, by children from 8 to 11 [47]. Reassurance was more effective with this group than with younger children. These findings suggest that the violence shown on news programs may be very frightening to children, as indeed it often is to adults. Children's fright may be modified by parents who view the violence with children and offer some comfort to them.

Commercials, as well as many programs, often portray restrictive gender-role stereotypes. "Men will like this shirt for its good looks, women for its easy care!" The exciting role of detective or doctor is most often performed by a man, the duller role of secretary or assistant by a woman. Another analysis of children's weekend programs showed 3 times as many male characters as female [36]. The average male gave and received more approval and disapproval than the average female. The programs therefore indicated to children that males were more significant persons than females. When a comparison was made between children who were heavy viewers (25 hours or more per week) and light viewers (10 hours or less), heavy viewers of both sexes were found to have stronger gender-typed preferences [21].

Although television acts as a direct pipeline communication of macrosystem values and beliefs, microsystem interactions can modify its effects. Parents can supervise selection of programs and amount of time spent viewing. They can also discuss programs with their children and make themselves available for sharing children's reactions. Television is sometimes used in schools, where teachers and peers can also modify interpretations and reactions.

Microsystems

In the previous chapter we discussed the microsystems of school, church, and recreational settings in terms of children's mental development. Here we are concerned with social-emotional development at school, with other children, and most of all, at home.

School. A list of conflicts in educational values and goals appears in Chapter 11. Although recognizing conflict, we believe that most teachers, parents, and children would affirm the following goals for children in schools: learning the basics; nondisruptive behavior; happiness. (*Happiness*, like *love*, is an unscientific word, very hard to define. We could say instead, lack of anxiety, or satisfaction, but happiness means more, and Americans are guaranteed the right to pursue it.) Disagreements occur over how to achieve these goals, whether to add more goals, and if so, which ones. We believe that movement toward these three goals is facilitated by social-emotional development in the following areas:

1. Prosocial behavior—helpfulness, cooperation rather than competition.
2. Self-esteem—a concept of self as adequate, successful, and worthy.
3. Intrinsic motivation—wanting to learn and to find out.

One approach to improving learning of basic subjects is *attribute-treatment-interaction* [27]. Special attributes or characteristics of children are matched with learning experiences or treatments designed to be effective. The most common example of this scheme is separating boys and girls and using different educational methods thought to be gender-appropriate. Or, slow learners might be separated from fast learners, and the slower groups given a longer time to learn the same material. Or, children may be separated on the basis of impulsivity and reflectivity, social class, ethnic group, or language spoken in the home. The success of a

program of attribute-treatment-interaction is usually judged on the basis of achievement scores, or perhaps IQ. A problem with such programs is that children are usually grouped on one attribute, but in reality, many processes are operating. If classrooms are thought of as microsystems, it becomes clear that each one is unique. A classroom has its own setting and a particular teacher interacting with a group of individual children. Suppose an improvement program tries to change the behavior of all teachers in a desired direction. The results will differ from one classroom to another. From personal experience as a Girl Scout leader, I (MSS) can testify to group differences. I thought that I brought the same knowledge and values to each microsystem, but one troop was highly cooperative with each other and with me, full of creative ideas, and enthusiastic about all of our projects and adventures. The other troop was full of interpersonal conflicts and tensions. They never agreed fully on what to do. We went from one crisis to another. My third troop was active and enthusiastic but rather barren of new ideas.

Another approach to classroom learning is to focus on the group, on the interactions in the microsystem and its relation to other groups. As a cooperative member of a group, the child derives self-esteem from the group success and feels motivated to work for the good of the group. Failure as an individual is softened by experiencing prosocial behavior (help and sympathy) from group members. Group rewards, rather than individual rewards, are reportedly given in schools in the Soviet Union. American Indian children will often try to work as a group in school, even when individual competition is the norm. Children compete more vigorously in highly industrial societies as compared with agricultural societies, and in urban as compared with rural areas. Group rewards are experienced by North American children who play on athletic teams. In order to find out what peer support would do to children's academic performance, classroom behavior, and interpersonal relationships, an experiment was carried out at The Johns Hopkins University [45]. The program was called Teams-Games-Tournament (TGT). In TGT four or five children are put into a team that is heterogeneous in academic ability, sex, and race. Teams are equated on average ability level. Individuals compete with individuals who are members of other teams. Each person's game score is added to that of her teammates to form a team score. Team members study as a group and help each other to prepare for the tournament. TGT has had positive effects on mathematics achievement in the junior high school, language arts achievement in the elementary school, and attitudes toward subject matter and classroom process and climate. Increases have occurred in cross-race and cross-sex helping, friendship choice, peer tutoring, peer-group mutual concern, importance to peers of individuals doing well, and class cohesiveness. It seems likely that TGT increases peer pressure to do well and the concern of children for each other's performance. Sociometric status of successful individuals increased under conditions of team reward, whereas it did not when persons were rewarded as individuals. That is, achieving children were

liked more when they succeeded as team members, but not when they achieved by themselves.

Peers and Other Children.　Playmates may be younger, older, or the same age.　As we saw in Chapter 9, interactions differ in these three relationships.　The essence of child behavior in each of the relationships is indicated by the words that follow them:

Older toward younger: Help, care, support, sociability, comfort, teaching, control.
Younger toward older: Watching, imitating, asking, dependence, sociability.
Peers: Reciprocity, sharing, negotiation, rule construction, aggression regulation.

FRIENDSHIP AS A RELATION.　Friendship is a relation in which two persons like each other.　The bond of affection or liking endures over a period of time, but it must be maintained by mutual actions, according to rules.　Children's concepts and understanding of friendship change with age.　Several studies, including some from Canada and Scotland, show consistent findings as to ways in which concepts of friendship develop [13, 29, 57].　The following three stages of friendship development are typical.

Level 1.　Six or 7 years.　Friends are persons with whom one plays or whom one sees often.　Liking is shown by doing something with the friend.　Friends interact according to shared rules that say children should be nice to one another, play together, and share goods.　The following quotations from 6- and 7-year-olds were given in answer to questions about what a friend is [57]:

"Like somebody you know. . . . Play with them; games like hide-and-go-seek."
"They always say yes when I want to borrow their eraser."

Establishing and terminating friendships can be quick and easy. The children sit together on the bus. They exchange names. They start playing. If a child does not play, does not share, or hits the other, the friendship may dissolve. Or a rule may be violated and the relationship repaired by following a rule, such as playing nicely. For example, A hit friend B. A became angry. B did nothing. After a time lapse, they played together again. Subjects explained, "They just forget it"; "They just laugh it off"; "They just play together." Another way of repairing the relationship was for *both* to apologize, as though the breaking of a rule required reparation from both members of the friendship.

Level 2. Nine or 10 years. The rules are the same, but connected with the needs of friends. Friends can trust one another to help when needed, and not to harm one another. Liking is shown by doing something for the friend. Personal characteristics are seen as contributing to liking. Friends are persons who are alike in some ways and who share interests, ideas, and feelings. An action in response to the need of a friend was shown in these statements: "You're lonely and your friend on a bike joins you. You feel a lot better because he joined you." "If you get in trouble, he won't say you did it but stays with you." Equality and reciprocity as requirements of friendship are shown in these statements: "Shared everything they had. One wouldn't have more than the other." "They'd have everything equal." "If one was better than the other one, he wouldn't brag that he was." If a friendship rule is violated, the fact must be acknowledged before it can be repaired.

Level 3. Twelve or 13 years. Friends understand each other more deeply. They share thoughts, feelings, secrets, and interests, help one another with psychological problems, and avoid hurting each other's feelings. Friendships last longer than in middle childhood.

FRIENDS IN DYADS AND GROUPS. Some children play with several children at a time and have a fairly large number of friends, whereas others prefer to play with one at a time, often with a best friend who may be one of a few friends or even the only one. Like-sex friendships are the usual type, girl-boy friendships being relatively infrequent. Girls are more

likely than boys to be involved in exclusive dyads; boys are more likely than girls to be in nonexclusive triads [29]. Waldrop and Halverson observed 7-year-olds playing in dyads and groups and obtained further information from tests and from interviews with the mothers [50]. Outstanding social maturity was frequent in girls who were oriented toward dyadic friendships or best friends, and in boys who often played outdoors with a group. The socially mature girls and boys were friendly, assertive, and involved with peers. One third of the girls, and 9 per cent of the boys were highly involved in both dyads and groups.

Looking for explanations for these sex differences in patterning of friendships, sex typing probably comes to mind first. Girls would gain approval for quiet social activity that would be conducive to intimate get-togethers at home. Boys would be pushed toward vigorous, competitive play outdoors that would require a group. Already established behavior would also contribute. When playing with peers, preschool boys are more active than girls. Waldrop and Halverson suggest, "These active, noisy, peer-oriented boys may frequently be told to go outside and play and there they would be attracted to other active, noisy boys who have also been told to go outside and play" [50, p. 25]. Girls, being less boisterous, would be permitted to play more often in their homes, where quiet play with one friend would be more likely.

LEADERSHIP. Comparisons on a large number of physical, sociological, intellectual, and social variables were made between 6- to 11-year-old children [28]. One group of 278 subjects had been frequently chosen as leaders. The contrast group of 416 had rarely or never been chosen as leaders. Leaders, as a group, were significantly healthier, more active, more aggressive, more intelligent, higher achievers, more gifted, more likely to be Caucasian, more socially adept, and better adjusted. The individual leader excelled in at least one of the areas of physical, mental, and social development, but not necessarily in all three.

POPULARITY. Sociometric status, or popularity, is determined by asking a group or classroom of children to indicate the names of the children whom they like, or with whom they would like to do specified activities. The number of times chosen indicates popularity. Characteristics of very popular children include physical attractiveness, higher social class, certain kinds of names, intelligence, friendliness, and assertiveness [29].

Age-related changes in valued characteristics were found in a study of middle-class children from fourth to eleventh grade [18]. Conformity steadily declined in value. Cooperation was highly valued in the fourth and fifth grades and declined thereafter. Brighter children in the youngest group placed cooperation higher, whereas the less bright children valued it most highly in the sixth and seventh grades. Independence and forcefulness were evaluated more positively with age, and by brighter children at younger ages than by the less bright children. Kindness and sociableness decreased in value. Leadership was highly valued throughout the age levels and self-centeredness was disvalued. Several sex differences were apparent. Girls valued kindness and sociableness more than boys. Girls disvalued self-centeredness more. These differences were consistent with sex-typed cultural expectations.

Attractiveness as a factor in popularity has often been studied in terms of body build and fatness or thinness. When asked, children almost always say that they dislike fat figures, and report negative stereotypes about fat children. However, when children in grades 2, 4, and 6 in Melbourne, Australia were questioned about liking their own fat, medium, and thin classmates, there was no relationship of liking to body build [34]. Although the children held the usual stereotypes against fatness, they did not apply them in real situations, to their classmates and friends.

ISOLATION. Some children are reared in relative isolation. Others are exposed to peers but are avoided, and chosen last or not at all in playing games. The interactions of last-chosen boys were observed on a playground [24]. They stayed on the edge of the group, at a distance from the other children. The isolates were not targets for aggression, but simply did not interact with the others. They were not experiencing mutual regulation of aggression, nor, indeed, of any reciprocal action. Lacking the rich experiences of building and maintaining friendships, isolates are at risk for social and emotional problems in adolescence and adulthood.

Origins of isolation may be in the temperament of the child (see "Temperament" in Chapter 6), in the isolated setting of a family, or in family interaction. The young child's experience with peers depends largely on whether the mother permits and arranges for peer play.

An intervention experiment with young social isolates was carried on successfully in day care centers [23]. The isolate played with a younger child, half of them children 15 months younger and half with children 3 months younger. A control group received no treatment. Both experimental groups increased in sociability, but the one with younger therapist-playmates increased the most. It is not known whether similar treatment of school-age children would increase their sociability.

Family. For all its members, a family provides protection from the rest of the world and opportunities for learning how to cope in the outside world. Adults in the family play double roles in regard to the children. Parents, and older siblings, interpret society's demands, insisting that children behave in socially acceptable ways outside the home. At the same time, parents defend children from those demands when they are in the privacy and safety of home. Indeed, all family members may put on their best behavior outside and express themselves more freely at home.

PARENTS. Throughout this chapter there are many instances of parental correlates of child behavior, and some of the parental influences on child behavior. Table 12–1 gives a quick review of the related child and parent behaviors. Parent-child relations have many facets. Attachment and love have been the subject of much research in infancy and early childhood, but of little in middle childhood. Companionship and enjoyment have received little attention, as have the parental function of pro-

TABLE 12–1
Child Characteristics and
Related Parental Behavior.

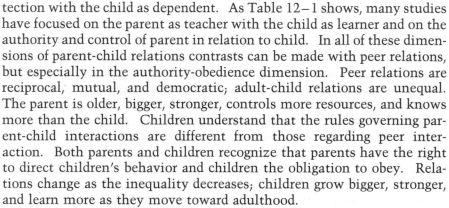

Child	Parent
High self-esteem	Warmth, supportiveness, authoritativeness
Internal locus of control	Acceptance, granting of autonomy
Rule attunement	Warmth, authoritativeness
Social sensitivity	Role-taking, person-oriented regulation
Restitution	Demonstration, teaching
Prosocial behavior	Inductive discipline, low power-assertion
Positive influence of television	Supervision, sharing, discussion
Having friends	Facilitating social play

Peer relations are reciprocal, mutual, and democratic
Child-adult relations are unequal

tection with the child as dependent. As Table 12–1 shows, many studies have focused on the parent as teacher with the child as learner and on the authority and control of parent in relation to child. In all of these dimensions of parent-child relations contrasts can be made with peer relations, but especially in the authority-obedience dimension. Peer relations are reciprocal, mutual, and democratic; adult-child relations are unequal. The parent is older, bigger, stronger, controls more resources, and knows more than the child. Children understand that the rules governing parent-child interactions are different from those regarding peer interaction. Both parents and children recognize that parents have the right to direct children's behavior and children the obligation to obey. Relations change as the inequality decreases; children grow bigger, stronger, and learn more as they move toward adulthood.

GENDER. In Chapter 9 we discussed gender differences in behavior, the development of gender concepts, influences on gender concepts and behavior, and the Freudian view of sexual development. The child enters the school years with a newly established concept of gender constancy, knowledge of gender-appropriate behavior, and an identification with the same-sex parent.

Children's lives are structured differently, according to whether they are boys or girls. Gender defines some of the ways in which parents and siblings interact with a child. When Whiting and Edwards compared mothers' behavior with boys and girls in samples from thirteen societies, they found some differences that held throughout all or most of the societies: Girls did more housework; girls took care of young children more; girls interacted more than boys with adult women; boys more often played alone or with other children; boys were more often idle [54]. Girls therefore had more opportunities to be responsible and nurturant, to cooperate in female dyads, learn mothering skills, and get more satisfaction from mutuality in social interaction.

SIBLING INTERACTION. Interaction is affected by the sex of the siblings and the age spacing; outcomes of sibling interaction are shown in intelligence, achievement, teaching, learning, helping, and use of power. Although a sibling pair may share some characteristics with any twosome of difference ages, siblings are special in that they belong to the same family. A sibling relationship is part of the family system, affecting other

relations within that system and being affected by them. The following studies show that a sibling relationship can affect a child's interaction with the mother, and that a mother-child relation affects sibling interaction.

Cicirelli, who has studied sibling relations extensively, measured first-grade children's problem-solving alone and with help, in different family structures [8]. He found that children who had older sisters were able to accept and use help from the older sister or the mother, but children with older brothers worked better alone. Cicirelli had shown previously that older sisters are more effective teachers of younger siblings than are older brothers. The present study indicates that the younger child's experience with the older sibling affected the former's interaction with the mother as helper.

Bryant and Crockenberg studied prosocial behavior and its correlates in 50 first-born girls in grades 4 and 5, their mothers, and their sisters, who were 2 or 3 years younger [4]. The pairs of sisters played games at home and in the laboratory, with and without their mothers participating. Mothers described their daughters on a check list. When a mother met the expressed needs of both her daughters, as in helping when the child asked for help, the two girls were most likely to share with and comfort each other. If the mother met the expressed need of only one of the sisters, both did more disparaging and discomforting of the other than they did when the mother met the expressed needs of both sisters. Siblings' prosocial and antisocial behavior toward one another was thus correlated with the mother's interaction with each daughter.

Family Transition. In Chapter 9 we discussed two family transitions commonly experienced by the young child, the birth of a sibling and divorce. Here we shall deal with the transition that frequently follows divorce, the reconstitution of a family through remarriage. A remarriage, like a birth, adds one or more persons to a family microsystem, whereas a divorce—like death—subtracts one or more persons. Either addition or subtraction upsets the interactions in the system and requires all members to work out new relations with each other. The transitions of birth, divorce, and remarriage differ in many ways, but significantly in this way: Our macrosystem has long-established customs and beliefs for coping with birth, but there are few ground rules for managing the changes of divorce and family reconstitution. It is predicted that by 1990 over 7 million children will be living in families with one natural parent and one stepparent [26].

Clinicians Carter and McGoldrick present their own experience as family therapists along with results of research on family reconstitution [5]. Children of school age adjust to a step-family better than adolescents, but with more difficulty than preschool children. The following issues are the most significant ones for children entering a family formed by the remarriage of a parent.

1. DEALING WITH LOSS OF A PARENT. Whether a parent is lost through

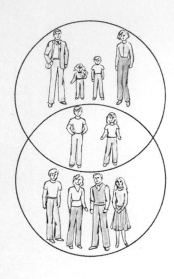

death or divorce, a quick remarriage may not give the child enough time to mourn the departed parent. As well as time, the child needs recognition of the loss, and support in coping with feelings of loss.

2. COPING WITH DIVIDED LOYALTIES. Parents, stepparents, grandparents, and other relatives can help by not requiring the child to take sides, and by recognizing the child's desire to maintain relations with both parents.

3. SHIFTING POSITIONS AND ROLES. When combining with step-siblings, a child may have to shift from eldest to middle position, from head kitchen assistant to minor helper, or from only child to caregiver for young children. New relations must be built with grandparents and kin. The child may have four sets of grandparents. It takes time to build new relationships, especially when there are no traditional guides to the new roles.

4. LIVING IN NEW HOMES. Some children divide their time between two remarried parents. There may be a set of step-siblings in each home. The child must shift between two microsystems, including physical settings and interacting members. If the shift does not require shifts in other microsystems, as in school and peer groups, the child has some stable, ongoing experiences.

5. MEETING NEW EXPECTATIONS. Parent and/or stepparent may expect too much, or so may the child. The child-stepparent relationship takes time to develop. It will not be the same as the relationship with the absent parent. The stepmother role is more difficult than that of the stepfather.

6. HOPES FOR REUNION OF NATURAL PARENTS. During and after a divorce, children often fantasize that their parents will resolve their conflict and remarry. It helps all around if parents can separate their parental roles from their spousal roles, continuing to cooperate in caring for their children, but making it clear that they have stopped being husband and wife. The child is helped to recognize the permanence of the new marriage when the parent supports the stepparent's decisions and actions, including those on matters of discipline and conflict.

7. GUILT OVER THE DIVORCE. Children often feel responsible for the marital breakup. If parents can be frank with the child concerning their own responsibility, a child may be reassured. As with all the issues listed, professional help may be needed.

Although the issues discussed may give the impression that family reconstitution is a difficult and negative experience, reports of step-families show a more positive side. Family integration, or feeling and acting like a family, was rated excellent or moderate in 79 per cent of reconstituted families in a sample of 88 families [17]. In 82 per cent of these families, stepparent-stepchild relations were rated good or excellent. Step-sibling relations were good or excellent in 62 per cent. Step-siblings got along better together if they all lived in the same household.

Stepfather-stepchild relations were examined in 106 families, and compared with relations in families with both natural parents [3]. Stepchildren were just as happy and successful with school and friends as were natural children. The stepchildren got along as well with their stepfathers as did the other children with their natural fathers. Children and mothers saw the stepfathers as just as good as natural fathers, but the stepfathers themselves had some doubts about their own fathering.

Social Networks

A child is born into a social network, consisting of persons "outside the household who engage in activities and exchanges of an affective and/or material nature with members of the immediate family" [10]. The people in the network include the parents' and siblings' friends, some relatives, significant co-workers, neighbors, and persons in other relationships. Grandparents and other kin are often important network members. The child experiences the network through its effect on parents, siblings, and any other members of the microsystem, and directly, through the child's own interactions and observations. We have already mentioned that the support of relatives and friends is very important to a family in the transition of divorce. At such times of crisis, the network may give more than the family is able to give in return, but over the long run, network interactions are reciprocal.

The child sees reciprocity in action between mother and her network, father and his network (which overlaps with mother's but is not identical), and perhaps with siblings and their networks. The child takes part in some of the reciprocal actions, delivering a cake and flowers to the home of a sick neighbor, going to Grandma's for Sunday dinner, or getting sympathy and a bandaid from an older friend. The child may hear parental discussions about which family is to drive the children to the Scout meeting today, or who owes whom an invitation. In this way, the network supplements peer play in children's learning of reciprocity. The network gives opportunities for interaction with a variety of people who start with a favorable attitude. These social experiences contribute to concepts of gender roles, occupational roles, and age roles. They may give work experience, knowledge of different family forms, and of class-related social customs, ethnicity, different child-rearing methods. The child's social world expands through network interactions, and with the development of the child.

Networks expand and contract. They are disrupted by moving and other family transitions. The child takes increasing responsibility for building and maintaining his own social network.

Summary

The development of the sense of industry is the key to healthy social development in middle childhood. Acquiring the knowledge and technology of his macrosystem successfully, the child can esteem himself as an adequate person. A sense of inferiority and inadequacy may often result if success is defined in ways that make it unattainable to the majority of children. Locus of control is a conviction of being or not being in charge of one's life. Gender concepts include gender constancy and well-developed gender-role stereotypes. Gender-typed occupational stereotypes have become more flexible for girls.

Moral development takes place in rule attunement and development of social sensitivity. The child learns the rules of home, school, neighborhood, and social network. Rules are developed with peers. Experiments on rule-following have shown effects of types of punishment, and of reasoning and modeling. Children distinguish between moral rules and social conventions. Social sensitivity has a biological base that is indicated by group control of aggression and by perceptions of facial expression and voice tone. Social sensitivity is enhanced by increasing role-taking skill and verbal communication skill. Style of parental communication is related to children's communication skill.

Moral knowledge increases and judgments mature with cognitive development and social experience. In judging goodness or badness of an act, outcome and intentions are considered. Cognitive maturity limits judgment of complex problems. Moral, or prosocial, behavior has been studied in terms of generosity and helping. Generosity is influenced by mood, modeling, presence of model, preaching, and discipline. Helping is influenced by strictness and permissiveness of rules, experimenter warmth, and gender.

Social-emotional development is affected by macrosystem beliefs, values, organization, and mode of transmittal. Political structure and socioeconomic factors are felt in physical care and development, as well as in child rearing and education. Children feel the impact of television's transmittal of values, beliefs, information, and misinformation. Aggression and gender-role concepts are particularly affected. Socioeconomic status and ethnic membership influence many aspects of self-concept.

Bare-minimal goals for school are suggested: learning the basics, nondisruptive behavior, and happiness. Movement toward these goals is facilitated by prosocial behavior, self-esteem, and wanting to learn. Attribution-treatment-interaction is a way of trying to help children learn by teaching or treating them according to particular child characteristics. Another approach treats children as group members rather than as individuals.

A child interacts differently with older, younger, and same-age playmates. All of these varied experiences contribute to normal social development. With peers or equals, who are friends of the same age or same ability level, interactions are reciprocal. Through sharing, taking turns, and negotiating, peers can make rules cooperatively and can regulate their aggression. Friendship is an enduring relation of affection, maintained by rule-governed reciprocal actions. Concepts of friendship develop in age-related levels: Friends play; friends play and help each other according to need; friends play, help each other according to need, and can be trusted. Most children have friends, but they vary in number of friends. Girls play more in dyads, boys more in groups. Social isolates may be helped by playing with younger children.

Child-adult relations are regulated by adult-imposed rules. Parental behavior has many correlates in child behavior. Family interaction involves more than two people. Sibling relations are affected by mother-child relations, and mother-child by sibling.

Family reconstitution is a transition experienced by almost 7 million children in the United States. A successful transition requires dealing with these issues: loss of a parent; divided loyalties; changing roles and positions; living in two homes; unrealistic expectations; hoped-for remarriage of natural parents; guilt over the divorce. Most reconstituted families do well in terms of their own evaluations.

A child's social network is made up of persons outside the family microsystem who give and receive support and help of goods, services, and understanding and sharing of experiences and feelings. The network provides the child with many positive social-emotional experiences as well as information and intellectual stimulation. The network demonstrates reciprocity to the child and gives protected opportunities for participating in the reciprocal action.

References

1. Barcus, F. E., and R. Wolkin. *Children's television: An analysis of programming and advertising.* New York: Praeger Publishers, Inc., 1977.
2. Bearison, D. J., and T. Z. Cassel. Cognitive decentration and social codes: Communicative effectiveness in young children from differing family contexts. *Developmental Psychology,* 1975, **11,** 29–39.
3. Bohannon, P., and R. Erickson. Stepping in. *Psychology Today,* 1978, **11:8,** 53–59.
4. Bryant, B. K., and S. B. Crockenberg. Correlates and dimensions of prosocial behavior: A study of female siblings with their mothers. *Child Development,* 1980, **51,** 529–544.
5. Carter, E. A., and M. McGoldrick. *The family life cycle: A framework for family therapy.* New York: Gardner, 1980.
6. Chan, I. Letter to the Editor: *Newsletter of the Society for Research in Child Development,* Winter, 1975, 3.
7. Children's television. *Newsletter of the Division of Developmental Psychology of the American Psychological Association,* Winter, 1973.
8. Cicirelli, V. G. Effects of mother and older sibling on the problem-solving behavior of the younger child. *Developmental Psychology,* 1975, **11,** 749–756.
9. Cline, V. B., R. G. Croft, and S. Courrier. Desensitization of children to television violence. *Proceedings, 80th Annual Convention, American Psychological Association,* 1972, 99–100
10. Cochran, M. M., and J. A. Brassard. Child development and personal social networks. *Child Development,* 1979, **50,** 601–616.
11. Coles, R. *Privileged ones: The well-off and the rich in America.* Boston: Little, Brown, and Company, 1977.
12. Coopersmith, S. *The antecedents of self-esteem.* San Francisco: W. H. Freeman and Company, Publishers, 1967.
13. Damon, W. *The social world of the child.* San Francisco: Jossey-Bass, 1977.

14. Darley, J. M., E. C. Klosson, and M. P. Zanna. Intentions and their contexts in the moral judgments of children and adults. *Child Development*, 1978, **49,** 66–74.

15. Dlugokinski, E. L., and I. J. Firestone. Other centeredness and susceptibility to charitable appeals: Effects of perceived discipline. *Early Child Development and Care*, 1974, **10,** 21–28.

16. Drabman, R. S., and M. H. Thomas. Does media violence increase children's toleration of real-life aggression? *Developmental Psychology*, 1974, **10,** 418–421.

17. Duberman, L. *The reconstituted family.* Chicago: Nelson-Hall, 1975.

18. Emmerich, W. Developmental trends in evaluations of single traits. *Child Development*, 1974, **45,** 172–183.

19. Erikson, E. H. *Childhood and society.* 2nd ed. New York: W. W. Norton & Company, Inc., 1963.

20. Flavell, J. H. Role-taking and communication skills in children. *Young Children*, 1966, **21,** 164–177.

21. Frueh, T., and P. E. McGhee. Traditional sex-role development and amount of time spent watching television. *Developmental Psychology*, 1975, **11,** 109.

22. Fu, V. R., M. K. Korslund, and D. E. Hinkle. Ethnic self-concept during middle childhood. *Journal of Psychology*, 1980, **105,** 99–105.

23. Furman, W., D. F. Rahe, and W. W. Hartup. Rehabilitation of low-interactive preschool children through mixed-age and same-age socialization. Unpublished manuscript, University of Minnesota. Cited in W. W. Hartup. Children and their friends. In H. McGurk (ed.). *Issues in childhood social development.* London: Methuen & Co., Ltd., 1978.

24. Ginsburg, H. J., M. S. Wauson, and M. Easley. Of omega children: And the meek shall inherit the worst. Paper presented at meeting of the Society for Research in Child Development, New Orleans, 1977.

25. Girgus, J. S., and J. Wolf. Age changes in the ability to encode social cues. *Developmental Psychology*, 1975, **11,** 118.

26. Glick, P. C. Children of divorced parents in demographic perspective. *Journal of Social Issues*, 1979, **35,** 170–180.

27. Gordon, E. W., and S. Shipman. Human diversity, pedagogy, and education equity. *American Psychologist*, 1979, **34,** 1030–1036.

28. Harrison, C. W., J. R. Rawls, and D. J. Rawls, Differences between leaders and non-leaders in six- to eleven-year-old children. *Journal of Social Psychology*, 1971, **84,** 269–272.

29. Hartup, W. W. Children and their friends. In H. McGurk (ed.). *Issues in childhood social development.* London: Methuen & Co., Ltd., 1978.

30. Hoffman, M. L. Development of moral thought, feeling and behavior. *American Psychologist*, 1979, **34,** 958–966.

31. Hogan, R., J. A. Johnson, and N. P. Emler. A socioanalytic theory of moral development. In W. Damon (ed.). Moral development. *New Directions for Child Development*, 1978, No. 2.

32. Israel, A. C., and P. A. Raskin. Directiveness of instructions and modeling: Effects on production and persistance of children's donations. *Journal of Genetic Psychology*, 1979, **135,** 269–277.

33. Kraus, R. M., and S. Glucksberg. The development of communication competence as a function of age. *Child Development*, 1969, **40,** 255–266.

34. Lawson, M. C. Development of body build stereotypes, peer ratings, and self-esteem in Australian children. *Journal of Psychology*, 1980, **104,** 111–118.

35. Lifshitz, M. Internal-external locus-of-control dimension as a function of age and the socialization milieu. *Child Development*, 1973, **44,** 538–546.

36. Nolan, J. D., J. P. Galst, and M. A. White. Sex bias on children's television programs. *Journal of Psychology*, 1977, **96,** 197–204.

37. Nowicki, S., and B. Strickland. A locus of control scale for children. *Journal of Consulting and Clinical Psychology*, 1973, **40,** 148–154.
38. Piaget, J. *The moral judgment of the child.* London: Kegan Paul, 1932.
39. Piaget, J., and B. Inhelder. *The psychology of the child.* New York: Basic Books, Inc., Publishers, 1969.
40. Prawat, R. S., S. Grissom, and T. Parish. Affective development in children, grades 3 through 12. *Journal of Genetic Psychology*, 1979, **135,** 37–49.
41. Rohner, E. C., C. Chaille, and R. P. Rohner. Perceived parental acceptance-rejection and the development of children's locus of control. *Journal of Psychology*, 1980, **104,** 83–86.
42. Rosenhan, D. L., and G. M. White. Observation and rehearsal as determinants of prosocial behavior. *Journal of Personality and Social Psychology*, 1967, **5,** 424–431.
43. Selman, R. L., and D. F. Byrne. A structural-development analysis of levels of role taking in middle childhood. *Child Development*, 1974, **45,** 803–806.
44. Shantz, C. U. Communication skills and social-cognitive development. Paper presented at meeting of the Society for Research in Child Development, Denver, 1975.
45. Slavin, R. E., R. L. DeVries, and B. H. Hulten. Individual vs. team competition: The interpersonal consequences of academic performance. Baltimore: The Johns Hopkins University Center for Social Organization of Schools, Report No. 188, 1975 (mimeo).
46. Staub, E. A child in distress: The effect of focusing responsibility on children on their attempts to help. *Developmental Psychology*, 1970, **2,** 152–153.
47. Surbeck, E., and R. C. Endsley. Children's emotional and cognitive reactions to television violence: Effects of film character, reassurance, age and sex. Paper presented at meeting of the Society for Research in Child Development, Denver, 1975.
48. Turnure, C. Cognitive development and role-taking ability in boys and girls from seven to 12. *Developmental Psychology*, 1975, **11,** 202–209.
49. Underwood, J. E., W. J. Froming, and B. S. Moore. Affect, attention and altruism. Paper presented at meeting of the Society for Research in Child Development, New Orleans, 1977.
50. Waldrop, M. F., and C. F. Halverson. Intensive and extensive peer behavior: Longitudinal and cross-sectional analysis. *Child Development*, 1975, **46,** 19–26.
51. Weissbrod, C. S. The effect of adult warmth and rules on male and female children's rescue latency. Paper presented at meeting of the Society for Research in Child Development, New Orleans, 1977.
52. Weston, D. R., and E. Turiel. Act-rule relations: Children's concepts of social rules. *Developmental Psychology*, 1980, **16,** 417–424.
53. White, K. M., and P. L. Ouellette. Occupational preferences in children's projections for self and opposite sex. *Journal of Genetic Psychology*, 1980, **135,** 37–43.
54. Whiting, B. B., and C. P. Edwards. Mutuality in mother-daughter and female diadic interaction: A cross-culture comparison. Paper presented at meetings of the Society for Research in Child Development, San Francisco, 1979.
55. Williams, J. E., S. M. Bennett, and D. L. Best. Awareness and expression of sex stereotypes in young children. *Developmental Psychology*, 1975, **11,** 635–642.
56. Winnick, R. H., and J. A. Taylor. Racial preference—36 years later. *Journal of Social Psychology*, 1977, **102,** 157–158.
57. Youniss, J., and J. Volpe. A relational analysis of children's friendships. In W. Damon (ed.). Social cognition. *New Directions for Child Development*, 1978, No. 1.

V

The Adolescent

13

Puberty:
From Child
to Adult

407

You're all grown up?" "He's a young man now!" "I hardly knew her. She's not a little girl any longer." Everybody recognizes the transformation of child into adult. Even though it happens to every girl and boy, it often surprises family, relatives, and friends, perhaps because they realize that they are changing their own responses and modes of interaction.

The physical changes of puberty trigger changes in the individual's feeling, thinking, and behaving. The physical changes also serve as cues to other people, to parents, siblings, relatives, teachers, and members of the social network, who begin to react in new ways to the person who is beginning the transformation from child to adult.

Puberty is a period of physical change; adolescence is a period of physical, intellectual, emotional, and social change that begins with the start of puberty and ends when the individual is socially defined as an adult. In some macrosystems adulthood is conferred as soon as one or more puberal changes occur, as when a girl begins to menstruate. In complex societies, such as our own, adolescence stretches out over several years and ends vaguely, with no one definitive mark to end it.

The same boy before and after puberty.

1. What sequence of bodily changes occurs during puberty?
2. How do females and males differ in puberal growth?
3. How do individuals differ in puberal growth?
4. How are differences in puberal growth rates related to differences in cognitive functioning?
5. To what types of injury and illness are adolescents most vulnerable?
6. How are health care and health problems related to different levels of the adolescent's ecology?
7. What implications for physical education programs are there in male and female variability in motor development?
8. How do patterns of growth and health relate to self-concepts?

Puberty

The period of puberal growth, or puberty, is a time during which a series of specific physical changes create the sexually mature body. The signs of puberty noticed by family and friends include changes in bodily size, shape, skin, hair, facial structure, and voice. Growth researchers have identified timing and sequences of changes both external and internal. They note changes in size, structure, and function of the body and its organs and systems. They chart the sequence of puberal changes in the reproductive organs and in secondary sex characteristics. This sequence is used as a measure of progress toward sexual maturity. Although the general plan of puberal changes is the same for both sexes, there are, of course, sex differences.

Female Puberal Sequence

The first sign of puberty is the appearance of the breast bud, a slight elevation of the breast and enlargement of the area around the nipple [45]. Five stages of breast development have been defined. The breast bud appears at 11 on the average, but it may come as early as 9 and as late as 13. Stage 5 is reached at between 12 and 18 years. Rapid increase in height begins at about the time when the breast bud appears, but of course the beginning of the height spurt cannot be seen. It is pinpointed only when longitudinal records are analyzed. The average duration of girls' height spurt (data from the Berkeley Growth Study and Guidance Study) was 2.82 years, the shortest being 1.51 years and the longest 4.03 [13]. Peak velocity comes at about 12 years for average European and Northern American girls [45].

Pubic hair begins to grow a little later than does the breast bud in ⅔ of girls, and shortly before the breast bud in ⅓ [45]. The growth of pubic hair has been divided into 5 stages, according to texture, color, and distribution. Menarche, the first menstruation, bears a close relation to the spurt in height; it occurs after peak velocity has been reached, when speed of growth is slowing down. The average menarche takes place at the point of maximum deceleration of height velocity [45]. Average growth after menarche is only 6 centimeters. Breast development and

Order of onset of puberal changes: Breast bud, pubic hair, axillary hair, height spurt, menarche, ovulation

pubic hair development are not related as closely to menarche as is the height spurt. Although the average girl is in breast bud stage 4 and pubic hair stage 3 or 4, some are earlier and some later. The median age of menarche in the United States, calculated from the National Health Survey, was 12.76 for all girls, 12.8 for white, and 12.5 for black (28). The range in median age at menarche is large, from 12.3 to 18.0, when populations from all over the world are compared [45].

Although menarche is the traditional sign of sexual maturity, the reproductive system still has some developing to do. The early menstrual cycles are often irregular; the ovaries may not ovulate (shed an egg). Some girls are not fertile for a year or a year and a half after menarche.

Male Puberal Sequence

Order of onset of puberal changes: Testicles enlarge, penis enlarges, pubic hair, height spurt, ejaculation, axillary hair, facial hair, body hair

The first sign of puberty in males is enlarging of the testicles, along with changes in color and texture of the skin of the scrotum [45]. Next, the penis grows and pubic hair appears. The average age for beginning penis growth is 12.5, with a range of 10.5 to 14.5. The average initiation of the height spurt is a year after the beginning of testicle growth; the point of highest velocity of height growth comes about a year after the start of the height spurt. At peak height velocity, the penis is also growing at maximal rate, and pubic hair has reached stage 3 or 4. Boys' height spurt occurs later in the puberal growth sequence than does girls' height spurt. The sexes are 2 years apart in peak of height velocity. They are only a few months apart in some parallel changes, such as appearance of breast bud and beginning of testicular changes.

Axillary hair appears when pubic hair is almost mature. Facial hair and bodily hair then appear, facial hair beginning with the mustache and ending with the beard. Voice changes occur relatively late in puberty. Breast tissue increases during puberty, sometimes embarrassing a boy. The enlargement usually disappears after a year or so, but if it remains, it can be perceived as a problem. Surgical removal is an option.

Fertility is established gradually. The first ejaculation of seminal fluid occurs about a year after the penis starts to grow. Sperms are usually fewer and less viable at first than later.

Figure 13–1 shows growth curves of two fairly average children. On the basis of the previous paragraphs about males' and females' puberal growth spurts, is Dana a girl or a boy? Which is Robin?

Increase in Height

Prepuberal child's height correlates 0.8 with adult height

Just before children start to spurt in growth, they are growing very slowly, boys more slowly than girls. At this point, a child's height gives a good indication of what the adult height will be. The correlation between the two heights is 0.8 [45]. With the onset of the height spurt, the future becomes cloudier in regard to eventual height. The length and intensity of the growth spurt are difficult or impossible to predict, and the puberal spurt determines 30 per cent of the variability of adult height. Differ-

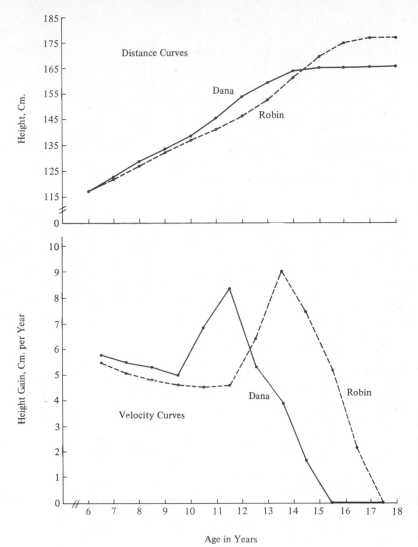

FIGURE 13-1
Two hypothetical growth records. The upper curve shows Dana's and Robin's height on successive birthdays (distance curves). The lower curves show the amounts Dana and Robin grew in the year between their birthdays (velocity curves).

ences in adult height can be traced to four types of differences in growth, as shown in Figure 13–2.

Because of the wide variation in both height and weight during adolescence, percentile tables are not so useful at this time as they are earlier for assessing an individual child's status. However, for their value in showing how height and weight are distributed during the teen years, height and weight percentiles (Tables 13–1 and 13–2) are included here, as such tables are included in the other sections of the book that have to do with physical growth. These figures were calculated from data of the National Health Survey which used a carefully chosen sample representing the United States population.

We suggest that the reader use the height measurements on Dana and

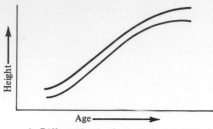

1. Different levels of growth during childhood; same pattern of growth spurt.

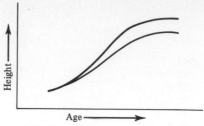

3. Difference in velocity of puberal spurt.

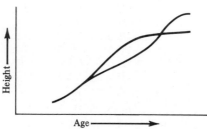

2. Different timing in start of puberal spurt; same pattern of childhood growth.

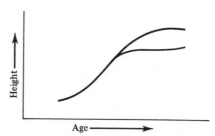

4. Difference in duration of puberal spurt.

FIGURE 13-2
Differences in height between two adults can be the result of any or all of the differences shown above.

Robin in Figure 13–1 in conjunction with the percentiles of Table 14–1. Suppose first that Dana is a girl. What are her approximate percentiles for height at each birthday? Suppose Robin is a boy. How does he rank with other boys each year? Next compare Dana's measurements with the boys' percentiles. If Dana is a boy, how does he compare at each birthday to his age mates? Similarly, consider Robin as a girl. Only for Dana as an adult male, and Robin as an adult female, are their heights in the extreme percentile ranks; and note how each year after age 14 or 15, when they are average, do a male Dana and a female Robin move further away from the average.

Actually, the figures for Dana were chosen to be typical of height measurements for females, and those for Robin were chosen as being typical for males. The differences between the distance curves for Dana and Robin at ages 12 and 13 are the differences that show up in fifth and sixth grades in school, where many of the girls are taller than many of the boys.

Increase in Weight

The curve of increments of weight begins to rise earlier than does the curve of increments of height. This difference can be explained in part by the earlier increase in the width and depth measurements of the chest and hips. The preadolescent increase of subcutaneous fat and muscle also contributes to the earlier increase in weight.

There are times when fat increases, and times when it decreases. Skinfold thickness, the usual measure of subcutaneous fat, is found by grasping a fold of skin and applying calipers to it. The clinician's favorite site

TABLE 13–1
Percentile Distribution of
Stature (in Centimeters) of
Males and Females from
Age 11½ Through 18
Years, United States.

Sex and Age	Stature in centimeters, percentile						
	5th	10th	25th	50th	75th	90th	95th
Male							
11.5 years	135.0	137.7	141.5	146.4	151.1	155.6	158.5
12.0 years	137.6	140.3	144.4	149.7	154.6	159.4	162.3
12.5 years	140.2	143.0	147.4	153.0	158.2	163.2	166.1
13.0 years	142.9	145.8	150.5	156.5	161.8	167.0	169.8
13.5 years	145.7	148.7	153.6	159.9	165.3	170.5	173.4
14.0 years	148.8	151.8	156.9	163.1	168.5	173.8	176.7
14.5 years	152.0	155.0	160.1	166.2	171.5	176.6	179.5
15.0 years	155.2	158.2	163.3	169.0	174.1	178.9	181.9
15.5 years	158.3	161.2	166.2	171.5	176.3	180.8	183.9
16.0 years	161.1	163.9	168.7	173.5	178.1	182.4	185.4
16.5 years	163.4	166.1	170.6	175.2	179.5	183.6	186.6
17.0 years	164.9	167.7	171.9	176.2	180.5	184.4	187.3
17.5 years	165.6	168.5	172.4	176.7	181.0	185.0	187.6
18.0 years	165.7	168.7	172.3	176.8	181.2	185.3	187.6
Female							
11.5 years	136.6	139.0	143.5	148.2	152.6	156.9	159.5
12.0 years	139.8	142.3	147.0	151.5	155.8	160.0	162.7
12.5 years	142.7	145.4	150.1	154.6	158.8	162.9	165.6
13.0 years	145.2	148.0	152.8	157.1	161.3	165.3	168.1
13.5 years	147.2	150.0	154.7	159.0	163.2	167.3	170.0
14.0 years	148.7	151.5	155.9	160.4	164.6	168.7	171.3
14.5 years	149.7	152.5	156.8	161.2	165.6	169.8	172.2
15.0 years	150.5	153.2	157.2	161.8	166.3	170.5	172.8
15.5 years	151.1	153.6	157.5	162.1	166.7	170.9	173.1
16.0 years	151.6	154.1	157.8	162.4	166.9	171.1	173.3
16.5 years	152.2	154.6	158.2	162.7	167.1	171.2	173.4
17.0 years	152.7	155.1	158.7	163.1	167.3	171.2	173.5
17.5 years	153.2	155.6	159.1	163.4	167.5	171.1	173.5
18.0 years	153.6	156.0	159.6	163.7	167.6	171.0	173.6

Source: P. V. V. Hamill, R. A. Drizd, C. L. Johnson, R. B. Reed, and A. F. Roche. *NCHS growth curves for children birth–18 years.* Vital and health statistics: Series 11, Data from the National Health Survey; no. 165. (DHEW publication No. (PHS) 78-1650.) Washington: U.S. Government Printing Office, 1977. Table 13.

for measuring skinfold is just below the right shoulder blade, an easy spot to reach, and one that yields measurements consistent with other fat measurements.

Fat thickness increases during the last three prenatal months and until nine months after birth, decreases until about age 6 and then increases slowly until just before the time of greatest increase in height. The median measurement of fat thickness for girls is at all times greater than the median for boys. From puberty on, the subcutaneous fat of females is always thicker than that of males, not only in the well-noticed places (hips and breasts), but everywhere. The increase in subcutaneous fat continues for both sexes until the fifth or sixth decades [21].

Fat thickness throughout childhood is closely related to weight at maturity [14]. By measuring fat thickness semiannually, it was shown that

TABLE 13–2
Percentile Distribution of Weight (in Kilograms) of Males and Females from Age 11½ Through 18 Years, United States.

Sex and Age	Weight in kilograms, percentile						
	5th	10th	25th	50th	75th	90th	95th
Male							
11.5 years	28.24	29.72	33.08	37.46	43.00	49.61	54.73
12.0 years	29.85	31.46	35.09	39.78	45.77	52.73	58.09
12.5 years	31.64	33.41	37.31	42.27	48.70	55.91	61.52
13.0 years	33.64	35.60	39.74	44.95	51.79	59.12	65.02
13.5 years	35.85	38.03	42.40	47.81	55.02	62.35	68.51
14.0 years	38.22	40.64	45.21	50.77	58.31	65.57	72.13
14.5 years	40.66	43.34	48.08	53.76	61.58	68.76	75.66
15.0 years	43.11	46.06	50.92	56.71	64.72	71.91	79.12
15.5 years	45.50	48.69	53.64	59.51	67.64	74.98	82.45
16.0 years	47.74	51.16	56.16	62.10	70.26	77.97	85.62
16.5 years	49.76	53.39	58.38	64.39	72.46	80.84	88.59
17.0 years	51.50	55.28	60.22	66.31	74.17	83.58	91.31
17.5 years	52.89	56.78	61.61	67.78	75.32	86.14	93.73
18.0 years	53.97	57.89	62.61	68.88	76.04	88.41	95.76
Female							
11.5 years	28.83	30.71	34.48	39.23	45.48	53.03	57.42
12.0 years	30.52	32.53	36.52	41.53	48.07	55.99	60.81
12.5 years	32.30	34.42	38.59	43.84	50.56	58.81	64.12
13.0 years	34.14	36.35	40.65	46.10	52.91	61.45	67.30
13.5 years	35.98	38.26	42.65	48.26	55.11	63.87	70.30
14.0 years	37.76	40.11	44.54	50.28	57.09	66.04	73.08
14.5 years	39.45	41.83	46.28	52.10	58.84	67.95	75.59
15.0 years	40.99	43.38	47.82	53.68	60.32	69.54	77.78
15.5 years	42.32	44.72	49.10	54.96	61.48	70.79	79.59
16.0 years	43.41	45.78	50.09	55.89	62.29	71.68	80.99
16.5 years	44.20	46.54	50.75	56.44	62.75	72.18	81.93
17.0 years	44.74	47.04	51.14	56.69	62.91	72.38	82.46
17.5 years	45.08	47.33	51.33	56.71	62.89	72.37	82.62
18.0 years	45.26	47.47	51.39	56.62	62.78	72.25	82.47

Source: P. V. V. Hamill, R. A. Drizd, C. L. Johnson, R. B. Reed, and A. F. Roche. *NCHS growth for children birth-18 years.* Vital and health statistics: Series 11, Data from the National Health Survey; no. 165. (DHEW publication No. (PHS) 78-1650.) Washington: U.S. Government Printing Office, 1977. Table 14.

between 1.5 and 12.5 years of age, children in the top 14 per cent in fat were advanced by about half a year's growth. Fat thickness was associated with skeletal maturity. The authors suggest that overnutrition or supernutrition results in speeded maturation, and general dimensional growth, in addition to subcutaneous fat.

Endocrinology of Growth

In addition to stature and weight, other dimensions of the human body have been studied in similar ways. These include sitting height and dimensions of the chest and head. Even diameters of the head show increments that follow the same kind of pattern of increments, although the curve for each dimension is unique in some way. The puberal growth spurt is the result of the complicated but interrelated ebb and flow of endocrine substances in the bloodstream.

Because every cell extracts materials from the bloodstream and gives up substances to it, every cell is *endocrine,* which means that it secretes internally. But the endocrine glands have specialized functions in relation to growth. The most important of these is the anterior portion of the *pituitary* gland, which is located in the center of the head, near the *hypothalamus,* a part of the brain. The hypothalamus sends hormones through the portal veins to the pituitary, which is then activated to produce hormones, each of which has specific functions.

Growth Influencers. Five hormones originating in the anterior pituitary have been identified as regulators of growth (Figure 13–3); four of these hormones stimulate other endocrine glands to function. The fifth, or perhaps first in order of importance, is called *growth hormone.*

1. Growth hormone (GH) affects all body tissues, except the central nervous system and possibly the adrenal glands and the gonads. It operates at the cellular level, influencing DNA synthesis and cell multiplication. GH has been found in the blood of fetuses as young as 15 weeks. It is produced throughout life, with bursts and pauses [19]. Related to quiet

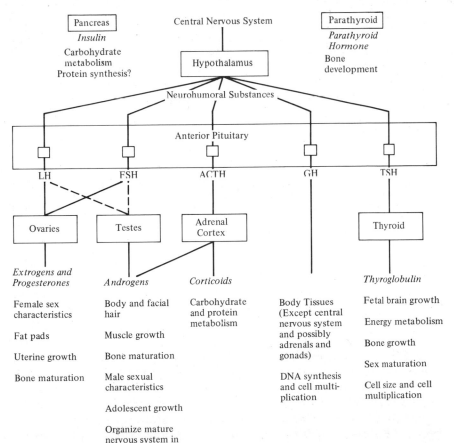

**FIGURE 13–3
Endocrine influences on development.**

sleep, GH is released soon after the onset of sleep [2]. During the puberal growth spurt, the secretion of GH is increased by 7½ times what it was during prepuberal growth.

2. Thyroid stimulating hormone (TSH) stimulates the production of *thyro-globulin* directly into the blood. The thyroid hormone is related to the growth of the fetal brain, to bone growth, sexual maturation, and to energy metabolism through its effects on cell multiplication and cell size.

3. Adrenocorticotropic hormone (ACTH), as its name implies, stimulates the production in the *adrenal cortex* of three groups of hormones, the water electrolyte hormones, the corticoids, and the androgens. The first influence water, sodium, and potassium balance in the body. The corticoids control the carbohydrate-protein balance. The androgens are produced in the adrenal glands of both sexes. They influence muscle growth, bone maturation, and adolescent growth.

4. and 5. Luteinizing hormone (LH) and follicle stimulating hormone (FSH) are the other two tropic hormones from the anterior pituitary. They stimulate the production of hormones in the gonads. In the ovary, FSH causes the secretion of *estrogens*, which produce the female sex characteristics and growth of the uterus; in the male it stimulates the tubular cells to produce sperm. The ovary responds to LH by producing *progesterones*, which bring about changes in the lining of the uterus; the testes produce androgens. Thus males have two sources of androgens, the testes and the adrenal cortex. In the postpubescent male there are, therefore, higher concentrations of androgens than in the postpubescent female. This higher concentration results in the male sexual characteristics, body and facial hair typical of males, the greater male muscle growth, and the longer duration of growth in size.

6. Parathyroid hormone affects bone development. It is, therefore, related to growth, but it is not controlled by a hormone from the anterior pituitary.

7. Insulin, also not controlled by the anterior pituitary, has to do with carbohydrate metabolism and possibly with protein synthesis. It is produced in the pancreas.

The maximum effect of GH occurs when there is some thyroglobulin present. Both of these hormones influence the growth and duplication of cells. GH and insulin have opposing and balancing effects within the body. Growth-influencing hormones, with the possible exception of GH, have feedback mechanisms that depress the secretion of the pituitary tropic hormones. Stress on the individual stimulates the production of ACTH. This mechanism results from the close linkage of the hypothalamus and the anterior pituitary.

GH was so named because its growth-promoting activity was its first discovered function. Its influence at the cellular level, and its continued presence throughout life are more recent discoveries. Still to come is the discovery of what process or mechanism dampens its effect after puberty. Of course, new cells are formed throughout life, but obviously at a replacement, not a growth, rate.

The different timings of the adolescent growth spurts of the various organs and tissues can be explained by differential sensitivity to the androgens. For instance, the sequence of appearance of pubic, axillary, and facial hair is probably caused by different thresholds of stimulation and reactivity to either adrenal or testicular androgens [45]. The skin of the pubis thus responds to the smallest increase of androgen, and grows hair in early puberty. The skin of the axilla requires a larger amount of androgen before it produces hair, and the skin of the face requires an even larger amount.

Changes in Proportions

In addition to changes in the distribution and thickness of fat, the human body changes in the ratios of linear measures to each other. The ratios change because the various bones grow at different rates, some growing longer slowly while others are growing relatively fast. One example is the Sitting Height/Stature ratio, the proportion of sitting height to standing height. The changes in average ratios for black and white boys and girls are depicted in Figure 13–4. From 6 to 12 the average ratios decrease, showing that the legs are growing faster than the upper parts of the body. There is not much difference, on the average, between boys and girls, but as is true throughout the age range shown, the legs of black children contribute slightly more than those of white children to total stature. But from 12 to 14 for girls and 13 to 15 for boys, the ratios become slowly larger, as the upper part of the body grows faster than the legs.

The ratio of hip width to shoulder width changes little from 6 to 12 years [4], although the average ratio for girls increases slightly faster than for boys. After puberty, the girls' average ratio continues to go up as the hips grow broader faster than the shoulders, but in boys the growth of the

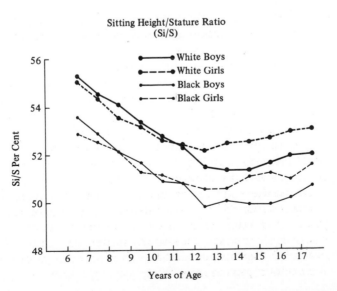

Sitting Height/Stature Ratio (Si/S)

White Boys
White Girls
Black Boys
Black Girls

Si/S Per Cent

Years of Age

FIGURE 13–4
Changes in proportions from 6 to 18 years of age, as shown by the ratio of sitting height to standing height. (SOURCE: R. M. Malina, P. V. V. Hamill, and S. Lemeshow. *Body dimensions and proportions: White and Negro children 6 to 11 years.* Data from the National Health Survey. Series 11. No. 143. DHEW publication no. (HRA) 75–1625. Washington,: U.S. Government Printing Office, 1974. P. V. V. Hamill, F. E. Johnston, and S. Lemeshow. *Body weight, stature, and sitting height: White and Negro youths 12 to 17 years.* Data from the National Health Survey. Series 11. No. 143. DHEW Publication No. (HRA) 74–1608. Washington,: U.S. Government Printing Office, 1973.)

hips slows down in the width dimension while the growth of the shoulders speeds up, thereby reducing the boys' average hip/shoulder ratio.

Puberal changes can be seen in almost every part of the body. The growth spurts of the various parts of the body do not coincide exactly with one another but are spread throughout the pubertal period. For instance, the peaks for growth in weight and head circumference come after the peaks for growth in height and hand length.

If a child grew in the way that a balloon blows up, he would keep the same proportions all the way along, but he does not. Spurting now in one measurement, now in another, he often looks different from the way he looked just a short time before. Spurts in head length and breadth makes the eyes look smaller. The nose and lower jaw grow more than other parts of the face, changing its proportions from childish toward adult. The ways in which a boy grows out of his suits are predictable, since the spurts of the various parts of the body follow a sequence. First the trouser legs become too short. If his mother can lengthen them, they will last for another four months until his hip growth makes the trousers too tight. Since chest breadth increases at the same time as hip width, a new suit is in order. It is a good idea to buy it wide in the shoulders, since the spurt in shoulder breadth comes just a few months after the spurts in chest and hip width. This suit will become too short in the jacket with the peak of growth in trunk length that comes about a year after the peak of growth in leg length. A filling-out process will make the jacket too tight just after it becomes too short, since the peak in muscle growth comes soon after the peak in trunk length. (Although boys' suits illustrate these changes better than girls' clothing, the same sequence of changes takes place in girls.)

Both boys and girls tend to worry as their feet spurt in growth. This spurt happens when the height spurt gets under way or before it [30]. The earlier it happens, of course, the larger the youngster's feet seem to him and to his family, who tend to be concerned about the frequent need for new shoes as well as about what looks like awkwardness.

Individual Differences in Proportions. Children's bodies differ in slimness, roundness, proportion of shoulder width to hip width, and in other dimensions and ratios that make one person look different from another. Many of these differences are produced by differences in the timing of growth of various bodily organs and systems. The onset of puberty is one such timing. As we shall show later, the onset of puberty is quite strongly genetic.

Linear children, those who look slim, tall, and narrow, tend to go through the sequence of puberal change later than do children of rounder shape. From the age of 2, children who will mature late weigh less for their height than children who will mature early. A late puberty allows more time for the legs to grow than does an early puberty. Consequently, the late-maturing boy or girl, already linear, increases in linearity in comparison with the early maturer.

Puberal growth spurts take place in internal organs and systems, each having its own time table.

Cardiovascular System. The cardiovascular system has been studied in terms of blood pressure, pulse rate, capacity for athletic and work effort, and recovery from work. Blood pressure rises gradually and continuously throughout childhood, adolescence, and, indeed, through the seventh decade [26]. The small sex difference, found in childhood, with the girls having higher median pressure, is reversed during adolescence [47]. During adulthood males have higher blood pressure, both systolic and diastolic. Pulse rate decreases during pubescence [26].

Respiratory System. Chest cavity and lungs increase, while rate of breathing decreases. Along with the increase in the size of the body, however, puberty brings a steady increase in the volume of air taken in. The sex difference grows in favor of boys, who develop a much larger lung capacity than girls.

The Brain. The brain spurts in weight at the same time that the whole body spurts. Head circumference spurts at around 11 and again at 15 years. Increases in girls' head circumference are about twice that of boys at ages 10–12, whereas the reverse is true at about ages 14–16 [11]. Girls' earlier puberty, then, is reflected in differences in head circumference and presumably in brain growth. There is some evidence that the spurts in brain growth at puberty are not merely part of general bodily growth, but represent some growth particular to the brain.

The puberal spurt in brain growth occurs at the same time that cognitive growth transforms concrete operations into formal thought. (The Piagetian stage of formal thought will be discussed in the following chapter.) There may be another cognitive stage corresponding to the brain growth spurt between 14 and 16. As we mentioned in Chapter 10, right and left hemispheres are specialized for various functions, such as speech in the left and spatial synthesis in the right. Two pieces of evidence suggest that adolecent girls and women are more strongly lateralized for language. First, females do better than males on several verbal tests, and second, the language area is usually in the left side of the brain. Similarly, males' superior visual-spatial and mathematical abilities, together with the fact that these functions are mainly in the right hemisphere, suggest that males are more strongly lateralized in the right side than females.

Looking for processes underlying the sex difference in spatial ability, Waber studied early-maturing and late-maturing boys and girls at two grade levels [46]. She found that late maturers, both girls and boys, performed better than early maturers on tests of spatial ability. Sex was less important than maturational rate in determining differences in spatial ability. Verbal ability was not closely related to maturational rate. This study suggest that the lateralization of the brain for spatial functions is stronger in persons who grow for a longer time before entering the puberal spurt. Because the average boy enters puberty 2 years later than the average girl, the average boy develops more spatial ability.

Ecology of Puberal Growth

Mechanisms underlying growth are strongly hereditary. The timing of the puberal growth spurt is one of these mechanisms. Its genetic nature can be shown by the degrees of similarity in menarcheal age between women of varying closeness of relationship. Average difference in menarcheal age between identical twins is 2.8 months, between fraternal twins 12.0 months, between sisters 12.9 months, and between unrelated women 18.6 months [18]. Differences in menarcheal age are also found between macrosystems and over time. In prosperous environments, children grow bigger and mature earlier than in poor ones.

Macrosystem Differences

Time of menarche differs with nutrition, hygiene, ethnicity, rural or urban status, and socioeconomic status

A cross-cultural comparison of median ages for menarche gave no evidence that menarche is directly affected by warmth of climate [18]. Both early maturers and late maturers live in hot climates. Five African groups' medians were reported in this study; they were all late in reaching menarche, with Afro-Cubans being the earliest. The three earliest median menarches were those of a black, a white, and a Chinese group.

Socioeconomic comparisons show that menarche is later at the low extreme than at the top level. Girls from the same ethnic stock can be compared under different conditions, as they were in Guatemala [39]. Girls of upper socioeconomic status menstruated at a median age slightly below 13, while girls from a lower level reached menarche at 14.5.

Differences in menarche occur between girls in rural and urban environments, menarche being earlier in the urban [45]. Higher levels of stimulation may promote earlier menarche. Another difference in all these environmental contrasts is in nutrition. When children receive nutrients in optimal amount and quality, they grow faster and mature earlier than when nutrition is less adequate. Hygiene also contributes to growth in preventing infections that interfere with growth.

The secular shift toward earlier menarche has, of course, followed the same course as the secular shift toward greater height. Records for Finland and Norway go back to 1860 and earlier. Together with more recently begun records from Europe and the United States, they show a steady drop in menarcheal age, averaging 0.3 years per decade from 1880 to 1960 [45]. The downward trend leveled during the 1960s in England and the United States, and before, in Norway. As with national and socioeconomic comparisons, secular shifts are influenced largely by nutrition and hygiene, and perhaps slightly by additional factors. Presumably, nutrition and hygiene did not advance beyond the high levels reached during the 1960s. Or it could be that levels were so adequate that genetic limits were approached, and further improvements would not be effective.

Like any period of rapid growth, puberty is a time when food needs are great, and changes must be made to accommodate transformations in all spheres of life. An important task is that of taking on responsibility for self-care.

Compared with other times of life, adolescence is less vulnerable to illness and death. Only 6 out of 10,000 persons between 12 and 17 died during a recent year. Table 13–3 shows the causes of those deaths. The

Health and Physical Problems

Illnesses

TABLE 13–3
Death Rates of Persons Aged 12 to 17 Years, United States.

Cause of death	Total	12–15 years	16–17 years
	Deaths per 10,000 persons		
All causes	6.0	4.4	9.1
Accidents and violence	4.2	2.7	7.0
Diseases and conditions	1.8	1.6	2.1
	Per cent of deaths due to specified cause		
All causes	100.0	100.0	100.0
Accidents and violence	69.9	62.5	76.8
Accidents	56.5	52.5	60.4
Motor vehicles	36.0	28.3	43.2
Fire and flames	1.6	2.2	1.0
Drowning	6.3	7.5	5.3
Suicide	5.4	4.0	6.7
Homicide	6.5	4.5	8.3
Diseases and conditions	30.1	37.5	23.2
Neoplasms	8.9	11.2	6.8
Malignant neoplasms	8.4	10.5	6.5
Leukemia	3.2	4.3	2.1
Congenital anomalies	2.5	3.4	1.6
Heart	1.3	1.7	0.8
Nervous system	3.3	4.1	2.6
Respiratory system	2.9	3.8	2.1
Pneumonia	1.8	2.3	1.3
Circulatory system	4.5	5.4	3.7
Infective and parasitic	1.4	1.9	0.9

Note: Deaths are coded according to the Eighth Revision of the International Classification Classification of Diseases Adapted for Use in the United States.

Source: M. G. Kovar. Some indicators of health-related behavior among adolescents in the United States. Public Health Reports, 1979, **94**, 109–118.

leading causes of death among adolescents, by rank, are accidents, malignant neoplasms, homicide, and suicide. The rates are lower for females than males and for whites than for nonwhites.

United States adolescents see themselves as having good health [41]. Only four in 1,000 rated their health as poor. Parents rated 4 per cent of this age group as having poor health [35]. Physical examinations showed more than 20 per cent of adolescents to have an illness, deformity, or handicap. Apparently neither parents nor children consider all of these conditions as indicating poor health. The poorer the results of the examination, however, the more likely parents were to realize that something was wrong. According to parents' reports, 72 per cent of the adolescents had had a serious illness. Although the severity of illness was the same for girls and boys, fewer girls (70 per cent) than boys (74 per cent) had had a serious illness.

Infectious Diseases. In the National Health Survey careful health histories were taken from the adolescents. Mumps, chicken pox, and measles were the most frequently reported of the childhood infectious diseases. During the years from 12 to 17 the percentages of persons reporting having had them were above 65 per cent, but did not increase with increasing age. This finding suggests that most individuals who will ever have these "childhood" diseases have them during childhood. The curves for whooping cough and scarlet fever were also almost horizontal during the teen years, but at a much lower level, between 5 and 20 per cent.

Sexually transmitted diseases pose a serious health problem in adolescence. Gonorrhea, the most common venereal infection, reached epidemic proportions in the 1970s and then stabilized [24]. According to estimates for one year, gonorrhea infected 3 out of 1,000 adolescents under 15, and 20 out of 1,000 older ones. This disease is more serious for girls than for boys, because it is more difficult to diagnose in the female and more likely to do permanent damage.

Chronic and Other Conditions. Respiratory problems were most commonly reported by teenagers in the health survey. They suffered most often from colds and also from sore throats, coughs, hay fever, and asthma. Smaller numbers had heart conditions and kidney trouble [35].

Sensory Imperfections

Glasses were worn by 35 per cent of the age group 12 to 17, a total of 8 million, according to the National Health Survey [36]. Four per cent wore contact lenses. Another 12 per cent, or 2.6 million, said that they needed to wear glasses but did not do so. Proportionately more black youth (19 per cent) than white (10 per cent) needed, but did not wear, glasses. Figure 13–5 shows percentages of boys and girls wearing glasses at each year of age from 6 to 17. Another 1.5 million between ages 12 and 17 had had eye troubles other than those corrected by lenses. Severe vi-

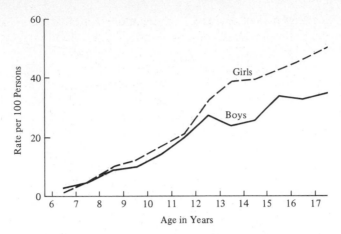

FIGURE 13-5
Girls and boys wearing corrective lenses at years from 6 to 17. (SOURCE: J. Roberts. *Eye examination findings among youths 12-17 years.* Vital and health statistics; Series 11, Data from the National Health Survey; no. 155. D.H.E.W. publication no. (HRA) 76-1637. Washington: Government Printing Office, 1975.)

12-17 years:
Worn = 35%
Needed but not
worn = 12%

12-17 years = 3.7%

Skin Problems

sual handicaps were estimated to occur at a rate between 1 and 4 per thousand.

About 934,000, or 4.1 per cent of the population from 12 to 17, have deficient color vision, 12 boys to one girl showing some defect. Red-green deficiencies were more common than blue-yellow deficiencies, affecting 6.6 per cent of boys and 0.4 per cent of girls. The affected girls were likely to have milder deficiencies than were the boys [43].

Trouble with hearing was reported for 3.7 per cent of 12- to 17-year-olds in the National Health Survey [37]. When tested for hearing, this group was found to have a higher threshold of hearing than those who reported no trouble. The most frequent abnormalities reported and found on ear examinations were earaches and running ears. Among the adolescents reporting earaches and loss of hearing, only half the cases were also reported by parents, indicating that parents were not very aware of the ear problems of their teenage children.

As children advance through the puberal growth spurt, most of them endure some facial acne. Mild cases consist mostly of blackheads. Acne is rated according to severity, the worst grade involving secondarily infected cysts, extensive distribution, and scarring. Fortunately, 60 per cent of youths afflicted with acne have the mildest type. Acne increases with age, but other skin problems remain at the same level throughout adolescence, as shown in Figure 13–6. The nonacne skin conditions include tumors, birthmarks, allergic and nutritional disorders, abnormal skin growth, injuries, infections, and others [38]. Acne is less prevalent among adolescents whose parents are more educated, among adolescents whose health was rated high, among those who rated themselves as nervous, and among those reported to eat too little rather than too much. Only 11 per cent of those bothered with acne had seen a doctor about it. It is unfortunate that acne becomes prevalent just as adolescents become more self-conscious about appearance and more concerned with establishing their identity.

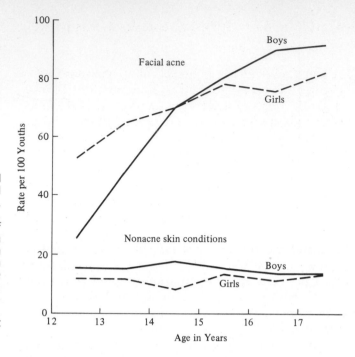

FIGURE 13–6
Percentage of boys and girls having facial acne and nonacne skin problems.
(SOURCE: J. Roberts and J. Ludford. *Skin conditions of youths.* Vital and health statistics: Series 11: Data from the National Health Survey. Data from the health examination survey; no. 157. D.H.E.W. publication; no. (HRA) 76-1639. Washington: Government Printing Office, 1976.)

Dental Problems

Dental health only gets worse as children and adults grow older, or so say the results of the National Health Survey. The average number of teeth filled, decayed, or missing in 12- to 17-year-olds is 6.2, compared with 4.4 in the previous age level, and 14.9 in young adults [23]. Periodontal disease follows the same pattern of increase. Dental deterioration can be slowed or prevented by oral hygiene, professional services, and fluoridation where natural fluorides are insufficient. Degree of oral hygiene is related to income, education, and sex [40]. Girls had cleaner teeth than boys!

Injuries

The survey of 12- to 17-year-olds found that 21.1 per cent of boys and 13.1 per cent of girls had had broken bones, 10 per cent of boys and 7.8 per cent of girls had been knocked unconscious, and 15.9 per cent of boys and 8.6 per cent of girls had had other accidents [35]. For every 100,000 15- to 19-year-olds, during one year, accidents caused the death of 88 boys and 26 girls. The totals represent 61 per cent of all male teenage deaths and 48 per cent of female [32]. As in childhood, males had many more accidents than females, probably reflecting greater activity and aggression in the male, as well as the greater restrictions placed upon the activities of females. Motor vehicle accidents were much more frequent for males than for females, 59 per 100,000 for males and 20 per 100,000 for females. Even though motor vehicles rate first as a cause of accidental deaths in the United States, the rate has declined over a 10-year period [20]. What is more, the United States ranked lowest among 11 prosperous, industrialized countries in mortality from motor accidents per 100 million vehicle-miles.

Family Violence. Teenagers, as well as younger children, are sometimes abused by parents. During one year, over half of children 10 to 14, and one-third of those from 15 to 17, were struck by their parents [15]. One-fifth of reported cases of child abuse were of teenagers. Older children are more likely than younger ones to be hurt by a knife or gun.

Violence between siblings is even more common than violence between parents and children [44]. The majority of sibling pairs fight, even those 15 years and older. Sibling violence is considered normal and acceptable by many people, even those who would call the actions abusive or criminal if they were done by and to persons who were not siblings.

Suicide. Adolescent suicide has increased rapidly in the past decade. Some of the contributing factors are very low self-esteem, failure at school, learning disabilities, loneliness, and inability to communicate [31].

Conditions related to suicide include low self-esteem, failure at school, learning disabilities, loneliness, and inability to communicate

Childbearing

Although the peak velocity of the puberal growth spurt is almost always past before conception is possible, "teenage" mothers still have some growing to do, especially the 12,000 girls between 10 and 14 who gave birth during a recent year. Nor are the 237,000 mothers between 15 and 17 fully mature [24]. The nutritional drain of pregnancy is added to the demands of their own growth. Pregnancy complications and death rates

are higher for adolescents than for mothers in their 20s. However, cross-cultural research indicates that when prenatal care is excellent, and social conditions support the pregnant teenager of 15 or older, she does as well physically as the older mother in giving birth [3].

Nutrition

Childhood nutrition affects the timing of the onset of puberty. During the growth spurt, of course, the body needs more nutrients than during the previous period of slow growth. For present growth and health it is important for adolescents to have sufficient quantities of high-quality food. For the health and growth of the next generation, it is important that girls eat the nutrients that will prepare their bodies for excellent reproductive performance. When pregnancy occurs, it is too late to repair nutritional deficiencies in the woman.

The food needs of an individual vary from time to time, with the speed of growth and the amount of energy expended. At the height of the puberal growth spurt, an adolescent may feel hungry very frequently. Unless he eats often, a fast-growing boy's stomach may be too small to hold all the food he needs.

Table 13–4 shows amounts of calories and proteins consumed by boys and girls, in terms of a standard used by the government team that analyzed the findings of a dietary survey [1]. The authors say that the standard does not necessarily represent exact requirements and that its use is in comparing groups. The table shows that girls receive relatively fewer calories and proteins than boys. This finding confirms the conviction of some nutritionists that teenage boys are more adequately nourished than girls. Recently accumulated evidence, however, indicates that the energy requirements of adolescents have decreased [9]. Teengers have become more sedentary during the years from 1947 through 1979. It takes fewer calories to ride on the school bus and to sit in front of a television set than to walk to and from school and to play games outdoors.

TABLE 13–4
Mean Calorie and Protein Intake of Boys and Girls Age 12 to 17, Expressed as a Percentage of Standard Requirements

| | Intake of nutrients, Percent of standard | | | |
| | Boys | | Girls | |
	Age 12–14	Age 15–17	Age 12–14	Age 15–17
Calories	82	85	73	69
Protein	158	154	120	99

Source: S. Abraham, M. D. Carroll, C. M. Dresser and C. L. Johnson. Dietary intake findings, United States, 1971–1974. Vital and health statistics; Series 11, Data from the National Health Survey; no. 202. (DHEW publication No. (HRA) 77-1647.) Washington: U.S. Government Printing Office, 1977.

Vegetarianism. Although vegetarian diets can be adequate, it takes careful planning to provide adequate protein and other nutrients. Certain vegetarian cults expose their followers to physical dangers. The Vegan diet does not supply enough vitamin B_{12}, but its effects may be masked by folic acid until irreparable damage has been done to the spinal cord [12]. The Zen macrobiotic diet may lead to scurvy, anemia, starvation, and kidney failure. Some of the adolescents who have been damaged by these diets have accepted nutritional counseling. Few lay people know enough about nutrition to provide an adequate diet within severe restrictions, but nutritionists can help them to do so.

Obesity. Being overweight is likely to be a psychological hazard as well as a serious physical liability to the adolescent. The causes and treatment of excess fat are complex. The fat adolescent may be expressing a genetic potential, in that the child of two obese parents has an 80 per cent chance of being too fat. With one obese parent, the child's chances of being fat drop to 40 per cent [48]. Of course, environmental factors are no doubt at work here, also. Some fat adolescents have been destined for obesity since infancy, when they grew more than the normal number of fat cells. The peak periods for the onset of obesity are late infancy, early childhood, and adolescence. There is evidence from animal studies to suggest that later onset arises from the enlarging of fat cells, rather than from growing new fat cells. The effects of poverty have been observed to differ between the sexes. In males, poverty is likely to result in thin children and thin adults but in females, the result tends to be thin children and fat adults. Affluence is more likely to produce heavy girls and slim women.

Weight reduction is as complex as are the reasons for obesity. Some studies suggest that obese adolescents eat no more than their normal peers, but they exercise less and are more likely to eat when they are bored rather than when hungry. However, a recent observational study in homes found fat adolescents eating more than nonobese teenagers. The role of exercise in adolescent obesity is not clear [17]. Although the attention of a specialist may be required by some fat adolescents, others have been helped to achieve normal weight by diet control, increased exercise, and psychological support. Clubs, camps, and other groups are often successful in providing the right combination of guidance and support. Since fat children are likely to be rejected and to suffer discrimination, it is important to give them adequate help.

Drug Use

A World Health Organization study group concluded that drugs are being taken earlier at all ages and that more and more people are trying dependency-producing drugs [50]. Physical and mental health problems arise from this world-wide tendency of youth to use chemical substances to induce changes in body and mind.

TABLE 13–5
Current Use of and Lifetime
Experience with Selected
Drugs, Youth aged 12 to 17

Drugs	Per cent ever used	Per cent current use
Alcohol	54	31
Cigarettes	48	23
Marihuana/hashish	29	16
Inhalants	9	1
Hallucinogens	5	2
Other opiates	5	1
Cocaine	3	1
Heroin	1	less than 1

Source: I. Cisin, J. D. Miller, and A. V. Harrell. *Highlights from the National Survey on Drug Abuse: 1977.* National Institute on Drug Abuse. (DHEW publication No. (ADM) 78-620.) Washington: U.S. Government Printing Office, 1978.

Table 13–5 shows results from a United States national survey on drug abuse [5]. The table indicates percentages of 12- to 17-year-olds who have ever used selected drugs, and percentages currently using them. Alcohol and cigarettes, both legal, are used more than any other drug. Cigarettes were formerly used more by teenage boys than by teenage girls, but in 1979, boys' smoking had decreased and girls' had increased to the point where girls' smoking exceeded boys' [49]. Marihuana use is approaching the frequency of the use of legal drugs. Among those who had ever used marihuana were 11 per cent of 12- to 14-year-olds and 42 per cent of 15- to 17-year-olds. Five per cent of the younger ones were current users, and 28 per cent of the older youth. Drug experience and use expanded greatly in the next age level, 18 to 21 [5].

Although hallucinogens, opiates, and inhalants may be more damaging to their users than alcohol, cigarettes, and marihuana, the latter three affect many more adolescents than the former group. Research, prevention, and treatment are, of course, needed in relation to all of these drugs. All have negative effects on physical and mental health. Although some individuals stop using a drug, many continue when once they have started.

Ecology of Health Care

All levels of the ecology contribute to the maintenance of adolescent health, the structuring of problems, and the solution of problems.

Macrosystem Influences

The macrosystem structures adolescence itself and consequently the problems of the period. Where adolescence is nonexistent, and completion of puberal growth brings adulthood, then there is no such thing as adolescent pregnancy. When adolescence is long and arrival at adulthood a vague point, defined in various ways, then the possibilities for problems are extensive. The values of the macrosystem create certain problems. For example, being a fat girl is difficult in the United States, but not in some West African macrosystems, where plumpness is desired in a bride. The health problems of injuries, sexual activity, and drug use will be discussed in relation to macrosystems.

Injuries. Violence, whether accidental or intentional, is related to attitudes and beliefs about the use of force. Injuries are more likely in macrosystems that support beliefs such as these: Everyone has the right to carry a gun; a real man fights physically for his rights; parents have the right to hit their children; it is all right to exceed the speed limit if a policeman does not see you. Such beliefs influence the amount of violence people use.

Control of violence depends to some extent on laws and their enforcement. The decrease in motor vehicle deaths (mentioned earlier) is thought to result from more stringent traffic laws, better enforced. Similarly, drownings are less frequent off supervised beaches than where lifeguards and regulations are lacking. Because beliefs about violence vary within the United States, laws regulating gun use and family violence are subjects of controversy.

The physical setting of a macrosystem also influences type and frequency of injuries. New Zealand, for example, provides bountifully for playgrounds, but its ski slopes are prone to avalanches, its dark, thick forests are easy to get lost in, and its many miles of lonely beaches offer dangerous swimming.

Sexual Acitivity. Adolescent sexual activity is promoted by a macrosystem that emphasizes sex and permits boys and girls to be together unsupervised. In the United States sexual themes are prominent in television, movies, advertising, and books. Coeducation is usual. Chaperones went out when the automobile came in. By drawing children's attention to sex and then letting them follow their impulses, the United States has achieved the highest rate of teenage pregnancies of any prosperous country. In contrast, sex is regarded as powerful and important in India, but boys and girls are usually segregated in school and watched over by adults when together. Pregnancy and disease could still be largely prevented even though sexual activity is encouraged by the media and permitted by offering opportunities. Children could be educated about reproduction, contraception, and prophylaxis, and provided with birth control services. This topic will be discussed further in Chapter 15.

If sexual desires are to be stimulated, sexual activity permitted, and pregnancies not prevented, the health of pregnant girls could still be improved by a careful program of nutritional care during childhood and the puberal growth spurt, in addition to extensive care in pregnancy. There are already government programs that seek to provide nutritional supplementation and adolescent prenatal care. Programs must draw upon educational and medical institutions to succeed widely.

Drugs. Ideology, laws, and law enforcement are all pertinent to the way in which everyone, including children and youth, will use drugs. As

Table 13–5 showed, legal drugs are used by many more people than are illegal ones. The more commonplace a drug seems, the more it is likely to be used. A social climate conducive to drug use (or any other behavior) is one in which friends and acquaintances use the drug (or perform the activity) and in which opportunities for doing so are prevalent. Over a 15-year period, United States teenagers increased steadily in acquaintanceship with users of marihuana [5]. Opportunities for using marihuana also increased steadily.

Some macrosystem conflicts or countertrends can be seen in the ideology of cigarette smoking. Since the medical dangers of smoking have become clear, nonsmokers have proclaimed their right to clean air and those who hate smoke have found the courage to say so. Nonsmokers have launched an ideological offensive. Through the Surgeon General's office, official advice in 1964 to Americans was to avoid smoking. The Surgeon General's report of 1979, based on 30,000 studies, confirms and extends the judgment that smoking causes illness and death [34]. Research with prevention has given new leads for dealing with teenagers. Adolescents, therefore, are exposed to a variety of beliefs and practices: the media, peers, and relatives who promote smoking versus nonsmokers and prevention programs. Similarly with drinking, strong antialcohol programs provide counter-ideology to the social climate that promotes the use of alcohol.

Microsystem Influences

Adolescents make many or most of the decisions that determine their own health. Those decisions are influenced by the important microsystems of family, school, peer groups, and perhaps jobs. For example, teenagers are more likely to use alcohol and illegal drugs if their mothers smoke cigarettes, drink even moderately and/or have ever used a psychotherapeutic drug even under a doctor's prescription [5]. Teenagers are more likely to smoke if their friends smoke. A later chapter is devoted to the complex and important topics of adolescent sexuality, values, and relationships with parents and peers. The creation and outcome of health problems described in this chapter are better understood in terms of the adolescent's interactions in home, school, and other microsystems.

Motor Development

At the point of entering the puberal growth spurt, children have accumulated experience, skills, and interests in many motor coordinations. They know how to perform the fundamental motor tasks of running, jumping, balancing, and throwing, although they will continue to improve in these skills throughout adolescence, especially those who train and practice. Adolescents build on what they have already achieved, according to their interests and to the opportunities offered them.

Exercise can be used to promote health and excellent physical development. Fitness is measured by performance tests and by physiological measures, such as heart rate and oxygen intake [6]. Health-related aspects of fitness include endurance, flexibility, strength, and muscular endurance. Skill-related aspects are agility, reaction time, balance, coordination, and speed. When adolescents improve in fitness, their self-concepts also improve [28].

Endurance. Stamina or endurance refers to being able to keep up an activity for a considerable length of time. Endurance is developed by muscles and also by the circulatory system. For example, hopping tests the endurance of feet and leg muscles, whereas running a mile requires considerable endurance from the circulatory and respiratory systems, as well as from feet and leg muscles and other muscles [7, p. 90]. Analysis of cardiovascular endurance has shown that at least eight measurable factors are involved, including such conditions as velocity and force of heart ejection stroke, vagus tone, pulse rate in the quiet state and after moderate exercise, and blood pressure adjustment to hard work. Thus, stamina and its improvement can be measured not only by noting how long a person can keep at a given activity but also by the use of laboratory measurements.

Endurance is developed through an overall program of optimal nutrition and adequate rest, combined with cycled activities, monitored and adjusted to fit the growing stamina of the individual. During the puberal growth spurt, boys develop larger hearts and lungs and more red blood cells than girls do [45]. Systolic blood pressure becomes higher and resting heart rate lower in boys. These sex differences make for greater endurance during heavy exercise in boys.

Strength. As they enter puberty, boys and girls are very similar in strength [45]. Strength normally increases during the puberal period and in boys during the postpuberal period [13]. Boys gain even more strength after puberty than they do during the spurt in height. Both girls and boys have a puberal spurt in muscle growth, but it is higher in boys [45]. Not only do boys have more muscle, but it is likely that male adolescent muscle tissue is stronger than female. Sex differences in proportions, especially the shoulder-hip ratio and the greater length of male limbs, also contribute to greater strength in the mature male. The timing of strength gain, as well as the amount, is different between the sexes. Boys' apex of strength increase consistently comes after apex of gain in height and weight; girls' apex of strength gain is quite variable in timing [13]. Therefore in planning a fitness program for boys, an instructor can know quite well what to expect in strength gain, according to a boy's puberal development, whereas a physical education program for girls would have to be more flexible.

Skills. Physical education and training, along with puberal growth, make for improvement in specific motor skills and in the sports and games that use the skills. To strength and endurance must be added flexibility, agility, balance, coordination, reaction time, and speed. Body movement is also used to express emotion, to communicate feelings, to cooperate with the movements and aims of others. Although the competitive side of sports and games is often emphasized, there is also a cooperative side of team play and group performances.

In the many qualities needed for motor skills, men have some advantages, including strength and endurance, and women others, such as expressiveness, flexibility, balance, precision, delicacy and speed of small movements. Differences between individuals are greater than differences between the averages of the sexes. There are some women who are stronger than the average man; certain men are more flexible and expressive than the average woman. Instead of expecting only some skills in women and others in men, it would benefit both sexes if wide opportunities for skill development were open to everyone, regardless of sex.

Macrosystem Influences

Two great changes have taken place in the climate for motor development in the United States. Interest in health and fitness have spurted. Changes in woman's role have opened opportunities in athletics to women.

In the 1950s American boys and girls between 10 and 18 were compared with British, Swiss, Austrian, Italian, Swedish, Japanese, and others in various measures of fitness and athletic performance [7]. United States children showed up very poorly on almost all measures. Girls made little or no improvement after puberty in body strength and running, although British girls did so. President Eisenhower took an interest, through his Youth Fitness Council and Citizens' Advisory Committee. The media cooperated and the nation was deluged with publicity about physical fitness. President Kennedy supported and extended fitness programs. Adults became interested in their own fitness, as well as in children's. Private and public programs multiplied.

The Women's Movement focused attention on all sorts of situations in which women did not have equal opportunities with men. Athletics was one of these. Girls and parents began to ask that girls have equal chance at team sports, even when it meant playing on teams with boys. High school athletic budgets were shattered and readjusted to provide space and equipment for girls that would be fair to them. The poor showing of girls on the cross-national comparisons during the 1950s was obviously related to lack of opportunity for fitness training and participation in sports. There were other reasons, too, that lay in the macrosystem beliefs, the stereotypes of male and female roles.

Bias can be seen in the events that were selected for comparisons between male and female: pullups, situps, shuttle run, standing broad jump, softball throw, 50-yard dash, 600-yard run-walk. These events require strength and endurance, in which boys have the advantage. The stan-

dards were largely male standards, and the early excellent fitness programs were male.

Today, with greater equality and cooperation between the sexes, there are broader opportunities for choice and participation in athletics. Although football and hockey, traditional male sports, are still popular, tennis has gained enormously, as have gymnastics and figure skating, all sports in which women can do well. Noncompetitive jogging and swimming are also gaining participants.

Physical-Psychological Relationships

Growth and health affect the adolescent's concept of self. The young person must come to terms with a new body, updating the body image, its boundaries and powers, its beauty or ugliness, its continuity with the childish body that it used to be. In the process of adjusting body image, face image, and feelings about them, the teenager makes comparisons with peers and with ideals. Attempts to make a better appearance include diets, cosmetics, beauty treatments, exercise programs, and peer-approved clothing.

Stereotypes of Body Build

Boys between 10 and 20 years showed certain expectations of various male physical types, in their ratings of photographs [25]. On a list of desirable characteristics, such as leadership, popularity, not smoking, and enduring pain, strong, athletic-looking boys were rated highest. Stereotypes associated with other physical types, such as skinny or fat, are generally negative. Thus, the nonpreferred type of boy (and girl, too) may have the destructive experience of low expectations from peers.

Effects of Illness on Body Image

The body image includes internal, as well as external structures. Even if a person has never seen a liver or a lung, he may have some notion of how it looks. In a children's hospital, teenagers discussed their illnesses and drew pictures of them [22]. Their explanations and descriptions bore

some relation to reality and also revealed their feelings and imaginings. A 15-year-old diabetic boy drew a normal pancreas as an oval and then drew his own, as an oval with half deleted. He believed that a portion of his pancreas was missing, that it had been violently broken away from him. The painting shown in Figure 13–7 is the work of a 13-year-old boy who was being treated for eye lacerations. In some cases, the drawings showed the patient's ideas of how his health could be restored and with it, his self-esteem. Studies such as this give clues as to how to help adolescents deal with the psychological trauma of illness.

Early and Late Maturity

Puberty brings new feelings about the self, as well as new attitudes in other people who relate to the maturing child-adolescent. The nature of these feelings has been a topic of interest ever since puberal growth has been studied. Special interest is aroused by the question of feelings and behavior connected with early and late puberty.

The first studies of early-maturing boys and girls indicated that, compared with their less mature peers, they were healthier in personality and had greater prestige with peers [10]. An Australian study, done two decades later, found no relationship between physical maturity and esteem of peers [16]. An American study found more negative self-concepts in early adolescent girls than in boys [33]. A British study showed that early-maturing girls had more negative attitudes toward school than did late developers [8]. If these findings seem to conflict, they are more understandable in the light of Simmons' study of adolescent self-esteem under different conditions of school and social life [42]. Children were followed from sixth into seventh grade in two types of schools. In each year, children were interviewed to establish measures of self-esteem and examined to judge puberal status. The greatest loss in self-esteem occurred in girls who experienced three changes at about the same time: reaching menarche, going from elementary to junior high school, and beginning dating. Of all three conditions, going to the junior high school (rather than continuing to eighth grade in the elementary school) had the most depressing effect on a girl's self-esteem. Girls increased in self-esteem if they stayed in the same school. For boys, type of school had no effect, but reaching puberty elevated their self-esteem. From this study it can be seen that the social environment modifies the effect of puberty, whether it be early or late. What is more, even though the physical environment is the same (the junior high school), the social environment may differ for boys and girls. In other words, social interactions differ for individuals in a microsystem, even though the setting is the same for all.

Summary

The sequence of puberal changes and the changes themselves occur in children everywhere and in all times, transforming them into adults. The sequence has been described in detail for primary and secondary sex characteristics, providing a method of estimating an individual's progression through puberty. Menarche usually occurs after the apex of the spurt of growth in height. Because of the variation in timing of spurt in velocity of height and weight growth, height and weight tables are of marginal use with adolescents. All organs and systems spurt in growth, having patterns peculiar to themselves. Puberal growth is initiated and controlled by the hypothalamus, which links the nervous and endocrine systems.

Many sex differences in appearance, abilities, and behavior can be traced to differences in growth patterns during the puberal period. The brain, as well as the rest of the body, is affected by sex-related growth.

The timing of the changes varies between individuals, sexes, ethnic groups, socioeconomic levels, and historic periods.

Although the timing and patterning of puberal growth is strongly genetic, ecological influences can be seen. Puberty, as indicated by menarche, is earlier in prosperous times and places, probably through the direct influence of nutrition and hygiene.

Although adolescents are unlikely to die, or even to be ill, they do have special health problems, one of which is taking over responsibility for self-care. Accidents pose the greatest threat to life and limb. Problems with skin, eyes, and teeth have implications for self-image, as well as for health. Health problems resulting from sexual activity are childbearing and diseases, both of which have psychological and social ramifications as well. Drug use is damaging to health in the present and future.

The macrosystem defines adolescence and structures its problems. The special problems of sexual activity, drug use, and violence can be traced to roots in the macrosystem. Contributions to solutions can also be found there. Microsystems are the settings in which individual adolescents develop and solve their problems.

Puberal growth leads to increased resources for motor behavior, as well as to greater differentiation between the sexes. Strength, endurance, and skills can be increased and enhanced by physical education and fitness programs. Although males have had a more favorable environment for motor development, ideological and legal changes have resulted in more equality of opportunity for girls and boys. Puberty requires a reorientation to self and others, which varies under different circumstances, and differently for boys and girls.

References

1. Abraham, S., M. D. Carroll, C. M. Dresser, and C. L. Johnson. *Dietary intake findings.* Vital and health statistics; series 11, Data from the National Health Survey; no. 202. (DHEW publication No. (HRA) 77-1647.) Washington: U.S. Government Printing Office, 1977.

2. Anders, T. Biological rhythms in human development. Paper presented at meetings of the Society for Research in Child Development, Boston, 1981.

3. Baldwin, W., and V. S. Cain. The children of teenage parents. *Family Planning Perspectives,* 1980, **12:**1, 34–43.

4. Bayer, L. M., and N. Bayley. *Growth diagnosis.* Chicago: University of Chicago Press, 1959.

5. Cisin, I., J. D. Miller, and A. V. Harrell. *Highlights from the National Survey on Drug Abuse: 1977.* (DHEW publication No. (ADM) 78-620.) Washington: U.S. Government Printing Office, 1978.

6. Corbin, C. B. (ed.). *A textbook of motor development.* Dubuque, Iowa: William C. Brown Company, Publishers, 1973.

7. Cureton, T. K. Improving the physical fitness of youth. *Monographs of the Society for Research in Child Development,* 1964, **29:**4.

8. Davis, B. Attitudes toward school among early and late maturing adolescent girls. *Journal of Genetic Psychology,* 1977, **131,** 261–266.

9. Dwyer, J. Nutrition requirements of teenagers. Paper presented at meeting of the Society for Research in Child Development, Boston, 1981.

10. Eichorn, D. Biological correlates of behavior. In J. Kagan and C. Spiker (eds.). *Child pshychology.* The 62nd Yearbook of the National Society for the Study of Education, Part I. Chicago: University of Chicago Press, 1963.

11. Epstein, H. D. Growth spurts during brain development: Implications for educational policy and practice. In J. S. Chall and A. F. Mirsky (eds.). *Education and the brain.* The 77th Yearbook of the National Society for the Study of Education. Chicago: University of Chicago Press, 1978.

12. Erhard, D. The new vegetarians. *Nutrition Today,* 1973, **8:**6, 4–12.

13. Faust, M. S. Somatic development of adolescent girls. *Monographs of the Society for Research in Child Development,* 1977, **42:**1.

14. Garn, S. M., and J. A. Haskell. Fat thickness and developmental status in childhood and adolescence. *American Journal of Diseases of Children,* 1960, **99,** 746–751.

15. Gelles, R. S. Violence toward children in the United States. *American Journal of Orthopsychiatry,* 1978, **48,** 580–592.

16. Harper, J., and J. K. Collins. The effects of early or late maturation on the prestige of the adolescent girl. *Australian and New Zealand Journal of Sociology,* 1972, **8:**2, 83–88.

17. Heald, F. Obesity: An update. Paper presented at meeting of the Society for Research in Child Development, Boston, 1981.
18. Hiernaux, J. Ethnic differences in growth and development. *Eugenics Quarterly*, 1968, **15**, 12–21.
19. *How children grow.* Clinical Research Advances in Human Growth and Development. (DHEW publication No. (NIH) 72–166.) Washington: U.S. Government Printing Office, 1972.
20. International variations in mortality from motor vehicle accidents. *Statistical Bulletin*, 1979, **60**:2, 9–11.
21. Johnston, F. E., P. V. V. Hamill, and S. Lemeshow. *Skinfold thickness of youths 12–17 years, United States.* Vital and health statistics; series 11, Data from the National Health Survey; no. 132. (DHEW publication No. (HRA) 74–1614.) Washington: U.S. Government Printing Office, 1974.
22. Kaufman, R. V. Body-image changes in physically ill teen-agers. *Journal of the American Academy of Child Psychiatry*, 1972, **11**, 57–70.
23. Kelly, J. E., and C. R. Harvey. *Basic dental examination findings of persons 1–74 years.* Vital and health statistics: Series 11, Data from the National Health Survey; no. 214. (DHEW publication No. (PHS) 79–1662.) Washington: U.S. Government Printing Office, 1979.
24. Kovar, M. G. Some indicators of health-related behavior among adolescents in the United States. *Public Health Reports*, 1979, **94**, 109–118.
25. Lerner, R. M. The development of stereotyped expectancies of body-build-behavior relations. *Child Development*, 1969, **40**, 137–141.
26. Lowrey, G. H. *Growth and development of children.* 6th ed. Chicago: Year Book Medical Publishers, Inc., 1973.
27. McGowan, T. H., II. Marihuana: The grass may no longer be greener. *Science*, 1974, **185**, Aug. 23, 683–684.
28. McGowan, R. W., B. O. Jarman, and D. M. Pedersen. Effects of a competitive endurance training program on self-concept and peer approval. *Journal of Psychology*, 1969, **39**, 27–39.
29. MacMahon, B. *Age at menarche, United States.* Vital and health statistics; series 11, Data from the National Health Survey; no. 133. (DHEW publication No. (HRA) 74–1615.) Washington: U.S. Government Printing Office, 1973.
30. Meredith, H. V. Human foot length from embryo to adult. *Human Biology*, 1944, **16**, 207–282.
31. Morgan, L. Suicide now No. 3 cause of teenage deaths. *Providence Evening Bulletin*, March 5, 1980.
32. Mortality from accidents by age and sex. *Statistical Bulletin*, 1971, **52**:5, 6–9.
33. Offer, D., and K. I. Howard. An empirical analysis of the Offer self-image questionnaire for adolescents. *Archives of General Psychiatry*, 1972, **27**, 529–533.
34. Pinney, J. M. The largest preventable cause of death in the United States. *Public Health Reports*, 1979, **94**, 107–108.
35. Roberts, J. *Examination and health history findings among children and youths, 6–17 years, United States.* Vital and health statistics; Series 11, Data from the National Health Survey; no. 129. (DHEW publication No. (PHS) 74–1611.) Washington: U.S. Government Printing Office, 1973.
36. Roberts, J. *Eye examination findings among youths aged 12–17 years, United States.* Vital and health statistics: Series 11, Data from the National Health Survey; no. 155. (DHEW publication No. (HRA) 76–1637.) Washington: U.S. Government Printing Office, 1975.
37. Roberts, J. and E. M. Ahuja. *Hearing sensitivity and related medical findings among youths 12–17 years, United States.* Vital and health statistics: Series 11, Data from the National Health Survey; no. 154. (DHEW publication No. (HRA) 76–1636.) Washington: U.S. Government Printing Office, 1975.

38. Roberts, J., and J. Ludford. *Skin conditions of youths, United States.* Vital and health statistics; Series 11, Data from the National Health Survey; no. 157. (DHEW publication No. (HRA) 76–1639.) Washington: U.S. Government Printing Office, 1976.

39. Sabharwal, K. P., S. Morales, and J. Mendes. Body measurements and creatinine excretion among upper and lower socio-economic groups of girls in Guatemala. *Human Biology,* 1966, **38,** 131–140.

40. Sanchez, M. J. *Oral hygiene among youths 12–17 years, United States.* Vital and health statistics: Series 11, Data from the National Health Survey; no. 151. (DHEW publication No. (HRA) 76–1633.) Washington: U.S. Government Printing Office, 1975.

41. Scanlon, J. *Self-reported health behavior and attitudes of youths 12–17 years, United States.* Vital and health statistics; Series 11, Data from the National Health Survey; no. 147. (DHEW publication No. (HRA) 75–1629.) Washington: U.S. Government Printing Office, 1975.

42. Simmons, R. G., D. A. Blyth, E. F. Van Cleave, and D. M. Bush. Entry into early adolescence: The impact of school structure, puberty, and early dating on self-esteem. *American Sociological Review,* 1979, **44,** 948–967.

43. Slaby, D., and J. Roberts. *Color vision deficiencies in youths.* Data from the National Health Survey, Series 11, No. 134. (DHEW Publication No. (HRA) 74–1616. Washington: U.S. Government Printing Office, 1974.

44. Steinmetz, S. K. Investigating family violence. *Journal of Home Economics,* 1980, **72:**2, 32–36.

45. Tanner, J. M. *Fetus into man: Physical growth from conception to maturity.* Cambridge, Mass.: Harvard University Press, 1978.

46. Waber, D. P. Sex differences in mental abilities, hemispheric lateralization, and rate of physical growth at adolescence. *Developmental Psychology,* 1977, **13,** 29–38.

47. Weiss, N. S., P. V. V. Hamill, and T. Drizd. *Blood pressure levels of children 6–11 years: Relationship to age, sex, race, and socio-economic status, United States.* Vital and health statistics; Series 11, Data from the National Health Survey; no. 135. (DHEW publication No. (HRA) 74–1617.) Washington: U.S. Government Printing Office, 1973.

48. Winick, M. Childhood obesity. *Nutrition Today,* 1974, **9:** 3, 6–12.

49. Women catch up on lung cancer rates. *New York Times,* Jan. 20, 1980.

50. *Youth and drugs.* Technical Report Series, No. 516. World Health Organization, 1973.

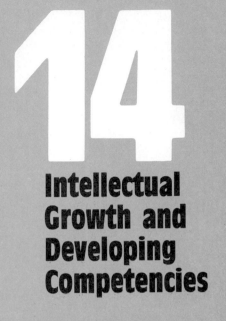

14

Intellectual Growth and Developing Competencies

As a thinker, the adolescent has some special characteristics. Compared with the school-age thinker, the teenager is more powerful, controlled, and logical. Piaget and his colleagues call adolescent intellectual development the stage of *formal thought* or *logical operations*. Other approaches to understanding the adolescent's mind include measuring a variety of mental abilities, studying creativity, and examining cognitive processes.

Thinking and other mental abilities are, of course, used vocationally when a person holds a job and carries on a work career. In this chapter we discuss not only adolescent intellectual characteristics, but the relation of intelligence and other personal characteristics and experience to moral and vocational development.

QUESTIONS TO THINK
ABOUT WHILE READING
THIS CHAPTER

1. In what ways does adolescent thinking differ from that of school-age children?
2. What is the meaning of freedom in thinking?
3. Which processes are increasingly controlled as thinking matures?
4. How can formal operations be tested?
5. How do macrosystems limit development of formal operations?
6. What are some dimensions of cognitive style?
7. What is the present secular shift in language learning?
8. Are there real sex differences in mental development and behavior?
9. How does Hogan's theory of moral development differ from Kohlberg's?
10. How do education, ability, and experience contribute to vocational development?
11. How does the social ecology influence education and vocational development?

Characteristics of Adolescent Thinking

Compared with elementary school children, high school students can do more difficult work in all the school subjects. Their vocabularies are larger. They know more facts. They deal with mathematical and scientific problems that younger children cannot solve. The following are ways in which adolescent thinking is more mature than school-age thinking.

The teenager can process information faster than the child. Not only does reaction time (time taken to react to a stimulus) decrease with age, but time required to make a decision about information also decreases. For example, boys between 4 and 18 years were asked to make judgments as to whether tones were high or low [48]. Five-year-olds took 3 times as long as 17-year-olds to process one bit of information. If this result applies to the usual thinking of children and adolescents, it is easy to see why teenagers can do all sorts of mental work faster than children.

Having lived longer than a child, an adolescent has more to remember. More information and experiences are stored in his mind. And as the adolescent stores an item in his memory, he can make more elaborate connections with what is already stored there, giving the item more meaning, and making it easier to retrieve. Not only does the teenager have more information, he can think of more ways of retrieving stored information and can retrieve it better, thus making more use of his memories. A number of studies have shown that younger children are able to retrieve information from memory when given strategies for doing so, and that those strategies are used spontaneously by older children or teenagers without any suggestions being given to them. An example of such a study is one by Keniston and Flavell [23], in which subjects in grades 1, 3, 7, and college were asked to write letters and numbers on cards, and then were asked to remember which numbers and letters they had and had not written. Older subjects more often thought of using the alphabet as a strategy for ordering the letters for recall. When instructed to use the alphabet, however, nearly all of the first-graders gave a perfect performance, showing that they were able to use the strategy just as well as adolescents.

Each new stage in thinking brings greater freedom and stronger control in intellectual operations. The infant is confined to her own sensory perceptions and motor acts of the present. The preschool child uses words and symbols to represent actions and perceptions, thus speeding up her dealings with the world, but she is still dealing with individual objects and events. Egocentric in being tied to one perception or another, her thought is not free and mobile enough to weigh and balance various aspects of an experience with each other and with other knowledge. The school-age child's thought is free in that she can delay response while considering and judging much information. She can also think an act and then think it undone, for thought is reversible at this age. The adolescent can think in terms of abstract symbols, instead of having to base thought on concrete things and events. She is thus freed from restraints of time and space, able to range throughout the universe, entertaining concepts with which she has had no real experience, such as the notion of infinity.

Speed

Memory

Freedom

Thinking About What Is Possible. A child thinks mostly about the present situation, the immediate future, practical problems, and concrete reality; an adolescent thinks about all this plus possibilities, how things could be different, what might be, and the relation between the real and the possible.

Child describes —Adolescent explains

Making and Testing Hypotheses. A child is likely to describe a phenomenon and then to think that he has explained it correctly. When he makes a hypothesis, he assumes that it is true, because he thinks it comes from the data rather than from his own mind [31]. If challenged, he fits the data to the hypothesis, rather than the hypothesis to the data. An adolescent seeks further for causes, and makes the explanation more tentative, making it a hypothesis rather than a statement of fact. A hypothesis can be tested and changed to fit as new facts are revealed or discovered. For example, take the physics experiment of boiling water in a tin, sealing, and cooling the tin. The child will describe the collapse of the tin. The adolescent is more likely to try to explain what he saw, relating it to a vacuum being produced and atmospheric pressure acting on the tin. He will attempt to make as complete an explanation as he can, possibly using concepts of boiling, gaseous state, condensation, vacuum, pressure, and strength. Then he may test the explanation by varying the conditions he thinks relevant.

Metacognition: Thinking About Thinking. As we have already shown, children can think about their own mental activities. Adolescents, however, think much more about their own cognitive and affective processes, and about the thoughts and feelings of others. When 12-year-olds think about other people's thinking, they often infer that the person is thinking about the objects and actions of the concrete world. A 16-year-old is more likely to infer that the person is thinking about thinking [2].

According to Elkind, thinking about thinking enables an adolescent to construct an imaginary audience for himself [12]. He gets the feeling of being the focus of attention, being on-stage. When he is critical of himself, he imagines his audience as critical, also. When he is self-admiring, his audience admires him. He often imagines other people as having thoughts that they do not have and that are, in reality, his own. Herein lies the basis of egocentrism in adolescence: failing to distinguish between his own thoughts, feelings, and wishes and those of others. The loud, show-off, faddish behavior of an adolescent group is easier to understand when one realizes that every member is both actor and audience. The ability to imagine the thoughts of others is also the basis for the sense of intimacy, which develops in late adolescence. As the adolescent differentiates more and more between other people's thoughts and his own, he interprets theirs more realistically.

Another result of confusing his own thoughts with those of other people is that he develops magnificent ideas about how society can and should be improved. He assumes that his fellow citizens want these improvements and makes vague plans for his own future that encompass the changes. Thus, he does not distinguish between his own point of view as a person organizing his future and the point of view of the social group to which he belongs [21, pp. 343–345]. The confusion disappears gradually as the young person assumes adult roles, especially the work role in a real job. When he meets the realities of dealing with the society that he has considered reforming, he learns the difference between what he can actually do, what he wishes could happen, and what society wants.

This special kind of adolescent thinking is very enduring in Western culture. Adults expect young people to be idealistic and impractical in their dreams of remaking the world. There is general belief that this type of thought has value for both the adolescent and society, in opening up possibilities for his future development and for social innovations.

The young adolescent often regards himself, particularly his feelings, as very special and unique [11]. His imaginary audience probably contributes to this notion. Sometimes the conviction of personal uniqueness results in a "personal fable," expressed in a very private diary, a personal relationship with God, a belief that one cannot die or that one cannot become pregnant. The personal fable, along with grandiose schemes for improving society, is gradually transformed into more manageable proportions. As the adolescent differentiates the thoughts of others from his own, he also becomes able to regard his own thinking more objectively. As thought grows more mobile and flexible, he can stand off and look at himself as a person. He can consider himself as a physical specimen, as a person-among-persons, as an intelligent being or as a person in any one of the numerous roles he plays—son, friend, sweetheart, student, and so on. He sees himself as a person-in-relation.

Self-cognition makes it possible for the adolescent to see himself as continuous with the child he once was, how he differs and how he is the same. He can see his continuity with the adult that he is becoming. He can look at himself in the ways in which other people and the community see him. Integrating all of this information and all of these points of view, he strengthens his sense of identity. At the same time, he begins to grow beyond the limits of adolescent thinking as he differentiates between his own plans and hopes and those of his social groups.

Control

Along with thinking about thinking, the adolescent increases in ability to control mental processes. Control is a necessary part of planning and of logical thinking.

Planning. An adolescent can organize the ways in which she will use mental processes. We have already mentioned storing memories systematically and trying out different strategies for retrieval. These processes can be monitored and adjusted as they go along. Plans can be made for keeping attention focused on a problem and away from potentially distracting stimuli. Plans for problem solving may include orderly steps, such as gathering information, grouping, comparing, and testing hypotheses. Planning is essential to scientific experiments.

Logical thinking includes accepting premises and reasoning within the information given

Accepting Premises. Strict control of thought is required for reasoning within the information given. The adolescent can cope with problems of logic in which a set of premises is given and all necessary information contained. The premises may even be untrue when judged by other information and experience, but the adolescent can act as though they were true. Children, of course, can accept untrue premises in games, and act within them. For example, "Let's pretend that we have no hands and so we have to pick things up with our feet." Adolescents are more able to think and reason within what is given.

In her study of children's thinking, Donaldson [10] found that between 12 and 14, children increased sharply in being able and willing to accept the given conditions and to reason within them, but even the sharp increase did not mean that a child *always* reasoned formally. She tells of Robin, when faced with this problem:

> Five boys, Jack, Dick, James, Bob and Tom go to five different schools in the same town. The schools are called North School, South School, East School, West School, and Central School.
> Jack does not go to North, South, or Central School.
> Dick goes to West School.
> Bob does not go to North or Central School.
> Tom has never been inside Central School.
> What school does Jack go to? What school does Bob go to?
> What school does James go to?
> What school does Tom go to?

Robin eliminated North, South, and Central to deduce that Jack went to East or West. He then apparently could not see how to combine the negative information about Jack with the positive statement about Dick. "You would have to find out the district he was in," Robin suggested. Unable to deal with the problem as stated, he added his own experience. He knew that children usually went to schools near their own homes and so pulled in this information with disregard for the premises as given. Difficulty in solving a problem increases the tendency to ignore premises.

Combining Abstractions. During the stage of concrete operations, a child can consider two or more dimensions when classifying or when solving conservation problems. The child is then dealing with concrete experiences, the height and width of a glass, or the sizes and colors of objects. The adolescent can compare two or more ideas, thoughts, or hypotheses, all of which are abstract. She can also compare and order in terms of relative statements. One of Piaget's examples is this:

> Edith is fairer than Susan.
> Edith is darker than Lily.
> Who is the darkest of the three?

Piaget says that children younger than 12 rarely solve this problem because they think of dark and light as qualities, rather than as dimensions. Children give answers like this one: Edith and Susan are fair. Edith and Lily are dark. Therefore Lily is darkest, Susan is fairest, and Edith is in between.

Conceptual Development

Concept formation reflects the increasing intellectual power of the adolescent. Compared with school-age children's, differences can be seen in adolescents' concepts of space and time.

Space Concepts. Although children in the stage of concrete operations (see Chapter 11) can solve conservation problems with mass, weight, and length, conservation of volume is usually too difficult for them. Indeed, less than half of adolescents can cope with conservation of volume, and many adults also fail such tests. A variety of tests are used to assess conservation of volume. An example of such a test is done with 2 same-size test tubes, filled with equal amounts of water. The examiner shows 2 cylinders the same size, but of different weights, places the heavier one into one test tube until it is covered with water, and asks, "Will the water in the second test tube rise equally to the water in the first tube when the lighter cylinder is immersed in the tube? Please explain your answer." [40]

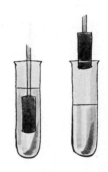

This test cannot be solved by concrete thinking because it requires combining two abstractions, identity and reciprocity. The subject must realize that nothing has been added or taken away (identity) and that an increase in one area may be canceled by a decrease in another area (reciprocity).

Another spatial task is presented by a drawing of a partly filled container of liquid, shown in an upright position. The subject is asked to choose a drawing that shows the correct orientation of the surface of the water when the container is tipped. When university undergraduates tried this test, the women got 59 per cent of questions right and the men 84 [15].

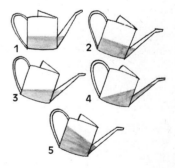

Time Concepts. During adolescence a mild diffusion of time perspective is common, according to Erikson [13, p. 169]. The young person feels a sense of urgency and yet acts as though time were of no importance. She finds it hard to start and stop activities, to go to bed, to get up, to get her work done. Eventual coming to terms with time is essential for the development of a sense of integrity, which means accepting one's place in time and space, one's own particular life cycle [13, p. 139]. Enabled by cognitive growth to consider a new time perspective, the adolescent may become intrigued with the overwhelming importance of the present moment or the mysterious joys of merging with an eternal entity.

The ability to delay before responding to a problem is correlated with success in solving certain kinds of problems. Being able to delay immediate gratification in order to achieve more gain and pleasure in the future is an aspect of *future orientation*. Whereas different cultures vary in time orientation, North Americans generally esteem future orientation as an attitude necessary for achievement. Mainstream children become more future-oriented as they mature, as shown by an analysis of stories written in response to pictures [30]. Subjects included five age groups: school children, adolescents, college students, businessmen, and senior citizens. There was an age trend up to college age, adolescents being more future-oriented than children, and college students more than adolescents. The adults were less future-oriented than the adolescents and college students.

Future-time orientation is functional for adolescents who can realistically look forward to a future in which they are rewarded for delaying gratification. Studies on economically depressed groups, such as American Indians and Mexicans, have found them to be more present-oriented than middle-class Americans [44]. The author suggests that present orientation is not a cause of poverty but a mentally healthy adjustment to it. He notes that future-oriented American Indians have been found to have more personality disturbances than their present-oriented peers.

Formal Operations

According to Piaget, a new stage of thinking follows the stage of concrete operations, beginning at 11 to 12 years of age, and reaching equilibrium at 14 to 15 [39]. He calls the new stage formal operations, or logical thought. As with entrance into the stage of concrete operations, the mind is restructured or reorganized. A new ability emerges, the ability to reason in terms of verbally stated hypotheses, rather than only in terms of concrete experience. Reasoning is formal when the person accepts premises, whether true or not, and deduces the consequences that follow from them. What is possible is considered, along with what is real, and all possibilities are linked in thought. The formal thinker isolates variables and uses the combinatorial system.

Isolation of Variables

Piaget and his associates test children's thinking by problems using the swing of a pendulum, weights on a balance beam, and objects sliding down inclined planes. Children between 7 and 10 act on the materials by trial and error, trying to classify what happens. Children on the formal operations level soon stop experimenting, list all possible factors involved, make hypotheses and test them, studying the effects of one variable while keeping all others constant.

An example of a problem in isolating variables in a lifelike situation is the plant problem, given to children and adolescents by Kuhn and Brannock [29]. They showed the subjects 4 plants, 2 of which were healthy and 2, dying. Beside each plant were a glass of water, either large or small, and a dish containing plant food, either light or dark. A bottle of leaf lotion was beside each of 2 plants. (See the sketches in the margin.) The task was to isolate the variable responsible for the health of the plants and to exclude the inoperative variables. Four levels of reasoning were found—concrete, formal, and 2 transitional levels in between. In grade 4 there were children at each of the 4 levels. Most of the college freshmen had reached formal operations, but a few were in the transitional level below formal operations. Examples of answers at each level are these:

1. First it's sick and then healthy. The last one was sick so this one will be healthy. (No concept of variable isolation.)
2. Sick because it doesn't have enough water. It depends on how much water. (Some notion of isolation of variables.)
3. Healthy, because it will get light, powdery stuff, and half a glass of water. Number 1 didn't have any lotion and it turned out healthy (hence lotion not involved). (Failure to isolate operative variable, but success in eliminating inoperative.)
4. (Isolated operative variable, the plant food, and excluded inoperative lotion.)

Using a Combinatorial System

The formal thinker uses all possible ways of combining variables, and does so in a systematic way. One of Piaget's tests for this capability is a chemical test, in which he gives 5 bottles of colorless, odorless liquid, 3 of which combine to make a yellow liquid. The fourth is a reducing agent, the fifth, water.

The comments of a 13-year-old, working on the chemical problem, went like this: "You have to try with all the bottles. I'll begin with the one at the end. . . . It doesn't work any more. Maybe you have to mix them. (He succeeds in making yellow.) But are there other solutions? I'll try . . . [21]. This boy used a systematic way of combining. He did not stop when one combination succeeded, because he was interested in all possibilities, and wanted to find the rules that governed the changes.

The acquisition of the combinatorial system has been studied in children 10 and 13 years old, who could be expected to be in a transition between concrete and formal operations [45]. Subjects were given different degrees of help in learning to plan and execute factorial experiments. The task was to learn the proper combination of four switches to run an electric train, requiring that the child generate 16 combinations. The first and second groups were given a conceptual framework that included teaching about factors, levels, and tree diagrams. The first group in addition was given training in solving analogous problems but the second group was not. The control group was given neither conceptual framework nor examples. Figure 14–1 shows the successes (measured in number of combinations made) by younger and older children under the three conditions. Thus, the more help that was given, the better both ages did at using the combinatorial system, but the older children did better than the younger. Another significant difference between the age levels was that the older children made more use of written records in problem solving, even though all children had equal opportunities to make such rec-

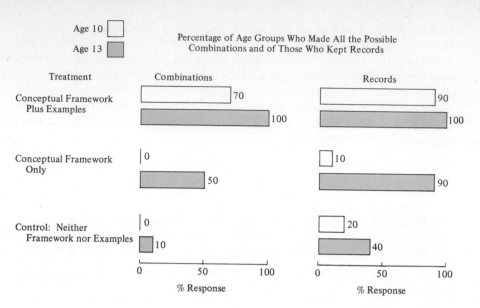

FIGURE 14–1
Performances of 10- and 13-year-olds on combinatorial problems: Percentages making all combinations and percentages keeping records. (SOURCE: Data from R. S. Siegler and R. M. Liebert. Acquisition of formal scientific reasoning by 10- and 13-year-olds: Designing a factorial experiment. *Developmental Psychology*, 1975, **11**, 401–402).

ords. Probably the 10-year-olds had less foresight in regard to the difficulty of remembering and therefore did not see the need to write down what they did as they went along.

Piaget points out that the combinatorial system of thinking can be used not only with chemicals, but with propositions. Logic involves combining propositions. An example of a problem in logic is the one used by Donaldson, mentioned earlier in this chapter, in which she asked which schools various boys attended.

Formal reasoning and logical thought employ all the cognitive powers that we described in the first part of this chapter: increased speed and memory; freedom to think about the possible as well as the real; making and testing hypotheses; thinking about thinking; control of thought processes in planning; accepting premises; and combining abstractions. Formal thinking is different in quality from concrete thinking because in formal thought form is abstracted from content.

Correlates of Formal Thought

Formal thought is related to other measurable characteristics of adolescents. We comment on three of these variables, IQ, cognitive style, and locus of control.

Measured Intelligence. Although studies do not agree well on how highly tests of formal operations correlate with IQ, there is evidence that the two measures do correlate. In fact, there is no evidence that they are measuring different processes [22].

Cognitive Style. Field independence and reflectivity were measured along with children's transition from concrete to formal operations [36].

Field independence was assessed by finding out how quickly and accurately a child could identify figures embedded in pictures. Reflectivity, as opposed to impulsivity, was measured by the child's matching one of six pictures with a standard after delaying his choice. Both field independence and reflectivity were associated with cognitive development. There was some suggestion that reflectivity was more influential in concrete operations and that field independence was more influential in formal operations. Field independence or dependence and reflectivity-impulsivity seem to be quite enduring characteristics of individuals. There are some training procedures known to promote reflectivity, but little has been done to show how to increase field independence.

Locus of Control. Individuals vary in how much they feel themselves to be in charge of what happens to them. When a person believes strongly that he controls many significant events, he is said to have an internal locus of control. A person with an external locus of control believes that what happens is the result of luck, fate, or the actions of other people and things. When 14- and 15-year-olds were tested for degree of formal thinking and locus of control, the internal-control subjects scored higher in formal thought than the externals [41].

Ecology of Formal Operations

Although almost all children attain concrete operational thought, it is not certain that everyone becomes a formal thinker. Piaget notes that his subjects, from the better schools of Geneva, achieved formal operations at between 11 and 15 years of age, but that slower progress has been seen in less privileged groups in many parts of the world [39]. Although he thinks it likely that all normal persons are capable of developing formal operations, experience determines the ways in which they develop. "However, the formation and completion of cognitive structures imply a whole series of exchanges with a stimulating environment; the formation of operations always requires a favorable environment for 'co-operation,' that is to say, operations carried out in common (e.g., the role of discussion, mutual criticism or support, problems raised as the result of exchanges of information, heightened curiosity due to the cultural influence of a social group, etc.)." [39, pp. 7–8.]

In her review of cross-cultural studies of formal operations Werner notes that formal thinking does not occur in all individuals in a given society, nor does it occur in all societies [52, pp. 223–227]. Formal thinking is less likely to be used in non-Western, nonindustrialized societies, as in New Guinea and in parts of Africa. She agrees with Piaget that probably all human beings have the capacity for learning to think formally, but that only certain social environments provide the intellectual give-and-take, as well as the motivation for developing formal operations. Logical thought is an advantage in dealing with science, technology, education, and urbanization. When no advantage is gained by formal thinking, few individuals are likely to achieve it or to use it.

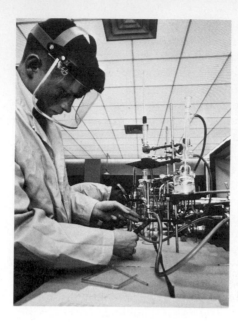

The acquisition of formal operations occurs, as Piaget has pointed out, in face-to-face settings, in microsystems. The value placed upon formal operations is a macrosystem variable, closely connected with the industry and education of the society. A highly scientific and technological macrosystem, such as our own, may require larger numbers of formal thinkers, whereas a different macrosystem, such as that of Tibet, may need only a few formal thinkers. In the mythical (or perhaps real) community of Shambhala, the model for Shangri-La, scholars study and preserve the best of human knowledge and thinking [5]. They have developed advanced science and technology. Only a few scholars are needed in Shambhala. Most Tibetans are peasants, wresting a living out of barren mountain soil, lucky if they learn to read and write.

Language Development

Adolescents continue to learn new words, new structures, new concepts, and the symbolic organization presented by the culture in which they live.

Relation of Language to Thought

Young children's private speech was discussed in Chapter 8. Adolescents rarely speak aloud to themselves, but speak silently, with inner speech. The relationship between thought and speech that adolescents achieve includes three functions: external speech, inner speech, and thought, according to Vygotsky, the Russian authority on thought and language. External speech is usually interwoven with thought, although it can occur without thought. Inner speech, derived from both external speech and thought, can be simply reciting, but rarely is it just that. It can be largely thinking in pure meanings, but it is not just that. "It is a dynamic, shifting, unstable thing, fluttering between word and thought . . ." [50, p. 149].

Thought itself does not have to be put into words. Sometimes a thought cannot be put into words. There are no units of thought, unlike speech, which has words as units. A thought is global, present at one time, but to be expressed in speech, it has to be developed in a succession of words. Vygotsky has likened a thought to a cloud shedding words. Words rarely express the whole thought, since a thought has a feeling and willing part to it. These subtle aspects are communicated somewhat through words, but largely through gesture, intonation, and context.

Many words have fuller and more abstract meanings for adolescents than for younger children. When asked to define words, the more complete definitions of adolescents indicate the more complex thought processes at work. Formal thought tries to take account of all possibilities inherent in the situation. Hence a word definition must encompass all meanings of the word. A child might say "Poverty means you're hungry"; an adolescent might say, "Poverty is a state of being without desirable goods and/or qualities." Interpretations of pictures, like definitions of words, show a progression from concrete to abstract and from limited to complete as the child progresses through the stages of thinking. The preschool child names objects ("Dog, mommy, basket"), the school-age child describes the picture by relating some of the elements ("The lady is chasing the dog. The dog has a shirt in his mouth.") The adolescent interprets the picture ("It's washday. The lady's cross at the dog for running off with the clean clothes. The dog is only playing.")

Elaboration of Concepts

Use of More Difficult Structures. Certain complex, infrequently used structures are acquired rather late in life or, by some people, not at all. One such situation involves certain uses of the words *ask* or *tell*. An exception to the regular use of such words provided the basis of research on the age of its acquisition [28]. An example of regular use is "Tanya asked Yvette to play." Here *Yvette*, the subject of the complement verb phrase, is placed next to the complement, *to play*. The irregular use occurs in "Tanya asked Yvette what to play." Here the subject of the complement is *Tanya*. A test of use and understanding of this irregular structure was given to 122 subjects between 8 and 19 years of age, all of average or superior IQ. Even at the college-age level, some subjects failed. More successes occurred in children over 12 than in children under 12. When told "Ask Ben which book to read," the subject who failed would say, "Ben, which book do you want to read?" Another response, more frequent among younger children, was telling instead of asking, as in "Read this one." When retested two years later, some but not all of the unsuccessful subjects were able to use the exceptional structure. It thus seems that some adolescents and some adults do not achieve full use of complex language structures.

Increase in Vocabulary. Although averages tell little about an individual and nothing about the mechanisms by which words are acquired, the size of average vocabulary at various ages gives an indication of the course of mental development. And for a quick estimate of IQ, there is nothing better than a vocabulary test.

The number of words understood far exceeds the number used in speech. When children were given a recognition vocabulary test, the average number of words understood in grade 1 was 23,700, with a range from 6,000 to 48,000, and in grade 12, the average was 80,300, with a range from 36,700 to 136,500. Figure 14–2 shows the results of this study for grades 2 through 11, indicating the steady rise in number of words understood. In a study that dealt with university students, their recognition vocabulary was estimated at an average of 156,000 words [46]. An individual's vocabulary continues to grow throughout his life span [42].

To figure out how many words an adolescent actually uses is an almost impossible task. An estimate of the average English child's active vocabulary at age 14 is between 8,000 and 10,000 words, a number similar to estimates made for American children [51]. Between 7 and 14, the English child is judged to increase his vocabulary by about 700 words a

FIGURE 14–2
Average sizes of understood vocabulary and active vocabulary (estimated) at various ages. (SOURCES: M. K. Smith and A. F. Watts. *The language and mental development of children.* London: George G. Harrap & Co. Ltd., 1944. Measurement of the size of general English vocabulary through the elementary grades and high school. *Genetic Psychology Monographs*, 1941, **24**, 131–345.)

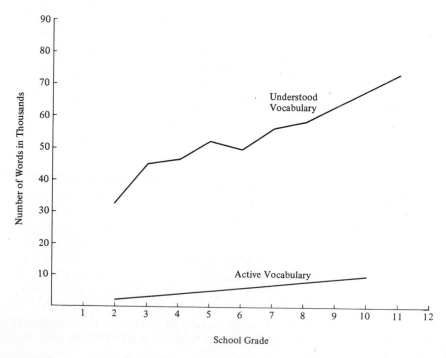

year. The increase from 14 to 20 averages about 10,000 words, resulting in an adult vocabulary of 18,000 to 20,000 words.

A particular kind of vocabulary develops during adolescence, especially in subcultures of crime and delinquency. *Argot* is the term for the special words devised and used by participants in these cultures and, to a certain extent, by other adolescents as well. Knowledge of argot increases during adolescence.

Secular Shift

Parents and teachers have recently become concerned as to whether children are reading as well as children used to read, and indeed, if today's children are as well educated as yesterday's. A study by Alvin Eurich provides some answers that are not reassuring [17]. In 1928 Eurich gave vocabulary and reading tests to 4,191 high school seniors and 1,313 freshmen at the University of Minnesota. In 1978 Eurich gave the same tests to college freshmen at the same university. In every comparison made, the 1928 high school and college students did better than the college students of 50 years later. Table 14–1 shows some of the ways in which the present-day students fell behind. The downward trend in language scores was confirmed by a study of SAT (Scholastic Aptitude Test) scores between 1970 and 1977 [54]. Both average verbal and quantitative scores declined, but verbal more than quantitative.

Ecology

The macrosystem makes more or fewer demands for language development. One relevant change in our macrosystem is in communications. Television gives children more visual experience, along with very simple verbal experience, pulling them away from books and more complex thinking. Talking on telephones and tape recorders may substitute for writing. Textbooks have become simpler and more visual. Institutions in our macrosystem have pushed for simplification of language. The educational institution has required the simpler textbooks. The Roman Catholic and Episcopal churches have revised the language of their services. Insurance companies advertise that the ordinary person can now read and understand their simplified policies. Within the government,

Tests	1928	1978
Vocabulary (out of 100)		
Average score	34.9	28.7
Highest score	95	75
Scoring near 60	5%	1%
Scoring below 26	40%	50%
Comprehension score Below 12	30%	50%
Speed score Below 20	54%	81%

Source: F. M. Hechinger. 1978 freshmen score poorly on 1928 exam. *New York Times*, March 3, 1980.

TABLE 14–1
Comparisons of Students in 1928 and 1978 on Vocabulary and Reading Tests

attempts are made to reduce bureaucratic writing to common language.

Although the microsystem of the school usually receives credit or blame for students' language development, the schools and teachers are responding to macrosystem demands in their teaching. They are also responding to what the students bring to the classroom. Today's high school seniors, and presumably freshmen, sophomore, and juniors, are not prepared to study as difficult language lessons as were the students of 50 years ago. And yet they know all sorts of things of which the older cohort had never heard.

The microsystem of the family, of course, is where a child begins to develop language and continues throughout adolescence. Families provide models and the setting for cooperative interchange in which cognitive and language development take place. Some family positions are more favorable than others. Early-born children and children from small families tend to score higher in intelligence than later-borns and children from large families. Among over a million National Merit Scholarship participants, the summed scores of first-borns from small families were highest and those of last-borns from large families lowest [6]. These results were because of verbal subtests and not the mathematical subtests. Eldest siblings scored higher than only children. When children were spaced far apart, both (or all, in three-child families) did better than when children were spaced closely. The authors suggest that the first child benefits in the beginning from talking with parents and having their full attention. Then when a sibling is born and the first child is already a good talker, the elder child benefits from her own efforts in explaining and teaching, adapting her language use to the younger child and children.

Creativity

Just as inner speech flutters between word and thought, so does thought itself shift between controlled thinking and fantasy or imaginative thinking. Adolescence sees a resurgence of imagination in many forms. Having greater control over her intellectual processes, the adolescent can move more rapidly and easily between purposeful thinking and fantasy. Unlike the preschool child who loses herself in a dramatic role, the adolescent can imagine herself into a role and then stand off to observe herself in it.

Whereas creativity is the breath of life to the preschool child, the school-age child is concerned with industry, duty, and accomplishment, with matters of fact, with learning what reality is and how to cope with it. The adolescent, thinking about what is possible, not just what is, creates new situations and original solutions in her imagination. Some teenagers are exploring different modes of thinking and feeling in order to integrate themselves with the universe and eternity. Creativity is thought to be involved not only in artistic expression but also in meditation, peak experiences, and dreams. High-creative and low-creative students, selected by tests, dreamed quite differently [49]. High-creative students' dreams were more unusual, contained more elements, and contained more words. The settings were more varied. Whereas 60 per cent of the dreams of low creatives were set at home, only 8 per cent of high creatives' dreams were located there.

Assessing Creativity

Much of creative thinking is divergent (see "Intelligence Testers" in Chapter 1.). In creating a solution, convergent thinking may be used to select the best answer from the many possibilities produced by divergent thought. Factors in divergent verbal thinking include fluency, flexibility, and elaboration. Tests for *fluency* focus on easy recall of information, words that fit certain classes, words or phrases that make certain relationships, and connected discourse in phrases or sentences. An example of a *flexibility* test is thinking up clever titles that give new interpretations, such as "snake and sidney pie" for "steak and kidney pie." *Elaboration* means building up or rounding out what is given. The fluency, flexibility, and elaboration factors just mentioned had to do with verbal information. Other parallel factors pertain to visual and symbolic information. Some people are creative verbally, others artistically, and still others are creative mathematically. Tests based on these concepts have been used to study creativity in children, adolescents, college students, and adults. Everyone is creative to a certain extent, but some people are more so than others. The tests give quantitative comparisons.

Relation of Creativity to Other Measures

Many kinds of social and personal characteristics have been investigated in efforts to find out what makes for creativity.

IQ. Many studies have been concerned with the relationship between creativity and tested intelligence. Results generally support the commonsense point of view, that the two have something in common but are not exactly the same. Intelligence of a certain level is necessary for creativity, but does not guarantee it. In a group of students with high scholastic aptitude, academic achievement was not related to creative achievement [18].

Socioeconomic Status. When measured by fathers' education and occupation, socioeconomic status of high school students showed a low but significant correlation with measures of divergent thinking [38].

Personality Characteristics. Research on creative people indicates that they are high in flexibility, fluency, drive, involvement, openness, curiosity, autonomy, independence of judgment, self-confidence, self-acceptance, humor, empathy, desire for complexity, and easy tolerance of ambiguity. Characteristics related to low creativity include rigidity, premature judging, defensiveness, contentedness, gentleness, conservatism, patience, virtuousness, and concern for others [3].

Self-concepts of adolescents, as shown by responses on an adjective check list, showed a distinctive picture of creative adolescents [43]. Chosen for creativity through testing and rating of productions, these high school students showed awareness and acceptance of opposing forces in their personalities. More often than controls, they saw themselves as imaginative, original, uninhibited, outspoken, rebellious, complex, reflective, cynical, idealistic, and aloof. The control group more often described themselves as dependable, cooperative, conventional, quiet, and silent.

Creative minds use unconscious memories, primitive ways of thinking, keen observation, and rational thought

A study of creative artists points out that these people often see what other people do not observe, in addition to what people ordinarily see. They often call attention vividly to unnoticed phenomena, using their powers of accurate observation not only for their own satisfaction but also for the benefit of others. With their greater mental capacity, creative people can hold many ideas at once, compare more ideas and hence synthesize more than the ordinary person. Often extremely vigorous, both mentally and physically, they lead complex lives, in touch with a complex universe. They contact and use the unconscious life liberally, with broad and flexible self-awareness. They can easily regress to primitive fantasies, naïve ideas, and tabooed impulses and then return to rationality and self-criticism. "The creative person is both more primitive and more cultured, more destructive and more constructive, crazier and saner, than the average person." [3, p. 159]

Brain Waves. Highly creative people differ from average people in the patterning of their brain waves [35]. *Alpha waves* are slow, high-amplitude waves that are characteristic of states of relaxation and drowsiness in the average person. Rational work requires medium arousal levels, with faster, lower-amplitude brain waves. When male college students were tested for alpha waves in a resting state, low-creatives produced alpha waves about 55 per cent of the time, whereas high-creatives produced alpha waves about 40 per cent of the time. When a creativity test was given, the former reduced alpha wave output by about one half, but the latter increased their output of alpha waves. This result suggests that the high-creatives were more able to get in touch with unconscious memories and primitive ways of thinking. In addition, the high-creatives were more able to block out alpha waves, suggesting that they could focus their attention more rigorously. Thus, it seems that the brain-wave patterning fits with studies of the behavior of highly creative people, in which they use both primitive thought and highly rational thought. The unconscious nature of some available material is consistent with experiences reported by composers who wrote down symphonies they heard in their heads, by mathematicians who suddenly became aware of new formulas, and by the more usual creative person who sleeps on a problem and wakens with the solution.

Family experiences are different from the average among persons of high creativity and of high measured intelligence. Creative persons are likely to have been born when their parents were older (in their thirties) and to have been given respect, freedom, and autonomy [1]. Their parents were nonpossessive, emotionally open, nurturant, unconcerned with status, involved in their work, and ready to deal with tensions verbally. Mothers were likely to have careers and fathers tended to be involved in activities with children, and confident in their occupations. Among the most eminent, including geniuses, parental death during childhood was three times as likely as among creative college students. The children probably often felt a sense of aloneness, because of parents who were busy with work, or even dead, and also because the values and standards of their families differed from those of other families. Being on their own, and trusted, they had plenty of opportunities to think, to imagine, and to make their own decisions. Values were more important than specific pieces of behavior.

Gender Role. On tests of divergent thinking and other creativity tests, there are no consistent differences between males and females. How can this be, when many more men than women are known for their creative achievements in science and the arts? Opportunities and restrictions are, of course, very different for men and women, boys and girls. A narrow, rigid gender role requires a person to limit all sorts of behavior, including creativity. It seems that females have been more restricted than males, but actually, both have had limitations on where, when, and how they were permitted to create. A loosening of gender stereotypes means that males are free to be sensitive and tender in addition to the traditional masculine modes of aggressive achievement, while females are allowed to assert themselves, to compete, and to relish success frankly, in addition to being sensitive and nurturant.

Adolescents carry with them their childhood experiences in gender-role training. Although they benefit from the freedoms recently won by women and the consequent freedoms for them, adolescents continue to be influenced by the old stereotypes. There may be many girls who believe, for example, that men do not like women, and boys do not like girls, who are creative, competent, and successful. When creativity tests are correlated with other tests, results suggest that although males and females may have equal potential, the patterning of their creativity may take different courses of expression and development. Girls were more affected than boys by the external situation in which a creativity test was given [24]. Retested five years after tests given in grade 5, girls showed stability of creative performance when they were tested by one nonevaluative female examiner, but not when they were tested in a group. Boys showed more stability when they were tested in a group. Further analysis suggested that the girls' creativity was depressed by anxiety, but not the boys'.

Creative persons are likely to have had older parents, respect, autonomy, solitude, unusual values

TABLE 14–2
Sex Differences in Mental
Performances

Males superior	Females superior
Mathematics, especially geometry and trigonometry	Verbal behavior
Conservation of horizontality	Reading
Pendulum problem	Remembering names and faces
Daylight vision	Sensitivity to touch
Perception of depth in space	Night vision
Reaction time	Hearing
Interest in objects	Resisting distractions while listening
Large motor coordination	Rapid information processing
	Fine motor dexterity
	Empathy

Source: Various references cited in this chapter, especially D. Goleman. Special abilities of the sexes: Do they begin in the brain? *Psychology Today,* 1978, **12**:6, 48ff.

Sex Differences in Mental Development and Behavior

Differences between the sexes have been found in several areas of intellectual life. Reasons for the differences can be found within individual development and in the ecology. Table 14–2 shows areas of male and female superiority that are well established by adolescence. Sex differences have been summarized by saying that man is a "manipulative animal whose chief mode of expression is action," whereas "woman is a communicative animal" whose style is to perceive, to remember, and to receive and transmit meaning through signs and symbols [14]. The quest for sex equality has led some persons to believe that sex differences in behavior are caused entirely by differences in bringing up boys and girls. Although differences in experiences between the sexes no doubt increase differences in their abilities, interests, and behavior, we believe that there is a physical base for those differences. As we have said earlier in this

book, the brains of male and female are different at birth and in the patterning of development. The genes and hormones controlling brain development are different in male and female. As we have also said before, a sex difference is a difference between the average performance of girls and the average performance of boys. Some girls do much better than the average of boys in areas where boys excel, even sometimes as well as the highest performance of boys. The same is true of boys in areas where girls excel. Therefore, it is unfair to individuals, and a waste to the community, if girls are not allowed to be architects and engineers, and boys are excluded from nursing and teaching young children.

Moral Development

Moral development involves intellectual and social development

Moral development is an outcome of intellectual and social development. Adolescent thinking makes possible a more advanced phase in reasoning and judgment about moral issues. Moral action has its roots in social interaction. The first theory that we discuss is the socioanalytic theory of Hogan and his associates. It is concerned with both intellectual and social aspects, with thinking, feeling, and action. Then we describe the cognitive developmental theory of Kohlberg, whose views on moral reasoning have stimulated a wealth of research and discussion.

Hogan's Socioanalytic Theory

According to Hogan's theory of moral development, described in Chapters 9 and 12, the young adolescent is involved in the second phase, social sensitivity, until about 16 years of age [19]. The third phase, beginning at around 14 to 16 years of age, is *autonomy* or *self-awareness*. (The phase of developing moral autonomy is *not* the same as Erikson's concept of the sense of autonomy, whose crisis is reached at around 2 years of age.) Moral autonomy means commitment to what is consciously chosen as highest in one's culture, despite the demands of family, peers, and conventional authority. Self-awareness, an aspect of metacognition, which increases with adolescent cognitive development, makes it possible for the young person to move toward moral autonomy. Increasing powers of metacognition enable the adolescent to think critically about her own motives, to appreciate the relativity of values and the limitations of philosophies, and to realize that injustice exists. Then the person does not accept rules and values blindly, but through conscious decision. The values of her culture are seen as valid for her.

Moral autonomy is like Fidelity

It seems to us that Erikson's concept of the virtue of *fidelity* is similar to Hogan's notion of moral autonomy. In developing a sense of identity the young person needs a community to which she can be faithful [13, p. 235]. When that community is found, and the person committed, the result is the virtue of fidelity. Both Hogan and Erikson are talking about a commitment made after a critical search and a choice made in awareness of self.

TABLE 14–3
Three Examples of
Nonautonomous Moral
Conduct

Uneven phase development	Moral behavior
High in rule attunement; low in social sensitivity and moral autonomy.	Obeys authority and follows rules without question.
High in rule attunement and social sensitivity; low in moral autonomy.	Lacks perspective, champions one moral cause after another.
High in social sensitivity; low in rule attunement and moral autonomy.	Terrorist, aggressive toward authority in the name of justice.

Source: R. Hogan, J. A. Johnson, and N. P. Emler. A socioanalytic theory of moral development. In W. Damon (ed.). Moral development. *New Directions for Child Development*, 1978, No. 2.

Hogan points out that people differ in how they manage the three phases of moral development. Adolescents who have developed well in all three moral phases have characteristics from each of the three. From success in *rule attunement,* they can be easily taught, coached, and depended upon; their morality is consistent with demands of their culture and religion. From success in *social sensitivity*, they are perceptive of others' thoughts and feelings, are understanding and tactful; they become concerned with fairness, justice, civil rights, and such issues. From success in *moral autonomy,* they are self-aware, inner-directed, task-oriented, and more interested in approval from adults than from peers; as adults, they live according to self-chosen principles that are consistent with the values of their culture.

Uneven development, or lack of balance, produces various results. A well-developed adult accepts authority easily, reacts sensitively and acceptably to others, and thinks objectively and critically on moral issues, and integrates all this in action. Hogan gives three examples of unbalanced moral development, which we summarize in Table 14–3.

Kohlberg's Cognitive Developmental Theory

Kohlberg is concerned with the ways in which children think about moral questions, in how they use their minds to judge right and wrong actions and to justify their conclusions. His method is to tell a story that poses a moral dilemma and then to question the child about what the characters ought to do and why. Through use of a special scoring system, which has been revised in recent years, a child is placed in a level and at a stage of moral development. The child's thinking is held to be the result of mental structures that develop in sequence, as Piaget's structures of thought develop in stages. Kohlberg maintains that his sequence of moral stages is invariant, that they are always achieved in the same order. Development takes place as the child interacts in his social environment. Kohlberg has said, "Moral development involves a continual process of matching a moral view to one's experience of life in a social world." [27]

The Story of Heinz. The first story in Kohlberg's moral dilemmas is this:

In Europe a woman was near death from cancer. One drug might save her, a form of radium that a druggist in the town had recently discovered. The druggist was charging $2000, ten times what the drug cost him to make. The sick woman's husband, Heinz, went to everyone he knew to borrow the money, but he could only get together about half of what it cost. He told the druggist that his wife was dying and asked him to sell it cheaper or let him pay later. But the druggist said "No." The husband got desperate and broke into the man's store to steal the drug for his wife. Should the husband have done that? Why? [25]

Levels and Stages of Moral Judgment. Six types of moral judgment are distinguished, grouped in twos, making three general levels of moral development.

I. *Preconventional level, on which impulse gratification is modified by rewards and punishments.*

Stage 1. Punishment and obedience orientation. The reason for doing anything or for not doing something is to avoid punishment. "Being right" means obeying an authority. There is no concept of *a* right.

Stage 2. Instrumental relativist orientation. The reason for behavior is to get pleasure for oneself, often in the form of rewards from another person. Everyone has a right to do what he wants with himself and his possessions, even though his behavior conflicts with the rights of others. Reciprocity is pragmatic and has nothing to do with loyalty or gratitude or justice.

II. *Conventional level where conduct is controlled by the anticipation of social praise and blame. Meeting the expectations of family or nation and maintaining such groups is valuable regardless of consequences.*

Stage 3. Good-boy, nice-girl morality, or maintaining good relationships and the approval of other people. Conformity to stereotyped notions of majority or "natural" behavior. Intention becomes important in judging behavior. The concept of everyone's rights is the same as in Stage 2, with the addition that nobody has the right to do evil.

Stage 4. "Law and order" orientation. Right behavior consists of following fixed rules, respecting authority, maintaining the established social order for its own sake. When legitimate authorities disapprove or punish, the youngster feels guilty. A right is a claim on the actions of others, usually an earned claim, such as payment for work.

III. *Postconventional, autonomous, principled level. Morality of self-accepted moral principles, in which the person regulates his behavior by an ideal which he holds, regardless of immediate social praise and blame.*

Stage 5. Social-contract legalistic orientation. Morality of contract and of democratically accepted law. Community respect and disrespect are powerful motivators. The concept of human rights emerges here. There are rights linked to role and status and also unearned, universal, individual rights as a human being.

Stage 6. Morality of individual principles of conscience. Motivation is feeling right with oneself. The idea of rights includes all that ex-

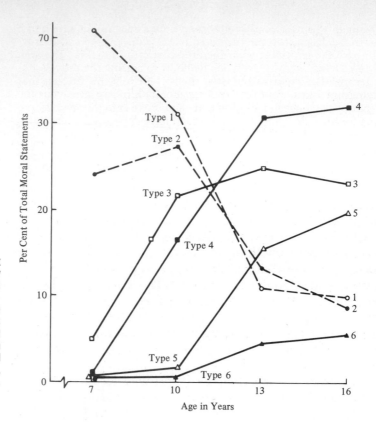

FIGURE 14–3
Frequency of use of six types of moral judgment by boys at ages 7, 10, 13, and 16. (Reprinted by permission from L. Kohlberg, The development of children's orientations toward a moral order: I. Sequence in the development of moral thought, *Vita Humana*, **6**, 11–33. Copyright © 1963, S. Karger, Basel/New York.)

pressed in Type 5 plus the notion that the life and personality of every individual are to be respected. Acceptable principles, such as the Golden Rule, have logical comprehensiveness, universality, and consistency.

Age Patterning of Stages of Moral Judgment. Kohlberg's first findings are shown in Figure 14–3. Between ages 7 and 16, boys showed changes in their use of the 6 types of moral thinking. Premoral thinking decreased rapidly up to 13, leveled off, and accounted for about 20 per cent of judgments at 16. Conventional role conformity rose rapidly in middle childhood and became the most frequent type of judgment during the years studied. Principled thinking rose rapidly between 10 and 13 and accounted for about 20 per cent of judgments at 16. During early adolescence, then, the most frequent type of moral judgment was made in order to serve social relationships, to receive praise, and to avoid disapproval by authorities and consequent guilt.

Universality of Kohlberg's Sequences and States. Kohlberg's early work and recent follow-ups on American and Turkish boys have shown his invariant stage sequence [26]. Further confirmation comes from a study on an American male group using more sophisticated statistical techniques [8].

Other studies do not find the sequences to be invariant [20]. Baumrind, from a dialectical point of view, states that because there are no moral universals, there are no culturally invariant stages of moral development [4]. Baumrind points out that in all cultures that socialize children in a family or familylike group, Stages 1, 2, and 3 will probably appear in that order, but that the higher stages will not occur in cultures where that type of reasoning is not needed for survival. Kohlberg himself has not found a Stage 6 in his recent studies of American and Turkish boys [26]. He suggests that Stage 6 should be viewed as an elaboration of a substage of Stage 5.

Sex Bias. Kohlberg's basic research was done on boys. So were many of the studies stimulated by this research. When the method was applied to girls and women, they usually scored lower than boys and men. Holstein, like others who have studied both males and females, found Stage 4 to be most typical of 16-year-old boys and Stage 3 most frequent for girls the same age [20]. Female moral reasoning is sometimes different from male, but is it inferior, as Kohlberg's theory suggests? Holstein says, "The problem of where to categorize irrational but morally relevant emotions, such as compassion, sympathy, and love will remain a problem, especially in the light of consistent sex differences produced by scoring standards for these moral passions." [20, p. 61]

The problem described by Holstein does not arise when one uses Hogan's socioanalytic theory of moral development. Moral passions have a necessary place in moral development, and that place is neither higher nor lower than the other essential components.

A government pamphlet on antisocial behavior starts thus:

> For no apparent reason, a youth grabs an 85-year-old woman in front of her doorstep and chokes her to death. A 15-year-old boy steals a neighbor's car and is picked up 3 weeks later, hundreds of miles away, because he has parked on the wrong side of the street. A middle-aged woman is jumped by a gang of teen-age girls—avid for money, of which she has none—and winds up in the hospital.[53]

Nobody doubts that these acts are antisocial and wrong. The adolescents who commit them are called delinquents. Through its laws, a macrosystem defines behavior that is intolerable, and the punishments appropriate for transgressors. The courts provide the setting in which offenders are judged and sentenced, or plans made for punishment and/or rehabilitation, but only if they are caught and arrested by the police. Delinquent acts of lower-class adolescents are more likely to be recorded by police than the same acts when committed by middle-class youngsters. The government pamphlet goes on to say that 2 million young people, 20 per cent of them girls, were arrested during one year for offenses that included murder, burglary, larceny, vandalism, arson, and assault. What

Delinquency: Problems of Moral Development

do theory and research have to say about the sources and treatment of juvenile delinquency?

Moral Development Theory. When moral behavior is poor, cognitive theory would predict retarded development of moral judgment. Socioanalytic theory would predict deficient development in one or more phases. Let us assume low development in all three of Hogan's phases. Low rule attunement would lead to breaking laws if desires and impulses were contrary to law. The girls ignored the laws against assault and theft because they wanted the woman's money. Low social sensitivity means not caring about how a victim feels. The girls did not care whether they hurt the woman while trying to take her money. Low autonomy means giving no thought to the relation between self and the highest values in the culture. The girls showed no concern for their part in upholding human rights, sanctity of person, the Golden Rule, or other high principles. The theory can be used in preventive programs, to guide child-rearing practices that will enhance development in all three phases. In order to prevent and treat delinquency, however, it must be understood in context of the whole person developing in the ecology.

Characteristics of Delinquents as Shown by Research. Delinquents have been found generally to have IQs below the average range, to read below their grade level, to attend school less often than average, and to cause disturbances in school [47]. A series of longitudinal studies by Robins has shown the childhood characteristics of delinquents by following over 500 child guidance clinic patients into their 40s, as well as control groups of normal children [53]. For most of the boys, symptoms began early in childhood, but not until 12 to 14 for most girls and a few boys. The chief symptoms were poor academic performance even with adequate IQ, stealing, truancy, and discipline problems. Causes included a deprived environment, usually of lower class, deviant parent or parents, lax and non-love-oriented discipline, hostile behavior in the family, and disturbed neuromuscular development. These symptoms can be traced to individual development, microsystems, and the macrosystem.

Treatment. Little success has been achieved by treatment programs. The Robins studies showed that only 16 per cent of child guidance clinic antisocial patients recovered by age 18. No success at all, even some negative results, were found 30 years after the termination of the Cambridge-Somerville Youth Study [33]. This well-designed program started with boys at age 10½ and tried different methods of intervention, including family visiting by counselors, academic tutoring, medical and psychiatric treatment, and going to camp. The Robins results suggest that 10½ was too late, because symptoms are well established in most boys at the beginning of school, and even for children whose treatment starts early, results have not been highly successful. Returning to Hogan's theory, we recall that the roots of moral development lie in infancy, in the attachment of babies to parents. The preschool years are crucial for rule attunement and social sensitivity. The older the child, the more gigantic the task of compensating for poor development in those early years.

Vocational Development

Intellectual development is only part, but an important part, of preparation for learning how to do useful work, finding a job, and working to support oneself. Specific skills have to be learned, some of them at school, some at home, and some on the job. The whole person takes part in the work career, including the maturing body and mind, social skills, moral orientation, and the self that directs efforts toward plans and goals. Vocational development takes place within the ecology, in microsystems of family, school, recreation groups, and work places.

Plans and Goals for Education and Career

Young children try on various occupational roles in their dramatic play. Of course they will play the parts of workers of whom they have some knowledge, a mother homemaker, perhaps a father homemaker, storekeepers, bus drivers, and characters from familiar stories. As children grow up, they contact more types of occupations and learn more about how work roles fit into the social ecology. When children are asked about their job preferences, their answers reflect their knowledge and experience. Two developmental trends were found in a study of white, middle-class students in grades 5, 7, 9, and college [37]. The subjects were asked to choose between jobs that represented stereotypic male and female occupations on 4 status levels, professional, skilled, semiskilled, and unskilled. The jobs were these: captain in the Air Force and registered nurse; auto mechanic and secretary; house painter and drapery sewer; porter and hotel maid. Sex stereotypes affected choices less as children grew older, especially girls. Money and prestige became more important than sex appropriateness when children realized which jobs would yield highest financial gain and status.

Adolescent aspirations are related to educational and financial outcome [34]. High school students' planning to go to college is of course strongly related to later college attendance. Indeed, those who do not plan to go are likely to take a program that will not fit them for college entrance. Occupational plans of high school seniors were related to their actual achievement 7 years later. Because high occupational status requires high educational achievement, students who aim toward high prestige and earnings usually have high educational goals as well. Research supports the common belief that more years of education will result in more earnings later on [16]. A follow-up of Wisconsin men high school graduates showed an additional 10 per cent of earnings for each year of college education for those who had bachelors degrees. For those who did not have degrees, the return was 6 per cent per year for each year of education beyond high school. The additional earnings varied between cohorts.

Influences on Plans and Goals. Academic aptitude and achievement, closely related to each other, affect the plans that an adolescent makes, as well as the encouragement parents give. Socioeconomic status of the family also affects plans through opportunities offered and the concepts of self formed by the child. Teachers, counselors, and peers also influence young persons' plans. These influences vary according to race and sex.

Some Ethnic Differences. Aspirations of black and white students were studied in 23 public schools in Mississippi [9]. For white students, parental encouragement was the most important influence on plans, followed by socioeconomic status of the family, and then the student's own academic performance. Black girls were also most influenced by their parents' encouragement, and next by their own performance. It was different with black boys. Their own academic aptitude was the first influence on their plans, and next came teachers and counselors.

Some Sex Differences. Girls used to set lower aims for themselves than boys, and no doubt some still do. The traditional women's occupations command less money and less prestige than men's. The Women's Movement has made some changes in what women are allowed to do, how much they earn, and how they are regarded. Therefore, women's vocational goals and plans would logically change.

A review of research up to 1978 came to the following conclusions [34]. Occupational goals of boys were more affected than those of girls by socioeconomic background, academic ability, and parental encouragement. At low socioeconomic levels, but not at high, boys were more likely than girls to plan to go to college, to be encouraged to do so, to go to college, and to graduate. Number of siblings had a negative affect on boys' goals, but not on girls'. When mothers were employed, girls were more likely to commit themselves to careers. Girls set educational goals lower when anticipating marriage. For boys, educational and occupational aspirations were more closely linked, probably because for them, education was (and is) the path to achievement. For girls, the connection between education and occupation was weaker, probably reflecting the reality of women's status coming through their husbands instead of through their own vocational achievements.

A recent report of freshman women indicates some changes in aspirations that have recently been made by adolescents, at least by those who go to college [32]. Comparing these young women with those of 10 years earlier, important differences in goals appear. Some of these differences are shown in Table 14—4. Most of the changes resulted in decreasing differences between male and female. However, this study says nothing about sex differences in youth who are not in college and not planning to

Goals increased in importance	Goals decreased in importance
Affluence	Developing philosophy of life
Recognition by peers	Interest in public affairs
Theoretical contribution	Personal development
Being an authority in field	Raising a family
Business career	
Career in medicine or law	

TABLE 14–4
Differences in Goals
Between Women Freshmen
in 1969 and 1979

Source: J. Magarrell. Today's new students, especially women, more materialistic.
Chronicle of Higher Education, Jan. 28, 1980.

go to college. We expect that on lower socioeconomic levels the older sex stereotypes would have more influence.

Cohort Differences. Whether we think of a cohort as all those born in one year, or all born during a longer period of time, there are differences between cohorts. Each has a different social environment in which to develop aspirations. A cohort growing up in a depression will experience economic matters in a different way from one that grows up amid prosperity. War and peace make different environments. Desegregation changes the environment. The influences we have mentioned, such as parental encouragement and number of siblings, may operate differently with different cohorts.

Work Experience. In recent years, the numbers of employed adolescents have increased. Not only are more young people working, but they are working longer hours. In Colonial days, of course, few teenagers went to school and most worked all day, just as adults did. Many children worked in factories and on farms during the nineteenth century. Few people would repeal the child labor regulations of 1938 that protected

TABLE 14–5
Benefits and Costs of
Jobs to Adolescents

Benefits	Costs
Practical knowledge of business world	Decline in school grades
Money to spend	Dissatisfaction with school
Learn how to find and hold a job	More use of marihuana and alcohol
Budgeting time	Opportunities for cheating employers
Assessing goals	Less time with family
Pride in achievement	Little time for self-exploration
Self-control	Cynicism and apathy if exploited
Coping with emergencies	

Source: S. Cole. Send our children to work? *Psychology Today,* 1980, **14**:2, 44ff.

children from full-time employment, but many people believe that it is good for adolescents to hold part-time jobs. Recent studies of working teenagers give some insight into the benefits and costs of part-time jobs [7]. Table 14–5 shows benefits and costs of jobs to adolescents. Significant technical skills and knowledge are not usually acquired by teenagers on part-time jobs. They are not apprentices, because most of their jobs are not highly skilled—in food service, retail sales, cashiering, manual labor, clerical work, and cleaning. A few jobs are in skilled labor.

Ecology of Education and Vocations

The macrosystem structures opportunities for both education and employment, as well as ideology to support the structures. Figure 14–4 shows percentages of boys and girls in secondary schools in a sample of countries of varying affluence. Politics and economics influence government aid to schools, educational research, job programs, and child labor laws. Political and legal action can limit or extend equality of opportunity to the sexes and to ethnic groups. Education may be related to the politics of defense, as were efforts to improve intellectual achievements after the Soviets launched the first space satellite. During the 1960s the

FIGURE 14–4
Per cent of males and females aged 12–17 enrolled in secondary schools, selected countries. (SOURCE: H. C. McHale, J. McHale, and G. F. Streatfeild. *Children in the World.* Washington: Population Reference Bureau, 1979.)

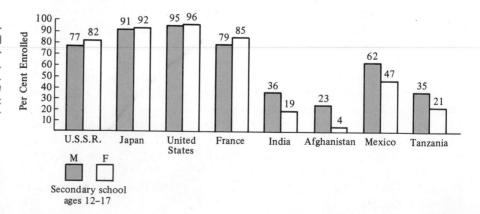

United States government underwrote scholarships for students to learn Asian and African languages. The United States macrosystem is in frequent ferment over educational issues. At present the traditional separation of religion and public education is being challenged by fundamentalist groups.

Adolescents develop intellectually and vocationally in their microsystems of family, school, and jobs. We have already commented on family influences on goals and achievement, and on benefits and costs of jobs. Here we shall discuss schools only briefly. The topic of schools and education is a field in itself.

School

Educators disagree over age-level organization of schools. Should the break between childhood and adolescence come between grades 8 and 9? Should it be a junior high school of grades 8 and 9, and senior high school of grades 10, 11, and 12? Or should the grades be divided 6–3–3? Presently popular, the middle school includes grades 7 and 8 and at least one grade below.

The purpose of trying out different organizations is to find one that will fit the majority of young adolescents. As we have shown in Chapter 13, puberty comes at a wide variety of ages, and the average for girls is 2 years earlier than the average for boys. When school groupings are made by chronological age, each grade from 7 through 10 contains students in a wide range of physical, intellectual, and social maturity. Over the years the problem has been intensified by the factors within individual development and within the social ecology. The secular shift toward earlier puberty means that if a grade organization worked well at one time, it has gradually become out of date. The social ecology also changes. In times of high unemployment it may seem desirable to keep adolescents in school and out of the job market. A particular social problem, such as adolescent childbearing, may call for a particular grade organization. And, of course, grade organization is not the only aspect of schooling that responds to individual and societal needs. When technological workers are in demand, certain subjects are emphasized in school. When vandalism and aggression are problems, the social organization and the curriculum may require overhauling. Integrated schools were established in order to solve problems of racism.

The mesosystem is very important to the adolescent's development and integration into the society. Vocational development is tied to educational, and educational to intellectual and social development. In putting together all parts of self and experience, it helps to have communications between family, community, school, and job. Some communities have experimented with combining school and job experiences, enlisting the cooperation of industry and unions in giving students experience as apprentices and contacts with a variety of workers in industries, trades, and professions.

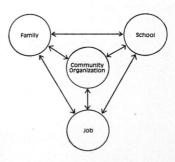

Summary

During adolescence, intellectual processes mature in terms of speed, elaboration, and efficiency of memory, freedom from dependence on concrete experience, and increased control. Freedom and control make it possible to test hypotheses and to delay conclusions until facts are obtained and weighed. Increasing metacognitive ability results in concern with thoughts and feelings of self and others, and the construction of an imaginary audience, a personal fable, and plans for improving society. Control improves planning the uses of mental processes and facilitates the accepting of premises, necessary for logical thinking. Abstractions can be compared and combined in thinking. New ways of thinking are applied to concepts of space and time.

Piaget's stage of formal operations is achieved by reconstruction of the mind in early adolescence, resulting in the ability to reason in verbally stated hypotheses, to accept premises as given, and to deduce consequences from them. Tests of formal thinking require the subject to isolate variables and to use a combinatorial system. Formal thinking develops in an environment where people think, discuss, exchange, and criticise together, in cooperative ways.

Closely related to thought, language is both external and internal. Language reflects the more complex and abstract thinking of the adolescent. Increasingly difficult grammatical structures are understood and used. Vocabulary continues to expand. A secular shift has been shown, that vocabulary and reading ability have decreased during the past 50 years, most likely because of changes on all ecological levels.

Creativity, as either divergent thinking or creative achievement, is different from tested intelligence. The two forms of intelligence are combined in those whom society defines as genius, or highly creative. Very creative people differ from others in personality characteristics, gender-role concepts, self-concepts, and self-awareness, powers of observation, complexity of life, control between states of consciousness, brain waves, and characteristics of family microsystem.

Intellectual sex differences are rooted in biology and experience. Males are typically manipulative and action-oriented; females are typically communicative and receptive. Differences between individuals of the same sex are greater than differences between averages of the two sexes.

Both intelligent and social development contribute to moral development, which includes thinking, feelings, and acting. Hogan's socioanalytic theory, based on the idea that moral behavior is a product of evolutionary adaptation, proposes three phases of development: rule attunement, sensitivity, and autonomy. Kohlberg's cognitive developmental theory is concerned with sequential development of mental structures of moral reasoning. He distinguishes 6 types of moral judgment, grouped into 3 levels. Juvenile delinquency is a problem of moral development with roots in the individual and his interactions at all ecological levels.

Vocational development consists of moving toward integration of the self into the community, in a work role. Planning and goal-setting are important vocational activities during adolescence. They are related to educational and vocational achievement. Plans and goals are influenced by academic aptitude and achievement, parental encouragement, teachers, counselors, and peers. Influences vary by sex and race, and can be expected to change along with plans and goals as sex equality and racial equality increase or decrease. Work experience contributes to vocational development but may also bring disadvantages in adolescence. All levels of the ecology influence a student's education and vocational development. Macrosystems make demands and give opportunities according to the political and economic climate, changing frequently in a rapidly changing society. School microsystems change with macrosystem ideology and with the realities of secular changes in adolescents. The mesosystem is very important to vocational development, as well as to adolescent development in general.

References

1. Albert, R. S. Cognitive development and parental loss among the gifted and exceptionally gifted, and the creative. *Psychological Reports,* 1971, **29,** 19–26.
2. Barenboim, C. Development of recursive and nonrecursive thinking about persons. *Developmental Psychology,* 1978, **14,** 419–420.
3. Barron, F. The needs for order and for disorder as motives in creative activity. In C. W. Tyler and F. Barron (eds.). *Scientific curiosity: Its recognition and development.* New York: John Wiley & Sons, Inc., 1963.
4. Baumrind, D. A dialectical materialist's perspective on knowing social reality. In W. Damon (ed.). Moral development. *New Directions in Child Development,* 1978, No. 2.
5. Bernbaum, E. *The way to Shambhala.* New York: Anchor Press/Doubleday, 1980.
6. Breland, H. M. Birth order, family configuration, and verbal achievement. *Child Development,* 1974, **45,** 1011–1119.
7. Cole, S. Send our children to work? *Psychology Today,* 1980, **14:**2, 44ff.
8. Davison, M. L., S. Robbins, and S. B. Swanson. Stage structure in objective moral judgments. *Developmental Psychology,* 1978, **14,** 137–146.
9. DeBord, L. W., L. J. Griffin, and M. Clark. Race and sex influences in the schooling processes of rural and small town youth. *Sociology of Education,* 1977, **42,** 85–102.
10. Donaldson, M. *A study of children's thinking.* London: Tavistock, 1963.
11. Elkind, D. Egocentrism in adolescence. *Child Development,* 1967, **38,** 1025–1034.
12. Elkind, D., and R. Bowen. Imaginary audience behavior in children and adolescents. *Developmental Psychology,* 1979, **15,** 38–44.
13. Erikson, E. H. *Identity, youth and crisis.* New York: W. W. Norton & Company, Inc., 1968.
14. Goleman, D. Special abilities of the sexes: Do they begin in the brain? *Psychology Today,* 1978, **12:**6, 48ff.
15. Harris, L. J., C. Hanley, and C. T. Best. Conservation of horizontality: Sex differences in sixth-graders and college students. In R. C. Smart and M. S. Smart (eds.). *Readings in child development and relationships.* New York: Macmillan Publishing Co., Inc., 1977, pp. 375–387.
16. Hauser, R. M., and T. N. Daymond. Schooling, ability and earnings: Cross-

sectional findings 8–14 years after high school graduation. *Sociology of Education,* 1977, **50,** 182–206.

17. Hechinger, F. M. 1978 freshmen score poorly on 1928 exam. *New York Times,* March 19, 1980.
18. Hogan, R. The gifted adolescent. In J. Adelson (ed.). *Handbook of adolescent psychology.* New York: John Wiley & Sons, Inc., 1980.
19. Hogan, R., J. A. Johnson, and N. P. Emler. A socioanalytic theory of moral development. In W. Damon (ed.). Moral development. *New Directions for Child Development,* 1978, No. 2.
20. Holstein, C. B. Irreversible, stepwise sequence in the development of moral judgment: A longitudinal study of males and females. *Child Development,* 1976, **47,** 51–61.
21. Inhelder, B., and J. Piaget. *The growth of logical thinking.* New York: Basic Books, Inc., Publishers, 1958.
22. Keating, D. P. Thinking processes in adolescence. In J. Adelson (ed.). *Handbook of adolescent psychology.* New York, John Wiley & Sons, Inc., 1980.
23. Keniston, A. H., and J. H. Flavell. A developmental study of intelligent retrieval. *Child Development,* 1979, **50,** 1144–1152.
24. Kogan, N., and E. Pankove. Creative ability over a five-year span. *Child Development,* 1972, **42,** 427–442.
25. Kohlberg, L. Stage and sequence: The cognitive-developmental approach to socialization. In D. A. Goslin (ed.). *Handbook of socialization theory and research.* New York: Rand McNally & Company, Inc., 1969.
26. Kohlberg, L. Revisions in the theory and practice of moral development. In W. Damon (ed.). Moral development. *New Directions for Child Development,* 1978, No. 2.
27. Kohlberg, L., and R. Kramer. Continuities and discontinuities in childhood and adult moral development. *Human Development,* 1969, 12, 93–120.
28. Kramer, P. E., E. Koff, and Z. Luria. The development of competence in an exceptional language structure in older children and young adults. *Child Development,* 1972, **43,** 121–130.
29. Kuhn, D., and J. Brannock. Development of isolation of variables scheme in experimental and "natural experiment" contexts. *Developmental Psychology,* 1977, **13,** 9–14.
30. LeBlanc, A. F. Time orientation and time estimation: A function of age. *Journal of Genetic Psychology,* 1969, **115,** 187–194.
31. Looft, W. R. Egocentrism and social interaction in adolescence. *Adolescence,* 1971, **6,** 485–494.
32. Magarrell, J. Today's new students, especially women, more materialistic. *Chronical of Higher Education,* Jan. 28, 1980.
33. McCord, J. A thirty-year follow-up of treatment effects. *American Psychologist,* 1978, **33,** 284–289.
34. Marini, M. M. Sex differences in the determination of adolescent aspirations: A review of research. *Sex Roles,* 1978, **4,** 723–753.
35. Martindale, C., and J. Armstrong. The relationship of creativity to cortical activation and its operant control. *Journal of Genetic Psychology,* 1974, **124,** 311–320.
36. Neimark, E. D. Longitudinal development of formal operations thought. *Genetic Psychology Monographs,* 1975, **91,** 171–225.
37. O'Bryant, S. L., M. E. Durrett, and J. W. Pennebaker. Developmental and sex differences in occupational preferences. *Journal of Social Psychology,* 1978, **106,** 267–272.
38. Olive, H. The relationship of divergent thinking to intelligence, social class and achievement in high-school students. *Journal of Genetic Psychology,* 1972, **121,** 179–186.

39. Piaget, J. Intellectual evolution from adolescence to adulthood. *Human Development*, 1972, **15**, 1–12.
40. Protinsky, H. O., and G. Hughston. Adolescent conservation abilities: A comparison of three tests. *Journal of Psychology*, 1980, **104**, 27–30.
41. Reiling, A. M., and D. J. Massari. Internal versus external control and formal thought. Paper presented at meeting of the Society for Research in Child Development, Philadelphia, 1973.
42. Riegel, K. F. Speed of verbal performance as a function of age and set: A review of issues and data. In A. T. Welford and J. E. Birren (eds.). *Behavior, aging and the nervous system.* Springfield, Ill.: Charles C Thomas, Publisher, 1965, pp. 150–190.
43. Schaefer, C. E. The self-concept of creative adolescents. *Journal of Psychology*, 1969, **72**, 233–242.
44. Shannon, L. Development of time perspective in three cultural groups: A cultural difference or an expectancy interpretation. *Developmental Psychology*, 1975, **11**, 114–115.
45. Siegler, R. S., and R. M. Liebert. Acquisition of formal scientific reasoning by 10- and 13-year-olds: Designing a factorial experiment. *Developmental Psychology*, 1975, **11**, 401–402.
46. Smith, M. K. Measurement of the size of general English vocabulary through the elementary grades and high school. *Genetic Psychology Monographs*, 1941, **24**, 311–345.
47. Sobel, S. B. Psychology and the juvenile justice system. *American Psychologist*, 1979, **34**, 1020–1023.
48. Surwillo, W. W. Developmental changes in the speed of information processing. *Journal of Psychology*, 1977, **96**, 97–102.
49. Sylvia, W. H., P. M. Clark, and L. J. Monroe. Dream reports of subjects high and low in creative ability. *Journal of General Psychology*, 1978, **99**, 205–211.
50. Vygotsky, L. S. *Thought and language.* Cambridge, Mass.: The M.I.T. Press, 1962.
51. Watts, A. F. *The language and mental development of children.* London: George C. Harrap & Co. Ltd., 1944.
52. Werner, E. E. *Cross-cultural child development: A view from the planet Earth.* Monterey, Calif.: Brooks/Cole, 1979.
53. Yahres, H. *Why young people become antisocial.* Alcohol, Drug Abuse and Mental Health Administration. (DHEW Publication No. (ADM) 79–642.) Washington: U.S. Government Printing Office, 1979.
54. Zajonc, R. B., and J. Bargh. Birth order, family size, and decline of SAT scores. *American Psychologist*, 1980, **35**, 662–668.

15

Self and Sociosexual Development

Laura S. Smart

Getting it all together is the task of the adolescent. Erikson calls it developing a sense of identity. In the two chapters that have gone before this one, we have described the rapid and complex changes that take place in children's bodies and minds as they enter puberty and live through the years that follow. How can these changes be accepted and put to use?

The task of developing a sense of identity is not to be done alone, but in cooperation with others, and sometimes in conflict with them. Social interaction, both real and imagined, is the mode through which an adolescent integrates body, mind, and feelings into a whole person, and the person into the social ecology. The period of integration, or establishment of the sense of identity, may stretch out beyond the high school years. It must continue for a while after body and mind have made their most dramatic changes, since those changes are what require integration. This chapter, therefore, must deal with a longer age span than do the two previous chapters. We shall include some research on college students that deals with their sense of identity. We shall also look briefly ahead to the next stage, the sense of intimacy, when pertinent.

In this chapter, we draw upon previous chapters, trying to picture the adolescent as a whole person in the ecology. Chapter 13 describes the physical development that results in a sexually mature body, changed in size and shape, stronger, better coordinated, endowed with new powers, and yet bearing a resemblance to the child's body from which it was built. Chapter 14 discusses the developing intellectual powers that underlie new ways of thinking about the self, other people, and the social order. New feelings accompany physical and mental growth and change. We have discussed ecological influences on physical and mental development. Here, we shall go further into the adolescent's interactions within her particular macrosystem and microsystems. The issues in developing a sense of identity include establishing the sociosexual self, working out more mature relationships in the microsystems of family, peer group, and school, preparing for work and gaining some job experience, and developing values and a moral code.

QUESTIONS TO THINK ABOUT WHILE READING THIS CHAPTER

1. How can many aspects of adolescent development be integrated in Erikson's concept, the sense of identity?
2. How is the adolescent's sense of identity related to the macrosystem and to family and school?

3. At which ecological level or levels would you look for sources of a generation gap, or conflict between adolescents and parents?
4. What is the nature and function of friendship during the teen years?
5. What sort of male-female relationships are usual at junior high and high school ages?
6. What are the directions of present-day trends in sexual behavior of adolescent males and females?
7. Why are large numbers of teenage females exposed to risk of pregnancy?
8. At which ecological levels are adolescent pregnancy and childbearing serious problems?
9. What are some of the problems associated with marriage during adolescence?

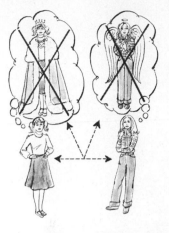

The Sense of Identity

A person's sense of identity answers the question, "Who am I?" It involves a core of sameness that comes from the past and is projected into the future. The sense of identity is constructed by the individual, organizing his beliefs, values, abilities, thoughts, and history. In spite of a thread of sameness, the identity undergoes modifications throughout life, and may shift greatly, as roles are dropped and added, or as the environmental context changes. The person with a weak sense of identity has trouble distinguishing himself from others, and feels confused when called upon to evaluate his own actions [38].

Intellectual Growth and Identity

Intellectual characteristics are described in the section "Characteristics of Adolescent Thinking" in Chaper 14. It is especially important here to review the section on metacognition.

It is through social interaction that the adolescent gradually learns that others are not as obsessed with her behavior as she herself is, and that the laws of the universe apply equally to her as to others. In the first case, the adolescent learns by testing reactions of real audiences. That is, she notices that peers are more concerned with their own behavior than with hers. Elkind [17] believes that the personal fable is eroded by the establishment of an intimate relationship. By sharing her own feelings of uniqueness with another, she comes to learn that the other has similar feelings of uniqueness. Thus, the development of cognitive structures give rise to new kinds of interactions, which in turn modify the cognitive structures.

Identity Statuses

Starting with Erikson's theory of the sense of identity, James Marcia and his associates have analyzed identity into 4 types, or *identity statuses* [38]. They have developed a method of classifying people by the way in which they deal with the issues of identity. The four identity statuses

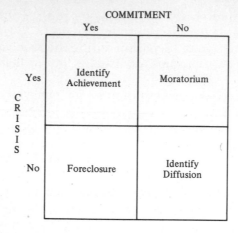

COMMITMENT

	Yes	No
Yes	Identify Achievement	Moratorium
No	Foreclosure	Identify Diffusion

(CRISIS on left vertical axis)

Identity Status	Correlated Behaviors	
	Females	Males
Achievers	Take charge of own life	
	Anxious	
	High Self-esteem	
Foreclosed	High Self-esteem	
	Authoritarian values	
	Not anxious	
	Externally oriented	
Moratorium		Anxious
Identity diffuse	Externally oriented	

FIGURE 15–1.
Possible identity statuses, according to Marcia. (Source: J. E. Marcia. Identity in adolescence. In J. Adelson (ed.). *Handbook of adolescent psychology.* New York: John Wiley & Sons, Inc., 1980.)

are these: identity achievement; foreclosure; identity diffusion; moratorium.

Individuals are classified on the basis of whether or not they have gone through a particular kind of decision-making period, and if so, whether they have come out of it with commitment to their choices. The kinds of decisions explored are choices that involve taking charge of one's own life. In adolescent males, the decisions have to do with occupation and political ideology. These two decisions plus a third one are used in classifying females' identity statuses. Figure 15-1 illustrates the four identity statuses.

Male Identity Statuses. An Identity Achiever is an individual who has actively made choices regarding occupation and ideology, and who has reached a decision to which a commitment is made. The Forecloser, by contrast, has made a commitment, but the decision was made by someone else, usually by parents. For example, one of my (L.S.S.) respondents in an unpublished study, when asked why he had chosen his future occupation, wrote, "I want to be a doctor because my Mom wants one of her kids to make good—not because I'm particularly interested in it."

Moratorium is the identity status of a person who is currently in crisis, but has not yet made a commitment to an ideology or to an occupation. The college sophomore who can't make up his mind what to major in is an example. Such a person is "having an identity crisis." The identity diffusion status also refers to a person with no commitment, but not actively searching for one. Like the sophomore in the previous example, the Identity Diffuse individual has not chosen a major, but he is unconcerned.

As would be expected from the definition of foreclosers, these individuals are most likely to hold authoritarian values. Foreclosure and Identity Diffusion types are more externally oriented, whereas Identity Achievement and Moratorium individuals are more likely to take charge of their own lives. Moratorium males, who are "in crisis," experience the most anxiety, and Foreclosures the least.

Women's Identity Statuses. Female decision-making was explored in the areas of occupation, ideology, and sex. The third area was added because the establishment of intimate relationships has been found to be important for the development of female identity. The crucial issue was whether the girl had chosen her own standards for sexual behavior rather than adopting her parents' without question. Just as in the choice of an occupation, an Identity Achiever might or might not have chosen what her parents wanted for her, but what she decided was right after careful thought. It was found that women who had high self-esteem were either Foreclosers, who had adopted their parents' standards without questioning them, or Identity Achievers, who had experienced a crisis and had chosen a standard for themselves. Achievers, however, were more anxious than Foreclosed individuals.

Erikson suggested that the process of identity formation differed for males and for females, and the identity status research seems to uphold this idea. Marcia concluded [38] that for the *average* female, interpersonal relationships take precedence over the establishment of a career. The woman who forms a separate identity around career issues loses social support, which contributes to mixed results of Identity Achievement women on anxiety and self-esteem. As achievement outside the family becomes more acceptable for women, it will be interesting to observe whether the identity formation process in women becomes more similar to the process in men.

Body Image

The child enters puberty with a body image that has not needed to change very much. Slow growth during childhood allows for a stable body image. Suddenly height shoots up, proportions change, breasts, testicles, and pubic hair suddenly spurt. The child of last summer may unwittingly crush the ribs of his grandmother in a bear hug when he greets her this summer. Surely the young adolescent asks now and then, "Can this

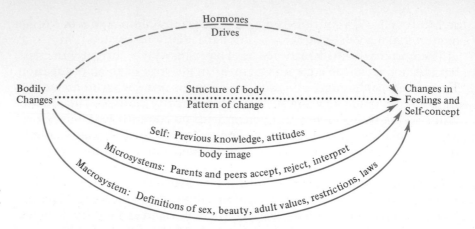

FIGURE 15–2.
Development of body image and sexual self-concept in early adolescence.

be I?" At this time, we suggest rereading the section on Characteristics of Adolescent Thinking in Chapter 14, thinking about the adolescent's task of knowing and accepting the new body while still feeling like the same person who is also a new person. The meanings of the changes are strongly influenced by the feedback that the adolescent gets from others, by earlier learning, by information picked up from the macrosystem, and by the adolescent's own creative thinking. Figure 15–2 illustrates some of the variables that may influence the adolescent's feelings about her changing body. In the following sections, we will discuss these variables.

Physiological Bases of Changed Feelings. Changes in hormones may produce mood changes in the adolescent, but it is difficult to prove the relationship, in spite of widespread belief that a connection exists [41]. Before firm conclusions can be drawn about the direct effects of hormones upon adolescent sociosexual development and self-concept, further study is needed.

Another explanation of direct effects of bodily changes upon the adolescent's psychological functioning is the *drive hypothesis,* offered by Freud and others. From this viewpoint, adolescent growth triggers rapid changes in sexual and aggressive impulses or drives. Adolescent conflict and rebellion are seen as inevitable consequences of the fluctuations of emotional states brought on by mushrooming drives. Because a drive is not measurable in itself, we have no research evidence that can confirm or disconfirm the existence of drives. Drive theories of adolescence refer to variations in behavior as results of the strength of drives, but the reasoning is circular. If one individual is observed to act more aggressively than another, the first is said to have a stronger aggression drive than the second.

Modification of Intervening Variables. A second major way of explaining the effects of bodily changes is represented in the lower portion of Figure 15–2. This model proposes that a number of factors, some internal to the individual and some external, influence the adolescent's developing body image and sexual self-concept.

1. INDIVIDUAL VARIABLES. The individual brings with her to puberty attitudes and feelings about her body and about the meanings of puberty. These self-attitudes and feelings have been developed throughout years of interaction in the family and peer microsystems. Family customs about nudity and use of the bathroom, sexual play between family members, parental handling of bodily self-exploration and masturbation in childhood, and of the child's play with peers, all will influence how the child feels about her body. The achievement of an adult body may be seen as a source of pride, shame, or both. Similarly, being a woman (or man) may be viewed as an asset or liability. The adolescent who has a positive view of what it means to be an adult of his or her sex should view evidence of individual sexual development with more pride than a person who has learned that adults of his/her sex are at a disadvantage. This topic will be further discussed in the section on gender role in this chapter.

2. MICROSYSTEM INFLUENCES. Persons close to the adolescent communicate to her their feelings about her developing body, either directly or indirectly. Physical contact between the opposite-sex parent and the child frequently is markedly decreased. The parent is responding to the sexual potential of the situation. From the parent's point of view, the child's sexual maturation causes a change in definition of behaviors from "affectionate" (for example, the child sitting on the parent's lap) to "potentially sexually stimulating" either to the parent, child, or both. The child is more likely to experience the parent's change in behavior as withdrawal of affection and support, and may feel badly about her developing body as a result.

Parents and siblings may make direct comments about the child's body. Information given about menstruation or nocturnal emissions has a covert meaning which is as important as the information given. The covert meaning may be that it is good to be an adult, or that it is bothersome and shameful. A parent or sibling may warn a girl whose figure is developing that she must now "watch out" for boys, or may point out in an approving way that she is becoming an attractive woman. Early and late puberty have social effects, as well as physical and mental. Social effects of the timing of puberty are discussed in Chapter 13, under Physical-Psychological Relationships.

Bodily attitudes influenced by parents, siblings, actions, comments

3. MACROSYSTEM INFLUENCES. The research on early versus late maturation has yielded varied results for girls, but it suggests that early maturation is an advantage psychologically and socially for American boys. Because girls as a group mature before boys do, the earliest maturing girls begin to develop before any boys have started the puberal growth spurt. Cultural stereotypes dictate that a "feminine" woman be small, especially in relation to men, and the early-maturing girl is likely to be taller than anyone in the class, female or male. The female body matures in a way that is defined as overtly sexual, since North Americans highly value

Early maturation is a plus for boys

the female breast as a sexual stimulant to men. The male body, by contrast, gains height and muscular mass, which are defined in terms as strength and manliness, rather than primarily as a sexual stimulant to women.

The early-maturing female must cope with the sexual advances of older boys at a time when she is socially still a child. A well-developed twelve-year-old is less equipped to deal with sexual interaction than is the fourteen-year-old who has a newly developed figure. In the study by Simmons [46] cited earlier in Chapter 13, girls who had been early daters with low self-esteem in seventh grade were interviewed in ninth grade. The interviews suggest that the girls experienced sexual pressures from boys as stressful. These girls did not want to kiss or hold hands with the boys that they were dating, and did not know how to handle such encounters with their dates. It would be interesting to know why these girls continued to date in spite of their negative reactions to dating.

Chilman [10] suggests another factor that may influence girls' reactions to early maturation. For girls, maturation means the beginning of menstruation, which is viewed ambivalently by most adolescent and adult females. Menstruation is viewed negatively in many societies, and such attitudes influence the thinking of many females in North America. Dealing with the menstrual flow is a nuisance. To women who highly value childbearing, the negative impact of menstruating is compensated for by menstruation's symbolizing the individual's potential to have a baby. If a woman's highest accomplishment is to produce a baby, menstruation is a small price to pay. However, 30 years of menstrual periods may seem like a large price to pay when production and rearing of children are devalued.

Cultural stereotypes about the desirability of certain body types exert strong influences upon adolescents and adults as well. In the United States, preference for large-breasted women leaves many adolescents and adults dissatisfied with their bodies. In modern Brazil, however, the

ideal body is one just past puberty. Current preferences in Brazil illustrate the interplay between genetics, environment, and culture. The average age of the population is under 18, making Brazil extremely youth-oriented. The environment is warm, and miles of beaches attract sunbathers. Thus, bodies are exposed, and it is difficult to hide defects. "Older" (that is, over 18) women struggle to meet the cultural ideal of a slim, immature body. For the wealthy, this means plastic surgery to firm up breasts and decrease their size, remove facial wrinkles, and remove excess fat from thighs [29].

Sexual Identity

In describing Marcia's classification of identity statuses, we touched on the role of sexual decisions in developing the female sense of identity. Now we discuss the identity of both males and females as sexual beings. Concepts of the self as female or male, feminine or masculine, are built through social interaction, observation, input from the media, and thinking. The foundations are laid in childhood, but acquire new meanings in the adolescent years, and continue to develop throughout the lifetime of the individual. Sexual identity also includes one's relationships as a sexual being within the whole social ecology. The following three aspects of sexual identity will be considered:

1. The self as *erotic*, or capable of having sexual feelings and desires.
2. The individual's standards of moral and immoral behavior for self.
3. Gender role, answering the question, what does it mean to be a boy or a girl, a man or a woman?

The Self as Erotic. Building on a foundation learned in childhood of what is sensually pleasing, the adolescent becomes aware of what is erotically pleasing and displeasing. Situations become defined as potentially sexually arousing, neutral, or distasteful. Actions by the self or by another, such as the stroking of a cheek or nipple, are similarly experienced and defined. Whether one is aroused by males, females, or both is another component.

SEXUAL ORIENTATION. Sexual orientation refers to the choice of sexual objects: either an individual of the same sex (a homosexual choice), one of the opposite sex (a heterosexual choice), or choosing individuals of both sexes (a bisexual choice). Many adolescents are attracted only to members of the opposite sex, and have relatively little concern about their sexual orientation. However, individuals who are not attracted to the opposite sex in adolescence or who feel attracted to members of both sexes very often are quite concerned about themselves as sexual persons. Males are more likely to be concerned than females, because male homosexuality is more feared and more condemned by society than is female homosexuality. Lack of interest in the opposite sex does not always mean interest in the same sex. Erotic interests develop at different paces in different individuals, and may not appear until the teen years have passed.

It is not uncommon for North American adolescents to become confused when they have feelings of love and tenderness for a friend of the same sex, and to fear that they are homosexuals. I (L.S.S.) recall reassuring a 16-year-old male friend that his feelings of love for his best male friend did not mean that he was a homosexual. In some cultures, the open expression of physical affection between members of the same sex is considered normal and desirable. In India, for example, high school and college age individuals stroll down the street holding hands with their best (same-sex) chum.

LEARNING WHAT IS EROTICALLY PLEASING. In North America, adults do not formally instruct children in the erotic arts, as is done in some societies, such as Mangaia. However, the adolescent has received sexual socialization in his family since he was brought home from the hospital. Whether he enjoys being held and stroked depends upon his prior experiences and upon genetic tendencies. Young children explore their own bodies freely unless parents punish them or express disapproval. They also will explore the bodies of their friends. However, these behaviors are not considered appropriate by most persons in our society, and are usually stopped.

In adolescence and young adulthood, North Americans must learn how to share their bodies with another person. With little previous experience of touching and being touched, and with little experience in seeing another person nude or being seen nude, learning how to share one's body can be a difficult task in our society. The touching of same-sex chums has been defined as potentially sexual and therefore threatening. Thus, the individual must learn about touching with an opposite-sex peer in a situation that is more likely actually to be sexually charged.

Although sexuality has been explored in college students, little research has been done with high school and junior high school populations. Therefore, we know little about how they express themselves through looking and touching. Lorna and Philip Sarrel, sex counselors who work with and have studied college students, suggest that the ideal situation would be one in which the individual's experiences increase in intensity and intimacy over the years, always in harmony with the person's level of emotional maturity, attitudes, and values, and within a supportive relationship or relationships [42, p. 60]. Within this framework, sexual intercourse might be saved for marriage, or might not be, according to the individual's beliefs and feelings.

We further suggest that the ecology in which the experience takes place is important. If sexual interactions take place in an atmosphere of fear of discovery, the meanings of the interactions and feelings associated with them will be different than if the individuals believe that their actions are acceptable to persons important to them. Much learning about one's sexuality takes place in social relationships. Another means of learning what is erotically pleasing is through masturbation. The Sarrels suggest that masturbation has potential for helping women to become more comfortable with their bodies and their sexual response patterns. However,

Sorensen [49] found that few adolescents who reported masturbating said that they got a great deal of enjoyment out of it and many reported feeling at least some guilt. Interestingly, those who felt worst were those whom Sorensen called "sexual adventurers," individuals who had sexual relations with a variety of partners in the absence of a stable relationship.

Personal Sexual Attitudes. Another aspect of sexual identity is the incorporation of sexual attitudes and values. The adolescent develops standards of behavior for herself in a number of ways answering the question, "What kinds of sexual behavior are acceptable for *me*, and under what circumstances?" These personal standards may be the same as those held for other people, or they may be different. Thus, a person might believe that it is all right for two people to have intercourse as long as they both want to do it, but to feel that *she* would not think it right for herself unless she were in love. A study of liberal college students and noncollege youth suggests that positive feelings about the self are more closely related to personal standards of behavior than to standards held for others [37].

Standards differ for self and others

Gender Role. The development of the sense of identity includes the development of identity as a man or a woman. As noted in previous chapters, sex typing occurs from birth onward. By the time a child reaches adolescence, he or she has done a great deal of growing toward becoming what is culturally defined as "masculine" or "feminine."

The adolescent has a clear idea of herself as female or himself as male. In other words, the gender identity of the adolescent is well-formed. However, in modern societies the role behaviors that express femininity or masculinity are not always clearly defined. For example, working outside the home traditionally has been defined as the primary task of the adult male. And yet, a majority of American women now work outside the home, and do not consider themselves to be "unfeminine" or to be "masculine." The adolescent seeks an answer to the following question: Just what does it mean to be an adult of my sex and what sort of acceptable adult am I capable of becoming? Both personality characteristics (such as "tenderness" and "competence") and role behaviors (such as "earning money" and "taking care of children") must be considered.

Early studies of masculinity and femininity conceived of the two as opposite ends of one continuum, or bipolar. The very masculine person was someone who was not at all feminine, and the feminine person was someone who lacked masculine qualities. In traditional societies, this bipolar conceptualization is more accurate than it is in postindustrial societies such as our own. More recently, researchers have broadened their view of masculinity and femininity in recognition of persons who are high (or low) on personality characteristics that are commonly seen as masculine or feminine. However, men (and adolescent males) as groups still score higher on "masculine" personality characteristics and lower on feminine ones than do women and adolescent females [50].

Traditionally, the definition of masculinity has included activity and achievement. Boys have been (and in most cases still are) encouraged to develop assertiveness and independence. A boy has to come to terms with authority while maintaining autonomy, neither submitting nor fighting too much. He has to come to terms with assertiveness, becoming neither timid nor cruel but controlled and purposeful. He has to come to terms with his sexuality, which he experiences directly as sexual desires. In order to control and gratify his sex impulses, he must loosen his family ties and make new ones. But before he can develop a sexual identity in relation to the opposite sex, he needs a foundation in the identity that requires achievement and assertiveness. Some sort of vocational success, perhaps a plan or commitment, will serve.

The adolescent boy knows and has known from early childhood that he must achieve and produce. Even though the high school peer group in general rewards athletes more than it does scholars, the adult male's vocational role is that of breadwinner, both before and after marriage. This fundamental is clear, even though expectations of husbands are not so definite. Also, there is continuity between the two roles. Research shows that husband-wife relationships are strongly influenced by the husband's vocational role. The very importance of work as part of a man's role makes vocational decisions serious and problems anxiety-producing.

Gender role stereotypes vary

For some individuals, the ideal masculine role has become less intensely competitive, with more emphasis upon sensuality, reflection, and passivity [14]. Feminist men such as Warren Farrell [20] have pointed out the pitfalls of the traditional masculine role. For most adolescent males, however, it seems likely that there will be a continued emphasis upon traditionally masculine forms of striving and achievement, including sports and preparing for an occupation. We now turn to an examination of feminine identity.

In the late 1950s, Douvan and Adelson [15] studied the gender identity of adolescent boys and girls. Autonomy, assertion, and occupational goals had no significance for feminine identity. Interpersonal competence was important for girls, and it was within a framework of interpersonal relations that they came to understand their sexuality. Girls who measured high on a femininity test measured high on ego strength. Whereas the boy gained masculine identity by focusing on a future job, the girl gained feminine identity by projecting herself into the future as wife and mother, carrying on nurturing interpersonal activities. The girls who were most feminine were responding to the cultural stereotype of woman as nurturant, centered on relationships involving love, reproduction, homemaking, and dependent upon a man to define her status in society.

Since Douvan and Adelson did their classic study, the relationship of women to work has changed dramatically. Most young women now expect to work outside the home after marriage and childbearing, thus combining domestic and occupational roles [1, 9]. However, adolescent and young adult females who want to be full-time housewives differ in a number of respects from those who want to have full-time careers. Desire for marriage at some time is still almost universal, as is the desire for at least one child. However, those who want to combine careers in non-typically female fields want to marry later and have fewer children than those females who prefer to be housewives [1]. Higher commitment to a career is related to endorsement of women's equality with men [47]. Career development was discussed in Chapter 14.

To conclude our discussion of feminine and masculine identity in adolescence, today's adolescent has more gender role choices, and is somewhat more likely to choose a nontraditional future role, especially if female. As women continue to enter occupations that were formerly open only to men, we can expect less concern about "sex-appropriate" behavior to be reflected in research. Indeed, it is currently thought that the androgynous adult, who combines both masculine and feminine personality characteristics, is the best-adjusted.

The Adolescent in the Family Microsystem

The adolescent moves from childhood dependence upon parents to adult independence from them. However, the route is not direct, and the destination is difficult to define. As most adults maintain relationships of mutual assistance with their parents, "adult independence" does not mean that ties are cut when the younger generation reaches adulthood. Rather, it is one of many stages that the parent and child pass through between the conception of the child and the aging and death of the parent. The relationship of parent and child is continuously redefined as the child grows up and the parent grows through the stages of adulthood. During adolescence, the child needs considerable independence, and yet still needs the love, security, and limit-setting provided by the parents.

Conflict and Closeness

A major controversy in the field of adolescence revolves around the question of the universality of adolescent rebellion. Is the adolescent inherently at odds with his parents? There is considerable evidence to the contrary showing that parents and children continue to be close and to be similar in many of their views, even throughout adolescence.

Psychoanalytic Perspective. According to the psychoanalytic viewpoint, the adolescent *must* conflict with his parents in order to strive toward an identity as a distinct and independent being. At the same time, he still wants the love, comfort, and protection that his parents have provided. Thus, to the adolescent, parents are almost always wrong, and children have to pick fights with them. This point of view is often comforting to bewildered parents, since it helps to reduce their guilt and feelings of inadequacy. If adolescents have to go through a difficult stage, then par-

ents simply have to wait patiently, confidently, and lovingly until the young people grow out of it into civilized adulthood.

Conflict as Avoidable.   Another point of view is that conflict is neither essential nor inevitable.   Most studies of adolescents and their parents have not found severe conflict between generations.   When parents have unhappy marriages or are extremely permissive or restrictive, adolescents are more likely to rebel [2].   Parents who reason with their adolescents, rather than dictating what is right and wrong, foster greater responsibility and less rebelliousness in their children [4].   When conflict does exist, it most often centers around activities that directly concern the adolescent, such as curfews.

Feelings of Love and Closeness.   Attachment is of vital importance throughout life, although attachment figures change.   Adults, as well as infants, seek proximity and contact with people they love at times when they feel threatened or weakened.   Adolescents normally continue to be attached to their parents, but not so strongly as they were as children. Girls are often more attached than boys.   Although boys are more likely than girls to report feeling closer to their father, the mother is most often the first choice of both boys and girls.

When comparisons are made of the responses of the parent generation and their college-age children, the older generation consistently overestimates the closeness, communication, and understanding that exists between them, and the younger generation underestimates it [6].   These differences in point of view reflect the younger generation's need for distance, and the older generation's need to feel that they have done an adequate job in rearing their children and that their views will be carried on to some extent by the youth.

The Generation Gap.   A "generation gap" exists when great value differences divide younger individuals from older ones.   There is considerable controversy about whether or not there is a generation gap in our society.   However, the term *generation* is vague, and can be used in a number of ways.   When *generation* refers to large groups of people, a more accurate term is *cohort* (see Chapter 1).   Another way of looking at generations is within the same family, the lineage type of generation [5]. When we use the word *generation*, we refer to the lineage type.   When studying lineage generations, the researcher compares the responses of parents with their own child's or children's responses.

Not surprisingly, when "the generation gap" is defined in terms of cohorts, larger value differences are found than when lineage generations are studied [6].   Parents and children rarely agree completely, but their views are closer to each other's views than are the average views of the parent cohort and the youth cohort.

Parents and children influence each other's development in complex ways from the conception of the child until the death of one generation. (In fact, the memory of the deceased can continue to be an influence upon the bereaved individual.) At some times during development, the strength of influence is stronger in one direction than the other. During adolescence in our society, the adolescent is often a powerful socializing agent of the parent. However, some parents are more responsive than are others to the attempts made by adolescents to introduce new ideas and behaviors. Such families, which are relatively open to change, have been called *forerunner families* by Bengston and Troll [6]. The parent generation is ahead of its time in holding certain important values, which are passed on to the children. The children, in their turn, pick up another theme in society, called a "keynote effect" by Bengston and Troll. For example, the forerunners of one cohort may experience a shift in values from a religious orientation to a secular orientation, and their children may be more concerned about changing sexual values. The parents socialized their children in a way that is different from the way that the parents were socialized. The children, aware that their parents have innovated, feel relatively free to bring home new ideas to the parents. When the new ideas are discussed within the family, there may be considerable conflict. Just as the children did not turn out exactly like the parents, the parents are unlikely to change their views completely. However, they are likely to change sooner than are nonforerunner parents, who are not as open to change.

In general, youth are more likely than older adults to pick up on a keynote effect. Forerunner youth would be first to change, followed by forerunner parents and by nonforerunner youth. Nonforerunner parents would be the last to change. By the time the forerunner parents change, if they do, the forerunner youth are on to a new keynote issue, starting the process all over again. Figure 15–3 illustrates the process.

It is not just in the realm of ideas that the younger generation attempts to influence the older. A teenager may suggest a new hairstyle for a parent, a solar-hot water system, or a more efficient way of washing dishes. Parents do not always notice all the ways in which their children are trying to influence them. The greatest number of attempts to influence parents are made by the most autonomous adolescents [3]. It seems that the adolescent gains autonomy through interactions with the parents, as well as gaining independence from them [3].

By now, it should be clear that adolescents and parents share similarities and influence each other. And yet, the peer group plays an increasingly important role in the life of the adolescent. The relative importance of parents and peers has been explored by asking the following questions.

How Close Do Adolescents Feel to Parents and Peers? Adolescent

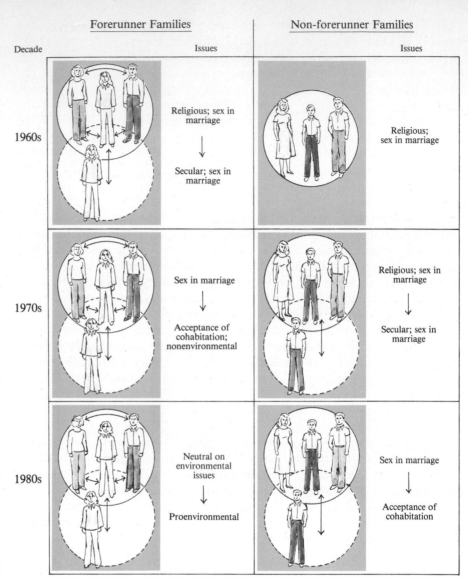

Forerunner Families | Non-forerunner Families

| Decade | Issues | Issues |

1960s — Religious; sex in marriage → Secular; sex in marriage | Religious; sex in marriage

1970s — Sex in marriage → Acceptance of cohabitation; nonenvironmental | Religious; sex in marriage → Secular; sex in marriage

1980s — Neutral on environmental issues → Proenvironmental | Sex in marriage → Acceptance of cohabitation

FIGURE 15–3
Social change in forerunner and nonforerunner families. (The issues in the 1980s' example is hypothetical.)

girls described their mother, father, and a friend using sets of descriptive adjectives. Mothers were rated most favorably. Fathers and friends received similar scores, with the father's score slightly more favorable [40].

With Whom Do Adolescents Discuss Problems? In a Toronto study [7], 13- to 20-year-old high school students were asked with which persons they were most likely to discuss their problems. Females were most likely to select their same-sex peers first, and males were most likely to select their mothers first. Mothers were the second choice of the females, and fathers were the second choice of the males. Boys were much more likely to choose fathers than were girls. Table 15–1 shows the results in greater detail.

Helper chosen first	Females		Males	
	No.	%	No.	%
Same-sex peers	71	41	20	24
Mothers	55	32	29	35
Opposite-sex peers	33	19	12	16
Other adults	7	4	7	8
Fathers	6	3	14	17
Totals	172	99%	82	100%

**TABLE 15–1
First Choice of Helpers by
Male and Female
Adolescents**

Source: Adapted from R. J. Burke and T. Weir. Sex differences in adolescent life stress, social support, and well-being. *Journal of Psychology,* 1978, **98,** 277–288.

Whose Wishes Would Prevail in a Conflict? Adolescents were asked what they would do if their friends wanted them to do one thing and their parents wanted them to do something else. Larson [34] found that most adolescents took into consideration not only what the others thought was right, but their own future needs and goals. The adolescents recognized that parents and peers each had areas of expertise. The opinions of parents were valued more in areas such as choosing a school curriculum, and peers' opinions carried more weight in areas such as deciding whether to go to a party. Parents were more influential when the affect between adolescent and parent was high [35]. Parent-adolescent affection was more important for boys than for girls, and more important in grades 9 and 12 than in grade 7.

In thinking about influences of parents and peers, it is not a case of *either-or.* Although every individual no doubt experiences times when conflicting demands are placed on her by members of her various microsystems, there are many other times of harmony. A study of adolescent peer groups indicates that adolescents are keenly aware of the standards set by parents of individual members, and that they compare the individual standards to a norm that is a composite of the parental standards for the entire group. Thus, the peer group actually reinforces parental values for group members, although the group parental values are not exact copies of those of the parents of any one individual [45].

The stronger the mesosystem between the adolescent's family and peer group, the less deviance there should be from parental norms. When the relationship between the parents and the adolescent is weak, the mesosystem of parents and peers is very likely to be lacking as well. Figure 15–4 illustrates this relationship. Although today's adolescents are more equipped to be independent from parents than were past cohorts, parental guidance is needed still. The individual adolescent, and her peer group as well, benefit from a strong mesosystem. And yet, it is unlikely that the parental standards of any peer group will be entirely uniform. Thus, the adolescent is exposed to some variance in standards and values, which is an aid to identity formation. And because socialization flows

**An Ecological
Perspective on
Parents and Peers**

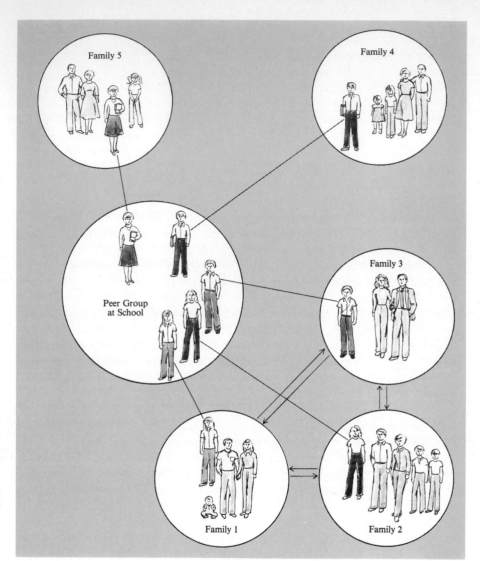

FIGURE 15-4.
The peer and family microsystems and mesosystems. Arrows indicate relationships between microsystems. The adolescents in families 1–5 form a clique at school. Families 1, 2, and 3 know each other. The adolescents in these families should be more similar to each other than they would be similar to the adolescents in families 4 and 5.

from child to parent as well as from parent to child, the parents as well are exposed to new ways of handling situations and perceiving the world.

The Peer Group

For most adolescents, peers (age-mates) play an even more important part in life than they did during childhood. A few adolescents remain outside the social swim from preference, pursuing studies, hobbies, or athletics, perhaps with one or two friends. Some youngsters, rejected by the peer group, exist in isolation or with other isolates in smaller groups of two or three. Among peers, there are two main kinds of groups: *crowds* and *cliques.* Friends, of course, are individuals.

Both boys and girls belong to "the crowd," but there are occasions when groups of one sex get together. The like-sex crowd is not always identical with the group of boys or girls that participates in the boy-girl crowd. Especially at the younger ages, late maturers and certain nonconforming, independent individuals are unacceptable or uninterested in boy–girl affairs, but they may be cherished members of a like-sex group. Within the crowd are cliques, small groups of close friends, and pairs of best friends.

The crowd is usually based on the school, although neighborhood has some influence. School is the place where most social interaction takes place, in the classroom and library, at basketball and football games, clubs, interest groups, parties, in the corridor and yard (or campus, as it is sometimes called).

One of the basic functions of the crowd is to provide a group identity that separates adolescent from parent, a "we" feeling apart from the family. The adolescent thus strengthens his own sense of identity by being a member of a group that defines his difference from his parents. Joe gets his hair cut (or not cut) like the other boys do, but different from Dad's. The girls wear pretty much the same shade of lipstick and nail polish, as well as standardized coiffures, but if adults adopt those fashions, the fashions are soon dead and are replaced.

The crowd is also for fun and comfortable feelings, for doing things together like bowling and strolling, for hanging around the soda fountain, for just talking and talking and talking. And giggling and shouting. The output in decibels is very large in comparison with the intellectual content of conversation, but with good reason. Everybody is trying out a variety of roles, uncertain and tentative as to what kind of person he can be. There is security and warmth in the company of people who face the same problems, feel the same way, behave the same way, and wear the same symbols of belonging. It feels good to giggle and shout, to be silly and to stand together against those who do not understand.

The Clique

Smaller and more intimate than the crowd, although often called "the crowd" by its members, a clique is a highly selected group of friends. Usually alike in social background, interests, and experience, the clique members are emotionally attached to each other. Members' feeling for one another is the basic factor holding them together. Some cliques become formalized into clubs, even fraternities and sororities, but most adolescent cliques remain informal and small. Just as the adolescent generation differentiates itself from adults by many symbols, and one crowd from another, so a clique is likely to have ways of proclaiming its difference from others and solidarity within itself. "Everybody" wears blue on Tuesdays. The turn of a phrase. A food fad.

Compared with boys, girls show a wider range of emotional needs in peer relationships [31]. Belonging to a clique or peer group is more related to status values for girls than it is for boys [12, 31]. Since high status is relative, excluding others from a high-status clique can make the

members feel important.   Boys, however, are more influenced by clique standards than girls are [45].

Year-long observations of ninth-graders revealed most boys and girls as belonging to cliques of three to eight members, with an average size of five [13].   As in earlier studies [15], the girls had closer friendships than did the boys.   Girls were much more likely than boys to interact socially only with other members of their cliques.   Nine girls and three boys were not accepted into cliques and did not form new cliques at the beginning of the year.   Eight of the girls were new students.   Unlike the new girls who tended to remain loners, the new male students formed a new clique. Only 20 per cent of the students studied were black.   Three black females formed a clique; four more remained loners.   No social interaction was observed between the black females and white females or males.   By contrast, black males dated both black and white females.

Erikson [18, pp. 92–93] tells how clique members can be petty, cruel, and intolerant in order to defend themselves against a sense of *identity diffusion*.   By excluding others who are "different" in skin color, religion, class, abilities, or even such trivialities as dress and appearance, the youngster gains some sense of identity from the group to which he belongs.   Erikson stresses the importance of understanding this mechanism without condoning the behavior.   Adolescents have to be helped to grow beyond the point where they feel the necessity for defending themselves by these cruel methods.   (These are the methods of totalitarian systems.)   Erikson implies that it can be done by adults living so as to demonstrate "a democratic identity that can be strong and yet tolerant, judicious and still determined."

Friends

The term *best friend* usually indicates a member of the same sex.   The best-friend relationship is an important one for the sense of identity, as anyone who shares a telephone with an adolescent will testify.   The long conversations are between like-sex friends, especially best friends, and longer for girls than boys.   A best friend is the best audience on whom to project all the roles and identities that an adolescent wants to test as possibilities, because this audience is just as concerned with testing and trying. In early adolescence, each is likely to be more concerned with herself than with the other.

A pair may try a role together. "We'd both look better minus ten pounds. Let's go on the same diet! We just won't let each other eat more than 1,100 calories a day." They may play at building a common identity, each gaining security from feeling stronger as a pair than as an individual. "Teri is part of me and I'm part of her. We think the same things. Each of us knows what the other one is thinking. We wear the same kind of clothes and we trade clothes." Communication is easy with someone who faces the same succession of changes—fluctuations in physical balance, emotional upsets, new mental powers, problems with parents, and all the rest.

In an upper-middle class community in a midwestern city, high school respondents were asked about their friendships [44]. These adolescents discriminated between "good," "best," and "casual" friends. One girl distinguished among types of friends in this way:

Q. What are some of the things you expect of a friend?
A. When you leave (a group), when you walk out, they don't all of a sudden start stabbing knives in your back. It all depends upon the degree of friendship you want (in response to the question).
Q. What are the various degrees of friendship?
A. With some girls you just have a casual friendship, and she's got her friends and I've got mine, but we'll sit down and talk. Then like the girls in my club, we are pretty good friends. We know who we are going out with. With the casual friend you don't sit and talk about your boyfriend to them. I have one best friend.
Q. Are there certain things you share with a best friend that you don't share with a fellow club member (that is, a "pretty good friend")?
A. You talk about your boyfriends if you had an argument, but you wouldn't tell them personal things (that is, to a "pretty good friend"). I could tell my best friend anything, and she wouldn't think badly of you. You don't have to worry that, will she tell anyone else? While the members of my club, I expect them not to stab knives in my back when I leave, but my best friend, if someone else does, I expect her to stand up for me. My club members, I wouldn't expect them to stand up for me.

Friendships tend to become more stable with increasing age, from 11 to 18 [30]. Choice stability probably reflects increasing personality maturity. In turn, stability in choice of friends makes possible more opportunities for the development of the sense of intimacy, because intimacy grows within permanent relationships. Erikson writes of the sense of intimacy as "the condition of a true twoness in that one must first become oneself" [18, p. 95]. Just as all the senses have early beginnings before their periods of critical growth, so we would expect the sense of intimacy to show some expression in childhood and adolescence. In its fullest meaning, intimacy between two people exists on all planes of contact, including sexual, but here, in its beginning stage, it is largely a meeting of minds. Bob tells Tom what he thinks and feels, trying to express it in ways that Tom will understand. Tom listens carefully to Bob and asks pertinent questions, trying to put himself in Bob's place. Each tries to understand and to make himself understandable. Each cares what the other thinks and feels. The stronger a person's sense of identity, the more he can care about the other person's thoughts and feelings. Released from the constant necessity of searching for his identity, he is free to enter into an intimate relationship. As identity develops slowly throughout the period of adolescence, it is reasonable that it should gradually make way for intimacy.

The years 1946 and 1947 were the dates of studies showing that the best-friend relationship became more stable through the teen years. If the studies were to be repeated today, we wonder (1) would best friend still continue through the teens to mean a member of the same sex? and (2) would friendships with the same sex show increasing stability? Adolescents have less time and energy for like-sex best friends because they are turning increasingly to the opposite sex for companionship. Comparing adolescents of the 1940s and 1960s there was an increase in the choice of cross-sex companions for nine activities, such as studying and going to the movies [33]. Earlier dating, earlier going steady, and fears of being labeled a "homosexual," have shortened the period when adolescents can form deep friendships within their own sex. Very early, they come to compete with one another for dating partners, thus lessening the trust they can put in each other. At the age when dating begins, the junior high school age, boys are, on the average, two years behind girls in physiological maturity. Boys and girls of the same age are less suited to be together at this time than at any other time of life. Thus neither can grow at his own pace, in the way that a boy could in male society and a girl in female. The recent increase in identity diffusion, the failure to develop a healthy sense of identity, is attributable to a complex of factors. This could be one of them, the deprivation of a period dominated by strong, deep friendships with members of the same sex.

Sex Differences in Friendship. Douvan and Adelson's [15] nationwide survey of 14- to 16-year-olds revealed important differences in the ways in which boys and girls needed friends and related to them. In order to solve his crucial problem of asserting his independence and resisting adult control, the boy needs a gang or at least a group of friends who band together to present a solid front. The girl's problem is more to understand her own sexual nature and to control and gratify her impulses in the context of interpersonal relationships; for this she needs a few close friends. Girls want friends to be loyal, trustworthy, and reliable sources of emotional support; boys want friends to be amiable, cooperative, and able to control aggressive impulses. Like preadolescent girls, boys between 14 and 16 are not concerned with warmth, sensitivity, and close relationships. The support that boys want from friends is against concrete trouble, especially conflicts with authority, whereas girls want help with their own emotional crises. As the study did not go beyond age 16 with boys, it is possible that older boys change in the direction of developing warmer and closer relationships with friends.

Girls need: close friends— Boys need: a gang or group

Reporting his earlier studies, John Coleman [11] noted that he found sex differences similar to those reported by Douvan and Adelson. When girls aged 11, 13, 15, and 17 were compared to boys the same ages, girls were more anxious about their friendships than were boys. Girls expressed more negative feelings about their friendships at all ages, especially at age 15. At all ages, but especially 15, girls were more afraid of being rejected than were boys. Coleman suggests that these sex differences are found because girls are more concerned with intimacy and dependency, and boys are more concerned with friendships based around shared activities.

Popularity. A popular person is one who is chosen or liked by many peers. A youngster may achieve popularity at some expense to his integrity because he may have to make many concessions in order to please a variety of people. He does not necessarily have a deeply satisfying "best friend" with whom he develops intimacy and strengthens his identity. Popularity is a strong value, however.

Although done in the late 1950s, James Coleman's study [12] probably still has relevance for adolescents today. From the feminine point of view being a leader in activities and being in a leading crowd and cheerleading were consistently important. A girl's grades and family background influenced her popularity more in relation to girls than to boys. Attractive clothes, on the other hand, were more important to her popularity with boys than with girls. As popularity with boys was important in the status system of girls, the importance of personal attractiveness was increased. Boys saw being an athlete, being in a leading crowd, and being an activities leader as important criteria. Scholarship, though relatively unimportant, appeared to boys as even less important in their popularity with girls, whereas having a good car was more important.

To the extent that success is measured by popularity and membership in the leading crowd, there is widespread threat to the sense of adequacy of many youngsters. There are not enough places at the top. Nor is there free access to the top for anyone who is willing to work hard for it.

The system does have its democratic aspects, however. Social position of families counts for considerably less than athletic achievement. Motor skill is distributed much more evenly throughout the socioeconomic hierarchy than is scholarship. If scholarship and class position were more important than athletics, then the youngsters from more privileged families would have a greater advantage than they do. Furthermore, it may be that the effects of attributes that determine popularity are strongest at the extremes. The most good-looking or most athletic are likely but not certain to be the most popular, and the least good-looking or least athletic are likely to be the least popular [11]. However, for the majority of adolescents who are at neither extreme, popularity is determined by a number of other factors. Researchers have paid little attention to individuals who are in the middle range of popularity [11], just as they have tended to ignore children of average IQ. Even for those adolescents who are at the extremes, possession of a valued attribute such as good looks or superior athletic ability does not guarantee popularity.

The Opposite Sex: Patterns of Association

"I want to ride my bike to the coffee shop across the street from Tommy's dad's service station in Centerville. He works there sometimes, and I want to see if he's there. Will you go with me?" Sally asked her best friend.

"Are you kidding? It's five miles—all uphill!" Josie gasped.

"Please!" Sally begged. "I just *have* to see him! Besides, it's downhill on the way home!"

The two girls having this dialog are in the eighth grade. Sally likes Tommy, a classmate, but he doesn't know it. Over the course of a month, the two friends will ride to Centerville several times, so that Sally can sit in the coffee shop and watch Tommy while he pumps gas.

Young adolescents may use a best-friend relationship as a bridge to the opposite sex. For Sally, it was enough just to watch Tommy at work, but she needed Josie's support while she did so. Sally is a long way from dating, but she has taken a step in that direction. In grades 7 and 8, some youngsters show no interest in the opposite sex, or no interest other than avoidance. Others move toward each other. In one middle-class suburban junior high school in Rhode Island, for example, seventh- and eighth-grade boys and girls voluntarily sit at opposite ends of the lunch room. Two or three tables are coed, chosen by the most mature of the eighth-graders [48]. Many young adolescents begin their heterosexual careers with group dates to movies or by "hanging out" in mixed sex gangs at bowling alleys or similar gathering places.

Dating. The next step in heterosexual social development is dating: the pairing off of opposite-sexed individuals for social activity that lasts for several hours, usually for an evening. For the past 25 years, most American adolescents have begun to date by 14 or 15 [27].

Dating, a custom developed by middle-class North American youth, is more of a social relationship than a courtship one. An informant in the study quoted earlier [44] in the section on "Friends" described dating as a game:

> It's one of the most fun games around, too. Because you never know what's going to happen. . . . It's up to you. There are no rules really. There might be a couple of rules that you take for granted . . . (like) not to do anything really nasty. Like go out with his best friend—break a date with him and go out with his best friend or something like that. Nothing really drastic, but aside from that there aren't too many rules, and you've just always got to make sure that you're on top, that you're winning because otherwise if you're not winning you're losing and there's no tie. So you always make sure you're winning.

However, there is evidence that dating is not viewed as cynically by all adolescents. When asked what they considered to be important attributes for a date to possess, white middle-class high school students chose attributes such as "pleasant and cheerful," "dependable," and "considerate." Items such as "has access to a car" and "knows how to dance" were considered most important by black working-class high school students in the same study [27]. Perhaps the more privileged white students took for granted having a car. In another study by the same author [28] college students were found to be unconcerned with whether a date had a lot of money or access to a car, concentrating instead upon the same kinds of attributes that the white high school students considered important. In older studies of college youth done between the late 1920s and the early 1970s, at least some importance was placed upon the more external attributes. All of these studies suggest that as youth become older and presumably more mature, internal qualities become more important. It may be also that a cultural shift is taking place.

In the 1950s and before, rigid rules kept girls from asking boys on dates. Some girls would refuse dates if the boy asked them only a day or two before the event, lest the boy think that she was unpopular. Traditionally, it was considered wrong for girls to call boys. By the 1970s, these patterns had faded or disappeared in some communities. Influenced by women's liberation, some females, particularly at the college level but in some instances at the high school level as well, began to ask males for dates and no longer to be as concerned about accepting a date a

day or two before it was to occur. In other high schools, the old patterns of female coyness and manipulation in order to get a boy's attention still continue, with little change from previous generations. The change toward female assertiveness represents a broadening of the spectrum of behavior that takes place, rather than an abrupt change.

Personality Development and Dating. Just what is the effect of early dating on personality development? Although much attention has been given to this question in the media, by members of the clergy and by parents, the exact effects are not known. Although some adults disapprove of early dating, others think that dating is educational, giving adolescents experience in human relationships, promoting social skills, and enhancing their ability to choose a mate wisely.

Erikson does not deny the possibility of developing the sense of identity through association with the opposite sex. In fact, he describes such a boy–girl relationship: ". . . such attachment is often devoted to an attempt at arriving at a definition of one's identity by talking things over endlessly, by confessing what one feels like and what the other seems like, and by discussing plans, wishes and expectations" [18]. The danger implied in a boy–girl relationship of this sort is not that it is inadequate for promoting identity. The danger is that the relationship will include sexual intercourse before the sense of identity is firm, and when the sense of intimacy cannot build on identity. And one concern that many adults have about early dating, is, of course, this increased opportunity for sexual intimacies at early ages.

Trends in Adolescent Sexual Behavior

Adolescent sexuality remains a highly controversial topic, arousing as much passion in the nonforerunner parent cohort as in the adolescents themselves. In spite of a recent increase of research on adolescent pregnancy, many important questions about adolescent sexuality remain unanswered. Research on sexuality of both adults and adolescents traditionally has concentrated on the female, with an emphasis upon counting the numbers of women who are engaging in sexual intercourse. Sexual behavior involves a great deal more than sexual intercourse, and the meanings of all of these behaviors to the individuals and couples themselves, to their families, and to the larger society seem to me (L.S.S.) to be more important than a mere "body count." In the following section, we will explore the question of "who is doing what" and then consider the implications of these behaviors.

Noncoital Sociosexual Behavior

Throughout the junior high school and high school, the majority of adolescents probably are more concerned with sexual behaviors that stop short of sexual intercourse. Holding hands, kissing, and petting are all forms of sexual behavior which among adults are called "foreplay" but which adolescents (particularly females) may find satisfying in themselves, or perhaps even more than they want. Many males as well do not really want to rush headlong into sexual intercourse, but enjoy being physically close to a girl. Adolescents are given little, if any, help in pacing their sexual careers. The assumption that "necking" leads swiftly to "petting," and that "petting" leads even more rapidly to sexual intercourse may become a self-fulfilling prophecy. Some couples are able to pace themselves with apparent comfort. Lorna and Philip Sarrel report that it is not uncommon for Yale students to sleep in the same bed for weeks or months before they decide to have sexual intercourse [42].

Premarital Coital Behavior

Research conducted in the 1970s indicates that increasing numbers of adolescent females have experienced sexual intercourse (coitus) [51]. Figure 15–5 illustrates the increases for both races combined. At all ages and during both years, black adolescent females were more likely to have had premarital intercourse than were whites. In 1979, 53 per cent of white and 76 per cent of black unmarried 18-year-olds were nonvirgins [51]. By contrast, research conducted between 1925 and 1965 indicates that about 10 per cent of white high school senior women, and 25 per cent of white college senior women, were nonvirgins. Rates of premarital intercourse experience for males were higher in the older studies, and have shown a less drastic increase in recent years [10]. By 1979, slightly more than three-quarters of black and white metropolitan males had experienced premarital intercourse by age 19 [51]. A 1981 report places the number of sexually active teenagers at 12 million [46a].

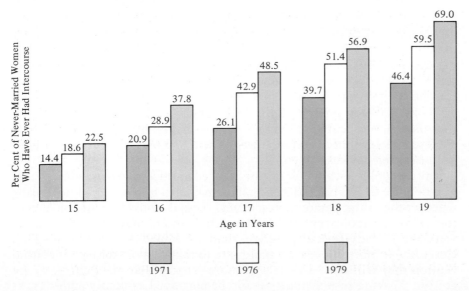

FIGURE 15–5.
Percentage of never-married women who have ever had intercourse, by age, 15–19 years, in 1971, 1976, and 1979. (SOURCE: Melvin Zelnik and John Kanter. Sexual activity, contraceptive use and pregnancy among metropolitan-area teenagers: 1971–1979. *Family Planning Perspectives*, 1980, **12**, 230–237.)

Exposure to Risk of Pregnancy

In Chapter 3, we were concerned with teenage childbearing from the standpoint of infants born to adolescents. In Chapter 13, we considered the impact of pregnancy and birth on the health and growth of teenagers. In this section, we focus on the meaning of sex, pregnancy, and birth to personality development and to the adolescent's present and future life style. First, we look at all levels of the ecology for factors promoting adolescent pregnancy. In Chapter 13, we touched upon macrosystem factors, and here, we add to them. We begin at the level of the individual.

Factors at the Individual Level. Reasons for having sexual intercourse vary for adolescent males and females. Boys experience a stronger sex drive, and yet, the extent to which the drive is innate or largely culturally determined is not known. Boys also receive more pressure from peers to "score" sexually. Girls, on the other hand, are more likely to report using sex as a way of getting close to their partner and of maintaining the relationship with him [10]. Many girls report that their boyfriends put considerable pressure on them to have sexual intercourse [25] and those girls who manage to resist this pressure have more power in relation to their boyfriends [32].

Many studies have shown that fewer than half of unmarried females used contraceptives the first time they had sexual intercourse [10]. Fewer than one-third of sexually active teenagers use contraceptives every time they have intercourse [51]. In view of the fact that the majority of sexually active adolescents do not wish to become pregnant or to impregnate, this behavior seems puzzling. Some reasons, however, have been identified.

High school age adolescent females who have premarital coitus are likely to have lower self-esteem than their virgin peers [10]. Low self-esteem and feeling out of control of one's life are associated, as well, with nonuse of contraceptives [10]. Some adolescents become pregnant because they don't understand how pregnancy occurs, or because they are misinformed about the probabilities of conception at different times during the menstrual cycle. In other cases, adolescents think that they are somehow immune to pregnancy. When asked why they did not use contraceptives, pregnant adolescents were likely to say, "I thought I would be lucky and not get pregnant" [10]. Such fatalistic attitudes suggest that these adolescents are living "the personal fable." Thus, the female adolescent's level of cognitive development is a factor in her use or nonuse of contraceptives.

Among adolescent males, failure to use contraceptives may be a result of ignorance or fatalistic thinking, but may also be a result of not caring whether they impregnate their partner. Less is known about use of contraceptives by adolescent males. One study found that inner-city whites were more likely to use condoms than were blacks or Hispanics [21]. Certainly, if more adolescent males are to take responsibility for contraception they will need a great deal more support than they currently are getting. Taking responsibility could be portrayed as manly and sexy, as well as safe. Such support would have to come from the macrosystem level, and also from the microsystems of family and peers. Before the use of birth control pills and intra-uterine devices (IUDs) became widespread, protection for intercourse was considered to be more the man's responsibility. Although female-controlled contraceptives add to women's autonomy, their widespread use has contributed to a cultural norm that protection for intercourse is solely the job of the female [10].

Factors at the Microsystem Level: Parents and Peers. The family microsystem influences the sexual development of the growing child in many ways. Attitudes about the relationships between men and women, about one's acceptability as a person, and feelings about one's body are learned in part within the family. Parents and siblings provide information about sexuality, either directly or indirectly. The peer microsystem provides input as well, which may conflict with or complement input from the family.

Direct teaching about sexuality is relatively rare in our society. Many parents find it impossible to discuss sexuality with their preadolescent and adolescent children, and resort instead to providing reading material, laying down a few prohibitions about sexual activity, or doing nothing. Several studies have found that fewer than half of parents of high school and junior high school age adolescents explain intercourse to them, and even fewer parents discuss birth control [22]. White, middle-class parents are more likely to provide their children with reading material about sex, and black, low-income mothers are more likely to discuss birth control with their children. Women who are not currently married to the father of their adolescent are more likely to have discussed sex and birth control with their child. Such adolescents are more likely to have initiated sexual intercourse before the age of 15. Women who themselves had premarital intercourse are more likely to discuss sex with their daughters, as are women who have positive attitudes toward birth control. Although adolescents at different ages need different kinds of information about sex, the age of the child has not been found to make much of a difference in the kinds of parent-child discussions held [22].

Most parents and teenagers agree that information about sex and birth control should come from parents [19]. Why, then, do many parents fail to do what they think is right? Discussing birth control is difficult for many parents because it forces them to deal directly with the developing sexuality of their children. Many parents are not well informed themselves. There is evidence that when mothers are able to discuss sexuality and birth control with their daughters the daughters are able to contracept effectively [22]. Having accurate information about birth control is a help, but parent-adolescent discussions about sex do more than provide information. Crucial to the effective use of contraceptives is acceptance of one's sexuality. There is a pervasive myth in our society that female sexuality is most acceptable when the woman is carried away by her passions, especially if she is unmarried. To take contraceptives along on

PR: Parental guidance recommended

a date routinely is to admit an interest in sex to oneself and one's partner. When parents stress to a child that contraceptives must be used when having sex outside of marriage, they enable the child to take responsibility for nonmarital sex.

Peers as well play an important role in responsible adolescent sexuality. When peers are seen as approving of the use of contraceptives, adolescents are more likely to use them consistently [32]. Thus, support for use of contraceptives can be effective whether from family members or from peers. The most advantageous situation, of course, would be support from both microsystems, either to avoid premarital intercourse entirely, or to use contraceptives effectively when having coitus.

Another very important factor in effective contraception is the quality of the dyadic relationship. Being in a stable, committed relationship increases the chances of having sexual intercourse, but it also increases the use of effective contraceptives [10, 32]. The adolescent (or adult) female who is not in a committed relationship, or who has been in one for fewer than six months, is less likely to use contraceptives. Although it may seem irrational for women to discontinue use of contraceptives when they are not in a stable relationship, discontinuation is motivated by a need to protect a view of oneself as nonpromiscuous and as not "looking for sex" [36].

Macrosystem Influences. Thus, the macrosystem value that a woman must not look for sex has a direct influence upon the risks that females are willing to take. These values are taught by and mediated through the peer and family microsystems, and can be circumvented at the microsystem, dyadic, or individual levels. Many macrosystem influences are extremely pervasive and subjective. Sex is used to sell countless products, even in magazines for teenagers. The macrosystem influences adolescent sexuality indirectly as well. Because most mothers of adolescents work outside the home, few adolescents are supervised after school.

Exposure to Risk of Pregnancy: Conclusions. Our society does much to promote adolescent sexual activity without providing the skills, knowledge, motivation, and safeguards needed to avoid pregnancy. Another grave problem is venereal disease. The dominant view regarding sexual activity seems to be that if an individual wants to engage in sex, he or she should take the risk of paying the price of disease or pregnancy. Over the years, family life educators have tried to get parents to provide information to their children, but with small results.

If adolescents are to avoid exposure to pregnancy, they need help in dealing with their sexuality. This help can come from family members, or from peers, and still have some positive effects. Nonetheless, only abstinence from sex will enable an individual entirely to avoid risk of pregnancy. Most adolescents remain virgins until the end of high school or beginning of college, but 12 million or more are sexually active. The results of adolescent sexual activity are a massive problem for our society.

Sexual
Intercourse
No / \ Yes
Contraception
Yes / \ No
Pregnancy
No / \ Yes
Abortion Infant
No / \ Yes
Adoption Parenting

The percentage of teenagers who give birth to an out-of-wedlock infant tripled between 1940 and 1975. In 1975, 1.2 per cent of white 15- to 19-year-olds, and 9.5 per cent of blacks, gave birth outside of marriage. Because fewer teenagers are giving up their babies for adoption, adolescent parenting has become a national problem. It is a problem because adolescents are not ready to take on the burdens of child care, and always need the help of either their families or the welfare system. Detriments to the infants are detailed in Chapter 3. In this section we will discuss the apparent causes of adolescent childbearing and its outcome for the adolescent.

The factors that cause an adolescent to have unprotected sexual intercourse are, of course, some of the same factors that result in adolescent pregnancy. Getting pregnant on purpose is relatively rare among adolescents. But are there other motivaters for adolescent childbearing, at an unconscious level, or at the microsystem or macrosystem levels? Many people think that there are.

Unconcscious Motivations. The inability to find a direction for one's life, or anger at one's parents, may result in the adolescent seeking a pregnancy, according to a psychoanalytic view. The adolescent who is in the midst of an identity crisis may use motherhood as a way of resolving the crisis temporarily. And yet, it is questionable whether the adolescent actually seeks the pregnancy, or whether she "falls into" the pregnancy as a result of low self-esteem and then uses the pregnancy as a focus for her life. If she feels unloved and unneeded by her parents, having sexual intercourse is likely to be an attempt to find love from her partner. When pregnancy results, she may hope that the baby will love her in a way that neither her parents nor her boyfriend seem to do.

Microsystem Influences. It is unlikely that many families actually want their teenage daughter to become pregnant and produce a child out of wedlock. However, once a pregnancy has begun, the parents (especially the mother) of the pregnant teenager have the potential for influencing the outcome of the pregnancy. If the pregnancy is discovered early enough, parents may insist on or forbid an abortion or, later, adoption. Mothers of the pregnant teenager may object at first to caring for a new baby, but if the mother has spent her life rearing children, she may welcome a new baby. To say that the grandmother motivates the young mother's pregnancy is an exaggeration, but the pregnant adolescent who has grown up in such a household may perceive few alternatives to motherhood for herself.

Macrosystem Influences. In truth, there may be few alternatives for such an adolescent. If she was raised in a culture of poverty, she has few of the necessary tools for escaping to a better life. Especially if she be-

Causes of Adolescent Childbearing

longs to a poor minority, good job opportunities are few. Motherhood is a familiar path to adult status, and provides a welfare income as well. For her boyfriend, too, becoming a father may provide status, for it proves that he is potent and fertile.

Outcomes of Adolescent Childbearing

Thus, the motivations for childbearing and the outcomes have a circular nature. The adolescent, her mother, and her boyfriend may not intend for a pregnancy to occur, but when it does, they derive certain benefits from it [24]. Of course, the benefits are only one side of the picture. The costs are high.

Costs to the Individual. Teenage childbearing has a long-term impact upon the adolescent parents, especially upon the female. At age 29, women who had become mothers while still in their teens had lower educational attainment, lower-status jobs and lower job satisfaction than those who had not become mothers. The young fathers were similarly affected, although the impact was not so great. Adolescent parents were less likely to marry, and if they did marry, more likely to divorce than their classmates who avoided early pregnancy [8].

Costs to the Family Microsystem. The addition of a new member to a family is always stressful, even when the addition is desired and planned for by other family members. One outcome of unplanned adolescent pregnancy is marriage, which creates a new nuclear family unit. Very often, however, the mother and infant, with husband/boyfriend or without, remain in the household of the mother's family, or at times, the father's. The arrival of an infant means that a new division of labor must be set up in the family. Who will care for the infant? Who will provide the additional income that is necessary to support the infant? Decisions must be made about allocations of space. If the teenage mother has younger siblings, the youngest of these is likely to be displaced by the infant, especially if the grandmother assumes responsibility for the infant's care.

The young mother may grow through the experience of parenthood, if she is guided by her own mother and permitted (or pushed) to take on responsibility. Some grandmothers, however, engage in a struggle with their daughters for control of the child care [24]. Other mothers resent the intrusion into their own lives. If they were looking forward to the time that their childrearing responsibilities would be over, a new infant delays the coming of their freedom.

Costs to the Macrosystem. Adolescent pregnancy is costly to society. Over $10 billion per year is spent upon Aid to Families with Dependent Children, half of this upon households in which the mother was in her teens when her first child was born [39]. It is thought by many that the availability of welfare is an incentive for adolescents to become pregnant, but there is no firm research evidence to substantiate this belief. However, the availability of welfare funds may encourage a pregnant teenager to continue with the pregnancy and keep the infant, especially when welfare funds pay for delivery and support of a child but do not pay for abortions. Welfare also makes it possible for women to avoid marrying the father of their child because they have an alternate means of support [39].

Another cost to society is an increased population because people who begin childbearing early have more children than those who start later. Furthermore, early starters bear more children than they actually want [8]. Because the birth rate in the United States is low, some people are not concerned about the effects of extra births. However, the extra births are to the individuals who are least equipped to cope with additional children. Unwanted children are more likely to be abused and neglected.

Costs of teenage child-bearing: money cost to society, population increase, unwanted children, greater likelihood of neglect, greater likelihood of abuse

Programs for Sexually Active Adolescents

We have suggested that there are a number of costs associated with adolescent pregnancy. And yet, not all persons in our society agree with us that preventing adolescent pregnancy is a desired goal. Tremendous controversy exists concerning the acceptability of providing educational, preventive, and supportive services for sexually active adolescents.

Sex Education in the School and Community

The controversy of longest standing has to do with sex education in the schools. At the present time, however, a vocal minority of 3 per cent of parents oppose sex education in the schools, while 70 per cent of Americans believe that contraception should be taught in the schools. The actual extent of sex education in the schools varies by state. In 1974, approximately 70 per cent of public school systems in the United States provided at least some sex education, and 10 per cent provided full sex education. In the late 1970s, about 35 per cent of public and private schools offered sex education courses [43].

Despite the controversy over sex education, there is no evidence that sex education increases rates of adolescent sexual activity, and none that it decreases rates of teenage pregnancy [10]. It may be that the courses, as taught, are inadequate to deal with the problem.

An alternative method of providing sex education for youth is to use the community rather than the school as the setting. In the community, parents can be more easily involved. The Red Cross and the National Congress of Parents and Teachers (PTA) have both taken part in developing sex education programs at the community level. The Red Cross, for example, provides sex education for parents [43]. When parents are involved, they have more knowledge of and control over what their children learn, and thus feel less threatened. Because discussing sex and contraception with parents is related to starting sexual activity at a later age and to more effective contraceptive use by adolescents, parent participation is important.

Contraceptive Services

Adolescents can receive contraceptive counseling and devices through Planned Parenthood clinics. For adolescents who live in rural areas, however, transportation to and from the clinics may be a problem. A school system in Minnesota has implemented an innovative program of contraceptive information and counseling, venereal disease testing and treatment, and prenatal and postpartum care [16]. The clinic provides other kinds of medical treatment and a weight-control program. Thus, the student who attends the clinic does not have to feel that doing so is an announcement of his or her sexual activity. Pregnancies have declined by 40 per cent in three years.

Programs for Pregnant Adolescents and Adolescent Parents

Throughout the country in 1977, a thousand programs existed to help the pregnant adolescent and the adolescent parent [23]. The programs provided a wide range of services, including contraceptive counseling, accredited education, counseling, financial assistance, housing aid, and medical care. The goals of the programs are to improve the health of the mothers and their infants, advance the mothers educationally, and promote employment of the mothers. Unfortunately, the programs have not achieved their goals, probably because they are too little, and too late [10]. Few of them are able to provide long-term follow-up services to the young families. A recent study of the programs suggests that involvement of the young mother's family could greatly improve the program's effectiveness [23].

Early Marriage

From the standpoint of personality development, one would expect adolescent marriages to be less satisfactory than those between adults. With one partner or both in the crisis of developing a sense of identity, the relationship cannot be one of mutuality and intimacy, which is the essence of the ideal North American marriage. Both partners expect happiness from marriage, and yet their own immaturity prevents the establishment of the relationship that yields lasting happiness. This theory is borne out by research. Divorce is twice as likely to end the marriage of a teenage bride as it is to end the marriage of a woman who waits to marry until she reaches her twenties [26]. Early marriage is associated with lower educational aspirations and lower educational attainment. Especially when babies are born soon after marriage, economic pressures may force the young couple out of school. The chances for divorce become compounded, because higher divorce rates are found among the poor and among persons with little education.

Many factors contribute to early marriage. The insecurity of modern life leads to a desire for loyalty, warmth, and affection that an adolescent hopes to find in marriage. Personal happiness is understood as inherent in family life. A bandwagon effect may operate, as friends marry young. Marriage is overvalued because of the romantic, glamorous image promoted by the mass media. Economic restraints are reduced by prosperity, employment of wives, contribution of parents, and occupational fringe benefits. Increased heterosexual behavior at younger years, earlier dating and going steady, plus increased stimulation of sex drives by mass media, lead to increased premarital sexual intercourse, pregnancy, and forced marriages. Some early marriages are precipitated by the desire to escape from unhappy situations in home, school, or community or to solve other emotional problems. Happily, most adolescents wait until adulthood for marriage.

Summary

The central task of adolescence is to develop a sense of identity, which answers the question, "Who am I?" Newly developing intellectual powers enable the adolescent to ask that question, to begin to integrate past and present, and to look toward the future, asking, "What might I become?" The person who is asking these questions is said to be in the midst of a normal identity crisis. In finding answers, a commitment is made that nonetheless leaves room for further questioning and change throughout life. For males, issues center around careers and political ideology; for females, interpersonal relationships are included as an issue, taking precedence over the other issues.

Rapid physical growth requires that the adolescent integrate a new body image into the identity structure. The meaning of bodily changes is interpreted by the individual, with input from family members and peers within the individual's macrosystem context. Girls tend to feel more ambivalence about bodily changes, in part because female maturity is interpreted as more overtly sexual than is male maturity, but also because girls mature before boys do, and because negative feelings are associated with menstruation.

Another aspect of the sense of identity is sexual identity, which includes a sense of the self as erotic, standards of moral behavior, and masculine or feminine roles and identity. Knowledge is gained about what is and is not sexually pleasing, and ways of sharing one's body in an intimate context are learned. Role behaviors that denote masculinity or femininity are tried on. The development of a masculine identity requires a boy to come to terms with his assertiveness, independence, and sexuality. Vocational interest is basic. Boys are pushed to strive, and are not encouraged to develop their tenderness, emotion, and sensuality. Traditionally, girls' identity remained more fluid than did boys' and often was defined in relation to their husbands once they married. Adolescent girls are now more egalitarian than boys in their view of gender roles.

During adolescence, the family remains an important influence but the importance of the peer group grows. A major task for the adolescent's parents is to know when to set limits. Although adolescents often appear rebellious, there are fewer differences of opinions between adolescent and parent generations in the same family than between members of adolescent and parent cohorts. Although all adolescents influence their parents, adolescents from forerunner families are more likely than their peers from nonforerunner families to introduce social change into their families. Adolescents perceive both parents and peers to have special areas of expertise. In many cases, values of parents and peers are mutually reinforcing.

Peer interaction provides opportunities essential to the growth of the sense of identity. The crowd offers the adolescent a group identity that helps him to separate himself from his family. Because he feels comfortable when identified with the crowd, he can try out a variety of roles. The clique is a small, select group of friends, usually alike in interests and background, giving one another security and status, often behaving cruelly to outsiders.

Friendship contributes to the sense of identity, especially the close relationships of best friends. When the sense of identity has reached a certain strength, friends can achieve true intimacy. It is easier and safer to develop the first intimate friendships with members of the same sex. Boys need a group of friends for support in resisting adult authority. Girls need close individual friends for emotional support in understanding themselves. Girls are more anxious about their friendships than boys are. Popularity is greatly valued by many adolescents, but it may exact a price from those who achieve it.

Early dating has been the norm for at least 25 years, but recently the age at first marriage has risen. High school students often view dating as a game, and may be manipulative in cross-sex relationships.

Until graduation from high school, sexual activity for most adolescents is restricted to kissing and petting. However, increasing numbers of adolescents are having sexual intercourse, usually without use of contraceptives. Motivation for having coitus differs for boys and girls. Adolescent males experience both a stronger sex drive and more peer pressure to initiate sex. Girls are more likely to use sex to get close to their boyfriends. High school age girls who have coitus usually have lower self-esteem than their virgin peers. Low self-esteem is associated with nonuse of contraceptives. Other reasons for failure to use contraceptives include the belief that one will not get pregnant. Although parents and teens agree that parents should provide information about sex, most parents do not do so. Both parents can play a role in responsible adolescent sexuality.

The percentage of teenagers who gave birth out of wedlock has risen dramatically over the past 40 years. More adolescents use contraceptives than was true in the past, but many more adolescents are having sexual intercourse. And today, though not in the past, almost all adolescent mothers keep their babies, causing strains on the young mother's family and decreasing the adolescent's chances for educational and occupational success. Programs that deal with adolescent sexuality exist in the schools, the community, and private agencies. Parental involvement in community programs is helpful. However, access to contraceptive services and venereal disease treatment programs that protect the adolescent's anonymity are also important.

Marriages begun in the teen years are especially likely to end in divorce. Especially when the marriage is begun because of pregnancy, marital partners have fewer chances to develop the senses of identity and intimacy. Economic insecurity contributes to the instability of young marriages, as does marrying in order to escape the parental home.

References

1. Aneshensel, C. S., and B. C. Rosen. Domestic roles and sex differences in occupational expectations. *Journal of Marriage and the Family*, 1980, **42**, 121–131.
2. Balswick, J. O., and C. Macrides. Parental stimulus for adolescent rebellion. *Adolescence*, 1975, **10**, 252–259.
3. Baranowski, M. D. Adolescents' attempted influence on parental behaviors. *Adolescence*, 1978, **13**, 584–604.
4. Baumrind, D. Authoritarian vs. authoritative parental control. *Adolescence*, 1968, **3**, 255–272.
5. Bengston, V. L., and K. D. Black. Intergenerational relations and continuities of socialization. In P. B. Baltes and K. W. Shaie. *Life span developmental psychology: Personality and socialization*. New York: Academic Press, Inc., 1973.
6. Bengston, V. L., and L. Troll. Youth and their parents: feedback and intergenerational influence in socialization. In R. Lerner and G. Spanier, (eds.). *Child influences on marital and family interaction*, New York: Academic Press, Inc., 1978.
7. Burke, R. J., and T. Weir. Sex differences in adolescent life stress, social support, and well being. *Journal of Psychology*, 1978, **98**, 277–288.
8. Card, J. J., and L. L. Wise. Teenage mothers and teenage fathers: The impact of early childbearing on the parents' personal and professional lives. *Family Planning Perspectives*, 1978, **10**, 199–204.
9. Cherlin, A. Postponing marriage: The influence of young women's work expectations. *Journal of Marriage and the Family*, 1980, **42**, 355–365.
10. Chilman, C. Adolescent sexuality in a changing American society: Social and psychological perspectives. U.S. Department of Health, Education, and Welfare, (DHEW Publication No. (NIH) 79-1426). Washington: U.S. Government Printing Office, 1979.
11. Coleman, J. C. Friendship and the peer group in adolescence. In J. Adelson, *Handbook of adolescent psychology*, New York: John Wiley & Sons, Inc., 1980.
12. Coleman, J. S. *The adolescent society*. New York: The Free Press, 1961.
13. Damico, S. B. The effects of clique membership upon academic achievement. *Adolescence*, 1975, **10**, 93–99.
14. Douvan, E. Sex differences in the opportunities, demands, and developments of youth. In R. J. Havighurst and P. H. Dreyer (eds.). *Youth*. The seventy-fourth yearbook of the National Society for the Study of Education. University of Chicago Press, 1975.
15. Douvan, E., and J. Adelson. *The adolescent experience*. New York: John Wiley & Sons, Inc., 1966.
16. Edwards, E., M. E. Steinman, K. A. Arnold, and E. Y. Hakason. Adolescent pregnancy prevention services in high school clinics. *Family Planning Perspectives*, 1980, **12**, 6–14.
17. Elkind, D. Egocentrism in adolescence. *Child Development*, 1967, **38**, 1025–1034.

18. Erikson, E. H. Identity and the life cycle. *Psychological Issues*, 1959, **1**:1.
19. *Family Planning Perspectives*. Parents and teens agree: Teenagers should get birth control information from parents primarily. 1979, **11**, 200–201.
20. Farrell, W. *The liberated man*. New York: Bantam Books Inc., 1975.
21. Finkel, M. L., and Finkel, D. J. Male adolescent contraceptive utilization. *Adolescence*, 1978, **13**, 443–451.
22. Fox, G. L. The family's role in adolescent sexual behavior. Washington: Family Impact Seminar, George Washington University, 1979.
23. Forbush, J. Adolescent parent programs and family involvement. Washington: Family Impact Seminar, George Washington University, 1979.
24. Furstenberg, F. F. Burdens and benefits: The impact of early childbearing on the family. Washington: Family Impact Seminar, George Washington University, 1979.
25. Furstenberg, F. F. *Unplanned parenthood: The social consequences of teenage childbearing*. New York: The Free Press, 1976.
26. Glick, Paul C., and Norton, Arthur J. Marrying, divorcing, and living together in the U.S. today. *Population Bulletin*, **32** (5), 1977. Updated, 1979.
27. Hansen, Sally. Dating choices of high school students. *Family Coordinator*, 1977, **26**, 133–138.
28. Hansen, Sally, and Mary Hicks. Sex role attitudes and perceived dating-mating choices of youth. *Adolescence*, 1980, **15**, 83–90.
29. Hoge, Warren. Doctor vanity: The jet set's man in Rio. *New York Times Magazine*, June 3, 1980.
30. Horrocks, J. E., and G. G. Thompson. A study of the friendship fluctuations of rural boys and girls. *Journal of Genetic Psychology*, 1946, **69**, 189–198.
31. Horrocks, J. E., and S. A. Weinberg. Psychological needs and their development during adolescence. *Journal of Psychology*, 1970, **74**, 51–69.
32. Jorgensen, S. R., S. L. King, and B. A. Torrey. Dyadic and social network influences on adolescent exposure to pregnancy risk. *Journal of Marriage and the Family*, 1980, **42**, 141–155.
33. Kuhlen, R. G., and N. B. Houlihan. Adolescent heterosexual interest in 1942 and 1963. *Child Development*, 1965, **36**, 1049–1052.
34. Larson, L. E. The influence of parents and peers during adolescence: The situation hypothesis revisited. *Journal of Marriage and the Family*, 1972, **34**, 67–74.
35. Larson, L. E. The relative influence of parent-adolescent affect in predicting the salience hierarchy among youth. *Pacific Sociological Review*, 1972, **15**, 83–102.
36. Luker, K. *Taking chances: Abortion and the decision not to contracept*. Berkeley: University of California Press, 1975.
37. MacCorquodale, P., and John DeLamater. Self-image and premarital sexuality. *Journal of Marriage and the Family*, 1979, **41**, 327–339.
38. Marcia, J. E. Identity in adolescence. In J. Adelson (ed.). *Handbook of adolescent psychology*. New York: John Wiley & Sons, Inc., 1980.
39. Moore, K. A. Government policies related to teenage family formation and functioning: An inventory. Washington: Family Impact Seminar, George Washington University Press, 1979.
40. Niles, F. S. The adolescent girls' perception of parents and peers. *Adolescence*, 1979, **14**, 591–597.
41. Petersen, C., and B. Taylor. The biological approach to adolescence: Biological change and psychological adaptation. In J. Adelson (ed.). *Handbook of adolescent psychology*. New York: John Wiley & Sons, Inc., 1980.
42. Sarrel, L., and P. Sarrel. *Sexual unfolding*. Boston: Little, Brown and Company, 1979.
43. Scales, P. Sex education and the prevention of teenage pregnancy: An over-

view of policies and programs in the United States. Washington: Family Impact Seminar, George Washington University Press, 1979.

44. Schwartz, G., and D. Merten. The language of adolescence: And anthropological approach to the youth culture. *American Journal of Sociology,* 1967, **57,** 453–468.

45. Siman, M. L. Application of a new model of peer group influence to naturally existing adolescent friendship groups. *Child Development,* 1977, **48,** 270–274.

46. Simmons, R. G., D. A. Blyth, E. F. Van Cleave, and D. M. Bush. Entry into early adolescence: The impact of school structure, puberty, and early dating on self-esteem. *American Sociological Review,* 1979, **44,** 948–967.

46a. Slade, M., and E. Hoffman. Continuing tragedy of teenage pregnancy. *New York Times,* March 15, 1981.

47. Smart, L. S. Gender role identity, feminist ideology, and career and family commitment of twelfth-grade girls in New England. Unpublished Doctoral Dissertation, University of Connecticut, Storrs, Conn., 1979.

48. Smith, Robert. Personal communication. July, 1980.

49. Sorensen, R. C. *Adolescent sexuality in contemporary America.* New York: World Publishing Company, 1973.

50. Spence, J. T., and R. L. Helmreich. *Masculinity and femininity: their psychological dimensions, correlates, and antecedents.* Austin: University of Texas Press, 1978.

51. Zelnik, M., Y. J. Kim, and J. F. Kanter. Sexual activity, contraceptive use and pregnancy among metropolitan-area teenagers: 1971–1979. *Family Planning Perspectives,* 1980, **12,** 230–237.

A

Height and Weight Interpre- tation Charts

The charts* that follow on pages 518–525 make it possible to show graphically a child's *status* as to height and weight for any one measurement of size. If two or more measurements are made, separated by a time interval, the child's *progress* will also be shown graphically.

How to Measure Weight and Height Accurately

Use a beam-type platform scale. Weigh the child without shoes, barefoot, or in stockings, wearing minimal clothing, underwear or gym clothes. For children under 24 months, recumbent length is measured between the crown of the head and the bottom of the heel, with the back flat, the knees extended, and the soles of the feet at right angles with the ankles. For children above 2 years, stature is measured as standing height. Without shoes, the feet should be together. Have the child stand normally erect, chin tucked in, eyes looking straight ahead. Stature is the distance between the floor and a horizontal board or bar firmly touching the crown of the head. Up to 36 months, record weight to the nearest quarter kilo (250 grams) and height to the nearest centimeter. At older ages, the nearest kilogram and the nearest centimeter are close enough.

Graphing Height and Weight Status

On the day he was measured, Carl was 7 years and 4 months old. His stature was 122 centimeters and his weight 22 kilograms. To plot his growth status, first find on the age scale of the weight graph a point one-third of the way between 7 and 8 years. Imagine a line drawn vertically upward to the point where it intersects with another imaginary horizontal line drawn through a point on the weight scale at 22. Put a dot on the graph at this point. Similarly, find the imaginary vertical line at the bottom of the height scale. Put a dot at the point where that line intersects with an imaginary horizontal line through 122 centimeters. Each of these dots falls just below the 50th percentile line on the graph. These show that Carl is slightly below the average child of 7 years and 4 months, slightly lighter and slightly shorter; he is neither heavy nor light for his height.

Graphing Height and Weight Progress

On his eighth birthday Carl weighs 25 kilograms and is 126 centimeters tall. As in the earlier measurement, put a pencil dot on the 8 year vertical line where it intersects with the imaginary line through 25 kilograms on the weight graph, and the imaginary line through 126 centimeters on the height graph. Lines connecting the two pairs of dots are roughly parallel with the printed 50th percentile lines. In the 8 months between measurements Carl grew proportionately in height and weight.

* SOURCE: P. V. V. Hamill, *NCHS growth curves for children.* Vital and health statistics: Series 11, Data from the National Health Survey; No. 165. (DHEW publication No. (PHS) 78–1650.) Washington: U.S. Government Printing Office, 1977.

If the points representing a child's height and weight are not about the same distance above or below the same percentile curve, the difference may indicate that the child is normally slender or normally stocky. If the difference between the stature and weight percentile is more than 25 percentiles, a further check on his or her health should be made.

Normal progress in height and weight gives lines for such a child that stay roughly the same distance from adjacent printed lines on the graph. When the lines go steeply up, or if one goes up and the other is nearly horizontal, a medical investigation of the child's health or nutritional condition is called for. Around the age of 11, a child's lines may cross the printed percentile lines, because there are individual differences in the timing and strength of the puberal growth spurt. A child's lines may go up more steeply for a period of time, or be more nearly horizontal than the printed lines.

Length by age percentiles for girls aged birth to 36 months.

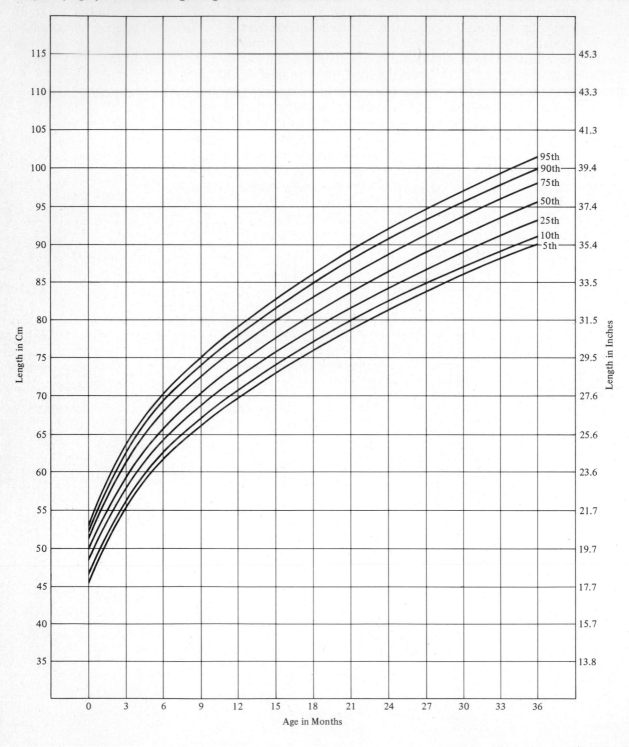

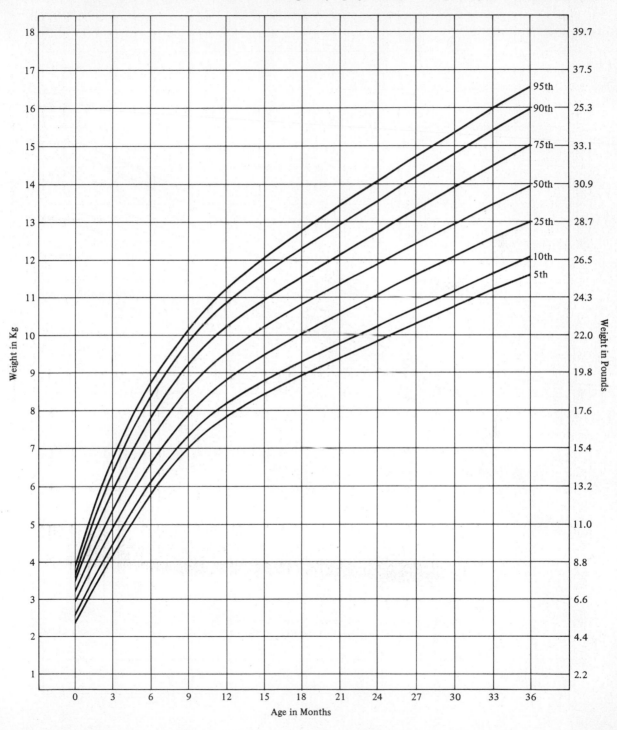

Length by age percentiles for boys aged birth to 36 months.

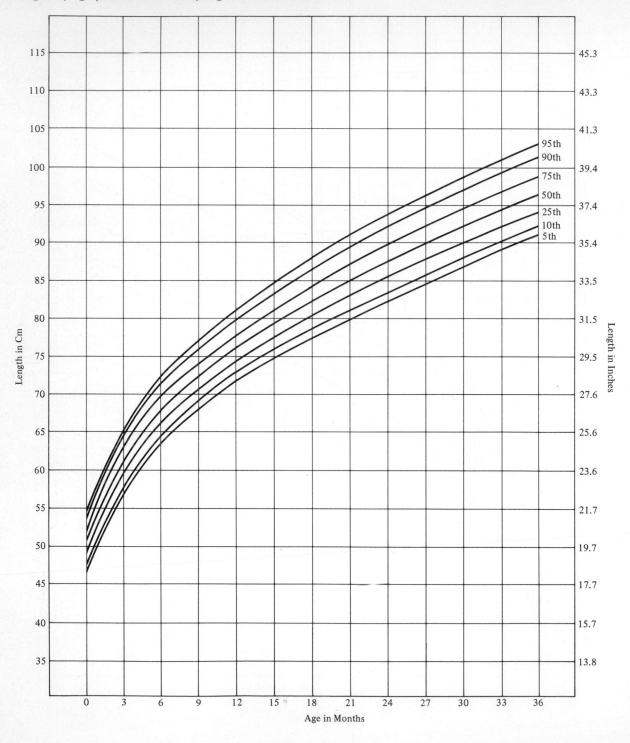

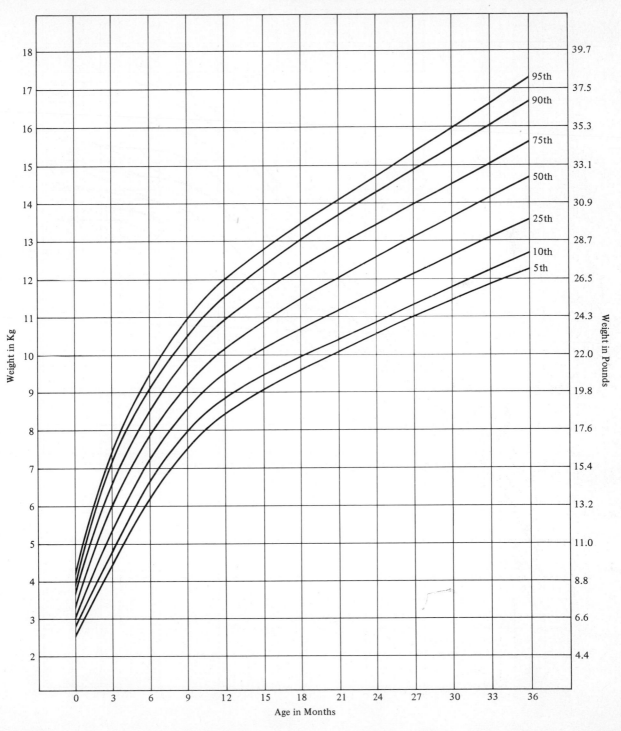

Stature by age percentiles for girls aged 2–18 years.

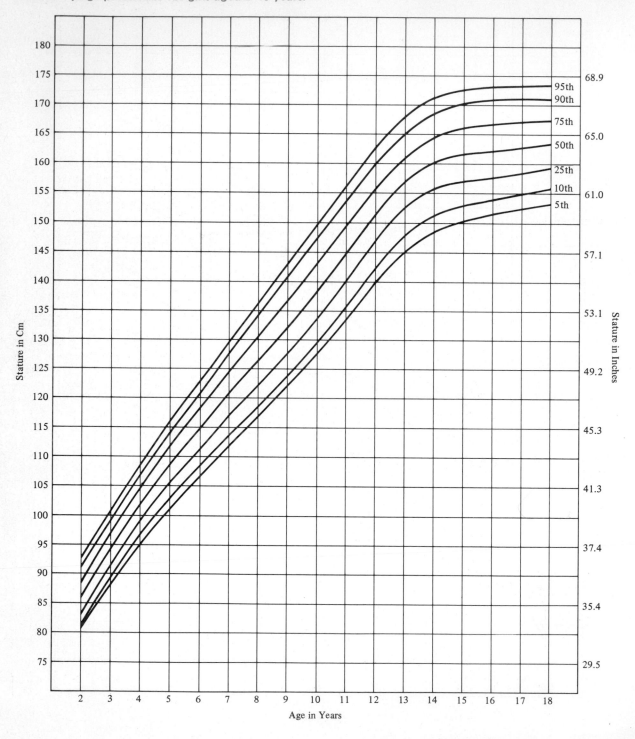

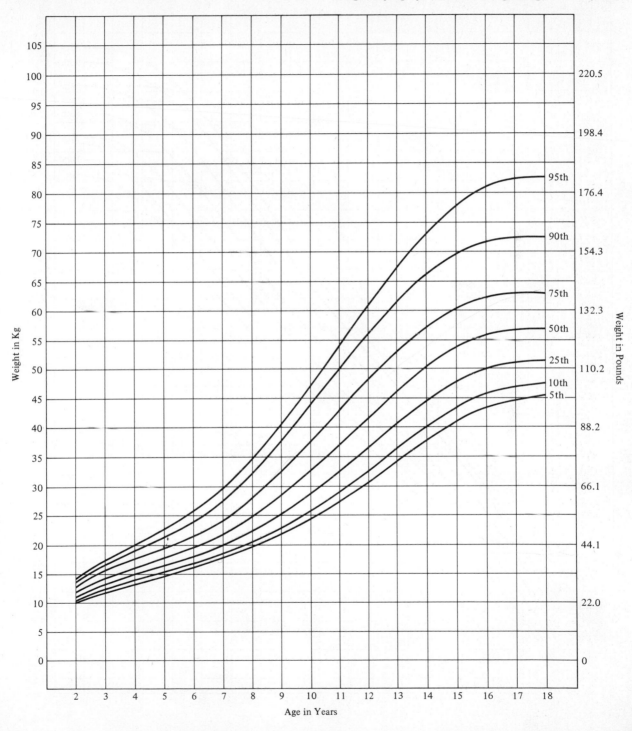

Stature by age percentiles for boys aged 2–18 years.

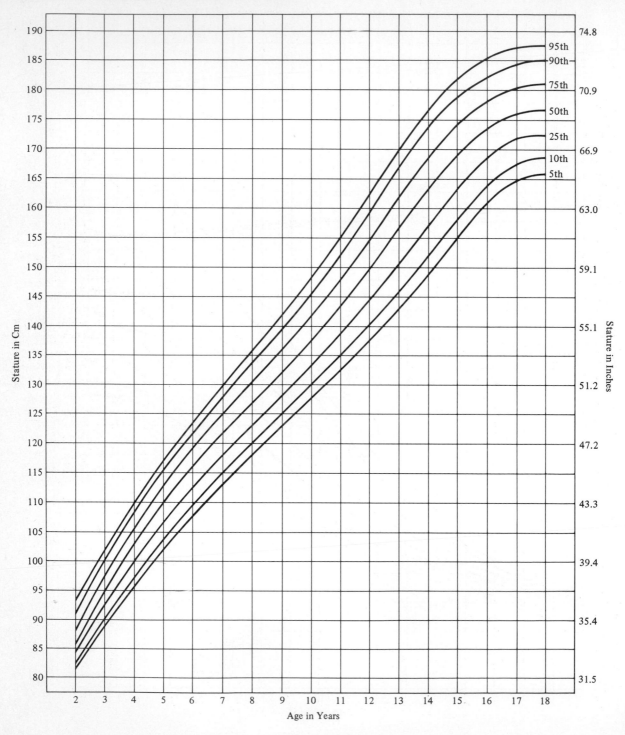

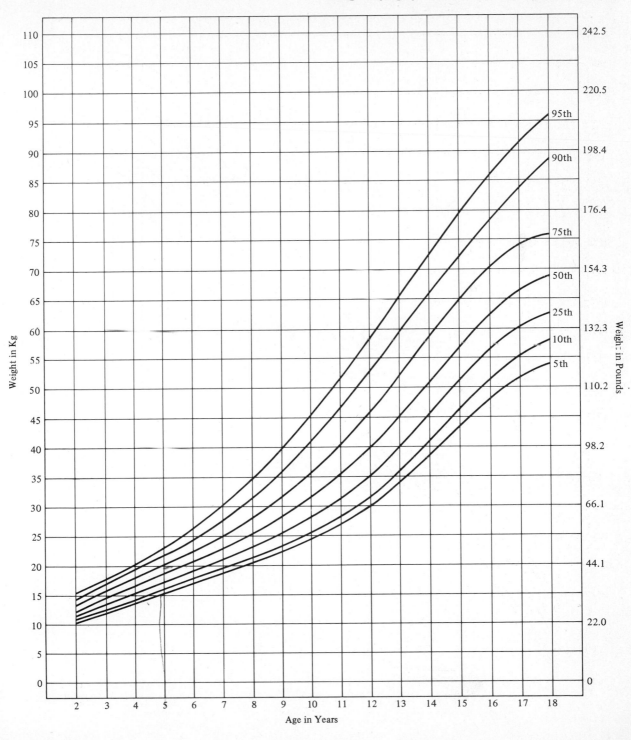

B

Communica-ble Diseases of Childhood

	Chickenpox	Diphtheria	Measles	Mumps	Polio
Cause	A virus: Present in secretions from nose, throat, and mouth of infected people.	Diphtheria bacillus: Present in secretions from nose and throat of infected people and carriers.	A virus: Present in secretions from nose and throat of infected people.	A virus: Present in saliva of infected people.	3 strains of polio virus have been identified: Present in discharges from nose, throat, bowels of infected people.
How spread	Contact with infected people or articles used by them. Very contagious.	Contact with infected people and carriers or articles used by them.	Contact with infected people or articles used by them. Very contagious.	Contact with infected people or articles used by them.	Primarily, contact with infected people.
Incubation period (from date of exposure to first signs)	13 to 17 days. Sometimes 3 weeks.	2 to 5 days. Sometimes longer.	About 10 to 12 days.	12 to 26 (commonly 18) days.	2 to 21 days
Period of communicability (time when disease is contagious)	From 5 days before, to 6 days after first appearance of skin blisters.	From about 2 to 4 weeks after onset of disease.	From 4 days before until about 5 days after rash appears.	From about 6 days before symptoms to 9 days after. Principally at about time swelling starts.	Apparently greatest in late incubation and first few days of illness.
Most susceptible ages	Under 15 years.	Under 15 years.	Common at any age during childhood.	Children and young people.	Most common in children 1 to 16 years.
Seasons of prevalence	Winter.	Fall, winter, and spring.	Mainly spring. Also fall and winter.	Winter and spring.	June through September.
Prevention	No prevention.	Vaccination with diphtheria toxoid (in triple vaccine for babies).	Measles vaccine.	Mumps vaccine.	Polio vaccine.
Control	Exclusion from school for 1 week after eruption appears. Avoid contact with susceptibles. Immune globulin may lessen severity. (Cut child's fingernails.) Immunity usual after one attack.	Booster doses (see Appendix C). Antitoxin and antibiotics used in treatment and for protection after exposure. One attack does not necessarily give immunity.	Isolation until 5 days after appearance of rash. Immune globulin between 3 and 6 days after exposure can lighten attack. Antibiotics for complications. Immunity usual after one attack.	Isolation for 9 days from onset of swelling. Immunity usual after one attack but second attacks can occur.	Booster doses (see Appendix C). Isolation for about one week from onset. Immunity to infecting strain of virus usual after one attack.

	Rheumatic Fever	Rubella	Strep infections	Whooping cough (Pertussis)
Cause	Direct cause unknown. Precipitated by a strep infection.	A virus: Present in secretions from nose and mouth of infected people.	Streptococci of several strains cause scarlet fever and strep sore throats: Present in secretions from mouth, nose and ears of infected people.	Pertussis bacillus: Present in secretions from mouth and nose of infected people.
How spread	Unknown. But the preceding strep infection is contagious.	Contact with infected people or articles used by them. Very contagious.	Contact with infected people; rarely from contaminated articles.	Contact with infected people and articles used by them.
Incubation period (from date of exposure to first signs)	Symptoms appear about 2 to 3 weeks after a strep infection.	14 to 21 (usually 18) days.	1 to 3 days.	From 5 to 10 days.
Period of communicability (time when disease is contagious)	Not communicable. Preceding strep infection is communicable.	From 7 days before to 5 days after onset of rash.	Greatest during acute illness (about 10 days).	From onset of first symptoms to about 3rd week of the disease.
Most susceptible ages	All ages; most common from 6 to 12 years.	Young children, but also common in young adults.	All ages.	Under 7 years.
Seasons of prevalence	Mainly winter and spring.	Winter and spring.	Late winter and spring.	Late winter and early spring.
Prevention	No prevention, except proper treatment of strep infections. (See Strep Infections.)	Rubella (German measles) vaccine.	No prevention. Antibiotic treatment for those who have had rheumatic fever.	Immunization with whooping cough vaccine (in triple vaccine for babies).
Control	Use of antibiotics. One attack does not give immunity.	Isolation when necessary, for 5 days after onset. Immunity usual after one attack.	Isolation for about 1 day after start of treatment with antibiotics—used for about 10 days. One attack does not necessarily give immunity.	Booster doses (see Appendix C). Special antibiotics may help to lighten attack for child not immunized. Isolation from susceptible infants for about 3 weeks from onset or until cough stops. Immunity usual after one attack.

Source: The Control of Communicable Diseases, American Public Health Association, 1975, *Report of Committee on Control of Infectious Diseases*, American Academy of Pediatrics, 1974. Courtesy of Metropolitan Life, and Rhode Island Department of Health, 1978.

C

Immunization Recommendations

This schedule for immunizations is that recommended by the Rhode Island Department of Health. A physician may suggest a slightly different schedule suitable for any individual child. And recommendations change from time to time as new discoveries are made.

Recommended Schedule for Normal Infants and Children		
Age	Vaccine	Comment
2 months	DTP-TOPV	DTP—diphtheria, tetanus, pertussis combined
4 months	DTP-TOPV	TOPV—trivalent oral polio vaccine
6 months	DTP	
15–18 months	MMR*-DTP-TOPV†	MMR—measles, mumps, rubella combined‡
4–6 years	DTP-TOPV	Should be given prior to school entry
Every 10 years	Td	Td—tetanus, diphtheria (adult type)

Recommended Schedule for Children Not Immunized in Infancy		
	15 months to 6 years	6 years and older
First visit	DTP-TOPV-MMR*	Td-TOPV-MMR*
2 months later	DTP-TOPV	Td-TOPV
4 months later	DTP	none
6–12 months later	DTP-TOPV	Td-TOPV

* Any child having a history of tuberculosis exposure should be tuberculin skin-tested before immunizations with measles vaccine. Most children born outside the U.S. should be tuberculin tested. Vaccine should be withheld from a child who is a tuberculin reactor until appropriate therapy for tuberculosis is begun.

† Give DTP, TOPV, MMR simultaneously at 15 months if visits are uncertain; otherwise at 15 months give MMR and at 18 months give DTP and TOPV. The PHS Committee on Immunization Practices have approved simultaneous administration of combined MMR vaccine with TOPV. This practice is particularly fitting when an immunization-delinquent child over 15 months of age presents himself for immunizations. Fever rates after simultaneous vaccine administration are not greater than the sum of fever rates following the separate administration of the vaccines.

‡ Yearly screening for lead poisoning is recommended for children 1–5 years of age, particularly those living in older dilapidated housing, i.e., with peeling or flaking surfaces.

Entries in *italics* refer to pages on which bibliographic references are given.

Guilleminault, C., 88, *92*
Guthrie, H. A., 215, *226*
Gutteridge, M. V., 219, *226*
Guttmacher, A. F., 74, *93*

Hagen, J. W., 343, *368*
Hakason, E. Y., 508, *511*
Hale, G. A., 343, *368*
Hall, B., 117, *127*
Halliday, M. A. K., 152, *159*
Halonen, J. S., 171, *190*
Halton, A., 134, 138, *160*
Halverson, C. F., 221, *226*, 282, *295*, 394, *403*
Halverson, L. E., 321, *329*
Hamill, P. V. V., 197, *226*, 302, 305, 322, *329*, 330, 413, 419, 437, *438*
Handler, P., 24, *36*
Hanley, C., 445, *471*
Hansen, J. D. L., 109, *128*
Hansen, S., 498, 499, *512*
Harlow, H. F., 14, *36*
Harlow, M. K., 14, *36*
Harper, J., 434, *436*
Harper, L. V., 219, *226*
Harrell, A. V., 428, 430, *436*
Harrill, I., 215, *226*
Harris, L. J., 353, *368*, 445, *471*
Harrison, A., 87, *91*
Harrison, C. W., 394, *402*
Harrison, D. M., 261, *263*
Hartup, W. W., 277, *296*, 392, 394, 395, *402*
Harvey, C. R., 311, 312, *329*, 424, *437*
Haskell, J. A., 413, *436*
Hauser, R. M., 465, *471*
Heald, F., 427, *437*
Hechinger, F. M., 453, *472*
Heinstein, M. I., 74, *92*
Hellman, L. M., 70, 82, *92*
Helmreich, R. L., 485, *513*
Hetherington, E. M., 291, 292, *296*
Hicks, M., 499, *512*
Hiernaux, J., 420, *437*
Higgins, A. C., 73, *92*
Hildreth, G., 222, *226*
Hinkle, D. E., 388, *402*
Hiscock, M., 221, 222, *226*
Hittelman, J. H., 141, *159*
Hock, E., 179, *190*
Hoffman, E., 501, *513*
Hoffman, L. W., 179, *190*
Hoffman, M. L., 270, 273, *296*, 378, *402*
Hogan, R., 270, 275, *296*, 378, 381, *402*, 455, 459, *472*
Hogarty, P. S., 154, *159*
Hoge, W., 483, *512*
Holland, W. W., 114, *127*
Holley, W. L., 70, *92*
Holstein, C. B., 462, *471*
Holt, E., 6, *36*
Honeyman, M. C., 76, *92*
Hood, L., 253, *262*

Hope, M. L., 134, *158*
Horn, J. C., 70, *92*
Hornung, M., 276, *296*
Horowitz, F. D., 83, *92*, 145, *160*
Horrocks, J. E., 493, 496, *512*
Houlihan, N. G., 496, *512*
Howard, K. I., 434, *437*
Hughes, M., 239, *263*
Hughston, G., 445, *473*
Hulsebus, R., 143, *159*
Hulten, B. H., 391, *403*
Hunt, J. McV., 154, *161*
Huntington, D. S., 187, *190*
Hutcherson, M. A., 261, *263*

Illsley, R., 70, 71, *92*
Inhelder, B., 48, 49, *58*, 146, 148, 149, *160*, 234, 244, 249, 250, *264*, 343, *369*, 379, *403*, 443, 447, *472*
Ireton, C. L., 215, *226*
Israel, A. C., 384, *402*
Ivanans, T., 155, *159*

Jacklin, C. N., 71, *93*
Jaffe, J., 150, *159*
Jarman, B. O., 322, *329*, 431, *437*
Jelliffe, D. B., 116, *128*
Jelliffe, E. F. P., 116, *128*
Johnson, C. L., 114, *126*, 302, 312, *328*, *329*, 426, *436*
Johnson, C. N., 235, *265*
Johnson, J. A., 270, 275, *296*, 378, 381, *402*, 459, *472*
Johnston, F. E., 197, *226*, 413, *437*
Jorgensen, S. R., 502, 504, *512*
Jusczyk, P., 143, *158*
Justice, E. M., 344, *367*

Kaban, B. T., 181, *191*, 231, *265*
Kagan, J., 155, *160*, 343, *368*
Kammeyer, K. C. W., 179, *190*
Kanawati, A. A., 206, *225*
Kantner, J. F., 501, 502, *513*
Karp, S. A., 336, *370*
Kaufman, R. V., 433, *437*
Kaye, K., 133, *159*
Kearsley, R. B., 142, *159*
Keating, D. P., 448, *472*
Keet, M. P., 109, *128*
Kellogg, R., 257, *263*
Kelly, J. E., 311, *329*, 424, *437*
Kelly, V. C., 110, *128*
Kemler, D. G., 248, *265*
Kendrick, C., 140, *190*, 289, *296*
Keniston, A. H., 344, *368*, 441, *472*
Kennell, J. H., 23, *36*, 98, *128*
Kermis, M. D., 355, *368*
Kern, S., 27, *36*
Kessen, W., 10, 17, *36*, 140, *158*
Killey, J. C., 344, *369*
Kilpatrick, A., 101, *128*
Kim, Y. J., 501, 502, *513*
Kimura, D., 309, *329*

Subject Index

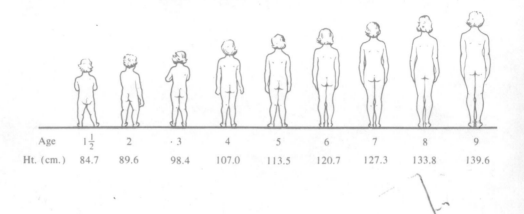

Age	$1\frac{1}{2}$	2	3	4	5	6	7	8	9
Ht. (cm.)	84.7	89.6	98.4	107.0	113.5	120.7	127.3	133.8	139.6

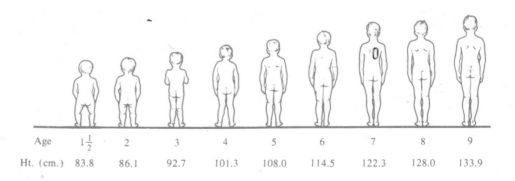

Age	$1\frac{1}{2}$	2	3	4	5	6	7	8	9
Ht. (cm.)	83.8	86.1	92.7	101.3	108.0	114.5	122.3	128.0	133.9